The Calvin Institute of Christian W.   .gICAL Studies
Series, edited by John D. Witvliet, is designed to   . reflection on the history, theology, and practice of Christian worship and to stimulate worship renewal in Christian congregations. Contributions include writings by pastoral worship leaders from a wide range of communities and scholars from a wide range of disciplines. The ultimate goal of these contributions is to nurture worship practices that are spiritually vital and theologically rooted.

Published

Resonant Witness

Conversations between Music and Theology

Edited by

Jeremy S. Begbie & Steven R. Guthrie

WILLIAM B. EERDMANS PUBLISHING COMPANY

GRAND RAPIDS, MICHIGAN

Wm. B. Eerdmans Publishing Co.
4035 Park East Court SE, Grand Rapids, Michigan 49546
www.eerdmans.com

26 25 24 23 22 21 20 19 18   8 9 10 11 12 13 14 15

Library of Congress Cataloging-in-Publication Data

Resonant witness: conversations between music and theology /
    edited by Jeremy S. Begbie & Steven R. Guthrie.
        p.   cm. — (The Calvin Institute of Christian Worship liturgical studies)
    Includes index.
    ISBN 978-0-8028-6277-8 (pbk.: alk. paper)
    1. Music — Religious aspects.   I. Begbie, Jeremy.   II. Guthrie, Steven R., 1967-

ML3921.R47   2011
261.5'78 — dc22

                                      2010027779

Contents

v

Part Four: Music and Worship

Acknowledgments

The editors and authors are profoundly grateful for the sponsorship of the Calvin Institute of Christian Worship at Calvin College, Michigan — without their support, this project would never have seen the light of day. In particular, we owe a debt of thanks to its director, Dr. John Witvliet, for his encouragement and his Afterword to the volume. Our thanks also go to Dona McCullagh for her meticulous attention to the numerous tasks that have come her way in the production of this volume: editing, proofreading, permissions, and the production of the glossary. We are all very much in her debt.

"Created Beauty: The Witness of J. S. Bach," by Jeremy Begbie is adapted from *The Beauty of God*, edited by Daniel J. Treier, Mark Husbands and Roger Lundin. © 2007 by Daniel J. Treier, Mark Husbands and Roger Lundin. Used with permission of InterVarsity Press, PO Box 1400, Downers Grove, IL 60515. ivpress.com.

"Music for the Love Feast: Hildegard of Bingen and the Song of Songs" by Margot Fassler was originally published in *Women's Voices Across Musical Worlds*, edited by Jane A. Bernstein (Boston: Northeastern University Press, 2004). © University Press of New England, Hanover, NH. Reprinted with permission.

Introduction

Jeremy S. Begbie and Steven R. Guthrie

"It is better to get a headache from exercises in canons, fugues and counterpoint than from confuting the Kantian confutation of the evidence for the existence of God. Enough of your theological spinsterhood!"[1]

So the music teacher, Wendell Kretschmar, attempts to lure Adrian Leverkühn away from theology into the study of music. For Leverkühn, the main character of Thomas Mann's *Doctor Faustus*, it seems these two cannot be pursued side by side. He writes to Kretschmar: "you consider [me] as 'gifted' for music and summon me to you and to its service, instead of leaving me humbly to tarry with God and theology."[2] To study the things of God is to refuse the study of music; to pursue music is to abandon theology. Indeed, Adrian's tuition in music will mean not only leaving seminary, but ultimately entering the realm of the demonic.[3]

---

1. Thomas Mann, *Dr. Faustus: The life of the German composer Adrian Leverkühn as told by a friend*, trans. H. T. Lowe-Porter (New York: Alfred A. Knopf, 1948), p. 135.

2. Mann, *Dr. Faustus*, p. 134.

3. Mann would later write: "It is a grave error on the part of legend and story not to connect Faust with music. He should have been musical, he should have been a musician. Music is a demonic realm; Kierkegaard, a great Christian, proved that most convincingly in his painfully enthusiastic essay on Mozart's *Don Juan*. Music is Christian art with a negative prefix. Music is calculated order and chaos-breeding irrationality at once, rich in conjuring, incantatory gestures, in magic of numbers, the most unrealistic and yet the most impas-

1

Or might it be that these two areas of study are not so fully set against one another? At one point Leverkühn concedes that his native "Lutheranism" even "sees in theology and music neighbouring spheres and close of kin."[4]

Certainly, in Western culture the dialogue between music and theology has often been lively and intense — a fact to which Mann's novel bears dramatic witness. Not only has music been ubiquitous, it also has had a persistent and virtually irrepressible place in the Christian church, pre-eminently in worship. To this day the vast majority of Christians sing or play instruments as part of their corporate encounter with God. This has provoked many, including some of the finest Christian thinkers in history, to explore how music might relate to Christianity's central convictions, to the shape and substance of the faith of Israel which climaxes in the person of Jesus Christ. The longest-lasting and most developed stream of thought in this regard stretches from Augustine and Boethius to the late Middle Ages, situating musical sounds amid a grand and highly distinctive vision of a divinely permeated cosmos. The emergence of modernity occasioned several fresh efforts to interweave theology and music — Leverkühn has already drawn our attention to the Lutherans, who offered a variety of ways of coming to terms with music theologically. A number of Enlightenment philosophers incorporated musical phenomena into the theological worldviews they believed appropriate to scientific discoveries.[5] Similarly, some of the nineteenth-century Romantics offered extended panegyrics of instrumental music, in effect, re-working and re-forming the grand medieval vision.[6]

For the last hundred years, however, the theological landscape has more closely reflected the pessimism of Leverkühn and Kretschmar. While no serious theologian to our knowledge has advocated a necessary connection between music and the demonic, relatively few have attempted any thorough

---

sioned of arts, mystical and abstract. If Faust is to be the representative of the German soul, he would have to be musical, for the relation of the German to the world is abstract and mystical, that is, musical – the relation of a professor with a touch of demonism." Thomas Mann, "Germany and the Germans," *The Yale Review* 35, no. 2 (1946): 227. As cited in Carroll E. Reed, "Thomas Mann and the Faust Tradition," *The Journal of English and Germanic Philology* 51, no. 1 (Jan. 1952): 20.

4. Mann, *Dr. Faustus*, p. 131.

5. Paul Henry Lang, "The Enlightenment and Music," *Eighteenth-Century Studies* 1, no. 1 (Autumn 1967): 93-108.

6. Daniel K. L. Chua, *Absolute Music and the Construction of Meaning* (Cambridge: Cambridge University Press, 1999), chs. 20-22.

integration of the theological and the musical.[7] Although we have witnessed a recent renewal of interest in theology and the arts in Europe and North America, the lion's share of attention has been given to the visual and literary arts. There are various reasons for this, among them the difficulty of using words to speak about something that so quickly eludes language ("In the face of music, the wonders of language are also its frustrations" [George Steiner][8]). There are also acute problems that arise from recognizing that "representation" and "reference" do not seem intrinsic to the way music operates — how can music be "meaningful" when it is so abstract, so semantically fluid?

Nevertheless, recent signs of fresh activity at the music-theology interface suggest that the difficulties are not insuperable,[9] and we hope that this

---

7. As far as major figures are concerned, the most obvious exceptions are the Congregationalist theologian P. T. Forsyth, Dietrich Bonhoeffer, Karl Barth, and Joseph Ratzinger.

See also Albert Blackwell, *The Sacred in Music* (Cambridge: Lutterworth, 1999); Christopher R. Campling, *The Food of Love: Reflections on Music and Faith* (London: SCM, 1997); William Edgar, *Taking Note of Music* (London: SPCK, 1986); Alfred John Pike, *A Theology of Music* (Toledo: Gregorian Institute, 1953). A few theological studies of composers have been offered: e.g., Jaroslav J. Pelikan, *Bach among the Theologians* (Philadelphia: Fortress Press, 1986); Hans Küng, *Mozart: Traces of Transcendence* (London: SCM, 1992); Harold M. Best, *Music Through the Eyes of Faith* (San Francisco: Harper, 1993). There have been forays into theology by musicologists: e.g., Wilfrid H. Mellers, *Bach and the Dance of God* (Oxford: Oxford University Press, 1981); *Beethoven and the Voice of God* (London: Faber, 1983); Eric T. Chafe, *Tonal Allegory in the Vocal Music of J. S. Bach* (Berkeley: University of California Press, 1991); *Analyzing Bach Cantatas* (Oxford: Oxford University Press, 2000). With regard to the potential of music to enrich theology, see Hans Urs von Balthasar, *Truth Is Symphonic: Aspects of Christian Pluralism* (San Francisco: Ignatius Press, 1987). See also Jon Michael Spencer, *Theological Music: Introduction to Theomusicology* (London: Greenwood Press, 1991); *Theomusicology* (Durham, NC: Duke University Press, 1994).

8. George Steiner, *Errata: An Examined Life* (London: Phoenix, 1997), p. 65.

9. See, e.g., Jeremy S. Begbie, *Theology, Music and Time* (Cambridge: Cambridge University Press, 2000); *Resounding Truth: Christian Wisdom in the World of Music* (Grand Rapids, MI: Baker, 2007); Leo Black, *Franz Schubert: Music and Belief* (Woodbridge, Suffolk: Boydell Press, 2003); David S. Cunningham, *These Three Are One: The Practice of Trinitarian Theology,* Challenges in Contemporary Theology (Oxford: Blackwell Publishers, 1998), pp. 127-64; Mark Hijleh, *The Music of Jesus: From Composition to Koinonia* (San Jose, New York, Lincoln, and Shanghai: Writers Club Press, 2001); Heidi Epstein, *Melting the Venusberg: A Feminist Theology of Music* (London: Continuum, 2005); Ann Pederson, *God, Creation and All That Jazz: A Process of Composition and Improvisation* (St. Louis: Chalice Press, 2001); A. R. Peacocke and Ann Pederson, *The Music of Creation* (Minneapolis: Fortress Press, 2006); Don E. Saliers, *Music and Theology* (Nashville: Abingdon, 2007).

volume will serve to carry forward such initiatives, stimulating fresh and fruitful interactions. Against the testimony of Adrian Leverkühn, the conviction of the authors and editors of this volume is that the study of theology and the study of music need not, and should not, be kept apart; that there is an enormous amount to gain from conversations between those who seek to explore and articulate the content and shape of Christian truth, and those who inhabit the world of Beethoven and Bruckner, Corinne Bailey Rae and Keith Jarrett.

Resonant Witness has arisen out of just such conversations among theologians, musicologists,[10] and philosophers with an interest in either or both fields. In 2002, a "Music and Theology Colloquium" was established as the result of a collaboration between the research project "Theology Through the Arts" at the University of St. Andrews, Scotland, and the Calvin Institute of Christian Worship at Calvin College, Grand Rapids, Michigan. It was chaired by Jeremy Begbie, and its participants, drawn largely from the United Kingdom and the United States, gathered for two residential meetings in Ely, Cambridgeshire. All but four of the essays in this volume arose directly out of these meetings and were revised through subsequent one-to-one discussions and email correspondence. This kind of extended exchange is time-consuming and demanding, but critical, we believe, for the success and fruitfulness of any multidisciplinary enterprise.

The aim of the Colloquium, and this book as a whole, is *to demonstrate the fruitfulness of theology for music, and the fruitfulness of music for theology, with a view to encouraging sustained engagements between musicians and theologians in the future.* We make no claim to be comprehensive. Many types of music, many historical periods, many doctrinal and philosophical issues, and many practical matters concerning music are not addressed. And there are types of music-theology dialogue not undertaken here, or even mentioned. The collection sets forth only a range of possibilities, a sample of different forms of engagement; no more.

10. In the English-speaking world, the term "musicology" can have different usages, and its definition is a much-debated issue. It is often used in a fairly narrow sense to refer to the history of (primarily Western) music. Here we use the term in the much wider sense of "the scholarly study of music."

Music in Action

To set the scene, it is worth saying something briefly about the terms "music" and "theology," about what shapes and conditions our use of these words in the essays that follow.

Although the word "music" may appear unproblematic, a moment's reflection reveals it to be highly multivalent. Not only are there are many forms of "music" worldwide, but even within a single category (such as "modern Western music") quite different activities and entities can be distinguished. In many scholarly circles, it has become a commonplace to urge that music is best conceived fundamentally in terms of *embodied practices* (rather than in terms of objects or theoretical disciplines), the primary practices being *music-making* and *music-hearing*. To pick up Christopher Small's expression, we should speak more of "musicking" than "music."[11] This seems a wise line to follow, given that the "products" of music (sound-patterns, pieces, works, scores) and its second-order disciplines are all dependent on the more basic practices of making and hearing music. For theology to come to terms with music, then, first and foremost means coming to terms with these actions or practices. (It is no accident that most of the contributors to this volume are keen music practitioners of one sort or another.)

"Music-making" we can understand as the intentional production of temporally organized patterns of pitched sounds, and "music-hearing" as the perception of temporally organized patterns of pitched sounds *as* "music" ("perception" covering everything from concentrated, attentive listening to unfocused, tacit awareness). (It may be that a distinct phase of "composing" precedes music-making, but this is certainly not always so: for most of human history, composing has been concurrent with music-making, and besides, many contemporary composers work at an instrument.)

Music-making gives rise to various objects or entities, first and foremost "temporally organized patterns of pitched sounds"; in other words, *musical sound-patterns*. This is the primary "text" of musical activity ("text" being understood here in the broad sense of the product of music-making, including a "form" such as the canon, or the blues). It may be that this text develops and solidifies into a particular "work," a "piece of music," often inscribed as a written "score," but this is not always so (works and scores are relatively recent phenomena in musical history).

11. Christopher Small, *Musicking: The Meanings of Performing and Listening* (Hanover: University Press of New England, 1998).

What emerges, then, is a threefold pattern — music-making/text/music-hearing[12] — a pattern that is met often in cultural studies (transferred to the persons involved, it works out as author/text/reader, producer/product/consumer, and so on). When we are dealing with what we call "music," even when concentrating on one of these elements, we need to be alert to this threefold pattern. Much scholarship has been hampered by ignoring or over-stressing one or more of the elements at the expense of others.

It is also important to be alert to the fact that these practices are *socially and culturally embedded:* the way we make and hear music is shaped by our relations to others — our social setting, all the way from one-to-one relationships to very large groupings.[13] And because of this, making and hearing music are shaped by the meaningful patterns and products that we fashion as we relate to others and the natural world — in other words, by "culture" (social institutions, images, books, customs, etc.).[14] Further, musical practices are *politically* entrenched: they are inevitably mixed up with the power relations that are necessary for social organization.

"Reading" Music — Resisting Reductionism

One of the perennial temptations in writing about music is what might be loosely termed "reductionism." One may, for instance, attend to only one type or aspect of musical practice (or musical text) without due regard for its relation to others. Or one may allow one discipline of inquiry to dominate so strongly that other legitimate modes are ignored, excluded, or perhaps subsumed under the master discipline.

To cite one example of reductionism, it has become routine in many academic music departments to stress that musical practices and products are socially, culturally, and politically conditioned — against the notion that

12. See Jean-Jacques Nattiez, *Music and Discourse: Toward a Semiology of Music* (Princeton, NJ: Princeton University Press, 1990); Nattiez speaks of the "poietic" and "esthesic" processes, and of "producer," "trace," and "receiver" (p. 17).

13. See Nicholas Wolterstorff, "The Work of Making a Work of Music," in *What Is Music? An Introduction to the Philosophy of Music,* ed. P. J. Alperson (University Park: Pennsylvania State University Press, 1987), pp. 109-12 for detailed discussion of the concept of "social practices," following Alasdair MacIntyre.

14. For a helpful survey of shifts in musicology toward seeing music chiefly as a human activity embedded in society and culture, see C. Michael Hawn, *Gather into One: Praying and Singing Globally* (Grand Rapids: Eerdmans, 2003), pp. 21-30.

music can exist in an a-temporal, "other-worldly" sphere, divorced from the strong and messy currents of human designs and interests. (This has been the predominant concern of the so-called "New Musicology," a largely Anglo-American movement emerging in the mid-1980s.)[15] However, problems arise if it is suggested that music can be *exhaustively* accounted for in these terms. We can lose sight of the fact that the temporally organized sound-patterns of music have their own distinct integrity and are not infinitely variable in their potential effects. They interact with features of our bodily make-up that are universally shared. It is one thing to say that music-making and music-hearing are humanly shaped, socially conditioned activities, intertwined with matrices of human relations and intentions; it is quite another to say that their significance for us is explicable solely in such terms.

An approach that is both *multidisciplinary* and *multileveled* is to be preferred — a "thick description" — and this volume is a modest contribution toward this end. An anti-reductionist reading of music will be *multidisciplinary* in that it recognizes that the multifaceted nature of "music" requires a variety of perspectives to do it justice. There are the disciplines of theoretical reflection that immediately surround music — musicology, in other words, which includes historical musicology (the history of music), music theory and analysis (of texts), ethnomusicology (the anthropology of music), performance practice and research, and acoustics (the science of sound and hearing). These disciplines, all of which are deployed to some extent in this book, employ their own *discourses*.[16] Further, there will be other, less proximate disciplines — such as physiology, psychology, sociology, aesthetics, semiotics, film studies, cultural studies, and so forth — that may also prove relevant. In fact, in the last twenty years or so, a wide variety of strategies, tools, and methodologies for the study of music has emerged, together with a sense that such variety is to be welcomed.[17]

Closely related to this, a thick description of music will be *multileveled.*

15. See, e.g., Joseph Kerman, *Contemplating Music: Challenges to Musicology* (Cambridge, MA: Harvard University Press, 1985); L. Kramer, *Classical Music and Postmodern Knowledge* (Berkeley: University of California Press, 1995); Alastair Williams, *Constructing Musicology* (Aldershot: Ashgate, 2001); Pieter C. Van den Toorn, *Music, Politics, and the Academy* (Berkeley: University of California Press, 1995).

16. We should perhaps note that the disciplines and discourses, though they reflect on musical practices, are *themselves* practices, and have themselves become the object of disciplines and discourses.

17. Nicholas Cook and Mark Everest, "Preface," in *Rethinking Music*, ed. Nicholas Cook and Mark Everest (Oxford: Oxford University Press, 1999), pp. xi-xii.

Musical practices, like any cultural reality, require explanations at different levels of complexity. When a violinist performs a concerto, we can describe what happens in terms of neurophysiology, but also in terms of the intentions of the performer, the society she lives in, the cultural values associated with the style, and so on. We can view this in terms of levels of ever wider explanation, each level drawing upon levels below it and opening up to higher levels.[18]

The essayists in this volume assume (and in some cases argue) that theology, with the levels of description it offers, has a legitimate place at the musicological round table without compromising the integrity of the particular responsibilities required by its truth-claims. The ultimate purposes and grounding of musical endeavor can hardly be dismissed as a non-question, nor theology be written off when it attempts to supply the beginnings of an answer. Indeed, numerous writers have contended that particular features of music-making and hearing, and the sound-patterns they involve, are able, even when no such intent is present, to intimate or gesture toward that infinite life which generates, upholds, and redeems all things, the life of the triune God made known in Jesus Christ. In fact, even in the arena of musicology, a sense of the "openness" of all levels of explanation to the theological can emerge quite naturally. Recently, two distinguished musicologists, reviewing a huge range of writing in their field, observed that in much of it we can discern the

> same underlying concerns: what are we doing when we analyse or contextualise music, and why are we doing it? What kind of truth can analysis or historical musicology reveal, and how might it relate to other kinds of truth about music? Should we be speaking of truth at all? Or does the act of engaging in analysis or the writing of history lock us into a predetermined epistemological stance?[19]

The status of truth-claims — whether viewed in terms of epistemology or otherwise — while traditionally an issue of concern among (at least

18. A much-discussed and highly fruitful way of regarding scientific inquiry is to see it as involving a conception of (a) reality as "stratified," as a "universe of levels," each operating under the influence of the levels above, and (b) explanation as similarly stratified, each level "knowing its limits" and opening up to the levels above. See Roy Bhaskar, *Scientific Realism and Human Emancipation* (London: Verso Press, 1986), p. 253; Michael Polanyi, *The Tacit Dimension* (New York: Doubleday, 1966), pp. 29-32, 37.

19. Cook and Everest, "Preface," p. xi.

some) philosophers, is one in which theologians are bound to have an interest and with which they can engage fruitfully, given the Christian commitment to the "givenness" of a material order which precedes all knowing, and to a Creator who graciously intends interactive relations of knowing with that order.

Theology in Action

What, then, of theology? In our discussions, we have made no attempt to settle on a definition that would command unanimous agreement. We come from a wide variety of traditions and viewpoints, and the major Christian figures discussed in the chapters do not share a single theology. On the other hand, it is fair to say we adopt as normative the broad perspective of Christian trinitarian orthodoxy, grounded in Scripture and classically expressed in the church's ecumenical creeds. At its heart, this entails being oriented toward, and being invited to share in, the gracious self-communication of the God of Jesus Christ. It finds its focus in the gospel — the announcement that in the life, death, and resurrection of Jesus, the triune Creator, the God of Israel, has acted decisively to reconcile the world to himself. The gospel finds its outworking in a reconciled people gathered by the Holy Spirit to share God's life and make known what God has done in Christ, a people of worship and mission, called to live in and for the sake of the world as a foretaste of the world to come. This gospel is testified to and mediated first and foremost through the Scriptures, writings that are themselves the outcome of God's reconciling work. Christian theology can thus be understood as the disciplined thinking and rethinking of this gospel, and as such, one dimension of the intellectual participation in the divine life that God has made possible.

Theology for Music

We seek to demonstrate the fruitfulness of theology for music, and vice versa. As far as the former is concerned — "what can theology do for music?" — all of the chapters in one way or another attempt to show ways in which the thinking and rethinking of the gospel can enable a richer description and deeper understanding of music. Two broad forms of this can be distinguished. (a) We may take *particular instances of music-making, music-*

hearing, and musical texts, and view them in the light of some aspect or aspects of the Christian proclamation. So, for example, when music has been made or heard with conscious theological intentions, theology can clarify the substance of those interests — as when Carol Harrison shows how Augustine interprets music in the light of the soul's return to God, or Robert Sholl explains the way in which Olivier Messiaen mines rich seams in Roman Catholic thought. These interests can be determined by a number of factors, such as sacred words (Richard Plantinga on Bach's Cantatas, Robert Sholl on Messiaen's *St. François d'Assise*) or the context of worship (Michael Hawn on the songs of South Africa). And even without such explicit theological concerns, certain musical practices and texts can be shown to benefit from close theological scrutiny (Daniel Chua's reading of musical developments in early modernity). (b) A second form of "theology for music" pays attention not so much to this or that instance of music as *to the processes of music-making and music-hearing in general, and to types of musical texts,* examining them from a theological perspective. (From the vantage point of the doctrine of creation, John Paul Ito inquires about the extent to which music can be said to have its roots in mathematical order; in the light of a theology of church unity, Steven Guthrie examines the practice of corporate singing.)

Music for Theology

But we can move in the other direction also. While still being firmly oriented to the same determinative reality, attentive above all to the reconciling self-revelation of God in Jesus Christ — we can ask: what can music bring to theology? (Indeed, in many of the essays, the traffic runs both ways.) When it comes to enriching theology, it is arguable that theologians in the West have been impoverished by restricting themselves to a fairly narrow range of conversation partners. Most notably, they have pursued a long and complex conversation with Western philosophy, and with great profit (though there are signs that natural science now occupies prime place in this respect). The essayists here believe that the world of music holds out considerable promise for theology today, by offering distinctive modes of apprehending, perceiving, and understanding its primary subject-matter (the gospel of the triune God), and — in that light — distinctive ways of "reading" the church's practices (such as worship and mission), and the wider world in which these practices are set.

Again, two major forms of this enterprise may be distinguished. (a) We may attend to *particular instances of music-making, music-hearing, and musical texts*. This may mean dealing with music with explicitly theological import. (Richard Plantinga shows how Bach's word-setting illuminates a Christian approach to death; Robert Sholl charts Messiaen's musical explication of human transformation in Christ.) Alternatively, much can be gained from music that does not carry explicitly theological agendas. (The appropriation of Mozart's works by Karl Barth is a case in point — discussed by David Moseley — as is the drawing on twentieth-century music for exploring eschatology, discussed by Hart, Monti, and Borthwick.) This approach may be undertaken with a theological interpretation of broad cultural movements in view, when music becomes a lens through which we read culture more broadly. (Catherine Pickstock and Robert Sholl view Messiaen as illuminating theological currents in modernist and postmodernist culture; Daniel Chua shows the way in which musical developments in the early modern period expose theologically resonant cultural shifts and transformations.) (b) Alternatively, we can concentrate on features of *the processes of music-making and music-hearing in general, and types of musical texts*. (Bruce Benson investigates musical improvisation as a model for biblical interpretation; Jeremy Begbie explains how the dynamics of emotion in musical experience can provide ways of uncovering and reimagining elements of a theology of Christian worship.)

Whether we are pursuing theology for music or music for theology, we aim to show that music might become a "resonant witness": bearing testimony to the richness and implications of the Christian gospel through a range of resonances with it. The theologian, with his or her well-tried languages, can release resonances, natural frequencies in the gospel to the benefit of the musician (theology for music); and the musician can release resonant responses, perhaps otherwise unhearable, to the benefit of the theologian (music for theology).

A Double Hazard

Like any conversation, ours is not risk-free. In particular, we have sought to be alert to two hazards that lie in wait for those working at the interface of theology and music — indeed, any of the arts. On the one side lies *theological instrumentalism*. Here music is treated as essentially, or no more than, a vehicle, a mere tool or instrument at the behest of theology. So, for example, the theologian will anachronistically read into this or that music all sorts of theological "meanings" or "messages" that serve the demands of some pre-given scheme of belief. Or, it will be insisted that all theologically legitimate music ought to direct our attention to "theological truths" whose proper mode of expression and communication is propositional (e.g., summative statements from Scripture ["God so loved . . ."], or the dogma of Christian orthodoxy). Indeed, it is sometimes assumed that the best that music can do for theology is provide an attractive gloss for such truths, secondary and colorful wrapping that can safely be tossed away once a specific "idea" has been grasped. Whether we speak of theology enriching music or music enriching theology, the danger is that the integrity, distinctiveness, and particularities of music will be stifled and distorted as they are made subservient to the requirements of an over-bearing theology.

The anxiety about instrumentalism often leads to a swing in the opposite direction, *theological aestheticism.* Here the overriding concern is with the "autonomy" of music. We are told that we must allow music to "speak for itself," meet it "on its own terms," without the potentially cramping effects of theological pre-understandings. This concern can take several forms. Some will see any kind of engagement with theology as detrimental to music, except when the theologian operates in a purely descriptive mode: for example, by helping us understand how a piece of church music of the past was theologically informed. Others are keen to integrate music and theology but want music to play a semi-independent role in relation to theology, to some extent conditioning the norms derived from Scripture and its testimony to God's self-revelation. This can be extended much further: as when music is presumed by its very nature to offer veridical access to the divine, providing a normative platform to relativize and critique other theological claims. History is not short of examples of music over-determining theology: among the most extreme versions, the Romantics' exaltation of music to quasi-religious status; among the subtler types, when the immense psychological power of music is taken to be evidence of its "spirituality" (i.e., its religiously loaded character) and theological claims developed accordingly.

We have attempted to steer clear of both these hazards. This depends on acknowledging that Christian theology is called to a distinct *orientation* as it engages with practices such as music — to the gospel, the dramatic movement of God by which he reconciles us to himself by the Spirit through the Son, witnessed to and mediated normatively by Scripture. This orientation need not ride roughshod over the particularities of music. Indeed, it should help us avoid instrumentalism. Just to the extent that it is oriented to a God who is dedicated to the flourishing of creation in its own order (the order out of which music is made), and to the flourishing of human cultural activities such as music, theology (properly practiced) will not suppress but *enable* a faithful honoring of music's integrities. We will be enjoined to take due regard of its distinguishing modes of communication, its distinctive engagement with the human body, the particular ways it intertwines with culture at large, and so forth. We will recognize that music is capable of being far more than a "varnish" on propositions, that it is undeniably "meaningful" yet not reducible to, for example, assertoric prose.

At the same time, aestheticism will be eschewed. For if it is properly oriented, theology's "pressure of interpretation" will come from the decisive self-communication of God in the history of Israel culminating in Jesus Christ. It cannot simultaneously come from a norm immanent to musical activity — nor indeed to a generic conception of religion or spirituality, or a foundational metaphysics or ontology elaborated prior to, or apart from, the specific dealings of the Christian God with the world. Thus, while we are keen in this volume to honor the integrity of music, we are not suggesting that music can provide its own independent measures of theological truth. When we speak of "music for theology," we do not mean to imply a relativizing of the normativity of scriptural texts or of the discourses of faith consonant with Scripture; rather we intend to allow music, in its own distinctive ways, to access the dynamic momentum of the gospel, of which these texts and discourses speak and in which they are caught up.

*   *   *

We have grouped the essays into four sections, each section comprising essays that relate to a particular area or field of theological concern.

Music and Cosmos

For centuries in the West, the close connection between music and the cosmos at large was taken for granted. It finds its strongest and most persistent expression in what is sometimes called "the Great Tradition," which ran from the half-legendary figure of Pythagoras, through Plato and into the church, and in one form or another pervaded the entire medieval era. While certainly not eclipsing all other traditions, and certainly not monolithic and continuous, it proved enormously influential. (A modern variation can be seen in J. R. R. Tolkien's *The Silmarillion,* which opens with a spectacular scenario of creation theology elaborated in musical metaphors.)

As it appears in Christian antiquity and medieval thought, the central notion is that musical sound, especially musical harmony, coincides with and gives expression to cosmic order, which in turn reflects and in some manner affords access to the Creator. **Carol Harrison** offers an account of one of this tradition's most illustrious representatives, Augustine (354-430). In his day, *musica* (as one of the "liberal arts") was first and foremost an intellectual discipline concerned with the measured relations between sounds (especially the sounds of poetic words), and as such was seen as far superior to the practicalities of singing and playing, which were commonly regarded as something of a distraction. It was one of Augustine's great achievements to appropriate and transform these long-standing views within a Christian framework, and in a manner that was to have a huge influence on succeeding centuries. Music enabled one to study the relations pervading God's creation, relations which have their source and supporting ground in the eternal God, who *is* music. The discernment of music can serve the ascent of the fallen soul toward God, from the temporal to the eternal, from the corporeal to the incorporeal, restoring the soul's lost harmony with God, who himself embodies the supreme, perfect, eternal, immutable music. Harrison defends Augustine against over-played charges of Platonism: his considerable stress on rational judgment, the subjection of the body, and his downplaying of the temporal and changeable need to be seen in relation to his overriding conviction that nothing created should be treated as an end in itself (the persistent tendency of fallen humans) but always referred to its origin in God. The world's harmony, unity, equality, and order are to be loved "toward" God, who himself is perfect harmony, unity, equality, and order. So when it comes to what we would today understand as "music" — music as sung and played — Augustine is understandably ambivalent: though beautiful, it is nonetheless only capable of being a temporal manifestation, imitation, or image of eternal beauty, order, harmony, or unity, and is of lasting value only insofar as, by God's grace, it serves to reorient us to him.

Whether or not Augustine gives adequate weight to the physically embodied, inherent beauty of creation (and thus music) is a much-debated matter. In any case, the nature of materiality and its relation to broader cosmological, metaphysical, and theological perceptions is the field opened up by **Nancy van Deusen** in her treatment of Philip the Chancellor (c. 1160-1236), the French theologian, poet, and (probably) composer. Philip's concern to coordinate biblically grounded teaching with Aristotelian learning generated philosophical writings that even today are regarded as highly complex. But what emerges clearly in van Deusen's essay is the key role that music plays in exemplifying and embodying his somewhat rarefied conceptual reflections. Widening her discussion, van Deusen comments that music in this period "constitutes a ministry discipline, making abstractions sensorially perceptible, making general principles plain, and thereby reinforcing the validity of unseen substantial reality."

Whatever its glories, the cosmic vision of the Great Tradition suffered serious criticism with the emergence of the modern era. For a variety of reasons, thinking about music in modernity has been marked by a shift from the cosmological to the anthropological, from justifying music in terms of creation at large to justifying it primarily in terms of human needs and aspirations — something that is simply taken for granted by most writers today. In sixteenth- and seventeenth-century Europe, some of the liveliest controversies about music were related to this shift. Loosened from its cosmic anchoring, music was frequently given validity by being tied to the order of words (by being linked to texts, for example, or by being shown to operate in language-like ways). The resulting tensions between the musical and verbal are brought out by **Joyce Irwin**, as she traces debates within early German Lutheranism concerning music's relation to the Word of God in preaching. It was widely believed that music had its own particular capacities to prepare the heart to receive the Word and instill it in the hearts of believers, special stress being placed on music's emotional potency. Some pushed this line further, arguing not only that music's powers are grounded in our physiological make-up, but that music can give voice to the order of the cosmos at large (as in the Great Tradition), bearing its own witness to creation's beauty and harmony — and, indeed, to the triune harmony of the Creator. This doubtless extended some of Luther's basic convictions (albeit in ways that would not always have convinced Luther himself). But it inevitably raised pointed issues about the indispensability of preaching and the space that should be allowed to instrumental music. Many felt bound to insist that whatever music's distinctive powers may be, it should never be cut loose from the theological constraint provided in revelation, manifest in the written and preached Word of God.

The underlying tension here is that between a view of music as achieving its meaning by virtue of its connections with the "givens" of creation on the one hand, and through humanly constructed and controlled activity on the other. Composing within the Lutheran stream, but after the debates

Irwin discusses, was J. S. Bach (1685-1750), whose music, according to **Jeremy Begbie**, can provide a striking testimony to music *both* as an honoring and exploration of creation's rich and variegated order *and* as a thoroughly arduous, human activity of construction — the latter by no means undermining the former. Begbie argues that some of Bach's output can afford a theological (trinitarian) perception and understanding of created beauty, in the sense both of the beauty directly given to the world by God and of the beauty that we are invited to fashion as God's creatures. Examining some of the ways in which this composer typically operates, a vision of beauty opens up that is highly consonant with a view of creation as the work of the triune God of Jesus Christ. If Bach does elicit cosmic beauty, Begbie argues, he is doing so by means of an active and arduous process of shaping and reshaping musical material. Thus musical composition need not be regarded as an activity inherently in competition with the affirmation of a beauty granted to the world by the Creator (as has so often been assumed in modernity). Rather, artistic creativity can be seen as a God-given means whereby something of creation's beauty can be brought to light precisely *in* and *through* the kind of strenuous formation and re-formation exemplified in Bach's music.

The potential "earthing" of music in the God-given arrangement of things is approached from a rather different angle by mathematician and musician **John Paul Ito**. As we have noted, the Pythagorean tradition came under considerable attack in early modernity. Ito believes that to a significant degree such censure was justified, but he cautions against dismissing Pythagoreanism too quickly. In fact, there is much that withstands critique — not least with respect to accounting for some aspects of musical experience; for example, our perception of consonance and dissonance and certain rhythmic configurations. Drawing upon contemporary "realist" theories of mathematics, Ito argues that the universe is characterized by an order that is at root mathematical, an order that humans seem to be constituted to apprehend and articulate. For the Christian, this can be read as witnessing to (though not proving) an ordering, purposeful Creator — with respect to both the creation of the world at large and the creation of human beings to interact fruitfully with their environment. Ito points to evidence suggesting there are innate, trans-cultural mathematical tendencies at work in the perception and production of music, regardless of musical training, even if such tendencies are realized in different ways in different cultures. Insofar as some aspects of musical experience can be shown to be mathematically grounded in this way, music can be regarded as partaking of fundamental dimensions of cosmic order (human and non-human) and thus as reflecting in its own way the ordering activity of the Creator. However, this does not lead to the reductionist claim that making and hearing music can be explained entirely in mathematical terms. Indeed, it would seem that humans are "hard-wired" for both mathematical order and deviations from that order, and that a large part of what we value in music is the interplay between the two — the given constraint and the results of "playing with" the constraint. Mathematical order, then, far from stifling creativity and human flourishing, provides the potential for it. This is part of our calling as God's creatures: in Ito's words, to respond to nature "with forms of creativity, agency, freedom, and love that echo those with which it was given."

Music and Culture

If there are good reasons to speak of music as embedded in realities that we did not construct, this need not lead us to overlook or downplay the extent to which it is also embedded in human culture. (There is every reason to reject the frequent opposition of "nature" and "nurture" that appears in some current debates about music.) Kevin Vanhoozer has spoken of culture as comprising "texts" and "worlds" of meaning — "texts" (a term we have already used) referring to the products of intentional human action, and "worlds" to the meaningful environments created by texts in which we dwell physically and imaginatively. Understood as such, a culture is a "lived worldview," a way of "being in the world."[20] Music-making and -hearing, together with musical texts (whether by intention or default), will communicate or reflect something of such "worlds" of meaning — values, concerns, and self-understandings that inform our "being in the world."

The story of the culture of Western modernity, and the theological dimensions of that story, has been told from a variety of perspectives, and with enormous erudition and subtlety. But it is fair to say that in the process, some perceptions have been uniquely privileged to the neglect of others: in particular, the history of philosophy and the history of science, intertwined with historical theology. Music, we submit, is capable of bearing its own distinctive witness to the development of the "worlds of meaning" that have formed mo-

---

20. Kevin J. Vanhoozer, "What Is Everyday Theology? How and Why Christians Should Read Culture," in *Everyday Theology: How to Read Cultural Texts and Interpret Trends*, ed. Kevin J. Vanhoozer et al. (Grand Rapids, MI: Baker Academic, 2007), pp. 26-27.

dernity, and, not least, to their theological import. Indeed, **Daniel Chua**, while keen to avoid certain models of music as theology's "mouthpiece," nevertheless argues that at least some music and some musical discourse has embodied in potent ways both modernity's ambitions and its futilities, and that music might thus be heard as a kind of "secular theology." He takes his cue from the sixteenth-century radical questioning of the "enchanted" universe of medieval tradition, and the subsequent emergence of an over-rationalized, technocratic account of humanity's attitude toward a natural world of mere "facts," from which God is marginalized to the point of exclusion. In early modernity, the rhetorical will of the human ego assumes center stage, and bifurcations open up between vocal music (the voice of humanity) and instrumental music, between will and reason, melody and harmony. With the Romantics, having lost its moorings in finite nature, music regains its cosmic significance but via the composer, the individual creative genius who works "out from inside" to produce "a new creation from nothing" (Schlegel). Music's validity is re-grounded in the universe's harmony (a modernized "music of the spheres"), and instrumental music is exalted as supreme, but this is a harmony that comes to expression supremely in the yearnings and strivings of the human ego, itself a microcosm of the transcendental ego of the cosmos. Such was one response to the deeply felt alienations of modernity between humans and their physical environment, between value and fact, freedom and necessity: music transmutes into a quasi-religion, with a mission to heal the dichotomies and aporias of its age. In contrast to this "divine displacement," in his closing reflections, Chua points the way to a vision of music set within a cosmos brought into being through trinitarian love, and thus to the possibility of a discourse about music that is marked by the language of difference rather than division, relation rather than alienation.

Moving to the twentieth century, there must be few composers as instructive as the Frenchman Olivier Messiaen (1908-1992) for exploring the ways cultural texts can elucidate "worlds of meaning" that are theologically charged, not least because he does nothing to conceal his theological commitments. Widely regarded as one of the most important voices in European music of the last hundred years, he sought to integrate a passionately held Roman Catholic faith with techniques from a modernist musical toolbox that were steeped in secular (and often negative) associations. **Robert Sholl** explores the subtlety and depth of this integration. Messiaen did not abstract himself from his surroundings. He engaged directly with some of the major movements of twentieth-century modernity and drew on many of the musical devices in which these concerns had been commonly tackled and articulated. And yet, as Sholl shows, we are presented with a theological transformation of modernity's aporias, achieved (to a significant extent) through reconfiguring and re-contextualizing modernist techniques. Messiaen clearly hoped that such a "refreshment" of modernism could serve as a vehicle through which God might graciously lure us back to himself. In this light, Sholl offers a detailed study of Messiaen's late and vast work, *St. François d'Assise*, arguing that this opera was intended to make possible not so much a *depiction* of the Christ-centered transformation at its center as a *participation* in that transformation. Taken seriously, such music will shock us. But this is not the negative shock of so much twentieth-century art, leaving a bitter hollowness in its wake; rather, it is a "positive shock," the shock of grace "breaking through" from beyond to "embrace humanity," the shock that can only be delivered by the God who is at work to make all things new.

Catherine Pickstock presses the theological-cultural examination of Messiaen further, but from a somewhat different angle and in a way that carries the discussion into "postmodernism." She notes that modernism in music may have largely shunned formal religion, yet at the same time it has rejected crude and depthless secularism, and this has led in some cases to music becoming a "substitute for religion" (Wagner) or at least a vehicle of sentiments that lean toward the religious (e.g., Vaughan Williams, Howells, Britten, Tippett, Maxwell Davies). Pickstock explicates what she sees as the close relation between religion and modernist music through the notions of sacrifice and tempo: music is perhaps the most central modernist art form, she argues, in that "It is best able to express self-abandonment to immanent mystery, and to a time that is more fundamental than the time which we can measure." Messiaen found features of certain modernist procedures to be vehicles well suited to his theological purposes, albeit features needing significant modifications. For example, like many modernists, he gestures strongly toward immeasurable time — the time of pure, "perpetual variation." Yet while other modernists "tended to gesture toward the impossibility of pure heterogeneity," for Messiaen it was mediated through regular, repetitive patterns. In this way, "surprising variations on [repeated patterns] could then point toward the Triune God in whom variation is absolute and yet self-identical."

Nevertheless, Pickstock argues that in certain respects Messiaen remained rather too constrained by modernism — in particular, he did not engage in reflection on history in a narrative mode. Seeking to do more justice to the contingencies of history, Pickstock gestures toward what she sees as a more fruitful "postmodern music," which would more fully "integrate the cosmic and the human, the spatially expansive with the narratively tem-

poral, and the tonal and the repeated with dissonance and continuous variation." Such music would be "more humanistic, historicist, and political than
the modern," yet still religious, not nihilistic (against much of the current
"postmodern"). And here she points to the works of Alfred Schnittke, Galina
Ustvolskaya, Sophia Gubaidulina, and James MacMillan. Such music claws
its way into suffering, exposing the abysmal depth of evil, yet embodies the
"arrival of musical grace." We live, she believes, in "an era of musical hope."

Music and Theology

The next group of essays takes a less cultural turn, exploring the potential
impact of music on some of theology's more immediate subject-matter and
methods. **Richard Plantinga** presents an account of J. S. Bach's musical-
theological treatment of death. Examining key works, including the remarkable *Actus Tragicus* (Cantata 106), Plantinga discerns an essentially Lutheran,
Christologically centered conception of death, articulated not only through
texts but also by means of a huge range of musical devices. He sets this
within a broader argument about the importance of theology to Bach. A
careful course is steered between, on the one hand, the now discredited view
of Bach as a person of quite exceptional and exemplary piety, for whom music was a mere tool of faith, and on the other hand, the view of Bach as a professional composer captive to opportunistic pragmatism, with little, if any,
theological interests. Plantinga contends that although Bach was first and
foremost a musician, his theological awareness and motivation were strong
and profound, and that there is ample evidence in his music of a serious intellectual engagement with biblically grounded theological themes. Not only
did theology inform the music, but the music "allowed him — and allows us
— to undertake fresh and sustained exploration of theological themes."

If Bach was a theological musician, then Karl Barth (1886-1968) and
Dietrich Bonhoeffer (1906-1945), two giants of twentieth-century thought,
were undoubtedly musical theologians. Whatever their differences, according
to **David Moseley**, both shared a common concern to orient theology rigorously toward the self-witness of God in Jesus of Nazareth, and to understand
humanity's status in the light of that self-witness. Within this orientation,
music — a passion they shared — becomes a "responsive form of 'witness'
that links worldly existence with its ground in God's reconciling self-
revelation in Christ." For Bonhoeffer, especially in his *Letters and Papers from
Prison,* written just prior to his execution, music (not least, polyphony) pro-

vides rich resources for discerning and articulating the nature of an authentically Christian engagement with a culture in which so much "religion" had proven void and impotent. Barth's engagement with music, far from being a form of "natural theology" (the attempt to discern the nature and activity of God apart from God's self-revelation in Jesus Christ as attested in Scripture), is better read as an instance of a "theology of nature" (the attempt to interpret the world in the light of divine self-revelation), one that can take seriously the world's "secularity." The music of Mozart (and Barth's devotion to the Salzburg composer was legendary) became for him a "parable of the Kingdom," a provisional and "secular" phenomenon, called forth by Christ as a means through which he bears witness to himself and his reconciling work. From this musical perspective, Moseley draws out a number of striking resonances between the two theologians. Among other things: neither lapses into an idolatry of music, and neither confuses "gospel" and "parable," or revelation and secondary witnesses *to* that revelation (such as music).

The distinction between natural theology and a theology of nature (or culture) is also crucial for **Alastair Borthwick**, **Trevor Hart**, and **Anthony Monti**, who invite us to find "eschatological resonances" in modern art music. They do not attempt to discern, apart from faith, the self-evidence of God in the world, but to read a particular dimension of musical culture with the eyes of faith. How might modern music be implicitly congruent with or evocative of the shape of Christian hope, even when the composer has no intention of conveying anything of the sort? With its clear and unambiguous closures, traditional tonality can instructively embody processes of hope and of achieving goals, processes that are integral to Christian faith. And yet, the authors argue, traditional tonality can also carry considerable drawbacks, not least "immanentism" (presuming the world to contain within itself the power to generate a future hope) and the suggestion that "closure" implies cessation, a "wrapping up" of everything such that there is no room for novelty, no ongoing flourishing. They suggest that some of Gustav Mahler's music, for example, embodies "non-cadential gestures of closure" that are rather more appropriate for conveying a sense of a "temporality with an open future," the kind of time that will, arguably, be appropriate to the final consummation, when all things (including time) will be renewed: "not a world where we finally 'arrive' and all loose ends are tied, but instead . . . one of infinite progression into the unfathomable mystery of God." In some of Michael Tippett's music, devices that might initially be heard as the rejection of teleology (purposive, forward-moving music) and closure (the reaching of goals) often turn out to be subtle re-conceptions of them. Such devices can serve to model, and help us comprehend more fully, the relationship between our present historical time and the time of the new creation.

The concern for a proper sense of "openness" links up with a discussion of improvisation by **Bruce Ellis Benson**. He argues that, properly understood and appropriately qualified, improvisation provides a fruitful and illuminating way of conceiving hermeneutics, the art of interpretation — and he has in view the interpretation of Scripture in particular. Scores are always imprecise; they are both "underdetermined," and "overdetermined" — they do not provide you with every detail for performance, and what they *do* specify provides *more* possibilities than could be realized in simply *one* interpretation. Thus the interpretation of a text always involves improvisation: it "says" both more and less than the original text. Benson demonstrates that both jazz and Christian texts take shape through improvisation and that subsequent interpretation of them is itself improvisational. However hesitant we might be in admitting it, in the church's interpretation of Scripture improvisation is simply unavoidable. And there is no reason to exclude the agency of God in this; indeed, Benson holds that the Spirit is active in both the improvisational writing and the improvisational interpretation of the texts by the Christian community. In the process, not only do multiple interpretations of texts arise ("polyphony"), but also differing and even conflicting ones ("heterophony"), the dissonance often being highly productive. However, as Benson points out, this improvisatory dynamic cannot be shapeless or infinitely pluriform, its polyphony and heterophony boundless. For ultimately it bears witness to, and is supported and guided by, a *cantus firmus* — supremely the self-revelation of God by way of the Scriptures, climaxing in Jesus Christ. Moreover, its dissonance cannot be final, but will give way to authentic *shalom*, a harmony of difference.

Music and Worship

It is in worship that people are most likely to encounter the intertwining of music and theology, and this forms the focus of our fourth section. Undoubtedly, many of the controversies about music in worship today revolve around music's emotional powers. **Jeremy Begbie** explores this area by asking two questions: What is it about musical sounds and the way they operate such that they become emotionally significant and valuable to us? And what can we learn from this theologically, with regard to music in worship? After offering some general comments about emotion, and setting these in the context of a trinitarian theology of worship, he goes on to argue that musical sounds become emotionally significant to us (at least in part) because they are processed by the same neurological systems as bodily behavior characteristic of emotions, and they become emotionally valuable because music can concentrate our emotional engagement with emotional objects, this dynamic being one of representation (in which music "speaks for us") and one of emotional education. This has remarkable resonances with the dynamics of trinitarian worship, whereby our emotional lives, having been representatively healed in Jesus Christ, are now "concentrated" — purified, compressed, and specified; in short, renewed through the ministry of Christ, the risen High Priest. The upshot is that music is seen to have singularly appropriate capacities for Spirit-driven emotional renewal in worship. More than that, not only does theology illuminate music, but music illuminates theology, in this case, the theology of worship. Indeed, the dynamic of representative concentration that Begbie delineates applies not only to our emotions but to every part of worship offered "through Jesus Christ our Lord."

Intensity of emotional involvement is a striking feature of the work of Hildegard of Bingen (1098-1179), a medieval composer and theologian of extraordinary depth whose music for communities of women in religious orders has attracted much attention in recent years. **Margot Fassler** explores the way Hildegard pursued a distinctively "female voice" for rendering praise to God. In particular, she demonstrates the subtlety and intricacy of Hildegard's multilayered engagement with Scripture, focusing here on the Song of Songs (which fascinated numerous medieval luminaries) and the book of Revelation. Some modern readers will doubtless want to ask questions about the composer's relatively free combination of metaphor systems and the extensive incorporation of erotic language and imagery into her vision of the divine-human relation. But there can be little doubt that in the striking juxtaposition of texts, in the subtle interplay of Scripture and liturgy, and in the music itself (which frequently extended the boundaries of what was commonplace in her day), we witness an immensely fertile mind at work, and one for whom theology and music were intimately intertwined.

The last three essays probe further what it means for a worshiping community to turn to song in the presence of the triune God. **Steven Guthrie** proposes that singing can make its own distinctive contribution to the growth of wisdom and understanding, and thus challenges the all too common relegation of music to the realm of emotional stimulation alone. Through exegesis of a key passage in Ephesians 5 (and its parallel in Colossians) he urges that singing in worship enacts the differentiated, free, and responsive unity of the church, and in this way, by the Spirit, deepens the church's wisdom and understanding. Further, deliberate and discursive reflection on the act of singing (of the sort undertaken in Guthrie's essay) can work to the same end: music provides not only "participatory knowledge" of church unity, but also conceptual resources that allow us to appreciate and articulate it more fully.

Bonhoeffer, in the midst of the Nazis' rise to power, famously said, "Only he who cries out for the Jews may sing the Gregorian chants."[21] Worship that has lost its public, social, and political conscience is not worthy of the name. With this in mind, **Michael Hawn** urges that we regard corporate singing amid an oppressive regime as potentially an act of resistance, indeed, as an intimation of hope for that final freedom of the new heaven and earth which sustains all Christian worship. He turns his attention to African freedom songs (and their precursors), tracing their formation, development, and adaptation in different contexts. He notes how they have been taken up in worship worldwide, thus providing "conditions for exchange" between radically different cultures, and enabling a type of encounter in which one society is opened up to the deeply held convictions and struggles of another. Music plays a key role here, facilitating direct and rapid communication: the songs are quickly learned, accessible, and easily harmonized. Corporate song can thus engender a deeper sense of belonging to one diverse and globally extended family of God. Not least, we are likely to become far more socially and politically attentive, not only with respect to other nations but also to our own.

At the center of the church's worship gatherings stands Jesus Christ, leading the congregation in song (Heb. 2:12). **Michael O'Connor** considers what can be gleaned about the singing of Jesus during his earthly life, as risen and ascended high priest, and as the last Adam of the new heaven and earth. He uncovers a wealth of material, references, and allusions in a wide variety of traditions and genres that illuminate and expand on what might seem at first to be a relatively thin and unpromising topic. His essay links up closely with Begbie's earlier one on emotion: both stress that our worship (and thus singing) is a participation, by grace, in the worship and song of the exalted human, Jesus Christ. It is also fitting that O'Connor closes the collection by linking the old and new creations, drawing out the cosmological significance of song, thus bringing us full circle to the theme of the opening essays.

21. Dietrich Bonhoeffer, as quoted in Eberhard Bethge, *Dietrich Bonhoeffer: Man of Vision, Man of Courage* (New York: Harper & Row, 1970), p. 512.

PART ONE MUSIC AND COSMOS

1. Augustine and the Art of Music

Carol Harrison

The Liberal Art of Music

In classical and late antique culture, music was generally understood not in terms of something composed, practiced, played, or performed, but as a mathematical discipline that was concerned with identifying, categorizing, and creating measured relations between sounds — usually the written or spoken sound of words in poetic rhythm, meter, and verse. Alongside the other mathematical-type disciplines of arithmetic, geometry, and astronomy, and the literary disciplines of grammar, rhetoric, and dialectic, music formed part of the "core curriculum" of the seven liberal arts: those disciplines which effectively formed a common culture shared by the governing elite of educated, free citizens among whom they were studied.

Of course, music as we would now commonly understand it did exist and was practiced, though we know very little about its precise form. Wind instruments such as pipes and horns; stringed instruments such as the lyre; percussion instruments such as the cymbals and drum — all of these were played, most often in a context associated with pagan cult, the theater, dinner parties, or brothels. In churches, vocal music, or more precisely, a type of simple, one-line chant, was increasingly used to recite the Psalms, although there is no evidence of instrumental music being used in a Christian context: it was most likely simply too tainted by its pagan associations. Instrumental or vocal music was, however, quite separate and distinct from the liberal discipline of music: the former was merely a craft or technical skill, working by imitation, in bodily, temporal, mutable media; the latter, on the other hand, was a rational discipline that studied the laws of spiritual, eternal, immutable measure and relation. The former was therefore merely an inferior distraction from the latter — and a potentially dangerous and misleading one at that — hardly worthy of being called "music." Only the latter could form and educate the mind in order to grasp the truth, if one was of a philosophical inclination — or, if one was more worldly minded, could form part of the educational formation that provided a passport to a career as a governor or military commander. Music, then, in its most acceptable, most widely acknowledged, highest, and purest form, was an intellectual discipline to be studied and acquired, much like geometry; it gave one a means of comprehending the eternal relations that govern reality and, more practically, a passport to higher culture and the society and occupations that went with it. No provincial governor, no lawyer, no general would be ignorant of "music," though none would think that accomplished playing of an instrument was something to boast about or really had anything to do with "music" in the proper sense.

Any attempt to consider what Augustine (354-430), or any other Christian author of antiquity, thought of music is therefore to pose a rather different question than one might think one was asking, and to invite somewhat unexpected answers. All Christian authors were, by definition, educated men (unfortunately there aren't any women authors from this period) — they were able to write, to preach, to catechize, to address letters and petitions, and (after Constantine) to act as legal arbitrators. In other words, they had benefited from a classical education: their intellectual, cultural formation was irrevocably that of the liberal arts; they were adept at dialectic or rational argument; they were proficient — sometimes consummate — rhetors; they could analyze and gut a text along with the best grammarians; and they understood the nature of reality in terms of measured relation or "music." All of these liberal arts or "disciplines" were therefore naturally, inevitably, applied to their understanding, exposition, and often defense of their Christian faith. This is not to say that the fathers were unaware of the potential ambiguities and dangers of such a procedure, but the question of how the liberal arts should be used and applied in a Christian context was no more, and no less, than the question of how they themselves understood and articulated their own faith: the liberal arts were not only the intellectual disciplines, but the preconceptions and prior understandings — the mind-set — that they brought to their faith. They could not simply be cast aside like an old or worn-out garment, but had to be carefully weighed, re-evaluated, and refashioned.

This is precisely what we find Augustine doing in his first works as a new Christian convert. The language of these works is that of the schools; the subjects — the happy life, order, the good, skepticism, evil, the soul, and so forth — are philosophical chestnuts. But this should not surprise: he believed, like all the fathers, that Christianity was the true, the ultimate, the consummate philosophy, which had superseded all the classical schools. Like them, it dealt with the nature of reality, the soul, providence, evil, the true, the good, the beautiful, the happy life, the ultimate good. . . . The questions were the same; the language remains very much the same too; but the answers are radically new and are shaped by Christian revelation, tradition, and Scripture. The new ontology, ethics, and aesthetics that emerge in a Christian context — and we see this happening dramatically in Augustine's works — were to be the crucible in which classical culture, and the liberal arts that had formed it, were dramatically transformed. It is in this context — which we must not ignore if Augustine is not to be misunderstood — that we might finally turn to consider Augustine on the art of music.

What place, then, did the liberal art of music have to play in a Christian context? Like the other arts, it certainly could not be ignored by an educated Christian. Just as it had formed the basis for analyzing and evaluating the nature of reality, for appreciating its essential harmony, unity, equality, and order, for generations of free citizens, Augustine obviously felt that it would be similarly appropriate in a Christian context. On a number of occasions in the early works, most notably in *On Order*, Augustine uses an analysis of the liberal arts as a sort of ladder in order to effect — or at least attempt to describe — a gradual ascent to grasp divine truth. Indeed, in a characteristically ambitious manner, as a new Christian convert he entertained the grand scheme of writing a commentary on each of the liberal arts in turn. It is not certain how far this project got, and all that is now extant are the works on dialectic (and possibly grammar) and music.[1] The latter, *On Music*, begun almost immediately after his conversion in 387 and completed around 391, is the most extended and perhaps the most revealing.

At the risk of stating the obvious, it is important to remember that when Augustine set out to write his projected series of works on the liberal arts, including music, he did so, not in the guise of his former profession as a teacher of rhetoric, but as a Christian — a positively enthusiastic and zealously evangelical one. They are evidently not intended simply as intellectual

---

1. The project was abandoned, not so much because Augustine lost interest, but because his clerical duties did not allow the time; see *Letter 101 (Patrologia Latina* 33).

exercises in order to tone his mental muscles, or, indeed as some sort of closely argued demonstration of Christianity's rational respectability. Rather, it is clear from the outset that they are careful attempts to further his understanding of his newly embraced faith, and most especially of how that faith should be lived: they are as much religious, ethical, and mystical works that seek self-knowledge and knowledge of God as exercises of the mind. What we find in *On Music* (in common with the other early works) is, in fact, a rather dramatic reassessment of the role of reason and the liberal arts, in the context of their application to a Christian doctrine of creation, the fall, and the work of God's saving grace, which leads to a rather more positive evaluation of the bodily, temporal, and mutable than one would ever have expected: careful rational analysis is used, rather disconcertingly, to demonstrate the role of faith; the liberal art of music is used, even more disconcertingly, to demonstrate the role of the created, temporal, and mutable (and thereby, perhaps to an extent, music as we would now understand it).

But this is to anticipate. What we find in books 1-5 of *On Music* is exactly what we would expect to find in any classical treatise by an ancient author on the liberal art of music:[2] a minute and painstaking analysis of the properties of number *(numerus)* or music *(musica)* — the two are synonymous — and the way in which it is manifest in measured relation, in rhythmic patterns and intervals, in meter, and in verse. The emphasis is firmly upon the rational quality of music: it is a knowledge *(scientia)* of how to measure and relate numerical properties well *(scientia bene modulandi)* — in other words, in a fitting, harmonious, unified manner that observes the inherent order of reality in all its aspects (1.2.2). The element of "fittingness," which the word *bene* suggests here, draws attention to the important fact that the liberal art of music was never "just" a matter of knowledge or *scientia* but, like all the liberal arts, had always been understood as an articulation of the nature of reality and, as such, a way of expressing not just quantitative judgments about — in this case — the nature of number, but also qualitative ones about the truth that number embodies and its ethical and aesthetic aspects.

The inextricable interrelation of the true, the good, and the beautiful was a presupposition of the liberal disciplines that was certainly not lost on Augustine, and in the final book, book 6, its implications are worked out in

---

2. In fact, *De Musica* tackles only one part of the classical treatment of music — rhythm. Augustine tells us he intended to write another work, on the other major aspect, harmony *(De melo)*, but his obligations as a bishop made it impossible (*Letter* 101 [*Patrologia Latina* 33]).

what virtually amounts to a small *summa* of Christian doctrine. The basic, but revolutionary, insight is that God *is* music: he *is* supreme measure, number, relation, harmony, unity, and equality. When he created matter from nothing he simultaneously gave it existence by giving it music, or form — in other words measure, number, relation, harmony, unity, equality. . . .

Thus, the whole of created reality exists because of its possession of music. It remains in existence, however, only by acknowledging its complete and absolute dependence upon its Creator, by understanding itself and all that is as existing only *in relation* to its Creator. Thus all that we are, all manifestations and embodiments of music, are from God and, in so far as we humbly, obediently, and lovingly turn toward him and acknowledge him as their source, they to some extent reveal him, allow us to know something of him and to relate to him aright. In book 6, therefore, in this new Christian context, music is no longer simply a liberal art that teaches us about the nature of reality through a rational analysis of numerical relation; it is an art that must be practiced in every moment of a creature's existence if it is to remain in right relation to God and not fall back into non-being; it has become a matter of ethics as much as a quest for truth. And we must not forget that God, the True and the Good, is also the Beautiful; that the music *(forma)* of creation is inherently beautiful *(formosus)*; and that this beauty is only preserved when it is loved in reference to its Creator. Both of these aspects of music — the ethical and the aesthetic — will become increasingly important in book 6 as Augustine analyzes the creature's failure to maintain a right relation with his or her Creator, and the way in which that relationship is restored by God's grace.

The previous paragraph is a summary of Augustine's teaching in *On Music*[3] — a necessarily brief and general summary, but important nevertheless in that, without an overview of the theological context, the seemingly remorseless rationalism, abstraction, and sheer intellectualism of the early part of *On Music* might certainly mislead — as indeed many scholars, who ought to know better, have been misled. A close reading of book 6 gives the lie both to the initial impression made by books 1-5 and to the often dismissive judgments of scholars that have been made on the basis of them.

3. It is succinctly and powerfully set forth in much the same terms in *On Free Will* 2.16.41–17.46 (*Corpus Christianorum Latinorum* 29, in *Works of Saint Augustine*, ed. John E. Rotelle, trans. Edmund Hill [New York: New City Press, 1990-], 1.3).

Book 6 of *De Musica*

The Ascent of the Soul — in Theory

Book 6 does not get off to a promising start, however — at least in terms of music as we now understand it. The reader is immediately caught up in a seemingly inexorable movement away from the bodily, temporal, and mutable toward the spiritual, eternal, and immutable. Augustine's avowed aim is to raise his reader, by means of a consideration of the art of music, from the corporeal to the incorporeal (6.2.2), from traces of music to music itself. What follows is a familiar, characteristically Augustinian, Neo-platonic-type ascent of the soul, couched in terms of a hierarchical categorization of the way in which, in this case, the soul perceives and knows a particular line of music (the first line of Ambrose's hymn *Deus Creator Omnium*). Each stage of the ascent is identified and labeled,[4] from the sound made by the body, to the reaction of the soul to sound in hearing, to that which produces the sound, to the memory that stores the sound, to that which has the power to judge it (6.2.2–4.7). As in many similar ascents, which punctuate the early works through to the *Confessions* and beyond, the movement is most definitely inward and upward — at least (and again, this is characteristic) in theory. As ever, the seemingly inexorable ascent, which is confidently set forth in theory, begins to waver and falter as soon as Augustine's actual attempt to pursue it, in practice, is examined more carefully. In this case the stumbling block takes the form of the relation between body and soul in the process of perception: in theory, and before the fall, the relation of the soul and body was characterized by the peaceful and harmonious subjection of the body to the soul; in practice, following the fall, the soul must suffer the distraction of the mortality and frailty of the body, which is no longer fully subject to it or obedient to it; the soul is thereby diminished and weakened, and experiences difficulty, labor, and pain in its operation — the characteristic *concupiscentia* of original sin (6.5.9–6.16).

Although the ascent falters, Augustine presses on to consider that power of the soul which has the ability to judge the different aspects of its perception of music that have formed the earlier stages of its ascent. He realizes that, to a large extent, its "judicial" power relies on memory, which both

---

4. We do not intend to present the technicalities of Augustine's argument here; he changes the labels or names in a rather complicated and confusing way as the argument is gradually refined.

contains the eternal rules according to which the soul judges (6.12.34), and which preserves the sounds which have gone before, so that they can be present to be evaluated and judged (6.7.17–8.22). But, as in the famous ascent in *Confessions* 10, he then proceeds beyond memory, to investigate what the *source* of the judicial power itself is. In doing this he makes a significant, but admittedly rather unsettling, distinction between that which enjoys and takes pleasure in the sound perceived by the soul and retained in the memory, and that which judges it by reason. It is as if the latter is an additional stage, ensuring that the soul does not simply remain at the stage of taking pleasure in well-measured, harmonious sound, but that it moves beyond it in judging it. He is emphatic that the taking pleasure and the rational judgment are both actions of the same soul, as were all the earlier types of perception of music he has enumerated and analyzed. "We are examining," as he puts it,

> the motions and states of one and the same nature, that is to say, the soul … [and he proceeds to summarize the different types or levels of perception:] as it is one thing to be moved towards the reactions of the body, which occurs in perceiving, another to move oneself towards the body, which occurs in an activity, yet another thing to retain what has been produced in the soul as a result of these motions, which is to remember, so it is one thing to approve or disapprove of these motions, when they are first set in motion or when they are revived by remembrance, which occurs in the pleasure of that which is convenient and in the dismay of that which is inappropriate in such motions or reactions, and another thing to evaluate whether it is right or not to enjoy these things, which is done by reasoning. (6.9.24)[5]

Thus, there is not so much a separation between pleasure and reason as a necessary warning that pleasure is not the end, but the *means* to the end, which is to know and love God, and that we need to be rationally aware of this and constantly judge all else against this end — even what is ethically right or aesthetically pleasing. This is not least the case because what pleases and delights us is a temporal, mutable manifestation and embodiment of eternal, immutable music. Reason and rational judgment make us aware of this (6.10.28).

If we are taken aback by Augustine's emphasis upon the need for ascent,

5. For the text and translation of book 6 I have used Martin Jacobsson, *Aurelius Augustinus. De musica VI* (Stockholm: Almquist and Wiksell, 2002).

upon hierarchy, upon the eternal, immutable archetypes of music, and upon the importance of rational judgment; if we are dismayed by his insistence on the subjection of the bodily, the temporal, the mutable, and even of that which gives enjoyment and pleasure, we must remember that behind it all lies not so much a philosophically inspired rejection of created matter, or a Neo-pythagorean obsession with perfect number, but his belief in the Creator God — the *Deus Creator Omnium* — in whom all music originates and on whom all music depends; his acute awareness of humanity's fallen state; his conviction that it is now incapable of either knowing or acting in accordance with eternal, ordered harmony, because it has become caught up, distracted, and diverted by its temporal, mutable, physical manifestations.

The Descent of the Soul — in Practice

The ascent that Augustine traces in *On Music* is, in fact, no different from all the other ascents that he describes: it is a theoretical ideal, a model set before fallen human beings in order to demonstrate the truth of God, the Creator, and the truth of the complete and utter dependence of every level of created reality upon him — from the physical world, to the senses, to the soul, to the mind, to the memory and reason — and of the dangers of taking anything other than God as an end in itself. And in practice, like all Augustinian ascents, the ascent through the levels of musical perception is a cogent demonstration of just how impossible it is for human beings, in their fallen, sinful state, to either undertake this ascent or ever achieve its goal in this life. Having theoretically traced the hierarchy of the soul's perception of music, Augustine immediately proceeds, in book 6, to demonstrate its present ignorance of it and its inability to observe it. Having turned away from its Creator to the temporal, mutable, physical order, the soul now finds itself part of that order, no longer able to appreciate the unity, harmony, and equality of the eternal music that is God, but only what is manifest to it from its own, now severely limited, perspective: it is like a statue in the corner of a beautiful building, or a soldier in the ranks, or a syllable in a poem; it can perceive only in part (6.11.30). Moreover, what limited perception of music the soul does have can tend to hinder and entrap it rather than point it toward the whole. Music is undeniably beautiful — it occasions pleasure, delight, and love — but unless this delight is rightly directed, it can simply become what Augustine describes as a "carnal pleasure" (*concupiscentia*), an "intimacy of the soul with the flesh" that vitiates the soul, creating in it a struggle or tension that renders it blind to the eternal music of God and impotent to order itself in accordance with it (6.11.33). Rather, it becomes preoccupied with temporal, mutable music, distracted and diverted by it, preferring it to its eternal source and Creator (6.13.37-40). Augustine sums up the reason for the soul's fall as pride: in taking created reality as an end in itself and in attempting to subject it — and other rational souls — to itself, it has failed to acknowledge its Creator and its complete and utter dependence upon him. In doing so it has fallen, not just from the truth, but from the source of its existence; it has literally diminished itself by self-destructive pride (6.13.40).

What Augustine is absolutely insistent upon is that every motion and movement of the soul, which he has here analyzed in terms of musical perception, must be ordered toward God and have God as its object, if it is not to fall back into the non-being from whence he created it: the *carmen uniuersitatis,* or hymn of the universe (6.11.29), will degenerate into meaningless dissonance if it does not continually refer to its source and sustainer, who is the source of all harmony, and without whom there would be no music at all:

> From where, I ask, do all these things [Augustine is talking about evidences of music at every level of created reality] come, if not from that supreme and eternal origin of rhythms and similarity and equality and order? But if you take these away from the earth, it will be nothing. Therefore God has created the earth, and it was created from nothing. (6.17.57)

> The soul by itself is nothing — otherwise it would not be changeable and admit any decrease of its essence — so, since it is nothing by itself and whatever it has of existence comes from God, if it remains in its own place, by God's own presence it is given life in its mind and conscience.... Therefore, to be inflated by pride, this is for the soul to proceed to the extreme exterior and, as it were, to become empty, which means to have less and less existence. (6.13.40)

Although Augustine's insistence on the importance of looking beyond the physical, temporal, and mutable realm of music is ultimately founded upon his identification of eternal, immutable music with God and the uniquely Christian doctrine of God's creation of all music (reality) from nothing, so that it exists only in relation to him, there were also, as we have just seen, more immediate and pressing reasons for this emphasis in his thought: the attachment of the soul to the realm of the physical, mutable, and temporal that occasioned its fall, and which it now suffers as a painful distraction and difficulty, which weakens and vitiates it, was no doubt at the forefront of his mind in his many warnings about taking any aspect of created reality as an end in itself. Having examined the reasons for this rather disconcerting judgment upon the bodily, temporal realm, we are perhaps now in a stronger position to ask whether his attitude is, in fact, quite as negative and world-denying as it might at first appear, and whether he allows any positive role for the manifestations of music that he has identified in the soul's perceptions of the temporal and bodily realm.

Delighting in the Music of Creation in Theory: Enjoyment or Use?

In fact, we do not have to wait until Augustine has completed his analysis of the soul's fallen attachment to the temporal to encounter a certain ambivalence in his attitude to the latter. At each step in his description of what traps, imprisons, and weakens the soul, he is careful to make clear that what is at fault is not so much created reality itself as the soul's mistaken attitude to and use of it. He is certainly not a Manichee, for whom the whole of material creation is substantially evil and at odds with the good: as he never tires of observing, creation is the good work of a good Creator; it is good in all its parts; it is — it exists, literally "stands out from nothingness" — because it possesses music, understood as form, unity, harmony, equality, and measured relation. In itself, therefore, creation is a beautiful, pleasing, delightful revelation of its Creator, and this is how it should be seen — and used: "what soils the soul is not something evil, for even the body is a creation of God and is adorned by its own form, however low . . . it is not the rhythms (music — *numeri*), which are inferior to reason and beautiful in their own kind, but the love of inferior beauty that soils the soul" (6.14.46; cf. 6.4.7). The answer to the manifest temptation that creation poses to the soul to love its music — its beauty and harmony — for itself, in a possessive, dominating, and ultimately destructive way,[6] is to love it in reference to its eternal, immutable

---

6. E.g., *On Music* 6.13.39, where Augustine analyzes the way in which the different levels of the soul's perception of music, which he has analyzed in the first part of book 6, can all be the cause of diversions and distractions. He frequently analyzes this in reference to 1 John 2:16: "Do not love the world, for all that is in the world is the lust of the flesh, the lust of the eyes, and worldly ambition." E.g., *On Music* 6.14.44.

source and Creator. The crucial distinction here is the characteristically Augustinian one between use *(uti)* and enjoyment *(frui):* we should only *enjoy* that which is eternal and immutable (in other words God, the Trinity) and we should *use* everything else toward that end, "like a plank in the waves, not by throwing them away as a burden, nor by embracing them as something well anchored, but by using them well" (6.14.45; cf. 6.11.29). The distinction is, of course, itself an ambiguous one — for how can we be said to *use* ourselves or our neighbor? — and it is one that Augustine is always at pains to refine and clarify in terms of love, so that the right order becomes an order of love: a love of God and of neighbor, in which we love ourselves and our neighbor "on behalf of" *(propter)* or "in reference to" *(referre ad)* God (6.13.43–14.46) and might "enjoy [someone] in God" *(frui in Deo).*[7] As he writes, "The soul maintains its order by loving with its whole self what is superior to it, that is to say God, but its fellow souls as itself. For by this virtue of love the soul adorns everything that is inferior to it but is not soiled by what is inferior" (6.14.46). Despite the ambiguities, then, the basic insight and intention are clear: nothing should be taken as an end in itself, but should be referred to its source and Creator, God. It is no doubt this that Augustine had in mind when he introduced the final category of the soul's perception of music as the rational judgment of that which gives it pleasure (6.11.28-29); in other words, it must appreciate that what gives it pleasure is indeed beautiful, ordered, harmonious, and unified, but that it is not God; it is not eternal beauty, order, harmony, or unity, but simply a temporal manifestation, imitation, or image of it. It must not be loved and enjoyed for itself but toward God. What he actually says is worth quoting at length:

> Let us, therefore, not look askance at what is inferior to us, but let us place ourselves between what is below us and what is above us, with the help of our God and Lord, in such a way that we are not offended by what is inferior but enjoy only what is superior. For the pleasure is like a weight for the soul [*Delectatio quippe quasi pondus est animae*]. And so pleasure sets the soul in its place. "For where your treasure is, there will your heart be also," where your pleasure is, there will your treasure be, but where your heart is, there your beatitude or misery will be. But what is superior except that in which the highest, unshakeable, unchangeable, eternal equal-

---

7. These distinctions are famously rehearsed in their most systematic form in the first book of *On Christian Doctrine* (*Corpus Scriptorum Ecclesiasticorum Latinorum* 80, in *Works of Saint Augustine*, 1.11). We can, however, see the first detailed sketch of them here, in *On Music* 6.

ity exists, where there is no time, because there is no change, and from which times are created and set in order and modified in imitation of eternity. (6.11.29)

Augustine does not, therefore, deny that the temporal, mutable perceptions of music that the soul has are beautiful; nor does he dismiss them as *mere* imitations. Rather, he asserts that "to the extent that they imitate equality we cannot deny that they are beautiful in their own kind and order" (6.10.28). What is important is that they are judged — that they are perceived, loved, and enjoyed for what they are — not as ends in themselves, but as temporal manifestations and pointers to their source. When the soul fails to do this and falls, Augustine is insistent (again against the Manichees) that this does not mean that created reality itself is somehow thereby flawed and vitiated; rather, he argues that God's punishment of human sinfulness is comprehended by the order of his providence, which will not allow the beauty and order of the whole to be affected. Instead, fallen humanity becomes "sewn into the order" (6.11.30). While human beings might now enjoy only a limited perspective on the whole, the beauty of the hymn of the universe does not falter (6.11.29-30) but rather serves to revive the memory of what they have lost and of what they must now seek to regain (6.11.34).

How the original harmony of the soul with God is restored is the subject of the final part of *On Music*, and in keeping with what Augustine has already hinted in considering the fall of the soul, the role of the temporal beauty of the music of created reality is of the utmost importance, not least because it is within this realm that the soul has now fallen. Its beauty is the only beauty it recognizes; its music is the only music it can hear. It needs to be led from the temporal to the eternal, from the corporeal to the incorporeal. Temporal music must become no longer a diversion, distraction, and temptation for the soul, but a means of restoring its harmony and unity with its Creator. Augustine observes that this will happen only "when . . . by definite steps back from every lascivious movement, in which lies a decrease of the essence of the soul," human beings are able to overcome the habit of disordered delight and desire, of carnal pleasure *(carnalium sensum delectatione)* or concupiscence, and instead take pleasure in the "music of reason" *(rationis numeros)*. When this happens — and Augustine seems to imply that it will only finally pertain in the life to come, when, as he puts it, "the exterior man has been destroyed and his change for the better taken place" — the soul will once again be turned to God and will "give the music of health *(numeros sanitatis)* to the body without receiving any [sinful, misdirected] joy from it" (6.11.33; cf. 6.15.49). Meanwhile, in this life, he sums up "the activity" that "is prescribed for . . . [the soul] by God, by which it is purified and unburdened and may fly back to the quiet and enter into the joy of its Lord" as the double commandment of love of God and love of neighbor as ourselves. "If," he suggests, "we direct all these movements and rhythms of our human activity to this end, we will undoubtedly be purified." It is in this context that he has already discussed the importance of distinguishing between use and enjoyment, and toward the end of *On Music* he describes the role of the four virtues of patience, temperance, fortitude, and justice, which should determine the right attitude of the soul to the temporal (but which will also be perfected only in the life to come). It is also in this context that he considers every aspect of created reality, every act of human creation or craftsmanship, every plant, animal, element, or particle of earth, every hair on our head and every leaf which falls, as witnessing to the supreme, perfect, eternal, immutable music of God who has brought them into being from nothing. Their very existence, their beauty, proclaims his harmony, unity, equality, and order (6.17.57-58); together they form a hymn of the universe, the *Deus Creator Omnium*, to whom the soul must refer the delight or love that they occasion, as to their source and end. Using and loving them in this way, the soul will be purified, sanctified, and ordered and will itself participate in divine harmony.

It should be clear from the above summary of the final part of *On Music* that temporal, mutable, physical reality, or music, has a central role to play in reorienting the fallen soul and in effecting its reformation and return to God. The very existence of created reality or music, its form and beauty, witnesses to its Creator; its temporality points to his eternity, its mutability to his immutability, its imperfection to his perfection; and, if rightly loved, judged, and used by the soul, it can reorder and reform its fallen attachment to it, to become attachment to God. What is involved in this movement is, at the same time, an aesthetic appreciation of the undeniable beauty of created, temporal music, a virtuous life lived in accordance with the harmony and order the soul perceives,[8] and, above all, a rational judgment or an awareness

---

8. This is something which Augustine frequently emphasizes in these early works: virtuous action is an expression of right order or love and one cannot be had without the other, e.g., *On Music* 6.15.49–16.51; *On Order* 2.8.25; 2.19.50-51: "For the soul that diligently considers the nature and power of numbers, it will appear manifestly unfitting and most deplorable that it should write a rhythmic line and play the harp by virtue of this knowledge, and that its life and very self — which is the soul — should nevertheless follow a crooked path and, under the domination of lust, be out of tune by the clangour of shameful vices" (*Corpus*

expressed in faith and love that it is not, in itself, supreme, eternal beauty; that it must be loved for what it is, and looked in and through; that although it is beautiful in itself, it is, as yet, incomplete and finds its wholeness only in its Creator — God. It must, in short, be loved rightly — toward God. Augustine expresses these ideas in a number of ways.

Delighting in the Music of Creation in Practice: Faith, Hope, and Love

For those who do not possess a training in the liberal arts and who do not have the necessary rational powers to follow the sort of arguments he has set forth in *On Music*, Augustine is convinced that the way of Christian life that he has described — of rightly loving, judging, and using created reality or music for the sake of its Creator — can be attained more directly, and certainly with less discursiveness or mental effort, simply by believing in God and living a virtuous life. Right faith can dispense with rational argument since it has already attained what reason is used to effect: a *scientia bene modulandi* — a knowledge of how to measure and relate number (understood as the harmony, unity, measure, and beauty of creation) to its Creator well. He admits that in *On Music* he has been writing for intellectuals, for "those whom God has endowed with a good mind," in short, for those who, like himself, cannot refrain from the attempt to rationally understand, explain, expound, and evaluate reality in terms of the liberal arts. He has written in the hope that they will not "wear out their good minds with trifles, without any idea of what they enjoy in them," but be enabled to refer what they discover in their study of liberal arts to God (6.1.1). Whereas faith already "knows" that the music of the universe originates in God and must be loved in him and toward him, reason seeks to rationally demonstrate this in terms of the numerical, mathematical categories of the liberal discipline of "music." This is a contrast, or tension, that runs throughout Augustine's work from beginning to end, and it is one in which neither faith nor reason is devalued, but their respective roles and interrelation are carefully delineated and appreciated. Although faith is mentioned only at the beginning and end of book 6, very much as an aside, we should not, as Augustine clearly does not, underestimate its importance: the right relation between

---

Christianorum Latinorum 29, in *Fathers of the Church* 1, ed. R. J. Deferrari [Washington, DC: Catholic University Press, 1947-]).

the harmony, beauty, order, and unity of created reality and God is not only intuitively known but also practiced by the one who has faith in God the Creator; reason simply attempts to set forth the rational grounds for such a relationship. Faith does what reason demonstrates is necessary without the need for such demonstration.

To dismiss Augustine's treatment of music as overly intellectual, rationalistic, dry, or mathematical is therefore to misunderstand the nature of *On Music* and to ignore the fact that it is only one side of his appreciation of music. The other side, faith (which includes hope and love), does not need a treatise to describe it: it simply is, in practice, what *On Music* has attempted to describe in theory. As he comments in the concluding paragraph of the work:

> these things have been written for much weaker persons than those who, following the authority of the two testaments, venerate and worship the one supreme God's consubstantial and unchangeable Trinity, by believing, hoping and loving it, from whom everything, through whom everything, in whom everything exists. For they are purified not through the brilliance of human arguments but through the most powerful and burning fire of love. (6.17.59)

When Augustine dismisses the flute player or the nightingale, who simply perform music through imitation or intuition, because they do not possess a rational understanding of the liberal art of music, he is not dismissing their music as such, but their failure to understand that it originates in, and should be directed toward, God (1.4.5).[9] Faith, on the other hand, is able to do this without engaging with the rational categories of the liberal art of music. What is needed is not so much reason as an awareness that both faith and reason provide in their different ways: that the music of the universe, the admittedly beautiful harmony, unity, measure, equality, and relation of the music of creation, is but a temporal, mutable expression of the eternal and immutable music that belongs to God.

Delight "through" the Senses: The Ambivalence of Music

We have seen that beautiful music can be either a temptation that distracts and weakens the soul or something that inspires love and desire for its divine source. The inherent ambiguity of all manifestations of music is no doubt

9. Cf. *On Order* 2.18.48 (*Corpus Christianorum Latinorum* 29, in *Fathers of the Church* 1).

the reason for Augustine's highly ambivalent attitude toward "music" as we would now commonly understand it — as written, practiced, and performed by a musician. Various passages in the *Confessions* leave us in no doubt that Augustine was keenly aware of the beauty of such music and profoundly sensitive to its effects. In the days following his baptism in Milan he recounts, "How I wept during your hymns and songs! I was deeply moved by the music of the sweet chants of your church. The sounds flowed into my ears and the truth was distilled into my heart. This caused the feelings of devotion to overflow. Tears ran, and it was good for me to have that experience" (*Confessions* 9.6.14).[10] He refers to the recent innovation of using hymns and psalms in Milan, where "the brothers used to sing together with both heart and voice in a state of high enthusiasm" as a "method of mutual comfort and exhortation," introduced "to prevent the people from succumbing to depression and exhaustion" (*Confessions* 9.7.15). In book 10, however, he reveals his divided mind on the subject. Analyzing the temptations that still assail him, even after his conversion, in terms of 1 John 2:16, he includes the pleasures of the ear among the "lusts of the flesh": they are clearly compelling and attractive, but he tells us that, whereas he had once been held by them, God has set him free, and he can now take them or leave them. What he goes on to say, however, reveals that in practice, his response is somewhat less disinterested and rather more ambivalent: he still values such music but is unsure how to do so and is well aware that he might tend to overdo it:

> I feel that when the sacred words are chanted well, our souls are moved and are more religiously and with a warmer devotion kindled to piety than if they are not so sung. All the diverse emotions of our spirit have their various modes in voice and chant appropriate in each case, and are stirred by a mysterious inner kinship. But my physical delight, which has to be checked from enervating the mind, often deceives me when the perception of the senses is unaccompanied by reason, and is not patiently content to be in a subordinate place. It tries to be first, and in a leading role, though it deserves to be allowed only as secondary to reason. So in these matters I sin unawares, and only afterwards become aware of it. (*Confessions* 10.33.49)

Despite the risk of being temporarily overcome by the beauty of music he hears in church, however, Augustine cannot bring himself to reject or dis-

10. Cf. *Letter* 9 (*Patrologia Latina* 33).

allow it. Instead, he wonders whether it might not be better to follow Athanasius's more sober practice of having the psalms delivered more in the manner of a recitation than of singing. But he wavers: he is well aware of just how powerful the beauty of music can be when it is used rightly; he remembers its profound effect on his soul when he was first reconciled to the faith; he observes how one can be "moved not by the chant but by the words being sung, when they are sung with a clear voice and entirely appropriate modulation," and he is forced to admit that music can be of great use in worship. The risks remain, then, but he is prepared to run them rather than give up music in church altogether. "Thus I fluctuate," he comments,

> between the danger of pleasure and the experience of the beneficent effect, and I am led to put forward the opinion (not as an irrevocable view) that the custom of singing in Church is to be approved, so that through the delights of the ear the weaker mind may rise up toward the devotion of worship. Yet when it happens to me that the music moves me more than the subject of the song, I confess myself to commit a sin deserving punishment, and then I would prefer not to have heard the singer. (*Confessions* 10.33.50)

As with all temporal manifestations of music in the created realm, therefore, while appreciating the beauty of music as it is sung in church, Augustine never ceases to emphasize the need to move beyond and through it: beyond and through the temporal, mutable, and bodily toward the eternal, immutable, and spiritual. For as long as he is caught up in the sheer beauty, delight, and pleasure of the temporal manifestations of music, for that moment he knows that he is distracted from God and risks taking it as an end in itself.[11]

The key word in Augustine's assessment of music here is "through" *(per)*: it is not by rejecting and dismissing music that he moves toward God, but in and "through" it. Indeed, as we have seen above, in his fallen state he is acutely aware that this is now the only way to God: human beings have become part of the temporal, mutable realm and can return to God only from

---

11. We see precisely the same ambivalence in Augustine's reflection on the art of rhetoric, for example, in book 4 of *On Christian Doctrine* (*Corpus Scriptorum Ecclesiasticorum Latinorum* 80). There is a fine balance between rhetorical fireworks which delight and move the mind, and stating the truth in plain and simple words. The same applies to his allegorical exegesis of Scripture. The truth seems to be communicated more effectively when it also delights and moves the mind.

within it and through it. That music delights and moves and inspires is a positive thing if it is referred to God and not taken as an end in itself. We have seen that Augustine later formulates this crucial distinction in terms of use and enjoyment, but there are earlier distinctions, which he elaborates specifically in relation to the liberal arts, that go some way to clarifying what it involves. In *On Order* he distinguishes between delight *of* the sense and delight *through* the sense *(per sensum)* by giving the example of hearing: "whatever has a pleasing sound," he writes, "that it is which pleases and entices the hearing itself. What is really signified by that sound is what is borne to the mind through the messenger of our hearing . . . our praise of the meter is one thing, but our praise of the meaning is something else" (*On Order* 2.11.34). The distinction is between the sound and that of which it is a symbol, between sense and meaning, between musical relations in created reality and divine and eternal music. The second book of *On Order* offers an extended demonstration of this truth in a manner very similar to *On Music,* by describing an extended ascent through the seven liberal arts: from the "shadows and vestiges of reason" in the senses, which must be judged and passed beyond, to ultimate truth and wisdom in God (*On Order* 2.15.42).

We have encountered the same distinction in the sixth book of *On Music,* when Augustine insisted, in his analysis of the soul's perception of music, that the pleasure of the senses must be judged and evaluated by reason. He makes a similar distinction between what the senses "announce" and what reason "judges" in book 5 (*On Music* 5.1.1), and, as we have seen in relation to the *Confessions,* his attitude to music in church is also described in these terms. Indeed, this is an attitude that sums up his approach not only to music but to the whole of temporal reality, including his theology of creation, the incarnation, the sacraments, Scripture, and preaching[12] — all are temporal, mutable manifestations of eternal, immutable truth to fallen humanity; all occasion delight, but they, and the delight they inspire, must not be taken as ends in themselves; rather, their divine source must be believed, loved, and sought after, not by setting them to one side or rejecting them, but *within* and *through* them.

Whether this movement is one of faith, hope, and love, or whether it is

---

12. Augustine constantly emphasizes these aspects of divine revelation — especially the incarnation and the "mysteries" or sacraments — in relation to fallen humanity's dependence upon authority or faith, rather than reason, in early works written at the same time as *On Music,* e.g., *Against the Academics* 3.20.43 (*Corpus Christianorum Latinorum* 29, in *Works of Saint Augustine,* 1.3); *On Order* 2.5.15-16; 2.9.26-27 (*Corpus Christianorum Latinorum* 29, in *Fathers of the Church* 1).

one of reason, does not ultimately matter, although the overwhelming beauty of these manifestations of divine music ensures that it is love that is pre-eminent both as the way and as the goal. We must remember that although the language of measure, order, unity, and number might appear to be a somewhat abstract, technical, mathematical, and overly philosophical way of describing and discussing music, it is also the language in which Augustine describes the beauty that reveals the Creator, that inspires our delight in and love of him, and that he employs to express profound theological insights concerning the nature of God, his incarnation, and humanity's dependence upon and relation to him. Although Augustine, like all the ancients, primarily understood music as an intellectual discipline, as one of the liberal arts, he did not dismiss or reject its temporal, mutable manifestation, or even the music that he heard sung in church, but acknowledged its power to reorient and reform, move and inspire — a power that he identified as the work of God's grace,[13] working both outwardly and inwardly, to enable fallen humanity to relate, in love, to its source and end — in other words, to God himself.[14]

13. This is specifically identified with the trinitarian operation of grace in early works written around the same time as *On Music,* such as *On True Religion* 113 (*Corpus Christianorum Latinorum* 32, in *Works of Saint Augustine,* 1.8) and *On the Morals of the Catholic Church* 1.13.22–14.24 (*Corpus Scriptorum Ecclesiasticorum Latinorum* 90, in *Works of Saint Augustine,* 1.19).

14. I would like to thank Steven Guthrie for allowing me to read two chapters of his doctoral thesis relating to Augustine's *De Musica.* They were an enormous inspiration and help in the writing of this paper. For *Confessions,* see *Confessiones. Corpus Christianorum* 27, in Henry Chadwick, trans., *Saint Augustine: Confessions* (Oxford: Oxford University Press, 1991).

2. Material: Philip the Chancellor and the Reception of Aristotle's *Physics*

Nancy van Deusen

Medieval Perceptions — in Hungary

It was a Monday morning, and I was preparing to go to work in the archive of the Hungarian Academy of Sciences, Budapest. The downstairs doorbell rang. Expecting no one and busy with my attempts to get off, I ignored its insistence. There was silence for the moment; then the doorbell to my apartment began to ring. Again I repeated to myself that I was expecting no one, had no wish at that moment to see anyone, and, further, had the right to ignore that morning any pressure, no matter how urgent, to open the door. No sooner had I said this to myself, when the door opened and the owner of the flat appeared, explaining that he needed some papers he had left when he himself had moved out in some haste one month previously, and that, really, it would only be a matter of a few moments and he would be gone. Still in my bathrobe, I had only one short sentence for him: "But this is my home," I said.

It was a clash of cultures and an issue of private space, a conceptualization of intrusion, and, also, the perception of one person's imposition of his will upon another, simply because he had a key. I reflected on what seemed to me to be a radical sense of private space, and the right, now and then, to be *incomunicando, unansprechbar*. Most of the terms for this occurred to me in other languages, but it is certainly a basic and necessary concept within the English language as well. I had lived for many years in Switzerland, as well as in the United States, where I myself had once been a landlady, who, in California, had been prevented from entering the apartment I owned even though the tenant had not paid rent for four months previously, and, in the meantime, had been convicted of arson and committed to a mental hospital. But this incident in Budapest was not so much a question of legality, even of a perception of intrusion. Rather, the issue was rooted in a cultural understanding of space, held in common by people who had lived together for a long time — a shared description of mental and physical contiguity, of shared space, of place, of density and aggregation. It was a deeply ingrained cultural characteristic that paid no attention to customary boundaries of urban-village, wealth-poverty, higher-lower classes, or education and profession, but did involve an identifiable internal property, a defining characteristic. This could be characterized by the Latin *proprietas,* and these aspects could also be described as belonging to, ultimately, material — even if that material was invisible. Further, this unseen property reached over other customary separations. There was, according to my observations, no difference with respect to a perception of private space and community between my "village" near the Kosztolányi Deszö square — a crowded meeting point in Budapest for bus and tram transportation — and the villages everywhere on the countryside, where I had quite often spent weekends.

My university office in Budapest was another case in point. Upon arrival, I had been assigned an office, with a computer, and an agreement had been reached that I would have the use of the office two mornings and three afternoons per week for purposes of conferences with students, of use of the computer, of meeting with colleagues — all of the activities for which one customarily uses designated space that has been placed at one's disposal. It all sounded clear and sensible to me, and familiar, since the situation seemed comparable to that at my North American university. I left, pleased that everything had been settled, and a card was placed on my door identifying me as a visiting professor and indicating my office hours.

This was, however, by no means the end of it. I returned the next day at the appointed time to find a couple using the desk and computer, and also camping out, so to speak; their back-packs, papers, bottles of mineral water, and half-filled coffee cups had, along with themselves, taken over the entire available space in the room. The following day, as I was discussing plans for a conference with the departmental chair, another colleague appeared, stating brightly that, if "the two of you are only talking, maybe I can use the computer." At the beginning of the next week, as I was speaking with a dissertation student, the colleague appeared again and began to use the telephone on the other desk in the room.

One could have been outraged — particularly in view of the fact that there were several virtually unused offices, actually a good deal of unused space — but there was another way to understand what was happening. Conceptually, for them to assign an office to me for my sole and individual use during predictable and predetermined hours of the week was not only incomprehensible but impossible. It simply could not, in that particular culture, be done. And it would appear that my presence there generated an aggregate, a "clumping" phenomenon, a coagulation. I noticed that my American office-mate, who had grown up in the United States but was Hungarian by birth, quite without realizing it slid comfortably into the same way of thinking, appearing whenever she wished, and at any time of day, appropriating the office space as her own, quite irrespective of agreed-upon office times, simply because the office was there and so was I. In fact, although I had no way of proving it, it seemed to me that she incorporated herself into the office space *especially* when I was there, and that the case was even more so when there were two of us to begin with. I noticed as well that the Hungarian colleagues at the university worked mostly in groups, in teams. In fact none of them appeared to work in the typical North American manner of academic research life, which, especially within the humanistic disciplines, is by and large solitary. Indeed, it seemed to them unimaginable that one worked mostly all by oneself, and I realized that I aroused not only curiosity but suspicion, as my Hungarian colleagues wondered what I was really up to with respect to my own personal research, as I plugged away according to internally generated goals.

Philip the Chancellor

Although a world away in time and space from medieval France and the focus of our attention, namely Philip the Chancellor (c. 1160-1236), these vignettes from life in Budapest — a sample of many experiences — resonated with and sharpened my awareness of medieval perceptions of material (and cogent properties of material). Deriving his name from his position as chancellor, Philip's duties — of particular interest to our ensuing discussion — involved providing a liaison between the theology faculty of the newly formed university and the episcopal see of Notre Dame.[1] Further, of even

---

1. "In Paris, the chancellor of the cathedral chapter of Notre Dame was chancellor of the university. His most important and prestigious assignment was to grant the license to teach. The basis of the chancellor's authority was very complex. As a dignitary of the cathe-

more interest to us here, the principles expounded in Philip's writings, difficult as they were to understand, found their most apt expression and exemplification in musical composition (particularly using more than one voice, known today as "polyphony") during the period of his activity. Some of these compositions have come down to us as from Philip himself, and there appears to be good reason for this attribution.

Writing in Paris around 1220, Philip the Chancellor incorporated Aristotelian principles and vocabulary taken from the newly translated *Physics* into his own *Summa de bono*. In the *Physics,* Aristotle concerns himself with material itself: its properties, inherent movement, potential, and expression. That the *Physics* was translated from the Greek into Latin at least five times within the century between the mid-twelfth and the mid-thirteenth centuries attests to its enormous intellectual importance within the Latin readership during the formative period of the early universities, notably in Paris, and soon thereafter at Oxford and Cambridge.[2] The ensuing stream of commentary on the *Physics,* throughout at least the next three centuries, also attests to its importance,[3] but it points as well to the difficulties faced by this intellectual community in attempting to grasp its basic principles, particu-

---

dral chapter who had traditionally been responsible for the cathedral school, he acted under the authority of the bishop of Paris." See J. M. M. H. Thijssen, *Censure and Heresy at the University of Paris, 1200-1400* (Philadelphia: University of Pennsylvania Press, 1998), pp. 8-11, as well as Jacques Verger, "Les institutions universitaires françaises au Moyen Age: Origines, modèles, évolution," in *Università in Europa. Le istituzioni universitarie dal Medio Evo ai nostri giorni, strutture, organizzazione, funzionamento,* ed. A. Romano (Catanzaro: Rubbettino, 1995), p. 68.

2. The *Physics* was translated by James of Venice, c. 1125-1150, of which translation there are at least 139 extant copies; by an anonymous translator (the so-called *"Physica vaticana"* in the mid-twelfth century); by Gerard of Cremona before 1187; by Michael Scot, c. 1220-1235, 65 copies; and by William of Moerbeke, c. 1260-1270, 230 copies. The great commentary of Averroes on the *Physics* was also translated by Michael Scot, c. 1220-1235. These translations, clustered together from the mid-twelfth to the mid-thirteenth centuries, as well as the number of copies that remain even today, attest to the intense interest generated by the *Physics,* a work that also subsequently was commented upon more than any other Aristotelian work. See Bernard G. Dod's article, "Aristoteles latinus," in *The Cambridge History of Later Medieval Philosophy,* ed. Norman Kretzmann, Anthony Kenny, and Jan Pinborg with Eleonore Stump (Cambridge: Cambridge University Press, 1982), pp. 45-47, esp. p. 75 (hereafter *CHLMP*); and John E. Murdoch, "Infinity and Continuity," in *CHLMP,* pp. 564-92, esp. p. 565.

3. Latin commentary literature has only partially been identified, much less edited. See Albert Zimmermann, *Verzeichnis ungedruckter Kommentare zur Metaphysik und Physik des Aristoteles aus der Zeit von etwa 1250-1350,* vol. 1 (Leiden: E. J. Brill, 1971).

larly the nature of motion within material, which, as Aristotle himself stated more than once within the work, was extremely difficult to comprehend.[4] Each commentary is different, each one beginning with the primary difficulty as well as the principal focus within the *Physics* as the commentator himself perceived them. Further, the format, the agenda, and the order of inclusion of the principal subjects all differ according to the discipline in which the commentator is writing, and which he is addressing, as well as to the purpose he has placed before himself. During the course of the thirteenth century, the comments of Philip the Chancellor, Robert Grosseteste, and Roger Bacon are of particular interest, since their writings evidence an excitement, as well as an underlying tension, that is indicative of the intellectual foment that the *Physics* produced at this time.[5] As we shall see, Philip's work, *Summa de bono,* is especially telling of the intellectual impact of Aristotle's work. Instead of quoting and commenting on passages, Philip allows his deep reading of the text to both inform and provide the linguistic tools to formulate his arguments.

Aristotle's *Physics*

But first we need to widen the focus and ask: What is Aristotle's *Physics* about, and why was it so prominent at the onset of the thirteenth century, with its influence scarcely diminishing throughout the next two centuries? I address this question with some trepidation, justified by the fact that the *Physics* treats some of the most basic and far-reaching questions of material reality. But it is obviously important to provide a base for Philip's discussion.

First of all, the *Physics* was and is of great importance because it is about material reality and how to recognize and deal with it. Further, rather than contesting a philosophical tradition or presenting an Aristotelian doctrine, the *Physics* brings together an entire corpus of writing concerning fundamental questions of undifferentiated or chaotic nature, substance, move-

---

4. According to Simplicius (*De caelo,* 226.19), the first four books of the *Physics* were referred to as "Concerning the Principles," whereas Books 5-8 were called "On Movement." The distinction between "change" *(metabole)* and movement *(kinesis)* is consistently emphasized by Aristotle.

5. See N. van Deusen, "On the Usefulness of Music: Motion, Music and the Thirteenth-Century Reception of Aristotle's *Physics,*" *Viator* 29 (1998): 167-87; and "Roger Bacon on Music," in *Roger Bacon and the Sciences,* ed. Jeremiah Hackett (Leiden: E. J. Brill, 1998), pp. 223-41.

ment, the nature of movement, time — again as material — and place, as well as the propensity for aggregation or density within place. Many of the most important themes are presented in the first three books of the *Physics*. Arguments are prepared in the first two books and brought to conclusions in the third. For the purposes of contextualizing our discussion, there can be no better place to begin than with Aristotle himself. In order to help us understand the line of reason followed within the *Physics*, I have brought together here seven passages that are most relevant to our focus. Drawn from books 3 and 8, they deal (in order of their appearance in the *Physics*) with the far-reaching topics of nature, mass, part, and contiguity.[6]

> Nature is a principle of motion and change, and it is the subject of our inquiry. We must therefore see that we understand what motion is; for if it were unknown, nature too would be unknown.
>
> When we have determined the nature of motion, our task will be to attack in the same way the terms which come next in order. Now motion is supposed to belong to the class of things which are continuous; and the infinite presents itself first in the continuous — that is how it comes about that the account of the infinite is often used in definitions of the continuous; for what is infinitely divisible is continuous. Besides these, place, void, and time are thought to be necessary conditions of motion.
>
> Clearly then, for these reasons and also because the attributes mentioned are common to everything and universal, we must first take each of them in hand and discuss it. For the investigation of special attributes comes after that of the common attributes. (200^{b}12-24)

> The appropriateness to the science of this problem is clearly indicated; for all who have touched on this kind of science in a way worth considering have formulated views about the infinite, and indeed, to a man, make it a principle of things. (203^{a}1-3)

> Nevertheless for him [Democritus] the common body is a principle of all things, differing from part to part in size and in shape.
>
> It is clear then from these considerations that the inquiry concerns the student of nature. Nor is it without reason that they all make it a prin-

6. Passages are taken from the English translation by R. P. Hardie and R. K. Gaye, in *The Complete Works of Aristotle*, Revised Oxford Translation, ed. Jonathan Barnes, Bollingen Series 71.2, 2 vols. (Princeton: Princeton University Press, 1984), vol. 1, pp. 315-446. For the Greek text, see W. D. Ross, *Aristotle's Physics: A Revised Text with Introduction* (Oxford: Clarendon Press, 1950; reprinted 1966).

ciple. We cannot say that the infinite exists in vain, and the only power which we can ascribe to it is that of a principle. (203^b1-6)

But the problem of the infinite is difficult: many contradictions result whether we suppose it to exist or not to exist. If it exists, we have still to ask *how* it exists — as a substance or as the essential attribute of some entity? Or in neither way, yet none the less is there something which is infinite or some things which are infinitely many? (203^b31-35)

Our account does not rob the mathematicians of their science, by disproving the actual existence of the infinite in the direction of increase, in the sense of the untraversable. In point of fact they do not need the infinite and do not use it. They postulate only that a finite straight line may be produced as far as they wish. It is possible to have divided into the same ratio as the largest quantity another magnitude of any size you like. Hence, for the purposes of proof, it will make no difference to them whether the infinite is found among existent magnitudes. (207^b28-34)

Now like *existence* of motion is asserted by all who have anything to say about nature, because they all concern themselves with the construction of the world and study the question of becoming and perishing, which processes could not come about without the existence of motion. But those who say that there is an infinite number of worlds, some of which are in process of becoming while others are in process of perishing, assert that there is always motion (for these processes of becoming and perishing of the worlds necessarily involve motion), whereas those who hold that there is only one world, whether everlasting or not, make corresponding assumptions in regard to motion. . . . Mind introduced motion and separated them. (250^b15-23, 26)

We must consider then, how this matter stands; for the discovery of the truth about it is of importance, not only for the study of nature, but also for the investigation of the First Principle. . . . Each kind of motion, therefore, necessarily involves the presence of the things that are capable of that motion. (251^a5-7, 10-11)

So then, material contains qualities, especially of motion, the ability to aggregate, the capacity for breaking out and fragmentation, and of opacity. As I indicated above, when I introduced the theme of unseen properties, I am particularly interested in this concept of opacity, since it constitutes not

only a property of material that is easily and visibly identified but also of
more difficult to access innate cultural properties that separate one group of
people from another — a property I attempted to bring to mind and illustrate in the opening examples of this study.

Writing during the first generation of the thirteenth century, Philip the
Chancellor was one of the first to put the tools to be found in Aristotle's *Physics* to use in describing both overtly physical material realities and material
properties that were, in fact, *invisible.* The subject of material, aggregation,
mass, and opacity as a potential and capacity that could be expressed without
distinction within both outward and inward property is a topic that obviously fascinated him, since he brings it up in many contexts during the course
of his large-scale *Summa de bono.* One might easily miss the importance of
the *Physics* within this work, since it is not what would become a typical commentary on the *Physics,* with quotations from the text followed by comments.
Rather, Philip brings up a topic important for its theological implication and
exemplification and then proceeds to formulate his comments using vocabulary, as well as argumentation, that he had culled from his careful and
thoughtful reading of the *Physics.* Our discussion here will bring out some of
these key passages. Finally, we will observe how the pivotal, yet abstract, topic
of aggregated, opaque, pre-existent substance *(substantia)* was made intellectually and sensorily available by the exemplification of new music composition at approximately the time of Philip's writing, as well as during the early
reception of the *Physics.* This was a period when the conceptualization of
materia within the *Physics* would have been fresh, exciting, yet difficult to
comprehend. (The equivalence of *materia/substantia* has been introduced
here in line with Philip's own equivalence.) In the synopsis below we will look
at what he has to say on the subject of aggregation, conglomeration, and
opacity, leading on to the concept of pre-existent substance.[7]

7. The index to the two-volume edition of Philip's *Summa de bono* gives insufficient indication of the importance of the topic of *materia-substantia* within the entire work. In fact, the
subject comes up consistently and constantly; Philip has recourse to *materia* repeatedly, for example, within the first volume: as *substantia mobilis* (p. 106); *moveretur vel contraria in eodem*
(contrary motion, p. 107); with respect to the motion of time within place and according to
part *(secundum partem,* p. 108); with respect to *chaos/anima/*corruptibility (p. 117, also
informem materiam, p. 130), *substantie spirituales* (p. 118), *imperfecta/proprio/perfectiones/opus*
(p. 118); *materia sive in potentia* (p. 119); *in contrarium* (p. 120); modes of *materia* and opposition (p. 120); *substantia* arbitrated according to quantity of time (p. 120); *separatio inter
substantiam* (p. 120); *materia secundum via compositionis* (p. 122; see also p. 157); *de materiali
luce et spirituali* (p. 125); *prius et posterius in natura* (p. 125); *nam materialis esset lux* (pp. 137-
38); *substantia incorporea illuminationum que sunt a primo prima relatione perceptive* (p. 158);

Material and the *Summa de bono*

In the opening chapters of his *Summa de bono*,[8] Philip deals with material differences, notably between light and opacity. Bringing both Pseudo-Dionysius (late fifth to early sixth century) and Augustine (354-430) into the discussion, he contrasts opacity with light, as properties of both material that has been delimited corporeally and spiritual material. In this comparison, opacity initially takes on a negative aspect. The principal point, however, for our discussion here is that opacity contains within itself opaqueness, a point that is reiterated.[9] Opacity is by nature opaque, just as earth contains within itself the property of opacity.[10] Relating earth to opacity is an important if obvious connection that Philip subsequently extends into a concept of *firmamentum*. Opacity furthermore can be placed in a proportional relationship with *materia/natura*, that is, "what is there," before this pre-existent *materia* is dealt with, shaped, or organized in some way. Philip, in this context, appropriates the term *silva*, referring to Calcidius's translation of Plato's *Timaeus*, thereby accessing a crucial concept within that translation, namely, *silva* as a forest, thicket, or aggregation of heavy, inchoate, dense, but ultimately useable *materia*. It is a translational importance — that is, from the Greek *hylē* to the Latin *silva* — that the translator, Calcidius, makes much of in his commentary on the *Timaeus*.[11] On this subject of pre-

---

omnium que substantialiter etiam nature assunt contentiva voluntas (p. 160); and so on through the entire two volumes of Wicki's edition. *Materia-substantia-natura* constitutes a background for nearly every topic of discussion, and invisible *materia* is an important discussion point within his argumentation. Although this is clearly a subject that would require a separate study (and has generated a considerable literature in medieval studies) the discussion gives a background for ensuing argumentation concerning the topic of transubstantiation.

8. *Philippi Cancellarii Summa de bono ad fidem codicum primum edita studio et cura Nicolai Wicki*, Opera philosophica mediae aetatis selecta, volumen II-Pars Prior/Posterior (Bern: Editiones Francke, 1985), hereafter referred to as *Edition*.

9. See, for example, *Edition*, vol. 1, pp. 25-26 ("Nec est simile de luce et tenebra corporali . . . non distinguitur a materia"), which quotes from both Augustine's *City of God* (*De civitate Dei*, XI c. 13 [PL 41,329ff; CSEL 40-I, 532,27–533,2]) and Pseudo-Dionysius's *De divinis nominibus* in its translation by John the Scot (*De div. nom.* c.4:30 [PG 3,732; see also trans. Joh. Scoti [PL 122,1145C]), while also accessing Aristotle's *Physica* I^c.9.

10. "Distinctio autem lucis, tenebris intelligitur separatio in natura partis orbis. . . . Nam quinta essentia habet naturam lucis, ultima vero, scilicet terra, habet naturam opacitatis" (*Edition*, vol. 1, p. 138). We are reminded here of an oft-recurring medieval topos of the "opacity" of Sacred Scriptures or the comparison of the Scriptures to a dense thicket.

11. See *Timaeus a Calcidio translatus commentarique instructus*, ed. J. H. Waszink, *Plato latinus*, vol. 4 (Leiden: E. J. Brill, 1975), pp. 167, 273, 278, 282, 303, 309.

existent substance, Philip not only draws upon the Genesis commentary tradition, specifically bringing into the discussion Augustine's commentary on the first chapters of Genesis, but also uses a musical example to make his point. Sound *(sonus)* is *materia* that exists before it is manipulated, delimited, and fashioned into song *(cantus)*, Philip states. Thus while *materia* — as underlying earth, *firmamentum,* or pre-existent substance — can be both readily seen and observed in the world around us and imagined in the connotation of the Latin *silva* (that is, a forest full of trees), equally it is the case that unseen, invisible, but nonetheless still real pre-existent substance (such as time and sound) can be not only conceptualized but in fact worked with in similar ways. Both seen, quantifiable materials, such as wood, and unseen material, such as sound, respond to one's craftsmanly efforts in much the same manner.[12] Furthermore, ways of working with this pre-existent *materia* can be explained with terms such as *simplex, simplicior,* or *compositus,* as a single *punctum* or portion of material or as an aggregation of portions *(aggregatio punctorum).*[13]

It is well to note here that the important concept of *firmamentum* is a

12. In a key passage ("Item, Augustinus super Genesim . . . est enim sonus formatus cantus," *Edition,* vol. 1, p. 58), Philip makes the point of unseen substance such as time existing before the formation of the world, before proceeding to his musical analogy of *sonus* and *cantus.* (See also Augustine, *De Genesi ad litteram* I c.l.n. 2 [PL 34, 247; CSEL 28-I,4] as well as the *Glossa ordinaria in Genesim* I,22 D; and Peter Lombard, *Sententiae in IV Libris* II d.2 c.5 [Grottaferrata: Editiones Collegii S. Bonaventurae Ad Claras Aquas, 1971], p. 341I.) It is of importance here that time, duration, and the measurement of time are related closely to creation. On the topic of time measured and time *ultra mensuram,* the above cluster of quotations demonstrates *in nuce* Philip the Chancellor's pivotal role of bringing together the most influential texts of late antiquity and the earlier Middle Ages, that is, Augustine's commentary on Genesis as well as the *Glossa ordinaria,* with the *Sentences* of Peter Lombard — required reading for theology students of his own day — and, as we have noted, the most recent Latin translations of Aristotle. This occurs over and over within his *Summa,* as study of the excellent footnotes and indices published with the *Summa* demonstrates. (On the crucial and formative role Peter Lombard played in the education of theology students during this period — and much later as well — see the comprehensive study by Marcia L. Colish, *Peter Lombard,* 2 vols. [Leiden: E. J. Brill, 1994], esp. the preface, vol. 1, pp. 1-13, and Chapter II, "The Theological Enterprise," vol. 1, pp. 33-90.)

13. As a wider examination of Philip's text will show (see, for example, "Item, si est ex materia . . . esse illud habebit latitudinem," *Edition,* vol. 1, p. 68), the vocabulary of terms employed in his discussion of a topic (here the substance and intellection of angels) could be, and indeed was, illustrated by musical examples. Further, these musical examples could be used to present a topic of some abstraction, which in turn is to be placed within the systematic study of theology.

pivotal principle within Philip's discussion. According to Philip and others whom he cites (such as Augustine), the *firmamentum* is there, stands firm, is positioned *(positum)*, is opaque, and contains within itself hidden potential — a miraculous operational potency. Further, this pre-existent *firmamentum* has a latitudinal "above" *(superius)* and "below" within an ordered universe *(ordo)*.[14] Thus, capacities of *materia-substantia* (in terms of a pre-existent, undifferentiated, aggregated basis with untold possibilities for expression, differentiation, and operation — all key concepts within Aristotle's discussion of material) come to the fore in a systematic discussion of key theological issues such as creation and the composition of the material of the world. He deals especially with the material God had on hand, but his treatment reaches right into the "stuff" of angelic beings, the *materia* of the differentiated persons of the Trinity, and even the unseen conceptual substance resident within the mind of human beings, of God, and of angels.[15]

Philip the Chancellor's discussion of material brings together a nexus of principles and terms taken directly from his reading of the Latin *Physics*, so that his *Summa* can be considered to be one of the first commentaries on that

---

14. See *Edition*, vol. 1, pp. 140-41, in which the term *firmamentum* accrues significance as Philip proceeds. ("Si vero quis dicat quod ex divina Scriptura scimus . . . et communicatio est in hoc quod plus habet pervietatis, ut supra dictum est.") See also Augustinus, *De Gen. ad litt.* II c.5 (PL 34,267; II c.1; PL 34,263, CSEL 28-I,33; II c.4; PL 34,266; CSEL 28-I,37).

15. Augustine on the subject of "material" has frequently been misunderstood. Notions of a more recent "materialism" have intervened, so that writers commenting on Augustine tend to both excise short phrases from his writings in order to make a point, and to leap from one treatise, dealing with a delimited subject matter — such as Augustine's commentary on Genesis, the Gospel of John, or his treatises concerning free will or the Trinity — to the other. The subject — one with a vast literature — has been treated elsewhere, but here we can make the brief point that various doctrines of "materialism" from the seventeenth century to the present share a common differentiation. The seen, visible world and its "matter" as evident to the sense of sight in the phenomenological world around us are regarded as "material," whereas the unseen "world" of concepts, ideas, emotions, educational experiences, memories, and (most importantly for Augustine) sound, time, and motion, is "immaterial" or non-material. This point of view has influenced both translation and interpretation of Augustine's writing, as, for example, within John Rist's discussion of Augustine's view of body and soul. See John Rist, *Augustine: Ancient Thought Baptized* (Cambridge: Cambridge University Press, 1994), pp. 93-95. Augustine, however, in the group of treatises (written at the time of his conversion) on the subjects of the soul, the order that exists among the disciplines, and that concerning music, presents a point of view that is to be found — and which he perhaps influenced — in the *Timaeus* of Plato in its Latin translation and commentary by Calcidius. Augustine places the seen world in a directly proportional relationship with the unseen as co-equivalent, containing the same properties.

work. But his discussion is also contextualized within the subject of creation, thus placing his considerations within the ongoing, long-standing Genesis commentary tradition — a tradition of which he is very much aware, and which he takes care to identify. Indeed, what we have here is a distillation and coordination of a whole stream of writers, beginning with Basil, Ambrose, and Augustine, on this very subject of the origin, propensities, and properties of material, united with Aristotelian tools in order to articulate more pungently what it is that material actually is, particularly with respect to the material property of motion. Philip the Chancellor has been discussing the question of material used by God in the creation of the world, and what one might mean by the concept of "In the beginning" *(In principiis)*. From this logical entrance he goes on to consider the topic of God's work, accessing the important concept of equivalence, as well as the properties of materials such as light and time *(nam materialis esset lux)*. One is immediately tempted to ask, In what way is light material? The answer follows that light contains properties of material, at once manifesting and exemplifying these properties, and at the same time making available the characteristics and distinctions of other materials. One is instantly aware of these characteristics in the separation of light from darkness. From here Philip proceeds to measurement, and the varieties of measurement appropriate to individual things.

In the calm, ordered discussion that ensues, the attentive reader is particularly impressed with the recurrence of two or three topics that seem to constitute a structure for Philip's intellectual agenda. These are just the priorities to be found in the *Physics*, namely, the expression of material potency, potentiality, and property in terms of motion and variety and within aggregation. Time is of particular interest as a material because it displays motion, varieties of the measurement of motion, and the possibility of aggregation in terms of simultaneous times — a notion exemplified in "polyphony" — and yet is invisible. Further, there is always an implied contrast between motion and mutation — that is, what is the meaning of things that "stand firm" (for example, earth, the ground upon which we walk, the firmament), and conversely what is the meaning of things that are "in motion" (for example, flying things or even ourselves moving about upon the earth)? We learn about motion as an absolutely essential property of material by its contrasting and contradictory quality, that is, stability. At this juncture, Philip brings up several pairs of contrasts, all dealing with properties of material and their identification: transparency, such as in water, is contrasted with opacity; corporeality, which is formed, delimited, and shaped, is contrasted with inchoate substance *(natura)*. It is clear that while these properties must be identified, their differences must also be brought into consonance, not only as one thinks about them, but in actually dealing with them in very concrete ways.[16]

Music as Paradigm for the Abstract

And this is just it. How does one deal with motion, mutation, and aggregation in concrete ways? How might these abstractions be made accessible, in Philip's case, not only to those who would eventually become doctors of philosophy-theology at the newly formed University of Paris, but to those who as intellectually rather ordinary people would eventually become priests and/or teachers of students on the primary school level, now applying themselves to the study of principles of creation and material substance, and attempting to understand the physical universe and God's place within it? This, after all, was Philip's task, to bring together biblical principles with the new Aristotelian learning and attempt to make both comprehensible to those students who would ultimately be engaged in basic people-to-people contact within their respective parishes. Philip, I believe, was a good teacher — his office required that he make himself plain, but beyond this requirement he also possessed a real heart for making himself understood. This is evident in the patient manner with which he takes up one consideration after another, defining each one and presenting what would have been unfamiliar, such as the concept of coagulation, more than once. Taking up the concept of opacity, he states that *natura* is opaque, subject to being formed, but susceptible to the understanding — in other words, to be intellected, by division and distinction, by addition and accretion. The firmament is opaque and dense, but it can be divided from what is above and below. Philip quotes Augustine on this, bringing up the adjacent concept of ornament and decoration.

Music provides a paradigm for all of these qualities, hence its importance as attested by Augustine's writings on the order that exists among disciplines, and on into the thirteenth century and the early university intellectual milieu. Additionally, as a matter of interest, there is good reason to believe that Philip himself possessed a special sensitivity to music's position as an exemplary discipline, with its capacity to plainly display abstractions,

---

16. See *Edition*, vol. 1, pp. 63-65. One important feature for this discussion, to be illustrated below, is that whatever moves is divisible into parts. For the related concepts of *firmamentum, medium, superius,* and consonance among these three levels, see *Edition*, vol. 1, p. 141.

such as motion and aggregation, in sensorially apprehensible illustration. And in fact, significantly for our purposes, his name and person are connected with several music-textual compositions.

Let us match up the considerations we have been discussing with a contemporaneous musical-textual example. *Laudes referat* (fig. 1),[17] a three-part composition and an example of what would become known as "polyphony" (motet), exemplifies and summarizes the issues we have discussed, namely:

(1) Whatever moves is divisible into parts: not only can latitudinal *partes* be seen clearly, but "portions" of sound are clearly delineated by portion-shaped *figurae* of music notation *(puncta)*.

(2) The *firmamentum*, or ground, is aggregated together *(Quo-ni[am])* in one place at the end of the composition. This material is also "pre-existent," having an existence prior to its incorporation into this composition and previous to the other two layers or *partes*.

(3) All three *partes* occur simultaneously, thus exemplifying a simultaneity of times *(tempora)*.

(4) The three *partes* exemplify the *firmamentum*, a firm, structural pre-existent part, with two other *partes* moving with *figurae* characteristic to their respective positions. All three come together into consonance.

(5) Contrary motion, as a graphic as well as intellectual statement, that is, *partes* that pursue contrary directionalities, can be clearly seen, and are also made to be resolved within motion and time.

(6) The material dimensions of this composition are clearly seen in terms of "portions" of time and sound.

Note especially the visual impetus of the notational *figurae* on the page: density and aggregation of the pre-existent substance are exempli-

---

17. The so-called "Notre Dame" manuscript (Florence, Biblioteca Medicea-Laurenziana, Ms 29.1; facsimile, in Luther A. Dittmer, ed., *Publications of Mediaeval Musical Manuscripts*, 10-11, 2 vols. [Brooklyn, NY: Institute of Mediaeval Music, 1966-67]) provides musical-textual *exempla* for the most important theological concepts of this period, and the largest repository of *conductus* texts for which the case has been made for the authorship of Philip the Chancellor. See Hans Tischler, *The Earliest Motets (to circa 1270): A Complete Comparative Edition*, 3 vols. (New Haven: Yale University Press, 1982), vol. 1, pp. 109-111; vol. 3, pp. 4, 59-60 (see fig. 2). The edition makes comparison of the versions possible, as well as facilitating performance by singers today, yet the graphic statement giving the priorities described above is not available. We have, in a sense, a translation in which the text is made comprehensible on an immediate level, but the intention and mentality of the text are lost.

Figure 1. "Laudes Referat," from the so-called "Notre Dame" manuscript, now in the Medicea-Laurenziana Library, Florence, copied c. 1238.

Reproduced here from a facsimile in Luther Dittmer (ed.), *Biblioteca medicea laurenziana*; Manuscript, Plut. 29, I., 2 vols. (Brooklyn, NY: Institute of Medieval Music, 1966), vol. 11, f.386v, by kind permission of the Institute of Mediaeval Music.

fied in what was later known as a *cantus firmus*, at the bottom — or ground — of the composition. Note as well the germane *figurae* in their respective levels as illustrative of the world itself, with the "earth" on the bottom and more swiftly moving *figurae* on the upper levels. Everything about the "face of the page" of this manuscript example is important, even the initial "L" — these are characteristic of the Paris milieu during the first generation of the thirteenth century, quickly spreading, especially to other university centers, throughout Europe.

Figure 2. Contemporary transcript of the "Laudes Referat" manuscript (see fig. 1).
Reproduced here from Hans Tischler, *The Earliest Motets (to circa 1270): A Complete Comparative Edition*, 3 vols. (New Haven: Yale University Press, 1982), vol. 1, pp. 109-11, by permission of Yale University Press.

Music's Vital Place among the Disciplines

We can close our study with some concluding observations on music's integral position as a discipline in the period under scrutiny. Thirteenth-century intellectual life generally, and Philip the Chancellor's work in particular, brings together disciplines that are frequently separated today. Better stated, here we witness the logical fusion of disciplines. Rather than functioning principally as entertainment for passive listeners, music serves to embody and exemplify concepts. By means of the substance it uses — namely, unseen materials of sound and time, each displaying the properties of motion and measurement — it exemplifies the presence or absence of invisible material as a reality, the principles of movement itself, of disassociation and autonomy, and of their opposites, attraction and aggregation. Music, then, constitutes a ministry discipline, making abstractions sensorially perceptible, making general principles plain, and thereby reinforcing the validity of unseen substantial reality. In short, invisible substance is taken seriously, a persuasion that is in need of being revived today.

Augustine stated that nothing, really, could be understood without the exemplary power of music.[18] On this basis, therefore, music retained an established disciplinary place between the material and measurement sciences and the science of unseen substance, that is, theology. Taking Augustine at his word — as did Robert Grosseteste and Roger Bacon, among many others — I have attempted to understand and to demonstrate how this vital link between music and theology has informed Western music — intrinsically, within its very structure. Rather than simply connecting the arts and theology, Western music at crucial phases in its history drew its most significant stylistic principles from its clear ministry to make theological concepts comprehensible to the *mind* through the rationality of temporal time-lapse, to the *eyes* through musical notation, to the *ears* through the unseen substance of sound, and thus to the soul. In this particular case, what has become known as "polyphony" in the intervening centuries served as illustrative of the important theological principle of pre-existent material from which God created the world, and from which the composer fashioned a music-textual composition of more than one part. In short, it is

18. See *De musica* in *Augustine through the Ages: An Encyclopedia,* with foreword by Jaroslav Pelikan, compiled by Allan D. Fitzgerald, O.S.A. (Grand Rapids: Eerdmans, 1999), pp. 574-76. Obviously, here Augustine is dealing with a wider and very important topic, namely, how one "understands" anything at all. See, for example, D. Shapere, "The Concept of Observation in Science," *Philosophy of Science* 49 (1982): 485-525.

hard to imagine an integration more complete, or a mission more far-reaching, than that between the material and measurement art of music and the study of the nature of God.

3. "So Faith Comes from What Is Heard": The Relationship between Music and God's Word in the First Two Centuries of German Lutheranism

Joyce Irwin

In the New Revised Standard Version of the Bible, Romans 10:17 reads, "So faith comes from what is heard, and what is heard comes through the word of Christ." A somewhat different meaning is conveyed in the wording of the King James Version: "So then faith cometh by hearing, and hearing by the word of God." Martin Luther's translation of this verse, rendered in English, has yet another emphasis: "So faith comes by preaching, and preaching by the word of God."[1] At issue in these different translations is whether the content, the mode of communication, or the manner of receiving the message of faith is primary. For Martin Luther the centrality of preaching for drawing individuals to faith was crucial. Although the written word was also gaining new importance in the age of printing and increased literacy, it was the preached word that became a means of grace. At the same time, auditory communication in a broader sense was highly valued by Luther. His love of music was second only to theology, and in at least one instance he recognized music's potential for preaching. In a *locus classicus* for the proclamatory role of music, Luther, in his *Table Talk,* said, "Thus God has even preached through music, as is seen in Josquin."[2] Another juxtaposition of preaching and music is found in Luther's preface to Georg Rhau's *Symphoniae iucundae* (1538), where the term "sonora praedicatione" appears

1. Similar to Luther's version is the wording of the New English Bible: "We conclude that faith is awakened by the message, and the message that awakens it comes through the word of Christ."

2. Martin Luther, *Works,* ed. Jaroslav Pelikan and Hartmut Lehmann (St. Louis: Concordia Publishing House; Philadelphia: Fortress Press, 1955-86), 54:129.

in the process of Luther's advocacy of praise of God through voice and word. Although this term has been used to identify music's role in worship as that of a sermon in sound,[3] in the original context it is less clear whether the term refers to music or to the voice of the preacher. Similarly, as Josquin's music is being given as an example of grace rather than law, to focus on the reference to preaching through music is to divert attention from Luther's main purpose, that is, to distinguish between law and gospel. As Luther wrote no systematic theology, much less a theology of music, but rather responded to the dramatic events of the early Reformation as circumstances dictated, it is understandable that both his followers of succeeding generations and his interpreters of our own era have connected with his thought from different directions.

Interpretations of Luther

Overshadowing all other twentieth-century writings about the relationship of music to Protestant theology is Oskar Söhngen's *Theologie der Musik,* and central to his position is the kerygmatic role of music. Over against the Reformed tradition's restrictive acceptance of music as prayer and praise — as response to proclamation but never as sermon, Söhngen believed that for Luther the office of preaching included music.[4] To be sure, music in its preaching function must be connected to the Word, because what is preached is the Word of God. Through the marriage of text and music, the impact of the Word is intensified, and consequently it is through singing in worship that this kerygmatic role is fulfilled.[5]

While Söhngen's view of music's theological value and of Luther's historical position is widely accepted among German Lutherans, a few voices of dissent have been raised. Matthias Viertel, for example, believes Söhngen misinterpreted Luther's references to preaching and singing as if they were equivalent rather than serving the two functions of proclamation and praise. For Viertel, to identify music's theological role as that of proclamation is to

3. The question posed to several contemporary church music composers in "Musik — eine klingende Predigt?" *Musik und Kirche* 70 (2000): 392-95, was "Can your music or individual works be designated with Luther as a 'praedicatio sonora'?" Most responded affirmatively.

4. Oskar Söhngen, *Theologie der Musik* (Kassel: Johannes Stauda Verlag, 1967), pp. 228-29.

5. Söhngen, *Theologie der Musik,* pp. 91-98.

limit music to liturgical function, whereas Luther regarded all music, both religious and secular, as God's creature.[6]

Against the background of these two different opinions, Christoph Krummacher, in *Musik als praxis pietatis*,[7] takes a fresh look at Luther's view of music and its role in proclaiming the gospel. First of all, he writes, Luther's view of music is not primarily as a component of worship but as a gift of creation. As such, Luther refers most often to music in general, not specifically to church music or to vocal music. Yet he is not interested in abstract speculation on musical theory, nor does he regard music as an independent source of revelation. Rather, as Krummacher explains, Luther's approach may be characterized as existential and experiential, proceeding less from cosmic design than from the experience of faith.[8] The ability to recognize music as a gift of creation comes from the faith that is made possible through the person and work of Jesus Christ. Accordingly, an individual of faith will make use of the gifts of creation in a manner that honors the Creator, whereas a person without faith will abuse those gifts. Music used in faith is an example of the freedom of the gospel and an expression of the joy of the believer in response to God's goodness. Used properly in this way, music serves to preserve order as given by God in creation over against the disordered realm of sin and disbelief.[9]

Krummacher finds that Luther frequently connects "singing and speaking" *(Singen und Sagen)* in the context of spreading God's Word. In his prefaces to hymnals, Luther urges the singing of hymns as a means of instilling God's Word.[10] Krummacher notes that, while without doubt Luther regards the preaching office as the primary means of proclaiming the gospel, he also considers each baptized Christian to have the duty to proclaim the Word. Such proclamation is not limited to public worship or to a preached sermon; it applies to the many ways and situations in which the gospel can be communicated. When Luther says that God preached the gos-

6. Matthias Silesius Viertel, "Kirchenmusik zwischen Kerygma und Charisma," *Jahrbuch für Liturgik und Hymnologie* 29 (1985): 111-23.

7. Christoph Krummacher, *Musik als praxis pietatis* (Göttingen: Vandenhoeck & Ruprecht, 1994).

8. Krummacher, *Musik,* p. 18.

9. Krummacher, *Musik,* p. 16. British scholar B. L. Horne observes that for Luther music "was not only a sign of the possibility of order, but was an actual achievement of that order, a sure indication of the stability of God in a shifting and unstable world." "A *Civitas* of Sound: On Luther and Music," *Theology* 88 (January 1985): 27.

10. See "Preface to the Wittenberg Hymnal," in Luther, *Works,* 53:316.

pel through Josquin, he is not referring to a liturgical function of music but to the freedom from binding rules of composition that, like the freedom from religious law, enabled Josquin to give expression to the joy and grace of God's goodness.

In a conclusion that mediates between Söhngen and his critics, Krummacher determines that the proclamatory role of music for Luther is unmistakable but that this role is broader than the function of text-based music in worship. Krummacher thus distances himself from Söhngen, but neither does he agree with Viertel's distinction between the office of preaching and the office of music. Krummacher argues that such a distinction is not true to Luther's broad view of proclamation, which extends to all believers. He thereby helps to identify the different possible understandings of the ways in which music, sermon, and gospel may be linked.

In light of such divergent interpretations of Luther by scholars of our own era, it should not be surprising that Luther's followers, even those who lived less than a century after his time, found different points of emphasis in his comments on music, depending on the historical circumstances and intellectual milieu in which they were writing.[11] During the course of the seventeenth century, Lutherans disputed whether music could convey religious meaning without a text. The phenomenal growth of organ building gave urgency to this question to an extent not encountered in Luther's lifetime. Others disputed the value of music sung in languages that ordinary people could not understand or in musical styles that rendered the text difficult to discern. Toward the end of the century, the increasing professionalism of church musicians and the increasing prominence of non-religious music led to tensions between clergy and musicians. At that point the distinction between the office of preaching and the office of music in proclaiming the gospel takes on new significance.

Music, Emotions, and the Word

Whether or not Luther thought that music was a means of preaching the Word, there can be no doubt that he believed music could prepare the heart

---

11. My sources are primarily theological and theoretical works of the period. For a fascinating study based on research into church orders and visitation documents, see Joseph Herl, *Worship Wars in Early Lutheranism: Choir, Congregation, and Three Centuries of Conflict* (New York: Oxford University Press, 2004).

to receive the Word. A recurring theme in his comments on music is that it cheers the sad or sluggish spirit and thereby arouses devotion.[12] In his *Table Talk,* he is quoted as saying that music, as the "best gift of God," had often aroused his desire to preach. In the same passage he noted that this unqualified endorsement of music's emotional power differed from that of Augustine, though he was convinced that if Augustine had lived in Luther's time they would be in agreement.[13] Be that as it may, Augustine's scruples concerning the emotional power of music emerged from a different understanding of human nature. Where Luther regarded the human being as an integrated whole, not a mind and soul imprisoned in a body, Augustine, influenced by Neoplatonic thought, could — at least in some of his writings — express a distrust of the senses as appealing to the lower faculties and drawing the mind and soul away from nobler thoughts. This way of thinking undoubtedly had an impact on the Reformed tradition.[14]

According to Luther's understanding of creation, by contrast, humans were created with natural musical appreciation and ability, and thus music's appeal to the senses need not be regarded with suspicion. Granted, one must not deny the sinful propensities of humans after the fall, but this is explained not as a disorder of the various human faculties but as a disorientation of the whole person. Thus music's power to appeal to the emotions was described approvingly by Lutheran writers throughout this period. Nevertheless, in common with the Reformed tradition as well as late Renaissance musical thought, Lutherans regarded vocal music, with its ability to communicate through words, as superior to purely instrumental music.

Cyriacus Spangenburg, in *Von der Musica und den Meistersängern,* acknowledged that music is called a divine gift and art because (where it is used properly), it "stimulates to godliness and causes one to grow and increase in the praise of God, godly love and Christian devotion."[15] Further, music that is sung with a natural voice is by far to be preferred to any stringed instrument "because it not only fills the ears with a lovely sound

12. See, for instance, his commentary on Psalm 4 in Luther, *Works,* 10:42; and his letter to Ludwig Senfl, in *Works,* 49:426.

13. *D. Martin Luthers Werke: Tischreden* (Weimar: H. Böhlau, 1883-), IV:313, no. 4441.

14. It is this branch of Protestantism that best fits Daniel Chua's understanding of the "disenchantment" of the world. See his article in this volume and his book, *Absolute Music and the Construction of Meaning* (Cambridge: Cambridge University Press, 1999), esp. pp. 23-28.

15. Cyriacus Spangenburg, *Von der Musica und den Meistersängern* (Strassburg, 1598), p. 32.

and to some degree cheers the heart, but in addition it also gives good teaching, warning, and comfort with articulated words."[16]

Michael Praetorius, in the first of many chapters on the uses of psalmody or choral music, compares it to a channel of a river which "by the mystical grace of the sacred words, flows from the mouth of the singer into the heart of the like-minded listener," enabling the words to be easily recalled to mind.[17] In another chapter, Praetorius ascribes the grace and efficacy of choral music to the Holy Spirit, for it is through the singing of inspired texts that affections are moved and a remedy is found for sickness of the soul.[18]

In the middle of the seventeenth century, theologian Johannes Botsack published a compendium of knowledge that includes a summary of the commonly recognized effects of music. In listing the effects of singing, Botsack refers to the effects "on us and on others," including exhilaration and movement of the spirit, exciting devotion and driving away spiritual sadness.[19] Included in the same list are the more pedagogical purposes of edifying others and instilling truth. Botsack's list of music's effects is unremarkable, nor does he intend to do more than pass on received knowledge on the subject. What we can note is that the emotional effects of music are repeatedly grouped with the pedagogical effects.

Accordingly, Johann Conrad Dannhawer, prolific Strassburg theologian, commended the ability of music to "awaken the spirit, encourage devotion, divert the mind and emotions from worldly cares, make the heart calm and capable of receiving the divine afflatus and movement through the accompaniment of the Word."[20] He credits Luther with retrieving singing for the people and praises Luther's songs for being well written, for springing from a fervent spirit, and also for being instructive, explaining the articles of faith for those who cannot read.[21]

Significant in this statement is the conviction that the songs sprang from a fervent spirit; throughout these discourses on the effects of music, seventeenth-century writers insist that songs be sung from a sincere heart,

16. Spangenburg, *Von der Musica*, p. 35.

17. Michael Praetorius, *Syntagma Musicum I: Musicae Artis Analecta* (Wittenberg 1614-15), reprinted in *Documenta Musicologica* I:21 (Kassel: Bärenreiter, 1959), p. 17.

18. Praetorius, *Syntagma Musicum*, p. 21.

19. Johannes Botsack, *Moralium Gedanensium* (Frankfurt am Main, 1655), p. 138.

20. Johann Conrad Dannhawer, *Catechismusmilch, oder Der Erklärung deß Christlichen Catechismi* (Strassburg, 1642-72), VIII: 547.

21. Dannhawer, *Catechismusmilch*, VIII:544.

not with the voice alone. The pedagogical value of music is not separate from its emotional power. Music does not simply communicate doctrinal truths in a way that reinforces memory of them, as if it affected only the mental faculties; nor does music simply appeal to the senses, which would lead to an insistence that the hearer rise above the aural appeal. Rather, music combines the emotional power of sound with the spiritual power of God's Word in such a way as to affect the soul. For music to convey this power, both the singer and the listener must be in tune with God.

Music without Texts

Though all could agree that the combination of music and words was the surest path for encouraging devotion and communicating the Word, Lutherans had continued to use organs in worship, whereas Calvinists had rejected instrumental music and, in many churches, destroyed organs. As Calvinist influence spread in German territories, organ music became more controversial. At the same time, however, organ builders were producing more and more magnificent instruments for churches, a situation that called for a theological defense of organ music.

One of the most influential sermons in support of organ music in worship was the *Ulm Organ Sermon* preached by Conrad Dieterich in 1624.[22] Drawing on evidence from the Old Testament, he argues that musical instruments were used in temple worship for the praise of God. The case is harder to make from the New Testament, he realizes, but he finds that instrumental music contributes to improvement and to good order in church, as prescribed in 1 Corinthians 14.[23] Instrumental music has the power to move minds and spirit: by means of the different musical modes, music can effect such responses as joy, sorrow, mercy, and empathy. It can awaken Christian devotion, drive away melancholy, calm the restless spirit, and thereby prepare a person to praise God joyfully. More directly related to the question of whether instrumental music can communicate meaning is his use of the citation attributed to Justin Martyr: "Verbum Dei est, sive mente cogitetur, sive canatur, sive pulsu edatur" ("God's Word is God's Word, whether one thinks it in the mind, or sings it, or produces it by striking").[24]

22. Conrad Dieterich, *Ulmische Orgel Predigt* (Ulm, 1624).
23. Dieterich, *Ulmische Orgel Predigt*, p. 16.
24. Dieterich, *Ulmische Orgel Predigt*, p. 19.

Dieterich does not use this quotation, however, to argue a role for music in proclaiming God's Word but rather to show evidence from the early church supporting the use of instruments. In fact, Dieterich dismisses the objection that worshippers cannot understand the meaning of organ music, responding that the Israelites could not have understood any words that were being sung while the trumpets, cymbals, drums, and strings were being played in the temple. It is enough that one understand the *genus,* the kind of music that is being played. If one knows that it is done to the glory of God, then it has the power to move the heart and arouse the spirit to Christian devotion and joy. Similarly, one can understand the sound of a trumpet as calling to battle or the sound of strings as the sign of a wedding.[25] As a component of worship, instrumental music is not essential,[26] but it is a gift of God that adorns the essential components of Word and sacrament and should therefore be received with gratitude and used to honor God.

Dieterich represents the orthodox Lutheran view of music for the early seventeenth century as it had been shaped over the course of the preceding century. While it may be consistent with Luther's viewpoint, the complex of arguments derives from disputes between Lutheran and Reformed theologians toward the end of the sixteenth century.[27] In defending the use of organs against Reformed objections, the Lutheran position became much stronger in affirming the liturgical position of organ music and its ability to communicate. When the leaders of the Saxon territory of Anhalt-Zerbst rejected the Formula of Concord and turned to Reformed theology, they still argued from within Lutheran thinking against organs. Luther himself had not always been positively inclined toward organs. The Anhalt theologians saw that organs were included in Luther's list of ceremonial items added to the "first, simple institution" of the sacrament which should be set aside in

25. Dieterich, *Ulmische Orgel Predigt,* p. 32.
26. Dieterich, *Ulmische Orgel Predigt,* p. 34.
27. See chapter 1 of Joyce L. Irwin, *Neither Voice nor Heart Alone: German Lutheran Theology of Music in the Age of the Baroque* (New York: Peter Lang, 1993), pp. 11-22. I regard the struggles between Lutheran and Reformed thought, particularly the colloquy of Montbéliard at which Lutheran theologian Jakob Andreae debated Calvinist Theodore Beza concerning music, as formative in the development of the Lutheran orthodox theology of music. For this reason, I have not attempted a thorough study of Lutheran theology of music in the sixteenth century, as Christopher Boyd Brown rightly points out in *Singing the Gospel: Lutheran Hymns and the Success of the Reformation* (Cambridge, MA: Harvard University Press, 2005), p. 231. His study is a valuable addition to the literature on Lutheran hymnody and will contribute to a more complete understanding of the role of music in the Reformation.

order to return the sacrament to the form which Christ instituted.[28] On that basis they rejected organs and used Luther's authority to argue against them. Also, they pointed to those exegeses of Psalms where Luther interpreted music allegorically. In such cases music is related to sermon as a type or foreshadowing of the preaching of the gospel: "The old Jewish string music to which they sang in such a way that one could still understand all the words is in truth only a type or image of the joyful sermon of the gospel which in the New Testament would sound quite loudly throughout the whole world, as Dr. Luther explains on Psalms 47 and 150."[29] Over against the position that music is a beautiful ornament of worship, the Anhalters assert that "the pure preached Word of God and the true use of the Holy Sacrament according to the Lord's institution, together with the untarnished fear of God and Christian love of neighbor which shines forth from one's entire life and action — that is the proper ornament of the church and the decoration that is pleasing to God."[30] Latin motets — which neither the singers nor the hearers understand — do not fulfill Paul's admonition of 1 Corinthians 14 that the words spoken in church be understood by others,[31] and organs belong to the list of superstitious, idolatrous ceremonial ornaments that detract from a proper understanding of the sacrament.[32]

While the overall position of the Anhalt writers toward music does not in any way reflect Luther's high regard for music, nevertheless they rightly point to Luther's unenthusiastic comments about organ music. Not only had Luther listed organs among things practiced in the "pretended church";[33] he had also in his "Exposition of the Lord's Prayer" compared people who pray with their lips but not their hearts to "lead organ pipes which fairly drawl or shout out their sounds in church, yet lack both words and meaning."[34] Used here as an analogy, this observation can hardly be taken as a general statement about organs, but it does indicate that Luther did not regard organ music by itself as

28. Martin Luther, "Pagan Servitude of the Church," in *Martin Luther: Selections from His Writings*, ed. John Dillenberger (New York: Anchor Books, 1961), p. 271.

29. *Erinnerungsschrifft etlicher vom Adel und Städten, An den Durchleuchtigen Hochgebornen Fürsten unnd Herrn, Herrn Johann Georgen, Fürsten zu Anhalt, Graven zu Ascanien, Herrn zu Zerbst und Bernburg* (Amberg, 1597), p. 74. Söhngen, *Theologie der Musik*, p. 111, discusses Luther's allegorical exegeses in the context of his early monastic views.

30. *Erinnerungsschrifft*, p. 73.

31. *Erinnerungsschrifft*, p. 25

32. *Erinnerungsschrifft*, p. 89.

33. Luther, "Exhortation to All Clergy," in *Works*, 34:55.

34. Luther, "An Exposition of the Lord's Prayer," in *Works*, 42:39.

capable of engaging the heart spiritually. Even if it is true, as Krummacher argues, that for Luther the proclamatory power of music is not necessarily tied to texted music, it would be difficult to find support in Luther for the seventeenth-century position that organ music can stimulate devotion in a listener who simply recognizes its devotional purpose.

The Music of Nature

Some writers of the seventeenth century defended instrumental music not on the basis of its ability to communicate but on the basis of its natural powers. With words reminiscent of Luther's preface to Georg Rhau's *Symphoniae iucundae*,[35] Philipp Arnoldi wrote, "Nature itself shows that vocal and instrumental music, in whatever way it occurs, is implanted and instilled in humans to refresh them."[36] Wolfgang Silber saw a physiological basis for the human response to music: "The natural spirits of our heart and blood are so related to and fond of the lovely song and sound of music that a person is easily moved thereby, yes even enraptured."[37] That music works through the natural physiology is evident in the response of infants to music: "It can be seen that even the little children in the cradle are moved by sweet song and sound, so that they look around, listen with great wonder, open their mouths and eyes, and lose themselves in it, even if they do not understand what it is or what it means."[38]

These descriptions of music's natural powers are very much in keeping with Luther's view that humanly made music, a wondrous and mysterious art, is grounded in God's creation. Yet Luther was not inclined to engage in philosophical explanations of the wonders of music, leaving that to "better men with more time on their hands."[39] Although none would dare claim

---

35. "Looking at music itself, you will find that from the beginning of the world it has been instilled and implanted in all creatures, individually and collectively." Luther, *Works*, 53:322.

36. Philipp Arnoldi, *Caeremoniae Lutheranae, Das ist, Ein christlicher Gründlicher Unterricht von allen fürnembsten Caeremonien so in den Lutherischen Preussischen Kirchen . . . adhibirt werden . . . den Calvinischen Ceremoniestürmern entgegengesetzt* (Konigsberg, 1616), p. 167.

37. Wolfgang Silber, *Encomion Musices: Lob der edlen Kunst der Musicen* (Leipzig, 1622), p. 15.

38. Silber, *Encomion Musices*, p. 15.

39. Luther, "Preface to Georg Rhau's *Symphoniae jucundae*," in *Works* 53:322-23.

that appellation, music theorists of the late sixteenth and early seventeenth centuries did attempt to ground music in philosophical and cosmological systems. As baroque monody began to compete with Renaissance polyphony and the modal system was replaced by the major/minor system, music theorists found theological significance in the emphasis on triads and harmony. The analogy of a musical triad and the divine Trinity was too obvious to be ignored, and various theoreticians and theologians reinforced their positions by making this connection. Writing in 1588, Rudolf Schlick saw the Trinity reflected in the design of creation. The harmony of the triad was as essential to music as the Trinity is essential to the universe: "If the combination of three notes in either type of *cantus* deviates from the legitimate way, is mutilated, or ruined, you will also see the entire harmony arising from it immediately disturbed, vanish, and utterly fall apart, just as everything in the expanse of the whole world would perish and return to nothingness, if it were bereft of the power and awesomeness of the Holy Trinity."[40] Joannes Lippius, in his *Synopsis Musicae Novae* of 1612, was even more explicit in regarding harmony as the fundamental basis of the universe. "There is a most beautiful harmony in God the triune original source of all, in the choir of good spirits, in the physical macrocosm, in heaven, in the elements, in mixed meteors, metals, stones, plants, animals and in the human microcosm. All things remain standing through harmony. In disharmony all things fall."[41]

The writers cited in the previous paragraph were writing music theory, though they were also trained in theology. Theologians and writers of devotional books sometimes took the theme of harmony as a metaphor for inward, spiritual harmony. Philipp Nicolai, who is best known for his hymns "How brightly shines the morning star" and "Sleepers, wake, a voice is calling," was the first spokesman for this new spirituality. In his *Frewdenspiegel des ewigen lebens,* he describes God as singing with the loveliest and sweetest voice surpassing the sound of "harps, drums, trumpets, pipes, lutes, zither, strings, cymbals, or any other such pleasant-sounding instruments." The elect "hear joy and delight as the Lord speaks and preaches peace to his people and the saints"[42] Johann Arndt, perhaps the most influential devotional writer of this period, was clear in stating that the instruments used in Old

40. Rudolph Schlick, *Exercitatio qua Musices Origo Prima* (Speyer, 1588), as translated in Benito V. Rivera, *German Music Theory in the Early Seventeenth Century* (Ann Arbor: UMI Research Press, 1974), p. 140.

41. Joannis Lippius, *Synopsis Musicae Novae* (Strassburg, 1612), p. ii.

42. Philipp Nicolai, *Frewdenspiegel des ewigen lebens* (1599), reprinted with foreword by Reinhard Mumm (Soest: Westfälische Verlagsbuchhandlung Mocker & Jahn, 1963), p. 72.

Testament times should be understood as metaphors for "our heart, spirit, soul, mind and mouth."[43] His advocacy of musical practice was limited to hymns and psalms sung in praise of God. Yet cosmic harmony, not in the sense of audible music of the spheres but in the orderly relationships between earthly and heavenly bodies, was intrinsic to his spirituality. He believed there was "a very mysterious and great consonance" between the microcosmic firmament and the macrocosmic.[44] Christoph Frick, a preacher whose *Musica Christiana* combines the spirituality of Arndt and Nicolai with an advocacy of musical practice, applied the microcosm/macrocosm principle to the musical triad. Quoting Valerius Herberger, another devotional writer, Frick remarks, "Music is God's gift. I am often amazed that in the whole keyboard no more than three keys harmonize together. The rest are simply octaves. Is that not a manifest mystery of the highly praised Trinity?"[45] The connection between music and human design is such that those who refuse to use their God-given capacity for singing reveal thereby their scorn for God and destine themselves to damnation.

The issue that concerns this circle of devotional writers is not whether words can be understood in the vocal music of their churches but whether the individual, living in spiritual harmony with God, was using his or her natural faculties for the praise and honor of God. Although they would not deny the power of music to prepare a listener to devotion, the real preparation takes place in the heart, which must be open to God's indwelling presence. Music's power is not so much tied to the communication of the Word of God as it is to the indwelling harmony of the universe. Herberger asked, "Is it not amazing that, when something is out of harmony in a song, one feels it in the ear at the same time?"[46] Because humans are created with lungs, arteries, windpipe, mouth, and tongue that make voice and song possible, writes Frick, a person so equipped should "use all the members around his heart so that God, who wants to dwell in the temple of our heart, will be praised and addressed in song out of true thankfulness."[47]

43. Johann Arndt, *Vier Bücher Vom Wahren Christenthumb* (Lüneburg, 1670), p. 546 (Book 2, ch. 41). The work was published in 1606 and reprinted many times.

44. Arndt, *Christenthumb*, p. 681 (Book 2, ch. 58).

45. Valerius Herberger, *Paradisz-Blümlein/Aus dem Lustgarten der 150 Psalmen* (Leipzig, 1670), pp. 71-72; Christoph Frick, *Music-Büchlein, Oder Nützlicher Bericht von dem Uhrsprunge, Gebrauche und Erhaltung Christlicher Music* (Lüneburg, 1631), p. 35.

46. Herberger, *Hertz Postilla* (Leipzig, 1613), p. 481.

47. Frick, *Music-Büchlein*, p. 58.

Music and Preaching

As the seventeenth century progressed, the devotional application of the concept of harmony came more directly into conflict with music theorists' application as a foundation for musical composition. A new reform movement known as Pietism began to scrutinize the spiritual life of individuals to a degree not previously seen in Lutheranism. Furthermore, cultural changes brought a shift in musical style and new professional awareness on the part of musicians. Before 1650 the office of cantor frequently served as a stepping stone to the pastorate, a situation which indicated a primary vocational commitment to the church. After 1650 such vocational transitions were less frequent than cases in which one cantorate served as a stepping stone to a larger one.[48] This, together with the rise of operas and musical styles that featured operatic-style soloists, brought into the church those whose primary vocational commitment was to music. This is not to say that cantors no longer were fully committed to the church — far from it — but there is increasing evidence of tension between pastors and cantors, and there was strong resistance in some circles to those singers who were hired on the basis of vocal ability without regard to religious belief. Furthermore, organists were often perceived to be showing off their prodigious skills rather than enhancing the worship of the congregation.

When, therefore, Pietists complain of music that merely tickles the ears, of texts in languages that the congregation does not understand, and of musicians who exhibit un-Christian behavior, they may be deviating from an orthodox Lutheran view of music, or they may be making a conservative attempt to retain an authentic Lutheran approach to music.[49] This is a question that leads to the very nature of Pietism and its relation to the Reformation, a larger question than we can address here. What is significant for the question of music's relation to the reception of faith is that the controversies about musical style and musical leadership led the writers of the late seventeenth and early eighteenth centuries to analyze the relationship of composer, performer, listener, and Holy Spirit more precisely than had previously been done.

One of numerous critics of the church music of the time, Christian Gerber, a Pietist writing in the early eighteenth century, complained about

48. Dieter Krickeberg, *Das protestantische Kantorat im 17. Jahrhundert* (Berlin: Verlag Merseburger, 1965), p. 175.

49. For a fuller discussion of this topic, see Joyce Irwin, "German Pietists and Church Music in the Baroque Age," *Church History* 54, no. 1 (1985): 29-40.

those whose outward lives were not in harmony with the devotion expected of a church musician. First, he wrote, there are the Italian Catholics who perform in Lutheran churches to earn money but scorn the form of worship, leave as soon as they have performed, and go drinking and courting women until it is time to perform again. Second, there are musicians who belong to the church but are whores, adulterers, or drunkards. They think all that matters is that they play or sing well.[50]

Responding to Gerber, cantor Georg Motz took the orthodox teaching on the office of priest and applied it to the office of musician: "The office of priest is and remains holy, even if he himself is evil and godless. And thus singing and making music is likewise good in and of itself, even though sometimes the person who sings and makes music is evil and godless."[51] The attempt to purify the church will fail because no one can look into another person's heart; outward observances must be retained as commanded by God, even if there is corruption.

Even though Motz's position seems to be good Lutheran theology, his explanation of the divine role in music differs from that of previous interpreters. Whereas earlier writers had said that the Holy Spirit works through the words of Scripture as set to music, Motz regards the Holy Spirit as coming directly to the composer. He compares composing to preaching and refers to God as the "highest Harmonicus of all."[52] For Motz this has less to do with the internal state of the soul, which is Gerber's concern, than with the fundamental reality of the universe, which is implanted into leaves, trees, birds, and planets, as well as the soul. Such a view of harmony can bypass the revealed Word and connect directly to the divine source. Gerber's approach to music, on the other hand, is text based; just as worship should be "reasonable," so "we should sing like reasonable humans, not like birds."[53] Motz, however, does not place the highest priority on connecting with the listener; it is the responsibility of each member of the congregation to listen with the right intention. Just as preachers are not to blame if their words fall on deaf ears, neither are composers to blame if their God-given skills are scorned.

Gerber's view of the duty of the congregation was not that it listen attentively to inspired music but rather that it express corporate praise of God. Artistry was of little importance if the people could not understand what

50. Christian Gerber, *Unerkannte Sünden der Welt* (Dresden and Leipzig, 1705-1719), I:1061-62.

51. Georg Motz, *Verteidigte Kirchenmusik* (n.p., 1703), p. 37.

52. Motz, *Kirchenmusik*, p. 39.

53. Gerber, *Unerkannte Sünden*, p. 345.

was being sung. Even then, the participation of all is to be preferred to a performance by a few.

> Furthermore, I can assure [Motz] that the singing of a whole congregation, which he scornfully calls "a vile chorale clamor," is far more pleasing to the Highest than an artistic piece where the listeners can understand nothing because of the noise of the instruments or else hear a word only now and then. I do not deny that God's deeds can be praised also in lovely and reverent [figural] music if it is rightly arranged for edification. But through the singing of chorales it happens just as well and even better, because the whole congregation is praising the greatness of God with one mouth.[54]

Motz was not alone in placing the musician on a level with the preacher. Johann Mattheson criticized Luther and Lutheran tradition for not admitting the ability of music, like that of the preached word, to convey faith through hearing. Luther should have translated Romans 10:17 as did the translators of the King James Version: "So then faith comes by hearing, and hearing by the word of God." This would have been more faithful to the original Greek, Mattheson argues, and it would have prevented an overemphasis on the sermon in Lutheran worship. "Saving faith comes not from the sermon alone but equally from listening to a beautiful piece of sacred music, which may then be called a main sermon."[55]

The aspect of music that enabled it to be compared to a sermon was its affinity to rhetoric. Early in the seventeenth century, Seth Calvisius had asked whether music and oratory have something in common and had responded that music was closer to poetry and painting than to oratory.[56] A century later, musicians were more inclined to respond differently. As operas became more popular, composers learned how to elicit emotional responses from the audience by means of musical rhetoric. When the cantata form was introduced in church by Erdman Neumeister, it was based on operatic forms of aria and recitative. Gottfried Scheibel explicitly advocated that the same musical affections cultivated in opera be carried into church music as a

54. Gerber, *Die Unerkannten Wolthaten Gottes* (Dresden, 1704), fol. B7.

55. Mattheson, *Das Forschende Orchestre, oder desselben Dritte Eröffnung* (Hamburg, 1721), pp. 132-33 and footnote pp. 134-35. Significantly, the Pietists also criticized the overemphasis on the sermon in the worship practices of their day, but their solution was not to add something more for the congregation to hear but to involve them in singing and praying.

56. Seth Calvisius, *Exercitatio Musica Tertia* (Leipzig, 1611), pp. 34-35. By contrast, Johann Matthaeus Meyfart, in a work on German rhetoric, writes that a complete speech must be like music with many songs (*Teutsche Rhetorica oder Redekunst* [Coburg, 1634], p. 12).

means of evangelization. While Scheibel's intent was to bring people into the church, his means were thoroughly naturalistic and involved an imitation of opera through rhetorical devices, not divine inspiration.[57]

Caspar Ruetz, writing in the middle of the eighteenth century, took the line of thought further and noted that the means that a preacher uses are thoroughly natural and therefore in no way superior to those of the musician: "For why should this movement, when a preacher opens and closes his jaw, moves his lips and tongue in a natural manner common to all people, lets few tones be heard without the beauty of the melody with the words, lets some movements of hands and body be seen as a customary expression of the fitting affect; or when a person praying moves his lips and repeats with soft voice or whispers the formula being read; why, I say should these movements in and of themselves be more holy and pleasing to God than when in music a singer lets himself be heard by putting his throat in all sorts of forms in an artistic manner, or when an instrumentalist moves fingers, hands and arms artfully or uses his breath for the artful sound of his wind instrument? It all depends on the inward disposition that must make our ministrations in worship pleasing to God."[58] In summary, figural music is just as pleasing to God and just as central to worship as sermon and prayer.

In his treatment of musical practice, Ruetz defends the repetition of words, which to some critics was a cause for mockery, by referring to rhetorical devices that provide decorative emphasis. The writers of the psalms made use of such repetitions. The difference between oratory and music, Ruetz notes, is that "in a speech one uses the tones of the voice for the sake of the words . . . but in music the words are there for the sake of the tones, because in the latter one speaks more through tones than through words."[59]

Conclusion

With Motz, Mattheson, Scheibel, and Ruetz, we can say that music has proclamatory power and that the role of music is considered of equal importance to the sermon. Even if we admit that Luther regarded music as having a

57. Gottfried Ephraim Scheibel, *Zufällige Gedancken von der Kirchen-Music Wie Sie heutiges Tages beschaffen ist* (Frankfurt and Leipzig, 1721). See my translation: "Random Thoughts about Church Music in Our Day," in *Bach's Changing World: Voices in the Community*, ed. Carol Baron (Rochester, NY: University of Rochester Press, 2006), pp. 229-46.

58. Caspar Ruetz, *Widerlegte Vorurteile von der Beschaffenheit der heutigen Kirchenmusic und von der Lebens-Art einiger Musicorum* (Lübeck, 1752), preface.

59. Ruetz, *Widerlegte Vorurteile*, p. 65.

kerygmatic role, the difference in worldview between Luther and these eighteenth-century writers must not be overlooked. The naturalism of the eighteenth-century writer who analyzes the rhetorical methods of preacher and musician is different from Luther's appreciation of divine revelation in nature. The difference is even clearer between Luther and those who pursued the cosmological foundations of music. For Luther the concept of the music of the spheres was metaphorical: when the church fathers used the concept, Luther says, it was not their intention "to be understood as though sound were given off by the motion of the celestial bodies. What they wanted to say was that their nature was most lovely and altogether miraculous."[60] Lutheran music theorists of the late baroque era, on the other hand, would not settle for a metaphorical grounding of their art. Drawing on Johannes Kepler's *Harmonica Mundi* (1619), Robert Fludd's *Monochordum Mundi* (1623), and Athanasius Kircher's *Musurgia Universalis* (1650), musicians such as Andreas Werckmeister and Johann Heinrich Buttstedt portrayed the universe as ordered according to musical proportions and the harmony of the heavenly bodies as exerting real influence on earthly music. Werckmeister expressed his affinity to Luther by pointing out that Luther understood the connection between music and the order of creation and valued music because it contributed to good order.[61] When Buttstedt uses the terms "Eternal Harmony" and "Eternal Foundation of Music" in the title of his book, however, he gives ontological significance to the foundations of music in a manner foreign to Luther's thought.[62]

Although rejecting Buttstedt's ontology, Johann Mattheson shared the view of music as existing prior to the creation of the physical universe, admitting, "One does not do injustice with the thought that harmony is something uncreated and is from eternity to eternity."[63] Because of this, humans, at least before original sin, had an unmediated connection to music through the process of creation: "For my part, I am certain that right at the beginning, when God created heaven and earth, yes, in the moment that the almighty *Fiat* sounded, music flowed and was imparted *eo ipso* into the created being and

---

60. Luther, "Commentary on Genesis 2:21," in *Works* 1:126.

61. Andreas Werckmeister, *Der Edlen Music-Kunst Würde, Gebrauch und Mißbrauch* (Frankfurt and Leipzig, 1691), p. 9.

62. Johann Heinrich Buttstedt, *Ut, Mi, Sol, Re, Fa, La, Tota Musica et HARMONIA AETERNA, Oder Neu-eröffnetes, altes, wahres, eintziges und ewiges Fundamentum Musices* (Erfurt, 1716).

63. Mattheson, *Das Neu-Eröffnete Orchestre, Oder Universelle und gründliche Anleitung/ Wie ein Galant Homme einen vollkommenen Begriff von der Hoheit und Würde der edlen Music erlangen . . . möge* (Hamburg, 1713), pp. 302-3.

human; and indeed before the Fall it was a large part of his happiness and blessedness."[64] Indeed, music in this life is preparation for the blessed life that is to come, which will consist of eternal music-making with the angels. Mattheson was so convinced of the reality of heavenly music that he devoted an entire book to the defense of this belief.[65] Whether Luther would have dismissed Mattheson's speculations on angelic music as "idle and useless human ideas" in the same way that he derided Pseudo-Dionysius's angelic hierarchies we can only guess.[66]

What we can recognize is that Mattheson and all the other writers in this chapter believed themselves to be writing from within the Lutheran tradition. Neither they nor we have any doubt that Luther held music in high regard, both for its beneficial effects on emotions and for its ability to serve the gospel. Changing circumstances in culture and intellectual history led Lutherans of the seventeenth and eighteenth centuries to discuss music in terms that sometimes seemed to diverge from Luther's theology. Yet, from a broad perspective, their goals were the same as Luther's. Over against a scientific naturalism that threatened to deny the role of God in the natural world, they asserted the divine basis of music. In the face of changing musical styles and shifting allegiances of musicians that threatened the primacy of church music over other kinds of music, they upheld the importance of music in worship as a means of spreading the Word of God.

Returning to the Bible verse cited at the beginning of this essay, we can observe that the NRSV emphasizes the content of the message of the gospel. It is fair to say that, in spite of Luther's wish to place music next to theology, the predominant tendency of Protestantism has been to rely chiefly on words to convey the Good News. Preaching has been central, as Luther intended, and has often been a powerful means of grace, but music, while given a large role in worship, has not generally been recognized as having theological significance. Fortunately, this situation is changing, as is evident in the articles in this volume. The challenge for our time is to recognize and cultivate the many modes of proclaiming the gospel, in accordance with Luther's theology, but also, following the lead of eighteenth-century Lutherans, to affirm music's divine origin and spiritual power with arguments that respond to the challenges of changing cultures and ideologies.

64. Mattheson, *Orchestre*, p. 302.
65. Mattheson, *Behauptung der Himmlischen Musik aus den Gründen der Vernunft, Kirchen-Lehre und heiligen Schrift* (Hamburg, 1747).
66. Luther, "Commentary on Genesis," in *Works*, 1:235.

4. Created Beauty: The Witness of J. S. Bach

Jeremy S. Begbie

Among the millions of words spoken and written about J. S. Bach's *Goldberg Variations* of 1741, few are as intriguing as those of the musicologist Peter Williams when he stands back from this dazzling *tour de force* and reflects:

> I think myself that it "feels special" because, whatever antecedent this or that feature has, its beauty is both original — seldom like anything else, even in Bach — and at the same time comprehensible, intelligible, coherent, based on simple, "truthful" harmonies.[1]

Most of what I want to say in this chapter is suggested by that observation (even though Williams himself would probably demur at the theological slant I shall be putting on his words). The matter he brings to the surface is the interplay between two types of beauty: on the one hand, the beauty that is in some sense already "there" in the nature of things (the beauty of "truthful" harmonies), and on the other, the beauty human beings make (the "original" beauty of a piece like the *Goldberg*). Put more theologically, there is the beauty directly given to the world by God, and that which we are invited to fashion as God's creatures. Taking our cue from Williams, the question we shall be pursuing in this chapter is: How might an engagement

1. Peter F. Williams, *Bach: The Goldberg Variations* (Cambridge: Cambridge University Press, 2001), p. 1.

I am very grateful to Dr. Suzanne McDonald and Dona McCullagh for their very valuable comments on an earlier draft of this chapter.

with Bach's music, especially as considered in its time and place, assist us in gaining a clearer theological perception and understanding of these two senses of created beauty and of the relation between them?

Theological Bearings

We shall turn to Bach in due course. The first task, however, is to say something about the concept of "beauty" itself, to clarify what we might intend by this fluid and much-contested notion and, in particular, what might be entailed in a specifically *theological* perspective on it. With limited space, I cannot attempt anything like a comprehensive "theology of the beautiful," but we do at least need to gain some theological bearings — that is, highlight key features of the theological landscape that are especially relevant to a responsible Christian account of beauty and the ways in which such an account is affected by them.

Our primary orientation, of course, will not be to an experience of the beautiful, nor to an aesthetics, but to the quite specific God attested in Scripture — the gracious, reconciling, self-revealing God of Jesus Christ. If an account of beauty is to be *theo-logical* in Christian terms, its *logos* or rationale will take its shape primarily from the being and acts of this *theos*. Crassly obvious as this may seem, even a casual survey of religious treatments and theologies of beauty over the last thirty years will frequently show a marked lack of attention to the identity of the deity or deities being presumed. Difficulties are compounded if the de facto basic allegiance is to some prior and fixed conception of beauty, especially if it is allied to a metaphysical scheme whose consonance with the testimony of Scripture is anything but clear. If we are to think of the phenomenon of beauty, at least initially, in terms of the main strands that inform the so-called "great theory" (and I see no compelling reason not to do so) — in other words, *proportion and consonance of parts, brightness* or resplendence, *perfection* or integrity, and as *affording pleasure upon contemplation*[2] — then these strands need to be constantly re-

2. See Wladyslaw Tatarkiewicz, "The Great Theory of Beauty and Its Decline," *The Journal of Aesthetics and Art Criticism* 31 (1972): 165-80. (Nicholas Wolterstorff rightly points out that, although Tatarkiewicz sees consonance of parts as identical with due proportion, not all the writers Tatarkiewicz cites presume this [Nicholas Wolterstorff, *Art in Action: Toward a Christian Aesthetic* (Grand Rapids: Eerdmans, 1980), p. 162].) I am not suggesting, of course, that these strands together constitute a *definition* of beauty — but they do at least indicate some of the most prominent lines or themes in mainstream Western thinking about

formed and transformed, purged and purified by a repeated return to the saving self-disclosure of Scripture's God.

Needless to say, this will sound to some like an appeal for a sectarian retreat into a Christian ghetto, an isolationist "fideism" that rules out conversation with all but Christians. Nothing of the sort is intended. The point is not to close down dialogue about beauty with those outside or on the edges of Christian tradition, nor with the vast corpus of philosophical writings on beauty. The issue is at root about the norms shaping our language. If a conversation about "beauty" is to be fruitful, one cannot *but* care about the criteria governing the deployment of such a historically loaded and polysemous word — for how can speech bear fruit if it has ceased to care about its primary responsibilities? And to care about these criteria, for the Christian at any rate, is ultimately to care about the God to whom the church turns for the reshaping of all its words.

A Christian account of beauty, then, will be oriented to a particular God. Let me press the matter. According to the Christian tradition, this God has identified himself as irreducibly *trinitarian.* The deity celebrated in Christian faith is not an undifferentiated monad or blank "Absence," but a triunity of inexhaustible love and life, active and present to the world as triune and never more intensively than in the saving life, death, and resurrection of Jesus Christ. If, then, we are to speak of God as primordially beautiful — however we may want to qualify this — then strenuous care must be taken to ensure it is *this* God of whom we speak.[3] If we speak of divine pro-

---

beauty. See also Jerome Stolnitz, "'Beauty': Some Stages in the History of an Idea," *Journal of the History of Ideas* 22, no. 2 (1961): 185-204; Edward Farley, *Faith and Beauty: A Theological Aesthetic* (Aldershot: Ashgate, 2001), ch. 2.

3. It was a rigorous concern for the specificity of theology's God that made Karl Barth so circumspect about ascribing beauty to God — perhaps excessively so (Karl Barth, *Church Dogmatics,* ed. T. F. Torrance and G. W. Bromiley [Edinburgh: T&T Clark, 1956-75], II/1, pp. 650-66). As so often with this theologian, the fear is of an intrusive a priori that in some manner constrains God, a "transcendental" to which God is made answerable — and the particular anxiety here is Hellenism. So Barth insists: "God is not beautiful in the sense that he shares in an idea of beauty superior to him, so that to know it is to know him as God. On the contrary, it is as he is God that he is also beautiful, so that he is the basis and standard of everything that is beautiful and of all ideas of the beautiful" (*Church Dogmatics,* II/1, p. 656). Hence Barth will not allow beauty to be a "leading concept" in the doctrine of God. It is secondary to God's glory, an "explanation" of it; beauty is the "form" of God's glory — that about his self-revealing glory which attracts rather than repels, which redeems, persuades and convinces, evokes joy rather than indifference. One might wish Barth had developed these views rather more extensively, and especially in relation to creaturely beauty, but his

portion and consonance, can these be any other than the proportion and consonance of this triune God? If we speak of divine brightness, integrity, or perfection, can these be any other than the brightness, integrity, and perfection of the trinitarian life? Everything depends here on refusing all a priori abstractions and maintaining a resolute focus on the saving economy of God in Jesus Christ. Divine beauty is discovered not in the first instance by reference to a doctrine (still less to a philosophy of beauty) but by strict attention to a movement in history enacted for us — supremely the story of Jesus Christ the incarnate Son, living in the Father's presence in the power of the Spirit. Trinitarian beauty has, so to speak, been performed for us.[4]

To begin to unfold the implications of this: if beauty is to be ascribed primordially to the triune God, and the life of God is constituted by the dynamism of outgoing love, then primordial beauty is *the beauty of this ecstatic love for the other.* God's beauty is not static structure but the dynamism of love. The "proportion and consonance" of God, his "brightness" or radiance, his "perfection," and his affording "pleasure upon contemplation" are all to be understood in the light of the endless self-donation of Father to Son and Son to Father in the ecstatic momentum of the Spirit. Hence we find Balthasar insisting that it is to the economy of salvation that we must go to discover God's beauty (and thus the ultimate measure of all beauty), since the incarnation, death, and raising of Jesus display God's love in its clearest and most decisive form; here, above all, we witness the mutual self-surrendering love of Father and Son in the Spirit for the healing of the

---

methodological concerns, I would suggest, are to be seriously heeded. (One of the most puzzling things about David Bentley Hart's substantial book on the aesthetics of Christian truth — *The Beauty of the Infinite: The Aesthetics of Christian Truth* [Grand Rapids: Eerdmans, 2003] — is that he is frequently very close to Barth methodologically, yet what few remarks he makes about Barth are extraordinarily dismissive. Among the reviews I have read, only Robert Jenson's points this out ["Review Essay: David Bentley Hart, *The Beauty of the Infinite: The Aesthetics of Christian Truth,*" Pro Ecclesia 4, no. 2 (2005): 236].)

4. So Hans Urs von Balthasar writes that we "ought never to speak of God's beauty without reference to the form and manner of appearing which he exhibits in salvation-history." And later: "God's attribute of beauty can certainly . . . be examined in the context of a doctrine of the divine attributes. Besides examining God's beauty as manifested by God's actions in his creation, his beauty would also be deduced from the harmony of his essential attributes, and particularly from the Trinity. But such a doctrine of God and the Trinity really speaks to us only when and as long as the *theologia* does not become detached from the *oikonomia*, but rather lets its every formulation and stage of reflection be accompanied and supported by the latter's vivid discernibility" (see Hans Urs von Balthasar, *The Glory of the Lord: A Theological Aesthetics,* vol. 1, *Seeing the Form,* trans. Erasmo Leivà-Merikakis [Edinburgh: T&T Clark, 1982], pp. 124, 125).

world.[5] This linking of beauty with outgoing love requires giving a full and crucial place to the Holy Spirit in connection with beauty — as we shall see many times. Insofar as the Spirit is the personal unity of the mutual outgoingness of Father and Son, the impulse toward self-sharing in God's life, we might well describe the Spirit as the "beautifier" in God.[6]

Giving the trinitarian character of God its formal and material due means *we will resist the temptation to drive apart beauty and the infinite,* something that is so much a mark of modernity and postmodernity. Here we can have some sympathy with John Milbank and others who lament what they see as the modern rupture of beauty and the sublime, evident especially since the eighteenth century.[7] As understood in the tradition represented by Kant, the experience of the sublime is an awareness of being overwhelmed by something uncontainable, beyond our grasp. In Kant this is either mainly "mathematical" — when we are overwhelmed by size and are

5. Speaking of God's saving economy, Balthasar writes: "should we not . . . consider this 'art' of God's to be precisely the transcendent archetype of all worldly and human beauty?" (*The Glory of the Lord,* vol. 1, p. 70). In this respect we can also join Jonathan Edwards when he writes of "primary beauty," whose chief instance is God's own triune benevolence, the mutual generosity and "infinite consent" that constitutes the life of God. See Roland A. Delattre, *Beauty and Sensibility in the Thought of Jonathan Edwards: An Essay in Aesthetics and Theological Ethics* (New Haven: Yale University Press, 1968), chs. 7-8; Amy Plantinga Pauw, *"The Supreme Harmony of All": The Trinitarian Theology of Jonathan Edwards* (Grand Rapids: Eerdmans, 2002); Farley, *Faith and Beauty,* ch. 4.

Balthasar's approach, of course, presses us to relate the crucifixion to God's beauty, for here God's love reaches its fullest intensity. We cannot enter into this matter in any depth here, but see Jeremy Begbie, "Beauty, Sentimentality and the Arts," in *The Beauty of God,* ed. Daniel J. Treier, Mark Husbands, and Roger Lundin (Downers Grove, IL: InterVarsity Press), pp. 63-67; and Stephen Fields, "The Beauty of the Ugly: Balthasar, the Crucifixion, Analogy and God," *International Journal of Systematic Theology* 9, no. 2 (2007): 172-83.

We recall the woman pouring expensive ointment over Jesus' head. Jesus rebukes his disciples for complaining: "She has done a beautiful thing to me" (Matt. 26:10). Her "giving everything" has been provoked by, and perhaps even in some manner shares in, the divine self-giving in and through Jesus.

6. For a thorough exposition of the Spirit in relation to beauty, see Patrick Sherry, *Spirit and Beauty: An Introduction to Theological Aesthetics* (London: SCM Press, 2002).

7. John Milbank, "Beauty and the Soul," in *Theological Perspectives on God and Beauty,* ed. John Milbank, Graham Ward, and Edith Wyschogrod (Harrisburg, PA: Trinity Press International, 2003), pp. 1-34; "Sublimity: The Modern Transcendent," in *Religion, Modernity and Postmodernity,* ed. Paul Heelas (Oxford: Blackwell, 1998), pp. 258-84; Frederick Bauerschmidt, "Aesthetics: The Theological Sublime," in *Radical Orthodoxy: A New Theology,* ed. John Milbank, Catherine Pickstock, and Graham Ward (London: Routledge, 1999), pp. 201-19; Hart, *Beauty of the Infinite,* pp. 43-93.

confronted with the limits of our sense perception (such as we might experience under a starry sky or when suddenly faced with a mountain massif), or
"dynamical" — when we are overwhelmed by a power that makes us acutely
aware of our own finitude and physical vulnerability (such as we might feel
in a raging storm).[8] On this reading, it should be stressed, the sublime is
unrepresentable to the senses and the imagination, and as such can provoke
not only awe and wonderment but also unease and even terror. Beauty, by
contrast, is radically tied to the ordering of the mind. The experience of
beauty, for Kant, is the experience of the cognitive faculties of the imagination and the understanding engaging in free play; the pleasure of the experience is derived from those powers which enable us to arrange a plurality of
sense data.[9] The Milbankian argument is that, in its approach to beauty and
sublimity, the logic of postmodernism is essentially Kantian.[10] Beauty is
downplayed (even "annihilated") as formed, tame, ordered, and controlla-
ble, affecting us through harmony and proportion, whereas the sublime is
extolled as formless, untamable, indeterminate, and uncontrollable. Transposed into theology: infinite divine transcendence is understood in terms of
negation: "modernity and postmodernity tend strictly to *substitute* sublimity for transcendence. This means that all that persists of transcendence is
sheer unknowability or its quality of non-representability and non-
depictability."[11] As such, the sublime is a *formless* divine presence,[12] devoid
of love or goodness, and thus potentially oppressive.[13] In response to these

8. Immanuel Kant, *Critique of the Power of Judgement,* trans. Paul Guyer and Eric
Matthews (Cambridge: Cambridge University Press, 2000), pp. 128-59. See Paul Crowther,
The Kantian Sublime: From Morality to Art (Oxford: Oxford University Press, 1991).

9. Kant, *Critique of the Power of Judgement,* pp. 89-127.

10. "Even when Kant's sublime is not directly invoked, its logic (at least, construed in a
certain way) is always presumed" (Hart, *Beauty of the Infinite,* pp. 44-45).

11. Milbank, "Sublimity," p. 259. According to Hart, the key metaphysical assumption is
"that the unrepresentable *is;* more to the point, that the unrepresentable . . . is somehow
truer than the representable (which necessarily dissembles it), more original, and qualita-
tively *other;* that is, it does not differ from the representable by virtue of a greater fullness
and unity of those transcendental moments that constitute the world of appearance, but by
virtue of its absolute difference, its dialectical or negative indeterminacy, its no-thingness"
(*Beauty of the Infinite,* p. 52).

12. "It is just this attempt at once to reconcile and preserve a presumed incompatibility
between form and infinity that recurs, almost obsessively, in postmodern thought" (Hart,
Beauty of the Infinite, p. 47).

13. Hart argues that the entire pathology of the modern and postmodern can be diagnosed in terms of "narratives of the sublime": the differential sublime, the cosmological sublime, the ontological sublime and the ethical sublime (Hart, *Beauty of the Infinite,* pp. 52-93).

lines of thinking, it is rightly insisted that the sublime should never have been divorced from beauty in the first place, that *beauty* should be thought through first of all in terms of infinity, but that, since this infinity is none other than the infinity of the Trinity, it is not formless or shapeless or wholly unrepresentable, but the form-full beauty of intratrinitarian love revealed in Jesus Christ, and as such can never be oppressive or dehumanizing but only life-enhancing. To quote Rusty Reno, "we are not overpowered by God as a sublime truth; we are romanced by God as pure beauty."[14]

With this primary orientation to the triune God in mind, whose own life is primordially beautiful, we can now turn more specifically to created beauty — and at this stage we will concentrate on created beauty in the first of our two senses, the beauty of the world as created by God.

First, a theological account of created beauty will speak of creation as *testifying to God's beauty, but in its own distinctive ways.* Much here turns on doing full justice to a double grain in Scripture's witness: the Creator's faithful *commitment* to the cosmos he has made, and his commitment to the cosmos *in its otherness.* Creation testifies to God's beauty, but *in its own ways;* or better: God testifies to his own beauty through creation's own beauty.

To take each side of this in turn: there is God's irreversible dedication to all that he has fashioned, a dedication grounded in the intratrinitarian love, "the love that moves the sun and the other stars" (Dante). Basic to this is the Creator's commitment to physical matter, something that blazes forth above all in the incarnation and resurrection of Jesus, where God's first "and it was good" in Genesis is stupendously and decisively reaffirmed. This means spurning any gnosticism that devalues created beauty (including that of the body) on the grounds, say, of its physicality, or out of a mistaken belief in the inherent formlessness of matter. We will resist treating physical beauty as something through which we ascend to immaterial beauty if this means leaving creation's physicality behind as something supposedly lacking reality or essential goodness in the sight of God. Creation's beauty is not, so to speak, something that lives in a land beyond the sensual or behind the material particular or beneath the surface or wherever — *to which* we must travel. Creation's beauty is just that, the beauty *of creation.* The beauty of a coral reef *is* its endless variegation, play of color, patterned relations; its beautiful forms are the forms *of its matter.*

No less important, however, is acknowledging God's commitment to the

14. R. R. Reno, "Return to Beauty," a review of *The Beauty of the Infinite: The Aesthetics of Christian Truth* by David Bentley Hart, *Touchstone* www.touchstonemag.com/archives/article.php?id=17-07-048-b.

flourishing of the world *as other* than God, this otherness arising from and testifying to the otherness of the trinitarian Persons.[15] Creation is indeed "charged" with divine beauty because the Creator is at work through his Spirit bringing things to their proper end in relation to the Father through the Son. But it is charged in its own creaturely ways, according to its own rationality and ordering processes.

There is therefore no need to deny a priori that the beauty of creation can correspond to God's beauty, can reflect and bear witness to it, but care is needed if we are to do justice to creation's integrity. Special caution is needed if we find ourselves thinking along Platonic lines: of God as the Form of beauty in which beautiful particular things participate. If we do attempt to discern creaturely signs of God's beauty in creation, we should be careful not to do so on the basis of some presumed *necessity* of created beauty to resemble God's beauty or to resemble it in particular ways, but only on the basis of what God has actually warranted us to affirm by virtue of his particular and gracious acts, climaxing in Jesus Christ. The naivety of assuming we may simply "read off" God's beauty from creation is most obvious when we are confronted with creation's corruptions and distortions (however we are to understand these), and when we forget that our perception of creation *as* reflecting God's beauty depends on the work of the Holy Spirit.

It is for these reasons that, if we are to speak of creation's beauty "participating" in God's beauty (on the grounds of creation as a whole "participating" in God), we will do so with some hesitation, despite the popularity of this language in some circles.[16] John Webster has drawn attention to the hazards of

15. Hart, *Beauty of the Infinite*, pp. 249-60. Wolfhart Pannenberg is one of many who want to trace the roots of the distinctiveness of the created world from God in the differentiation of God's intra-trinitarian life. See Wolfhart Pannenberg, *Systematic Theology*, vol. 2, trans. Geoffrey W. Bromiley (Grand Rapids: Eerdmans, 1994), pp. 20-35.

16. The notion of participation is central to the "Radical Orthodoxy" movement, with its commitment to a rehabilitated, Christianized Platonism, and its eagerness to overcome any implication that a part of created territory can be thought of as independent of God. However, it is far from clear that Radical Orthodoxy's notion of the "suspension of the material" in the divine can do justice to a biblical, dynamic ontology of grace that upholds the irreducible Creator-creature distinction. For discussion, see James K. A. Smith, *Introducing Radical Orthodoxy: Mapping a Post-Secular Theology* (Grand Rapids: Baker Academic, 2004), pp. 74-77, 189-95; "Will the Real Plato Please Stand Up? Participation Versus Incarnation," in *Radical Orthodoxy and the Reformed Tradition*, ed. James K. A. Smith and James H. Olthuis (Grand Rapids: Baker Academic, 2005), pp. 61-72; Adrienne Dengerink Chaplin, "The Invisible and the Sublime: From Participation to Reconciliation," in *Radical Orthodoxy and the Reformed Tradition*, pp. 89-106.

the "participation" metaphor, especially insofar as it is allowed to carry inappropriate Platonic overtones: for instance, that we will overlook the irreducible Creator-creature distinction and the asymmetry of the God-world relation, that we will fail to understand God's ways with the world through the lens of the particular saving acts of God in the history of Israel and Jesus Christ, that we will forget that any capacity of creation to reflect or witness to the Creator is graciously given by the Creator.[17] Nevertheless, it is not at all obvious that we need to reject the participation model altogether, for arguably there are ways of employing it (as history shows) that can highlight very effectively the gracious, prior agency of God, and the contingency of the world upon God's triune life, without falling into the traps Webster fears.[18]

Second, a theological account of created beauty will return repeatedly to *Jesus Christ as the one in whom creation has reached its eschatological goal.* If Christ is the measure of divine beauty, so also of created beauty. In Jesus Christ, divine beauty has, so to speak, got to grips with the wounded and deformed beauty of the world; in the incarnate Son, crucified, risen, and now exalted, we witness God's re-creation of the world's beauty. The one through whom all things are upheld (Heb. 1:3), by whom all things are held together (Col. 1:17), by whose blood all things are reconciled to God (Col. 1:20), is "the

17. Webster's objections to the language of "participation" as applied to humans' fellowship with God are succinctly set out in "The Church and the Perfection of God," in *The Community of the Word: Toward an Evangelical Ecclesiology,* ed. Mark Husbands and Daniel J. Treier (Downers Grove, IL: InterVarsity Press, 2005), pp. 91-92.

18. See the trenchant treatment of Calvin's handling of the theme in Julie Canlis, "Calvin, Osiander and Participation in God," *International Journal of Systematic Theology* 6, no. 2 (2004): 169-84; and the wider discussion of participation in relation to theological language in Alan J. Torrance, *Persons in Communion: An Essay on Trinitarian Description and Human Participation* (Edinburgh: T&T Clark, 1996), ch. 5. The critical point is this: the first and primary control on the semantics of "participation" should be the New Testament notion of *koinonia,* not the Platonic concept of *methexis* (the participation of particulars in eternal forms) — whatever wisdom may be justifiably gleaned from the latter notion. The massive issue lurking in the background here is that of the "analogy of being" *(analogia entis),* of purported analogical correspondence between divine and created reality, a matter that in various forms has exercised considerable influence on philosophies and theologies of beauty. For an exceptionally clear-headed treatment, see A. Torrance, *Persons in Communion,* pp. 356-61. Torrance properly urges that we do not presume an ontological continuity between the divine and created realms that is conceptualized apart from and independently of God's self-revelation in Christ. There are subtle and important differences between Balthasar and Barth on this matter; see John Webster, "Balthasar and Karl Barth," in *The Cambridge Companion to Hans Urs Von Balthasar,* ed. Edward T. Oakes and David Moss (Cambridge: Cambridge University Press, 2004), pp. 248-50.

firstborn of all creation . . . the beginning, the firstborn from the dead" (Col. 1:15, 18), the one in whom all things will finally be gathered up (Eph. 1:10). In the risen and ascended Christ, creation's beauty has reached its culmination. Here we see physical matter transformed into the conditions of the age to come, granting us a preview of that age when the earth will be filled with the glory of God as the waters cover the sea (Hab. 2:14).

Third, a theological account of created beauty will return repeatedly to *the Holy Spirit as the one who realizes now in our midst what has been achieved in the Son, thus anticipating the future*.[19] A Christian account of created beauty is thus charged with promise. It is not chiefly determined by a sense of a paradise lost but of a glory still to appear, the old beauty remade and transfigured, the beauty of the future that has already been embodied in Christ: "the beautiful is only the pre-appearance of the coming truth . . . [it] carries within itself the *promise* of truth to come, a future *direct* encounter with truth . . . the beautiful is a *pre-appearance directed to a goal*."[20] Here there is much to be said for the ancient wisdom of Basil the Great (c. 330-379), for whom the Holy Spirit "perfects" creation, enabling it to flourish in anticipation of the final future.[21] Beauty we apprehend now is a Spirit-given foretaste of the beauty still to be given, in the midst of a creation that languishes in bondage to corruption, groans in anticipation of a glory not yet revealed (Rom. 8:20-22). Hence the dazzling mountain scene that takes our breath away should not provoke us to try to seize and freeze the moment, but to give thanks and look ahead to the beauty of the new heaven and the new earth, of which this world's finest beauty is but a miniscule glimpse. We delight in the world's beauty *as* we lament its transience. To borrow William Blake's words:

> He who binds to himself a joy
> Does the winged life destroy;
> But he who kisses the joy as it flies
> Lives in eternity's sunrise.[22]

19. This dimension is brought out strongly in Eberhard Jüngel's penetrating essay on beauty, "'Even the Beautiful Must Die' — Beauty in the Light of Truth: Theological Observations on the Aesthetic Relation," in *Theological Essays II*, ed. John Webster (Edinburgh: T&T Clark, 1995), pp. 59-81.

20. Jüngel, "'Even the Beautiful Must Die,'" p. 76.

21. See Sherry, *Spirit and Beauty*, ch. 7. For a recent treatment of the Holy Spirit as the one who frees creation, see Sigurd Bergmann, *Creation Set Free: The Spirit as Liberator of Nature* (Grand Rapids: Eerdmans, 2005).

22. "Eternity," in *The Complete Poems*, 2nd ed., ed. W. H. Stevenson (London: Longman, 1989), p. 189.

What is true of joy is no less true of beauty.

Fourth, a theological account of created beauty, oriented to Christ and the Spirit, and thus to a trinitarian God, will delight in a *diversity of particulars*. If beauty's integrity involves a "proportion of parts," these parts are just that, distinct parts or particulars in various measured relations with each other. And these particulars, in order for beauty to be manifest, are not normally identical but will manifest diversity as they relate to each other, at least at some level. In Gerard Manley Hopkins's words, creation's beauty is a "pied" beauty: "dappled things," "skies of couple-colour as a brinded cow," "rose-moles all in stipple upon trout that swim," "Fresh-firecoal chestnut-falls; finches' wings" — all these things "Praise him."[23] Creation sings *laus Deo* in and through its ineffaceable diversity of particularities. Here again the ministry of the Spirit comes to the fore. The Spirit is the "particularizer" (sadly, something not seen strongly in Hopkins): unifying and uniting, certainly, but in so doing liberating things to be the particular things they are created to be. The beautiful unity that the Spirit generates is not one of homogenized harmony or bland replication, but one in which the unique particularity of things is enabled and promoted; it is the Spirit's office "to realise the true being of each created thing by bringing it, through Christ, into saving relation with God the Father."[24] The spring of this is of course to be found in the Godhead, whose unified life is not monadic sameness or an undifferentiated oneness more fundamental than the trinitarian persons, but a life of divine "particulars-in-relation," in which the Spirit (we may tentatively suggest) "particularizes" the persons of Father and Son, constituting and realizing them as persons-in-communion.

Fifth, a theological account of created beauty will be *wary of closed harmonies*. We may indeed articulate beauty in terms of proportion and perfection or integrity, but if beauty is to be rethought out of a center in the being and acts of the triune God, we will be guarded about accounts of created beauty that interpret such notions primarily or exclusively in terms of balance, symmetry, and equivalence. As far as divine beauty is concerned, if the "measure" of beauty is outgoing love for the sake of the other, it will not be long before we are forced to come to terms with *excess* or *uncontainability*, the intratrinitarian life being one of a ceaseless overflow of self-giving. There

23. Gerard Manley Hopkins, "Pied Beauty" (1877).

24. Colin E. Gunton, *The One, the Three and the Many* (Cambridge: Cambridge University Press, 1993), p. 189. This is a strand of pneumatology explored very fully by Gunton (see esp. ch. 7).

is still proportion and integrity, but it is the proportion and integrity of abundant love.

Creation, by grace, is given to share in this "excess" — indeed, creation's very existence is the result of the overflow of divine love — albeit in its own creaturely ways. So God's beautiful extravagance takes creaturely form in the oversupply of wine at Cana, the welcome Jesus shows to outcasts and sinners, the undeserved forgiveness in the first light of Easter Day. This is how creation's deformed beauty is remade, not by a repair or "return to normality," but by a re-creation exceeding all balance, by a love that is absurdly lavish and profligate, surplus to all "requirement," overflowing beyond anything demanded or expected, generous beyond measure.

This in turn means taking creation's *contingency* seriously, giving due recognition to the unpredictable, to that which does not simply flow out of the past but which is nonetheless consistent and fruitful, to the new developments that God is constantly bringing forth from his world. Those working at the borderlands of contemporary science and theology have not been slow to engage with such ideas, giving rise to various proposals for a metaphysics of "contingent order."[25] Whatever weight we give to this or that emerging cosmology, the widespread questioning of closed mechanistic models in the natural sciences should at least give us pause for thought. Once again, a danger often lurking here is a defective account of the Holy Spirit, in which we describe the Spirit's role chiefly (solely?) in terms of effecting return and closure, completing a circle. This has the unfortunate effect of neglecting the Spirit's role as improviser, bringing about a faithful novelty, fresh improvisations consistent with what has been achieved "once and for all" in Christ.[26] The other great danger of overharmonious models of beauty is that they will be singularly ill-equipped to take the evilness of evil seriously, its sheer irrationality.

25. For different examples, see T. F. Torrance, *Divine and Contingent Order* (Edinburgh: T&T Clark, 1998); J. C. Polkinghorne and Michael Welker, *The End of the World and the Ends of God: Science and Theology on Eschatology* (Harrisburg, PA: Trinity Press International, 2000), ch. 1; A. R. Peacocke, *Creation and the World of Science* (Oxford: Clarendon, 1979); Jean-Jacques Suurmond, *Word and Spirit at Play: Towards a Charismatic Theology* (Grand Rapids: Eerdmans, 1994).

26. In this regard, with respect to human history, Ben Quash makes some pointed critical comments about Balthasar, especially in relation to his theodramatics, questioning whether he has allowed the "epic" character of his thought to engender an approach to history that cannot do justice to the humanly contingent (*Theology and the Drama of History* [Cambridge: Cambridge University Press, 2005]).

Sixth, an account of created beauty will recognize that beauty *elicits desire* — a desire to dwell with and enjoy that which we experience as beautiful. This links up with those currents in the "great theory" that speak of beauty's brightness (and thus attraction), and the pleasure it affords upon contemplation. There is, of course, a massive literature in Christian history on the attractiveness of God's beauty, and the love and desire *(eros)* that God's beauty evokes in us. Understandably, many are nervous about an alliance of beauty and desire, especially in a theological context. From a philosophical perspective, those in the Kantian tradition will suspect that desire spells the end of aesthetics (and, indeed, ethics), for to allow "interest" a constitutive role in aesthetic enjoyment is to destroy its character as contemplative dispassion. From a theological perspective, the suspicion may well derive from a sharp contrast sometimes made between "desire" and "love," *eros* and *agape,* the former understood in an instrumentalist sense as possessive and consuming, the latter as selfless self-giving for the sake of the other as other. To permit *eros* a place in Christian faith, it is said, is to open the door to the subjugation of the other, to an inevitable violation of the other's integrity.[27]

Much recent writing has sought to counter these suspicions. Without space to enter a complex field, we might at least say the following. Just as the triune God lives as an endless movement of attraction and delight, so God does not make himself available as an object for dispassionate scrutiny but in an overture of enticement, through which by the Spirit's agency we are made to long for God's presence, indeed, thirst for him. God "attracts our attention" by the outgoing Spirit, enabling us to respond, catching us up into the divine life. Indeed, can we not say that to experience the allure of God *is* nothing other than to experience the Spirit reconciling us to the Father through the Son, and thus reordering our desires?[28] No wedge need be driven between *agape* and *eros* provided the latter is not allowed to introduce notions of subsuming the "other" under manipulative restraint; indeed, as David Bentley Hart puts it, God's love, and hence the love with which we come to love God, is "eros and agape at once: a desire for the other that delights in the distance of otherness."[29] As far as created beauty is concerned, beauty in the world that glorifies this God will also evoke desire — a yearn-

27. Hart, *Beauty of the Infinite,* pp. 19-20, 188-92.

28. See Balthasar, *Glory of the Lord,* vol. 1, p. 121. Balthasar is rightly eager to reshape certain Platonic and Neo-Platonic conceptions of *eros* in the light of God's own self-communication in the economy of salvation.

29. Hart, *Beauty of the Infinite,* p. 20.

ing to explore and take pleasure in whatever is beautiful. There need be no shame in this provided our delight is delight in the other *as other,* and as long as we regularly recall that our love for God is the *cantus firmus* that enables all other desires to flourish.[30]

Bach and Created Beauty

With these theological bearings in mind, expressed all too briefly, we may turn to the music of J. S. Bach (1685-1750). How might an engagement with Bach's music, especially as considered in its time and place, help us gain a clearer theological perception and understanding of created beauty — beauty of the sort we have just been adumbrating? To avoid methodological confusion, two preliminary points need to be made. First, in an exercise of this sort, the controlling truth criteria are not provided by music; Bach's music does not and cannot be allowed to provide norms for beauty that are more ultimate or determinative than those given in the self-disclosure of the triune God in Jesus Christ. Nevertheless, and this is the second point, it is quite legitimate to ask whether, *within* the theological bearings provided by these criteria (some of which we have just outlined), music might make its own unique contribution to the perception and understanding of created beauty. And this is my concern here. Such an approach depends on (1) acknowledging that music is an art that is irreducible to the verbal forms of theological discourse, yet (2) allowing for the possibility that it might nevertheless be able to engage the realities with which that discourse deals, and in ways that afford genuine discovery and truthful articulation of them.[31]

We can focus down our concern by asking, first of all: What kind of cosmos, under God, might Bach's music provoke us to imagine, and thus what vision of created beauty? Is there anything to support Hart's bold claim that "Bach's is the ultimate Christian music; it reflects as no other human artefact ever has or could the Christian vision of creation"?[32]

---

30. Dietrich Bonhoeffer, *Letters and Papers from Prison* (London: SCM Press, 1972), p. 303.

31. For discussion of what is entailed here, see Jeremy Begbie, *Theology, Music and Time* (Cambridge: Cambridge University Press, 2000), ch. 10; "The Theological Potential of Music: A Response to Adrienne Dengerink Chaplin," *Christian Scholar's Review* 33, no. 1 (2003): 135-41.

32. Hart, *Beauty of the Infinite,* p. 283. In this section I am greatly indebted to Hart's short but masterly discussion of Bach (pp. 282-85).

To begin with, we need to clarify some of the features of the way this composer typically operates. Of special importance is something that Laurence Dreyfus has recently argued was central to Bach's art, namely, "invention" *(inventio).*[33] Many pianists' first introduction to Bach will be one of his two-part "inventions."[34] The composer tells us these were designed to serve as models for "good inventions" and "developing the same satisfactorily." What does he mean?

The word *inventio* derives from classical rhetoric and in Bach's time was widely used as a metaphor for the basic musical idea, the unit of music that formed the subject matter of a piece. Not only this, it denoted the process of discovering that fundamental idea. The key for Bach was to find *generative* material, an idea that was capable of being developed in a variety of ways, for "by crafting a workable idea, one unlocks the door to a complete musical work."[35] So the method of finding an invention was inseparable from thinking about how it might be developed — *elaboratio,* to use the rhetorical term. Hence Bach's concern to show us models of good inventions *and* of their development.

So, for example, the first of the two-part inventions begins:

Figure 1. The first of Bach's two-part inventions (BWV 772)

Section "A" marks an invention.[36] Bach has found that the opening figure of this invention can be turned upside down (inverted) in a musically convincing way. So the seven-note figure in the first measure

---

33. Laurence Dreyfus, *Bach and the Patterns of Invention* (Cambridge, MA: Harvard University Press, 2004).

34. See J. S. Bach, "Inventions and Sinfonias," *Aufrichtige Anleitung* (BWV 772-801).

35. Dreyfus, *Bach and the Patterns of Invention,* p. 2.

36. An invention is thus not a "theme" in the modern sense of the word — in this case the invention includes the same theme played twice. An invention is *the entire unit of music* that will provide material for development.

Figure 2. Seven-note figure in the first measure

in the third measure becomes

Figure 3. Inverted seven-note figure

Indeed, this inversion is itself part of a secondary invention (beginning in the third measure). Both these core inventions have been chosen with a view to what can be elaborated from them. They can be subjected very effectively to voice exchange, melodic inversion, switching from major to minor, and so forth — as Bach goes on to demonstrate. I cannot here trace all the elaborations displayed in this one piece.[37] What needs stressing, however, is Bach's intense interest and skill in this elaborative dimension. The evidence suggests that most of his contemporaries viewed *elaboratio* as among the most unexciting parts of composing and could treat it almost casually. Bach appears to have thought about extensive elaboration even from the start, when choosing the initial material. As Dreyfus puts it, "One might even be tempted to say that in Bach's works both invention and elaboration are marked by an almost equally intense mental activity. . . . In no other composer of the period does one find such a fanatical zeal directed so often toward what others considered the least interesting parts of a composition."[38] Indeed, Bach seems to have had an almost superhuman eye for how relatively simple sets of notes would combine, cohere, and behave in different groupings. His son, C. P. E. Bach, famously testified to how his father used to hear the main theme of a fugue played or sung by someone else, predict what would be done with it, and then elbow his son gleefully when he was proved right.[39] In short, as Christoph

37. For a full treatment, see Dreyfus, *Bach and the Patterns of Invention*, pp. 10-26.

38. Dreyfus, *Bach and the Patterns of Invention*, pp. 22, 24.

39. "When [J. S. Bach] listened to a rich and many-voiced fugue, he could soon say, after the first entries of the subjects, what contrapuntal devices it would be possible to apply, and which of them the composer by rights ought to apply, and on such occasions, when I was standing next to him, and he had voiced his surmises to me, he would joyfully nudge me when his expectations were fulfilled" (C. P. E. Bach, in *The New Bach Reader: A Life of Johann Sebastian Bach in Letters and Documents*, ed. Hans T. David, Arthur Mendel, and Christoph Wolff [New York: W. W. Norton, 1998], p. 396).

Wolff puts it, the principle of elaboration "determines like nothing else Bach's art and personal style."[40]

With these preliminary remarks about *inventio* and *elaboratio* in mind, we can begin to open up the theological dimensions of our inquiry by highlighting certain features typical of the musical fabric of a vast number of Bach's pieces.

First, we hear an *elaboration governed not chiefly by an external, pregiven logic but first and foremost by the musical material itself.* Dreyfus's research has shown that, whatever the precise order in which Bach composed a piece, it is highly inappropriate to envision him starting with a fixed, precise, and unalterable "form" and then proceeding to fill it with music; rather, we would be better understanding him *searching for inventions with rich potential, and accordingly finding an appropriate form.* In other words, this is an art in which the musical material is not forced into preconceived strict grids but structured according to the shapes that appear to be latent in it and thus apt for it. For Bach, we recall, *inventio* and *elaboratio* were the chief disciplines; *dispositio* — the disposition or arrangement of the elaborations in a particular order — was a subsidiary process (as was *decoratio,* the art of decorating or embellishing).[41] This is not, of course, to claim that Bach had only a passing interest in large-scale structure, or that he never worked with basic formal outlines. The point is rather that he does not seem to be driven chiefly by prior structural schemes that require strict adherence in advance, but far more by the local and specific material he handles. A fugue, for instance, is more like a texture with conventions than it is a PowerPoint template.[42]

It is this aspect of Bach that has been obscured by some scholars' fascination with number schemes and mathematics in his music. There is little doubt that Bach was greatly charmed by numbers, that he used some number symbolism in his music, and that some of this symbolism is theologi-

---

40. Christoph Wolff, *Johann Sebastian Bach: The Learned Musician* (New York and London: Norton, 2000), p. 469.

41. Dreyfus: "if a passage was to be transformed several times during the course of a piece, Bach must have planned at least some of its transformations in advance." In other words, "there is every reason to suppose that he composed some of it *out of order*" (Dreyfus, *Bach and the Patterns of Invention,* p. 13).

42. This is why genre was far more important than large-scale form for Bach and why so many of Bach's pieces modify and even disrupt traditional forms; "form was seen . . . as an occasional feature of a genre, and not the general theoretical category subsuming the genres that it later became" (Dreyfus, *Bach and the Patterns of Invention,* p. 28).

cal.[43] But this has not only led some scholars to construct vast and fanciful theories on the flimsiest of evidence;[44] it has also led to a neglect of the extent to which Bach, even in his most "mathematical" pieces, includes material that is anything but mathematically elegant. So, for instance, although we find ample evidence in the *Goldberg Variations* of mathematical sequences and symmetries, we find these interlaced with striking and surprising irregularity.[45]

In sum, Bach seems far more intent on exploring the logic and potential of the musical material in hand than on being driven by extramusical schemes of organization.[46] If we allow this aspect of his music to provoke a vision of creation as God's handiwork possessed of beauty, it is one in which creation is not, so to speak, a text that hides a more basic group of meanings. Rather than theological schemes in which forms are given an eternal status in God's mind,[47] or schemes in which God initially creates ideas or forms and then subsequently creates the world, or schemes in which matter is created first and then shaped into forms, is it not more true to the biblical affirmation of the goodness and integrity of creation to affirm that it is created directly out of nothing, such that *it has its own appropriate forms*, forms that

43. The "Sanctus" ("Holy, Holy, Holy") from the *Mass in B Minor*, to cite one instance, is pervaded with threeness. Calvin Stapert remarks: "if Bach did not use number symbolism, there are a remarkable number of remarkably apt coincidences in his music" (Calvin Stapert, "Christus Victor: Bach's St. John Passion," *Reformed Journal* 39 [1989]: 17).

44. Some, for example, hold that Bach frequently employs a number alphabet, each number corresponding to a letter, such that the number of notes, rests, and bars or whatever carry theologically coded messages or allusions. This has been roundly criticized, and in any case, the particular connections drawn between numbers and music in Bach are often of meager theological value. For further discussion, see Ruth Tatlow, *Bach and the Riddle of the Number Alphabet* (Cambridge: Cambridge University Press, 1991).

45. Williams helpfully lists some of them: "The opening and closing irregularity of the dance-arabesque-canon sequences; the sheer difference in musical genre between the movements, irrespective of their part in the sequence (e.g. whether or not they are canons); the exploring of both twos and threes, both to the ear and the eyes; the irregular placing of the minor variations and slow movements; the variety in the arabesques (not always two voices) and canons (not always threes); the absence of other symmetries that would have been easy to organize (e.g. if the canons at the perfect fourth and fifth are *inversus*, why not the canon at the perfect octave?)" (Williams, *Bach: The Goldberg Variations*, p. 46).

46. To borrow some words from John Milbank on baroque music, "Structural supports are . . . overrun by the designs they are supposed to contain" (*Theology and Social Theory: Beyond Secular Reason* [Oxford: Blackwell, 1990], p. 429).

47. On this, see the perceptive discussion in Colin E. Gunton, *The Triune Creator: A Historical and Systematic Study* (Edinburgh: Edinburgh University Press, 1998), pp. 77-79.

God honors and enables to flourish as intrinsic to the matter itself?[48] This links directly to what I have said about creation possessing its own creaturely beauty to which the Creator is wholly committed; created beauty testifies to God's trinitarian beauty, certainly, but in its own distinctive ways. Creation's forms are beautiful as the forms *of its matter;* only after acknowledging this can we ask about how these might witness to the beauty of the triune God.

Second, we are provoked to hear, in a way that has perhaps never been surpassed, *difference as intrinsic to unity.* Bach's skill in deriving so much music from such tiny musical units means that he can offer intense experiences of the simultaneous combination of extreme unity and extreme complexity. Even the resolutions in his music rarely neutralize its richness: the reconciliation at the end of the "Dona Nobis Pacem" fugue at the end of his *Mass in B Minor,* for example, does not compromise any of that work's immeasurable diversity. Indeed, Bach is adept at helping us perceive rich complexity *in* the apparently simple. In the *Goldberg Variations* we are given thirty variations on a lyrical and stately sarabande. After an hour and a quarter of *elaboratio,* he asks for the aria to be played at the end, *da capo,* note for note. Now we cannot hear it apart from the memory of all the variations in which it has been imagined. In other words, we now hear the aria *as* varied, replete with diversity, rich with light and shade, humor and sadness. At this point, the aria, we might say, *is* its elaboration; it is not more "real" than its diverse variations. (For Bach, we recall, *elaboratio* is no less important than the invention. If Dreyfus is right, Bach heard simplicity *as* elaborated simplicity.)

The links with our earlier theological material on creation's beauty — seen through the double lens of Christ and the Spirit — will be clear. The diverse particulars of creation are not an elaboration on some more profound, more basic, uniform simplicity, any more than the threefoldness of the Creator is the expression of a more basic singularity (as in modalism). In Hart's words, "The 'theme' of creation is the gift of the whole."[49] And this diversity of particulars-in-unity is not negated in the new heaven and the new earth, but finds there its full and final glory: the beauty of that endless day is surely not the beauty of one note but of an eternally proliferating "polyphony," whose elaborations are never a "return" to a state more original than the music itself.

Third, we are provoked to hear *the simultaneous presence of radical open-*

48. I am not, of course, suggesting Bach was creating out of nothing; the point is about "working with the grain of the universe," seeing form as intrinsic to matter.
49. Hart, *Beauty of the Infinite,* p. 282.

ness and radical consistency. With almost any piece of Bach — although perhaps most of all in the solo instrumental works — the music will sound astonishingly contingent, free of necessity. Not only does Bach constantly adapt and reshape the forms and styles he inherits; even within the constraints he sets for himself for a piece, there is a remarkable contingency — Peter Williams even uses the word "caprice" of this aspect of the *Goldberg Variations.*[50] There is a wildness about Bach's beauty.

This is why I have deliberately avoided the word *organic.* Tempting as it might be to say that the elaborations "organically" emerge from the inventions like plants from seeds, there is in fact rarely anything organic about Bach's music — in the sense of the quasi-inevitable, smooth, continuous unfolding of an idea or motif. Dreyfus ruthlessly exposes the inappropriateness of "organicism" as applied to Bach, arguing that such models are too closed, too prone to the logic of necessity, suppressing the place of human agency and historical circumstance.[51] Even without demonstration of this sort, however, we can perform a simple experiment to grasp the point: listen to almost any of the pieces for solo violin, stop the CD mid-way through a movement, and unless we happen to know the piece well, it is virtually impossible to predict what comes next. Yet what is heard is filled with sense: "each note is an unforced, unnecessary, and yet wholly fitting supplement" to the one that has come before it.[52]

It is this enticing interplay between constraint and contingency that has enthralled so many Bach scholars and players. An 1805 review of the first edition of Bach's works for solo violin described these pieces as "perhaps the greatest example in any art form of a master's ability to move with freedom and assurance, even in chains."[53] Put differently, much of Bach's music sounds improvised. This was one of the things about Bach that so intrigued the nineteenth-century composer and virtuoso Franz Liszt (1811-1886) — who himself transcribed and arranged many of Bach's works[54] — and that captivates many jazz musicians. (It is no accident that Bach was a brilliant improviser.) Again, I hardly need to point out the links with what I was say-

50. Williams, *Bach: The Goldberg Variations,* p. 46.

51. Dreyfus, *Bach and the Patterns of Invention,* esp. ch. 6.

52. Hart, *Beauty of the Infinite,* p. 283.

53. *Jenaische Allgemeine Literaturzeitung,* 282 (1805), as quoted in Wolff, *Johann Sebastian Bach,* p. 471.

54. Martin Zenck, "Reinterpreting Bach in the Nineteenth and Twentieth Centuries," in *The Cambridge Companion to Bach,* ed. John Butt (Cambridge: Cambridge University Press, 1997), p. 228.

ing earlier about the danger of thinking of beauty in terms of "closed harmonies," about the particularizing, proliferating ministry of the Holy Spirit, effecting faithful but unpredictable improvisations on the harmony achieved in Jesus Christ.

Fourth, a closely related observation: we are provoked to hear *the potential "boundlessness" of thematic development.* Even at the end of the *Goldberg Variations* — to take one of numerous examples — the music is by no means structured toward giving the impression that it *has* to stop when it does. Although these pieces do involve mathematical structures that require specifically timed closures (on both the small and large scale), as I noted earlier, there is much in the music that works against this.[55] The "logic" is "open," as if the variations were only samples from a potentially limitless range of options. It is thus not surprising that this has led some to speak of "infinity" being evoked in pieces of this sort. This would need careful qualifying, but, cautiously, we might say that insofar as there is an evocation of infinity to be heard here, it is not the infinity of monotonous continuation but much more akin to the infinity of proliferating novelty, the ever new and ever more elaborate richness and bounty generated by the Holy Spirit as creation shares in the excess of God's own abundant differentiated infinity, and this itself might be heard as a glimpse of the nontransient novelty of the future transformed creation, "in which new occurrences are added but nothing passes away."[56]

Fifth, Bach's music can provoke us to hear *a beauty that can engage with and transform dissonance.* I have already alluded to this aspect of creation's beauty. One of the marvels of Bach is the way in which he treats dissonance, in some pieces exploring it to quite unprecedented and alarming degrees (such as the famous twenty-fifth variation of the *Goldberg*), yet never in such a way as to grant it any kind of ultimacy.[57]

Sixth and finally, to state the obvious, and picking up on our earlier point about beauty and desire, Bach's music, as a creaturely reality, has proved an endless source of delight for three hundred years; its beauty has a rare attraction, provoking a desire among millions to be "with" the music whether as listener, dancer, jogger, singer, player, or analyst.

55. See n. 45.

56. Richard Bauckham, "Time and Eternity," in *God Will Be All in All: The Eschatology of Jürgen Moltmann*, ed. Richard Bauckham (Edinburgh: T&T Clark, 1999), p. 186.

57. For reasons of space, I have not treated the notion of the transformation of creation's "de-formed" beauty at length in this essay, but for a fuller discussion, see Jeremy Begbie, "Beauty, Sentimentality and the Arts," pp. 61-69 *et passim*.

Standing back, then, what kind of cosmos, under God, might this music provoke us to imagine, and thus what vision of created beauty? A cosmos and a vision, it would seem, highly congruent with the sort we brought into relief in the first part of this chapter. This is not to claim, of course, that all of Bach's music has this capacity (were the argument to be developed, we would need to be far more specific); nor is it to claim that no other composer's music could do similar things; nor is it to deny that there are features of some of Bach's music that move in rather different directions. The claim is only that there is music here that can justifiably be said to embody some of the main features of a theological vision of created beauty and, as such, in its own musical ways, help us perceive and understand that vision more deeply and clearly.

It may well be asked: If we are on the right lines, are the links merely fortuitous? Bach, after all, even if not remarkably or exceptionally devout, was a strong Lutheran, biblically well-educated. Is there anything to suggest that he himself would have conceived his music as giving voice to creation's beauty, or indeed that this might have been part of what he intended? This kind of question, of course, is deeply unfashionable these days. And to demonstrate what Bach might have believed about his music does not of itself imply that such beliefs are correct. As we are constantly reminded, "the road to hell is paved with authorial intention."[58] Nevertheless, here we need only register that even a modicum of historical-theological research in the case of Bach does show that our invitation to hear his music in a certain way does at least have historical propriety — it would not have been fanciful to Bach himself and may in some cases reflect his intention — and this can be highly illuminating.[59] For the linking of music and the cosmos at large was anything but foreign to the Lutheranism of his period. As Joyce Irwin has

58. The phrase comes from N. T. Wright, *The New Testament and the People of God* (London: SPCK, 1992), p. 55.

59. If some are tempted to cry "intentional fallacy" at this point, it is worth remembering that when William Wimsatt and Monroe Beardsley offered their classic exposition of the intentional fallacy, their main point was that the "intention of the author is neither available nor desirable as a standard for judging the success of a work of literary art" (W. K. Wimsatt and M. C. Beardsley, "The Intentional Fallacy," in *The Verbal Icon: Studies in the Meaning of Poetry,* ed. W. K. Wimsatt [Lexington: University of Kentucky Press, 1954], p. 3). That is quite different from claiming that research into what a composer may have believed and intended is always doomed to failure or is invariably irrelevant for understanding or benefiting from a musical text. One of the refreshing things about Dreyfus's work is his refusal to be hidebound by theorists who turn limited, instructive insights into inflated, all-encompassing claims (the "death of the author," etc.). See Dreyfus, *Bach and the Patterns of Invention,* p. 171.

shown, among theologians the ancient tradition of seeing music as articulating the divinely gifted order of the cosmos may have weakened considerably
by Bach's time, but among musicians it was by no means dead.[60] Although
Bach was not a theorist or theologian of music (how interested he would
have been in detailed metaphysics is moot),[61] there is plenty to suggest that
the notion of music bringing to sound an engrained God-given cosmic
beauty and thus offering "insight into the depths of the wisdom of the
world" (words used on Bach's behalf),[62] would have been anything but foreign to him.[63] In this light it is not at all inappropriate to listen to the forty-

60. Joyce L. Irwin, *Neither Voice nor Heart Alone: German Lutheran Theology of Music in
the Age of the Baroque* (New York: Peter Lang, 1993), esp. chs. 4, 11.

61. Dreyfus, *Bach and the Patterns of Invention*, p. 9; Wolff, *Johann Sebastian Bach*, pp.
337-39.

62. J. A. Birnbaum, as quoted in Wolff, *Johann Sebastian Bach*, p. 338.

63. See John Butt, *Music Education and the Art of Performance in the German Baroque*
(Cambridge: Cambridge University Press, 1994), pp. 33-35; Wolff, *Johann Sebastian Bach*, pp.
1-11, 465-72. For example, there is a much-quoted saying attributed to Bach about the "thor-
oughbass" (a foundational bass line with accompanying chords, very common in baroque
music) which seems to relate this device to the God-given created order. John Butt calls this
a "late flowering of the Pythagorean view of well-composed music as natural harmony"
("Bach's Metaphysics of Music," in *The Cambridge Companion to Bach*, p. 54). Relevant also
is the witness of J. A. Birnbaum. Defending Bach's music in response to a criticism that it
leads us "away from the natural to the artificial," and likely reflecting the views of the composer himself, Birnbaum appeals to "the eternal rules of music" and speaks of polyphonous
music as an exemplar of the unity and diversity pervading the cosmos (Butt, "Bach's
Metaphysics of Music," pp. 55-59; Wolff, *Johann Sebastian Bach*, pp. 5-6). (There are elements
in the Birnbaum document, however, that suggest he believes nature is sometimes *lacking*
beauty, something that does not seem to trouble Wolff et al.) In 1747 Bach joined a learned
group, the Corresponding Society of the Musical Sciences, one of whose members wrote:
"God is a harmonic being. All harmony originates from his wise order and organisation. . . .
Where there is no conformity, there is also no order, no beauty, and no perfection. For
beauty and perfection consist in the conformity of diversity" (as quoted in Wolff, *Johann
Sebastian Bach*, p. 466). During his last years Bach wrote music that would seem to be highly
consonant with the theories current in this circle, especially that of music as "sounding
mathematics" — e.g., the *Canonic Variations on "Vom Himmel hoch da komm ich her"* and
most famously, the *Art of Fugue* (Malcolm Boyd, ed., *Bach* [Oxford: Oxford University Press,
2000], pp. 205-6).

Some have tried to align Bach's vision very closely with some of the rationalist
cosmologies of the German Enlightenment. Recently, Wolff has contended that Bach's output is usefully interpreted in the light of the concept of musical "perfection," a characteristically Enlightenment notion used in Birnbaum's defense of Bach (see Wolff, *Johann Sebastian
Bach*, pp. 466-67; see also John Butt, "'A Mind Unconscious That It Is Calculating?' Bach and
the Rationalist Philosophy of Leibniz and Spinoza," in *The Cambridge Companion to Bach*,

eight preludes and fugues of the *Well-Tempered Clavier*, for example, as a stunning exploration of the properties and possibilities of a God-given sonic order, for they are derived from that physical "universal" built into the physical world, the "harmonic series."

Yet matters cannot be left there. The implication would be that all Bach is doing, or thinks he is doing, is bringing to light and representing the order of the natural world. It is patently obvious that he is doing very much more. If he *is* eliciting creation's own beauty, he is doing so *through an active process of making:* principally through *inventio* and *elaboratio*, both of which are themselves constructive exercises, involving combining tones, making music. Inventions do not tumble out of nature like apples off a tree; they have to be worked at, constructed, and the elaborations likewise. Indeed, frequently we find Bach having to adjust the elaborations slightly to make them "fit" his constraints. Even at the very basic acoustic level, there are modifications: the *Well-Tempered Clavier* is indeed based on the twelve-note chromatic scale that does indeed derive from the "natural" fact of the harmonic series, but the scale he used and the slightly differently tuned one we commonly use today are in fact adjustments, "temperings" of what nature has given us.[64]

In fact, Bach reshaped almost everything he touched: from simple motifs to whole styles and genres. He is one of the least "passive" composers in history. Thus we are led to the second main sense of "created beauty" I distinguished at the start — the beauty humans make. If "natural" beauty is being discovered and turned into sound by Bach, this happens *as* it is shaped

ed. John Butt [Cambridge: Cambridge University Press, 1997], pp. 60-71; Ulrich Leisinger, "Forms and Functions of the Choral Movements in J. S. Bach's *St. Matthew Passion*," in *Bach Studies 2*, ed. Daniel R. Melamed [Cambridge: Cambridge University Press, 1995], pp. 70-84). However, Dreyfus argues that these lines of argument pay insufficient attention to the role of human agency in Bach's practice — I have already spoken about the dangers of interpreting Bach in terms of "closed" systems. See Dreyfus, *Bach and the Patterns of Invention*, pp. 26-27, and ch. 8. We cannot enter the complexities of this case here; I can only register that I find arguments that Bach would have leaned heavily on thinkers such as G. W. Leibniz and Christian Wolff speculative and unconvincing, however commonplace the ideas of harmony, unity, natural laws, and the like might have been in some of Bach's circles. Even Leisinger admits that "no documentary evidence can be presented that Johann Sebastian Bach ever possessed or read any of Leibniz's or Wolff's treatises" (Leisinger, "Forms and Functions," p. 84). As far as aesthetics is concerned, Dreyfus argues that Bach is better understood as a subtle *critic* of Enlightenment thought than a staunch supporter of it (see *Bach and the Patterns of Invention*, ch. 8).

64. For explanation, see Stuart Isacoff, *Temperament: How Music Became a Battleground for the Great Minds of Western Civilization* (New York: Alfred A. Knopf, 2001).

and reshaped, formed and reformed, through the ingenious use of a vast array of often highly sophisticated techniques.

We are thus confronted with perhaps the central paradox of a Christian view of creativity: in and through the act of strenuous making we discover more fully what we have not made. The inability to hold these two together in our thinking — "given" beauty and "generated" beauty (in this case, artistic beauty) — the tendency to see them as inherently opposed, is, I submit, one of the cardinal marks of modernity, captivated as it has so often been by the notion of the godlike artist, forging order where supposedly none can be trusted or even found. Postmodernity has fared no better, typically collapsing "given" beauty into "generated" beauty without remainder (for what beauty could there be except that which we construct?). Reactions to both of these visions sometimes take the form of a "return to nature," as if any modification of nature is to be seen as a corruption of it. But this trades on essentially the same competitive, bipolar outlook — human creativity as necessarily pitted against the natural world. Bach's music would seem to point us toward — and, arguably, embodies — a vision of the relation between natural and artistic beauty that does not assume an intrinsic tussle between them. Significantly, Bach's obituary spoke of his "ingenious and unusual ideas" *and* his extraordinary grasp of the "hidden secrets of harmony" without so much as a hint that the two had to be at odds.[65]

This is why attempts to line up Bach with the German Enlightenment's aesthetics of his day are so questionable, with its ideals of transparency and representation, where music is thought to be best when it shows least human artifice. Bach seems less interested in representing than he is in shaping his materials respectfully, and *in that way* expanding our awareness of those materials, the world we live in, and our place in it.[66] At the same time, though of course Bach was astonishingly "original," we should avoid interpreting him through the lens of the self-conscious creativity of the Roman-

---

65. *The New Bach Reader: A Life of Johann Sebastian Bach in Letters and Documents,* ed. Hans T. David, Arthur Mendel, and Christoph Wolff (New York: W. W. Norton, 1998), p. 305.

66. This is arguably where Christoph Wolff comes unstuck *(Johann Sebastian Bach).* He acknowledges that Bach shows astonishing novelty and originality, but he is still *over*enamored with trying to show Bach's supposed indebtedness to certain Enlightenment notions of music's transparency to nature's harmony and order, and with these the notion that Bach's elaboration is a quasi-scientific exploration and discovery of nature's beauty (fueled by a comparison with Newton that is perhaps more questionable than illuminating). For discussion, see John Butt, "The Saint Johann Sebastian Passion," *The New Republic* 10 (2000): 33-38, and of the wider issues, Dreyfus, *Bach and the Patterns of Invention,* ch. 8.

tic *Künstler,* the individual genius who mediates order to the world through his unique art.

What Bach's music provokes us to imagine, then, when set in its context, is a subtle relationship between natural and artistic beauty, where the two are not seen as fundamentally incompatible, but where natural beauty is the inhabited environment, trusted and respected, in which artistic beauty is born, even if born through sweat and struggle. The vision of making beauty is not one that sees the artist as striving for creation out of nothing, fashioning and foisting order where none is given, or pursuing a fetish for originality (the wholly underived act); still less is it one of defiantly challenging God.[67] But nor is it one in which we simply "let nature be," merely follow its resonances and rhythms the way one might follow a river through a valley or the grain of a piece of wood. The vision is rather of the artist, as physical and embodied, set in the midst of a God-given world vibrant with a dynamic beauty of its own, not simply "there" like a brute fact to be escaped or violently abused, but there as a gift from a God of overflowing beauty, a gift for us to interact with vigorously, form and (in the face of distortion) transform, and in this way fashion something as consistent and dazzlingly novel as the *Goldberg Variations,* art that can anticipate the beauty previewed and promised in Jesus Christ.

67. In a review of Wolff's book, Edward Said suggests that Bach (however unconsciously) appears to be engaged in a kind of rivalry with God. Is there not a "cosmic musical ambition" here, Said asks, "epic" in nature, even "demonic," especially in the late pieces where the composer unleashes such an awesome array of creative powers that we are bound to question (or at least qualify) traditional views of Bach's devotion to and reverence for God? "One can't help wondering whether all the piety and expression of humility before God weren't also Bach's way of keeping something considerably darker — more exuberant, more hubristic, verging on the blasphemous — at bay" (Edward Said, "Cosmic Ambition," *London Review of Books* [2001]: 13). Said does not seem to notice how anachronistic the guiding assumption behind this kind of suspicion is: Bach and most of his contemporaries would not have seen anything unusual in holding at one and the same time that God provides the already-structured materials for the composer *and* that this same God *invites* and *delights in* an energetic elaboration of these materials on the part of a composer. And why should *we?*

5. On Music, Mathematics, and Theology: Pythagoras, the Mind, and Human Agency

John Paul Ito

The fortunes of a possible link between music and mathematics have been varied. For around two millennia, from the time of Pythagoras until the beginning of the seventeenth century, a great many thinkers in the West saw music and mathematics as inextricably intertwined both with each other and with the ordering of the natural world. And during the second of those millennia, Christian thinkers found the link robust enough to carry a good deal of theological freight. Today the issue is contested. Some believe that music is very mathematical, some on the basis of specialized knowledge of both fields and some, in an interesting remnant of Pythagoreanism, as a sort of folk belief; others see no meaningful connection between the two. And just what might make a connection "meaningful" is itself up for debate. If mathematics are seen as fundamental to the natural world, then the question of whether music is mathematical is a question about the degree to which music as a cultural product may have been shaped by aspects of physical reality. But if mathematics are themselves viewed as culturally constructed, then the question is one of cultural history, not of science or psychology.

I believe that some relatively recent developments in theology and in the psychology of music make the time ripe for a reexamination of this old question of the interrelationships among music, mathematics, and theology.

This essay has benefited from comments on earlier drafts by Kenneth Bozeman, Alan Parks, and John Polkinghorne. Above all, I am indebted to the editors, without whose patient guidance this music theorist would not have been able to publish in theology.

I shall argue that the role of mathematics in music is limited, but I shall also argue that it is real. In particular, recent theological proposals by Alister McGrath and John Polkinghorne, when brought to bear on research in music psychology, reveal a limited form of Pythagoreanism to be strongly consonant with the Christian doctrine of creation, allowing us to see deep connections between music, mathematics, and the ordering of the natural world. Furthermore, human tendencies toward mathematical thinking — according to McGrath and Polkinghorne an important aspect of our created nature — may surface not only explicitly in the work of mathematicians but also implicitly in the historical development of some culturally situated musical systems. Finally, I shall attempt to show that mathematical ordering is not all-pervasive in music, so that it does not impose a straitjacket upon musical practice. Rather, musical practice is consistently found to be in constructive tension with mathematical aspects of order, so that the mathematics do not stifle but rather engender and enrich human musical agency.

Pythagoras Reaffirmed

Before assembling the tools that I shall need to rehabilitate Pythagoras, let me briefly survey the first two millennia or so of Pythagorean thought, with particular focus on the reasons for its rise and for its fall.

It is Pythagoras who is credited with discovering, in the sixth century B.C., that when musical consonances are produced by vibrating strings, the lengths of the strings relate to one another by small integer ratios (assuming that the strings have the same composition, thickness, and tension). This was a remarkable link between a simple, everyday musical phenomenon on the one hand and simple mathematics on the other. It is a commonplace, easily confirmed by anyone who presses the keys of a piano at random, that when two pitches sound simultaneously, they may either sound like they fit well together or else they may clash with each other. The fitting well is called consonance (con + sonare), the clash dissonance. Pythagoras found that the orderliness of sound corresponded to a simple mathematical order.[1]

1. Throughout the musical history of the West, consonance and dissonance have not always been perceived in the same ways, but the variation has basically corresponded to moving the point of demarcation between consonance and dissonance along a spectrum of ratios, with the more restrictive views of consonance admitting only those intervals that correspond to ratios among the smallest integers (from 1 to 3) and more permissive views including ratios involving numbers as large as 6.

This would prove to be a crucial link in an extremely influential cosmology. In this cosmology number and ratio were the ultimate constituents of order and relationship. The movements of the heavenly bodies and consonance in music were alike reflections of a fundamentally numerical order, an order that could be (and was) described as *harmony*. In English, "harmony" has both a technical, specifically musical meaning, as well as a more general meaning. Similarly, the word "rational" has a precise mathematical meaning (a number that can be expressed as a ratio of integers) but also denotes a combination of intellectual clarity with emotional balance. These words are a linguistic residue of a Pythagorean perspective in which these meanings all fused: mathematics were harmonious and music was rational. All order was seen as mathematically structured and musical in nature.

With significant contributions by Plato (c. 429 B.C.–347 B.C.)[2] and by Boethius (c. 480–c. 524),[3] these ideas would display their staying power for another millennium to come, with discussions of the harmony of the spheres occurring in treatises on music by Zarlino (*Le istitutioni harmoniche*, 1558) and on astronomy by Kepler (*Harmonices mundi*, 1619). From antiquity through the middle ages and on to the end of the Renaissance, many citizens of the Western world believed in a connection between mathematics and music in which not only was music mathematical but also mathematics musical.[4]

This worldview rested on the following core beliefs. The first was that the universe possessed an elegant order that was at root mathematical, having to do with number and ratio. Today, some hold that the universe is either disorderly or else ordered in some fundamentally non-mathematical way,

2. See especially in the myth of Er from the *Republic*, and *Timaeus* (the primary representative of Plato's works to the medieval world), section 14.

3. Boethius's treatise on music, *De institutione musica*, was one of the two main works on Greek musical thought widely available to medieval readers. In it he codified three distinct forms of music: *musica mundana*, the music of the spheres, primarily produced by the ratios inherent in the motion of the heavenly bodies, but also present in interrelationships among the seasons and among the four elements; *musica humana*, which represented the orderly interrelationship of body and soul; and *musica instrumentalis*, actually sounding music, whether produced by instrument or by voice. That all of the forms of music were fundamentally mathematical was for Boethius a matter of first principles, as he included music in the quadrivium of mathematical sciences, together with arithmetic, geometry, and astronomy.

4. For a somewhat journalistic survey of the Pythagorean tradition, with a helpful emphasis on interactions between science and music, see Jamie James, *The Music of the Spheres: Music, Science, and the Natural Order of the Universe* (New York: Grove, 1993). For a survey more focused on the history of musical aesthetics, see Wayne D. Bowman, *Philosophical Perspectives on Music* (New York: Oxford University Press, 1998), pp. 19-68.

and that the success of mathematical descriptions is a meaningless coincidence. This position reacts against the older worldview, which affirmed that the success of mathematical descriptions reflected the ontology of the cosmos. The second core belief was that the human ability to apprehend this order indicated that we had been tuned to resonate with the world. And the third core belief was that human musical activity also reflected this much larger order. For the Christian heirs of the Pythagorean tradition, these forms of order — of the cosmos, of humanity, and of music — were seen as the workmanship of the creator God.

Late in the sixteenth century, however, a number of developments, especially in astronomy, began to shake this ancient view of the cosmos, ultimately dislodging it altogether. From the perspective of music, the rejection of Pythagoreanism resulted most directly from a crisis of consonance, having to do with the development of means of measuring frequencies of vibration precisely and the evolution of musical style in a way that highlighted inherent limitations of the Pythagorean system.[5] The stylistic developments would take a century to complete, and the debates about tuning they sparked would rage into the nineteenth century; for the sake of simplicity, the following discussion will be unapologetically anachronistic, viewing the issues as they are usually seen today.

The most fundamental issue in this crisis was the internal consistency of musical systems built on Pythagorean consonances. Understanding this will require us to do some simple mathematics.

The most fundamental of Pythagoras's consonances are musical intervals called the octave, the perfect fifth, and the perfect fourth, which have frequency ratios of 2/1, 3/2, and 4/3, respectively.[6] When the use of thirds and sixths as consonances became impossible to ignore by theorists, it was a straightforward matter to add major (5/4) and minor (6/5) thirds to the list. These consonances have the important feature of internal consistency: a fifth plus a fourth is an octave, and indeed $(4/3) \times (3/2) = 2/1$. Similarly, a major third plus a minor third is equal to a perfect fifth: $(6/5) \times (5/4) = 3/2$. This consistency is important. In Western music since the beginning of the Renaissance, the most basic chord, the fundamental building block of har-

5. For an extremely engaging account of the beginning of this crisis and its consequences for the prevailing worldview, see ch. 3 of Daniel K. L. Chua's *Absolute Music and the Construction of Meaning* (Cambridge: Cambridge University Press, 1999).

6. Higher-pitched sounds correspond to faster vibrations of air molecules, and thus to higher frequencies of vibration. Frequency ratios are the ratios of the higher frequency to the lower.

mony, has been the "triad." In its simplest form, the triad consists of three notes: a lower note and two notes added on top of the lower note, each one either a major or a minor third above the one immediately below it. Because consonant triads use one of each kind of third, major and minor, the resulting fifth (i.e., between the lowest and the highest notes) is always perfect. And because the Pythagorean consonances are internally consistent to this point, each note in the triad can be perfectly in tune with both of the others.

The problem with the Pythagorean system is that, in the musical system that has been in place in the West since the seventeenth century, this consistency disappears as soon as we move beyond the triad. What is crucial to grasp here is that the limitation is one of *internal* consistency. It is *not* that nature was disappointingly found not to be in accord with a beautiful theory, but that the beautiful theory is inherently limited, unable *in principle* to do what was asked of it. *Pace* some theologians who have written on this topic, the failure of the Pythagorean system cannot be attributed to the imperfections of a fallen world — that attribution makes sense only if some fundamental arithmetic truths are also a product of the fall. I shall explain this briefly.

The heart of the matter is that the frequency ratios cannot be used to reach the same pitch by means of different intervals. Take the fifth, with frequency ratio $3/2$. If we start with some low note on the keyboard and ascend by fifth twelve times, we will arrive at a higher member of the pitch-class with which we started; if we start with the lowest C, we will end up at the highest C.[7] If we started with the same low note and ascended by octave seven times, we would arrive at the same destination. But if we work out the (Pythagorean) frequency ratios, we discover a problem. $(3/2)^{12}$ is $531,441/4096$. This is close to but not the same as 2^7, which is 128. A moment's mathematical reflection shows that there is no way that they could be the same, as no power of 3, containing only 3's and powers of 3 as factors, can ever equal a power of 2, containing only 2's and powers of 2 as factors. Thus a fraction with a numerator of 3 can never equal a power of 2 if the denominator is not also a multiple of 3. Thus $3/2$ raised to the power of any integer (except 0) will always be a fraction, so that it cannot be equal to a positive integer

---

7. The concept of "pitch class" unites all notes called F, regardless of which octave they sound in, just as the clock unites all hours called 11, regardless of whether they are A.M. or P.M., and of what day they fall on. This is a very significant abstraction from specific pitches sounding in specific octaves, and it is justified on the grounds of octave equivalence — the principle that two notes separated by exactly one or more octaves sound somehow "the same." Octave equivalence allows men and women to sing a single melody "in unison," even though they are singing in different registers.

power of 2, which will always be a whole number. Given these basic mathematical realities, the problem is not confined to the fifth — we can choose any of the intervals defined by small-integer ratios and ascend by that interval until we reach "the same" note some number of octaves higher, and in no case will the resultant frequencies agree with an octave defined as 2:1.[8]

In time, a tidy solution to this problem would arise: as the octave is divided into twelve semitones, let each semitone be an equal portion of the octave. This is known as equal temperament, and it results in a semitone that is the 12th root of 2. With this step, all of the inconsistencies of different interval combinations disappear, but so too do the small-integer ratios. In place of 3/2, or 1.5, the perfect fifth is now an interval of 2 raised to the 7/12 power, approximately equal to 1.4983. And that "approximately" is precisely the problem. 2 to the 7/12 power is a nonterminating, nonrepeating decimal; it is in an irrational number. Though the difference seems hardly significant when expressed as digits on a page, it signaled, as Daniel Chua has so compellingly argued, the end of the Pythagorean system of rationality.[9]

In what state were the basic beliefs left? Most significantly, the crisis of consonance showed that Pythagorean ratios had limited utility in describing actual musical practice. Music and mathematics, previously closely linked, were split apart, divided by the beginnings of a Cartesian wall that would be built between interior and exterior worlds, music being on one side and nature and (usually) mathematics on the other. Music, seen as one of the sciences in the Pythagorean tradition, had been relegated to the humanities. And the order of the universe, previously an article of faith, would be a matter to be demonstrated empirically.[10] In time some would even question if genuine order *could* be demonstrated empirically, claiming that mathematical descriptions of nature were a matter of predictive utility, lacking ontological connections to the phenomena described.

8. Again, brevity forces anachronism. The basics of this problem had been known since antiquity, but the issue came to a point of crisis in the late sixteenth century because of a confluence of stylistic and technological developments.

9. Chua, *Absolute Music,* ch. 3.

10. At first blush this development has more to do with the scientific revolution, which began around the same time, than with the crisis of consonance. For suggestions that investigations of tuning had an influence on the development of modern science, however, see Stillman Drake, "Renaissance Music and Experimental Science," *Journal of the History of Ideas,* 31, no. 4 (1970): 483-500, and Penelope Gouk, "The Role of Harmonics in the Scientific Revolution," in *The Cambridge History of Western Music Theory,* ed. Thomas Christensen (Cambridge: Cambridge University Press, 2002), pp. 223-45.

Science through the Lens of Creation: Polkinghorne and McGrath

Before music may be placed back into relationship with mathematics and nature, this question of how phenomena of the natural world relate to scientific theories stated in mathematical terms must be addressed. Of the questions raised, the most fundamental is the question of the status of mathematics.

Those who have pressed farthest in questioning the link between mathematics and nature have come to stark anti-realist positions: mathematics are invented by human beings and have no reality outside of the minds of mathematicians; and scientific theories do not approach a true description of nature as it really is, but rather represent some combination of good luck and powerful imagination in finding a formulation that (for a while) resists flat-out empirical contradiction. For the antirealist, nature is not truly mathematical because nothing (outside of human imagination) is truly mathematical. The fact that mathematics has, so far in human history, provided helpful tools for the manipulation of the natural world is a coincidence that has no larger meaning. Clearly, if nature and mathematics are to be meaningfully related, it will be necessary to defend realist stances on these issues: scientific theories *do* converge toward a true description of nature as it really is;[11] and the mathematics employed in these theories do have some kind of ultimate reality, being discovered — not invented — by mathematicians.[12]

A number of thinkers have vigorously defended the realist position in recent decades, with lines of argumentation frequently including the elegance of the theories; the aesthetic and philosophical depth of the implications later discovered to reside in apparently simple ideas, implications that, in the case of science, are empirically confirmed; and skepticism about the number of "meaningless coincidences" that must be accepted in many antirealist views.[13] For our purposes the writings of John Polkinghorne will be

11. For a survey of prominent positions on this question, see Clark Glymour, "Realism and the Nature of Theories," in *Introduction to the Philosophy of Science,* ed. Marrilee H. Salmon et al. (Englewood Cliffs, NJ: Prentice-Hall, 1992), pp. 104-31.

12. For an overview of the mathematical questions, see Stewart Shapiro, *Thinking about Mathematics: The Philosophy of Mathematics* (Oxford: Oxford University Press, 2000), esp. pp. 201-56.

13. As examples of such arguments, see Roger Penrose, *The Emperor's New Mind: Concerning Computers, Minds, and the Laws of Physics* (Oxford: Oxford University Press, 1989), pp. 74-116, and John D. Barrow, *Theories of Everything: The Quest for Ultimate Explanation* (Oxford: Oxford University Press, 1991), pp. 172-93.

particularly helpful. He writes lucidly, and as a significant particle physicist he has firsthand experience from which to argue that fitting data with math is too difficult to dismiss as lucky coincidence. Above all, he is helpful because he situates his arguments within a Christian theological worldview. Polkinghorne is able to go beyond arguing that a merely coincidental fit between math and nature is too strange to be true; he has a story to tell about why this is and how it came to be, namely, the Christian story of creation.[14]

A central part of the argument against the idea of successful mathematical descriptions as coincidence involves pointing out an even larger "coincidence," namely, that there are any sentient beings around to think about the question at all — something that cosmologists call the "anthropic principle." When contemporary physicists consider the basic laws that govern the physical world, they observe that the hospitality of the universe to life requires these laws to take very particular forms. In the great majority of the alternative ways in which the cosmos could rationally be imagined to be structured, the development of systems having the complexity of living organisms would be extraordinarily improbable. It would seem that the universe has been fine tuned in order to make life possible.[15]

The anthropic principle can take several forms, some very consonant with theism and some quite dissonant. For me, one of Polkinghorne's most helpful contributions has been the charting of a particularly promising path through the maze of anthropic options, in the process arguing convincingly against those that conflict with theism.[16] Older natural theological arguments often appeared to be weak intellectual supports that could only bear the weight of those already at least strongly disposed toward be-

14. A good place to start is John Polkinghorne, *Belief in God in an Age of Science* (New Haven: Yale University Press, 1998), pp. 1-24. He takes the argument somewhat further in John Polkinghorne, *Science and Creation: The Search for Understanding* (London: SPCK, 1988), pp. 69-83.

15. John D. Barrow and Frank J. Tipler, *The Anthropic Cosmological Principle* (Oxford: Oxford University Press, 1986), and John Leslie, *Universes* (London and New York: Routledge, 1989).

16. John Polkinghorne, *Belief in God in an Age of Science* (New Haven: Yale University Press, 1998), esp. pp. 1-24; John Polkinghorne, *Reason and Reality: The Relationship between Science and Theology* (Valley Forge, PA: Trinity Press International, 1991), esp. pp. 74-84; and John Polkinghorne, *Beyond Science: The Wider Human Context* (Cambridge: Cambridge University Press, 1996), esp. pp. 75-93. The discussion in *One World: The Interaction of Science and Theology* (Princeton: Princeton University Press, 1986), pp. 79-81, is less meaty scientifically but reflects more on the relationship between the anthropic principle and the character of God.

ing convinced. In Polkinghorne's telling, however, the story of an anthropic universe does seem to make considerably more sense with an orderly creator driving the narrative; strange as theism may be, the other options start to look significantly stranger. This may well point the unconvinced toward more seriously considering the existence of God. If so, well and good. But it is not news to Christian theologians that the world is orderly, or that that order is a reflection of divine order. What Polkinghorne offers is some assurance for the theologian who fears that in seeing the mathematical ordering of the world as part of God's ordering of creation she is merely taking a result from science and claiming that that is what her (much vaguer) Scriptures are really alluding to — who fears that *any* scientific result would be as easily appropriated, which, if true, would empty the claim of significance. Polkinghorne argues that Christian theology is not merely appropriating and relabeling here, but rather adding distinctive content of its own — as it happens, content that is capable of making a strong case to the unconvinced.

So far we have dealt with the connection between mathematics and the natural world; but what about the connection between humans and mathematics? Is it just good luck that we have come up with the very tool that allows us to understand significant aspects of the structure of the universe? This question is raised by Polkinghorne and explored in greater depth by Alister McGrath in his *Scientific Theology*.[17] As McGrath explains, "mathematics [as an apparently human construction] offers a puzzling degree of correlation with the natural world — puzzling, that is, unless one operates with a Platonic notion of 'recollection' or a Christian doctrine of creation."[18] To show just how strange this correlation between mathematics and the world really is, he offers the following extended quote from Roger Penrose:

> There is the mystery of why such precise and profoundly mathematical laws play such an important role in the behaviour of the physical world. Somehow the very world of physical reality seems almost mysteriously to emerge out of the Platonic world of mathematics. . . . Then there is the second mystery of how it is that perceiving beings can arise from out of

17. The source of the mathematical inclinations of the human mind is stated most clearly in Polkinghorne, *Belief in God*, p. 122, but it is also strongly suggested on p. 4 of that work and in *Reason and Reality*, p. 76.

18. Alister E. McGrath, *A Scientific Theology*, vol. 1: *Nature* (Grand Rapids: Eerdmans, 2001), p. 213.

the physical world. How is it that subtly organized material objects can mysteriously conjure up mental entities from out of its material substance? . . . Finally, there is the mystery of how it is that mentality is able seemingly to "create" mathematical concepts out of some kind of mental model. The apparently vague, unreliable and often inappropriate mental tools, with which our mental world seems to come equipped, appear nevertheless mysteriously able (at least when they are at their best) to conjure up abstract mathematical forms, and thereby enable our minds to gain entry, by understanding, into the Platonic mathematical realm.[19]

McGrath shows that Penrose's mysteries are harmonized by the Christian understanding of creation. Under the doctrine of creation, the action of a rational, omnipotent God explains the fact that there is consistent rational patterning behind the universe. And human beings are able to discover aspects of the terms of that patterning because of a created link between the physical world and the human mind: human powers of reason have been designed to seek forms of order that actually exist. As McGrath puts it, this results from the action of "the God who created both the reflecting mind and the orders of creation upon which that created rationality reflects."[20]

McGrath demonstrates that in relation to other ways of thinking that hew to realist stances on mathematics and nature on other grounds, Christian theology offers a significant explanatory gain. In making this argument, McGrath takes pains to emphasize that the picture he develops relies critically upon doctrines that Christians accept as foundational — that is, as a post-foundationalist, he understands his foundation as chosen; it is not, like the chimerical Enlightenment "view from nowhere," a foundation which all rational people would be compelled by their own intellect to ac-

19. Roger Penrose, *Shadows of the Mind: A Search for the Missing Science of Consciousness* (London: Vintage, 1995), pp. 413-16, quoted in Alister E. McGrath, *A Scientific Theology,* vol. 2: *Reality* (Grand Rapids, MI: Eerdmans, 2002), p. 80.

20. McGrath, *A Scientific Theology,* 2:78. McGrath seems frequently to go beyond the claim that an orderly, rational God has formed creation in *some* rational, orderly way, making the much stronger claim that the rationality of creation directly reflects God's own rationality itself. It seems to me that the evidence for the weaker claim is strong and the evidence for the stronger claim is weak; I therefore make only the weaker claim. Those who embrace the bolder position should find nothing in the present discussion that contradicts their views, just as McGrath's argument seems to me to stand perfectly well if the rationality of God is understood to be reflected more directly in the way in which God created than in the particulars of what was created.

cept.[21] Building on the work of Alasdair MacIntyre, he acknowledges that his argument only functions in its entirety when placed within the Christian theological tradition. Displaced from that tradition, the arguments are likely to lose their coherence. For readers who are less at home with the discussions of math and science, this is an important point. The less scientifically literate in our culture often find themselves compelled to accept the pronouncements of scientists as if they came from high priests: it is generally agreed that such pronouncements rest on a (reasonably) solid epistemological foundation, but the layperson may have no resources with which to confirm or disconfirm any given result for himself. It must be understood that the foregoing arguments are not among such pronouncements. Cosmology and the philosophy of mathematics do not prove the existence of God, much less any specifically Christian doctrines of creation. Rather, Christian doctrines of creation give us a new perspective on the link that mathematics provides between the exterior natural world and the interior world of the mind. What would otherwise be the sort of mystery that demands to be solved becomes instead a harmonious relationship — still a mystery, but now the sort that provokes awe and wonder rather than baffled curiosity.

Polkinghorne and McGrath prepare us to address the question of Pythagorean thought. The renewed Pythagoreanism that I propose here takes the form of four propositions, three foundational and one derivative. First, the universe possesses an elegant order that is at root mathematical, not merely conveniently described by mathematics. This is the realist stance in the philosophies of science and mathematics. Second, this order is meaningfully connected to the ontology of the cosmos; it reflects an orderly God creating in an orderly manner. This has been Polkinghorne's main point. Third, the human ability to apprehend this order is a result of God's work in creation; we have indeed been tuned to resonate with the world. This is the point that McGrath has made so forcefully. Fourth, on the basis of these three claims we may conclude, *if* we are able to observe mathematics at work in "natural" aspects of music, that music does indeed partake in the rational ordering of the cosmos, that music reflects the handiwork of the creator God in making an orderly universe and in making creatures who would be able to apprehend that order. Essentially the fourth point is that human musical activity participates in and bears witness to the contents of the first three points. What remains, then, is to remove the crucial "if."

21. McGrath, *A Scientific Theology,* 2:55-120.

Music, Mathematics, and the Psychology of Music

In talking about the collapse of the Pythagorean tradition, I was exaggerating somewhat, for Pythagoras has continued to have his adherents.[22] And how could it be otherwise? Although the difficulties are significant, are we to dismiss as mere coincidence the close (if not always exact) correspondence between the consonances and the simple integer ratios? In this section I shall look at what music psychology has to say about these sorts of relationships. The materials discussed will serve as primary data for the renewed Pythagoreanism that I am proposing. I shall consider first pitch materials and then rhythmic materials.

Pitch Materials

Our question is why the intervals we use as consonant are still so close to the simple Pythagorean intervals. Why should there be any relationship at all (even if often only approximate and imprecise) between the sounds we tend to consider pleasing and those elegant ratios of integers? The answer involves fitting together two basic aspects of acoustics: beat frequencies and overtones.

Hermann von Helmholtz is generally credited with being the first to suggest that dissonance might have something to do with beat frequencies.[23] When two different notes sound at the same time, having almost — but not quite — the same pitch, they produce what are called "beat frequencies." Pitched sound results from regular fluctuations in the pressure of air, called "pressure waves." If two tones had exactly the same pitch, and they were produced so that the crests of the two pressure waves matched up, they would result in a louder sound — both sounds would be making increases in air pressure at the same time. On the other hand, if two tones of the same pitch were produced so that the crests of one lined up with the troughs of the

22. For a brief discussion of a number of Pythagoreans since the Renaissance, see the end of James Haar, "Music of the Spheres," in *The New Grove Dictionary of Music and Musicians*, ed. Stanley Sadie, 2nd ed. (New York: Grove, 2001), vol. 17, pp. 487-88.

23. Hermann L. F. Helmholtz, *On the Sensations of Tone as a Physiological Basis for the Theory of Music*, trans. Alexander J. Ellis, orig. pub. 1885 (New York: Dover Publications, 1954). According to R. Plomp and W. J. M. Levelt, "Tonal Consonance and Critical Bandwidth," *Journal of the Acoustical Society of America* 38 (1965): 548-60, Sorge made a similar proposal more than a hundred years earlier.

other (and if they had the same loudness), the result would be silence. Because one sound would be increasing air pressure at the exact moment that the other was decreasing it, and vice versa, they would cancel each other out. When two pitches are very close but not the same, their pressure waves have slightly different frequencies, and as a result they shift in and out of phase, going back and forth between reinforcing each other and canceling each other out.[24] This results in the sound growing and fading in intensity with a regular frequency. This is called "beating," and it is quite clearly audible.[25] The beat frequency is always equal to the frequency difference between the two tones, so that the beats get faster as the frequencies move farther apart.

Helmholtz observed that when the beats reach around 20 vibrations per second (around the lower limit for humans to hear vibrations as pitched sounds), the sound acquires an unpleasant quality that he described as "roughness." Subsequent work found that roughness — also often called "sensory dissonance"[26] — is most intense within the "critical bandwidth," a range of frequencies around 10-20 percent of the center frequency at which the ear has been found to respond in special ways to a number of aspects of sound.[27] This provided an explanation for the dissonance of small intervals such as minor and major seconds; understanding the dissonance of larger intervals rests on an understanding of overtones.

Because of the physics of most sound sources used in music, tones con-

---

24. Imagine two people walking at slightly different rates. Sometimes their feet will come down exactly together, sometimes they will be exactly out of sync, and much of the time they will be somewhere in between.

25. At the time of this writing, an Internet search found a number of websites offering examples of the sound of beating. The best that I found, http://qbx6.ltu.edu/s_schneider/physlets/main/beats.shtml (accessed Feb. 6, 2008), allows the user to adjust the frequencies of two tones; as we shall see, this changes the frequency of the beating, and it eventually leads to roughness.

26. "Sensory dissonance" is dissonance as a product of the central nervous system; the term is used to distinguish it from consonance and dissonance as employed in actual music, which always has a cultural component.

27. On the critical bandwidth, see E. Zwicker, G. Flottorp and S. S. Stevens, "Critical Bandwidth in Loudness Summation," *Journal of the Acoustical Society of America* 29 (1957): 548-57; and R. Scharf, "Complex Sounds and Critical Bands," *Psychological Bulletin* 58 (1961): 205-17. At this time work on the critical bandwidth tended to be couched in terms of the frequency response of hair cells on the basilar membrane. As the basilar membrane is still not well understood, these explanations should be regarded as provisional. For work linking sensory consonance to the critical bandwidth, see R. Plomp and W. J. M. Levelt, "Tonal Consonance and Critical Bandwidth," *Journal of the Acoustical Society of America* 38 (1965): 548-60.

sist not only of the pitch primarily heard, called the fundamental, but also of higher pitches, called "overtones." These higher pitches are not usually heard as separate pitches, but rather as part of the color of the main note. It is possible, though, both to demonstrate the reality of the overtone series to an untrained listener and to learn to "hear out" overtones within complex sounds.[28] Example 1 shows the lower portion of the overtone series for a low C; with the exception of bells, almost all musical instruments produce this pattern of overtones including, significantly, the human voice.[29] As indicated in the example, the frequencies of the overtones are all integer multiples of the fundamental frequency; this will be a key point.

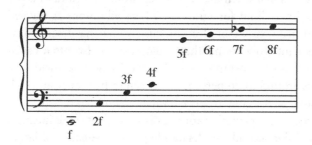

Example 1

Overtones unlock the problem of widely spaced dissonances like sevenths because roughness can arise not only between two fundamentals, but also between two overtones. As illustrated in Example 2, the second overtone of the lower note in the tritone is rough against the first overtone of the upper note, and the first overtone of the lower note of the major seventh is rough against the fundamental of the upper note. Conversely, a fifth will be

28. To demonstrate the overtone series for yourself, silently depress as many keys as possible in the upper half of a piano's keyboard using your arm. Then strike and release a low note; you will hear overtones of that note ringing. This is because the air vibrations at the frequencies of the overtones induce sympathetic vibrations in the undamped strings of the same frequencies.

29. For any pitch, the overtone series will consist of the same intervals above the fundamental. It should be noted that Example 1 contains a few idealizations. The F-sharp and the B-flat are approximations, as the overtones are rather out of tune relative to our scale. Furthermore, the frequencies are only exact integer multiples when we make idealizations about the physics involved (such as perfect elasticity of strings). In a real sound, the frequencies of the overtones will vary to some extent from exact integer multiples of the fundamental. This phenomenon is called "inharmonicity."

heard as consonant at least in part because of the coincidence of so many of the overtones, especially the more salient lower overtones (Example 3). Indeed, analysis of roughness between complex tones with six overtones shows sharply defined minima of total roughness for intervals corresponding to the simple Pythagorean consonances used in Western (and much other) music.[30] At the most basic level, Pythagorean ratios are consonant because the overtone series is based upon the same ratios.

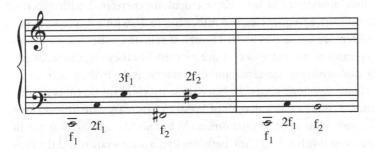

Example 2

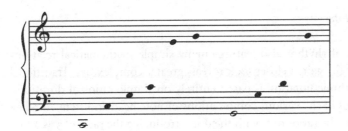

Example 3

Much more recently, Helmholtz's guess about dissonance having to do with beat frequencies has received remarkably strong confirmation. Experiments have been performed on humans and on monkeys in which brain activity was monitored while subjects heard intervals ranging from the minor second to the octave, with each of the two tones consisting of a fundamental plus nine harmonic overtones. When difference frequencies between overtones (or between fundamentals) fell in the range of 10-300 Hz, the primary auditory cortex tended to respond with phase-locked neuronal activity *at*

---

30. Plomp and Levelt, "Tonal Consonance," pp. 555-56.

the difference frequency.[31] Phase locking greatly increases the collective power of small stimuli; familiar examples of its effects include the laser beam and the large vibrations of London's Millennium Bridge before it was retrofitted with special damping mechanisms. In the case at hand, the spikes of neuronal response at the difference frequencies tower above the rest of the neural activity, including responses at the frequencies that are actually acoustically present.[32] The strong response at the difference frequencies indicates that dissonance is not just accidentally correlated with a certain range of difference frequencies, but rather has to do with a response to (and at) the difference frequency itself. Though it remains to be discovered why these responses occur and why they are perceived as they are, this work conclusively ties sensory consonance and dissonance to the Pythagorean consonances via the overtone series. To trace these psychoacoustic roots of many dissonances is not to claim that all of Western dissonance treatment can be derived solely from natural phenomena.[33] But we do see that science has been able to establish a direct link between Pythagoras's ratios and the experience of consonance.

Rhythmic Materials

The domain of rhythm also features many simple mathematical relationships, although again a closer look reveals greater complexities. Traditional Western rhythmic notation is based entirely on simple ratios of durations. The durations of the various combinations of note head and stem all relate to one another by ratios of 2, with the dot introducing the ratio of 3 as a further possibility. All of the standard meters group beats at various levels in

31. Yonatan I. Fishman, Igor O. Volkov, M. Daniel Noh, P. Charles Garell, Hans Bakken, Joseph C. Arezzo, Matthew A. Howard, and Mitchell Steinschneider, "Consonance and Dissonance of Musical Chords: Neural Correlates in Auditory Cortex of Monkeys and Humans," *Journal of Neurophysiology* 86 (2001): 2761-88.

32. To make this more concrete, one of the dissonant intervals was the major second between middle C and the D immediately above it. The two fundamental frequencies were 256 and 288 Hz, and the two first overtones had frequencies of 512 and 576 Hz. The two strongest responses observed were at 32 and 64 Hz, the differences in frequencies between the two fundamentals and the two first overtones respectively. There was no sound present at the frequencies of 32 or 64 Hz.

33. To see just how far this possibility can be taken, though, see David Huron, "Tone and Voice: A Derivation of the Rules of Voice-Leading from Perceptual Principles," *Music Perception* 19, no. 1 (2001): 1-64.

two's and three's, and rhythmic ratios involving larger prime integers, such as 5 or 7, started to appear only in the beginning of the nineteenth century and remained fairly rare until early in the twentieth. Indeed, the traditional Western system of rhythmic notation is incapable of dealing precisely with any relationship not based on whole-number ratios.[34]

If we move beyond the notational system to actual human perception, simple ratios continue to be central to rhythm. There is very extensive experimental evidence that people think of durational relationships in terms of simple ratios. Durational relationships are more consistently categorized and reproduced when they are close to simple ratios, and durational relationships that are most unstable in their perception and reproduction are those that aren't close to any simple proportion. Though the presented durations may not actually have a simple proportion, it is clear that they are perceived in terms of categories that are defined by ratios of small integers.[35]

It seems quite possible that the importance of simple ratios in rhythm perception may be related to the importance of simple mathematical relationships in rhythmic movement. In one of the more prominent current theories of motor behavior, simple patterns of phase relationships, most frequently involving 1:1 ratios of durations but in certain circumstances also other simple ratios, arise as stable solutions to complex nonlinear systems of equations that are posited to govern motion. If this theory is correct, patterning based on simple durational ratios in music performance and perception may be a result of the nature of organization of bodily movement.[36] Eric Clarke has made a similar suggestion. In one of his experiments he asked performers to reproduce rhythmic patterns that had been transformed, some of them in very unusual ways. He observed that some of the performers, when playing the most unusual rhythms, contorted their bod-

---

34. Though freighted less than pitch ratios, simple temporal ratios were also significant in the music of antiquity, serving as the basis for rhythmic patterning. This seems to have been a natural outgrowth of the rhythmic patterning of spoken Greek. See M. L. West, *Ancient Greek Music* (Oxford: Clarendon, 1992), pp. 129-59, and Lionel Pearson, *Aristoxenus: Elementa Rhythmica: The Fragment of Book II and the Evidence for Aristoxenean Rhythmic Theory* (Oxford: Clarendon, 1990), pp. xxiii-liv. Steven Guthrie discusses the ratios behind Augustine's theory of rhythm in *Carmen Universitatis: A Theological Study of Music and Measure* (PhD diss., University of St Andrews, 2000), pp. 209-50.

35. See Dirk-Jan Povel, "Internal Representation of Simple Temporal Patterns," *Journal of Experimental Psychology: Human Perception and Performance* 7 (1981): 3-18.

36. J. A. Scott Kelso, *Dynamic Patterns: The Self-Organization of Brain and Behavior* (Cambridge, MA: MIT Press, 1995).

ies, using strange postures and gestures. As a result he hypothesized some form of bodily encoding of rhythm.[37]

We see, then, with regard to both pitch and rhythm materials, that music is structured in terms of simple, whole-number ratios, and that these ratios are not merely culturally contingent choices but have roots in human neurophysiology, the rest of the physical world, and the ways in which the two interact. If we accept the work that McGrath and Polkinghorne have done in integrating science with the doctrine of creation, then we may indeed affirm that some aspects of music's order are related to fundamental aspects of the ordering of the cosmos, and that music reflects God's workmanship in creation — both in the creation of the natural world at large and in the creation of human beings to interact productively with the larger world in thought and in deed. Making music and listening to music, then, bear witness to the ways in which God acted in creation.

In what follows I discuss the extent of and the boundaries around music's mathematical ordering, each of which possesses theological resonance of its own.

Mathematics on Our Minds

So far I have considered mainly very basic aspects of music that cross boundaries of culture (and even of species, in the case of the monkeys' responses to dissonance). In further pursuing the mathematical structuring of music it is necessary to deal with specifics, and to move gradually from the trans-cultural to the culturally situated.

Up to this point we have been leaving unexamined the assumption that intervals, our main locus of mathematical investigation so far, are significant to musical experience. In fact, they are the bedrock of our experience of pitch, and this is something that ought not be taken for granted. When hearing in terms of intervals, the primary manner in which most people perceive pitch, we give attention to the *relationship* between two pitches, largely ignoring their *absolute* frequencies.[38] Note how different the situation is with

37. Eric F. Clarke, "Imitating and Evaluating Real and Transformed Musical Performances," *Music Perception* 10, no. 3 (1993): 317-41.

38. See Edward M. Burns, "Intervals, Scales, and Tuning," in *The Psychology of Music*, ed. Diana Deutsch, 2nd ed. (San Diego: Academic, 1999), p. 219. For a discussion of absolute pitch, see W. Dixon Ward, "Absolute Pitch," in *The Psychology of Music*, ed. Deutsch, pp. 265-98.

color. There, also, we are dealing with a continuously variable physical quantity (rather than frequency of air vibration, frequency of electromagnetic radiation), and there also we use the simplifying strategy of dividing the spectrum into a manageable number of categories. But if color perception were like relative pitch perception, the following would hold: we would be unable reliably to identify colors, unable to say for sure that a color was green and knowing only that it would be green if another color were given as red; we would be able to perceive relative distances between colors (based on the ratios of their frequencies) with precision, making judgments such as whether particular shades of mauve and magenta were closer together or farther apart than particular shades of seafoam and aquamarine; and, if given some means of continuously adjusting color, we could tune certain color relationships by eye, so that given light with a wavelength of 500 nanometers, we could tune a second color to 600 nanometers with an accuracy of approximately 1 percent.[39]

Because most people hear primarily in terms of relative pitch, hearing not in terms of the particular notes used (G3-C4-E4) but in terms of the intervals between them (up a perfect fourth, up a major third), we can sing the same melody starting on any pitch — our understanding of the tune is based on relationships among notes, and it is not tied to specific note names. We have already noted that when men and women are singing "in unison," they are singing in different octaves and yet sound somehow "the same." Similarly, the same familiar melody can start on a different pitch class and still be recognizable as the same melody. This property of being in some sense the same despite clear differences is described by mathematicians as invariance under transformation, or symmetry, and it is a concept that generalizes across different branches of mathematics in fascinating ways. This elementary, universal aspect of human musical experience, that we can start a tune on any given note, turns out to be deeply mathematical.[40]

39. This accuracy is based on extrapolations from research cited by Burns, "Intervals, Scales, and Tuning," p. 220. It is interesting to speculate about why perception of color and pitch might be so different. One possible reason has to do with octave equivalence; if we generalize the octave as a 2:1 frequency ratio, the entire visible spectrum extends barely beyond a single octave. The lowest frequencies are shades of red, and the spectrum gradually moves to blue and finally to violet, around the "octave" point, where we do indeed perceive blue as becoming reddish. How might we perceive colors if we could see a few more octaves?

40. The phenomenon of relative pitch may derive ultimately from the overtone series. The overtone series itself is a construct based on relative pitch: start with the fundamental and go up an octave, up a fifth, up a fourth, etc. As human beings hear this spectrum fre-

There even seems to be a fairly universal melody, the major scale. This statement requires several qualifications. It is not the major scale itself that may claim universality, but a more general class of scales to which the major scale belongs, namely, the "diatonic" scales. A diatonic scale may be thought of as any scale that can be generated by starting with some white key on the piano and ascending one octave using the white keys only. And diatonic scales are not universal, but they do generalize across cultures to a remarkable extent.[41] These scales consist of patterns of whole steps and half steps, and these patterns have a remarkable property: if you take a diatonic scale (e.g., C major), it will be possible to move either one of two notes in the scale (F and B in this case) by a half step (to F-sharp or B-flat) in such a way that a new instance of the same kind of scale will be created (G major or F major). This, again, is a symmetry property.

Though the current system of twelve pitch classes is undeniably a cultural construct, it derives in an elementary way from the cross-culturally prevalent diatonic scales. All that is needed is a system of temperament such as equal temperament or its predecessors in the seventeenth and eighteenth centuries. As it turns out, the symmetry discussed in the previous paragraph is just the tip of the iceberg when diatonic scales are examined in relation to the twelve pitch classes; the branch of music theory that explores such mathematical relationships, known as "diatonic set theory," has an entire litera-

---

quently, it makes sense that our hearing would be well adapted to extracting its invariant features, namely intervals. This may seem a bit of a stretch, given that most of us are not used to hearing out the overtones within a complex sound. But it turns out that the overtone series is fundamental to our main mode of communication, speech.

We all know that we can distinguish different vowel sounds in singing — and you can demonstrate this for yourself by singing this sentence on an arbitrarily chosen fixed pitch. What *is* the difference between vowels, then, if it is not one of pitch? The answer is that different vowel sounds correspond to the placement of bands of frequency amplification called "formants." When we distinguish between vowels, we are examining the overtone series, finding which overtones have been amplified, and analyzing the relationships among the regions of amplification. This analysis of the formant regions involves judgments of relative pitch. Understanding speech thus requires us to use relative pitch on two levels, as we examine the relative-pitch structure that is the overtone series and as we analyze the placement of the formant regions. Thomas D. Rossing, *The Science of Sound* (Reading, MA: Addison-Wesley, 1982), pp. 281-99, 315-21. For some complications to this basic picture, see Stephen Handel, *Listening: An Introduction to the Perception of Auditory Events* (Cambridge, MA: MIT Press, 1989), pp. 141-62.

41. See Burns, "Intervals, Scales, and Tuning," and Edward C. Carterette and Roger A. Kendall, "Comparative Music Perception and Cognition," in *The Psychology of Music*, ed. Deutsch, pp. 725-91.

ture of its own.[42] The set of twelve pitch classes even has interesting mathematical properties of its own, apart from its relationship to diatonic scales. Several of these are a consequence of the many divisors of the number 12; 12 $= 2 \times 6 = 3 \times 4 = 4 \times 3 = 6 \times 2$. In musical terms, this means that there are a number of symmetrical means of traversing the octave: as six whole steps, four minor thirds, three major thirds, or two tritones. Starting with Beethoven, composers in the nineteenth century became increasingly interested in the musical possibilities of such symmetries, and they made extensive use of them in structuring relationships among chords and among keys.[43] While I believe (and intend to argue elsewhere) that music theorists have often overrated the explanatory value of mathematics, there is no denying that many otherwise puzzling aspects of nineteenth-century music make much more sense when viewed mathematically.

We see, then, that as small steps are taken from the innate and universal toward the culturally contingent, more and more interesting mathematical features appear in the structures by means of which we organize the perception and production of music. At least in Western music ca. 1600-1900, mathematical shaping of music comes not only from the exterior world and from our neuropsychology, but from higher-order mental processes as well.

Above I stressed the central place that McGrath and Polkinghorne assign to the orderliness of human thought, and especially to its mathematical orderliness — this is seen as a reflection of God's work in creation. Especially when dealing with the level of mathematics required to understand recent advances in cosmology, though, this may seem a curious choice as an example of God's work being manifest in humanity generally. Few of us have much understanding of higher mathematics, and of those who understand it, fewer can contribute to it — if mathematical advances do uncover new as-

---

42. For an entry-level introduction to diatonic set theory, see Timothy A. Johnson, *Foundations of Diatonic Theory: A Mathematically Based Approach to Music Fundamentals* (Emeryville, CA: Key College, 2003). For an enthusiastic survey of the ways in which mathematics have been used more generally in music theory, see Catherine Nolan, "Music Theory and Mathematics," in *The Cambridge History of Western Music Theory*, ed. Thomas Christensen (Cambridge: Cambridge University Press, 2002), pp. 272-304. Music and mathematics are also explored in two more recent books, Leon Harkleroad, *The Math Behind the Music* (Cambridge: Cambridge University Press, 2006), and David J. Benson, *Music: A Mathematical Offering* (Cambridge: Cambridge University Press, 2006).

43. Analyses that reveal such relationships are found in any advanced undergraduate harmony textbook; see, for example, Edward Aldwell and Carl Schachter, with Allen Cadwallader, *Harmony and Voice Leading*, 4th ed. (Boston: Schirmer, 2011), chs. 32-33; or Steven G. Laitz, *The Complete Musician*, 2nd ed. (New York: Oxford University Press, 2008), chs. 34-37.

pects of God's action in creation, this seems to be something in which only a few geniuses in each generation can significantly take part. It would seem fascinating, then, if it turned out that mathematical tendencies of human thought were to be found not only in the discoveries of great mathematicians, but also in the workings of ordinary minds not attempting anything mathematical at all — more specifically, if some culturally contingent system, not painstakingly designed but evolved in community over a large period of time, turned out to have significant mathematical properties. I have suggested that Western music in the period c. 1600-1900 may be such a system. Of course, it is one thing to observe mathematical properties in a cultural system, another to demonstrate that they result from innate mathematical tendencies of human thought. Indeed, it isn't clear that such a demonstration would even be possible in principle. The foregoing should be taken not as a proof but as an intriguing possibility — that this one case *may* not be a coincidence, but rather the result of a basic human tendency toward mathematically structured thought.[44]

Music, Mathematics, Freedom, and Constraint

Having charted something of the reach of mathematics in explaining musical phenomena, I shall conclude by discussing some of its limitations — limitations that will resonate with some important conclusions about music and theology that Jeremy Begbie has already developed elsewhere.[45]

We have seen that our perception of consonance and dissonance is grounded in the phenomenon of beat frequencies, and that beat frequencies

44. If such a tendency exists, there is no reason to suppose that it fits *every* cultural product into a mathematical mold, nor need it imply any value judgment about mathematical vs. non-mathematical systems. Again, Western music of this period has been chosen for the focus because of the limits of my knowledge and because mathematical studies of music have been most extensive on this repertoire. But musics from other times and places — including African drumming, free jazz, and heavy metal — have also been subjected to probing mathematical analysis. For bold and imaginative explorations of how music and mathematics may illuminate thought, see Douglas R. Hofstadter, *Gödel, Escher, Bach: An Eternal Golden Braid* (New York: Basic Books, 1979), and Edward Rothstein, *Emblems of Mind: The Inner Life of Music and Mathematics* (New York: Times Books, 1995).

45. See, for example, Jeremy S. Begbie, *Theology, Music and Time* (Cambridge: Cambridge University Press, 2000), pp. 224-33, 246-47; and Jeremy Begbie, "Christ and the Cultures: Christianity and the Arts," in *The Cambridge Companion to Christian Doctrine*, ed. Colin Gunton (Cambridge: Cambridge University Press, 1997), pp. 108-12.

can be created not just by conflict between fundamentals but also by conflict between overtones. Because the overtone series embodies the Pythagorean ratios, hearing consonances that correspond closely to simple integer ratios is grounded in nature and not a mere coincidence. But because the simple ratios are internally inconsistent for a musical system of any complexity, musical pitch is an open system: because it is inherently impossible to consistently realize the highest good (of exclusive use of purely tuned intervals), there is not one perfect solution to the problem of musical pitch but rather an infinite number of compromises, ways of balancing competing goods.

To see this more clearly, let us imagine that our neurophysiology were such that we found equally tempered intervals to be the most perfectly pleasing sounds. This would solve the problem of consistency in tuning, because the system of equal temperament has, by design, perfect internal consistency. But we would then have a closed system: there would be no question that the best thing we could hear would always be equal temperament, and the universal goal of musicians would be to produce equally tempered intervals with the greatest precision possible.

But this is not the case, for purely tuned intervals have a raw sonic beauty that equal temperament can never match. Earlier I stressed the apparently miniscule difference between pure and equally tempered fifths. That difference is miniscule to the eye and to the general quantitive sense — but the ear is sensitive enough to find the difference quite salient. It seems remarkable that debates over tuning and temperament have almost entirely died out; probably this is because most people don't know what they're missing. I first encountered the sonic power of purely tuned triads in my early thirties, after the first of the gatherings of scholars that would eventually lead to the production of this book. After our meetings in Ely, I spent a day as a tourist in Cambridge and attended evensong at St. John's College. It was an overwhelming experience. I had heard excellent intonation before, but never before applied so well to purely tuned thirds and fifths, never before with vibratoless voices resonating in a magnificent neogothic space. I was a PhD student in music theory with a brief career as a professional orchestral musician already behind me, and I had never before experienced the full glories of a purely tuned triad. Suddenly a bunch of dusty old treatises, filled with comparisons between the triad and the perfection of the Trinity, were making much more sense.

But it is not for no reason that so few musicians use these pure tunings today. When groups try to make extensive use of purely tuned consonances, and also are punctilious about consistent pitch levels, they encounter the costs of this approach. This can be heard in recordings of Hilliard Ensemble; as they make extensive use of pure tuning, they must allow some chords and melodic intervals to be extremely out of tune in order to make it possible for others to be perfectly in tune. Triads that use Pythagorean ratios can be overpoweringly beautiful, but mathematics and psychoacoustics have given us this beauty in limited measure. We can alternate perfect beauty and great harshness, or we can attenuate this beauty altogether, but we cannot, in a musical system of any complexity, experience this kind of beauty all of the time. (Of course, the alternation of extremes of consonance and dissonance can have aesthetic value of its own.) Mathematics are behind our desire to hear pure triads, but those same mathematics declare that it is impossible for us to use pure triads within our musical system with any consistency; we must either banish them entirely or else buy them in some places at the cost of great dissonance in others. In other words, we must make subjective choices about how we wish to balance the competing goods of the purely sonic beauty of individual sounds and the consistency of our sonic experience over time. We are in a richly open system.

If rhythm followed the pattern of interval, we could imagine that the durations that conformed to simple ratios might be perceived as most pleasing, with durations that failed to fit the ratios seeming disturbing in some way. In many musical styles, however, a metronomic performance is the farthest thing from preferred. Without some rhythmic flexibility, much music sounds sterile and lifeless. Carl Seashore, who oversaw the most comprehensive early empirical studies of musical performance, stated as a general rule that "beauty in music lies largely in artistic deviation from the exact or rigid."[46] In most styles of Western tonal music, the performances that are felt to be most pleasing and expressive involve a perceptible degree of deviation from simple small-integer durational ratios.

Beyond being merely preferred, timing deviation seems also to be built into our perception of music at a deep level. Going beyond previous experimenters who demonstrated that most pianists are unable to give a metronomic performance when instructed to, Bruno Repp has shown that the structure of a musical score creates very strong expectations about how the tempo (and thus the durational ratios) will fluctuate. Listening to computer-generated performances, his experimental subjects found it much easier to detect lengthenings inserted into an otherwise deadpan performance when

46. Carl Seashore, *Psychology of Music* (New York and London: McGraw-Hill, 1938), p. 249.

those lengthenings occurred in unexpected places. Where lengthening is customary, listeners were often unaware that the sequence of durations had not been metronomic. Musical structure, then, effectively warps time for listeners, so that their ability to judge equal intervals of time is impaired. In further experiments, Repp showed that an average of the timing profiles of a great many commercially recorded performances yielded a timing profile that was found pleasing by listeners and that was similar to timing profiles of graduate student performers. But the performances by the artists who had the biggest reputations as interpreters were found to be among those most at variance with the average timing profile. This means that we have a preference for a double deviation. The most usual timing profile is a systematic deviation from a strictly metronomic performance, and the most striking interpretations are themselves deviations from the usual timing profile, thus fulfilling Seashore's theory of musical beauty at two hierarchically nested levels.[47]

Small-integer durational ratios form the basis for the performance, perception, and notation of rhythm. But most musicians are unable to produce exact durational ratios in real musical contexts, and, most interestingly, listeners may well not like it if they come too close to succeeding.

These results strongly confirm two points that Jeremy Begbie has made in relation to music and theology.

The first is that in music, there is a very rich form of interaction between freedom and constraint, in which freedom is not the opposite of constraint, but rather is engendered by constraint.[48] As we have seen, research into the psychological functioning of very basic materials of music gives us just such a picture. With respect to both pitch and rhythm, very simple mathematical relationships are fundamental to the most basic materials of music, both in production and in perception. But while simple ratios provide a basic framework, giving form and organization to what would otherwise be a chaotic jumble of

---

47. See Bruno H. Repp, "Probing the Cognitive Representation of Musical Time: Structural Constraints on the Perception of Timing Perturbations," *Cognition* 44 (1992): 241-81; Bruno H. Repp, "The Detectability of Local Deviations from a Typical Expressive Timing Pattern," *Music Perception* 15, no. 3 (1998): 265-89; Bruno H. Repp, "A Microcosm of Musical Expression: I. Quantitative Analysis of Pianists' Timing in the Initial Measures of Chopin's Etude in E Major," *Journal of the Acoustical Society of America* 104, no. 2 (1998): 1085-1100; and Bruno H. Repp, "Variations on a Theme by Chopin: Relations Between Perception and Production of Timing in Music," *Journal of Experimental Psychology: Human Perception and Performance* 24, no. 3 (1998): 791-811.

48. Begbie, *Theology, Music and Time*, pp. 224-33, 246-47; see also Guthrie, *Carmen Universitatis*, pp. 141-56, 298.

infinite possibilities, they do not pervade those basic materials to the extent that could be imagined. Just as Begbie has argued, we see "the given" as constraint as inseparable from "the given" as a gift that gives us the means to exercise freedom. It would be most ungrateful to view the constraints on our musical perception primarily as limitations that bar our access to what we might otherwise hear, as if we encountered in them the boundaries around God's generosity to us — "just so much and no more." Rather, these constraints are opportunities to take imaginative and fruitful action.

And this is the second point of contact with Begbie, for he emphasizes that part of the overflowing abundance of this gift, part of its great potential, is the richness of opportunity embedded within the constraints. With respect to both pitch and rhythm, we see human activity both making use of and deviating from a simple, given order; in the case of pitch, we even see that the deviation is demanded by limitations intrinsic to the given order. In nature we are not given a children's book in which we may connect the dots or color between the lines, the overall design being determined in advance. Rather, we are given the opportunity to respond to nature musically in ways that allow us to grow into the fullness of the image of God. Of all the aspects of this gift's plenitude, the greatest may be that it invites us to respond to it with forms of creativity, agency, freedom, and love that echo those with which it was given.[49]

Back to Pythagoras

Pythagoras comes out of this survey strongly reaffirmed. The structure of music is indeed significantly mathematical in a number of respects. For those who agree with the theology of McGrath and Polkinghorne, this mathematical structure resonates with fundamental aspects of how God has ordered both the cosmos and human beings. Music may even allow us to glimpse aspects of the mathematical ordering of human thought at work in a domain that is not explicitly mathematical. Even where we encounter the limitations of mathematical ordering in music, we find strong confirmation of Jeremy Begbie's work on freedom and constraint in music as illustrative of larger theological principles. In antiquity, the harmonious ordering of the cosmos could be heard in music. I have argued that those who have ears for the song of creation may rationally hear the same thing today.

49. Begbie, "Christ and the Cultures: Christianity and the Arts," pp. 108-12; see also Guthrie, *Carmen Universitatis*, pp. 162-208, 298.

6. Music as the Mouthpiece of Theology

Daniel K. L. Chua

Nietzsche once accused Wagner of being the "ventriloquist of God." Too much Schopenhauer had turned the composer into "a telephone from beyond," he said, as if his music were some kind of metaphysical channel.[1] Wagner was under the delusion that his music spoke divinely when, in fact, he was merely manipulating it like some Teutonic Wizard of Oz. Nietzsche's polemic is a warning: music does not simply speak, it is often spoken for. So what is going to prevent the theological speculation on music in this book from being another act of ventriloquism? After all, in the West we have inherited a music that is not unlike a ventriloquist's dummy; there is an inherent "muteness" in the nineteenth-century notion of "absolute music," where the meaning of music is located in the emptiness of its sign.[2] An inarticulate

1. Friedrich Nietzsche, *On the Genealogy of Morality*, ed. K. Ansell-Pearson, trans. C. Diethe (Cambridge: Cambridge University Press, 1994), p. 78.

2. On the nineteenth-century idea of absolute music, see Carl Dahlhaus, *The Idea of Absolute Music*, trans. R. Lustig (London and Chicago: University of Chicago Press, 1989); Mark Evan Bonds, "Idealism and the Aesthetic of Instrumental Music at the Turn of the Nineteenth Century," *Journal of the American Musicological Society* 50, nos. 2-3 (1997); and Daniel K. L. Chua, *Absolute Music and the Construction of Meaning* (Cambridge: Cambridge University Press, 1999). The idea of "absolute music" emerged from the philosophy of the early Romantics at the turn of the nineteenth century, although the term was coined retrospectively by Wagner in an attempt to expose music's mendacious claims to purity. See Richard Wagner, *Das Kunstwerk der Zukunft* (1850) and *Oper und Drama* (1851), in *Sämtliche Schriften und Dichtungen* (Leipzig, 1911-16), 3:42-177 and 222-320; also see Klaus Kropfinger, *Wagner and Beethoven: Richard Wagner's Reception of Beethoven* (1974), trans. P. Palmer (Cambridge: Cambridge University Press, 1991), p. 115; and Thomas S. Grey,

DANIEL K. L. CHUA

music bereft of words is championed as the purest music, the most abstract of systems, whose self-referentiality creates a language so inchoate as to be ineffable if not universal. But this metaphysical blank only serves to hide the controlling voice on the other end of the phone. An uncritical reflection on music might unwittingly end up lip-reading the kind of ventriloquism that Nietzsche accused Wagner of doing.

One way of escaping music's "absolute" power is to discard the notion of purity and to redefine music as something "contaminated" by discourse, that is, to contextualize it as an object that is both culturally constructed and embedded within deeper epistemological structures. From this perspective, music becomes a highly contested site of meaning that plays an essential role in the way modern society has made sense of itself. At first, such contextualization may seem to dilute the meaning of music, but far from diminishing music's significance, it actually demonstrates music's centrality in the construction of modernity. In particular, music, with its god-like aura, is employed by the ventriloquists to articulate the theological consequences of modern thought. Indeed, the resonances between music and its discourses are like harmonics to the "fundamental bass" of theology.

Theology persists in secular thought for at least two reasons. First, intrinsic to the historical development of modernity is the progressive marginalization of God as the source of explanation. On the one hand, this allows humanity to take center stage as the autonomous agent that shapes the world; yet on the other hand, in defining itself against God, the modern world finds its identity bound to him, albeit as a negative image or anti-theology. Second, despite its rebellion, modernity ends up replicating the old theological structures as its new modes of thought; its "grand narratives" are often a rehearsal of the biblical ones — creation, fall, redemption, apocalypse — all revised without God, of course. What is important is that all these (anti-)theological consequences reverberate within the structures of music, which, in fact, can barely contain the inevitable crises that result from such delusions of autonomy. Music, acting as a kind of divine surrogate, is elected to exemplify both the possibility and the ultimate futility of these human projects. Thus music can be heard as a mode of "secular theology" that exposes some of the major theological issues of our times.

There are, of course, far too many "divine" ventriloquists in the history of modern music to unmask in the cramped spaces of this chapter. The strat-

---

Wagner's Musical Prose: Texts and Contexts (Cambridge: Cambridge University Press, 1995), pp. 1-2.

egy here is merely to pull out *one* thread from a complex texture in order to examine a fissure that has frayed the identity of modern music, a division that has caused the status of music to oscillate between the physical and the metaphysical in humanity's search for meaning. This thread is not the *only* history of modern music; neither is it a unifying thread. What follows should be understood as three selected splices in time[3] — or, to use Nietzsche's metaphor, snatches of conversation tapped from music's invisible telephone lines.

Vincenzo Galilei

In the history of Western music, the birth of the modern world was signaled by an apparent collapse of the ancient cosmos. This world, as modernity conceives it, was one in which the universe was indeed a *universe*; it was a static, unified environment in which humanity was at one with the cosmos. Unlike the modern world, this universe was not natural — or at least, what was called natural was in fact *super*natural. Nature was not a ground of knowledge, but was embedded within a supernature, an enchanted cosmos of divine, immutable essences where all things found their ultimate coherence in God. This was a Christian world bursting with theological symbols, but it was equally a Neo-Platonic world and an occultic one — indeed, in practice, the three were often interchangeable.[4] What held this magical universe together was music. The ancient cosmos was literally en*chant*ed — it

---

3. For a more detailed discussion of such discourses see Chua, *Absolute Music and the Construction of Meaning*. This article has been adapted from various sections of the book. The three "splices" of music history here reflect the "archeological" method of my book which explores the underlying epistemic shifts that construct meaning in Western instrumental music with opera as its antithesis. This is a very specific archeology. The history of music, in its broadest sense, is an overlapping and multi-layered discourse with as much activity at its peripheries as at its center. Since my book focuses on the center, tracing the musical discourses at the heart of modernity, it is an archeology of *secular* music; indeed, the secular, as the chapter will explain, is a mark of modernity. Church music, of course, continued to flourish, at times intersecting with modern discourses. However, it is not surprising that those older epistemic layers should persist or even re-surface in the discourses of various religious groups. An example is provided by Joyce Irwin's chapter in this volume, " 'So Faith Comes from What is Heard': The Relationship between Music and God's Word in the First Two Centuries of German Lutheranism" [pp. 65-82], where the notion of a cosmic music was revived, a notion that was no longer a dominant belief.

4. See Gary Tomlinson, *Music in Renaissance Magic* (London and Chicago: University of Chicago Press, 1993).

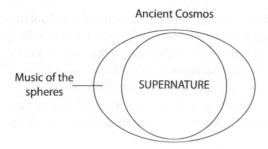

Figure 1. The Supernatural Cosmos

sang (Fig. 1, above). The music of the spheres ordered the universe with its inaudible harmonies. It was truly an absolute music.

This cosmic harmony came to be pictured as a monochord that connected the stars to the earth like a long piece of string; its harmonies imposed a unity over creation, linking everything along the entire chain of being (fig. 2). When music moved, the earth moved with it. Thus music was not simply an object in a magical world, *but the rational agent of enchantment itself*.

It is precisely the question of enchantment that is pivotal to modernity's identity, for according to the German sociologist Max Weber (1864-1920) modernity is marked by "the disenchantment of the world" *(Entzauberung der Welt)*, whereby Western society exorcises itself of its fear of demons, ghosts, and ultimately God.[5] Once desacralized, the world becomes *natural* matter amenable to the interrogation and technological control of human rationality. The modernization of society is therefore its secularization. Disenchantment, according to Colin Gunton, results in a "displacement" in which the divine will is usurped by a human one; man becomes like God — albeit a pseudo-deity reduced to nothing more than a monistic force.[6] As if to register the theological ramifications of this, Weber describes the process of secularization in terms of the fall: "The fate of an epoch which has eaten of the tree of knowledge," he writes, "is that it must know that [it] cannot learn the meaning of the world from the result of its analysis."[7] Humanity

5. Max Weber, "Science as Vocation" (1917), translated in *From Max Weber*, ed. H. H. Mills and C. Wright Mills (New York: Oxford University Press, 1946), p. 155.

6. See Colin E. Gunton, *The One, the Three and the Many* (Cambridge: Cambridge University Press, 1993), pp. 1-40.

7. Max Weber, *Methodology of the Social Sciences*, ed. E. A. Shils and H. A. Finch (New York: The Free Press, 1949), p. 57.

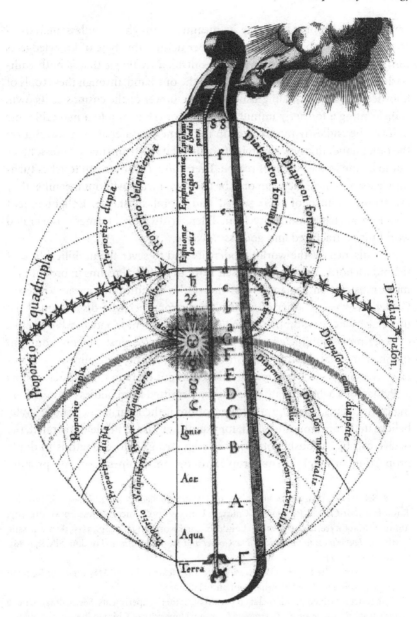

Figure 2. Robert Fludd, a monochord from *Utriusque cosmi* (1617-19). Instrumental sound as divine order: the hand of God tunes the string of the cosmic monochord that stretches from heaven to the earth to embrace all the elements within the unity of its harmonic ratios.

DANIEL K. L. CHUA

gains knowledge only by losing its meaning through an endless analysis of *facts* that have no binding *values*.[8] Weber defines this type of knowledge as *instrumental reason;* it is a *means* of control, a *technique* that is both ruthlessly direct and relationally remote. On the one hand, through these tools of knowledge, humanity can grasp the divine power of the cosmos as its own, transforming a formerly immutable world of essences into a malleable one that can be endlessly modernized in the name of material progress. But on the other hand, this new sovereignty, with all its instrumental prowess, turns out to be the Midas touch of reason. Everything the sovereign touches turns into facts; and these facts can only be used as a means without meaning; they are truths drained of their sacred and moral substance. Enlightenment therefore alienates humanity from Eden. It divides a formerly integrated world into a fractured and godless universe.

To disenchant the world, modernity had to sever the umbilical link of the monochord, disconnecting itself from the celestial realms in order to remove music as an explanation of the world. Significantly, it was Vincenzo Galilei (1520-1591), father of Galileo, the astronomer who disenchanted the universe,[9] who was among the first to cut the ancient monochord in a series of experiments conducted in the 1580s;[10] he subjected instrumental sound to the instrumental reason of empirical science. Music, he claimed, does not exist as some perfect numerological system out there in the celestial realms as Pythagoras believed; rather, sounds are emitted from bodies whose differing components color the aural perception of their harmonic ratios.[11] Why believe in the ancient ratio of 2:1, for example, if, as Galilei demonstrated, the octave can be variously obtained between strings whose length is in duple proportion, or weights in quadruple proportion, or pipes in octuple propor-

8. See Weber, "Science as Vocation," pp. 141-56; Michael Polanyi, *Personal Knowledge: Towards a Post-Critical Philosophy* (Chicago: University of Chicago Press, 1958), pp. 3-17; Alasdair MacIntyre, *After Virtue* (London: Duckworth, 1981), pp. 35-59; and Lesslie Newbigin, *Foolishness to the Greeks: The Gospel and Western Culture* (London: SPCK, 1986), pp. 21-41 and 65-94.

9. See Alexandre Koyré, "Galileo and Plato," in *Metaphysics and Measurement: Essays in Scientific Revolution* (London: Chapman and Hall, 1968).

10. Indeed, Galileo may have taken part in his father's experiments. See Stillman Drake, *Galileo at Work: His Scientific Biography* (Chicago: University of Chicago Press, 1970), pp. 15-17; "Renaissance Music and Experimental Science," *Journal of the History of Ideas* 31 (1970): 497-98; and Claude V. Palisca, *The Florentine Camerata: Documentary Studies and Translations* (New Haven: Yale University Press, 1989), p. 163.

11. Vincenzo Galilei, "A Special Discourse Concerning the Diversity of the Ratios of the Diapason," in Palisca, *The Florentine Camerata*, pp. 183-85.

142

tion?[12] Empirical reality simply did not match up with the ancient ratios that were supposed to organize the universe. By conducting these experiments, Galilei instigated a line of reasoning that grounds music theory in the acoustical nature of the external world, with calculations based on physical reality. Music became an audible *fact* divorced from celestial *values*. From now on music was to live by sound and not by faith.

With the collapse of the musical cosmos, music became just another object under the gaze of the human eye/I. This was not so much an incarnation — the musical *logos* made flesh, as it were — but an incarceration that robbed music of its significance; as a natural phenomenon, music was reduced to a set of meaningless vibrations that oscillated along strings, reverberated in pipes, and jangled the nerve fibers of modern man. But these empirical facts, for all their material veracity, had no value. Music had lost its magic. Its necessary disenchantment triggered a sense of meaninglessness, rekindling a desire for the re-enchantment of music. Modern music required a modern magic. But how?

One telling symptom of this desire was the attempt toward the end of the sixteenth century to transfer music from the medieval quadrivium of music, geometry, astrology, and arithmetic to the rhetorical arts of the trivium.[13] By collapsing the music of the spheres into the rhetorical will of the human ego, the magic of the cosmos could reconfigure its power in the voice of humanity, bestowing the subject with divine possibilities. The shift split the nature of sound. Music, modernized in the quadrivium as a scientific fact of external nature, found itself pitted against music as the interior, moral power of human nature, setting music in opposition to itself as object and subject. This epistemic division is the source of a historical dialectic in music history, pitting tone against word, voice against instrument, and harmony against melody (see Fig. 3 on p. 144).

Indeed, this division is already evident in Galilei's theories; his scientific interrogation of music runs parallel with his attempt to reinvent a modern "magic" through a new type of singing — monody — which imitates a form of bardic incantation where the musical tone, by adhering to the contours of the text, empowers the words to affect the soul. Music's celestial influence upon our humors was now transferred to the human voice. The invention of

12. Galilei, "A Special Discourse."

13. See Claude V. Palisca, "The Alterati of Florence, Pioneers in the Theory of Dramatic Music," in *New Looks at Italian Opera: Essays in Honor of Donald J. Grout,* ed. W. W. Austin (Ithaca, NY: Cornell University Press, 1968), p. 14.

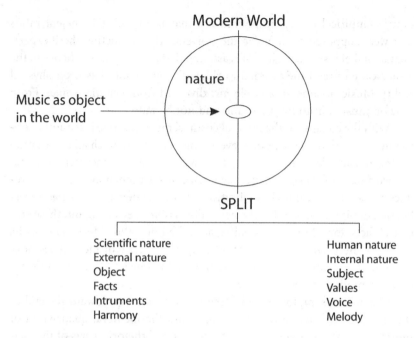

Figure 3. The Modern World

monody toward the end of the sixteenth century famously gave rise to an elaborate spectacle designed to re-enchant the world through purely human means, and the name of this magic is "Opera."

After all, to dis-*enchant* the world is literally to leave it un-*sung.* Opera sings in an unsung world as nostalgia for an ancient age enchanted by music. This is why the earliest operas were all Arcadian pastorals.[14] The pastoral is nature as a garden, a secular Eden conjured by the desires of the urban imagination. And the figure who dramatizes the Arcadian landscape is Orpheus, the son of Apollo, the god of music. His song is the ecosystem of the enchanted world. What distinguishes early opera from other forms of pastorals is that the subject of enchantment, music, is also the *medium* of enchantment; the content is the form. Opera is music about music, and, just to make it clear, the music tells you. In the prologue of Monteverdi's *Orfeo* (1607), "Musica" is personified on stage. She defines herself: "I am music," she sings,

14. See Nino Pirrotta, "Early Opera and Aria," in *New Looks at Italian Opera,* pp. 72-89; Ellen Harris, *Handel and the Pastoral Tradition* (London: Oxford University Press, 1980), p. 25; and Ruth Katz, *The Powers of Music: Aesthetic Theory and the Invention of Opera* (New Brunswick: Transaction Publishers, 1994), pp. 142-48.

after which she proceeds to elaborate the theory of her own powers; she moves, she allures, she enchants. The magic on stage is the magic you experience, presented and demonstrated before your very ears; she is both the content and the intent of opera, as though she brings the reality of an ancient magic into a modern practice.

The group who allegedly created opera, the so-called "Florentine Camerata" of Giovanni Bardi (1534-1612), which included Vincenzo Galilei, were driven by the need to regain an ancient power. If music is still magical, argues Galilei, then where are the "miracles" today that are described in the ancient texts?[15] "Pythagoras cured alcoholics, and Empedocles the mad, and Xenocrates someone possessed of a devil," says Bardi, but modern music is merely a polyphonic confusion that cannot work its magic on the soul.[16] Although it would be simplistic to claim that the Camerata invented opera,[17] the theories they espoused in the 1580s register the disenchantment of music that is the *anxiety* behind opera. Whereas a hundred years earlier magic was a musical practice,[18] by the time of the Camerata such powers could only be proposed as a *theory* for the re-enchantment of empirical reality. Their discussions testify to a disenchanted world disenchanted with itself, and so mark a critical moment of self-realization in modernity's progress. From now on, music's future becomes a matter of recovery; its drive toward the new is haunted by an idealized past. Thus the Camerata forged a new strategy for modernity: it denounced the present as a pale imitation of music's "first and happy state,"[19] to quote Galilei, in order to propel the ancient strains back to the future. With the disenchantment of the world, music becomes a site of both nostalgia and anticipation, where Arcadia and Utopia, fixed at either end of history, yearn for harmonization. It becomes a secular retelling of the biblical narrative of a paradise lost and the hope of a paradise

15. Vincenzo Galilei, *Dialogo della musical antica e della moderna* (1581), in Oliver Strunk, *Source Readings in Music History* (New York: Norton, 1950), p. 305. Much of Galilei's argument here is taken from a letter he received in 1572 from his mentor, Girolamo Mei; see Palisca, *The Florentine Camerata*, pp. 45-77.

16. Giovanni Bardi, *Discourse Addressed to Guilo Caccini, Called the Roman, on Ancient Music and Good Singing*, in Palisca, *The Florentine Camerata*, p. 111. Again, the material is adapted from Mei's letter to Galilei; see footnote above.

17. See, for example, Claude V. Palisca, "The Alterati of Florence, Pioneers in the Theory of Dramatic Music," in *New Looks at Italian Opera*, pp. 9-11. The theories of the Camerata were not unique; however, I shall use the Florentine Camerata as a focus for the new theories of music discussed within the humanist circles of sixteenth-century Italy.

18. See Tomlinson, *Music in Renaissance Magic*, p. 144.

19. Galilei, *Dialogo della musical antica e della moderna*, p. 310.

regained. Or, to adopt Gunton's phrase, music becomes the focus of a "displaced eschatology." "Responsibility for the end of things as well as for their beginning is displaced from divine to human agency," he writes. "It thus falls on the human agent not only to impose patterns of rationality on a recalcitrant nature, but to determine its future also. . . . [This] illusion of modernity . . . generates an incapacity to live in the present."[20] Thus, in the discourse of opera, whatever good music had in creation was now lost in the present by the creature in his delusion as the creator of the future.[21]

Rameau and Rousseau

Bereft of a unifying theology of creation, the division of music that preoccupied both sides of Galilei's brain became an epistemic rift that widened with the progress of the physical sciences on one side and the exploration of human identity on the other. Music's split-personality caused its discourses to fluctuate between a godless materialism and a self-deifying idealism that would leave its meaning ultimately empty. In the earlier years of the eighteenth century, this fissure found itself caught between the body and the soul, a split epitomized by Descartes' cogitating ego, which divided its identity from the flesh as a disembodied mind. From this dualistic perspective, instrumental music was relegated to the body because it had no concept for the mind to grasp; it was explained, instead, by Newtonian physics and was experienced as physiological vibrations that could quite literally slacken one's moral fibers. Vocal music, on the other hand, emanated from the inner sanctum of the human being; the alignment of word and tone provided clear and distinct concepts that signified the presence of the thinking "I am" that was the moral identity of the Cartesian self. Thus the voice had soul; instrumental music, in contrast, was just a "body without soul"; and since the body, prior to the birth of biology in the 1740s, was regarded as a mechanism of levers and pumps, this music was denounced as a "dead thing."[22] Indeed,

20. Gunton, *The One, the Three and the Many*, pp. 90-91.
21. This belief would find one of its most sinister and anti-Christian forms in Wagner's "music of the future." See Chua, *Absolute Music*, pp. 224-34.
22. Johann Christoph Gottsched, *Auszug aus des Herrn Batteux schonen Kunsten aus dem einzigen Grundsatze der Nachahmung hergeleitet* (Leipzig, 1754), p. 202. Nöel-Antoine Pluche shares the same opinion; see *Le Spectacle de la nature, ou Entretiens sur les particularités de l'histoire naturelle, qui ont paru les plus propres à rendre les jeunes-gens curieux, et à leur former l'esprit* (Paris, 1732-50), vol. 7 (1746), pp. 114-15.

without the imprint of God, which, for Descartes, connected the innate ideas of the mind with the objects of the world,[23] these empty tones had no divine identity; it was purely material and dangerously secular.

But with the increasingly secular reasoning of the eighteenth century, the soul lost its epistemological grip on reality. Its metaphysical status was put in doubt. And because music was tied to the fortunes of the soul, it was caught up in a battle between those who happily dispensed with it and those who desperately clung on to its metaphysical meaning. It did not take long for Descartes's divine realm of innate ideas to become an untenable assumption. Its metaphysics of the soul was abandoned for a natural history of it. The soul became disenchanted; "many philosophers [have] written the romance of the soul," says Voltaire; "a sage has arrived who has modestly written its history. Locke has set forth human reason just as an excellent anatomist explains the parts of the human body."[24] Instead of grounding the soul in some transcendental realm, the empirical twist located it in space and time. But where are the documents of its newly "displaced" history to be found? Not in the world, but in the sensations of the soul itself. The passions were given a history. And it was vocal music, as the passionate script of the soul, that provided the data for the linguistic and moral origin of humanity. "Each sentiment has its own tones, its accents and its sighs," writes Jean-Batiste Dubos,[25] and these sounds can be traced back in the mind to formulate the primal psychology of being. So it was no longer just the clarity of words that legitimized vocal music, but its prelinguistic utterances of pure expressivity. Hence almost all the conjectural histories of language written in the eighteenth century had their genesis in the voice, in a kind of *Ursprache* of passionate tones filled with sighs, groans, and expressive inflections that emanated from the purity of aboriginal existence.[26] Opera theory provided the secular soul with an Edenic anthropology. A theology of creation was no longer required, for the singing voice was now the "transcendental signifier,"

23. See Ernst Cassirer, *The Philosophy of the Enlightenment*, trans. F. C. A. Koelln and J. Pettgrove (Princeton: Princeton University Press, 1951), p. 95.

24. Voltaire, *Lettres sur les Anglais*, quoted in Cassirer, *The Philosophy of the Enlightenment*, p. 94.

25. Jean-Batiste Dubos, *Réflexions critiques sur la poésie, la peinture et la musique* (Paris, 1740), p. 470.

26. The classic example is Jean-Jacques Rousseau's *Essai sur l'origine des langues*. See also Jacques Derrida's discussion of the essay in *Of Grammatology*, trans. G. C. Spivak (Baltimore: Johns Hopkins University Press, 1976), pp. 144-307; and Downing A. Thomas, *Music and the Origins of Language* (Cambridge: Cambridge University Press, 1995).

to use Derrida's term, that fixed the identity of the ego.[27] Conversely, instrumental music had no presence except as a simulation of the voice and its representations.

But why believe in the soul at all if it cannot be found or verified by empirical science? The rise of experimental physiology in the 1740s threw a spanner into the anatomical works, replacing a system of blind mechanism with a dynamic of growth and regeneration. Life was no longer a matter of structure, but of vital function. Tissues and nerves, as the physician Théophile de Bordeu (1722-1776) claimed, contained invisible forces of "sensibility."[28] Thus "the faculties of the soul," suggested Ettiene de Condillac (1715-1780), "could have their origins in sensation itself."[29] Consequently, a vital materialist like Denis Diderot (1713-1784) had no problem with instrumental music, since he had no real soul to worry about in any metaphysical sense;[30] he could revel in the pure, secular sensation of its vibrations as the sounds oscillated violently through every nerve fiber of the body. Its power to excite was purely biological; it was not fixed by the authority of the rational soul, but depended on the particular disposition of a person's nervous system.[31] In effect, the divine mediation necessary in Cartesian epistemology between knowledge and reality is replaced by the *immediacy* of an aesthetic experience where sense and cognition could intermingle directly.[32] If the flesh could live without spirit, then life could aspire to the condition of music's isomorphic relation with the body. In fact, for Diderot, the body could become a living instrument. "We are all instruments endowed with

27. See Derrida, *Of Grammatology*, pp. 262-307; and Paul de Man, "The Rhetoric of Blindness: Jacques Derrida's Reading of Rousseau," in his *Blindness and Insight: Essays in the Rhetoric of Contemporary Criticism* (New York: Oxford University Press, 1971), pp. 102-41.

28. See Thomas L. Hankin, *Science and the Enlightenment* (Cambridge: Cambridge University Press, 1985), pp. 124-27; and Dorinda Outram, *The Body and the French Revolution* (New Haven: Yale University Press, 1989), p. 54. For a detailed study of the ideology of the body in the Enlightenment, see Barbara Maria Stafford, *Body Criticism: Imagining the Unseen in Enlightenment Art and Medicine* (Cambridge, MA: MIT Press, 1991).

29. Ettiene de Condillac, *Traité des animaux* (1755), quoted in Cassirer, *The Philosophy of the Enlightenment*, p. 101.

30. See Denis Diderot, "Soul," *Elements of Physiology* (1774-80), in *Diderot's Selected Writings*, ed. L. G. Crocker, trans. D. Coltman (New York: Macmillan, 1966), pp. 278-79; also see p. 271.

31. See Denis Diderot, *Lettre sur les sourds et muet a l'usage de ceux qui entendent et qui parlent* (1751), in *Œuvres complètes*, ed. H. Dieckmann and J. Varloot (Paris: Hermann, 1978), 4:206-7.

32. See Cassirer, *The Philosophy of the Enlightenment*, pp. 94-108.

feeling and memory," he writes. "Our senses are so many strings that are struck by surrounding objects and that also frequently strike themselves." Just give a harpsichord feeling and memory and it would be an animal capable of thinking, he claims.[33]

In a sense, this was exactly how Jean-Philippe Rameau (1683-1764), who corresponded with Diderot, viewed the human body. After all, as Diderot says, "there are bodies [*corps*] that I would certainly call harmonic."[34] In the 1750s, Rameau regarded bodies as resonators that emit the partials of the harmonic series as if they were literally the *corps sonore* that was so critical for his harmonic theory. By some kind of sensory transfer, the body could become harmonic, picking up the ratios of nature. But for those who wanted to save the soul in the eighteenth century, this sort of rampant materialism was eroding the moral fiber of society. French resistance to such desacrilization used vocal music as one of their moral weapons. It was Jean-Jacques Rousseau (1712-1778) who opposed Rameau most vehemently. For him, a harmonic ontology, because it is soulless, is not human by definition. Human conscience, claims Rousseau, arises from the voice of the soul — and the voice is *melodic*. Only instruments are harmonic, and in Rousseau's mind instruments are tools that merely alienate man from nature. Rameau's instrumental ontology is instrumental reason in disguise, disenchanting music with its harmonic calculations. It is made in the image of science instead of opera, substituting the passionate presence of the voice for the dead calculation of intervals.[35] For Rousseau, Rameau's harmonic genesis of humanity sounded too much like the cosmic *pneuma* (breath) of the vital materialists, as if instrumental sound could animate the body in the same way that the cosmic *pneuma* could inhabit matter.[36]

And perhaps Rousseau was right, for this is precisely what happens in Rameau's opera-ballet *Pygmalion*. Music breathes life into a stone statue and gives art both a body and a biology. Rameau himself, rather like that statue in his opera, had once possessed an inanimate body that his Cartesian mind had mechanized, as it were, into stone. His own conversion from a mechanistic to a sensationalist epistemology in the 1750s was nothing less than a

33. Denis Diderot, *D'Alembert's Dream* (1769), in *Diderot's Selected Writings*, 187-88. This philosophical work is in the form of a play, in which the main characters are Diderot, D'Alembert, and, pertinently, the physician Bordeu.

34. Diderot, *Lettre sur les sourds et muet*, 4:206.

35. See Derrida, *Of Grammatology*, pp. 199-215; and Thomas, *Music and the Origins of Language*, pp. 82-142.

36. On cosmic *pneuma*, see Hankin, *Science and the Enlightenment*, p. 127.

harmonic revelation. As an experiment, he had put himself into the state of a man "who had neither sung nor heard singing,"[37] in order to experience from within the first sounds that would strike his edenic ears — except that it was not a single sound, but a composite series of tones that resonated from the fundamental base of his being. Obviously, with such empirical evidence, the *corps sonore* had to become the stamp of nature for Rameau, and therefore the *pneuma* of biological instinct.[38] So what else should imbue the statue with life in the opera than the "composing out of the *corps sonore*" (see Example 1).[39] Having finished an air in G major, Pygmalion hears a magical harmonic disjunction as the music sinks into the natural vibrations of an E major chord, symbolically breathed out as life by the flutes. "Where do these concordant sounds come from?" cries the sculptor as some mysterious *pneuma* filters into his beloved statue. "What are these harmonies? A dazzling brightness fills this place." This "dazzling brightness" *(vive clarté)* that fills the stage is surely the same "flash of light" that Rameau speaks of in his memoires that had brought him to his senses.[40]

On entend une symphonie tendre et harmonieuse.
Le théâtre devient plus éclairé.

Example 1. Rameau, *Pygmalion*, scene 3: the breath of harmonic life.

37. Jean-Philippe Rameau, *Démonstration du principe de l'harmonie* (1750), pp. 11-12, quoted in Thomas Christensen, *Rameau and Musical Thought in the Enlightenment* (Cambridge: Cambridge University Press, 1993), pp. 217-18.

38. See the preface to Jean-Philippe Rameau, *Observations sur notre instinct pour la musique et sur son principe* (Paris, 1754).

39. Christensen, *Rameau and Musical Thought in the Enlightenment*, p. 228.

40. Rameau, *Démonstration*, pp. 11-12, quoted in Christensen, *Rameau and Musical Thought*, p. 218.

Unwittingly perhaps, Rameau had become the mouthpiece of the new body; the desacralized body, severed from its theological scaffolds, became an autonomous, self-regulating, sovereign structure and produced an aesthetic in its own image.[41] But the problem of such an image for Rousseau is that it robs humanity of its moral freedom.[42] "My will," he writes, "is independent of my senses."[43] If music is to reflect humanity, then it must arise from the moral autonomy of the will and not the passive responses of motor neurons.[44] To discover this will, music had to return to its anthropological origins in Neolithic man, to an emotive state of nature where musical tones were innately moral. Thus the fall of modern civilization is described as the estrangement of music from its natural origins, as it severs itself from speech to become the artificial harmonies that can no longer touch the heart.[45] "This is an age," complains Rousseau, "that seeks to prove that the workings of the soul spring from material causes and that there is no morality in human feelings." This new philosophy, embodied in the harmonic theories of Rameau, is the moral undoing of music. "As music becomes increasingly concerned with harmony at the expense of vocal inflection it is rougher on the ear, and less pleasing to the heart. Already it has ceased speaking; soon it will cease to sing."[46] In a section entitled "How music has degenerated" in his *Essay on the Origin of Language*, Rousseau concludes:

> Thus we see how singing gradually became an art entirely separate from speech, from which it takes its origin; how the harmonics of sounds re-

41. See Outram, *The Body and the French Revolution,* pp. 48-51. Ironically, Rameau himself, in the dialectic of vital materialism, slipped back in his late years into the cosmic mysticism that concepts like the universal *pneuma* always threatens to return to.

42. Jean-Jacques Rousseau, *The Creed of a Priest of Savoy,* trans. A. H. Beattie (New York: Continuum, 1990), pp. 8-15. On the idea of moral will and moral sensibility in the writings of Rousseau, see Ernst Cassirer, *The Question of Jean-Jacques Rousseau,* trans. P. Gay (Bloomington: Indiana University Press, 1954).

43. Rousseau, *The Creed of a Priest of Savoy,* p. 25.

44. See Cassirer, *The Question of Jean-Jacques Rousseau,* pp. 123-27.

45. See Robert Wokler, *Rousseau on Society, Politics, Music and Language* (New York: Garland, 1987), pp. 344-47.

46. Jean-Jacques Rousseau, *Essai sur l'origine des langues* (1764): the translation is taken from Peter Le Huray and James Day, *Music Aesthetics in the Eighteenth and Early-Nineteenth Centuries* (Cambridge: Cambridge University Press, 1981), pp. 100 and 102. Complete translations of the essay can be found in *The Origin of Language,* trans. J. H. Moran and A. Gode (New York: Frederick Ungar, 1966) and in *The First and Second Discourses together with the replies to Critics and Essay on the Origin of Languages,* ed. and trans. V. Gourevitch (New York: Harper & Row, 1986).

sulted in forgetting vocal inflections; and finally, how music, restricted to purely physical concurrences of vibrations, found itself deprived of the moral power it had yielded when it was the twofold voice of nature.[47]

As with the Florentine Camerata, Rousseau's arguments are driven by the need to regain an ancient power in order to legitimize the "displaced" will of modern humanity. The future of civilization is again haunted by a magical past, but this time it is internalized as a history of the self. Thus for Rousseau what the statue in Rameau's opera needed was not so much a biology as some kind of prelapsarian soul. "Your figure must be given one," says Pygmalion in *Rousseau's* retelling of the story, for life is not simply a matter of sensation but self-consciousness.[48] Only then can the statue become remotely human. So when Rousseau's statue awakens, her life does not begin with the external perceptions that characterize Rameau's statue — "What do I see? Where am I?" Rather, for Rousseau, the statue first touches her own body and simply says "I" — that vital articulation of self-presence. This is an autonomy of the will rather than Rameau's autonomy of sound — a vocal rather than an instrumental consciousness, an internal rather than an external nature. Indeed, external nature is discarded by the living statue: "That's not me," she says, touching a block of marble. It is only as the statue touches her creator, Pygmalion, that she recognizes her consciousness in another: "Ah, still me," she says as if to acknowledge the moral autonomy innate within his being. When Pygmalion cries out, "I adore myself in what I have made," he reveals the prelapsarian narcissism that is at the heart of the sentimental aesthetic; and the divine miracle that realizes the impossible is nothing more than the conversion of a corrupt culture into the innocence of pure nature. In tapping into the soul of natural man, humanity can be made perfect in an art that is "without art."[49] Thus the musical voice is Eden as nature, the illusion of a world without artificial signifiers and without sin. With its operatic recovery, modern civilization might just save itself from itself, and so maintain the illusion of its autonomy.

47. Rousseau, *Essai sur l'origine des langues,* trans. J. H. Moran and A. Gode in *The Origin of Language,* pp. 71-72.

48. Jean-Jacques Rousseau, *Pygmalion,* in *Œuvres complètes* (Paris: Pleiade, 1959), 2:1224-31. The quotations in English are taken from Jean Starobinski, *Jean-Jacques Rousseau: Transparency and Obstruction,* trans. A. Goldhammer (Chicago: University of Chicago Press, 1988), pp. 70-80.

49. Jean-Jacques Rousseau, "Expression," in *Dictionnaire de musique* (Geneva, 1781), p. 293.

Together, Rameau and Rousseau represent the disjunction in modern thought between reason and will, with "a rational self on the one hand, which has a cognitive relation to reality, and the voluntative self on the other, which consists of affections, emotions and decisions." In theological terms, their discourse on music is split between "hearing and doing," a divorce that Oliver O'Donovan defines as the "malfunction of the moral life" that robs humanity of its freedom: knowing is no longer willing and believing is no longer loving. On the verge of an age in which the notion of freedom would become the new absolute of human identity, music's internal rupture already articulates "the alienation of freedom."[50] Rameau and Rousseau speak of this alienation as two types of living bodies — one biological, the other moral. Both claim an autonomy for the self — one purely material, the other based on the freedom of the will. Both authenticate their origins in nature — one scientific, the other emotive. Both claim an immediacy of communication — one bodily, the other innate within the soul. Both make music in their own image — one harmonic (rational calculation), the other melodic (human voice). To a certain extent, the development of instrumental music in the eighteenth century into the absolute music of the nineteenth century fused the rational sensationalism of the one with the moral sentiment of the other. If anything, it inclined toward the latter; the irony of Rousseau's thought was that its concepts were more fully realized by the Germans in their instrumental music than the French in their vocal music. But then, it was the Germans who systematically thought through the implications of Rousseau's philosophy — in Eric Weil's words, "It took Kant to *think Rousseau's thoughts*."[51] If the French gave instrumental music a living body, then it was the Germans who gave it a moral soul.

Early Romantic Philosophers

The delusions of moral innocence were not going to survive the age of revolution. The sensitive soul could not turn a man of feeling into a man of ac-

50. Oliver O'Donovan, *Resurrection and Moral Order: An Outline for Evangelical Ethics* (Grand Rapids: Eerdmans, 1986), p. 111.

51. Eric Weil, "J-J Rousseau et sa politique," *Critique* 56 (January 1952): 11, quoted in Starobinski, *Jean-Jacques Rousseau*, p. 115. Jean Starobinski, Ernst Cassirer, and Dieter Henrich also take the view that both Kant's ethics and aesthetics are indebted to Rousseau's ideas. See Starobinski, *Jean-Jacques Rousseau*; Cassirer, *The Question of Jean-Jacques Rousseau*; and Dieter Henrich, *Aesthetic Judgement and the Moral Image of the World* (Stanford: Stanford University Press, 1992), pp. 3-28.

tion. By the end of the eighteenth century, a new soul was required, one of unsentimental freedom and independence. And this new soul demanded a new aesthetic; to this end, the notion of "disinterested contemplation" was championed by philosophers such as Kant (1724-1804), to enable the subject to sever all sympathetic identification with the object in an act of formal alienation.[52] The fusion of body and soul on which the passive aesthetic of sensibility depended was split by the Kantian aesthetic in a replay of the body-soul duality of Descartes. The rational soul, transformed as the Kantian subject, became the precondition for the imperatives of moral freedom. The subject asserted its difference from nature as disembodied soul.

But this was precisely the problem. Where was the soul? The medical science of the eighteenth century had dispossessed the body of its spirit. And in German philosophy, the condition of the soul was becoming increasingly inaccessible and abstract. It was at this point that instrumental music became the quintessence of art, for it was elected to resolve the crisis of the soul's disappearance. Although Kant, in the Critique of Judgement, left instrumental music vibrating in the body, he actually hoisted the aesthetic out of the empirical world and relocated it in the transcendental realm.[53] The early Romantics merely carried further the logic of Kant's aesthetics to include instrumental music. For them, such music was a mysterious out-of-body experience; or as Wilhelm Heinrich Wackenroder (1773-1798) puts it, music has to demonstrate "the movement of our soul, disembodied."[54] The Romantics turned a music of lack into one of plenitude: the lack of rational concept became the logic of a language beyond language; and the lack of representation became the ineffable intimations of the noumenal self. By the turn of the nineteenth century, the early Romantics had moved instrumental music from body to soul.

"Now what do we mean by 'soul'?" asks Kant:

"Soul" [Geist] in an aesthetical sense, signifies the animating principle in the mind. But that whereby this principle animates the psychic substance [Seele] — the material which it employs for that purpose — is that which

52. Immanuel Kant, Critique of Judgement (1790), trans. J. C. Meredith (Oxford: Oxford University Press, 1973), pp. 50-60.

53. See Henrich, Aesthetic Judgement, pp. 29-56; and Paul Crowther, The Kantian Sublime: From Morality to Art (Oxford: Clarendon Press, 1989).

54. Wilhelm Heinrich Wackenroder and Ludwig Tieck, Phantasien über die Kunst für Freunde der Kunst (Hamburg, 1799), in Werke und Breife von Wilhelm Heinrich Wackenroder (Berlin: Verlag Lambert Schneider, 1938), p. 207.

sets the mental powers into a swing that is final, i.e. into a play which is self-maintaining and which strengthens those powers for such activity.[55]

Kant's aesthetic definition of *Geist* as "self-maintaining" is also his definition of the creative genius who "prescribes the law to himself."[56] And the definition of music by the early Romantics is the sonic reflection of this autonomy. Instrumental music "is independent and free," writes Ludwig Tieck (1773-1753), paraphrasing Kant; "it prescribes its own laws to itself."[57] The symphony becomes a self-generating object made in the image of the Romantic genius: "The modern artist," says Friedrich Schlegel (1772-1829), must "work out from the inside" to produce "a new creation from nothing."[58] And what could be a better representation of the metaphysics of nothing than the empty sign of instrumental music? It is the promise of a new creation, a Promethean counter-creation that imposes its will on the world in the name of freedom.[59]

Given such transcendental claims, any type of pictorial music was regarded as embarrassingly naïve, since it claims to know reality as empirical fact. The new aesthetic was therefore a kind of purifying agent that cleansed the emotional and pictorial representations that the eighteenth century had foisted on music. So whereas in the past instrumental music was forced into imitation, now under the new regime it disappeared into its own emptiness. Musical mimesis, as found in the symphonies of Dittersdorf, for example, was consigned by E. T. A. Hoffmann (1776-1822) "to total oblivion as ridiculous aberrations" to make way for a music that dematerializes into "the spirit-realm of the infinite."[60] The sudden invisibility of music was an epistemological move to support the subject's ailing powers to ground itself in the visible world. Music became invisible because the visual objects of knowledge that had structured the empirical thought of the eighteenth cen-

55. Kant, *Critique of Judgement,* p. 175.

56. Kant, *Critique of Judgement,* p. 168.

57. Wackenroder and Tieck, "Symphonien," in *Phantasien über die,* p. 254.

58. Friedrich Schlegel, *Gespräche über die Poesie* (1799-1800), in *Kritische Schriften und Fragmente,* ed. E Behler and H. Eichner (Munich, 1988), 2:201.

59. On the significance of "nothing" in music and the representation of human freedom, see Daniel K. L. Chua, "The Promise of Nothing: The Dialectic of Freedom in Adorno's Beethoven," *Beethoven Forum* 12, no. 1 (2005).

60. E. T. A. Hoffmann, "Review of Beethoven's Fifth Symphony," *Allgemeine musikalische Zeitung,* vol. 12 (1810), ed. D. Charlton, trans. M. Clarke; *E. T. A. Hoffmann's Musical Writings: Kreisleriana, The Poet and the Composer, Music Criticism* (Cambridge: Cambridge University Press, 1989), pp. 236-37 and 239.

tury had disappeared in an act of subjective reflection. The first thing to go was the subject itself. The thinking ego of Descartes had become a theoretical vacuum in Kantian philosophy; in its bid for autonomy, the subject became entirely without cause and content and was inaccessible to knowledge, despite being the first principle of knowledge. The noumenal existence that Kant bestowed upon it turned the ego into an abstract sign of absence, a logical necessity that accompanies all its representations, but was unable to represent itself to itself. The I in all its sovereignty was simply an empty form. But not only had the subject, along with the soul and its spirit, disappeared from the phenomenal world, but reason and its principles of freedom and morality had gone too; they were, in Kantian terms, supersensible ideas that were out of reach of empirical intuition. So music, following the subject, was made to empty its content in order to mime the noumenal world of Kantian freedom and morality. The autonomy of music is therefore tied up with the autonomy of the subject, and the aesthetic was a way of bringing them into recognition as brothers of invisibility.

In this way, music could reflect the invisible operations of the transcendental subject. It was called "a music of thought" because it traced the *movement* of the mind *before* speech.[61] Music is therefore not speech but consciousness itself, and as such, it is a "general language," says Johann Ritter, "the first of mankind"; all the languages of the world are merely "individuations of music" and relate to music "as the separate organs relate to the organic whole."[62] Thus the invisible signs of music were more than a representation of the subject; they were, in a sense, ingrained in the ego's transcendental processes, not merely depicting the I, but presenting it as real presence: "the activity and existence of man is tone."[63] That which accompanies all my representations, to paraphrase Kant, is no longer the subject as an abstract necessity, but an aesthetic reality. The empty ego knows the fullness of its existence in the empty sign of music.

Thus the Germans brought the moral subject of Rousseau and the natural order of Rameau into a unified theory, harmonizing the self-presence of the voice with the vibrations of the symphony. In effect, it was an attempt to heal the divisions of a disenchanted world, to merge the subject of the triv-

---

61. Friedrich Schlegel, *Literary Notebooks, 1797-1801,* no. 1116, ed. H. Eichner (London: The Athlone Press, 1957), p. 118.

62. Johann Wilhelm Ritter, *Fragmente aus dern Nachlasse eines jungen Physiker, ein Taschenbuch für Freunde der Natur* (1810), quoted in Charles Rosen, *The Romantic Generation* (Cambridge, MA: Harvard University Press, 1995), pp. 58-59.

63. Rosen, *The Romantic Generation,* p. 59.

ium with the universe of the quadrivium. The idea of absolute music was driven by the same sense of loss and alienation that had bedeviled Galilei and Rousseau. Indeed, the Romantics were acutely aware that modernity, in dividing to rule, risked possessing nothing but its own divisions, creating a world without God, without magic, and without meaning. Friedrich Schiller, in the final years of the eighteenth century, already spoke of the "disenchantment of the world"; in fact, Max Weber's narrative of disenchantment is a retelling of Schiller's aesthetics as sociology. For the poet, the "all-unifying nature" of the ancient world has been replaced by the "all-dividing intellect [*Verstand*]" of the modern age.[64] The machinery of state, the rationalization of labor, and the specialization of knowledge have brought modernity into a crisis of division. "Everlastingly enchained to a single little fragment of the whole," says Schiller, "man himself develops into nothing but a fragment."[65] And Hegel agrees: "Modern culture," he writes, has "driven [humanity] to the peak of harshest contradiction." Man has become "amphibious," split between himself and his environment, and unable in his self-styled sovereignty to mediate between object and subject, freedom and necessity, sense and reason, fact and value.[66]

What the subject needed was a "music of the spheres" for the modern age. For the Romantics, absolute music did not merely reflect the operations of the ego but was also an intimation of an unknowable cosmic force prior to consciousness, an impulse in which the subject participates in order to create a meaningful universe for itself; it was a transcendental movement both within and without. It is "pure motion," writes Friedrich Schelling (1775-1854), "born on invisible, almost spiritual wings," that lift it beyond the transcendental subject to embody the "aurally perceived rhythm and harmony of the universe itself." Music returns to the mathematics of the stars, but this cosmos is not the ancient spheres of earlier times, but a world created *for* the subject, who, in its desire to harmonize with nature, tries to relate music as "a substance counting within the soul"[67] with the abstract calculations of the

64. Friedrich von Schiller, *On the Aesthetic Education of Man: In a Series of Letters*, trans. E. Wilkinson and L. A. Willoughby (Oxford: Clarendon Press, 1967; reprinted 1985), p. 33.

65. Schiller, *On the Aesthetic Education of Man*, p. 35.

66. Georg Wilhelm Friedrich Hegel, *Aesthetics: Lectures on Fine Art*, trans. T. M. Knox (Oxford: Clarendon Press, 1975), p. 54.

67. Friedrich Wilhelm Joseph von Schelling, *Philosophie der Kunst* (1802-3), in *Music Aesthetics in the Eighteenth and Early-Nineteenth Centuries*, ed. Peter Le Huray and James Day (Cambridge: Cambridge University Press, 1981), pp. 280 and 275.

heavens. Humanity's musical logic is also a cosmic *logos;* and so the "starry heavens above" and the "moral law within" that Kant had left divided at the end of his second critique are united through music's invisible power.[68]

But this idea of "absolute music" is only an *aesthetic* totality and not a real one — an infinite yearning for reconciliation and not an actual condition. To re-enchant a rationalized world, the early Romantics could not reconstruct a system that would validate celestial truths that are eternal and external to their subjectivity; they only had an aesthetic system that searches for truths from the *particularity* of their own ego. The Romantic concept of "absolute music" is therefore Neo-Platonism in *subjective* form, the cosmology of a transcendental ego in search of an unattainable wholeness. This is why absolute music for the Romantics is posited as a *work* and not an inaudible cosmos of harmonic ratios; it starts from the particular because the modern subject, in its delusion of genius, tries to create a universe out of itself, hoping to find a global system that might restore its fragmented existence. Thus between the absolute music of the ancients and that of the Romantics, the absolute had changed irrevocably. The aesthetic system designed to retune the world was only a necessary figment of the Romantic imagination. For the ancients the metaphors of cosmic harmony were literal,[69] but for the Romantics they were literary; both believed in an absolute music, but for the Romantics the absolute was an "infinite yearning" for the "spirit realm"[70] that ancients knew as enchanted reality. Absolute music is therefore a regulative principle, doomed by the Romantics as a fictional "as if." The ancient idea of absolute music is not so much revitalized by the Romantics as brought into a modern condition.

In this way, music, in collusion with the subject, opened the way for a kind of divine displacement. It became like the Kantian deity, a "regulative" principle, as Gunton puts it, "merely an 'as if,'" a "blank unity." In its abstract and metaphysical forms, both man and music became like God — invisible and omnipotent. Indeed, according to Carl Dahlhaus, the veneration of instrumental music in the nineteenth century was itself a religion. Such divine attributes were a necessary consequence of grounding the subject in the subject itself with the absence of God as cosmic interpreter. But, of course, man is not God. The impossibility of making any sense of the world from the particular-

68. Immanuel Kant, *Critique of Practical Reason,* trans. L. W. Beck (Chicago: University of Chicago Press, 1949), pp. 258-60.

69. See Tomlinson, *Music in Renaissance Magic,* pp. 211 and 246.

70. E. T. A. Hoffmann, "Review of Beethoven's Fifth Symphony," pp. 238-39.

ity of one's subjective being, whether in social, moral, or political spheres, forced the subject to make an alliance with instrumental music. With music as its universal mirror, the subject could believe itself to be invisible and omnipotent like God, when in reality it was invisible and impotent like the aesthetic.

Concluding Remarks

The musical seesaw between the physical and metaphysical could continue with Wagner and Nietzsche, Schoenberg and Stravinsky, and so on. But let's stop the oscillation here and ask how theology today should participate in this process of ventriloquism. Any form of writing on music is bound to be an act of ventriloquism, although the bind is probably the consequence of a definition of music that is separate from speech. Music is more than its discourse, yet it is inseparable from it. Nonetheless, if theology today should lend its voice to music, then it has to provide a better act of ventriloquism than its secular counterpart; otherwise it may be denounced by modern-day Nietzsches as yet another fictional "telephone from beyond." So to conclude, I want to sketch some possibilities for further theological thought, not so much to give a definitive answer to the meaning of music as to suggest ways in which a theological perspective might turn the modern discourse on music into a meaningful conversation.

In tapping the historical phone-line for these snatches of musical ventriloquism, it is clear that music is already ladened with theological issues, albeit in negative forms. Thus music is not some tabula rasa for theology to inscribe its wisdom; it is encrusted with a history that has to be engaged with lest we inadvertently rehearse the anti-theological discourses of the ventriloquists and so contribute to music's oscillation between the metaphysical and the physical. Theology needs to go beyond this oscillation; after all, it ought to start from a different epistemic base. If God relates to the world, then the divorce between the natural and the supernatural that has bedeviled modernity cannot be sustained. Indeed, if God *relates* to the world, then knowledge itself ought to focus on the *relational* rather than merely the *rational* in the search for reconciliation.[71] Music understood in relational terms would be very different from its modern definition.

---

71. See John D. Zizioulas, "On Being a Person: Towards an Ontology of Personhood," in *Persons, Divine and Human,* ed. Christoph Schwöbel and Colin E. Gunton (Edinburgh: T&T Clark, 1991).

DANIEL K. L. CHUA

Absolute music's *ex nihilo* attempt at counter-creation would be sense-less in a world created without violence for the good of humanity. There would be nothing to purify itself against, no cage to free itself from, no material chaos outside to impose its will on.[72] Thus music's alleged purity, autonomy, or universality should not be assumed as its essence. And neither should its physicality or immateriality be pitted against each other as competing definitions. Such non-relational strategies are merely discursive constructions that require critique. Indeed, a theology of creation cannot simply equate the mind with the spirit, as if music were something pure, abstract, and disembodied; neither can it connect the materiality of music with the secular or its somatic affects with the purely sensual. Such binary oppositions result from the monistic will of modern freedom, which, in displacing the divine will, has merely enslaved itself in endless division.[73]

And, of course, music should not be forced to heal these divisions by re-creating the world as some kind of cosmic order or human origin. Such universal definitions tend to hide the possibility of music as a *particular* gift given in creation as a human activity. If music is an integral part of what it is to be human, then it ought to reflect something of the image of God in which we are made. If part of the *imago Dei* is the relationship of love that lies at the heart of the Trinity, then perhaps music can open up a way of thinking about how we relate to the world and to God in a manner where love rather than reason dominates. After all, music is inherently relational, both internally in the way its notes are put together and externally in the way in which it is used to communicate in everyday life. A relational discourse on

72. On the non-violence of creation in Christian thought, see the chapter "On Being Creatures" in Rowan Williams, *On Christian Theology* (Oxford: Blackwell, 2000), pp. 63-78; and also John Milbank, *Theology and Social Theory: Beyond Secular Reason* (Oxford: Blackwell, 1990), p. 329. Milbank, in fact, suggests the possibility of a relational understanding of music in his reading of Augustine's *De Musica* (pp. 424-25).

73. The freedom of the modern will has long been diagnosed by philosophers, feminists, and theologians as a delusion, and a dangerous one at that, inasmuch as its declaration of liberty hides an inherent unfreedom. See, for example, Georg Wilhelm Friedrich Hegel, *Phenomenology of Spirit,* trans. A. V. Miller (Oxford: Clarendon Press, 1977), pp. 355-63; Theodor W. Adorno and Max Horkheimer, *Dialectic of Enlightenment,* trans. John Cumming (London: Verso, 1979); Colin E. Gunton, "God, Grace and Freedom," and Christoph Schwöbel, "Imago Libertatis: Human and Divine Freedom," in *God and Freedom,* ed. Colin E. Gunton (Edinburgh: T&T Clark, 1995); John Milbank, *Being Reconciled: Ontology and Pardon* (London: Routledge, 2003), pp. 1-25; Christine Di Stefano, *Configurations of Masculinity: A Feminist Perspective on Modern Political Theory* (Ithaca, NY: Cornell University Press, 1991).

music would replace the gap of alienation native to monistic thought with the distance of relation fundamental to trinitarian thought, creating difference without division. Indeed, music might actually register some kind of transcendence inasmuch as it *gives distance* to such relationships instead of collapsing everything into the ego in its act of displacement. In this way, music's eschatology would no longer be the yearning of the displaced will for a wholeness that can only be posited in the future, but a celebration in the *present* that partakes in the goodness of creation and its redemption. With an alterior epistemology, music's meaning should be different.

What I have sketched as tentative alternatives are not arcane or peripheral issues, for the history of modern music is one that is embroiled in some of the most significant questions of our time. The challenge for theology is whether it can articulate the difference while engaging with the modern and postmodern world.

7. The Shock of the Positive: Olivier Messiaen, St. Francis, and Redemption through Modernity

Robert Sholl

Modernity Re-enchanted

The French Catholic composer Olivier Messiaen's statement that his mission had been "to revive the faith in the luminous and positive elements of the Christian religion" could not have been more portentous.[1] Only five years after this edict, Messiaen relinquished his spirit to the God he had spent some eighty years trying to reach through his music. If Messiaen's faith in the hereafter paid dividends, then it must have been a surprise to him, because in his extensive writings there is more than a hint of doubt about his own capacity to connect his music to God. At the heart of this anomaly is the problem of how the truths of Christianity can be expressed through a modern music saturated with secular aesthetic meanings. By addressing this issue, and its ramifications in one of his final works, the monumental opera *St. François d'Assise* (1975-83), we can attain a greater understanding of both Messiaen's astonishing music and the way that he must have hoped God would astonish him.

Perhaps it is because Messiaen's music takes Christian thought into such surprising regions that his music can help theology think through the searing heights and depths of the Christian faith. Like St. John the Baptist in Grünewald's Isenheim altarpiece (1515), Messiaen realized that he could only point humanity toward the presence of Christ:[2]

1. Interview with Olivier Messiaen by Patrick Szersnovicz on 29 May 1987 in *Le Monde de la Musique* (July-August 1987): 34.
2. The Resurrection panel of this altarpiece was one of Messiaen's favorite images.

I have tried to be a Christian musician and proclaim my faith through song, but without ever succeeding. Without doubt this is because I am unworthy of doing so (and I say this without any sense of false humility!). Pure music, secular [*profane*] music and, above all theological music (not mystical as my listeners believe) alternate in my production. I really do not know if I have an "aesthetic," but I can say that I prefer a music that is iridescent, subtle, even voluptuous (but not sensual, of course!). Music that is tender or violent, full of love and vehemence. A music which soothes [*berce*] and sings, which honours melody and the melodic phrase. Music that is like new blood, a signed gesture, an unknown perfume, an unsleeping bird. Music like a stained-glass window, a whirl of complementary colours. Music that expresses the end of time, ubiquity, glorified bodies and the divine and supernatural mysteries: a "theological rainbow."[3]

In order to create this theological rainbow, Messiaen needed a way of making the complex language of modern music, with its often negative associative meanings, a medium for theological thought. To do this he attempted to create an iconoclastic language that had the shock and freshness of "new blood," that had the originality of a "signed gesture," but that, although rich and strange, communicated the eternal mysteries of his Catholic faith in a way that not only drew people to them, but enabled his listeners to participate in and be transformed by his visions of glory.[4]

It may seem, however, that the religious ideology of transcendence implicit in Messiaen's "theological rainbow," a critical paradigm reinforced by the composer's voluminous writings, effectively masks its kaleidoscopic cultural makeup.[5] In fact, far from the "purity" ascribed above, Messiaen's music is sat-

3. Olivier Messiaen, "Résponses à une enquête," *Contrepoints* 1, no. 3 (March-April 1946): 73. All translations are my own, unless otherwise indicated. In the late 1940s, Messiaen counted himself a *"grand lecteur"* of various Surrealist writers. For more on this, see my "Love, Mad Love and the *'Point Sublime'*: The Surrealist Poetics of Messiaen's *Harawi*," in *Messiaen Studies,* ed. Robert Sholl (Cambridge: Cambridge University Press, 2007), pp. 34-62.

4. In his audaciously titled manifesto *Technique de mon langage musical* [hereafter *TMLM*] (Paris: Leduc, 1944), trans. John Satterfield (Paris: Leduc, 1956; reprinted 2001), Messiaen proclaimed his desire to create "a true music, that is to say, spiritual, a music which may be an act of faith: a music which may touch upon all subjects without ceasing to touch upon God; an original music, in short, whose language may open a few doors, take down some distant stars" (p. 7). For him, originality demanded not only that his music be modern, and yet outside the canon of modern music — Stravinsky, Ravel, *Les Six,* and to a lesser extent Schoenberg and Berg in the France of the 1940s — but that it must take God as its *fons et origo.*

5. Messiaen's *Traité de Rythme, de Couleur, et d'Ornithologie* [hereafter *TRCO*] was published in seven tomes (Paris: Leduc, 1994-2002) and is over 2,500 pages. For a current

urated with the theological reconfiguration of symbolism and surrealism, historical and cultural ideals of time and color, and the adaptation of historical and contemporaneous musical ideas. Furthermore, Messiaen's musical aesthetics take certain fundamental concerns of twentieth-century modernity — the utopian aspirations of modernism, a suspicion of and a fascination with progress, a rejection of materialism, and a renewed spiritual commitment to the future — but crucially continues and transforms these in a sacred vein.[6] If, as Daniel Chua states in his essay in this volume, the great theological narratives (creation, fall, death, and redemption) are sedimented in the narratives of modernity, all re-inscribed without God, the task of "a great artisan and a great Christian," was surely to absorb and transcend the diverse secular presences in his music through his faith, and thereby re-enchant modernity.[7]

In order to do this, Messiaen had to do more than simply put a thin varnish of theological gloss over his music: faith and art had to become one. The subjects of Messiaen's works form a kind of musical catechism of the life of Christ — his birth, his transfiguration, death and resurrection, ascension, and the expectation that he will return. Ironically, however, his desire to adorn his music with scriptural and theological material is a symptom of the difficulty of making his absolute or wordless instrumental music understood as religious.[8] For Messiaen, the search for this connection became like the perpetual exploratory quest for the horizon; each work precipitated another. Eventually he must have realized that nowhere could he dramatize theology more directly than through opera — in which instrumental music's indeterminate character is given theological focus and depth through the use not only of language, but gesture, dramatic character portrayal, stage

---

bibliography, see Peter Hill and Nigel Simeone, *Messiaen* (New Haven and London: Yale University Press, 2005), pp. 402-18.

6. For more on this, see "The Two Modernities" ("bourgeois" and "aesthetic" modernity) in Matei Calinescu's *Five Faces of Modernity* (Durham: Duke University Press, 1987), pp. 41-45. For a recent study of the intellectual history of the engagement between Catholicism and modernity in France see Stephen Schloesser's *Jazz Age Catholicism: Mystic Modernism in Postwar Paris, 1919-1933* (Toronto: University of Toronto Press, 2005).

7. Olivier Messiaen, *TMLM*, p. 7. Quoting himself in *TMLM*, Messiaen declares that " 'To express with a lasting power our darkness struggling with the Holy Spirit, to raise upon the mountain the doors of our prison of flesh, to give to our century the spring water for which it thirsts, there shall have to be a great artist who will be both a great artisan and a great Christian.' Let us hasten by our prayers the coming of the liberator."

8. This begins with Messiaen's first published composition, *Le Banquet Céleste* (1928), which has John 6:56 superscribed on the score: "Those who eat my flesh and drink my blood abide in me, and I in them."

craft, and so forth.[9] If Messiaen's work is centered on the life of Christ, it was entirely fitting that Messiaen would create a revelation of Christ's work through humanity for the stage.

Yet, it was only after considerable persuasion that Messiaen agreed to write an opera. Unsurprisingly perhaps, he chose St. Francis of Assisi as the subject, because "of all the saints, he most resembles Christ, by his poverty, his chastity, his humility, and, bodily, by the stigmata that he received on his feet, his hands, and side."[10] Messiaen wrote his own libretto, taken from a variety of sources, and worked consistently on the work for eight years (1975-83).[11] *St. François d'Assise* is over four hours long, it contains three acts divided into eight tableaux (3, 3, 2), and it is a summa of his technical and aesthetic preoccupations.[12] There are seven characters in the opera: Francis, the Angel, the Leper, and four brothers (Bernard, Elias, Leo, and Masseo), as well as the invisible presence of Christ sung by the chorus.[13]

For our purposes, this study will concentrate on the way in which Messiaen modifies the shape and meaning of Francis's leitmotif — a leitmotif being a short musical motive or phrase that usually signifies a nonmusical meaning. If the central figure of Francis can be interpreted as an allegorical figure for both the striving of Messiaen himself and humanity,

9. Messiaen thought that *St. François d'Assise* would be his last work. Hill and Simeone, *Messiaen,* p. 340.

10. "Entretien avec Olivier Messiaen" (Paris, January 1992) [Conversation between Messiaen and Jean-Christophe Marti], *Opera Aujourd'hui, L'Avant Scène, Programme du Festival de Salzbourg,* 1992, p. 15. This is referred to below as *L'Avant Scène.*

11. Messiaen cites "the *Fioretti, The Considerations on the Stigmata,* the writings of St. Francis himself, and the Canticle of the Creatures [*Cantique des Créatures*]." See *St. François d'Assise: Scènes Franciscaines,* Opéra en trois actes et huit tableaux, Poème et musique par Olivier Messiaen, Programme for a performance at the Opéra Bastille in 1992, pp. 18-20 (hereafter *Programme*).

12. *Tableaux* is a reference to the paintings of Fra Angelico, Giotto, and Cimabue that inspired the costumes in the opera.

13. The chorus does not always represent Christ, but comes increasingly to do so throughout the opera. For some recent work on this opera, see the articles by Stefan Keym and Robert Fallon in *Messiaen Studies,* ed. Sholl. Keym's monograph *Farbe und Zeit: Untersuchungen zur musiktheatralen Struktur und Semantik von Olivier Messiaens St. François d'Assise* (Hildesheim: Georg Olms, 2002) provides the most detailed account of the opera to appear thus far. See also Christopher Dingle's "Frescoes and Legends: The Sources and Background of *Saint François d'Assise,*" in *Olivier Messiaen: Music, Art and Literature,* ed. Christopher Dingle and Nigel Simeone (Aldershot: Ashgate, 2007), pp. 301-22, and Sander van Maas's "Messiaen's Saintly Naïveté," in *Messiaen the Theologian,* ed. Andrew Shenton (Aldershot: Ashgate, 2010), pp. 41-59.

then Francis's interior progression of grace toward God, charted through the harmonic, melodic, and timbral changes of his leitmotif, can be understood as a prism through which we can view the journey toward Messiaen's allegorical redemption of secular modernity and humanity through his opera.[14] An apposite embodiment of Messiaen's religious modernism, the aphoristic and enigmatic qualities of Francis's leitmotif belie its narrative depth and purpose. Francis's life is given a dramatic dynamic through this musical symbol as the audience witnesses Francis's cathartic realization of Christ's presence through the meeting with the Leper, the bodily confirmation of this in Francis's reception of the stigmata, and finally his death and redemption.

To create such a parable serves to reveal how humanity can encounter Christ, and through his transfigurative presence within, begin to conform to his likeness, in "imitation" of him.[15] Yet, almost despite the theologically rich text, this metamorphosis is dramatized through the absolute (wordless) music of the leitmotif. Moses' lament, "O word that I lack" at the end of Arnold Schoenberg's opera *Moses und Aron* (1930-32), is answered in the imaginative capacity of Messiaen's audience to perceive the meaning and depth-structure of a seemingly meaningless musical sign (the instrumental leitmotif), to perceive Messiaen's modernist musical language as religious, and to imagine that Francis's spiritual and eschatological progress transcends rather than mimics the progressive telos of modernity. As an instrument of God's loving grace and as a visible sign of an invisible reality, Francis's sacramental status seems to entice our participation in his drama, as we view Francis's movement from the ideological chrysalis of theology (understood

14. Leitmotifs are discrete iconic segments of musical material that are individuated by certain motivic, harmonic, melodic, or timbral characteristics. Through time they are able to change and thus narrate an element of the action. But, in order to do this successfully, they must retain certain features so that they are identifiable with their original character or idea.

15. The dramatic possibilities of confronting the audience with unusual and discomforting images, issues, and aspects of the human condition is of course fundamental to opera and very old. In the twentieth century, the operas of Alban Berg, Luigi Dallapiccola, Benjamin Britten, John Adams (among others) have explored this dramatic possibility.

St. Thomas à Kempis's *The Imitation of Christ* (one of Messiaen's favorite theological books), with its persistent topos of overcoming the self, is an important source for Messiaen's opera. By using the chorus to speak Christ's words, Messiaen neutralizes his physical presence and promotes his mythic, atemporal presence. The audience is given the sense of Christ (chorus) speaking to (and through) Francis's soul. Through his tangible presence, therefore, a desire for Christ is intimated. By becoming a physical symbol of Christ's grace, conforming to the imitation of Christ, Francis therefore begins to fulfill this desire.

merely as a formal knowledge of God), through a transformative encounter with God, to being with his God in heaven.[16]

Messiaen's Musical Aesthetics

It may seem, even for the casual listener, that the interface between the Christian faith and music in Messiaen's work is somewhat complex. They would not be wrong. The question of where one cuts this critical cake is crucial. For some, Messiaen's music may seem to subsume theology in its musical discourse, while for others, the overwhelming emotional quality and, indeed, the modernism of his music, for instance, in his *Turangalîla-Symphonie* (1946-48) or in parts of his opera, seem almost to marginalize the theological underpinning of his music.[17]

For scholars of his music, it may seem, for instance, that Messiaen's inculcation of theology into his music, especially through his own voluminous writings, is calculated somewhat to act as a counterbalance to the overwhelming effect of his music. But theology is surely more than just Messiaen's muse, and, at least because of the importance Messiaen attaches to it in his aesthetics, it cannot be lightly set aside.

As an active ingredient, as much as a discrete presence, theology seems to underpin the interaction between the circle of related concepts that inform Messiaen's modern music. For instance, the symbiosis of time (rhythm) and color (harmony) in his musical aesthetics, which sought to create a bridge between perception and intuition, between knowledge and faith, and between mortality and eternity, has at its root the presence and action of God.[18]

Nevertheless, when we come to examine specific features of Messiaen's

16. Brian Davies, *The Thought of St. Thomas Aquinas* (Oxford: Clarendon Press, 1992), p. 359, quoting Aquinas's *Summa Theologicae* 3a. 61.1: "Through the sacraments, therefore, sensible things are used to instruct people in a manner appropriate to their nature." Also p. 358, quoting Aquinas 3a.61.3: The sacraments "constitute certain visible signs of invisible things by which people are sanctified."

17. The so-called "Tristan trilogy," which comprises the song cycle *Harawi* (1945), the orchestral *Turangalîla-Symphonie,* and the *Cinq Rechants* (1948) for a cappella choir, are all works that subsume Christian symbolism in seemingly secular works. For more on this, see my "Love, Mad Love, and the *Point Sublime.*"

18. I am thinking here in particular of the *Strophe* I and II in *Chronochromie* (1959-60), where a quasi-serial ordering of durations is colored by the juxtaposition of different types of chords, and birdsong. For some recent research on this, see Amy Bauer's "The Impossible Charm of Messiaen's *Chronochromie,*" in *Messiaen Studies,* ed. Sholl, pp. 145-67.

music, the degree to which Messiaen's own writings have configured the meaning of his music must be carefully investigated: there is often a subtle difference between what he says and what he does. For example, when Messiaen adopted the conception of the separation of time and eternity from St. Thomas Aquinas — time is a property of creation, and eternity is a property of God — and connected God's immutability to his music through the idea of "staticism," such an idealized (and ideological) interpretation is brought into tension with the different temporal colorist paradigms in the music itself.[19] The relationship between musical staticism and God is therefore not really the *fait accompli* that Messiaen had in mind.[20] Upon investigating this further, the relationship between Messiaen's music and traditional (German) ideals of musical structure become a little clearer, while also revealing something of Messiaen's originality.

Staticism was tendentiously ascribed by Messiaen, at a fundamental level in his music, for instance, to a juxtaposition and recontextualization of small cells of musical material that he termed *personnages rythmiques*. Messiaen thus sought to differentiate the aesthetic and construction of his music from traditional musical development, in which formative ideas or motives undergo a gradual (or organic) process of change through the course of a work mediated by tonality and through patterns of tension and resolution. In Messiaen's music, by contrast, the dynamic and progressive role of tonality, as an overarching directional force, is minimized.

But the synergy between his music and traditional thinking is somewhat intricate. While tonality itself may be absent in most of his music, tonal centers may still have an (albeit weakened) localized polarizing force, and his complex harmonies may even imply different harmonic roots. Therefore, we can see that Messiaen created his own kinds of developmental discourse. Indeed, even if, as Messiaen (and many scholars) would have us believe, his "static" (or ecstatic) music were radically different from much traditional Western music, a closer inspection reveals that both ideals of musical development entail common features: the retention of certain characteristics or motives which undergo the essential processes of compositional manipula-

19. See Messiaen's *TRCO*, Tome I (Paris: Leduc, 1994), p. 7. Messiaen adapts St. Thomas Aquinas's *Summa Theologicae*, "The Eternity of God," 1a. q.10. art. 4.

20. Messiaen states: "I'll take this opportunity to plead my own case: Japanese music is static, and I myself am a static composer because I believe in the invisible and in the beyond; I believe in eternity. Now, Orientals are on much closer terms with the beyond than we are, and that's why their music is static. The music written by me, a believer, is equally static." Claude Samuel, *Musique et Couleur: Nouveaux Entretiens avec Olivier Messiaen* (Paris: Pierre Belfond, 1986); English translation by E. Thomas Glasow (Portland, OR: Amadeus Press, 1994), pp. 103-4.

tion (embellishment, augmentation/diminution, inversion, addition and subtraction of material, timbral and registral recontextualization).[21]

Certainly, in Messiaen's case, his use of different forms of development (sometimes barely perceptible) is musically and aesthetically designed to minimize the traditional linear and teleological ideal of development, so that while change occurs, it seems that it is not subject to the "progress" associated with secular music and modernity.[22] Nevertheless, the processes in Messiaen's music in many respects resemble traditional Western music.

In Messiaen's opera, for instance, his leitmotifs function like musical cells *(personnages rythmiques)* that enact a quasi-developmental narrative function. Indeed, it is because some identifiable elements remain and some are changed, that his leitmotifs can be understood as a metaphor for the instrumental action of God's changelessness in the midst of time: they change but essentially remain the same.

The way in which these musical motives change also implies the progression of human time, and this is why Messiaen adopts Henri Bergson's (1859-1941) thought to explain the interior interaction between time, man, and God. For Messiaen, the relative changelessness and non-development of his musical *personnages,* or leitmotifs in the opera, attempts to disrupt diachronic time, and confuse the mind, forcing it to break out of progressive time and inward toward an appreciation of a personal and intimate sense of time that Bergson calls *la durée.*

For an ardent Catholic like Messiaen, the implied rejection of rationality and materialism in favor of subjective intuition [*l'intuition sensible*] enabled him to connect his modern and original language with divine revelation.[23] Francis's journey to redemption through a language saturated with the aesthetic ramifications of modernity, therefore, becomes a progressive appercep-

21. Messiaen's *personnages* can be understood as a creative engagement with the German tradition of development, Berlioz's *idée fixe,* Wagnerian leitmotifs, and Stravinskyian cell manipulation. While Messiaen's *personnages* use repetition, variation, and juxtaposition, their differentiation from Beethovenian development is located in the extent to which motive forms reconfigure or even break with preceding motive forms, and whether there is an identifiable *Urform* or *Grundgestalt* of the motive to break from in the first place. St. Francis's leitmotif (ex. 2) does function as an *Urform,* so Messiaen's subsequent development of this through his leitmotifs approaches the idea of traditional musical development.

22. Olivier Messiaen, "Introduction to the Programme Booklet for Paris, 1978," in Almut Rössler, *Contributions to the Spiritual World of Olivier Messiaen* (Duisburg: Gilles und Francke, 1986), p. 10.

23. Messiaen writes about Bergson's *durée* in *TRCO,* Tome 1, pp. 9-12. See also Calinescu, *Five Faces of Modernity,* p. 5.

tion of this *durée* as Christ's presence in us. Time, rather than eternity, is therefore paramount in Messiaen's aesthetics, as it acts as the instrument of God's love, ineluctably drawing humanity both to imitate and to be with God.[24]

The subjective intuition of God's presence and love was, for Messiaen, manifested through his synaesthesia described in 1978 in words that prefigure the end of his opera:

> When I hear music, when I read music, I see colours, which are marvellous and impossible to describe because they are moving like the sounds themselves, and as the durations are in movement, these are the things that move and which interpenetrate. One is not able to write them down, but one is dazzled [*ébloui*]. And it is this dazzling which brings us closer to a leap beyond time, to a leaving of oneself that will be eternity.[25]

For Messiaen the effect of these colors in his music was analogous to that of the fractured light passing through stained-glass windows. But, given that Messiaen could not write down these colors that he saw, is it possible to understand Messiaen's music as a subjective vision that presupposes, but attempts to overcome, the alienation of humanity from God? For what Messiaen's colorist metaphors (rainbows, stained-glass windows, and the jewels of the New Jerusalem in the Apocalypse) imply is that humanity is placed, somewhat traditionally, below God searching for redemption through the diffuse radiance of music. It is almost as though Messiaen is exhorting humanity not just to bathe in his prismatic fireworks, but to realize a fundamental (and possibly unexpressed) desire to go back through the stained-glass window, and join the reconstituted white light of God.

What this process seems to suggest is that, through music, God is striving to connect to the center of the person. Put another way, this process seems to indicate that for Messiaen, music can be a way in which humanity is empowered to re-connect with God, and, perhaps, a means by which God is able to

24. For Messiaen this process of drawing humanity in was informed by his ideal of predestination. For Messiaen, predestination was based on his belief that his mother Cécile Sauvage's (1883-1927) poetry, written about a musician while Messiaen was still in her womb, formed and literally predestined his future as a musician. Messiaen combines this with the New Testament ideal that predestination is God's loving purpose to make people his sons and daughters. Therefore, for Messiaen, it comes to signify the ways in which, through the loving grace of God, we are brought to God by conforming to the perfect imitation of Christ. This is the path that is taken by St. Francis in Messiaen's opera.

25. Raymond Lyon, "Entretien avec Olivier Messiaen," *Le Courrier Musicale de France* 64 (1978): 132.

draw us into the dynamic of his redemptive and transforming grace. Both parties, God and man, however, fear that their efforts may be falling on deaf ears, drowned out by the clangor of modernity. A composer such as Messiaen then, even though he may feel inadequate, sits in the seat of the telephone operator, trying to improve the crackling line of his theological music.

As a musical-theological concept, Messiaen used the communication network of color in his music to attempt to displace the traditional paradigm of consonance and dissonance, and, more particularly, to usurp the negative aesthetic resonances of "dissonance" in modernist music. It is therefore not without a sense of irony that Messiaen's most dissonant and colorful music was that which employs birdsong (for him the voice of God in nature), which dominated his music from the early 1950s.[26] That Messiaen could create some of the most modernist, complex, and dissonant music of the twentieth century through birdsong is testament to his attempted reorientation of the aesthetics of modern music.

Color in Messiaen's harmony can be seen very clearly in the effect of the infusion of consonance (engendered by triads) and dissonance (non-triadic notes). Messiaen creates chords from hierarchically organized scales that he calls "modes of limited transposition," collections of pitches that can only be transposed a limited number of times before the original pitches return. Each mode used by Messiaen has a different type of harmonization, and this uniqueness makes his music instantly recognizable.[27] Messiaen's harmonization of mode 3/transposition 1 appears in Example 1 on page 172 (mode 3^1 in bold).

The infusion of triads with added notes and dissonances (a differentiation made by their degree of consonance) that are inside Messiaen's complex chord imparts color.[28] Messiaen manipulates this ideal of color, like the light that emanates from a stained-glass window, in the transformed appearances of St. Francis's leitmotif to chart his spiritual progress. For Messiaen, this color or light, as an image of God's glory in the musical sublime, reaches

26. Messiaen transcribed birdsong initially from recordings, and then increasingly "live" through his travels, from all over the world.

27. These harmonizations in turn differentiate Messiaen's music from that of other composers — in the case of what Messiaen calls mode 2, or the octatonic scale (a scale of alternating semitones and tones), from Stravinsky, Scriabin, Debussy, Ravel, Tournemire, Berg, and Webern, to name only a few composers.

28. Each voice in Messiaen's harmonization (top two staves) progressively articulates mode 3^1. It is, of course, not just triads (enharmonically respelled in ex. 1) that create Messiaen's harmony, but also the spacing and voice-leading of his chords. I am merely using this as a model for understanding his harmonic language.

Example 1. Messiaen's harmonization of Mode 3[1] (top two staves) with extrapolated triads

into Francis and breaks down his resistance to God's grace.[29] Thus, Messiaen's modernist, dissonant, and colorful music becomes the agent of Francis's redemption.

The metaphor that Messiaen often used in connection with the realization of God's grace and truth is that of the abyss [*l'abîme*], a concept he borrowed from the Bible and the nineteenth-century theologian and writer Ernest Hello (1828-1885).[30] This abyss of the modern soul of humanity is sunk in misery, and covered over by the deep waters of consciousness that awaits the call of God. If for both Hello and Messiaen, the *promesse de bonheur* of the Enlightenment had failed, then, rising from the ashes, the task of a theological music was to impart a veritable *éclairage de l'âme* (a cathartic awakening of the soul) to humanity. The shock of his modern music therefore

29. Messiaen likens his harmonies to the effect of stained glass in which the individual cannot easily identify the figures in the glass. Confused and dazzled by the kaleidoscopic movement of color, the individual is forced to move inward toward the dimension of *durée* and God.

30. See Hab. 3:10, Rev. 9:1-12, and Ernest Hello, *Paroles de Dieu: Réflexions sur quelques textes sacrés*, texte présenté par François Angélier (1875; Grenoble: Jérôme Millon, 1992), pp. 131-32. For more on the abyss, see Siglind Bruhn's "Religious Symbolism in the Music of Olivier Messiaen," in *Signs in Musical Hermeneutics* ed. Siglind Bruhn, *The American Journal of Semiotics,* special issue 13/1-4 (1998): 269-302.

could function like an aesthetic aversion therapy, and force humanity from the abyss of modernity toward a potential encounter with God.[31]

Thomas Merton (1915-68), one of the theologians that most inspired Messiaen, indicated that "From the abyss there comes, unaccountably, the mysterious gift of the Spirit sent by God to make all things new, to transform the created and redeemed world, and to re-establish all things in Christ."[32] Messiaen's opera looks forward to this moment by attempting to overcome the temporal, fallible, and human dimensions of music and modernity. This "holy departure" from the "deepest space *in* us" so that "the innermost point in us stands outside" outlines the transformation of subjectivity that defines the narrative and the meaning of Messiaen's opera.[33]

St. Francis and Theological Music

In this manifesto from 1978, Messiaen summarizes the connections between time and color that animate his model of modernity:

> Scientific research, mathematical proof, amassed biological experiments have not saved us from uncertainty. Quite the contrary, they have increased our ignorance by constantly revealing new realities within what was believed to be reality. In fact, the one sole reality is of a different order: it is to be found in the realm of Faith. Only by encountering another Being can we understand it.
>
> But to do that we have to pass through death and resurrection, and that implies the leap out of temporal things. Strangely enough, music can prepare us for it, as a picture, as a reflection, as a symbol. In fact, music is a perpetual dialogue between space and time, between sound and colour, a dialogue which leads into a unification: Time is a space, sound is a colour, space is a complex of superimposed times, sound-complexes exist at the same time as complexes of colours. The musician who thinks, sees, hears, speaks, is able, by means of these fundamental ideas, to come closer to the

31. Messiaen, *Quatuor pour la fin du Temps, Note de l'Auteur*, I. "The abyss, it is time, with its sadness, its lassitude. The birds, it is the opposite of time; it is our desire for light, the stars, rainbows and jubilant vocalises."

32. Thomas Merton, *Contemplative Prayer* (London: Darton, Longman and Todd, 1973), p. 28.

33. "An die Musik," from *Uncollected Poems* (1913-18), *The Selected Poetry of Rainer Maria Rilke* (1875-1926), ed. and trans. Stephen Mitchell (London: Picador, 1987), p. 147. Rilke is frequently quoted in Messiaen's *TRCO*.

next world to a certain extent. And, as St. Thomas Aquinas says: music brings us to God through "default of truth," until the day when He Himself will dazzle us with "an excess of truth." That is perhaps the significant meaning — and also the directional meaning — of music. . . .[34]

Is this then one of the rare and precious moments of documentation in which a composer provides evidence for his artistic vocation? Messiaen seems to imply that the ability to perceive the interlaced paradigms of each musical moment will provide humanity with the means to rise upwards through the stained-glass window.[35] It seems then that, in raising old Orphic questions about the power of music and the ontological status of humanity, Messiaen clearly equates our mortal state to a prison from which music, through its power to reorientate these elements, can release us, and give us a vision and even a certain experience of the "next world." If his "fugitive" theology can be identified with fallen humanity and with modernity, then surely the task of transforming humanity has to be achieved through a transformation of modernity and music. Alienation must be reconfigured in a new subjectivity based on faith, and this faith must reorientate "progress" toward a fresh realization of "divine and supernatural mysteries."[36]

However, this dynamic process is not, as Messiaen seems to posit, about timelessness or totally escaping time. Rather, the processes in his music, as distinct from the ways in which his own discourse seeks to configure them, seem to imply new and interesting ways to appreciate and live within this parameter, while also attempting to encapsulate a process of transformation

34. Olivier Messiaen, "Introduction to the Programme Booklet for Paris, 1978," in Rössler's *Contributions to the Spiritual World of Olivier Messiaen*, p. 10. This is Messiaen's adaptation of Aquinas, possibly from two sources. The first is from the *Commentary on the Sentences* (Super Sent., q. 1 a. 5 ad. 3): "To the third objection, I say that the poetic science concerns things that cannot be grasped by reason because of a shortage of truth; hence the reason must be seduced by certain likenesses; theology, however, is about things that are above our reason; and so the symbolic mode is common to both, since neither is proportioned to our reason" (http://www.vaxxine.com/hyoomik/aquinas/sent1.html). The second quotation is from the *Summa Theologiae* (I-II, q. 101, a. 2 ad. 2): "Just as human reason fails to grasp poetical expressions on account of their being lacking in truth, so does it fail to grasp Divine things perfectly, on account of the sublimity of the truth they contain: and therefore in both cases *there is need of signs by means of sensible figures*" (my italics). (http://www.newadvent.org/summa/210102.htm, accessed October 15, 2007). My thanks to Michael O'Connor for these references.

35. Messiaen's language in this statement is reminiscent of his former student Karlheinz Stockhausen (1928-). See Stockhausen's "Momentform" (1960), in *Texte zur Musik*, vol. 1 (Köln: DuMont, 1963), pp. 198-99.

36. Messiaen, "Résponses à une enquête," p. 73.

and looking forward to the moment (in Revelation) when the world, and presumably time, will be re-enchanted.[37]

Such a process is implied through St. Francis's leitmotif, where music becomes an heuristic tool, or what Aquinas might call a sensible poetic sign, that can conduct humanity to its own redemption.[38] For Aquinas, both poetry and theology use signs and figures, because both are disproportionate to the truth under consideration, poetry by defect, theology by excess. But Messiaen, in his manifesto quoted above, does not mention poetry or theology: his particular interest is in music, which can subsume and irradiate both poetry and theology, and in so doing reach toward God.

Francis's progression toward his own redemption dramatizes this telos. He becomes, following St. Augustine's thought, a sacred sign (a sign of Christ) who has the "character of divine revelation," and who allows the audience to participate vicariously in a threefold purpose.[39] Francis's life is "at once commemorative of that which has gone before, namely the Passion of Christ, and demonstrative of that which is brought about in us through the Passion of Christ, and prognostic, i.e. a foretelling of future glory."[40] In the opera, these moments correspond, respectively, to Francis's healing of the Leper, his reception of the stigmata, and his redemption.

As I have already indicated, Messiaen uses leitmotifs as his musical signs to narrate Francis's journey of grace. There are leitmotifs for characters (St. Francis, the Leper, and the Angel) and for ideas (*thème de la Joie, thème de la vérité*), but St. Francis's theme dominates and animates the drama through its interaction with the other characters. His leitmotif has three principal attributes: it is arpeggaic, self-reflexive (it turns back on itself), and principally associated with the strings. In its cross-like shape (reminiscent of baroque *Affektenlehre*), Messiaen indicates Francis's true nature, his effect on others, and his eventual destination (see Example 2 on p. 176).[41]

Francis's theme dominates the first tableau, *La Croix*, which is organized as a series of strophes that formally chart the expansion of Francis's self-awareness and his own interior progression to *la joie parfaite*. Messiaen inti-

---

37. See Rev. 10:5-7. I am grateful to Jeremy Begbie for pointing this out to me.

38. See Aquinas, *Summa Theologiae* (I-II, q. 101, a. 2 ad. 2), cited above.

39. Davies, *Thought of St. Thomas Aquinas*, p. 347.

40. Davies, *Thought of St. Thomas Aquinas*, pp. 354-55, quoting Aquinas's *Summa Theologicae* 3a. 60. 3.

41. *Affektenlehre* was a systematic method of using rhetorical expression through musical figures to direct the emotions (affects) of the listener. It is most associated with baroque music such as Bach's *St. Matthew Passion*.

Example 2. St. Francis's leitmotif, Tableau 1 — fourteen bars after fig. 8.
Reproduced by permission of Editions Alphonse Leduc, Paris/United Music Publishers Ltd.

mates through Francis that humanity must begin to follow and imitate Christ, and become transfigured in his image through suffering.

Tableau 2 foreshadows the appearance of the Leper in the third tableau. In depicting Francis's prayer that he may not only meet a leper but also be able to love him, Messiaen blends his theme and the Leper's (at fig. 77), and thereby links Francis's destiny to that of the Leper.[42] Messiaen signals, therefore, that Francis (and humanity) is in his own abyss from which he can only be redeemed by God, symbolized in the ubiquitous birdsong.

The first two tableaux reveal Francis's gradual recognition of the presence of Christ. Now comes the moment of catharsis. Even before Francis appears in Tableau 3, Messiaen intimates that Francis will be the agent of the Leper's transformation.[43] Like Kundry in Wagner's *Parsifal,* who laughed at Christ on the cross, the Leper scoffs at the brotherhood's piousness by using Francis's theme in this dissonant harmonization (see Example 3 on p. 177).[44]

Yet, Francis on his own lacks the power to transform the Leper. He has only a "knowledge" of the interior power of transformation.[45] According to

42. Francis's final words, asking that he be capable of loving the Leper, are set in C major (orchestrated with the tender sound of three Ondes Martenots and solo strings), the key that will ultimately represent the redemption of Francis and the glory of Christ.

43. Tableau 3 begins with a distorted version of Francis's theme which is followed at fig. 4 by extremely dense polytonal chords containing triads (including that of A flat, used in Tableau 1 at one bar before fig. 61 to signify Christ/God [*Lui*], and C major) that, through their color, tell of the presence of Christ, and his movement in the souls of the main characters.

44. In his appearance, behavior, and improprietous dialogue, Messiaen's Leper contains within his physiognomy the medieval suspicion that diseases of the body proceed from possession by demons (this image perhaps derives from Luke 8:27-39). Another source for Tableau 3 is the story of Christ's healing of ten lepers in Luke 17:11-19.

45. Francis's pious reminder to the Leper, "If the interior man is beautiful, he shall ap-

Example 3. Tableau 3 — four bars after fig. 15.
Reproduced by permission of Editions Alphonse Leduc, Paris/United Music Publishers Ltd.

Aquinas, sacraments derive their power from Christ. Through dissonant clusters (at figs. 42, 51, 53, 55, and 57), Messiaen intimates a dialectic between Christ's struggle to overcome the fears of Francis and the Leper, and their alienation from themselves (a symptom of modernity signified in the negative aesthetic resonances of the dissonance). The incorporeal is then made tangible in the presence of the Angel, who will act as the mediator of Francis's becoming and the healing of the Leper.

Like St. Thomas, who needs to touch Christ's wounds to believe, the Leper's internal wounds need to be soothed by the Angel. This character (sung by the only female voice) appears at a window and is only visible, we are told, to the audience. She speaks to Francis and the Leper in radiant A-major mode-3 string and Ondes Martenot halos: "Leper, leper, your heart accuses you, your heart accuses you, but God, but God, but God is greater, much greater than your heart." The Leper, alienated from himself and God, cannot understand this, enabling Francis to act as God's mediator:

> **Leper:** What did he say? I don't understand.
>
> **Francis:** He said: your heart accuses you, but God is greater than your heart.
>
> **Angel:** But God, but God, but God is all Love, and he who remains in love remains in God, and God in him![46]

---

pear glorious at the moment of the resurrection," reveals that his knowledge is still only intellectual. *Programme*, p. 89.

46. *Programme*, p. 90.

The Angel's words echo 1 John 4:16 ("God is love, and those who abide in love abide in God, and God abides in them"), and intimate Francis's sacramental essence; Francis is the medium through which God's love reaches the Leper. The Leper immediately asks for forgiveness and recognizes his mortal penury. His words: "Your Brothers call me: The Leper!" at fig. 75 are placed over dissonant choral chord clusters that again indicate the transformative power of Christ within his soul. This change has a profound effect on Francis, something we know from this strange and tortured harmonization of Francis's theme at fig. 76 that prefigures Francis's response: "Where sadness is found, there I sing of joy!"[47]

Example 4. Tableau 3 — fig. 76.
Reproduced by permission of Editions Alphonse Leduc, Paris/United Music Publishers Ltd.

Repentance and recognition of sin precede a cathartic transformation. The Leper calls Francis his friend and brother, once again to the dissonant music of Christ, and Francis's theme at fig. 84 (transposed from Example 4) is then continued upward to reveal his true trajectory (see Example 5 on p. 179).

Francis in return asks the Leper to forgive him.[48] At the moment when Francis embraces the Leper, the muted strings and Ondes Martenots play a set of chords in C major (the key of the Glory of the Resurrection at the end of the opera). The Leper is healed (complètement transformé) and his theme begins to take on the shape of the rising part of St. Francis's theme, now proximate to the Angel's key of A major-mode 3 (see Example 6 on p. 179).

For Messiaen, the abyss of the Leper's soul has raised its hands and

47. These chords are derived from another type of chord that Messiaen uses: "chords of transposed inversions on the same bass note." See *TRCO*, Tome VII, pp. 141-47. Messiaen adds notes to these chords here, and alters them so that there is a unison between the outside parts. This emphasizes the melody of St. Francis's theme (ex. 2).

48. St. Francis: "Where darkness is found, there I bring the light! Forgive me, my son: I have not loved you enough. . . ." *Programme*, p. 91.

Example 5. Tableau 3 — fig. 84.
Reproduced by permission of Editions Alphonse Leduc, Paris/United Music Publishers Ltd.

Example 6. Leper's theme: Tableau 3 — fig. 9 and at Tableau 3 — fig. 91.
Reproduced by permission of Editions Alphonse Leduc, Paris/United Music Publishers Ltd.

sought the profundity of Christ.[49] Francis comforts him while Christ (chorus) sings: "To those who have loved greatly: all is pardoned!" (to another version of Francis's theme), finishing in C major that prefigures the redemptive forgiveness of the resurrection at the end of the opera.[50]

Here the message to troubled humanity and modernity is clear: repent, turn to Christ, and all will be healed. Hans Urs von Balthasar encapsulated the theological drama of the gaze at the heart of this transformation:[51]

> It is only thus that the presentiment of the divine shining, which plays on man's face because of his origin (Ps. 8:6) . . . the mirror of his own being in the image of God, is brought to fulfilment. But the fulfilment takes place, not in the glory of paradise, but in the crucifying encounter of the crucified Lord in the sin-distorted face of one's fellow man. And it is in terms of this encounter that we shall be judged.[52]

Messiaen uses the association of keys with characters, and dissonance in his leitmotifs to speak the unspeakable. The Leper's appearance belies his predestination to draw Francis toward God through grace. Predestination follows as the subject of the next tableau *(L'Ange Voyager)* where the Angel visits the monastery, and is turned away brusquely by Br. Masseo and then by Br. Elias.[53]

Brother Elias is a symbol of humanity caught up in its own strife. Like the Klee/Benjamin *Angelus Novus* in which the storm of progress has got caught up in the angel's wings and he is being blown inexorably back, unable to attain the desired paradise, Br. Elias is caught up in the pile of debris before the Angel.[54]

49. After the Leper's dance he becomes penitent and weeps: "I'm not worthy of being healed." He sings these words to Francis's theme (at three bars after fig. 119), confirming that Francis is the catalyst of his change.

50. *Programme*, p. 91. The use of C major to depict light has a long history, ranging from *The Creation* by Haydn (1801) to Bartók's *Duke Bluebeard's Castle* (1913).

51. Claude Samuel, *Permanences d'Olivier Messiaen: Dialogues et Commentaires* (Arles: Actes Sud, 1999), p. 18. Messiaen describes Balthasar as *"le plus grand théologian actuel."*

52. Hans Urs von Balthasar, *The Glory of the Lord: A Theological Aesthetics*, vol. 7: *Theology: The New Covenant*, trans. Brian McNeil (Edinburgh: T&T Clark, 1989), pp. 469-70.

53. That the Angel knocks too loudly for Br. Masseo is an indication that the Angel is somehow out of humanity's sphere, and yet intent upon influencing humanity. This music is used later in Tableau 7 to indicate the stigmata.

54. Walter Benjamin, "Theses on the Philosophy of History," in *Illuminations*, ed. Hannah Arendt, trans. Harry Zohn (London: Fontana, 1992), p. 249. "A Klee painting named *Angelus Novus* shows an angel looking as though he is about to move away from something he is fixedly contemplating. His eyes are staring, his mouth is open, his wings are spread. This is how one pictures the angel of history. His face is turned towards the past. Where we perceive a

But Messiaen's Angel wants to calm Br. Elias's inner turmoil and shut off this storm from paradise.[55]

The Angel knocks again and asks Br. Bernard about predestination.[56] Bernard sings: "I have often thought, after my death, that our Saviour Jesus Christ will look at me as he regards the tributary money and say: 'Of whom is this image and this inscription?' "[57] Br. Bernard's vocal line is reminiscent of Francis's theme, revealing both Bernard's holiness, and that Francis has God's sacramental imprimatur. Through this moment, Messiaen reminds us that humanity must not only be watchful for the coming of Christ, but that it must seek for an encounter with Christ and to live in his image.

The fifth tableau *(L'Ange Musicien)* opens with Francis in his grotto praying the *Benedicite* (as in Tableau 2). But the pious monk of earlier days has undergone a transformation that is revealed in the complex harmonization of his leitmotif at fig. 14: Francis has begun "to reclothe the new man," and find his true visage in the "imitation of Christ." With this change, Francis is able now to recognize the Angel through the agency of birdsong.[58] Choral "chords of the total chromatic" alternating with mode 3 (at figs. 64 and 66) reveal the power of Christ, given to the Angel, to overcome Francis's alienation and humanity.[59] Paraphrasing Aquinas, the Angel speaks to Francis of the transfiguring power of music:

---

chain of events, he sees one single catastrophe which keeps piling wreckage upon wreckage and hurls it in front of his feet. The angel would like to stay, awaken the dead, and make whole what has been smashed. But a storm is blowing from Paradise; it has got caught in his wings with such violence that the angel can no longer close them. This storm irresistibly propels him into the future to which his back is turned, while the pile of debris before him grows skyward. This storm is what we call progress." Benjamin's fears about modernity echo Baudelaire, who warns of the dangers of progress. See Charles Baudelaire, "The Universal Exhibition of 1855: The Fine Arts," in *Baudelaire: Selected Writings on Art and Literature,* trans. with an introduction by P. E. Charvet (London: Penguin Classics, 1992), p. 121.

55. The Angel asks, "What do you think of predestination? Have you rejected the old man to reclothe the new man, and find your true visage . . . ?" *Programme,* p. 94.

56. Rev. 3:20 is perhaps in the background of this moment in the opera: "Listen! I am standing at the door, knocking; if you hear my voice and open the door, I will come in to you and eat with you, and you with me."

57. *Programme,* p. 95.

58. Figs. 61-63 inclusive: "My friend Gheppio calls me anew . . . he announces something to me . . . perhaps my prayer has been heard?"

59. "Chords of the total chromatic" are specific chordal arrangements of all twelve tones. Messiaen spaces these chords so that they have a great number of triads in them. They therefore sound radiant, rather than anodyne and colorless. For full tables of these chords together with their corresponding colors, see *TRCO,* Tome VII, pp. 187-90.

God dazzles us by an excess of truth. Music carries us to God by default of truth. You speak to God in music: He shall reply to you in music. Know the joy of happiness by the sweetness of colour and melody. And let it open for you the secrets, the secrets of Glory! Hear this music that suspends life from the ladders of heaven. Hear the music of the invisible. . . .[60]

These words confirm Francis's sacramental status. As if to highlight Francis's transformation, the Angel's viol is depicted in the irreal tones of the Ondes Martenot over shimmering strings at fig. 86, and then with Christ (at fig. 87) in C major, the key of glory and resurrection. As a radiant transformation of the Leper's and Francis's theme, Messiaen makes the invisible presence of Christ visible in Francis's dreams:

Example 7. Angel's solo viol Tableau 5 — fig. 87.
Reproduced by permission of Editions Alphonse Leduc, Paris/United Music Publishers Ltd.

Messiaen then reveals Francis's oneiric transformation in the most radiantly beautiful harmonization of his theme thus far; its increasing brightness intimates Francis's emerging synergy with Christ in the C major of redemption (see Example 8 on p. 183). Francis remains on earth and "dwells in Christ only because Christ and God dwell in him and remain in him, the formulae of indwelling [having] become reciprocal."[61] The conduit between Francis and God is then firmly established in the birdsong which dominates the sixth tableau *(Le Prêche aux Oiseaux)*.[62] Messiaen's birds sing

60. *Programme,* p. 97. Note the move from mode 3 to chords of the total chromatic to underline the word *"mélodie,"* and at *"invisible."*
61. Balthasar, *The Glory of the Lord,* 7:308-9.
62. Francis addresses the birds and in so doing becomes synonymous with Messiaen and his *mission universelle* to mankind: "In all times and places, praise your creator." God has given birds the gift of agility, so that they become images of resurrected bodies and light "waiting for the day. . . . The day when Christ will unite all creatures." *Programme,* p. 100.

Example 8. Tableau 5 — fig. 90.
Reproduced by permission of Editions Alphonse Leduc, Paris/United Music Publishers Ltd.

"*si merveilleusement,* speaking without words, like the locution of angels, only by music."[63] Their invisible absolute music becomes a utopian vision flying from the orchestral pit in groups of four: "the four directions of the cross."[64]

That Francis is now synonymous with the Angel is underlined in the A major quality (especially prominent at fig. 120) of the "*Grand concert d'oiseaux*" (figs. 118-24).[65] This key is directly connected, on the words *par surcroît* (in excess) at five bars before fig. 137, to chords of E flat major (associated with the Angel's *Thème de la Vérité*) and C major (Resurrection). This chord of C major is augmented by a quiet halo of all the remaining pitches

---

Agility is one of the properties ascribed to the resurrected bodies by St. Bonaventure. Messiaen's birds are given agility through his *Hors Tempo* technique in which instruments enter and leave in a controlled *ad libitum* (under the direction of the conductor who merely signals each instrumentalist to commence playing).

63. *Programme,* p. 100.

64. *Programme,* p. 101. St. Francis sings: "Towards the Orient, the Occident, the Midi and the Aquilon: the four directions of the cross! . . ."

65. Francis's words "*par la seule musique*" are sung to notes of his theme, thus making him synonymous with the birds' "invisible music" that follows at fig. 106. Francis's words before the "*Grand concert d'oiseaux*" are set to music that pre-empts his final words: "Deliver me, enrapture me, dazzle me for ever by your excess of truth. . . ."

to embrace the twelve-note chromatic: a dissonant but ecstatic musical pre-monition of completeness and redemption that both embodies and yet also attempts to placate the associations of traditional modernism.

The giant black cross behind the stage in Tableau 1 has burned its way into Francis's consciousness and become the musical and metaphysical cross of the birds. In the seventh tableau the cross marks Francis with the five wounds of Christ's stigmata that enable him to become sacramental "like a second host."[66] At this moment the chorus confirms the trans-figurative power of music in ecstatic chorale-like textures. The swirling en-tropy of strings, percussion, and Ondes Martenots, juxtaposed with the choir, dramatize the innermost turmoil of Francis's soul and propel him onward to receive the stigmata (fig. 54) to chords reminiscent of the Angel's knocking in Tableau 4. As the fifth ray of light strikes Francis's side, the cho-rus's stabbing vowels register aphasically the horror of Christ's spear wound. The immense black cross becomes gold and sparkling, making the audience witness the means of Francis's and their own redemption. Like one abyss calling to another, the chorus implores "François!" in E major (1st inversion) at fig. 56, a chord increasingly used by Christ to prefigure Fran-cis's death.[67]

In the course of the seventh, and the eighth and final tableau (la Mort et la Nouvelle Vie), the chorus becomes more and more pronounced, as the drama moves from the spiritual darkness of night toward the resurrection. Francis the redeemer is himself redeemed after he sees the Leper in heaven with the Angel,[68] who reveals this to Francis and sings: "Both of us will en-

66. Francis asks for two things in prayer: "that I may feel in my body that pain you en-dured at the moment of your cruel passion. The second, that I may feel in my heart the love with which you were fired, the love that allowed you to accept such a passion for us sin-ners." Francis's impending joy in God is marked by an extended ascending version of his theme that reflects his own inner radiance at fig. 17. The chorus (Christ) then sings of the transforming power of the transubstantiated host: "If you truly wish to love me, you must suffer in your body the five wounds of my body on the Cross, accepting your sacrifice and always surpassing yourself, like a higher music, becoming yourself a second host. . . ." Programme, p. 102.

67. The repetition of this call at fig. 58 is preceded at fig. 57 by one of the least musically characteristic passages in Messiaen's music. Francis sings: "My Saviour and my God," to music that fuses the E major of Christ at fig. 56 (and of Francis's death) with C major (Resurrection).

68. The allusion to the end of Wagner's Parsifal is tangible: "Redemption to the re-deemer!" (Erlösung dem Erlöser!). Messiaen tells us that the Leper and the Angel are only vis-ible to St. Francis. The fact that we do not see Francis resurrected implies that the audience is still in a temporal dimension awaiting this state.

circle you for your entry into Paradise, in light and brilliance [*clarté*] and glory! Today, in a few moments, you will hear the music of the invisible . . . and you will hear it forever. . . ." In these words, the final possibility of human transfiguration and destiny is glimpsed. Through dissonant chord clusters, colored by bells and gongs and higher resonances, the chorus (Christ) carries the listener to Francis's final words (paraphrasing Aquinas): "Saviour, Saviour, music and poetry have brought me towards you, by image, by symbol, and by default of truth. . . . Deliver me, intoxicate me, dazzle me with your excess of Truth . . . *(he dies).*"[69]

Francis's music vacillates between A major and C major before his final E dominant-seventh chord that seems to signify only a liminal hiatus before the music of his redemption, in which the chorus finally tells of the light of the resurrected in glory and *"la Joie!"*[70] Just before this denouement, however, Francis's theme is transformed into a radiant *Alleluia!* which uses chords reminiscent of those in Examples 4 and 5, and a melodic line that takes the notes of Example 2. In both examples (2 and 9), it seems that the traditional *diabolus in musica* meaning of the tritone is turned on its head; it now becomes an icon of praise.[71]

The rising tide of modernist dissonant color is subverted by C major; Messiaen's image of Francis's redemption triumphs through the dissonance of modernity, and allows the audience to participate vicariously in Christ's glory and the serendipitous gift of grace. Modernity therefore is both the catalyst and the spark that makes the cocktail of Messiaen's theological music flammable. It is not just that conservative Catholicism is evangelized and articulated through radical means so that Messiaen's art can move beyond the strictures of ideology that divide the church. Messiaen's opera is no mere depiction of theological action. Rather Messiaen takes risks that match his

69. *Programme*, p. 105.

70. *Programme*, p. 106. Trills are used throughout the opera to represent the light of God in the resurrection. Toward the end of the work they become increasingly persistent until, at the end of the opera, they are used to decorate a C major chord (with an added 2nd and 6th), an image of the light and triumph of Christ. Even the words at the end of the opera dissolve into a sound: A(h).

71. Throughout the opera Messiaen uses the tritone as a symbol of God's presence, which is a fascinating reversal of traditional symbolism. Some examples of this in the opera are to be found in Francis's interjections at figs. 5, 15, and 23 and fig. 65 (where he sets the words "Seigneur Jésus-Christ" to a tritone) in Tableau 1. The *thème de la Vérité* used by the Angel at figs. 67 and 104 of Tableau 3 uses the tritone at the words "par Dieu." The word "résurrection" is set to the tritone in Tableau 6 at fig. 71, and likewise "vers Toi" at three bars before fig. 102 in Tableau 8.

Example 9. Tableau 8 — fig. 142.
Reproduced by permission of Editions Alphonse Leduc, Paris/United Music Publishers Ltd.

extraordinary subject. In doing so, he demonstrates that both music and theology must seek unconventional and even uncomfortable paths in seeking to expound eternal truths.

The Shock of the Positive

Messiaen's desire for "music that is like new blood, a signed gesture, an unknown perfume, an unsleeping bird" is a call to art to refresh eternal mysteries through a reconfiguration of subjectivity.[72] By making the "mythic" drama of Christ's life appreciable through the changes in the character of St. Francis, Messiaen attempts through his opera to bind divided humanity back together with God.[73] On the surface, at least, this project of uniting and even redeeming humanity is reminiscent of the aspirations of Richard Wagner in the nineteenth century. But Francis/Messiaen's attempts to become more than Wagner's revolutionary and utopian "Artist of the Future" (i.e., Wagner himself) who endeavors to restore the vanished harmony between art and society. For Messiaen this quest is but a symptom, a secular manifestation of an underlying separation that cannot be breached just through ideology (or through the im-

72. Messiaen, "Résponses à une enquête," p. 73.
73. Aquinas (3a.79.5) comments that the Eucharist nourishes spiritually "through union between Christ and His members." Francis as a sacrament therefore binds humanity to a common root in Christ.

age of redemptive human agency as in Wagner's operas), but through the miracle and serendipity of God's grace breaking through art to embrace humanity, and the God-given human capacity to receive the grace of God.

Messiaen's opera therefore exposes an underlying anxiety in modernity about what lies beneath the layers of the various traditions of humanist anthropology. The inability, or perhaps ultimately the unwillingness, to find this, together with the need to redeem or explain the past has in recent years become an inspiration for a renewed interest in "spiritual music" — music that seems to gnaw at the wound of modernity as much as it desires the spear that might close the wound and overcome human alienation from God.[74] If we can sense an epigonal search for the absolute, perhaps a testament to (millennial) angst as much as a self-conscious search for the reconfiguration of humanity, such imperatives reflect a secular theology that, though it would like to transfigure the past, may, to varying degrees, question or simply remain open to an unknown outcome. The return to grand-narrative thinking in works such as John Adams's musical "memory space" *On the Transmigration of Souls* (2002) (the terrorist attacks on America on 11 September 2001), Steve Reich's video opera *Three Tales: Hindenburg, Bikini* and *Dolly* (1997-2001) (the Hindenburg disaster, atomic tests on Bikini atoll, and the cloning of Dolly the sheep), Harrison Birtwistle's opera *The Last Supper* (1998-1999) and Karlheinz Stockhausen's seven-day music drama *Licht* (1977-2002), not to mention other dramatic and instrumental works, seems to stem from an uncertainty about the claims of (post)modernity, and, in most cases, a belief that humanity itself cannot resolve its own issues.[75]

Like the Beethoven of the "Hammerklavier" sonata Op. 106 (a work that Messiaen played to his students), Messiaen's music holds out the hope that humanity can be raised above its present condition, and yet it acknowledges that this cannot be achieved through the artifice of human creation alone. While Messiaen certainly believed that we can access, experience, and understand the realities to which theological language bears witness much more fully through music, his music also seems to attempt to embody those reali-

---

74. Michael P. Steinberg, "Music Drama and the End of History," *New German Critique* (Fall 1996): 163-80. Steinberg interprets Amfortas's wound, in Wagner's *Parsifal,* an as allegory of modernity, examining the meaning of the claim that the wound has finally been closed.

75. For some recent musicological discussion of new theological music, see Arnold Whittall's "Echoes of Old Beliefs: Birtwistle's Last Supper and Adams's El Niño," *The Musical Times* 143, no. 1881 (Winter 2002): 16-26, and Richard Taruskin's "Sacred Entertainments," *Cambridge Opera Journal* 15, no. 2 (2003): 109-26.

ties in sound. Perhaps this explains something of why Messiaen felt that he had never succeeded in proclaiming his faith through song.[76] Indeed, it may have seemed to Messiaen that his own modern music only "increased our ignorance by constantly revealing new realities within what was believed to be reality" even as it pointed toward "the one sole reality" of faith.[77]

So how could music attempt to lead thought out of its own ideological and aesthetic aporias? Surely, the bridge between music having a "significant" or "directional meaning" and the "dazzlement" that Messiaen speaks of so often, could only really be achieved through shock.[78] This is not the shock of the negative that has animated and re-animated modernist music from Schoenberg and Stravinsky through to Ligeti and Carter — the various deaths of modernism throughout the twentieth century have left a heap of corpses and a large corpus of art in its wake — but the shock of the positive. Messiaen feels this shock in the moment of the Resurrection. When asked about this idea in the last tableau of *St. François,* Messiaen replied:

> . . . it acts as a pressing fundamental; the most considerable to take place since creation. At the opposite of certain representations, I do not see the resurrection as an effort made by Christ: it was sudden, like the explosion of an atomic bomb.
>
> The shroud of Turin is a witness. I believe in it, not because this appears to me to be like a miracle, but [because it is] a natural phenomenon. At Hiroshima, the bodies of the victims were found photographed on the walls. In the same way, the resurrection was an atomic shock. Christ was raised in one stroke [*coup*] and his effigy was imprinted on the shroud.
>
> I have tried in my music to render the resurrection — this very concrete and extraordinary thing — in multiple ways, without ever having achieved it. I am not able to render this moment as it was. The resurrection of Christ gives to us all the right to be resurrected also, and the presentiment of this moment particularly disturbs me [*m'émeut*].[79]

76. Messiaen, "Réponses à une enquête," p. 73.
77. Messiaen, "Introduction to the Programme Booklet for Paris, 1978," in Rössler, *Contributions to the Spiritual World of Olivier Messiaen,* p. 10.
78. When asked in 1961 by Claude Samuel what advice he would give to an enthusiast who was coming to hear one of his works that would be difficult at first hearing, Messiaen said that the public must come with no "a priorisms," and with a sort of "aural virginity" *(virginité d'oreille).* Samuel then asks: "He must hear a shock?" Messiaen responded (emphatically): "Yes! A Shock!" Claude Samuel, *Entretien avec Olivier Messiaen,* 11-13 October 1961, included with a recording of Messiaen's *Turangalîla-Symphonie,* Vega 30 BVG 1363.
79. "Entretien avec Olivier Messiaen," *L'Avant Scène,* p. 11. I translate *m'émeut* here as

Messiaen's shock of the positive is nonetheless articulated, as we have seen, through direct engagement with the shock of modernity, consciously placed in his music to redirect our gaze. His ecstatic visions are "sensible poetic signs" that, for him, can only approach the resurrection asymptotically by attempting through his leitmotif technique to conflate the transient, the fleeting, and the contingent within the eternal and immovable.[80] Yet because of this, the burning bush of his project of Christian revival is enabled to glow more fiercely.[81] Modernity is invoked as part of a historical endgame, so that after Messiaen's opera we are left with the task of its completion.

As in Grünewald's resurrection panel, our eyes are raised above the sin and drudgery of *la vie quotidienne*, to participate in Christ's glory. Messiaen's vision of humanity's destiny is clear. His opera is critical of the modern commodification of and division between spirituality and religion. Not only is Francis not free to choose his spirituality (God chooses him), but for Francis/Messiaen, alienation from God and ourselves is excised as we live through Francis's self-realization. Such an organic process brings together the sometimes alienated realities of art and religion, not into any sort of synthesis, but into an uncomfortable symbiosis. The discomfort and the strength of Messiaen's piece lies not entirely in any triumphalism, but in the serendipity of finding ourselves in a new emotional and spiritual arena. Messiaen's refreshment of modernism is a reminder that even an ideology that sees itself as being an end can be a new beginning when revived by the imagination: a message of hope to an unbelieving world.

"disturb" although it can just mean "move." This translation appears more germane in the context of Messiaen's comment on the shock of the resurrection.

80. Paraphrased from Charles Baudelaire, "The Painter of Modern Life," in *Baudelaire: Selected Writings on Art and Literature*, p. 403.

81. "The bush burned brighter because its interpreter was not allowed too near." George Steiner, *Errata: An Examined Life* (London: Wiedenfeld and Nicolson, 1997), p. 22.

8. *Quasi Una Sonata:* Modernism, Postmodernism, Religion, and Music

Catherine Pickstock

Initial Statement of Theme

One can detect an ambivalence concerning the relationship of music to the process of secularization.[1] Music appears to be more closely related to religion than the other arts; many of its forms are liturgical in nature, and its ordered expression of joy has been connected with the offering of praise. While music is also associated with the work of mourning, the very conversion of sorrow into song can seem to tilt away from the tragic toward resignation, consolation, and eschatological hope. It would seem that the inherent bias of music is toward synchronic harmony and diachronic resolution. Nevertheless, the wordless character of music and its relative freedom from representation can also suggest a certain urging toward a mystical, nondogmatic religion, or even a cult of music that would substitute for a cult of faith. It can be argued that the historical periods that have seen a gradual decline in the importance of church attendance have also seen the emergence of the public concert, opera, and ballet as quasi-sacral rites that are neither sacral liturgical music nor occasional music — such as "table music" and music for dancing — nor music for private performance.

1. Music has often been regarded ambivalently by theologians. Augustine, Aquinas, and many others have indicated that while music is a suitable vehicle for the worship of God, because it reflects a divine order and harmony, it should remain subordinate to word and doctrine, which articulate this order with greater exactitude. For example, see Thomas Aquinas, *Summa Theologiae,* II-II q. 91 a. 2 and 3; Edward Booth, "Thomas Aquinas," in *The New Grove Dictionary of Music and Musicians,* ed. Stanley Sadie (London: Macmillan Publishers, 1980).

Music in the twentieth century seems to sustain this double-facing. Modernism in music stems in part from the later Romanticism of Richard Wagner, who had already distanced himself from the structures of fixed keys and, with the invention of the *leitmotif,* allowed Romantic expressivism to drift further away from the dominance of harmonic relation and melodic development. In Wagner's operas, the inter-communication of the internal discourses of the *leitmotifs* constitutes a non-dramatic subplot that is the esoteric aspect of these works. Closely allied with this esoteric aspect is Wagner's deliberate attempt to create a new secular sacrality, a celebration of the possibility of absolute sacrificial self-commitment in erotic love: this enterprise reaches its consummation in his opera *Tristan and Isolde.*[2] In general, Wagner's music tends to reflect Schopenhauer's notion of a pure unteleological fated process undergirding reality, and this allows a liberation of modulation from the constraints of proportionate concordance and repeatable tune. But the *leitmotif* superimposes upon this the use of a superessential *intermezzo* in the form of little *ritornelli,* little melodic and rhythmic folds, which are then placed in juxtaposition with one another. This seems to anticipate the modernist literary interest in the "stream of consciousness" and a world made up not simply of a shared daytime plot but also of multiple and only obscurely intercommunicating nights of inchoate desire and dreaming.

As Roger Scruton has argued, artistic modernism as a whole continued and radicalized the Wagnerian enterprise.[3] On the whole, formal religion was eschewed; yet equally disdained was the modern totalized and desacralized world. The desire was to make of art a refuge and enclave for the hyperspecific symbol, form, or expression, whose secrecy and difficulty ensured that it could not be made banal or functional by an all-devouring marketplace. In the case of music, this process has perhaps been carried to its furthest extreme; music especially permits an extreme degree of abstraction and formalization. But the result of this, particularly with the rise of total serialism after the Second World War, has been to give the world of classical music the ethos of a small, diminishing sect, claiming to be able to hear beauties to which the public ear has remained tone-deaf.

In modern times, one could argue, music has tended to become a sub-

2. Roger Scruton, *Death-Devoted Heart: Sex and the Sacred in Wagner's* Tristan and Isolde (New York: Oxford University Press, 2004); Nick Nesbitt, "Deleuze, Adorno and the Composition of Musical Multiplicity," in *Deleuze and Music,* ed. Ian Buchanan and Marcel Swiboda (Edinburgh: Edinburgh University Press, 2004), pp. 54-76.

3. Scruton, *Death-Devoted Heart.*

stitute for religion. If, on hearing music, one is bound in some sense to inti-mate cosmic harmonies, then it seems nonetheless possible to halt at a cer-tain mystical agnosticism that will not countenance doctrinal formulas or metaphysical explanations. In accordance with this, many modern compos-ers, perhaps especially British composers, have remained close to religious practice and attitude without espousing formal belief: Vaughan Williams, Howells, Britten, Tippett, and Maxwell Davies all spring to mind.

Yet, at the same time, music remains a vehicle for the persistence of ex-plicit belief and of organized religion. This is not surprising because, to the reflective person, as the composer James MacMillan has pointed out, music presents a mystery: How is it that mathematically organized patterns of sound are capable of inspiring such great emotion, and also, as Hungarian education has tended to prove, of stimulating intellectual inquiry?[4] We are still confronted with the Pythagorean truth that music seems to link soul and body, reason and the passions, the individual with society and the cos-mos.[5] Moreover, any given musical tradition contains implicitly certain views about time, space, and eternity, or the emotional and the rational, and the individual and the general. Although music is without words and indeed *verbis defectis, musica incipit,* according to the Renaissance tag, it is itself an organized language capable of a degree of translation into other aesthetic id-ioms and other discourses. Asked whether he was a "mystical composer," Olivier Messiaen denied this and replied that, no, he was a theological com-poser. This comment is surely elucidated by Messiaen's other statement that, for him, music provides a more rather than less exacting means of saying things than the words of language.[6]

For these reasons, many musicians, including many popular musicians, have asked what the ground of the possibility for music is, and their answer is often an explicitly religious one. I have already cited British composers whom one might describe as "mystical agnostics," yet it is striking that these

4. James MacMillan has made this point in several unpublished and broadcast talks.
5. See Catherine Pickstock, "Music: Soul, City and Cosmos after Augustine," in *Radical Orthodoxy: A New Theology,* ed. John Milbank, Catherine Pickstock, and Graham Ward (London: Routledge, 1999), pp. 243-77.
6. Ian Darbyshire, "Messiaen and the Representation of the Theological Illusion of Time," in *Messiaen's Language of Mystical Love,* ed. Siglind Bruhn (New York: Garland, 1998), pp. 33-55; see also Roberto Fabbi, "Theological Implications of Restrictions in Messiaen's Compositional Processes," in *Messiaen's Language,* ed. Bruhn, pp. 55-84; and Theo Hirschbaum, "Magic and Enchantment in Messiaen's *Catalogue d'Oiseaux,*" in *Messiaen's Language,* ed. Bruhn, pp. 195-224.

(with the arguable exceptions of Vaughan Williams and Benjamin Britten), are scarcely to be counted among the major innovators in twentieth-century music. By contrast, it is still more striking that among the major innovators one finds perhaps a greater instance of continued adherence to some mode of Christianity or Judaism than in the case of any of the other arts: one can think here of Stravinsky, Schoenberg, Messiaen, Schnittke, Ustvolskaya, and Arvo Pärt. One could suggest that this is because the more self-conscious innovators (who are not necessarily, of course, thereby the best composers) are also those likely to inquire after the "ground of possibility" of music.

But this observation immediately raises the question of the relation between musical modernism and religion. As I have suggested, the former is a secular movement, or rather a movement that is, in the long-term wake of Wagner, seeking to discover an immanent musical cult that will substitute for formal religion. So how could the composer of "The Rite of Spring," so replete with the use of rhythm to establish "personality," later come to be a loyal communicant of the Russian Orthodox Church? There is surely no easy answer to that question, but the example immediately indicates two sites for rendering the question a more general one: and these are *sacrifice* and *tempo*.

After Wagner, modernism was concerned with sacrifice: with sacrifice as the primitive essence of religion in the wake of modern anthropological discoveries, and with the possibility of a purified, immanent sacrifice toward the human other, or the human community, or even the void. These thematics could be reintegrated quite easily into the framework of Christian typology, looking toward Christ's passion. The ecstasy of music can convey the going beyond oneself that such a notion requires, including its strange fusion of the ethical demand with an extra-ethical obsession. To lose oneself in the absolute is to lose oneself in that which exceeds the ethical, especially if the absolute is an immanent law, or totality, or process. The lure of eros is for the modern artist just a given, as is the succession of time or the social totality. To lose oneself in these things is to surrender to an extra-human rhythm, which pulses through the subconscious but expresses the natural in an aleatory mode that is more fundamental than anything that can be explored by natural science.

With respect to both sacrifice and tempo, music reveals itself to be perhaps the most central modernist art. It is best able to express self-abandonment to immanent mystery, and to a time that is more fundamental than the time that we can measure. Most of modernism was in one way or another influenced by Henri Bergson's philosophy, which hinged upon this distinction. For Bergson, a creative and spontaneous *élan vitale* sustains nature at a level prior to the emergence of the regular and spatialized processes that science can formulate as law. In the human being, this more fundamental process rises to the surface of full consciousness and allows a superrational experience of time as properly *durée,* in which past, present, and future are intensively fused, with a bias toward future creative action, rather than laid out as externally separate moments, according to a spatial model.[7] It is obvious that music would seem to be the art that can most naturally express pure "duration."

And something like the attempt to do just that was present in musical modernism after Schoenberg, Berg, and others. Traditional diatonic music was seen as "spatialized" music; musical flow was subordinate to vertical harmonies, fixed harmonic ratios, static scalar relations and formal regular metric patternings, and predictable continua of speed and dynamic. Beyond Wagner, the modernist revolutionaries undertook to set free a process of "continuous variation" for which there are no fixed tones and no fixed relations, but instead a pure becoming that is never for a single instant self-identical. With explicit reference or not, this was seen as akin to the absolute heterogeneity of Bergson's *durée* and Husserl's expression of ecstatic temporality, radicalized by Heidegger (probably in Bergson's wake) into an identity with Being as such. In the latter case, one is removed both from punctuality and from relation, a singular but self-differentiating process. The radical subjectivity of this process indicates also a development of Romanticism, but in the direction of subjective forces that exceed us from within. This lineage is relevant to the musical world also.

The new obsession with technique was subordinate to ultimate expressivist aims. One can see this above all with the idea of the twelve-tone scale, or "tone row." The goal here is to complete the work of equal-tempering by producing a scale taken from the traditional octave (itself the child of the yoking-together of two Greek tetrachords, comprising two single intervals and one half interval), but purged of any inequalities or supposed colorings of different keys. This results in twelve equal half intervals with no tonics or dominants: no home-base, no middle, and no higher aim that recapitulate the original base. This allows the composer to impose his own unique expressive hierarchy and also ideally permits an escape from all-too-totalizing notions of thematic development and final resolution. Beyond the modalism of

7. See especially Henri Bergson, *Creative Evolution,* trans. Arthur Mitchell (New York: University Press of America, 1983), pp. 186-272.

Debussy and Ravel (historicized and re-romanticized by Vaughan Williams and so "re-emplotted" with a great originality that now seems more "post-modern" than nostalgic), music could now become impressionistic, but, beyond Debussy, impressioned of itself and not anything else, and wandering in its own virtual space without either development or return.

One can observe two paradoxes. Despite the Bergsonian aim to liberate music from spatialization, time as narrative here disappears. This is because, in the first place, continuous variation, for which the variation of the original is in the condition of "always already," is a kind of simultaneity, and so seemingly "spatial" after all. Second, time as memory also disappears, as Pierre Boulez indicates: in a piece without development of a theme but only ceaseless juxtaposition and surprise, both the composer and the listener must continuously forget what has come before.[8] Yet both are strictly impossible: one has to hear music in laid-out measured time, and indeed music is, as Messiaen put it, a kind of "geometry of time." The most extreme modernist experimenters after the Second World War, such as Iannis Xenakis, sought to deploy the *glissando* in place of isolatable notes, yet even here one has to hear to some degree a "first" and then "what succeeds" it. The *glissando* has a narrative aspect. What comes later may be in some sense the same as what came earlier, yet for our hearing it is also different and so is "in relation" to a precedent.[9] Pure self-differentiation is simply not hearable, just as pure juxtaposition would be merely noise and not music. In this way, the endeavor to remove theme, development, measurable meter, and harmony is an impossible one. The modernist enterprise was often self-consciously stochastic: gesturing negatively toward the sublimity of *durée* beyond the bounds of musical reason. The twelve-tone scale was the boundary of musical finitude; although it held out the prospect of release from the diatonic octave, it also necessarily bound one back within it, since it is merely the abstraction of the purest degree of chromaticism that the octave pre-contains. For this reason, the somewhat "post-modern" philosopher Gilles Deleuze ar-

8. Pierre Boulez, "Eloge de l'amnésie," *Musique en Jeu* 4 (1974); and "J'ai horreur de souvenir," in *Roger Desormière et son temps,* ed. D. Mayer and P. Souvtchinsky (Monaco: Editions du Rocher, 1966).

9. For Xenakis's use of glissando, Iannis Xenakis, *Metastasis* etc, CD: Ensemble Instrumental de Musique Contemporain de Paris, Konstantin Simonovic; Orchestre National de l'O.R.T.F. Maurice le Roux (Paris: Le Chant du Monde, 2001) and *Anastenaria* etc, CD: Chor des Bayerischen Rundfunks, Christoph Adty; Symphonie Orchester des Bayerischen Rundfunksa, Charles Zacharie Bornstein (Munich: Musica Viva, Bayerischen Rundfunk, 2001).

gued that tonic experimenters such as Béla Bartók were more successful in creating something drastically new that genuinely broke with the bounds of previous convention.[10]

Does this mean that musical modernism was inherently secular and immanentist? Not necessarily. Schoenberg came to see the tone row, in a Neo-Pythagorean or Cabbalistic way, as the natural, divinely ordained grammar of music and the cosmos. Nevertheless, one could see this as a characteristically modern Jewish embrace of a post-Kantian position. The supposed finally identified bounds of finitude are identified with the laws of God. They gesture, negatively, to the unrepresentable infinite and even intimate it as a glimpsed chasm, yet they are unable to mediate this infinite to us.

Nevertheless, the example of Schoenberg, like that of Stravinsky (whose innovations were more percussive in character), shows that the modernist reinvention of the sacred in art as secret, subjective, temporal, and sacrificial could readily be deployed as a new means to safeguard and convey more traditional religious belief: examples of this in the literary field would include T. S. Eliot and David Jones. For the latter, one finds a fusion of modernism with elements of Thomism. A similar fusion applies also in the case of the composer Olivier Messiaen.

Messiaen is central to the topic of musical modernism, because it was his compositional and theoretical work that foreshadowed the "total serialism" of the post-war period, when the serial principle of de-hierarchization was applied not just to pitch but also to the other elements of musical composition: rhythm, dynamic, color, intensity, attack, duration, polytonality, and so forth. And yet, Messiaen himself developed a musical theology that was by no means "Kantian" in character, and that arguably dealt with the stochastic yearning in a different fashion. Moreover, while he helped to found the "Darmstadt" group along with Stockhausen and his own pupils Boulez and Xenakis in the 1950s, he eventually broke with its total serialism, in a way that perhaps has some connection with musical "post-modernism."[11]

If Messiaen is the pivotal figure in twentieth-century music and also the most explicitly theological, then his work merits some examination before we ask, What is musical post-modernism, and how does it relate both to modernism and to religion?

10. Gilles Deleuze and Félix Guattari, *A Thousand Plateaux*, trans. Brian Massumi (London: Athlone, 1987), pp. 349-50.

11. See Bruhn, ed., *Messiaen's Language;* also Iain G. Matheson, ed., *The Messiaen Companion* (London: Faber and Faber, 1995).

Development

For Messiaen, the relation of musical modernism to Bergson is clearly set forth at the outset of his multi-volume musical notebooks. Music is to do with *durée*, the dimension of continuous variation that is primordially heterogeneous and subjective. Rhythm, as opposed to measured meter, is defined by just these properties; it is "la succession de mêmes qui sont toujours autres [. . .] et d'autres qui ont toujours quelques parentés avec la même: c'est la variation perpetuelle."[12] This, according to Messiaen, is better recognized in Oriental than in Western music. Hindu rhythm is more complex than classical Western rhythm, while Chinese composers have attended to another factor outside the melodic and the harmonic: resonance or intensity, as shown in their use of the clangor and lingering of sounded bells. Properly speaking, Messiaen alleges, horizontal melody reduces to rhythmic interval in such a way that pitch and tone are less essentially musical elements of added "color." They belong inherently to the vertical scale of harmony, which melody simply runs through in temporal sequence. (Here, one might ask, can there also be rhythms of space?)[13] In attributing pitch more to the harmonic side, Messiaen sounds as if he were within the French tradition of Rameau rather than Rousseau, but, on the other hand, he gives a Rousseau-like priority to monodic melody reconstrued as rhythm, just as, in the wake of Rameau, the "classical" composers Haydn and Mozart gave a new role to the horizontal temporal line of music by a newly complex interest in the percussive.[14]

Nevertheless, there are at least two significant ways in which Messiaen departs from this Orientalist-Bergsonism, both of them suggestive of a specifically Catholic theological perspective.

First, Messiaen denies that *durée* can, as Bergson supposed, be an "immediate given" of consciousness and the object of a pure intuition. Rather, duration or "perpetual variation" is something that we have access to only through bodily and sensory experience and through sound itself. But sound, which mediates to us duration, is also and equally the point where duration is interwoven with measured and spatialized time. In this way, in effect,

12. Olivier Messiaen, *Traité de Rythme, de Couleur et d'Ornithologie*, Tome I (Paris: Leduc, 1994), p. 39.

13. Messiaen, *Traité de Rythme*, pp. 7-52. See further in this volume the more detailed account of Messiaen offered by Robert Sholl, "The Shock of the Positive: Olivier Messiaen, St. Francis, and Redemption through Modernity."

14. See Pickstock, "Music: Soul, City and Cosmos."

Messiaen was able to accept a post-Einsteinian time-space relativity that Bergson notoriously sought to refuse. For the composer, therefore, one finds far less dualism than for the philosopher.[15] This connects directly with the composer's belief in a transcendent Creator God. For Messiaen, even mundane measured time remotely echoes eternity, while duration echoes eternity to a still higher degree. However, it does not fully attain to its pure simultaneity, and duration as subjective memory still properly refers to a real external past and future even though it reimagines the former and actively anticipates the latter.

Messiaen grasps this in terms of a musical angle upon the Thomistic real distinction, which suggests that his musical composition and theoretical reflection sit easily within the central twentieth-century philosophical debate concerning Being, life, time, and symbolic expression that concerned not just Bergson and Heidegger, but also the Thomists, Etienne Gilson and Jacques Maritain.

Just as, in ontological terms, for Thomas, *esse* and *essentia* are distinguished for human beings but coincide in God, so also, as Messiaen points out, for Thomas, creatures are in time, and yet do not coincide with time, whereas God simply is his own eternity.[16] The vanishing-away of external time reveals that creatures entangled in time "are" also something else that points toward the eternal, while the subjective human being remains in excess of memory and projection. Even angels live in a non-passing duration that is *aevum;* and even with this they do not perfectly coincide. Their personality escapes their created "remaining," and here one has an angelogical refutation of Bergson's subjective impersonalism, for which the self is lost in ineffable heterogeneity. All this is expressed in Messiaen's music: the cosmic time of rocks; the biological time of birds; the human time of memory, contemplation, and eschatological expectation; the pure remaining of the angels. And all these things, by analogy, build up to the impossible expression of an eternal music that would represent only itself, as at the end of *Eclairs sur l'Au Delà.*[17] This latter would seem to be an aim of all musical modernism, but it is notable that Messiaen seems always to insist that finite music is programmatic, inevitably and properly evocative, for reasons that we shall presently see.

15. Messiaen, *Traité de Rythme,* p. 9.
16. Messiaen, *Traité de Rythme,* pp. 7-15.
17. Olivier Messiaen, *Eclairs sur l'Au Delà,* CD: Orchestre de l'Opéra Bastille, Myung-Whun Chung (Hamburg: Deutsche Grammaphon, 1994).

In the second place, Messiaen does not really subordinate the harmonic to the melodic, taken as essentially rhythm, which he defines as "continuous variation." In the end, as later in the case of Boulez, he is concerned with the mysterious "diagonal" that one hears between the horizontal and vertical coordinates.[18] Exploration of this diagonal or transversal is really proper to Western music alone, in the traditions of polyphony, counterpoint, use of the ostinato bass, and so forth. And such free-floating obliquity was only permitted by the stress upon punctual notes, pauses, and strict selection of modes or scales. Such abstract simplification, as compared with certain Eastern traditions, was the precondition of a new complexification (and the same sequence holds good for serialism).[19]

Nevertheless, Messiaen thought about the diagonal in a peculiar way, influenced by his possession of a physiological condition that permitted a constant experience of synesthesia: he heard sounds as colors. Or rather, it is more proper to say that he heard sequences of sounds as equivalent to a kaleidoscopic or cinematic transmutation of color. The seeing of an isolated sound as an isolated color was characteristic rather of a drug-induced psychedelic experience.[20]

While for Messiaen horizontal rhythm in time is the properly musical factor, nevertheless the "extra" of coloration is not extrinsic, and this suggests that music always invokes also the spatial domain; hence the dizzying geographical expansiveness of Messiaen's music, as well as its exotic and varied coloration. Nevertheless, just as Messiaen peculiarly sees melody as rhythm, so also he peculiarly sees harmony arising from color and intensity.[21]

18. See Fabbi, "Theological Implications of Restrictions." Fabbi mentions Messiaen's *Modes de Valeurs et intensités* for piano, where "entities appear as suspended in an oblique and fluctuating space-time dimension" (p. 66). See also Pierre Boulez, *Notes of an Apprenticeship*, trans. Herbert Weinstock (New York: Knopf, 1968), pp. 231-32, 295-301, 382-83; and *Boulez on Music Today*, trans. Susan Bradshaw and Richard Rodney Bennett (Cambridge, MA: Harvard University Press, 1971), pp. 55-59. See also Deleuze and Guattari, *A Thousand Plateaux*, p. 297; Gilles Deleuze, *The Fold: Leibniz and the Baroque*, trans. Tom Conley (London: Athlone, 1993), pp. 121-37.

19. See Pickstock, "Music: Soul, City and Cosmos." Here it is argued that Augustine in his *De Musica* theorized the grounds of polyphony in advance of the practice with his stress on the pause as linked with the notion of the inherent "nothingness" of created realities, as well as on the simultaneity of Pythagorean intervals.

20. Claude Samuel, *Entretiens avec Olivier Messiaen* (Paris: Editions Pierre Belfond, 1967), pp. 41-56. On Messiaen's synesthesia and the implications for his music, see further Sholl, "The Shock of the Positive," in this volume.

21. Messiaen, *Traité de Rythme*, Tome I, pp. 7-52.

For this reason, Messiaen undertook to extend further the Western rationalization of music, in order to permit a new complexity and a new operation of creative spontaneity. Alongside scales of pitches, he created scales of duration (not simply tempi but scales of variation of tempi), of color, of intensity, of dynamic, and of attack. This allowed him to add to his music polyrhythm and polycoloration as well as polyphony. For example, Messiaen's music often involves the coordination of several different speeds and volumes running alongside one another.

Beyond this, however, Messiaen's commitment to original heterogeneity (or perpetual variation, akin to Derrida's *différance*) encouraged him to go beyond certain tendencies within baroque music to permit simultaneous and concurrent polyphonies, where it seemed as if disparate pieces of music were running at the same time; a "polyphony of polyphonies," as Boulez put it, and then polyrhythm of polyrhythms, and so forth.

Messiaen was a "radical composer" in the most literal sense. He sought to conjugate the most disparate and newly invented forces. Like all Bergsonian modernists, he saw his art as a kind of higher scientific experiment that captured and exhibited through original exemplification the ultimate vital cosmic forces. However, for Messiaen, the possibility of this surprising holding-together lay in the co-incidence of beauty with eternity and infinity in God. Because this is reflected in the created order, the cosmic hymn can be revealed and created ever-anew.

But how does this stand in relation to musical modernism in general? For Messiaen, the release of a flattened chromaticism was not the crucial thing. Rather, as for Igor Stravinsky, it was the insistence upon rhythm as non-identical repetition. Yet, whereas the other modernists tended to gesture toward the impossibility of pure heterogeneity, Messiaen saw that it was always mediated through, and not contradicted by, selected regular formal patterns ("identical repetitions") of various sorts. Surprising variations on these could then point toward the Triune God, in whom variation is absolute and yet self-identical. Messiaen was a supreme innovator in that he sought to give an enhanced role to neglected musical elements, which he nonetheless subjected, in a craftsman-like and indeed scholastic manner, to the sort of rules and norms that had earlier in Western musical history been applied to melody and harmony.

In parallel with this approach, Messiaen held back from serialism with regard to pitch. He broke with the diatonic scale, but did so through a selection of certain modes and fixed rules for modal transposition, similar to, but not coincident with, those of Gregorian chant. This can be seen as relatively conservative, although there is a complicating factor. Serialism in a sense only further extends the rationalization carried out by equal temperament in the eighteenth century.[22] Its release of random chromatic slides further excludes the sense of intrinsic mood or color proper to modal music and still surviving somewhat in the baroque era, even in Bach, who probably favored "well" rather than "equal" tempering. By comparison with other modernists, Messiaen returned more to the predilections of Gregorian chant, which, prior to the Cistercian reform that took Western music on the road to strictly related "keys" by forbidding modal transpositions, not only embraced modes of different prevailing mood but also allowed complex slides from one mode/mood to another under certain rules.[23]

In this way, Messiaen's Thomistic modifications of Bergson's approach to time concur with his conservative revolutionism in music, his "radical orthodoxy." (Curiously, it might seem, he did not invoke Augustine, but this was not unusual for French Catholic thought during this epoch.)

And yet it was Messiaen who paved the way for the most drastic serialism of all. This was because his pupils, Boulez and Xenakis, along with Stockhausen and Berio, undertook to apply serial principles to all aspects of music, including those which Messiaen had newly brought to the fore. If Messiaen resisted this, then it was because, in the case of every variable, as with pitch, he did not choose to adopt serial parameters, but rather modal or quasi-modal ones. What was really at issue here?

Messiaen's pupils sought a purely self-referential, entirely musical music. The criteria here for what was to be selected had to be internal to musical considerations rather than programmatic, representative, social, or even emotional and subjective ones. A series simply offered a neutral repertoire or *mathesis* from which one could select a way or ways of organizing this series, as in mathematical set theory. But what dictates the choice? Purely formal considerations? Why go one way rather than another? Even mathematicians have to start talking about "intrinsic beauty" at this point, and in Xenakis's thesis defense, Messiaen asked where "love" entered into the business of selection. Xenakis was interestingly prepared to talk about "revelation" here, but the question for Messiaen seemed to be whether there can be, as for Xenakis, a clear distinction between pure mathematical technique, on the one hand, and the mysterious intervention of "revelation," on the other. This is the point at which John Cage was only prepared to talk about pure

22. Stuart Isacoff, *Temperament* (New York: Vintage, 2003).
23. Nesbitt, "Deleuze, Adorno and Musical Multiplicity," p. 60.

"chance." But for Messiaen there is no such technique/love duality; rather, it would seem, Messiaen saw his selection of formal rules and the creative operation of these rules as itself already guided by "love" or by "revelation."[24]

And this fits with his preference for mode over series. Messiaen's base is not a pure, flat, smooth, nomadic space but rather a pre-selection of something with a certain color, a certain mood, a certain tendency, a certain hierarchical bias or tilt. Is this then to prefer the striated, fixed, and arboreal to the labyrinthine vegetation of the rhizomatic in Deleuze's reworked Bergsonian terms? Not entirely, because for Messiaen each modal "tree" is constantly being qualified by intertwining with other modal "trees." By contrast, Xenakis is prepared to release total "dissonance" in every musical domain, in such a way that there are no more hierarchical biases toward base notes, themes, developments, resolutions, harmonies, and so forth. However, he can do this only by beginning with the arbitrary decision to prefer the Cartesian space of serial regularity, which is picked out just because it accords with a mood of cold neutrality. In fact, a more iron rule has been selected here than those which apply to the diatonic scale, and, as Deleuze himself indicates, this premature attempt to seize absolute deterritorialization can result in spiraling down a black hole of complete non-musicality. For any actual surviving music will always somewhat gesture toward the various idioms of hierarchization. Xenakis can avoid a black hole only by admitting to the moment of revelation. But if, in composing together disparate elements, one sees the way one should go, then this is tantamount to glimpsing a new and unexpected moment of harmony. And there is indeed nothing wrong with deployment of the serial principle (as sometimes undertaken by Messiaen himself, implicitly) in order to permit a freer sort of chromatic transition. Yet if one permits revelation to supervene upon seriality in the process of composition, why should it not intervene in the form of a prior selection of modes and favored sorts of transposition that are more intrinsically colored (as the word "chromatic" indicates)? The latter allows one to see that creativity has a social and traditioned dimension, which is indeed another aspect of modernism as such.

It was said above that musical modernism tends to suppress development, resolution, and memory. In the case of Boulez's work *Pli selon Pli*, this tends to mean that the music endlessly unfolds toward further and further

---

24. Iannis Xenakis, *Arts/Sciences Alloys: The Thesis Defense of Iannis Xenakis before Olivier Messiaen et al.*, trans. Sharon Kanach (New York: Pendragon Press, 1985), pp. 27-47; Samuel, *Entretiens avec Olivier Messiaen*, pp. 61-79, and *passim*.

horizons in such a way that the music advances no closer to an arrival and does not return upon itself. And yet in reality, in listening to this (very beautiful) piece of music, one cannot help hearing endless semi-arrivals and endless semi-returns.[25] The constant frustration of these and revelation of yet another turn in the non-plot is indeed delightful, and yet the constant drive to undo, not to arrive and not to return, means that one feels that anti-music has the last word. Irony triumphs: there may be music within non-music, but the whole piece is not music — in which case it falls apart and its elements seem arbitrary and non-revealed or non-loved. Despite all the beauty, it is ultimately more barrage than beauty, even allowing for a trained ear. I am not arguing against formal complexity here: modernist music is far more listenable to than is usually allowed, and denial of this is the disgrace of populist culture, not of skillful composers. But if more barrage than beauty, why just *this* barrage? There seems no reason to compose what is not a composition. But if there is more beauty than barrage, as with Messiaen, then one has an affirmation that beauty must be infinite.[26]

To go on composing outside the rules *requires* one to be theological. And this becomes much more evident when one considers avant-garde music, such as that of Messiaen and his pupils, than when one considers more strictly modernist music that remains within the compass of rules. Here one can, as it were, nostalgically feign faith.

Exactly how does Messiaen's music endlessly expand toward the cosmos and yet also intimate an infinite order rather than infinite chaos? One important consideration here is that order in some sense implies circularity; it implies that one can "return" on a course taken because there is a perceptible sequence. If the sequence is not yet complete, one can still know that there is a final order only because this incomplete sequence intimates an infinite and complete one. To favor non-return, like Boulez, is perhaps too arbitrary a choice for a meaningless cosmos, a denial that patterns one can intimate betoken a final patterning. Hence to resist memory, recapitulation, harmony (even of the discordant), and reversal is in effect to resist, for no musical or other reason, the lure of God, and to resist music as such.

Messiaen, by contrast, deploys three devices that intimate return, and so

25. Pierre Boulez, CD: *Pli selon Pli,* Christine Schafer, Soprano, Ensemble Intercontemporain, Pierre Boulez (Hamburg: Deutsche Grammaphon, 2002).

26. See David Hart, *The Beauty of the Infinite: The Aesthetics of Christian Truth* (Grand Rapids: Eerdmans, 2003), *passim.* The fundamental argument here is that Christian theology uniquely envisages the infinite itself not as disordered but as beautiful. A concomitant of this would seem to be that a Christian aesthetic can be aligned with aesthetic experimentation.

order.[27] The first of these has already been discussed: it is "modes of limited transposition." The second is "non-retrogradable rhythm." This concerns the following paradox. If one takes the series *1,2,3,4*, and reverses it as *4,3,2,1*, then the reversal has made it symmetrically different: a mirror image. Such a series is subject to retrogradation, and it is easy to envisage musical equivalents. But take instead the series *1,2,1*. Reversed, this is still *1,2,1*, and therefore it is said to be "non-retrogradable," despite its perfect symmetrical reversibility.

Messiaen makes great use of such non-retrogradable rhythms, which can also be described as palindromes; for example: crotchet (i.e., quarter note), dotted crotchet, crotchet. For him the significance of such a rhythm is that its reversible symmetry, which could be seen as its *absolute* retro-gradabality, is an example of time collapsing inward toward eternity. For where memory makes projection precisely equivalent to memory, one has an image of time itself sandwiched between the same eternity coming "before" and "after" time. Yet because the palindrome is non-retrogradable, it cannot really be reversed, and therefore it stands also for the pure forward-moving event. So here, time as *durée*, time in its most intimate fusion of past, pres-ent, and future, remains at once the creative forward-pressing pure event and yet as such the very thing that points to timelessness. But in contrast to Bergson, as we have seen, Messiaen saw the rhythmic patterning of time as music as crucial to the realization of *durée* as such.

But Messiaen deployed this device also with a further twist. If one re-verses a retrogradable series as follows: *1,2,3,4, 4,3,2,1*, then the entire unit of eight elements is itself non-retrogradable. In *Les Corps Glorieux*, Messiaen uses this device to suggest the raising up of temporal bodies to the "winged" character of angels in the resurrection. Here and elsewhere he employs this device to represent the substantive relations of the Trinity: the Son in receiv-ing all of the Father "reverses" him to form one symmetrical and non-reversible event that the Holy Spirit can only affirm and offer. In this way, Messiaen's music hopes to fulfill the prayer *enfoncez votre image dans la durée de mes jours.*[28]

His third technique is another way of trying to achieve this same goal. This is symmetrical permutation or "interversion." Whereas the first tech-nique is applied to pitch and the second to rhythm, this third technique be-

27. For the discussion concerning the three crucial devices, see Darbyshire, "Messiaen and the Representation"; Fabbi, "Theological Implications"; Messiaen, *Traité*, Tome III (Paris: Leduc, 1995), pp. 352-53; Samuel, *Entretiens, passim.*
28. Cited by Fabbi, "Theological Implications," p. 80.

comes a parameter for all the musical variables, although especially for the unit Messiaen called "neume," which means something like a melody of indeterminate rhythm. Using this technique, one modulates from one sequence to another and then to the next one, by way of a strictly proportionate analogy that folds the first sequence "inside out," and then the second sequence likewise, and so forth. It is like a constant emerging of butterflies from their chrysalises, and can be numerically exemplified thus:

$$1 \rightarrow 2 \rightarrow 3 \rightarrow 4$$
$$3 \rightarrow 2 \rightarrow 4 \rightarrow 1$$
$$4 \rightarrow 2 \rightarrow 1 \rightarrow 3$$
$$1 \rightarrow 2 \rightarrow 3 \rightarrow 4$$

In every case, one follows the rule: commence the next sequence with the third element of the first; then take the second element, then the fourth, and then the first. Finally, though, the inside becomes the original outside again, and once more the whole four-element unit constitutes a pure event that, in its circularity, nonetheless ascends with symmetrical wings toward eternity. Messiaen described this way of transposing as like the constant opening and shutting again of fans by a woman.

It should be mentioned that Messiaen was by no means the first Christian composer to deploy modes of retrograde motion for theological purposes. In medieval music such involutions were used to convey a sense of the world as a labyrinth into which the warrior Christ enters, constantly going back upon the traces of human sin in order harmonically to redeem them. This amounted to a musical presentation of the Irenaean notion of "recapitulation."[29] Moreover, in both Messiaen and the tradition, these palindromic devices were associated with magical conjuring formulas, and Messiaen spoke of a "good magic" that concerns the ability of music to invoke the cosmos in a new way and to evoke and alter human emotion. His free deployment of technical devices to these ends can indeed be seen, in the sense that is not mechanical, manipulatory, or sinister, as "theurgic" in character.[30]

Messiaen especially achieved "magical" effects by deploying all three of the fundamental formal techniques in conjunction, and particularly by

29. Craig Wright, *The Maze and the Warrior: Symbols in Architecture, Theology and Music* (Cambridge, MA: Harvard University Press, 2001).

30. See Samuel, *Entretiens*, p. 44: "there exists a good magic. . . ."

blending harmonic vertical palindromic sequences with "neumic" horizontal ones, often in such a way that a relative emphasis on one or the other itself took the form of an alternation between "opening the fan" on the melodic plane and "shutting the fan" on the harmonic one. In the "between" of the motion of this four-dimensional fan (operating in space-time) one hears or sometimes "almost hears," on the diagonal, something that is impossible mathematically to formulate, but yet something not simply stochastically reached out for; rather, it is as if something miraculously descends into time as an echo of the Incarnation, which Messiaen ceaselessly sought to present in his music.

In this way, Messiaen's Thomistic Bergsonianism overcame the "Kantianism" of musical modernism and to this degree anticipated the postmodern, as indicated also by his non-abandonment of a dominant modal tonality and the finality of at least a relative harmony. In affirming by faith the infinite beauty and so "compose-ability" of the cosmos, Messiaen had to deny that being is the violence of forgetting, or the constant leaving-behind of that which cannot be blended with what is to come. On the contrary, if there is beauty and order, then even the non-identically repeated must be beautiful in reverse, thereby constituting the palindromic sequence that can happen only "once" (1,2,1) and in moving backward still moves forward, but just in this respect as pure event is also entirely reversible and so intimates eternity beyond time.

Messiaen's blending of the thematic of "difference" or continuous permutation with a Thomistic metaphysics of eternity and time, which doubles the ontology of the real distinction, also suggests a "postmodern" element in his Catholic reflection that is absent from Gilson and Maritain (except for the latter's reflection on sign). Although this thematic was Bergsonian, and therefore in reality lay at the heart of modernism itself, Messiaen already gave it a postmodern twist by insisting that *durée* is mediated through spatial placement. Later, officially "postmodern" philosophy and art, however, have tended to view such mediation as an aporetic obscuration of that *durée* which it nonetheless discloses in its own inevitable self-deconstruction. In this way the sublimity of Bergsonian duration is newly sustained as continuous tensional violence. By contrast, Messiaen's musical presentation of difference as beauty through the deployment of devices of return is an argument for the harmony between eternity and time that distances itself more emphatically from the stochastic negativity of the pure modernists. In a certain sense, Messiaen was already more postmodern than the postmodernists, even if this verdict is somewhat problematic, as we shall later see.

Recapitulation?

For all his modalism, refusal of serialism, and final commitment to harmony in music, and for all his practical and theoretical commitment to a nonviolent, non-identical repetition, one cannot entirely describe Messiaen as "postmodern." He was a typical Thomistic modernist; he refused Romantic historicism and subjectivism in favor of formal technique and *claritas*, and he was concerned to reflect permanent natural order via a reflection of eternity rather than engage in a reflection upon history in a narrative idiom. Significantly, Messiaen composed almost no exclusively liturgical, as opposed to contemplative, music. Plainchant, he felt, was the only appropriate musical liturgical language. And apart from the Tristan myth, his music is not concerned in any way with temporal emplotment. Still less, then, does it seek to integrate worldly with divine drama in the fashion of much baroque and post-baroque liturgical music.

One can link this observation with another one. For all his criticism of Bergson and espousal of the idea that continuous variation must be mediated by fixed patterns, Messiaen still favored complex patterns and the mixture of such patterns because he was perhaps haunted by the notion of a stochastic yearning for continuous variation, even if this was for him the eternal music of the Trinity. To be sure, one should not push this observation too far, because Messiaen grasped the essential difficulty of this conception. He realized that non-identical repetition is not pure except in God; for human beings it has to be mixed always with deployment of identically repeated patterns. Or one could say that the mysterious one-to-one analogy of attribution with its unleashed yoking of disparate elements has to be combined with measurable analogy of proportion when one is conjugating the relations of this world, even if attribution is more fundamental and becomes still more so in the yearning toward the eternal.

Nevertheless, Messiaen seemed somewhat to scorn the deployment of simple repeated proportions, affirming that Bach and jazz swamp rhythm with meter and so are "unrhythmical."[31] In contrast to this perspective, it could be claimed that just the use of perpetual identical repetition allows one to spring surprises and exhibit continuous variation, and moreover to do so in a readily hearable and popular manner.

These two observations come together at the point of humanism: the regularly repeated, as in the case of a more regular tonal or modal range, lies

31. Samuel, *Entretiens*, pp. 65-80.

nearer to the capacities of the human voice and untrained ear. For this reason, it is well adapted to *narrative*. Like much modernism, there is something apolitical about Messiaen's music.

At the same time, one does not want to lose the range of Messiaen's new cosmic effects; one could argue that the aim of postmodern music would be to integrate the cosmic and the human, the spatially expansive with the narratively temporal, and the tonal and the repeated with dissonance and continuous variation.

This would mean, though, that some usual characterizations of the postmodern would not hold good of music. It would actually be more humanistic, historicist, and political than the modern. Moreover, in its aim to compose harmoniously, it would be religious and not nihilistic.

But such in fact is arguably the case. John Adams's minimalist use of repetition is often geared to music that boldly confronts the politics of our time: *Nixon in China,* for example, or *The Death of Klinghoffer* (which concerns the Israeli/Palestinian conflict). Other minimalists, such as John Tavener and Arvo Pärt (whose work partially develops the trajectory of Britten), are clearly concerned centrally with the religious realm.

Do they, however, qualify as postmodern? Not really, in the sense of seeking to integrate modernist with premodernist techniques, since modernist techniques are so largely abandoned — sometimes, in Tavener's case, along with all the dramatic, conflictual elements of post-medieval music.

The music that better qualifies did *not* emerge from the neo-liberal West, normally associated with the postmodern. Rather, it emerged from the old communist East in the compositions of Alfred Schnittke, Galina Ustvolskaya, and Sophia Gubaidulina. In Ustvolskaya's music, one has a wedding of yet more extreme dissonance with constant variation of liturgical themes. Indeed, all these composers push musical anguish, stridence, and ugliness to a new level, and yet they dramatically contrast this with the arrival of musical grace. Ustvolskaya makes "Dona nobis pacem" sound forth as peace through a terrible musical screeching.[32] One is reminded here, as James MacMillan says, that before Cecilia was the patron saint of music, it was Job on account of his patience. For, as he likewise says, it is in fact religious faith that exposes the greatest depth of suffering. If there is no ultimate meaning, then suffering is finally meaningless and so is not suffering. Suffering and evil are only terrible because there is good, which,

---

32. Galina Ustvolskaya, CD: *Preludes and Compositions,* Oleg Malov, The St Petersburg Soloists (Ghent: Megadisc, 1994).

to be good, must be more final than evil. Messiaen made a similar point, citing Ernest Hello: "the abyss of death must show death so that the abyss of height can show above itself life."[33] Yet the sense of a dramatic passage through death and evil on this earth is not strongly present in the French composer.

By contrast, the retrieval of a more tonal, regular (sometimes minimalist), narrative element in these composers permits this expression of suffering and its dramatic resolution or problematic semi-resolution. In the case of the German-Russian Schnittke, this is paradigmatically shown in his piece for violin and orchestra *Quasi una Sonata*.[34] Here the development and recapitulation radically break down, but in such a way as to show that any such things are only gestures toward an impossibly complete development and recapitulation (like praying in order to pray).[35] Yet in making such a gesture, somehow the reconciliation is all the more real even if more anguished and temporary.

In his other works, especially thinking of the *concerti grossi*, Schnittke offers a neo-baroque that runs into frenzied Faustian extremes and mixes tonality with atonality and the banality of popular music, which for Schnittke is demonically seductive and yet also somehow beautiful and redeemable.[36] His music always deals (after Thomas Mann) with the appeal of the Faustian lure for absolute musical control and easy aesthetic wealth: it squarely confronts the demonic in order to overcome it and redeem what must remain good in it if it is to be at all. Unsurprisingly, for the listener, one gathers that Schnittke became a Catholic to rescue himself from abysses opened up by involvement in the occult.[37] His music reflects with constant irony, pain, and nostalgia upon the course of human history from the early modern baroque era to the present: the Faustian age.

Sometimes the blend of tonal and atonal in Schnittke seems too constantly ironic and merely juxtaposed, as also in the nonetheless very fine

33. Samuel, *Entretiens*, p. 140.

34. Alfred Schnittke CD: "Quasi una Sonata" on *Concerti Grossi nos 1 and 5*, The Chamber Orchestra of Europe, Gidon Kremer (Hamburg: Deutsche Grammaphon, 1990/3).

35. See Catherine Pickstock, *After Writing: On the Liturgical Consummation of Philosophy* (Oxford: Blackwell, 1997), pp. 167-267.

36. Alfred Schnittke, CD already cited; also *Symphony no 6/Concerto Grosso no 2*, Russian State Symphony Orchestra, Valeri Polyanski (Colchester: Chandos, 2004).

37. Alexander Ivashkin, *Alfred Schnittke* (London: Phaidon, 1996). See also, for discussion of music and magic, Jonathan Harvey, *In Quest of Spirit: Thoughts on Music* (Berkeley: University of California Press, 1999), esp. pp. 171-76, regarding the spell of the palindrome.

work of the Finnish composer Einojuhani Rautavaara.[38] But not always, and certainly not in the music of Ustvolskaya, although in her case the development is of essentially atonal elements. The work of Sofia Gubaidulina also exceeds mere juxtaposition, and moreover develops a complicated theological integration of tonal with atonal elements. Like Messiaen (who continued the French tradition of the deliberately "non-Germanic" referential "symphonic poem," beginning with Saint-Saëns and César Franck), Gubaidulina refuses the "absolute" music of modernism. Her work is replete with the programmatic, from the representation of a tight-rope walker to the use of number symbolism and liturgical allusion. She sees musical rhythmic strategies — legato, pizzicato, glissando, vibrato, col legno, and so forth — as representing diverse spiritual states, and above all she contrasts the uneven and obscure staccato of the quotidian with the legato of the liturgical. The latter, however, emerges in her music only from a complex tensional interplay of different moods: the sensual, the anxious, the mournful, and the courageous in particular, which all offer their own partial "beatitude" and yet require a fusion in a co-incidence of opposites that lies at the heart of religion.

In her piano concerto Introitus, referring to the introductory chant of the Mass in the Roman Catholic liturgy, she conveys this interaction of moods by use of a complex polytonality in alternated succession and combination. The wind instruments play in a microchromatic idiom, often accompanied by pizzicato, to represent the natural restless state of humanity; the strings play a chromatic range to represent existential awareness of the human condition of loneliness and longing. Both of these ranges develop essentially horizontal melodic and rhythmic themes since they are concerned with human life in time. The piano, by contrast, plays in an austere pentatonic mode that conveys ascetic striving to overcome egotism and is concerned with the vertically chordal, expressed by an "iconic" deployment of fifths and major and minor thirds. Finally, all the instruments in combination at times play in a diatonic range to suggest an integration of all these elements of human life within a contrapuntal and surging diagonal, which still exhibits some of the early influence of Shostakovich upon this composer. However, the diatonic attempts at integration, sometimes heralded by a dramatic flurry of ultra-tonal diminished sevenths, keep musically breaking down, and in a rising spiral of intensity it is the pentatonic piano that has continuously to renew the reconciliatory impulse. There is a continuous li-

38. Einojuhani Rautavaara, CD: Piano Concertos nos 2 and 3, Laura Mikkola, Netherlands Radio Symphony Orchestra, Eri Klass (Finland: Warner Chappell, 2002).

turgical process of lapsing, starting again and rising once more to a new but provisional state of peace. In the end, a brightly flickering diatonic resolution dominated by the strings passes over into a prolonged pentatonic piano trill, which gradually diminishes and concludes the work.[39]

Likewise, in some pieces by James MacMillan, for example *Veni, Veni Emmanuel,* one hears a seamless fusion of the tonal, atonal, and percussive. In his case, there is an integration to some degree of Messiaen's use of complex polyrhythm, polydynamics, and polysonority, plus a complex sense of retrogradation and non-retrogradation.[40] His music is Catholic in a way that makes his espoused Catholicism seem almost incidental.

Thus we live in an era of musical hope. Time and space, narrative and simultaneous complex sonority are coming together with the human and the cosmic. A richer diagonal is being composed. A yet more glorious diagonal descends.

39. Sofia Gubaidulina, "Introitus" on CD: *In the Mirror,* Béatrice Rauchs, Vladimir Kozhukhar, Kyiv Chamber Players (Akersberga: BIS Records, 2002).

40. James MacMillan, CD: *Veni, Veni Emmanuel/Tryst,* Colin Currie, Ulster Orchestra, Takuo Yuasa (London: Naxos, 1997).

PART THREE   MUSIC AND THEOLOGY

9. The Integration of Music and Theology in the Vocal Compositions of J. S. Bach

Richard J. Plantinga

New Discoveries and Novel Perspectives

Writing in the mid-1960s, Karl Geiringer prefaced his well-known biography and study of J. S. Bach with the justificatory comment that "BACH [*sic*] research has made spectacular progress in recent years."[1] The second half of the twentieth century witnessed much change in the domain of Bach scholarship, ranging from new discoveries of material to novel perspectives on the historical person and his compositions. These discoveries and perspectives have in turn spawned a series of debates ranging from the seemingly minor (e.g., manuscript dating) to the major (e.g., rethinking the composer's views about music, religion, and life).

This paper will trace the main lines of one of the debates in Bach scholarship, namely, the animated discussion about the relationship between music and theology in Bach, especially in connection with his vocal compositions. Was Bach a pure musician who merely involved himself with things theological because his job, particularly during his Leipzig years (1723-50), demanded it? Or was he really a theologian and churchman who used musical means to express his Lutheran faith? After the music-theology debate as it exists in Bach scholarship has been briefly reviewed, some attention will be paid to the Lutheran theological and musical milieu in which Bach was raised and operated during his highly productive compositional life. There-

1. Karl Geiringer, *Johann Sebastian Bach: The Culmination of an Era* (New York: Oxford University Press, 1966), p. v.

after, the paper will explore one particular theme in Bach's sacred music, namely, his sustained interest in the subject of death. It is a theme he often explored musico-theologically in his passions and cantatas, particularly in the famous funeral cantata "Gottes Zeit ist die allerbeste Zeit" ("God's time is the very best of all times" [BWV 106]). The paper adopts the following line of argument: In much of his vocal music, and exemplarily so in those compositions that deal with death, Bach engaged theology regularly, thoughtfully, and skillfully, crafting compositions in which music and theology form an integrated whole. Implied in this argument is the recognition that Bach's music allows for insightful treatment of theological themes, including death — a subject that tends to provoke discomfort and is often avoided in the contemporary Western world.

The Music-Theology Debate

As every student of music history knows, Bach was not as famous as a composer during his own lifetime as some of his contemporaries. Neither was he renowned as a composer of a wide variety of music during the half a century following his death. Although some of his music was known to the likes of Mozart and Beethoven, it was the nineteenth century that inaugurated what music historian Donald Jay Grout has termed the Bach "resurrection." This resurrection was rooted in a number of factors: the publication of the first Bach biography by J. N. Forkel in 1802; Felix Mendelssohn's revival performance of the *St. Matthew Passion* in 1829; and the founding of the Bach Society in 1850.[2] Following these developments, during the next half century a certain mythical portrait of Bach came into prominence, created chiefly by the German musicologist Philipp Spitta and subsequently embellished by Albert Schweitzer.[3] According to Friedrich Blume, Spitta "turned Bach into the great Lutheran cantor, the retrospective champion of tradition, the orthodox preacher of the Bible and the chorale . . . [fostering] the conception of Bach as supremely the church musician, and the ascendancy of the churchman over the musician."[4] This Spitta-crafted portrait, Blume con-

2. See Donald Jay Grout, *A History of Western Music* (New York: W. W. Norton & Company, 1960), p. 400. See also Malcolm Boyd, *The Master Musicians: Bach* (London: J. M. Dent & Sons, 1983), pp. 209-21.

3. See Friedrich Blume, "Outlines of a New Picture of Bach," *Music and Letters* 44, no. 3 (July 1963): 214.

4. Blume, "Outlines of a New Picture of Bach," p. 216. See also Robin Leaver, *J. S. Bach*

tends, "was considered conclusive and unsurpassable"[5] well into the twentieth century.

In the 1950s, things began to change in Bach scholarship. Working independently of one another in Germany, Alfred Dürr and Georg von Dadelsen came to some surprising and similar conclusions about Bach's compositional chronology. As Dürr himself describes it, a new timeline was produced "based chiefly on research into the watermarks in the paper of the original manuscripts, and on the fact that the various copyists who shared the task of producing those manuscripts can be distinguished by their handwriting."[6] The most important result of the new timeline concerns the dating of the Leipzig church cantatas, most of which were now thought to have been composed in the first several years that Bach was in Leipzig (i.e., beginning in 1723). Gone was the old view that Bach worked on the church cantatas more or less consistently across the decades in Leipzig (i.e., from 1723 until his death in 1750). With this new conception came some rich conjecture. Dürr identifies the ends of the speculative spectrum as represented by the aforementioned Friedrich Blume on the one hand and Friedrich Smend on the other. Of Blume, Dürr writes:

> Blume accepts the new chronology, and concludes that although Bach fulfilled his duties with enthusiasm during his first years at Leipzig, his enthusiasm waned — this indicating that he was by no means so devoted to church work as previous scholars have believed — that indeed, at bottom, he found the duties of the Cantorate distasteful.[7]

---

and Scripture: Glosses from the Calov Bible Commentary (St. Louis: Concordia Publishing House, 1985), pp. 13-14. The Spitta-inspired portrait of Bach as the "fifth evangelist" seems to have taken various forms. The Swedish Lutheran theologian Nathan Söderblom, for example, referred to Bach as the author of "the fifth gospel." See Uwe Siemon-Netto, "J. S. Bach in Japan," *First Things* (June-July 2000): 16. Although she does not specify the origins of the Bach "legend," as she calls it, Joyce Irwin seems to have the Spitta portrait in mind in *Neither Voice nor Heart Alone: German Lutheran Theology of Music in the Age of the Baroque,* American University Studies, Series VII, Theology and Religion, vol. 132 (New York: Peter Lang, 1993), pp. xi, 141, 152.

5. Blume, "Outlines of a New Picture of Bach," p. 215.

6. Alfred Dürr, "New Light on Bach," *The Musical Times* 107, no. 1480 (June 1966): 484. See also Leaver, *J. S. Bach and Scripture,* p. 14; Calvin R. Stapert, *My Only Comfort: Death, Deliverance, and Discipleship in the Music of Bach* (Grand Rapids: Eerdmans, 2000), p. 24.

7. Dürr, "New Light on Bach," p. 484. In Blume's own words: "Did Bach have a special liking for church work? Was it a spiritual necessity for him? Hardly. There is at any rate no evidence that it was. Bach the supreme cantor, the creative servant of the Word of God, the staunch Lutheran, is a legend." "Outlines of a New Picture of Bach," p. 218.

Smend, on the other hand, disputed the propriety of the new chronology, favoring the traditional view that Bach worked steadily on the cantatas over some two and a half decades, and rejected Blume's conclusions. Dürr insightfully notes that the two seemingly diametrically opposed viewpoints have something fundamental in common, namely, the conviction that "a truly Christian church musician would not pack all his compositions into just a few years, but would spread them evenly over the whole of his life — otherwise, it seems, there would be something wrong with his faith, or at least with his vocation."[8]

Anyone holding a traditionalist position like that of Smend could be accused of denying new evidence in order to keep a cherished conviction, in the fashion of a Ptolemist in the face of a Copernican revolution. While the new chronology appears to be indisputable, the radical conclusions that Blume and his ilk have drawn from it are eminently debatable. Such debate has been fostered by the advancement of other theories that seek to account for Bach's compositional waxing and waning. One worthy alternative explanation for Bach's marked drop-off in cantata output is suggested by Robin Leaver, who argues that the change "is more likely to have been caused by the lack of understanding and sympathy on the part of the officialdom in Leipzig."[9] In proposing this theory, Leaver recognizes that Blume forced Bach scholars to ask a key question: "Where is the objective evidence, outside of the internal evidence to be discovered in his choral works, that will demonstrate clearly the composer's Christian faith and commitment?"[10] In answer to his question, Leaver presents some crucial and fascinating evidence, rediscovered but a few years after the publication of Blume's seminal essay. It is

---

8. Dürr, "New Light on Bach," p. 484. Needless to say, some Bach scholars find Blume's portrait attractive, seeing in it material to establish the view that Christianity, Lutheranism, and theology were at best tolerated by Bach as unfortunate grist for his compositional mill. Whether indebted to Blume or not, consider the following words by Lionel Rogg made with reference to Part III of Bach's *Clavierübung* (i.e., the "Deutsche Orgelmesse," BWV 552a, 669-89, and 552b): "The collection of preludes has been thoroughly examined by exegetists [*sic*] in an attempt to reveal the [trinitarian] symbolism of the series. . . . Bach probably never gave as much thought to the illustration or the defence of a religious concept as he did to creating a poetic and contemplative musical work. He is not a preacher who sets out to prove or to convince, but a creative artist, no doubt influenced by his religious background, but predominantly preoccupied with the problems of his art." Lionel Rogg, Accompanying Booklet, J. S. Bach, *Organ Works* (Arles, France: Harmonia Mundi Compact Disc HMX 290772.83, 1999), pp. 68-69.

9. Leaver, *J. S. Bach and Scripture*, p. 14.

10. Leaver, *J. S. Bach and Scripture*, p. 16.

well known that Bach possessed a rather large theological library, which included various works dealing with Scripture and its interpretation, as well as two sets of the works of Martin Luther.[11] After his death, his goods were distributed among his children. Unfortunately, in addition to lost compositions, the entire contents of Bach's library were lost — that is, until 1934, when the first volume of Bach's three-volume set of Abraham Calov's *Die heilige Bibel* (hereafter the Calov Bible Commentary)[12] turned up in Frankenmuth, Michigan. Eventually, the other two volumes were also discovered, and the three volumes were given to Concordia Seminary in St. Louis, Missouri, where they were stored for safekeeping and subsequently misplaced, resurfacing again in the 1960s and displayed at the *Bachfest* in Heidelberg in 1969.[13] Examination of these volumes — the only surviving volumes from Bach's theological library available to scholarship — indicates that Bach was a careful reader of Scripture. In addition to various underlinings in the text, the volumes contain some instructive handwritten comments made by its owner.[14]

In addition to Bach's possession of a respectable theological library, and his markings in the Calov Bible Commentary, there is biographical evidence to be considered. Bach grew up in a very Lutheran part of Germany and studied theology in his youth. Even after his formal schooling ended, he demonstrated an ongoing interest in the subject, evidenced in part by the fact of his theological library.[15] Moreover, Bach successfully sustained theological examinations as a condition of his being awarded the cantorate of the *Thomasschule* in 1723.[16]

In Leaver's terms, the "objective evidence" just briefly reviewed, coupled with the "internal evidence" in Bach's sacred compositions, do seem to demonstrate that Bach had a deep interest in Lutheran Christianity and theology — although judging his personal faith and beliefs remains methodologically difficult. How then should the music-theology relationship be adjudicated

---

11. See Hans T. David and Arthur Mendel, eds., *The New Bach Reader: A Life of Johann Sebastian Bach in Letters and Documents*, rev. and enl. by Christoph Wolff (New York: W. W. Norton & Company, 2000), pp. 253-54.

12. In this work, the text of Scripture is accompanied by commentary, mostly by Luther and occasionally by Calov. By virtue of his possession of the Calov Bible Commentary, Bach owned another substantial collection of Luther's writings.

13. See Leaver, *J. S. Bach and Scripture*, pp. 16-21.

14. See Leaver, *J. S. Bach and Scripture, passim.*

15. See Stapert, *My Only Comfort*, pp. 7-9.

16. See David and Mendel, eds., *The New Bach Reader*, p. 105.

in Bach's case? Perhaps it would be helpful at this juncture to construct a continuum, with two extreme postures and one mediating stance:

> Position 1: Bach was first and foremost a pure musician who had no real interest in theology. He engaged theology, which remained extrinsic to his work as a composer, only for the sake of necessity.
>
> Position 2: Bach was first and foremost a musician whose engagement with theology was deliberate, sustained, and carefully designed. Theology was intrinsic to much of his work as a composer, and the relationship between music and theology can well be described as a harmonious whole.
>
> Position 3: Bach was first and foremost a Christian theologian. In his work as a composer, he used music as a means of expressing theological positions.

To review the strengths and weaknesses of each position[17] briefly, it might be observed that Positions 1 and 3 bear respective resemblance to Blume's position and the Spitta mythical portrait. Position 1 seems unnecessarily one-sided, agenda-laden, and willful in its refusal to engage certain bodies of evidence now available to scholarship. It also has the weight of much internal evidence against it. Position 3 seems blinded by prejudgments, which make it unable to engage other bodies of evidence available to scholarship. It seems rather more hagiographical than historical. If Bach's sense of his own vocation was to compose music (both instrumental and vocal) to the glory of God, that sense of calling does not make him a traditional practitioner of theology (*fides quaerens intellectum*) comparable to Augustine, Anselm, Aquinas, Luther, or Calvin. It would seem that Position 2 has much to say for it, as it takes account of the objective evidence, as it was reviewed above and as the paper will further present below ("Bach and Lutheranism"). Position 2 also has much internal evidence in its favor, a sample of which can be found below ("Bach's Musico-Theological Conception of Death"). In order to bolster the case for Position 2 and the general argument of this essay, the discussion now turns to an examination of Bach's eighteenth-century Lutheran context.

---

17. One could easily add more mediating positions between 1 and 3 above, but so doing would take the present discussion too far afield and beyond the necessary limitations of space.

Bach and Lutheranism

Bach's orthodox Lutheranism steeped him in a tradition centered on Scripture. It was Luther's study of Scripture, after all, that allowed him to see God not solely as the awesome and terrible judge but also as the gracious God who justifies sinners through faith in Christ.[18] It is through Christ alone that the demanding and righteous God can be known as loving and forgiving. For Luther, therefore, Christ's atoning death on the cross is fundamental, insofar as the cross is the event where Christ graciously justified a sinful humanity that could not justify itself. Luther thus regarded the work of Christ on the cross both as satisfying divine righteousness and as effecting the ransom of fettered sinners — and central to this work is the resurrection on Easter Sunday.[19]

Given Lutheranism's high regard for Scripture, it is not surprising that Bach was a careful Bible reader.[20] As a premodern reader of the Bible, Bach did not read the text historically-critically (i.e., diachronically), as many moderns are disposed to do. Rather, he would have been inclined to read the text rather literally (i.e., synchronically) as realistic narrative. A narrative approach emphasizes typology; that is, it sees characters in the text as representatives or symbolic figures — and none more so than Christ. As Hans Frei argues, such an approach to the text of Scripture was favored by Luther and Calov, from whom Bach took his most important clues and hermeneutical

18. For a general summary of Luther's theology, see Bernhard Lohse, *Martin Luther's Theology: Its Historical and Systematic Development*, trans. and ed. Roy A. Harrisville (Minneapolis: Fortress Press, 1999). On the teachings of Lutheranism in its formative stage, see *The Book of Concord: The Confessions of the Evangelical Lutheran Church*, ed. Robert Kolb and Timothy J. Wengert, trans. Charles Arand et al. (Minneapolis: Fortress Press, 2000). For a general description of the Lutheran tradition and its significance for Bach, see Robin A. Leaver, "Music and Lutheranism," in *The Cambridge Companion to Bach*, ed. John Butt (Cambridge: Cambridge University Press, 1997), pp. 35-45.

19. The Christian tradition articulated the work of Christ with the use of different atonement theories. Of these theories, two are of importance for Bach, as they were for Luther. The classical or ransom theory, which came into prominence in Patristic Christianity, holds that Christ died on the cross in order to free sinners in bondage to sin, death, and the devil. The satisfaction theory, which came into prominence in the Middle Ages via St. Anselm, holds that Christ died on the cross in order to meet the demands of divine justice and righteousness. See "Atone; Atonement," in *The International Standard Bible Encyclopedia*, rev. ed., ed. G. W. Bromiley, vol. 1 (Grand Rapids: Eerdmans, 1979). On Luther's view of the work of Christ, see Lohse, *Martin Luther's Theology*, pp. 223-28.

20. See Leaver, *J. S. Bach and Scripture, passim.*

RICHARD J. PLANTINGA

strategies as a Bible reader.[21] In the New Testament in particular, the pre-
modern, orthodox Lutheran Bible reader would recognize the significance
of the paradigmatic second Adam — that is, Christ — the representative of
humanity who died for and justified all humanity.

Basic Lutheran teachings formed the bedrock of the theological world
in which Bach was born, raised, and worked.[22] But it was not theology
alone that made Lutheranism a hospitable environment for Bach's genius.
Among the Protestant Reformers of the sixteenth century, Luther stands
out for his devotion to music, which he regarded as a good gift from God.
Consider the following comments, drawn from various places in Luther's
corpus: "[m]usic is the greatest gift of God which has often induced and
inspired me to preach"; "next to the Word of God, music deserves the
highest praise"; "except for theology there is no art that could be put on
the same level as music."[23] With his radical theological ideas and exalted
estimate of music, Luther in the 1520s undertook a reform of the Roman
Catholic liturgy for the fledgling community which he led. In so doing,
Luther specified that worshipers should sing hymns, some of which he
himself adapted or wrote.[24] One of the chief factors in the general development of Protestant sacred music in Germany before the time of Bach,
then, is the theology of Luther. In particular, Luther's view of Scripture is
key, as Alfred Dürr notes: "The conviction that God's Word, as laid down
in the Bible, is dead and ineffectual unless it is proclaimed, that everything
depends on making it current, increasingly resulted in a new orientation
for church music."[25]

While there is not a straight line from Luther to Bach, and while the tradition that bears Luther's name did not develop a theology of music in a debate-

21. See Hans Frei, *The Eclipse of Biblical Narrative: A Study in Eighteenth and Nineteenth Century Hermeneutics* (New Haven: Yale University Press, 1974), pp. 19-25, 37-39. See also Eric Chafe, *Tonal Allegory in the Vocal Music of J. S. Bach* (Berkeley: University of California Press, 1991), pp. 10-19; Eric Chafe, *Analyzing Bach Cantatas* (New York: Oxford University Press, 2000), pp. 3-22.

22. Lutheran theological teachings can be seen in many of Bach's cantatas. Especially illustrative is Cantata 9 ("Es ist das Heil uns kommen her"/"Now to us salvation is come"),
which emphasizes sin, the need for justification, and the relationship between law and gospel. For the text, see http://www.bach-cantatas.com/.

23. Martin Luther cited in Leaver, "Music and Lutheranism," pp. 40-41.

24. See Leaver, "Music and Lutheranism," pp. 42-45. See also Frank C. Senn, *Christian Liturgy: Catholic and Evangelical* (Minneapolis: Fortress Press, 1997), pp. 267-98.

25. Alfred Dürr, *The Cantatas of J. S. Bach*, rev. and trans. Richard D. P. Jones (Oxford: Oxford University Press, 2005), p. 3.

free fashion,[26] there are unmistakable continuities between Luther's sixteenth-century Wittenberg and Bach's eighteenth-century Leipzig. In addition to the Lutheran theological and musical matters reviewed above, there is the matter of the Lutheran liturgical calendar, itself a theological device of which Bach was expected to avail himself. After arriving in Leipzig in May 1723, therefore, the new cantor of the Thomasschule planned cycles *(Jahrgänge)* of cantatas organized around the liturgical calendar, beginning four Sundays before Advent and ending as late as twenty-seven Sundays after Trinity. Well-schooled as he was in the biblical text and Christian theology, including the Lutheran leitmotif of the theology of the cross, the Christocentric Bach centered his focus in the Lutheran liturgical calendar on Good Friday. The magisterial passions that he composed for this day of days in the church year reflect Bach's sense of Christianity's epicenter. His passions should thus be regarded as the foundation (i.e., speaking not compositionally-chronologically but theologically) for his musico-theological conception of death, to which the discussion now turns.

Bach's Musico-Theological Conception of Death

Before turning to Bach's Christian conception of death, the general subject of death in modernity and pre-modernity needs to be briefly addressed, for modern persons encountering pre-modern conceptions of death often find themselves startled, puzzled, and even somewhat affronted. From the perspective of modernity, to encounter pre-modernity, with its non-cosmetic and often very religious conception of death, is to enter another universe. As a bridge to that universe from one rather more contemporary and familiar, Philippe Ariès's *Western Attitudes Toward Death* merits traversal.

In his classic study, Ariès characterizes the stance of the twentieth-century West on the topic of death as a radical departure from the centuries that preceded it. Whereas in earlier times, death was regarded as an ineluctable part of the order of being, to which humanity had to and did resign itself, death in the twentieth-century West became — and this is Ariès's key

---

26. On the complex developments relating to the theology of music in seventeenth- and eighteenth-century Lutheranism, see Irwin, *Neither Voice nor Heart Alone, passim.* See also Senn, *Christian Liturgy,* pp. 323-56. Interestingly, just as *The Book of Concord* warns against certain errors in Calvinist Christology (see, e.g., Article VIII of "The Epitome" of the "Formula of Concord" [*The Book of Concord,* pp. 508ff]), so too was fear of and opposition to Calvinism a key factor in the development of a Lutheran theology of music in the late sixteenth and seventeenth centuries. See Irwin, *Neither Voice nor Heart Alone,* pp. 11-22.

descriptor — "forbidden."[27] Death occurred not at home, as in times gone by, but at the hospital. At the moment of death, one was no longer necessarily surrounded by loved ones, including children, but more likely by technology dedicated to biological prolongation. Care for and disposal of the body was not conducted by families or small communities but rather managed by professionals, who make the embalmed departed look as alive as possible. Indeed, Ariès argues, in the twentieth century the subject of death was suppressed and rigorously censored; in other words, death has become a virtual pornography in the West.[28] Ariès roots this changed modern attitude to death in developments in America and England. Especially in the case of the former, which declared in its charter document its dedication to the pursuits of life, liberty, and happiness,[29] death became a first-order problem, having three strikes against it, for it is the obvious contradiction of life, rather constricting of liberty, and generally incongruent with happiness. Accordingly, the modern, Western world would seem to require not just a well thought out view of death, a *thanatology*, but an articulate and reasoned justification of death, a *thanatodicy*. Such, however, is conspicuously lacking in the West's public discourse, although private religious traditions have always offered and continue to offer philosophies and theologies of death. But in democratic societies, these remain emphatically private.

Given this interdict on the subject and reality of death in the contemporary West, it is not surprising that the modern person encountering the works of the decidedly pre-modern J. S. Bach may find him- or herself confused and perhaps even offended. One need spend but a little time with the music of Bach, especially his sacred music, in order to be impressed at the *absence* of interdict on the subject of death. Bach was clearly not uncomfortable with the topic of death or uneasy about the presence and reality of death. Indeed, as many commentators have noted, he seemed to be preoccupied, even obsessed, with it.[30] Moreover, his attitude toward death was any-

27. See Philippe Ariès, *Western Attitudes Toward Death: From the Middle Ages to the Present*, trans. Patricia M. Ranum (Baltimore: Johns Hopkins University Press, 1974), pp. 84-107.

28. Instructive in this regard is the great reversal in the case of children, who were once *not* protected from the specter of death but who were sheltered from the mysterious and powerful realm of human sexuality. Today's children are alarmingly literate and sometimes distressingly practiced in matters pertaining to sex, but tend to be rigorously shielded from the reality of death.

29. See the American "Declaration of Independence" (http://www.constitution.org/usdeclar.htm).

30. See Jaroslav Pelikan, *Bach Among the Theologians* (Philadelphia: Fortress Press,

thing but forbidden. In fact, Bach's posture in the face of death often seems rather compliant.

Ariès characterizes the predominant pre-modern attitude to death with the descriptor "tamed."[31] In times now long past, people approaching the end of their lives sensed that death was near, resigned themselves to it, prepared for it in ritual fashion, were attended by family and friends, and were finally laid to rest ceremonially but without great emotion or sense of tragedy. Ariès writes: "death was both familiar and near, evoking no great fear or awe."[32] This attitude toward death involved the attendant belief that death did not mean annihilation but sleep *(requies, dormitio)*, that is, a sleep which "presupposed a survivial [*sic*]."[33] Ariès argues that this attitude toward death persisted at least until the dawn of Romanticism. As a general characteristic of an age, then, it well fits the time of Bach in which "literature and art about death experienced phenomenal growth."[34] It also sums up the general attitude of Bach himself. In fact, in *Western Attitudes Toward Death*, Ariès cites Bach's own death on 28 July 1750 as an instance of "tamed death."[35]

Bach's tamed view of death was funded by at least two sources, namely, his orthodox Lutheran Christianity and his own experience. With respect to the latter, it bears pointing out that Bach was orphaned by the age of ten. It is also worth recalling that, as an adult, he lost his first wife and laid to rest several of his own children.[36] But such frequent grim reaping was not unprecedented in the seventeenth and eighteenth centuries and does not alone, it would seem, explain Bach's rather conciliatory view of death, which could even come to irreverent expression, as in the famous complaint once made

1986), p. 12. Further on Bach's attitude to death and the *ars moriendi,* see David Yearsley, *Bach and the Meanings of Counterpoint* (Cambridge: Cambridge University Press, 2002), pp. 1-41.

31. See Ariès, *Western Attitudes Toward Death,* pp. 1-25.

32. Ariès, *Western Attitudes Toward Death,* p. 13. Yearsley, however, indicates that death presented even orthodox Lutheran believers with hesitation and fear. See Yearsley, *Bach and the Meanings of Counterpoint,* pp. 6-7.

33. Ariès, *Western Attitudes Toward Death,* p. 104.

34. Pelikan, *Bach Among the Theologians,* p. 68.

35. See Ariès, *Western Attitudes Toward Death,* p. 6. Bach's attitude toward death, it might be argued, speaks to a modern culture too often in denial of death (an assessment that also seems to be true of much modern Christianity). Bach's view of death as expressed in his church music may thus be seen to function apologetically, as a therapeutic corrective that promotes engagement with a topic under prohibition.

36. See Christoph Wolff, *Johann Sebastian Bach: The Learned Musician* (New York: W. W. Norton, 2000), pp. 211, 396-98.

by Bach that not enough people were dying in Leipzig, depriving the music director of income normally earned at funerals.[37]

With respect to the Christian source of Bach's view of death, it is instructive to consider how Lutheran theological themes come to expression in his two surviving "oratorio passions," namely, the *St. Matthew Passion* and the *St. John Passion*.[38] Expressed in the first and final choral compositions that frame the *St. Matthew Passion*, that is, in the call to lament (No. 1) which opens it ("Kommt, ihr Töchter, helft mir klagen"/"Come you daughters, help me cry out") and in the declaration of teary devotion at the foot of the cross (No. 68) which ends it ("Wir setzen uns mit Tränen nieder"/"We here remain with tears") — and everything in between — Bach intends to summon up three responses in his listener: compassion (i.e., literal "suffering with" Christ in the face of his suffering);[39] conviction (i.e., of sin, which leads to death, and the consequent need for redemption); and imitation (i.e., cross-bearing). In other words, in eminent Lutheran fashion, Bach seeks to underscore the cost of human redemption *vis-à-vis* sin and to create a keen awareness of what Christ has undertaken on behalf of humanity. But he also endeavors to emphasize the importance of dying — and ultimately of rising — with Christ. How Bach connects the paradigmatic death of Christ with individual human death can be seen in the *St. Matthew Passion* in Bach's response to Jesus' last words. After the evangelist sings in No. 61 that Christ cried out and departed, Bach's immediate response is a chorale — a communal confession of faith[40] — which utilizes the melody of the famous passion chorale "O Haupt voll Blut und Wunden"/"O Sacred Head Now Wounded" (No. 62: "Wenn ich einmal soll scheiden"/"When I shall once depart"):

37. See David and Mendel, eds., *The New Bach Reader*, p. 152.

38. Unlike many of his fellow eighteenth-century composers, who set the events of Good Friday to music employing a poetic rendering of Scripture (i.e., the "passion oratorio"), in both the *St. Matthew Passion* and the *St. John Passion*, Bach used the actual words of the Gospel in question interspersed with chorales and arias (i.e., the "oratorio passion"). See Gerardus van der Leeuw, *Bachs Johannes Passion* (Amsterdam: Uitgeversmaatschappij Holland, 1946), pp. 10-13; Stapert, *My Only Comfort*, pp. 34-35. For the texts of Bach's vocal works referred to in the following, see the "Bach Cantatas Website" (http://www.bach-cantatas.com/).

39. *Affektenlehre* (doctrine of the affects) in baroque music sought to coordinate certain styles and types of music with human emotions and passions. See "Affections (affects), doctrine of," in *The New Harvard Dictionary of Music*, ed. D. M. Randel (Cambridge, MA: The Belknap Press of Harvard University Press, 1986); Claude V. Palisca, *Baroque Music* (Englewood Cliffs, NJ: Prentice-Hall, 1968), pp. 3-6.

40. See Gerardus van der Leeuw, *Bach's Matthaeuspassion*, 3rd ed. (Amsterdam: Uitgeversmaatschappij Holland, 1941), pp. 36-39, 41.

(Chor)	(Choir)
Wenn ich einmal soll scheiden,	When I shall once depart,
So scheide nicht von mir,	Depart not from me,
Wenn ich den Tod soll leiden,	When I shall suffer death
So tritt du denn herfür!	Then come and stand by me!
Wenn mir am allerbängsten	When the greatest fear
Wird um das Herze sein,	Shall surround my heart,
So reiß mich aus den Ängsten	So tear me from my fears
Kraft deiner Angst und Pein!	By the power of your fear and pain![41]

In the remainder of the work, Bach follows the post-mortem passion narrative in the Gospel of Matthew and then points out the connection between the two Adams in No. 64, and in so doing shows himself to be a good Pauline, Augustinian Lutheran: "Am Abend, da es kühle war, Ward Adams Fallen offenbar; Am Abend drücket ihn der Heiland nieder"/"In the evening, when it was cool, [the first] Adam's fall was made manifest; In the evening the Savior [the second Adam] overpowered it"). Bach ends the work with the believer clinging to the cross and calling to Christ in the grave, wishing him rest. Interestingly, there is no obvious indication of resurrection at the end of the *St. Matthew Passion*. This absence may well be rooted in the satisfaction theory of the atonement which the *St. Matthew Passion* embodies.[42] The satisfaction theory has a relatively lower estimate of the resurrection than the ransom theory of the atonement, which comes to expression in the *St. John Passion*,[43] and to which the discussion now turns.

In reflecting on the cosmic significance of Christ's death in the *St. John Passion*, Bach reflects cosmic themes in the Gospel of John itself. Bach begins this work (No. 1) with a threefold cry addressed to the Lord *(Herr)*, asking to be shown that even in suffering and lowliness, Christ will be shown to be the glorified and triumphant Son of the triune God. Here Bach hints at the ransom theory of the atonement, which emphasizes Christ's defeat of the powers of sin, evil, and death — a point Bach makes at various junctures in the *St. John Passion*. When he comes to the point in the narrative in the Gospel of John where Christ speaks his final words, Bach writes a most moving aria for alto on the last words spoken by Christ, accompanied by a sole, mournful viola da gamba (No. 30: "Es ist vollbracht"/"It is finished"). In this lament, there is a

---

41. Translations, aimed at literal accuracy, are my own.
42. See Pelikan, *Bach Among the Theologians*, pp. 89-101.
43. See Pelikan, *Bach Among the Theologians*, pp. 102-15.

sudden shift (tempo, dynamics) to the theme of triumph ("Der Held aus Juda siegt mit Macht"/"Judea's hero conquers with power"), consistent with the ransom theory of the atonement, and then a return to the lament. Then the evangelist declares that Christ bowed his head and departed. Here Bach masterfully pauses for a moment of deeply searching *individual* theological reflection accompanied by background choral singing (cf. the purely *communal* response of the *St. Matthew Passion*) dominated by a single, deep voice. In an aria for bass with choir, he indicates the intimate relation between the death of the incarnate Son of God and the deaths of all sons and daughters of God, and in so doing, he asks his own central question concerning the "last enemy" (1 Cor. 15:26), which is answered by the bowed head of the voiceless, crucified Christ — an image that Bach movingly reads as an affirmative answer to his line of questioning, to his faith in search of understanding (No. 32):

(Baß)
Mein teurer Heiland, laß dich fragen,
Da du nunmehr ans Kreuz geschlagen
Und selbst gesaget: Es ist vollbracht
Bin ich vom Sterben frei gemacht?
Kann ich durch deine Pein und Sterben
Das Himmelreich ererben?
Ist aller Welt Erlösung da?
Du kannst vor Schmerzen zwar nichts
    sagen,
Doch neigest du das Haupt
Und sprichst stillschweigend: "Ja!"

(Bass)
My precious Savior let me ask you,
Now that you are nailed to the cross
And yourself said: It is fulfilled
Am I now from death made free?
Can I through your pain and death
Inherit the kingdom of heaven?
Is all the world's salvation here?
You cannot even speak because of
    pain,
Yet you bow your head
And speak silently: "Yes!"

(Chor)
Jesu, du der warest tot,
Lebest nun ohn' Ende,
In der letzten Todesnot
Nirgend mich hinwende,
Als zu dir, der mich versühnt.
O mein trauter Herre!
Gib mir nur, was du verdient,
Mehr ich nicht begehre.

(Choir)
Jesus, you who were dead
Live now without end,
In the final despair of death
Never turn me anywhere,
But to you, who reconciles me.
O my faithful Lord!
Give me only what you have earned,
More I do not ask.

In the rest of the work, Bach completes his musical account of the passion narrative in the Gospel of John, emphasizing the cosmic proportions in the event that has unfolded and the sorrow of the believer in witnessing the death of Christ. He ends the *St. John Passion* with a theology of hope, in which there is a clear reference to the idea of resurrection. In the concluding movement (No. 40: "Ach Herr, laß dein lieb Engelein"/"O Lord, let your dear little angel") the text expresses a desire for the soul to be carried to Abraham's bosom, there to await awakening from death — a clear indicator of the Christian view that Christ's death *finally* (but only finally) spells the end of all death. In other words, Christ's resurrection guarantees the believer's resurrection.

The theological connection between Christ's death and resurrection and the believer's death and resurrection is also emphasized by Bach in what might be thought of as his *Summa Theologiae* in miniature, the *Mass in B Minor*.[44] In the Credo, his setting of the Nicene Creed, the Christocentric Bach depicts the mystery of the incarnation and laments the crucifixion, which Bach places at the very center of the Credo. The piece ends almost inaudibly. After a short moment of silence, he releases all the forces at his disposal and bursts out with *Et resurrexit:*

(Coro)	(Choir)
Et resurrexit tertia die	And the third day he rose again
secundum scripturas,	according to the scriptures,
et ascendit in coelum,	and ascended into heaven,
sedet ad dexteram	and sits at the right hand of
Dei Patris,	God the Father,
et iterum venturus est cum gloria	and he shall come again with glory
judicare vivos et mortuos,	to judge the living and the dead,
cuius regni non erit finis.	whose kingdom shall have no end.

When he ends the Credo with *Et expecto resurrectionem* ("And I look for the resurrection of the dead"), Bach clearly seeks to remind the listener of the connection between Christ's death and resurrection and the believer's own,[45] for the second part of this choral movement is melodically similar to

44. Although he assembled the *Mass in B Minor* near the end of his life, Bach worked on different parts of it at various points in his long compositional career. That said, it must be emphasized here that it is not the *compositional* order of things (i.e., order of composition and compositional type) but the *theological* order of things for Bach (i.e., Christocentrism that moves from paradigmatic divine realities to the human condition) that provides the structure for this section of the paper.

45. In this connection, also worthy of consideration is Cantata 4 ("Christ lag in

and composed in the same key as the *Et resurrexit*. And like *Et resurrexit*, the instrumentation of *Et expecto resurrectionem*'s second part prominently features trumpets and tympani:[46]

(Coro)	(Choir)
Et expecto resurrectionem	And I look for the resurrection of the dead
et vitam venturi saeculi,	and the life of the world to come.
amen.	Amen.

With his foundational Christological conception of death, then, Bach in his cantatas explores this sad vale in which Christians continue to dwell throughout history, church year after church year.[47] Given the different seasons of the church and of life itself, it is not surprising that one finds a variety of themes emphasized in Bach's cantatas. These range from the uncommon but nonetheless occasionally at hand theme of terror at the prospect of judgment that follows death, as in Cantatas 20 and 60 ("O Ewigkeit, du Donnerwort"/"O eternity, you thunderous word") to the more common and generally prevalent cluster of themes that focus on resignation, world-weariness, peacefulness, and even embrace, as expressed in the titles of the following cantatas:

8 ("Liebster Gott, wenn wird ich sterben?"/"Dearest God, when will I die?")

Todesbanden"/"Christ lay in the bonds of death"), an Easter Sunday cantata composed by Bach in his early twenties that seeks to connect Christ's death on Good Friday and the resurrection on Easter Sunday. This work's text and main melody are both by Luther. Drawing on St. Paul in 1 Corinthians 15:54-55 (death has been swallowed up in victory and lost its sting), Luther and Bach in the fourth and fifth verses of the text mock death on the basis of Christ's victory over it in the resurrection. Bach emphasizes the point of Christ's defeat of death with musical laughter, repeating the syllable "Ha" in "Hallelujah" and referring to death as a "mockery" ("Spott"). Because death was theologically laughable for Bach, he did not seem to fear it, avoid it as a subject of discussion, or refer to it with hushed tones of respect.

46. See Chafe, *Tonal Allegory*, pp. 82-83; Pelikan, *Bach Among the Theologians*, pp. 125-27; Stapert, *My Only Comfort*, pp. 96-101; George B. Stauffer, *Bach: The Mass in B Minor — the Great Catholic Mass* (New Haven: Yale University Press, 2003), pp. 125-44.

47. The *St. John Passion* was first performed in 1724 and the *St. Matthew Passion* in 1727 — that is, after the composition of many of the sacred cantatas. To argue, therefore, that the passions form a foundation for Bach is to make a theological claim — and not a compositional, chronological one. In other words, Bach's theology of the cross can be regarded as foundational, even if he had not yet expressed it musico-theologically. See note 44.

27 ("Wer weiß, wie nahe mir mein Ende"/"Who knows how close to me is my end")

72 ("Alles nur nach Gottes Willen"/"Everything only according to God's will")

73 ("Herr, wie du willt, so schick's mit mir"/"Lord, as you will, so let it be with me")

82 ("Ich habe genug"/"I have had enough")

95 ("Christus, der ist mein Leben"/"Christ, who is my life")

125 ("Mit Fried und Freud ich fahr dahin"/"With peace and joy I travel hence")

156 ("Ich stehe mit einem Fuß im Grabe"/"I stand with one foot in the grave")

161 ("Komm', du süße Todesstunde"/"Come, you sweet hour of death").

Citing Albert Schweitzer, Alec Robertson expresses Bach's characteristic attitude toward death as follows:

> How can it be doubted . . . that Bach's whole thought was transfigured by "a wonderful, serene longing for death? Again and again, whenever the text affords the least pretext for it, he gives voice to this longing in his music; and nowhere else is his musical speech so moving as in the cantatas in which he discourses on the release of the body from death."[48]

The particular expressions of this cluster of thanatological themes in Bach's cantatas are numerous, which is not surprising, for as Robertson estimates, at least twenty of Bach's cantatas deal centrally with death, and many more touch on the matter in one fashion or another.[49] Perhaps no better example of Bach's fundamental attitude toward death can be found than in what might be his best known cantata on the theme of death, Cantata 106 ("Gottes Zeit ist die allerbeste Zeit"/"God's time is the very best of all times"), composed for a funeral by Bach during his Mühlhausen years when he was but in his early twenties. The work would be a masterpiece if written by a mature composer; the fact of Bach's relative youth and inexperience as a cantata composer makes the *Actus Tragicus,* the other name by which Cantata 106 is known, a musico-theological marvel.

The internal evidence indicates that Cantata 106 was very carefully and

48. Alec Robertson, *Requiem: Music of Mourning and Consolation* (New York: Frederick A. Praeger, 1967), p. 201.

49. See Robertson, *Requiem,* pp. 183-201.

expertly designed. Accordingly, it lends itself to investigation on a variety of levels, and eminently so on the level of musico-theological analysis, as Eric Chafe has demonstrated.[50] The origin of its text, whether assembled by Bach (and perhaps partly written by him) or prepared by an anonymous librettist, remains unknown. Unlike the texts of many of Bach's later cantatas, especially the Leipzig cycles, the text of Cantata 106 contains no recitatives or arias; it is a "pre-Neumeister" cantata type.[51] Its greater part consists of biblical quotations assembled to illustrate the Lutheran theme of "death under the Law and death under the Gospel."[52] Its alternate title (or superscription), *Actus Tragicus*, is a Latin translation of the German *Trauerspiel* (tragedy play), a form of German drama in the seventeenth century which engaged in "'mourning' over the human condition."[53] From a Christian point of view, and particularly a Lutheran one, the desperate human plight as depicted by the *Trauerspiel* cannot be overcome by humanity on its own; for reversal of its tragic fall and fortunes, God must act, and human beings must have faith in God's action. As Luther expressed it in his commentary on Psalm 90: "The Law says 'In the midst of life we are in death' and the Gospel answers 'In the midst of death we are in life.'"[54] This chiasm[55] (life-death-death-life) finds expression in Cantata 106's text (and shape — see below), which, after its introduction of subject (instrumentally in No. 1 and textually in No. 2a) moves through the history of redemption in three stages — the Old Testament (the

50. On the following analysis of Cantata 106, see Eric Chafe, *Tonal Allegory in the Vocal Music of J. S. Bach*, esp. ch. 4 ("The 'Actus Tragicus'"). In this complex volume, Chafe "considers the figurative use of tonality and its association with theology in the music of J. S. Bach" (p. vii). Of his general approach, he writes: "Put simply, change of key within many cantatas reflects or allegorizes the spiritual development, its relation to established doctrine, personal experience, and the like. As such, it often introduces design of a kind that is relatively unfamiliar to modern listeners, who have assimilated post-eighteenth-century tonal theory and a more secular outlook" (p. viii). See also Chafe's *Analyzing Bach Cantatas*, where he continues with the line of thinking begun in *Tonal Allegory*. For the score of Cantata 106, see Johann Sebastian Bach, *Neue Ausgabe Sämtlicher Werke*, Series I, vol. 34 (Kassel: Bärenreiter, 1986), pp. 1-40.
51. See Dürr, *The Cantatas of J. S. Bach*, pp. 6, 758-65.
52. Dürr, *The Cantatas of J. S. Bach*, p. 760.
53. Chafe, *Tonal Allegory*, p. 94.
54. Martin Luther cited in Chafe, *Tonal Allegory*, p. 96.
55. A chiasm is a symmetrical device that hinges on a center point, in the pattern "abcba." The Christocentric Bach often used chiastic structures in his sacred compositions, for, among other reasons, the fact that in Greek the term "chiasm" begins with the Greek chi (χ) as does the name Christ (χριστος/*Christos*). The resemblance of the Greek χ (capital X) to the cross was also likely not lost on Bach.

old covenant, the time of the law, before Christ); the New Testament (the new covenant, the time of the gospel, the coming of Christ); and the Christian Church (the time of faith, between the two comings of Christ):

No. 1 Sonatina (flauto dolce I/II, viola da gamba I/II, continuo)

No. 2a (Chor und Soli)   (Choir and Soloists)
Gottes Zeit ist die allerbeste Zeit.   God's time is the very best time.
In ihm leben, weben und sind wir,   In him we live, move and have our
  [Acts 17:28]   being,
Solange er will.   as long as he wills.
In ihm sterben wir zur rechten Zeit,   In him we die at the proper time,
wenn er will.   when he wills.

No. 2b (Arioso — Tenor)   (Arioso — Tenor)
Ach Herr, lehre uns bedenken,   O Lord, teach us,
Daß wir sterben müssen,   that we must die,
auf daß wir klug werden. [Psalm 90:12]   in order that we may become wise.

No. 2c (Arie — Baß)   (Aria — Bass)
Bestelle dein Haus;   Set your house in order;
denn du wirst sterben   for you will die,
und nicht lebendig bleiben. [Isaiah 38:1]   and not remain living.

No. 2d (Chor)   (Choir)
Es ist der alte Bund: It is the old covenant:
Mensch, du mußt sterben! [Sirach 14:17]   Man, you must die!
(Arioso — Sopran)   (Arioso — Soprano)
Ja, komm, Herr Jesu! [Revelation 22:20]   Yes, come, Lord Jesus!

No. 3a (Arioso — Altus)   (Arioso — Alto)
In deine Hände befehl ich meinen   Into your hands I commend my
  Geist;   spirit;
du hast mich erlöset,   you have redeemed me,
Herr, du getreuer Gott. [Psalm 31:5]   Lord, you faithful God.

No. 3b (Arioso — Bass)   (Arioso — Bass)
Heute wirst du mit mir im   Today you will be with me in
  Paradies sein. [Luke 23:43]   Paradise.

(Choral — Chor-Alt)	(Choral — Choir-Alto)
Mit Fried und Freud ich fahr dahin	With peace and joy I travel hence
In Gottes Willen,	According to God's will.
Getrost ist mir Mein Herz und Sinn,	My heart and mind are comforted,
Sanft und stille,	Calm and tranquil,
Wie Gott mir verheißen hat:	As God has promised me:
Der Tod ist mein Schlaf worden.	Death has become my sleep.
[M. Luther]	

No. 4 (Chor)	(Choir)
Glorie, Lob, Ehr und Herrlichkeit	Glory, praise, honor, and splendor
Sei dir, Gott Vater	Be prepared for you, God the Father
und Sohn bereit',	and the Son
Dem Heilgen Geist mit Namen!	And the Holy Spirit named!
Die göttlich Kraft	The divine power
Macht uns sieghaft	Makes us victorious
Durch Jesum Christum, Amen.	Through Jesus Christ. Amen.
[A. Reusner]	

The text thus shows in human life an "internal progression from fear of death and acceptance of its inevitability to faith in Christ and in the promise of the Gospel, and, finally, to the willingness of the believer to die in Christ and his church"[56] in order once again to live (i.e., a chiasm: life-death-death-life). Bach employed a tonal plan for the various movements of the work to underscore the work's chiastic, theological (or poignant Christological) point. To comprehend his tonal planning, one must understand that according to certain baroque music theorists, keys with more flats were deemed suggestive of a downward direction, and keys with less flats were taken to be indicative of an upward direction.[57] With this piece of information in mind, consider the sections of Cantata 106, the keys in which they are composed, and the number of flats in each section:

56. Chafe, *Tonal Allegory*, pp. 92-93.
57. Chafe explains this matter in less than crystal-clear fashion in *Tonal Allegory*. For downward tonal direction, he employs the term "catabasis" (and also "descent"), and for upward tonal direction, he employs the term "anabasis" (and also "ascent"). See Chafe, *Tonal Allegory*, esp. pp. 15-19.

No.	Type	Key (Number of Flats)
1	Sonatina	E flat major (3)
2a	Choral	E flat major/C minor (3/3)
2b	Arioso for tenor	C minor (3)
2c	Arioso for bass	C minor/F minor (3/4)
2d	Choral with arioso for soprano	F minor (4)
3a	Aria for alto	B flat minor (5)
3b	Arioso for bass with choir	A flat major/C minor (4/3)
4	Choral	E flat major (3)

If one graphed on a horizontal grid the direction suggested by the number of flats across the sections of Cantata 106,[58] the shape would be, roughly speaking, parabolic. This shape traces out, among other things, the events of the incarnation: Christ's descent to the world of humanity; his birth; his life and ministry; his crucifixion and death; his descent into hell; his resurrection; and his ascension. Cantata 106 suggests that human beings must pattern their lives — and deaths, and hope — on this Christological shape. Accordingly, the point made earlier with reference to Bach's passions — that Christ, the second Adam, is the paradigm for humanity — is duly underscored.

Without knowledge of Cantata 106's tonal plan, it might seem as though the work centers and turns on No. 2d, where the choir sings a fugue intoning the stark reality of life under the old order ("Es ist der alte Bund"/"It is the old covenant [i.e., subject to law]"). Further in No. 2d, the soprano sings longingly for Christ's return with a clear eschatological reference ("Ja, komm, Herr Jesu!"/"Yes, come, Lord Jesus") and the recorders play a chorale melody ("Ich hab' mein Sach' Gott heimgestellt"/"I have brought my affairs home to God"). In light of its tonal plan, however, it becomes clear that the real center and turning point is found in No. 3a, where the alto repeats Christ's Psalmic words on the cross ("In deine Hände befehl ich

58. Due to complicated issues of baroque pitch and tuning — issues that would take the present discussion too far afield — it is important to note that some modern editions of Cantata 106 are centered on E flat major and others on F major. For example, the *Neue Ausgabe Sämtlicher Werke* referred to in the foregoing opts for F major. See Ryuichi Higuchi, *Kritischer Bericht* to Johann Sebastian Bach, *Neue Ausgabe Sämtlicher Werke*, Series I, vol. 34 (Kassel: Bärenreiter, 1990), p. 20. This paper follows Chafe's analysis in *Tonal Allegory* and indicates the various keys of Cantata 106 in relation to E flat major. It should also be noted that Bach did not change key signatures throughout the *Actus Tragicus* but simply provided accidentals where they were required.

meinen Geist"/"Into your hands I commend my spirit"). This is the moment of redemptive promise and hope in the work, theologically speaking, and the place that marks the transition from low point to ascent, tonally speaking.[59] Instructively, at the beginning of No. 3a, the continuo is assigned an ascending scale — a pattern found throughout the movement. The augmentation of hope and the tonal ascent continues in No. 3b, where the bass sings Christ's words on the cross addressed to one of the criminals crucified with him: "Heute wirst du mit mir im Paradies sein"/"Today you will be with me in Paradise"), joined by the choir singing Luther's hymn — representative of the church — about death and its promise of restful sleep ("Mit Fried und Freud ich fahr dahin"/"With peace and joy I travel hence"). Tonally speaking, having emerged from the dark valley of minor modes, Cantata 106 ends on a light, joyous, and upward note in a major mode (No. 4), with the choir praising the power of the Holy Trinity and the victorious work of Christ.

In accordance with Cantata 106's textual-theological message and tonal plan, it might also be pointed out that Bach's instrumentation contributes to the overall design of the work.[60] The *Actus Tragicus* is scored as follows: flauto dolce (i.e., recorder) I/II; viola da gamba I/II; soprano; alto; tenore; basso; continuo. After he has established the range of the work's orchestration (No. 1) and vocalization (No. 2a) at the beginning — which he combines at the end (No. 4) — Bach in the succeeding movements reduces his forces and then again augments them. He does so very much in step with the overall plan of the work and in clear congruence with the tonal plan; where the music is most flat tonally, the orchestration and vocalization is most sparse; and where the music is least flat tonally, the orchestration and vocalization is most rich. Again, the turning point in this connection is found at the transition from No. 2d to No. 3a. At the end of No. 2d, the soprano sings "Herr Jesu" ("Lord Jesus") completely unaccompanied; and at the beginning of No. 3a, the continuo alone plays an ascending scale leading up to the alto solo "In deine Hände" ("Into your hands"). Keeping in mind the movements' keys (with number of flats), consider the individual movements' particular orchestration and vocalization (rec = recorders; vg = violas da gamba; cont = continuo):

---

59. See Chafe, *Tonal Allegory*, pp. 100, 103-4.
60. See Bach, *Neue Ausgabe Sämtlicher Werke*, pp. 1-40. See also Chafe, *Tonal Allegory*, p. 110.

No.	Key (flats)	Orchestration//Vocalization
1	E flat major (3 flats)	2 rec/2 vg/cont//[none]
2a	E flat major/C minor (3 flats/3 flats)	2 rec/2 vg/cont//choir
2b	C minor (3 flats)	2 rec/2 vg/cont//tenor
2c	C minor/F minor (3 flats/4 flats)	2 rec/cont//bass
2d	F minor (4 flats)	2 rec/2 vg/cont//choir/soprano
3a	B flat minor (5 flats)	cont//alto
3b	A flat major/C minor (4 flats/3 flats)	2 vg/cont//bass/choir
4	E flat major (3 flats)	2 rec/2 vg/cont//choir

The design parallels between the tonal plan and the orchestration-vocalization seem clear and expertly contribute to the work's overall musico-theological plan. It is tempting and indeed seems fitting to go on to explore Bach's use of meter, tempi, and dynamics in Cantata 106, in order to see if yet greater evidence of design would emerge. Such an investigation does not, unfortunately, seem to bear as much fruit as does textual-theological, tonal, and orchestration-vocalization analysis.[61]

The Integration of Music and Theology

There are many more examples of the integration of theology and music on the theme of death in Bach's oeuvre. With his understanding of death in

---

61. With respect to meter and tempi, consider the following indications in the score:

No. 1   4/4 (Molto adagio at measure 1)
No. 2a   4/4, 3/4 (Allegro at measure 7), 4/4 (Adagio assai at measure 41)
No. 2b   4/4 (Lento)
No. 2c   3/8 (Vivace)
No. 2d   4/4 (Andante)
No. 3a   4/4
No. 3b   4/4
No. 4   4/4 (Allegro in measure 19)

Clearly, the prevalent time signature in the work is 4/4, "common time," as it known in musical circles. Bach's choice in this matter may well have been deliberate in a work with "Zeit" ("time") in its very title; it is perhaps symbolic of humanity's common plight — moving through time to a certain end: death.

On the matter of dynamics, indications in the score are few, with the majority of them occurring in No. 4, twice to indicate a contrast (i.e., *piano* to *forte* in measures 2 and 4/5). Interestingly, after the choral "Amen" in No. 4, Bach gives a dynamic indication in Cantata 106's final measure. The recorders and the violas da gamba have a quarter note and eighth note which they are to play *piano* — a fitting conclusion to a work that deals with death.

terms of a sleep-filled transition to a better reality, Bach seemed disinclined to trust this world and its snares, refusing to succumb to what Luther called *Anfechtung* (temptation). The theme of distrust of the world is often expressed by Bach in his sacred music. Consider the motet "O Jesu Christ, meins Lebens Licht"/"O Jesus Christ, my life's light" (BWV 118b). In this short motet, which makes use of an early seventeenth-century text by Martin Behm, Bach tells his listener the following:

(Chor)	(Choir)
Auf erden bin ich nur ein Gast,	On earth I am only a guest,
Und drückt mich sehr der Sünden Last.	And sore oppressed by the burden of sin.

Auf deinen Abschied, Herr, ich trau,	In your departure, Lord, I trust,
Darauf mein letzte Heimfahrt Bau,	On it I base my final journey home,
Tu mir die Himmelstür weit auf,	Open the door of heaven wide to me,
Wenn ich beschließ meins Lebens lauf.	When I close my life's course.

As should be clear by now, for Bach death is the door through which the believer must pass in order to have full communion with Christ. Bach expresses this idea in, among other places, Cantata 56 ("Ich will den Kreuzstab gerne tragen"/"I gladly carry the cross-staff"). In the opening aria of the work (No. 1), Bach reminds the listener that cross-bearing is required by God and leads to the promised land where God dwells. Throughout our earthly lives, likened by Bach to a journey on a ship, despair and death are constant companions. That yoke is finally removed at "the port of rest" ("Port der Ruhe" [No. 4]). Bach concludes with a chorale, which extends the nautical, journeying images (No. 5):

(Chor)	(Choir)
Komm, o Tod, du schlafes Bruder,	Come, o death, you brother of sleep,
komm und führe mich nur fort;	Come and lead me only forward;
löse meines Schiffleins Ruder,	loosen my little ship's rudder,
bringe mich an sichern Port!	bring me to the sure port.
Es mag, wer da will, dich scheuen,	Whoever wants to may cower before you,
du kannst mich vielmehr erfreuen;	but me you rather fill with joy;
denn durch dich komm ich herein	for through you do I enter the presence
zu dem schönsten Jesulein.	of the most beautiful little Jesus.

Bach seems in general to have regarded embodied life in the world as shadowy, destined for death, and redeemable only by the heartrending death of the Son of God on the cross. Death is thus the gate through which one must go in order to move from this sad world to a joyful one beyond.

Taking into account the objective evidence reviewed above as well as the internal evidence afforded by the compositions themselves, the general conclusion that music and theology were very closely connected for Bach seems irresistible. Theology was by no means extrinsic to his work as a composer. As the foregoing has attempted to demonstrate, Bach's engagement with theology was calculated and sustained. But the reverse is also the case. Bach's music allowed him — and allows us — to undertake fresh and sustained exploration of theological themes. This exploration can be instructively discerned in his treatment of the sensitive and often avoided subject of death.

In the musico-theological works that Bach crafted, both the music and the words contributed to the creation of a whole, of a unity. In terms of the old debate in Western music about the primacy of music or words — *Prima la musica e poi le parole? O prima le parole e dopo la musica?* ("First the music and then the words? Or first the words and after the music?")[62] — one imagines Bach being slightly perplexed about others' consternation over an issue that was not particularly vexing for him because he found the interface of music and theology to be natural. Perhaps in response to this famous dilemma thus posed, Bach would simply "keep silent and not chatter,"[63] preferring to leave to others the resolution of such paradoxes.

62. This issue has raged in Western music for centuries. Beginning with the invention of opera, prompted by the efforts of the Florentine Camerata in the late sixteenth century (e.g., Jacopo Peri's *Dafne* [1598]), and extending well into the twentieth century (e.g., Richard Strauss's last opera, *Capriccio* [1942], deals with this issue explicitly), the issue of the relationship of words and music has never been far from consciousness in Western music. Neither has it been definitively resolved.

63. "Schweigt stille, plaudert nicht" ("Keep silent, do not chatter") is the title of one of Bach's secular cantatas, BWV 211, the so-called "Coffee Cantata."

10. *"Parables"* and *"Polyphony"*: The Resonance of
Music as Witness in the Theology of Karl Barth
and Dietrich Bonhoeffer

David J. R. S. Moseley

Introduction

The legendary singer, Johnny Cash, passed away in September 2003. His
obituary in *Time* magazine reflected on the difficulty of categorizing someone like Cash — his colossal genius was hard to squeeze into the sub-
departments of a music store designed for strict categorization and commodification:

> The stature Cash embodies is not so much out of fashion as above it. His
> CDs are found in the country section of the music store, but he doesn't
> quite fit there. He came up with rockabilly phenoms like Elvis Presley,
> Carl Perkins and Jerry Lee Lewis, but few of his songs were hard-driving
> rave-ups. "I Walk the Line," "Ring of Fire," "Folsom Prison Blues" — these
> are, if anything, contemporary folk songs. Cash sang of specific injustices
> and eternal truths; he was the deadpan poet of cotton fields, truck stops
> and prisons. He was a balladeer, really, a spellbinding storyteller — *a wit-
> ness, in the Christian sense of the word.* Here was a man who knew the
> Commandments because he had broken so many of them. . . .[1]

Almost exactly a year earlier in the same publication, an interview with
Bruce Springsteen — as equally "unclassifiable" as other great musical artists

---

1. Richard Corliss, "Country Star, Christian, Rocker, Rebel: Johnny Cash Showed the
World How to Walk the Line," *Time Magazine,* 14 September 2003; my italics.

like Johnny Cash, Elvis Presley, Bob Dylan, or Van Morrison — reflected a similar characteristic of his music:

> When he is onstage, Springsteen says, he sometimes feels like a preacher, and on the last E Street Band tour, he did a mock monologue in a fire-and-brimstone voice about the power of music. "It was one of those things that was joking but serious at the same time," he says. Springsteen is a lapsed Catholic, but whether he is telling [his backup singer and wife, Patti] Scialfa that he wants her backup vocals to be "more gospel" or asking his listeners to "come on up for The Rising," he understands that spiritual revival is a necessity and that it has to be a communal experience. "*I think that fits in with the concept of our band as a group of witnesses,*" he says. "*That's one of our functions. We're here to testify to what we have seen.*" And to hear the testimony of others.[2]

The category of "witnessing" is central in the apostolic church,[3] and appears constitutive of the transformed life that results from an encounter with the resurrected Christ. It binds the believer to God as a proper response to the transformational encounter with the risen Lord, and it connects the believer to the world in the act of living testimony. In a broader sense, the incarnation represents God's own engagement and participation in human history as an act of self-authenticating witness to his own love. Moving from the appropriation of the vocabulary of "witness" in contemporary music to a key dispute in recent historical theology, this essay will attempt to show that the appeal to theological terminology in the passages quoted from above about Johnny Cash and Bruce Springsteen is not at all inappropriate. The theological dispute in question concerns Karl Barth and Dietrich Bonhoeffer.

Barth (1886-1968) and Bonhoeffer (1906-1945) were two of the — if not *the* — most significant figures in twentieth-century theology. Inextricably linked by the developments of modern Protestant thought, and the tragedy

---

2. Josh Tyrangiel, "Reborn in the USA," *Time Magazine,* Saturday, 27 July 2002; my italics. The occasion for this article — the release of Springsteen's album, *The Rising* — is also pertinent because many of the album's songs were the first attempt by a mainstream American artist in any medium to respond and "witness" to what had occurred on 11 September 2001. Springsteen's most recent album, *We Shall Overcome: The Seeger Sessions* (2006), is made up of cover versions of songs in a mixture of musical styles made famous by the folk singer Pete Seeger. Live performances of this music felt like a "revival meeting," and were frequently described as such in reviews.

3. For example, see Acts 1:22; 2:32; 3:15; 4:33; 5:32; 10:39.

of Nazi Germany, nevertheless, one much-discussed comment by Bonhoeffer about Barth has generated a great deal of controversy about the precise relationship of their theologies. One year away from his execution, contemplating the theological aftermath of World War II, Bonhoeffer wrote to a
friend from his prison cell about the rise of "religionless Christianity" in the
future, and apparently seemed to dismiss Barth's theology as "positivism of
revelation," which he considered to be a retreat from the path that post-war
Christianity ought to pursue.[4]

What exactly Bonhoeffer meant by this phrase — "positivism of revelation" *(Offenbarungspositivismus)* — is a matter of great controversy.[5] Barth's
detractors have taken it to imply an authoritarian, "top-down" assertion of
the precise content of theological truth within the *exclusive* confines of
Scripture and the church, specifically excluding the claims of speculative
metaphysics and the natural sciences. Bonhoeffer seems to fear that this
leaves no room for engagement with the "religionless" world of contemporary secularity — what he refers to in his prison writings as a "world come of
age."

Barth was certainly stung by this criticism, and expressed both diffi-
dence and confusion as to how he ought to respond to what he regarded as a
mysterious attack:

> But as always with Bonhoeffer one is faced by a peculiar difficulty. He was
> — how shall I put it? — an impulsive, visionary thinker who was sud-
> denly seized by an idea to which he gave lively form, and then after a time
> he called a halt. . . . Now he has left us alone with the enigmatic utterances
> of his letters — at more than one point clearly showing that he sensed,
> without really knowing, how the story should continue — for example,
> what exactly he meant by the "positivism of revelation" he found in me,
> and especially how the program of an un-religious speech was to be real-
> ized. . . . I am somewhat embarrassed by the thought that so sensible and

4. Dietrich Bonhoeffer, *Letters and Papers from Prison,* enl. ed., ed. Eberhard Bethge,
trans. Reginald Fuller et al. (New York: Macmillan, 1972), pp. 280, 286, 329.

5. See Simon Fisher, *Revelatory Positivism? Barth's Earliest Theology and the Marburg
School* (Oxford: Oxford University Press, 1988), which traces the historical antecedents that
might ground Bonhoeffer's accusation. See also Andreas Pangritz, *Karl Barth in the Theology
of Dietrich Bonhoeffer,* trans. Barbara and Martin Rumscheidt (Grand Rapids: Eerdmans,
2000), which sympathetically argues that there is more that unites Bonhoeffer and Barth
than divides, and laments the way in which the charge of "positivism of revelation" has been
accepted uncritically, and has then become an exclusive lens through which the relationship
between the two theologians has been perceived.

well-meaning a man as Bonhoeffer somehow remembered my books . . .
in terms of this enigmatic expression. The hope remains that in heaven at
least he has not reported about me to *all* the angels (including the church
fathers, etc.) with just this expression. But perhaps I have indeed on occasion behaved and expressed myself "positivistically," and if this is so then
Bonhoeffer's recollections have brought it to light. Without being able to
ask him personally, we shall have to make do with remaining behind,
somewhat confused.[6]

The purpose of this essay is not to resolve the many hermeneutical complexities that this controversy raises in post-war theology, but rather to explore the significant convergence that exists between Barth and Bonhoeffer
at precisely this point where they are supposed to diverge the most. Charles
Marsh points this out in a striking passage:

> [Bonhoeffer's] project is that of exploring the depths of revelation's
> worldly objectivity with regard to the event of God's being for the world
> in the concrete presence of Jesus Christ. This project is not at all incom-
> patible with Barth's explication of the Trinitarian identity of God. . . .
> Bonhoeffer's theology should be regarded as complementary with Barth's
> rejuvenation of the doctrine of the Trinity, although with varying nuances
> and emphases, yet still sharing the common concern of understanding the
> *self-witness* of the living God in Jesus of Nazareth and the relationship of
> humanity to that *self-witness* — of thinking after the God who has given
> himself to humanity as an expression of his own loving character.[7]

Indeed, it is submitted that a crucial way to open up the resonance of
Barth's and Bonhoeffer's theology regarding this "common concern" is to
examine the part that music plays in their theology during key periods.
From his prison cell in the dying months of World War II, Bonhoeffer uses
music to plot a route toward Christian engagement with a "religionless"
world. In his later theology, Barth uses music to move beyond "natural theology" toward a "theology of nature" that truly engages with the secular
world.[8] Both of these theologians explicitly understand music as a respon-

6. From a letter to *landessuperintendent* P. W. Herrenbrück, 21 December 1952, in *World
Come of Age*, ed. Ronald Gregor Smith (Philadelphia: Fortress Press, 1967), pp. 89-90.
7. Charles Marsh, "Dietrich Bonhoeffer," in *Modern Theologians: An Introduction to
Christian Theology in the Twentieth Century*, 2nd ed., ed. David F. Ford (Oxford: Blackwell
Publishers, 1997), pp. 37-51, at 49; my italics.
8. "Natural theology" refers to any theology that attempts to know God and God's rela-

sive form of "witness" that links worldly existence with its ground in God's reconciling self-revelation in Christ. A shared passion for music, then, is instrumental in generating this resonance in their theology.

Musical Existence

Karl Barth

Music was always of the utmost significance in the life of Karl Barth, but his preferences and tastes were subject to the vacillations and modulations that everybody experiences with the passing of the years. From his earliest childhood memories to his final dying moments, music was the constant accompaniment to Barth's life. The seminal childhood experience when Barth first became aware of great music was the famous recollection of his father playing "Tamino mein, o welch ein Glück" on the piano at home, from Mozart's *The Magic Flute*. This music "thrilled me through and through," Barth recalled, and he mentally noted at the time: "He's the one!"[9] From the age of ten he was taught the violin, learning to play "resounding Handel and cheerful Mozart" in the school orchestra.[10] But he was fonder of singing, possessing a steady baritone voice.[11] As a professor at Göttingen, Barth would sit at the piano singing raucous songs to his own accompaniment at exuberant student parties.[12] Throughout his life he displayed a Lutheran predilection for church hymns and the popular theology they embodied, from which he was never ashamed to quote in the *Church Dogmatics*.

As president of a student society at grammar school, he gave lectures on the theater and opera, likening theater-going to worship, and praising Wag-

---

tionship to the world through nature and human reasoning without any reference to revelation. On the other hand, "theology of nature" refers to theological reflections on the natural world and science premised upon the knowledge of God in revelation.

9. "A Testimonial to Mozart," in *Wolfgang Amadeus Mozart,* trans. Clarence K. Pott, foreword by John Updike (Grand Rapids: Eerdmans, 1986), p. 15; and "Music for a Guest — A Radio Broadcast" (interview by Roswitha Schmalenbach on German Swiss Radio in Basel dialect, broadcast 17 November 1968), printed in *Final Testimonies,* ed. Eberhard Busch, trans. Geoffrey W. Bromiley (Grand Rapids: Eerdmans, 1977), pp. 19-30. See also Eberhard Busch, *Karl Barth: His Life from Letters and Autobiographical Texts,* trans. John Bowden (Philadelphia: Fortress Press, 1976), p. 15.

10. Letter to E. Huber, 14 January 1951, in Busch, *Life,* pp. 25-26.

11. Busch, *Life,* p. 26.

12. Busch, *Life,* pp. 130-31.

ner's *Tannhäuser* as a piece of "powerful preaching": "Why shouldn't we see a divine spark in the genius of a Mozart or a Wagner?" The teenage Barth also wrote a "grand, spectacular romantic opera," *The Sixth-Former's Dream*, in which he set new texts to familiar arias by Mozart. For decades Barth's "Colour Song" was the society's song.[13]

As a young pastor in Geneva, Barth took part in a performance of Bach's *St. Matthew Passion* in June 1910, a piece of which he was very fond.[14] Dominated by the *Kulturprotestantismus* of his university teachers, Barth published a long article on "Faith and History"[15] including Francis of Assisi, Michelangelo, and even Beethoven as "sources of revelation" alongside Paul.[16] (Barth would later regard the article as something "which would have better remained unpublished.")[17] While in Geneva, Barth became engaged to Nelly Hoffmann, a seventeen-year-old violin student at the conservatory who had been a member of his first-year confirmation class.[18]

Following Barth's decisive shift away from liberalism in 1914-15,[19] he was inevitably more wary of giving any theological significance to music. He regretted ever having conceived of music and culture as a form of "natural theology" or revelation in his controversy with Emil Brunner in 1934.[20] But his infectious love of music was everywhere evident as a young professor.[21] In

13. Busch, *Life*, pp. 29-30.

14. Busch, *Life*, p. 56. Later, Barth criticized Bach's *St. Matthew Passion* as a "tragic ode culminating in a conventional funeral dirge ('Rest softly'). It is neither determined nor delimited by the Easter message, and Jesus never once speaks in it as the Victor," and it is only an "abstraction and not the real passion of Jesus." *Church Dogmatics*, ed. T. F. Torrance and Geoffrey W. Bromiley (Edinburgh: T&T Clark, 1956-75), IV/2, pp. 252-53.

15. "Die Christliche Glaube und die Geschichte" (1910), revised and printed in *Schweizerische Theologische Zeitschrift* 29 (1912): 1-18, 49-72.

16. Quoted in Busch, *Life*, p. 57.

17. Busch, *Life*, p. 57, from autobiographical sketch in the *Fakultätalbum der Evangelisch-theolgischen* at Münster, 1927.

18. Busch, *Life*, p. 59.

19. See Bruce McCormack, *Karl Barth's Critically Realistic Dialectical Theology: Its Genesis and Development 1909-1936* (Oxford: Clarendon Press, 1995), pp. 111-25.

20. "Nein! Antwort an Emil Brunner" ("No! Reply to Emil Brunner"), in *Natural Theology*, trans. Peter Fraenkel (London: Geoffrey Bles, The Centenary Press, 1946), pp. 65-128, at 70. Barth believed the Tambach Lecture of 1919 (in *The Word of God and the Word of Man*, trans. Douglas Horton [New York: Harper Torchbooks, Harper & Brothers Publishers, 1957], pp. 272-327) and his 1926 lecture on "Church and Culture" (in *Theology and Church: Shorter Writings 1920-1928*, trans. Louise Pettibone Smith, with an introduction by T. F. Torrance [London: SCM Press, 1962], pp. 334-54) betrayed such tendencies.

21. During the turbulent years in Bonn (1930-35), Barth still found time to play Mozart

lectures on Schleiermacher, Barth devoted considerable attention to his *Christmas Eve* dialogues,[22] one of the few hitherto published discussions of music by a leading Protestant theologian. Barth highlighted the fact that music — along with the theme of "women" — constituted the "real theological substance of this little masterpiece."[23] Barth's popular lectures on eighteenth- and nineteenth-century theology included a discussion of Rousseau's article on "Génie" in his *Dictionnaire de Musique*, which Barth thought unfortunately prophetic of the "delirium" of Romanticism, akin to the theology of Schleiermacher's *Speeches*, which could also be found in the music of Beethoven and Schubert.[24] But Barth exempts the "genius" of Bach and Haydn, and particularly Mozart. In his introduction, "Man in the Eighteenth Century," Barth went out of his way to commend the music of the baroque and the classical period — Bach and Haydn, again, along with Handel and Gluck.[25] In terms prophetic of the famous passage about Mozart and creation in *Church Dogmatics* III.3, he wrote:

> There was one musician who had . . . in addition something entirely personal to himself: the sadness or horror inherent in the knowledge of the border before which absolutist man, even and particularly when cutting his finest figure, stands in blissful unawareness. . . . He still fully belonged to the eighteenth century and was nevertheless already one of the men of the time of transition. . . . I am referring to Wolfgang Amadeus Mozart.[26]

The earlier volumes of Barth's masterpiece, the *Church Dogmatics*, written amid the *Sturm und Drang* of the 1930s and 1940s, have relatively little to say on the topic of music and culture generally. However, as far as the

---

string quartets, "discreetly in the background as a viola player." Letter to L. Kreyssig, 18 September 1950, in Busch, *Life*, p. 220.

22. *Weihnachtsfeier*, published as *Christmas Eve: Dialogue on the Incarnation*, trans. Terence N. Tice (Richmond: John Knox Press, 1967).

23. *The Theology of Schleiermacher: Lectures at Göttingen, Winter Semester 1923/1924*, ed. Dietrich Ritschl, trans. Geoffrey W. Bromiley (Grand Rapids: Eerdmans, 1982), p. 70. See also "Schleiermacher's *Celebration of Christmas*" (1924), in *Theology and Church*, pp. 136-58, at 156-57; and "Schleiermacher" (1926), in *Theology and Church*, pp. 159-99, at 161 and 185.

24. *Protestant Theology in the Nineteenth Century*, trans. Brian Cozens (London: SCM Press, 1972), p. 178.

25. *Protestant Theology in the Nineteenth Century*, pp. 69-73.

26. *Protestant Theology in the Nineteenth Century*, p. 73. In addition to a number of sideswipes at Wagner (pp. 69, 342, 567), there are other plentiful references to Mozart, clearly now established as the Barthian musical paradigm (pp. 34, 36, 269, 365, 549, and 567).

sources of revelation are concerned, Barth wrote: "God may speak to us through Russian Communism, *a flute concerto,* a blossoming shrub, or a dead dog. We do well to listen to him if he really does."[27] Nevertheless, one cannot stretch the interconnection of contemporary socio-political and cultural considerations with dogmatic expression too far, because Barth's theology in the third volume on the doctrine of creation demonstrates a greater generosity toward culture, a trend he had been developing in his secondary writings for some time — written while the European and world powers were ripping the created order to pieces. After another swipe at Wagner and other modern "neo-Marcionites,"[28] Barth surprisingly commended Leibniz's philosophy of eighteenth-century "optimism."[29] Despite reservations, Barth is able to commend Leibniz and his disciples for trying to "sing the unqualified praise of God the Creator."[30] "Nor is it an accident that this century of all others produced the finest music — J. S. Bach and G. F. Handel, Gluck and Haydn, and the incomparable Mozart."[31]

Barth's famous panegyric addressed to Mozart in §50.2 of the doctrine of creation synopsizes all that Barth finds most distinctive and theologically significant in the music of Mozart: his unique right to be taken seriously in theology; his music's non-synthetic dialectics of light and darkness; the fundamental orientation of praise in his music, on the frontier of the "shadow side" of creation; and his mediating agency of God's good and perfect creation.[32]

Barth's idiomatic discussion of angelology reiterates what he had earlier asserted when singling out Mozart's music for special theological treatment.[33] Playing music is an intelligent attempt to make creation sound, and articulate its praise: this is the reason why angels are often pictured with

---

27. *Church Dogmatics* I/1, p. 55; my italics. (Hereafter cited as *CD.*) Perhaps Barth had in mind the fact that Schleiermacher claimed to have been inspired to write the *Christmas Eve Dialogues* while returning home from a concert by the renowned flutist Dülon on 2 December 1805 in Halle — Barth was certainly aware of this (*Theology of Schleiermacher,* pp. 57, 70). Barth was very fond of Mozart's flute concerti (Mozart's *Flute Concerto in G* [K.313/286c] was performed at Barth's funeral), and *The Magic Flute,* the piece which sparked his life-long love of Mozart.

28. *CD* III/1, 334. Barth also highlights Wagner's negative influence on Nietzsche (*CD* III/2, pp. 232f).

29. *CD* III/1, pp. 388-414.

30. *CD* III/1, pp. 405-6.

31. *CD* III/1, pp. 405-6.

32. *CD* III/3, pp. 297-99.

33. *CD* III/3, pp. 369-531, at 461-76.

harps in their hands.[34] This flight of fantasy concerning angels led to one of Barth's most frequently cited comments regarding Mozart:

> Once upon a time I formulated my notion this way: it may be that when the angels go about their task of praising God, they play only Bach. I am sure, however, that when they are together *en famille*, they play Mozart and that then too our dear Lord listens with special pleasure.[35]

Distancing himself from Romanticism, Barth states that the best musician hears not only his own heart, but also what all creation says.[36] He assiduously distinguishes the harmonious cosmic praise of God (Revelation 5), and the singing of angelic hymns of praise, from the "wild shout of joy" at the conclusion to the finale of Beethoven's Ninth Symphony.[37]

In the doctrine of reconciliation,[38] Barth's approach to culture was liberalized enough to allow for a more significant engagement, particularly with regards to music and theology, as will be seen below. In addition to his analysis of the "parabolic" significance of the "true words" and the "lights" of creation, Barth also uses two of Mozart's operas to illustrate various theological points.[39] Finally, Barth uses Mozart as a litmus test for good theology in the prefaces to two later part-volumes of the *Church Dogmatics*,

---

34. *CD* III/3, p. 472. Barth conjectures that the harps signify the "prayers of the saints."

35. "A Letter of Thanks to Mozart," in *Wolfgang Amadeus Mozart*, p. 23.

36. "A Letter of Thanks to Mozart," in *Wolfgang Amadeus Mozart*, p. 23. Confusingly, Barth concludes that we are not to find any instruction in this concerning the form of divine service, and he emphasizes the distinction between a concert and a church service. As Timothy Gorringe points out, Barth never quite overcame his Calvinist suspicion of church music (*Karl Barth: Against Hegemony*, Christian Theology in Context [Oxford: Oxford University Press, 1999], p. 177). This is also reflected in his views on church architecture: "Since the organ and choir are accessories appreciated to a greater or lesser degree and may in principle be dispensed with, they should not appear in the field of vision of the assembled community" ("The Architectural Problem of Protestant Places of Worship," first published in no. 8/1959 of the review *Werk*; reprinted in *Architecture in Worship: The Christian Place of Worship* by André Biéler [Edinburgh: Oliver & Boyd, 1965], p. 93). And yet, Barth specifically ascribed doxological significance to Mozart's music earlier in the same part-volume (*CD* III/3, pp. 297-99), and was passionate about Mozart's masses and church music. See "Music for a Guest," p. 30; and "Wolfgang Amadeus Mozart" in *Wolfgang Amadeus Mozart*, pp. 38-40.

37. *CD* III/3, p. 476.

38. In particular, *CD* IV/3.1 §69.2.

39. The severity of the avenging god Neptune in *Idomeneo*, a *deus ex machina*, is to be distinguished from the softening resolve of *Yahweh* in the book of Job (*CD* IV/3.1, p. 427); Barth also critiques humanity's sinful attempt to invert its relationship with God, as if playing Leporello to God's Don Giovanni (*CD* IV/3.2, p. 665).

in which he fended off the attacks of Dutch Neo-Calvinists who had singled
out for special vitriol Barth's hymn to (Roman Catholic) Mozart in the doctrine of creation.[40] Later on in the doctrine of reconciliation, Barth is forgiving enough to be more favorably disposed toward the Neo-Calvinist
"fundamentalists," so long as they "do not say any more unseemly things
about Mozart."[41]

Hans Küng recalled that Barth had wanted Mozart's "Coronation Mass"
(*Missa Brevis* in C Major, K.317) played at the (Protestant) World Council of
Churches assembly in Evanston, Illinois, in 1954.[42] Barth's devotion to Mozart's theological significance was renowned enough to occasion an illustrated lecture that same year, entitled "The Music of Mozart in the Theology
of Karl Barth": Barth was able to attend, and described it as "a splendid affair."[43] Despite the celebrations of his own seventieth birthday in 1956, Barth
declared that "the year 1956 was more meaningful to me as the 200th anniversary of the birth of Wolfgang Amadeus Mozart. And the high point of
1956 for me was my invitation to give the memorial address on Mozart and
his work at the celebration held in Basel."[44] Barth threw himself into the fes-
tivities, as a member of the Swiss Mozart Committee, delivering lectures,
writing articles,[45] spending a great deal of money buying new recordings
that were issued for the bicentenary, and attending many of the celebratory
concerts.

> In one concert at the Basel Musiksaal, at which Clara Hackil was playing
> the F Major [Piano] Concerto [K.413], I even had a sudden vision of him
> standing there in front of the piano, so clear that I almost began to cry.
> That's quite a story isn't it — such a story that even Balthasar with his

---

40. "Preface" to *CD* III/4, p. xiii. Barth himself noted the seeming contradiction of
"proclaim[ing]" Mozart as an "evangelical Christian" when he was "so Catholic, even a Free-
mason" ("Mozart's Freedom," in *Wolfgang Amadeus Mozart*, pp. 56-57).

41. "Preface" to *CD* IV/2, p. xii.

42. In *Mozart: Traces of Transcendence*, trans. John Bowden (Grand Rapids: Eerdmans,
1993), p. 17.

43. Letter to U. Barth, 19 March 1954, in Busch, *Life*, p. 402. Jürgen Uhde, a musician
highly regarded by Barth, delivered the lecture in Swabian-Gmünd.

44. *How I Changed My Mind*, ed. and trans. John Godsey (Edinburgh: The Saint Andrew Press, 1969), p. 71. The memorial address was "Mozart's Freedom" (pp. 43-60).

45. "Wolfgang Amadeus Mozart" and "Mozart's Freedom" were first published in the
Festschrift edited by Walter Leibrecht, *Religion and Culture: Essays in Honour of Paul Tillich*
(London: SCM Press, 1959), pp. 61-78, later collected and published separately in *Wolfgang
Amadeus Mozart*, with a "Foreword" by the American novelist, John Updike.

DAVID J. R. S. MOSELEY

mystical experiences listened respectfully when I told him. At any rate, I know just what Mozart looked like in the last year of his life.[46]

The wide circulation and acclaim for his lectures, as well as his membership on the Swiss Mozart Committee, brought him the acquaintanceship of many leading musicians, conductors, and musicologists. He did not hesitate to make long journeys to the committee meetings, and would have counted the Swiss billionaire businessman, conductor, and musical patron Paul Sacher, a fellow resident of Basel, among his colleagues on the committee.[47]

To keep him occupied during his retirement, Barth's study contained a voluminous collection of books about Mozart, and his friends kept his library of gramophone records of all the latest Mozart recordings well stocked.[48] Despite deteriorating health, Barth was "thankful to God and man that I am still alive and can read, carry on conversations, smoke, sing

46. Letter to his son, Markus Barth, 21 April 1956, in Busch, *Life*, p. 409.

47. Busch, *Life*, p. 410. Paul Sacher commissioned two hundred or more works, which made his sponsorship of twentieth-century classical music unrivaled. Among them were major works by Bartók, Richard Strauss, Stravinsky, Honegger, Britten, Boulez, Harrison Birtwistle, Elliott Carter, and Wolfgang Rihm. Britten wrote for him the *Cantata Academica*, conducted by Sacher in 1959 in celebration of the five hundredth anniversary of Basel University, whose most distinguished employee at the time was the professor of theology, Karl Barth. Sacher's extravagant patronage made Basel one of the world's leading centers for contemporary music, a place of pilgrimage for composers and audiences alike in search of *avant-garde* excellence. Therefore, Barth is without excuse for failing to engage with contemporary classical music, living in the midst of a contemporary music renaissance that prompted jealousy throughout Europe and the world. Indeed, Barth's reluctance or inability to appreciate music beyond the confines of the eighteenth century was the cause of considerable regret and embarrassment to him. "[U]nfortunately I simply cannot make sense of any modern art (in all three forms). I am in no position to pass a negative judgment on it, which is why I don't think I have ever said a bad word against it. But it is a sad fact that I have no understanding of it, no eye or ear for it. . . . Perhaps I shall discover in heaven what is so hidden from me now. But it is lamentable that this has not happened to me yet" (letter to K. Lüthi, 22 June 1963, quoted in Busch, *Life*, p. 411). However, despite Barth's frequently expressed prejudices against nineteenth-century music, Eberhard Busch once reported a visit to Basel in the 1960s when he found Barth in his garden listening approvingly to a record of the late Romantic lavishness of Bruch on the gramophone (mentioned in a letter to the author by H. Martin Rumscheidt).

48. John Bowden, *Karl Barth* (London: SCM, 1971), p. 9. In a letter to Rudolf Bultmann in 1952, Barth mentions that "[T]here are hints that the Christ child has ready for me a whole set of Mozart records" (*Karl Barth-Rudolf Bultmann Letters 1922-1966*, ed. Bernd Jaspert, ed. and trans. Geoffrey W. Bromiley [Grand Rapids: Eerdmans, 1981], p. 108).

psalms and chorales, listen to Mozart, enjoy my fourteen grandchildren and exist from day to day in this positive kind of way."[49]

In a short interview in early 1963, Barth accused his Swiss compatriots of being "un-Mozartean" in their failure to engage the two sides of the Cold War in real dialogue: "But we Swiss lack the Mozartean element, the calm joyfulness so badly needed now in a torn and divided world. We lack the ability to see ourselves in our own relativity — it is that from which true peace comes."[50] Barth's letters from his last years of retirement are packed with references to Mozart, testifying to his continuing obsession.[51] In one letter, he recounted to a friend a recent occasion when he had lectured on church renewal with Balthasar, accompanied by various Roman Catholic bishops:

> Everyone was happy. And God's sun shone down in astonishment, but in a friendly way, over it all. Is the millennium really round the corner? The fact that Mozart was played twice could also be a pointer in this direction. I recommended that the Lord Bishops should do something about his beatification, if not canonization.[52]

Less than a month before he died, Barth recorded an interview for Swiss radio as part of a series called "Music for a Guest" — a Swiss version of

49. Letter to G. Schwenzel, 8 November 1965, in Busch, *Life*, p. 472.

50. "The 'Un-Mozartean' Swiss," an interview in Zürich's *Die Woche* in January 1963, published in *Fragments Grave and Gay*, ed. Martin Rumscheidt, trans. Eric Mosbacher (London: Fontana Library, Collins, 1971), pp. 48-53, at 52-53.

51. As a few examples of the more than twenty references to the music of Mozart in Barth's letters from the 1960s *(Letters)*, he refers to the music of Mozart as if it were a constant accompaniment in his twilight years (end of May 1968, p. 298), and to Mozart's contribution "throughout the years and decades" toward his own "relaxation" (6 June 1962, p. 48). He jokes to the theologian Paul Althaus that "I now have almost all the available Mozart records. So I do not need 'primal revelation' and am all the more sure of the order 'Gospel-Law'" (28 October 1962, p. 69). He attempts to explain the comparison between the music of Mozart and Beethoven as analogous to the relationship of *Agape* and *Eros* (9 January 1963, p. 86) in *Evangelical Theology: An Introduction,* trans. Grover Foley (New York: Holt, Rinehart & Winston, 1963), p. 201. He expresses excitement concerning a Bavarian student's dissertation (K. Hammer, *W. A. Mozart — eine theologische Deutung. Ein Beitrag zur theologischen Anthropologie* [Zurich 1964], supervised by Barth and Werner Bieder) that gives a theological interpretation of Mozart (4 April 1964, pp. 155f.).

52. Letter to K. P. Gertz, 29 February 1968, in Busch, *Life*, p. 493. Barth repeats this wish in a letter of 30 September 1968 on the subject of Mozart, citing the influence he might use through being on "good personal terms with the present pope [Paul VI]," in *Letters*, pp. 315-16.

Desert Island Discs — in which, characteristically, Barth chose all Mozart![53]
He attempted to distinguish the "secular" and "sacred" sides of Mozart's
music;[54] he commented on the "playfulness" of Mozart.[55] But he also made
extraordinary claims for the provenance of Mozart's music, which he considered to have originated from a place which agreed with the "harmony"
Barth himself heard and attempted to articulate in the *Church Dogmatics* —
namely, from Scripture.[56]

It is a well-established fact that in his fastidious daily routine while re-
searching and writing the *Church Dogmatics,* Barth would spend a considerable amount of time each day listening to records of Mozart's music on the
gramophone in his study before embarking on his work.[57] Having passed
away peacefully on the night of 9-10 December 1968, "his wife found him the
next morning, while in the background a record was playing the Mozart
with which she had wanted to waken him."[58] Barth had often expressed to
friends his desire to seek out Wolfgang Amadeus Mozart first before becoming acquainted with other celestial residents.[59] During the Memorial Service
on 14 December 1968 at Basel Cathedral — which was broadcast live on the
radio — a performance was given of Mozart's *Flute Concerto in G* (K.313/
286c) between the memorial speeches.[60]

---

53. "Music for a Guest," in *Final Testimonies,* pp. 17-30. Barth chose: (i) the third movement *(Allegretto)* from the *Quintet in E-Flat Major for Keyboard and Winds* (K.452); (ii) the
second movement *(Andante)* from the *Symphony in A Major* (K.201/186a); (iii) one of Mozart's art-songs, with the refrain, "Silence — I will say no more"; (iv) the finale from the opera *Die Entführung aus dem Serail* (K.384); and (v) the *Agnus Dei* from the *Missa Brevis in D
Major* (K.194).

54. "Music for a Guest," pp. 28, 30. Elsewhere Barth undermined any firm distinction
between the style and purpose of Mozart's "secular" and "sacred" music (see *Wolfgang
Amadeus Mozart,* pp. 38-40).

55. "Music for a Guest," p. 21.

56. "Music for a Guest," pp. 23-24.

57. "A Testimonial to Mozart," p. 16. See also Ved Mehta, *The New Theologian* (London:
Weidenfeld & Nicolson, 1965), p. 108, cited in Bowden, *Karl Barth,* p. 9.

58. Busch, *Life,* pp. 498-99.

59. "I even have to confess that if I ever get to heaven, I would first seek out Mozart and
only then inquire after Augustine, St. Thomas, Luther, Calvin, and Schleiermacher" ("A Testimonial to Mozart," p. 16). In a letter to Karl Rahner from the last year of his life, Barth, in
contradiction of his usually perceived hostility toward Schleiermacher, commends "a few
hundred years in eternity" in his company, but quickly adds, "so long as I could have a thousand years with Mozart first" (letter of 16 March 1968, in *Letters,* p. 288).

60. Busch, *Life,* p. 499.

Dietrich Bonhoeffer

If Barth's love of music was that of the passionate amateur, Bonhoeffer was such an accomplished pianist that for a while both he and his parents thought he might become a professional musician.[61] In contrast to Barth's somewhat provincial middle-class Swiss family background, Bonhoeffer grew up in an upper-class, highly cultured family environment in Berlin, one of the most artistically vibrant cities in the world at that time. Although he developed eclectic musical tastes in later life, he was grounded in the canon of Bach, Mozart, and Beethoven. By the age of ten he was playing Mozart sonatas, and soon began to compose songs, trios, and cantatas, and enjoyed accompanying his mother and sister on Saturday evening performances of songs by Schubert, Schumann, Brahms, and Hugo Wolf. By the age of seventeen he was also able to accompany his sister's singing on the lute. As a member of the German branch of the Boy Scout movement, he was also much in demand as a musical performer and accompanist. His family and friends recall that "he could never be thrown off by unevenness on the part of a singer."[62] Indeed, it was his prowess as a musician that distinguished the young Bonhoeffer among his school-fellows and his extensive family. Before making a final decision about pursuing theology and the church, his parents arranged for him to perform before the Viennese piano virtuoso, Leonid Kreuzer.[63]

While a student at Union Theological Seminary in New York (1930-31), Bonhoeffer spent a lot of time in Harlem, worshipping at an African-American Baptist church, and collecting gramophone records of "spirituals" and other roots music from the days of slavery.[64] Later in the 1930s, he would transport his students at the Confessing Church seminary in Finkenwalde to the cotton fields of the American Deep South by playing these haunting recordings.[65] Despite his classical musical education, Bonhoeffer's inquisitive artistic impulses were wide enough to enable him to absorb multi-cultural influences. Indeed, it was his much-admired extensive collection of gramophone recordings — which accompanied him to London in 1933, along with his Bechstein piano — as well as his newly discovered love of English choral

61. Eberhard Bethge, *Theologian, Christian, Man for His Times: Dietrich Bonhoeffer — A Biography*, rev. and ed. Victoria J. Barnett (Minneapolis: Fortress Press, 2000), p. 25.

62. Bethge, *A Biography*, p. 25.

63. Bethge, *A Biography*, p. 37.

64. Bethge, *A Biography*, pp. 150-52.

65. Bethge, *A Biography*, p. 427.

music that was often the occasion for striking up new acquaintanceships and friendships.[66]

In his earliest theological works, Bonhoeffer shows an appreciation of the subtleties of contemporary disputes about the connections between beauty and holiness, upon which much more would depend than mere questions of aesthetic judgment in the 1930s.[67] Indeed, he frequently distinguishes the music of Bach — which he regarded as an appropriate "witness" to the gospel in the church — from the Romantics (Beethoven and Wagner), which he enjoyed *outside* the church. Nevertheless, he resented the co-opting of the Romantics for the purpose of Nazi propaganda, and warned against the power of beautiful music which might prevent us from hearing the Word of God and truly praising God in the new song of our redemption in Christ.[68] Bonhoeffer's warnings against the seductions of the "outer beauty" of music at the expense of the "inner beauty" of music — which he connected to the struggle for faith and freedom against unjust authority in the Reformation[69] — account for the particular thrust of one of his most famous aphorisms: "Only he who cries out for the Jews may sing Gregorian chants."[70]

As was true with Barth's involuntary retirement, so it was also true of Bonhoeffer's involuntary confinement — both were constantly accompanied by music, real or imagined. During his years in prison — cut off from beauty, music, and friendship — we find references to art, and especially to music, proliferating in Bonhoeffer's writings. Without his beloved gramophone, he nevertheless preserves many works in his musical memory, and he reflects that "the music we hear inwardly can almost surpass, if we really concentrate on it, what we hear physically." He poignantly expresses sympathy for the pre-

66. Bethge, *A Biography,* p. 328.

67. For example, the twenty-one-year-old Bonhoeffer discusses forms of artistic expression that are, and are not, fitting for a church in *Sanctorum Communio: A Theological Study of the Sociology of the Church,* Dietrich Bonhoeffer Works, vol. 1 (Minneapolis: Fortress, 1998), pp. 128, 273 n. 430. Much of the following material on the place of music in Bonhoeffer's biography is indebted to John W. de Gruchy, *Christianity, Art and Transformation: Theological Aesthetics in the Struggle for Justice* (Cambridge: Cambridge University Press, 2001), ch. 4.

68. These sentiments are expressed in a sermon preached in London on Cantate Sunday, 29 April 1934, in Dietrich Bonhoeffer, *London 1933-1935,* Dietrich Bonhoeffer Werke, vol. 13 (Gütersloh: Chr. Kaiser/Gütersloher Verlagerhaus, 1994), pp. 351-55.

69. Andreas Pangritz, *Polyphonie des Leben: Zu Dietrich Bonhoeffers "Theologie der Musik"* (Berlin: Alektor-Verlag, 1994), pp. 15, 21-26.

70. Bethge, *A Biography,* p. 607.

dicament of Beethoven who could not even hear many of his greatest compositions.[71] A letter to his parents shows the impact and importance of his musical memory as he plays an extensive piece through in his imagination:

> For years now I've associated [the *Mass in B Minor*] with this particular day [Repentance Day, 17 November], like the St Matthew Passion with Good Friday. I remember the evening when I first heard it. I was eighteen, and had just come from Harnack's seminar, in which he had discussed my first seminar essay very kindly, and had expressed hope that some day I should specialize in church history. I was full of this when I went into the Philharmonic Hall; the great *Kyrie Eleison* was just beginning, and as it did so, I forgot everything else — the effect was indescribable. Today I'm going through it, bit by bit, in my mind . . . as it's my favourite work of Bach.[72]

Furthermore, it is while in prison that he begins to break down the artificial barriers that he had constructed between appropriate "church" music — for example, Bach, and Schütz, whose music Eberhard Bethge had introduced him to — and the Romantics. The compartmentalization of spiritual and worldly existence, characteristic of the traditions in which he was reared, was being undercut in prison — not only in the realm of ethics and politics, but also in his attempt to revive a form of "aesthetic existence" in the church that Kierkegaard had written off as mere sensualism.[73]

Dietrich Bonhoeffer: "The Polyphony of Life"

As we have seen, Bonhoeffer's last years of life are saturated by music, both in thought and reminiscence.[74] Music

71. Bonhoeffer, *Letters and Papers*, p. 240.
72. Bonhoeffer, *Letters and Papers*, pp. 126-27.
73. See Søren Kierkegaard, *Either/Or*, Kierkegaard's Writings, III, ed. and trans. Howard V. Hong and Edna H. Hong (Princeton: Princeton University Press, 1987). Included in the first part-volume is Kierkegaard's analysis in the "Seducer's Diary" of Mozart's *Don Giovanni*, interpreted as a parable of almost erotic beguilement, in which the form (music) perfectly expresses the opera's content (seduction for seduction's sake). See "The Immediate Erotic Stages or the Musical Erotic," in Kierkegaard, *Either/Or — Part I*, pp. 45-135.
74. The first writer to seriously consider Bonhoeffer as an aesthetic thinker was Theodore A. Gill, in "Bonhoeffer as Aesthete," *American Academy of Religion* (November 1975). The only monograph devoted to Bonhoeffer's reflections on music is Andreas Pangritz's

provided him with most of his aesthetic categories when engaged in theological reflection. Indeed, his theological thought in prison develops in
tandem with his reflection on musical concepts (Pangritz). Moreover, it is
through music that Bonhoeffer has his profoundest "aesthetic experience," undeniably religious, even mystical, in quality, yet profoundly
Christological in character.[75]

The means by which Bonhoeffer extends these theological reflections is
through a meditation in *Letters and Papers* on musical "polyphony."[76]
Polyphony is a musical texture consisting of two or more independent melodic voices. Polyphonic music is often expressed through "counterpoint" or
"contrapuntal" music, a broad organizational category involving the simultaneous sounding of separate musical voices. Thus, polyphony contrasts
with music consisting of just one voice (monophony), or music with one
dominant melodic voice accompanied by chords or interior harmonic voices
(homophony).[77]

Polyphonie des Lebens: Zu Dietrich Bonhoeffers "Theologie der Musik" (Berlin: Alektor-
Verlag, 1994); see also Pangritz's "Point and Counterpoint — Resistance and Submission:
Dietrich Bonhoeffer on Theology and Music in Times of War and Social Crisis," in *Theology
in Dialogue: The Impact of the Arts, Humanities, and Science on Contemporary Religious
Thought*, ed. Lyn Holness and Ralf K. Wüstenberg (Grand Rapids: Eerdmans, 2002), pp. 28-
42. Bonhoeffer scholar John De Gruchy offers a fine elucidation of Bonhoeffer's quest to revive "aesthetic existence" in *Christianity, Art and Transformation: Theological Aesthetics and
the Struggle for Justice* (Cambridge: Cambridge University Press, 2001), ch. 4. See also incidental, tangential treatments in David S. Cunningham, *These Three Are One: The Practice of
Trinitarian Theology* (Oxford: Blackwell Publishers, 1998), ch. 4; and David Ford, *Self and
Salvation: Being Transformed*, Cambridge Studies in Christian Doctrine (Cambridge: Cambridge University Press, 1999), ch. 10.

75. De Gruchy, *Christianity, Art and Transformation*, pp. 145-46.

76. Ironically enough, the index entry for "positivism of revelation" is right after the
entry for "polyphony" in Bonhoeffer's *Letters and Papers*.

77. Earlier in his career, in *Life Together* — a short book in which he outlines his vision
of the life of the seminary — Bonhoeffer advocates for the "unity, clarity and simplicity" of
unison singing in Christian worship as the ideal for any Christian community, and explicitly
rejects harmonization (Dietrich Bonhoeffer Works, vol. 5 [Minneapolis: Fortress, 1996], pp.
65-68, 123-24). Bonhoeffer's concern in these passages is to assert the primacy of the words in
worship over their musical accompaniment: as such, his argument for the subjugation of
music to words in unison singing concerns only the outward "form" of music as a feature of
worship, and a concern that harmonization might lead to "vanity or bad taste." But in the
passages on "polyphony of life" under discussion in *Letters and Papers*, Bonhoeffer's focus is
on the metaphorical and theological significance of music. The distinction is between the
role of music in worship in the life of an isolated Christian community, and the exploration

Bonhoeffer introduces this model in two letters from May 1944, at a point when he is feeling particularly alone. His friend, Eberhard Bethge — a student of his from Finkenwalde, married to his niece, Renate, and who would later become his biographer and leading expositor — had complained about his situation at the Italian front, and of not being included in the sharing of Bonhoeffer's correspondence with his family. He had even expressed envy for Bonhoeffer, protected from the fighting in his prison cell. Nevertheless — and in spite of his pitiful circumstances — Bonhoeffer replies with great magnanimity, and introduces a striking metaphor:

> There's always a danger in all strong, erotic love that one may love what I might call the polyphony of life. What I mean is that God wants us to love him eternally with our whole hearts — not in such a way as to weaken or injure our earthly love, but to provide a kind of *cantus firmus*[78] to which the other melodies of life provide the counterpoint.[79]

Previously, Bonhoeffer had mourned the fragmentary character of life during the war — uprooting and displacing friends and families. But this very fragmentariness

> may, in fact, point towards a fulfilment beyond the limits of human achievement; I have to keep that in mind, particularly in view of the death of so many of the best of my former pupils. Even if the pressure of outward events may split our lives into fragments, like bombs falling on houses, we must do our best to keep in view how the whole was planned and thought out.[80]

Bonhoeffer puts this experience of "fragmentation" into an eschatological perspective: some fragments will be consigned to the dustbin of history; but there are others

> whose importance lasts for centuries, because their completion can only be a matter for God, and so they are fragments that must be fragments —

---

of a fruitful theological metaphor regarding the complexities of life in, and engagement with, a post-Christian, "religionless" world.

78. Literally "firm chant," the principal or central theme, or pre-existing melody, in a piece of medieval polyphony (literally, "many voices"), providing coherence and enabling the other contrapuntal parts to flourish.

79. Bonhoeffer, *Letters and Papers*, p. 303.

80. Bonhoeffer, *Letters and Papers*, p. 215.

I'm thinking, e.g., of the *Art of Fugue*. If our life is but the remotest reflection of such a fragment, if we accumulate, at least for a short time, a wealth of themes and weld them into a harmony in which the great counterpoint is maintained from start to finish, so that at last, when it breaks off abruptly, we can sing no more than the chorale, "I come before thy throne,"[81] we will not bemoan the fragmentariness of our life, but rather rejoice in it.[82]

Thus, the metaphor of polyphony itself integrates contrapuntal material that Bonhoeffer had been considering three months earlier. Regarding the "polyphony of life," Bonhoeffer states that earthly affection is a counterpoint to the *cantus firmus* of our love for God as his beloved creatures. Such themes "have their own independence but are yet related to the *cantus firmus*" he continues in a subsequent letter to Bethge:

Where the *cantus firmus* is clear and plain, the counterpoint can be developed to its limits. The two are "undivided and yet distinct," in the words of the Chalcedonian Definition, like Christ in his divine and human natures. May not the attraction and importance of polyphony in music consist in its being a musical reflection of this Christological fact and therefore of our *vita christiana*? . . . Do you see what I'm driving at? I wanted to tell you to have a good, clear *cantus firmus;* that is the only way to a full and perfect sound, when the counterpoint has a firm support and can't come adrift or get out of tune, while remaining a distinct whole in its own right. Only a polyphony of this kind can give life a wholeness and at the same time assure us that nothing calamitous can happen as long as the *cantus firmus* is kept going. . . . [R]ely on the *cantus firmus*.[83]

This metaphor of the "polyphony of life" had clearly energized Bonhoeffer's theological thinking, for he returns to the same theme in another letter to Bethge the next day:

The image of polyphony is still pursuing me. When I was rather distressed today at not being with you,[84] I couldn't help thinking that pain and joy

81. Like Bonhoeffer's own life and work, Bach's consummate work of polyphony was incomplete, and handed down with this chorale as a conclusion.
82. Bonhoeffer, *Letters and Papers*, p. 219.
83. Bonhoeffer, *Letters and Papers*, p. 303.
84. Bonhoeffer is referring to the baptism of his godson, Dietrich Wilhelm Rüdiger Bethge, for whom he had written a baptismal sermon. In this sermon he had commended

are also part of life's polyphony, and that they can exist independently side by side. . . . I do want you to be *glad* about what you have: it really *is* the polyphony of life (excuse this riding around on my little invention).[85]

In this way, Bonhoeffer affirms that the *cantus firmus* of our love for God orders and brings coherence to the multidimensional and fragmentary nature of contrapuntal human life. Furthermore, he shows that the theological value of music lies precisely in the way that it binds together, without dissolving, the distinctive integrity of the spiritual and worldly realms of existence, nevertheless grounding the possibility of the latter in the reality of the former. In a real sense, the significance of the contrapuntal motifs of worldly life lies ultimately in their witness or testimony concerning — their *harmonizing* with — the *cantus firmus*. This theme has been understood by some Bonhoeffer scholars to be foundational in the anticipation of the religionless "world come of age" in his last, strange writings.[86]

Karl Barth: "Parables of the Kingdom"

George Steiner described Karl Barth's "laboring after Mozart" as an "exemplary instance" of an attempt to "communicate to others, in some lucid and scrupulous way, the quality, the intelligible ramifications of an aesthetic experience," comparable to Nietzsche's pursuit of Wagner, or Proust's of Vermeer.[87] As Barth wrote on the occasion of the bicentenary of Mozart's birth in 1956: "In the case of Mozart, we must certainly assume that the dear Lord had a special, direct contact with him. 'He who has ears, let him hear!'"[88]

However, Barth's legendary devotion to the music of Wolfgang Amadeus Mozart is both an obstacle and an opportunity. For those who

---

the musical life of his godson's home: "Music, as your parents understand and practice it, will help to dissolve your perplexities and purify your character and sensibility, and in times of care and sorrow will keep a *ground-bass* of joy alive in you" (my italics). Bonhoeffer, *Letters and Papers*, p. 295.

85. Bonhoeffer, *Letters and Papers*, p. 305. Note how Bonhoeffer expresses himself at the beginning ("the image of polyphony is still pursuing me"), as if he has been grasped by the metaphor of "polyphony" rather than it simply being a product of his imagination; but then how he modestly pulls back at the end ("excuse this riding around on my little invention").

86. See Pangritz, *Polyphonie des Lebens*.

87. George Steiner, *Real Presences* (London: Faber, 1989), p. 178.

88. "Wolfgang Amadeus Mozart," p. 26.

would interpret Bonhoeffer's observation regarding "positivism of revelation" as a dismissal of Barth's orientation toward, and engagement with, culture, there is a danger that Barth's love of Mozart might be evacuated of theological content, and relegated to a place equivalent to his enjoyment of a good pipe. But such dismissive strategies fail to appreciate the extent to which Barth's writings on Mozart demonstrate the depth and generosity of Barth's later theology, which opens out the freedom of God's ways with the world in categories that amplify the resonance of theology and music.

Rarely do Barth's commentators regard his treatment of Mozart as a serious matter of *theological* engagement with the significance of music.[89] But there is no reason to suppose that Barth is being facetious when he wrote in 1962: "Without such music [Mozart], I could not think of that which concerns me personally in both theology and politics."[90] The great theologian who taught with "the Bible in one hand and the newspaper in the other" was accompanied in this vocation by Mozart recordings on the gramophone in his study every morning while he prepared for the epic task of laboring at the *Church Dogmatics*.[91]

---

89. Very few scholarly publications are devoted solely to the theological implications of Barth's love affair with Mozart's music, and most of these are pitched at the level of synopsis and anthology rather than analysis and explication. Certainly the earliest written work is Arthur C. Cochrane's piece, "On the Anniversaries of Mozart, Kierkegaard and Barth" (in *Scottish Journal of Theology* 9 [1956]: 251-63). In *Karl Barth's Theology of Culture: The Freedom of Culture for the Praise of God* by Robert J. Palma (Allison Park, PA: Pickwick Publications, 1983), there is a concerted attempt to integrate Barth's writing on Mozart within a systematic engagement with his views on culture (see pp. 31-69). Theodore A. Gill's piece on "Barth and Mozart" (in *Theology Today* 43 [1985]: 403-11) makes some intriguing observations about theology and the arts using Barth's love of Mozart as a brief case-study. Hans Küng made a disappointing attempt to emulate Barth by commemorating the two hundredth anniversary of Mozart's death in 1991, in *Mozart: Traces of Transcendence*, trans. John Bowden (Grand Rapids: Eerdmans, 1992); the book's synopsis of Barth's comments on Mozart is swallowed up by Küng's thinly veiled attempts to canonize Mozart as a shining example of Roman Catholicism. As an antidote, Colin Gunton's Radio 3 broadcast, "Mozart the Theologian" (transmitted on Good Friday, 29 March 1991, reprinted in *Theology* 94 [1991]: 346-49), is a brief but more worthy tribute to the resonance of Mozart's music within Karl Barth's theology, on the occasion of the Mozart bicentenary. Most of the material in this section is taken from my unpublished doctoral dissertation, " 'Parables of the Kingdom': Music and Theology in Karl Barth" (Cambridge, 2001). Finally, Philip Stoltzfus, *Theology as Performance: Music, Aesthetics and God in Modern Theology* (Edinburgh: T&T Clark, 2006) examines the musical aesthetics of Schleiermacher, Wittgenstein, and Barth.

90. *How I Changed My Mind*, pp. 71-72.

91. "I confess that thanks to the invention of the phonograph, which can never be

Barth's detractors have interpreted Bonhoeffer's phrase as criticism of an authoritarian, "top-down" assertion of the precise content of theological truth within the *exclusive* confines of Scripture and the church, specifically excluding the claims of speculative metaphysics and the natural sciences. However, the great misconception about Barth is to interpret his uncompromising insistence on the exclusive primacy of revelation "from above," as witnessed to in Scripture and proclamation, as being ineluctably hostile to the world of culture "below." This leads to an equally correlative tendency to assume, falsely, that Barth rejects the notion that experience of the natural world can yield anything epistemically significant about God. Barth does acknowledge the possibility in his later theology of accepting some version of "general revelation" in our experience of the natural world that can yield unspecified but non-Christian conclusions about a deity. (Subsequently, Barth will develop this into a full-blown "theology of nature.") But before the full import of this foundational insight completely permeated Barth's methodology, he often resorted to the language of "parables" to vindicate his theological and political commitment to Christian socialism, and even as an indirect mediatory concept pointing toward the "infinite qualitative distinction" that exists between the world of humanity and the knowledge of God.[92] However, Barth perceived in this discourse a slippery slope toward natural theology, and all its attendant dangers.

While it is true that Barth goes to extraordinary lengths to safeguard the objectivity of God's self-revelation in Jesus Christ over and against the polluting cultural assimilation of liberal "religion" — indeed, it was this aspect of Barth that greatly attracted the young Bonhoeffer — nevertheless, as the "Christological concentration" in his theology intensified, Barth's approach to this issue mellowed. He understood culture to be less theologically determinative; and yet, if culture is interpreted as a task involving "the outer and inner shaping of human existence," Barth was comfortable enough to de-

---

praised enough, I have for years and years begun each day with Mozart, and only then (aside from the daily newspaper) turned to my *Dogmatics*" ("A Testimonial to Mozart," p. 16). The place of Mozart's music in Barth's daily working routine has been confirmed by his wife, Nelly Barth, as related to Ved Mehta, in *The New Theologian* (London: Weidenfeld & Nicolson, 1965), p. 108; also cited in John Bowden, *Karl Barth* (London: SCM Press, 1971), p. 9.

92. See, for example, "The Christian's Place in Society" (the "Tambach Lecture"), in *The Word of God and the Word of Man,* trans. Douglas Horton (New York: Harper Torchbooks, Harper & Brothers Publishers, 1957), pp. 272-327; and *The Epistle to the Romans,* trans. of the 6th ed. by Edwyn C. Hoskyns (London: Oxford University Press, 1968).

clare Christ "the one and only cultured man."[93] Given that Barth inverted Feuerbach's anthropological critique of religion by affirming that in Christ we are confronted with the "humanity of God,"[94] he was able to reintroduce the language of parables in his later dogmatic theology in his consideration of the prophetic office of Christ in witnessing to his own work of reconciliation.[95] He is able to generate the fruitfulness of Christological "parables of the kingdom" without any sense of betraying his central convictions concerning the grammar of the knowledge of God.

A decade after Bonhoeffer disparaged Barth's "positivism of revelation" while also declaring the coming of age of the "un-religious" world, Karl Barth — whether in deliberate response to Bonhoeffer's critique or otherwise — outlined the existence of Christological "parables of the kingdom," thus reviving a category that he used in his earlier theology to moderate the pretensions of Christian socialism which might mistakenly aspire to the "wholly other" kingdom of God. Almost forty years later, Barth was now using parable language to express the fruitfulness of Christ's prophetic witness to his own work of reconciliation, to which both the created and secular orders can testify within their particular limitations, according to God's will (*Church Dogmatics* IV/3.1, § 69.2).

While expounding the possibility of "true words" *extra muros ecclesiae* as "parables of the kingdom" in his late 1955 and early 1956 lectures which would later form *Church Dogmatics* IV/3.1, Barth resolutely refused to give any concrete examples of such "parables."[96] A number of theologians have speculated as to whether Barth is deliberately and specifically responding to Bonhoeffer's rebuke at this point concerning "positivism," which may be so — Barth does not explicitly say so himself.[97] But behind Barth's dogmatic abstractions lies

---

93. "Evangelium und Bildung" (Gospel and Culture), in *Theologische Studien*, vol. 2 (Zollikon-Zurich: Evangelische Buchhandlung, 1938), p. 6.

94. "The Humanity of God," a lecture delivered at the meeting of the Swiss Reformed Ministers' Association in Aarau, on 25 September 1956, in *The Humanity of God*, trans. John Newton Thomas and Thomas Wieser (Atlanta: John Knox Press, 1960), pp. 37-65.

95. *CD* IV/3.1, §69.2, pp. 38-165.

96. *CD* IV/3.1, §69.2, p. 135.

97. For example, Charles Marsh writes: "As the driving force behind theological discussions of worldliness and secularity, Bonhoeffer must be recognized, at the same time, as a primary inspiration of Barth's treatment of these themes in his discussion of 'secular parables' in *Church Dogmatics* IV.3" (*Reclaiming Dietrich Bonhoeffer*, p. 27). See also Pangritz, *Karl Barth in the Theology of Dietrich Bonhoeffer*, writing about Barth's "Doctrine of Lights" in *CD* IV/3.1: "The later volumes of *Church Dogmatics* clearly manifest how Barth accommodated Bonhoeffer's concern. . . . Barth's most substantive agreement with Bonhoeffer is

the paradigm of his beloved Mozart, which can clearly be demonstrated by examining the same deployment of parabolic language in contemporaneous works by Barth on the occasion of the 1956 Mozart bicentennial.[98]

Barth employed exactly the same parabolic terminology to describe his understanding of the theological importance of Mozart's music in a series of lectures and essays commemorating the bicentenary of Mozart's birth that were composed contemporaneously with the exploration of Christological parables in *Church Dogmatics* IV/3. It is submitted that, like a musical score, the linear, "horizontal" readings of these much debated passages in the *Church Dogmatics* — which many incorrectly interpret to be a relapse into "natural theology" — must be integrated "vertically" with the harmonic complexity of what Barth has to say about the parables of Mozart's music.[99]

In these disputed passages from his dogmatic theology, Barth claims that Jesus Christ, as the one true Word of God, bears witness to himself and his work of reconciliation by miraculously calling forth "parables" that tes-

---

found, however, in section 69, 'The Glory of the Mediator' (CD IV.3.1). Without directly referring to Bonhoeffer, Barth comes very close to Bonhoeffer's discussion of the 'world come of age,' the world that seeks to be taken seriously precisely in its 'religionlessness' and possibly even in its 'godlessness which is full of promise' in light of Christ, the Lord of the world" (pp. 133-34.)

98. As far as I can tell, no theologian who has connected the "secular parables" in Barth's *CD* IV/3.1 with Bonhoeffer's "positivism" charge has been able to extend this connection to the operative analogue of Mozart in Barth as the paradigm of "parables of the kingdom." It is particularly surprising that Pangritz does not make this connection in *Karl Barth in the Theology of Dietrich Bonhoeffer* given that he has also authored the only monograph on Bonhoeffer's use of "polyphony" *(Polyphonie des Lebens),* and has also written on Barth and Mozart; see Pangritz, "'Freie Zuneigung': Über Karl Barths Verhältnis zu Mozart" ("'Free Affection': Karl Barth in Relation to Mozart") in *Störenfriedels Zeddelkasten — Geschenkpapiere zum 60. Geburtstag von Friedrich-Wilhelm Marquardt* (Berlin: Alektor Verlag, 1991), pp. 187-202. The only author to approximately approach this connection is Stanley Hauerwas, whose 2001 Gifford Lectures — *With the Grain of the Universe: The Church's Witness and Natural Theology* (Grand Rapids: Brazos Books, 2001) — champions Barth's exegesis of Christological witness in *CD* IV/3.1, and makes passing reference to the appropriateness of Barth's employment of musical metaphors in this section, given his love of Mozart (p. 197 n. 51 and p. 216). Hauerwas also dismisses Bonhoeffer's "offhand" "positivism" rebuke as betraying "the deep continuity between Barth and Bonhoeffer, particularly in terms of their theological metaphysics," for it mistakenly assumes that "Barth is trying to answer a question that he thought should not be asked" (p. 190 n. 37).

99. Hauerwas's 2001 Gifford Lectures also refute the idea that Barth is relapsing into natural theology in *CD* IV/3.1. See also ch. 5 of my unpublished doctoral dissertation, *Parables of the Kingdom,* which attempts to demonstrate that Barth was reconfiguring a Christological "theology of nature" in *CD* IV/3.1.

tify to his glory — not only in the Bible and the church, but also in "secularity." Such "signs" and "attestations" are secondary eschatological forms, whose provisionality points to the unique and paradigmatic primacy of revelation and reconciliation in Christ who alone has the capacity to call them forth.[100] Barth also speaks of the "lights of creation" within the *"theatrum gloriae Dei"* (Calvin) of the cosmos that dependently testify to the reconciliation wrought in and through Christ, the "one true light of life."[101]

The hermeneutical key required to unlock these passages of dogmatic theology can be found in Barth's assessment of Mozart's music as "parables of the kingdom."[102] Barth refers to Mozart's music as "theology," a "miraculous" phenomenon akin to "revelation," "mediating" the praise of the cosmos, and in conformity with Scripture and proclamation. Mozart's music has a place in the doctrines of creation and eschatology, and witnesses to the theonomous *perichoresis* of the triune life. The themes of Mozart's music discerned by Barth correlate with the anticipated content of the secular "parables" discussed in his dogmatic theology. More precisely, Mozart testifies regarding the lights of creation, and brings to sound the constancy and praise of the created order.[103] Barth states the theological significance of Mozart in unambiguous terms:

> I am not . . . inclined to confuse or identify salvation history with any part of the history of art. But the golden sounds and melodies of Mozart's music have from early times spoken to me not as *gospel* but as *parables* of the realm of God's free grace as revealed in the gospel — and they do so again and again with great spontaneity and directness.[104]

Given that it appears highly likely that Barth had the musical analogue of Mozart in mind when exploring the possibility of secular "parables of the kingdom" in the *Church Dogmatics,* Barth is clearly allowing music to witness to God's reconciling act in Christ not just in the church, but also in the world of secularity.

100. *CD* IV/3.1, pp. 112-30.
101. *CD* IV/3.1, pp. 135-65.
102. "Mozart's Freedom," in *Wolfgang Amadeus Mozart,* pp. 56-57; and *How I Changed My Mind,* pp. 71-72.
103. See the 1956 bicentenary essays collected together in *Wolfgang Amadeus Mozart.* See also *CD* III/3, pp. 297-99, where Barth praises Mozart for voicing creation's praise even in the presence of the "shadow side" *(Scahttenseite)* of the universe, which signifies its temporal limits and finitude, including death.
104. *How I Changed My Mind,* pp. 71-72; my italics.

Resonance

If we can accept that Barth's analysis of "parables of the kingdom" in the *Church Dogmatics* assumes a musical paradigm, then a comparison with Bonhoeffer's conception of the "polyphony of life" produces great resonance.[105]

1. Bonhoeffer's description of the *cantus firmus* (our love for God) being the only limit of endless worldly counterpoint is paralleled in Barth's similar metaphor of Christology standing at the center of expanding concentric rings of prophetic witness in secularity and nature.[106] In both cases, it is our orientation to God and Christ as the center of gravity that anchors all human earthly existence. Both contrapuntal living and parabolic exposition point beyond themselves to the *cantus firmus* which give meaning and value to these secondary forms of witness. They possess their own integrity; nevertheless, the worldliness of both modes of existence has their identity constituted in God's gracious accompaniment.

2. Barth's designation of Mozart's music as "parables" mediates between Bonhoeffer's charge of "positivism of revelation" and Barth's own repudiation of "natural theology," much as Bonhoeffer understands "polyphony" holding together what he describes as "ultimate" (the divine) and "penultimate" (that which is worldly). Both categories link without synthesizing, preserving essential differences within a unity — a Chalcedonian unity, as Bonhoeffer expresses it. For Bonhoeffer, our love for God *(cantus firmus)* must not be confused with our love of the world (counterpoint); for Barth, "parables of the kingdom" in the natural and secular world are not to be mistaken for "natural theology." The wholeness into which the contrapuntal themes fit does not obliterate their own independent melodic beauty. So also, the parabolic witness to the mystery of God's kingdom is affirmed precisely in its vocation and limitation as witness. This is appropriate for the mediatory function of Christ in both Bonhoeffer's and Barth's theology. The *cantus firmus* is established as the ground of contrapuntal improvisation, permitting and enabling — yet they are not to be confused, just as the provisional parabolic testimony

---

105. It is worth pointing out that while Mozart's music is of course "polyphonic" in the broad sense of that term, in terms of compositional texture most of his music is not "polyphonic" but "homophonic." Bonhoeffer's exploration of "polyphony of life" clearly has the great contrapuntal music of Bach in mind as both paradigm and accompaniment. Nevertheless, both theologians are working with analogues of multi-voice music that resonate with similar models of Christian witness.

106. *CD* IV.3.1, pp. 118-25.

stands between the ultimate mystery of God and the worldly limits of human experience and understanding.

This is precisely what Barth means when he stresses that "gospel" should not be confused with "parable" in his discussion of Mozart.[107] The fallacy of carelessly treating music as "gospel" or "revelation" — which is so catastrophic and idolatrous in negligent musical discourse, whether within the theological discipline or in secular music criticism — is thereby corrected.[108]

3. The provisionality of parable language in Barth, and the fragmentariness of life that Bonhoeffer knits together with polyphony, connotes the demand to struggle and work on the connecting up of the narrative "whole" that music requires of its individual participants. Bonhoeffer describes this as the process of "conforming to Christ," our love for whom forms the *cantus firmus* of all other love and worldly engagement. The "freedom" and "responsibility" which both theologians emphasize in this context illustrates the constructivist — rather than "positivist" — nature of musical meaning that underlies their reasoning. In both Bonhoeffer and Barth, responsibility and a certain humility (self-deprecatory, in Bonhoeffer's case) condition the freedom of musical collaboration. The fragments of Bonhoeffer's prison writings, like the fragments of his own life, testify to the eschatological hope he placed in God's great act of recapitulation. And even Barth laments the fact that, like Mozart's *Requiem* and Schubert's *Unfinished Symphony,* the thirteen part-volumes, ten thousand pages, and six million words that make up the *Church Dogmatics* are, ultimately, incomplete.[109]

4. Parabolic language in Barth and polyphonic language in Bonhoeffer necessarily invites us to consider the "invitational" and "participatory" nature of the life of Christian witness. The natural images used by Jesus in his parables are not in and of themselves parabolic, but become such as God capacitates and enhances them as Christological events. Thus, we might speak

107. *How I Changed My Mind,* pp. 71-72.

108. An old Chinese proverb states: "When a man points to the moon, the idiot looks at the finger." This is very much what Barth has in mind when he refers to the "prodigious index finger" of John the Baptist in Grünewald's Isenheim altarpiece which points away from himself to the crucified Christ (*CD* I/1, pp. 112, 262; I/2, p. 125). A copy of this painting hung above Barth's desk in his study, and, from early days, he clearly understood this to be a paradigm of proper biblical Christian witness. "We think of John the Baptist in Grünewald's painting of the crucifixion, with his strangely pointing hand. It is this hand which is in evidence in the Bible" ("Biblical Questions, Insights, and Vistas," in *The Word of God and the Word of Man,* p. 65).

109. Which is appropriate, given the divine attribute of perfection — see preface to *CD* IV/4.

of Christ himself as a "self-enacted parable" (Austin Farrer).[110] The primary purpose of parables is not that we might understand the kingdom of God, but that we might *experience* it, as God invades our time and gifts us the temporality of narrative under the form of parables. Essentially, this underscores the performative and participatory nature of parables in theological discourse. Likewise, the *cantus firmus* calls forth the improvisation and transformation accomplished in contrapuntal invention, empowering and activating the latent possibilities in the *cantus firmus* itself. As such, parabolic and contrapuntal existence are both essentially "invitational" categories of experience, inspiring a striving after God as revealed in Christ that will always be penultimate. Indeed, Barth's terminology of "witness" and "testimony" is a summons to actively engage and transform the world that aligns with Bonhoeffer's vocational understanding of Christian life as simply "witness to Christ." Just as Christ's "witness" meets with the direct and indirect "witness" of Scripture and the church, so also the musician becomes the responsive covenant partner freed up by the Spirit of God to engage with the world — for musical experience is not passive, but requires active participation within the matrix of the musical performance.

5. Barth's celebration of the "exemplary listening" of Mozart corresponds to Bonhoeffer's requirement that the contrapuntal elements of the Christian life keep "in tune" with the *cantus firmus*. The thrust of Bonhoeffer's argument is that earthly loves must be in tune with our love for God: this primary responsibility requires us to always be attentive to God or else we will lose track of the "polyphony of life." In this regard, Barth's emphasis on *hearing,* and *listening to,* the Word of God comports with the gospel injunction and standard parabolic formulation: "He who has ears to hear, let him hear." To borrow a phrase from Thomas Merton, Barth's exposition of Mozart's theological significance embodies a lesson in the "sound of listening" that could serve as the motto for all Barthian theology. This is a double process: Mozart listens to, and then sets to music, the sound of creation's praise, which Barth in turn discerns in his music. Likewise, when counterpoint ceases to "listen" to the *cantus firmus,* it becomes chaotic noise.

6. The essentially "communitarian" conception of polyphonic living that Bonhoeffer advances conforms to Barth's parables of the "kingdom," also an essentially "social" category. Bonhoeffer identifies play and friendship as essential elements of a rediscovered "aesthetic existence." Barth's own

---

110. "Revelation" by Austin Farrer in *Faith and Logic,* ed. Basil Mitchell (London: George, Allen & Unwin, 1957), p. 98.

assessment of Mozart teems with the language of play, and thus sows the seeds for serious constructive engagement and dialogue between theology and music. In his dogmatic theology Barth makes clear that "play" is constitutive of the genuine joy derived from *fellowship* with God that should accompany all human activity. Mozart's music teaches us how to play for it responsively "simply sings and sounds," and thus becomes a parable of the liberated self-giving of perfect play in which we fulfill our creaturely task of singing together in witness. Bonhoeffer's "polyphony of life" is communitarian in the way in which it binds all earthly loves to the *cantus firmus* of our love for God; and Barth, even if he does not explicitly draw out the communal implications of his musical analogues, is nevertheless exploring musical parables of "kingdom" life which witness to, and enlarge the understanding of, the church community reconciled in Christ. Uniquely, the participatory relationality and sociality of music makes available to us a sonic model of individual and communal playing, where humanity freely improvises (within its limitations) its witness to God, who graciously makes humanity's active play and playful work a parable of his own Triune activity.

7. Finally, Barth's model of parabolic living speaks to Bonhoeffer's announcement of an era predicated on God's non-existence. Parables engage the imagination and experience of the hearer. Although Barth's exploration of Mozart's parables is pneumatologically impoverished, the logic of Spirit language is compelling in terms of the power of God to capacitate someone to have the "ears to hear" the parable, just as the Spirit inspires the creative artist who constitutes the parable in the first place. Parables reach through the commonplace to its alleged transcendent ground without evacuating the mundane and ordinary of its proper dignity. As such, they cannot be mere examples, but constitute an enlargement of our perception of the world, making new things familiar and familiar things new, enabling us to comprehend things as they truly are. The parabolic event is both informative and representative, disturbing and critiquing our assumptions about piety, bringing together profoundly theological and non-religious dimensions.

Barth's tribute to Mozart's music — "that which moves me most in theology and politics"[111] — concerns its "creatureliness," and therefore the humble awareness, and yet glorious affirmation, of its limitations. This does indeed speak to Bonhoeffer's deepest concerns about the shape of Christian existence in the "world come of age." His last writings break down the dualistic barriers erected between the "two spheres" of ethical-political exis-

111. *How I Changed My Mind*, pp. 71-72.

tence, within and outside of the church, just as he seeks to integrate his theological reflections about churchly and religionless music — for both partake in the "pain and joy" of polyphonic living.

Conclusion

This essay has sought to discuss the musical analogues that Barth and Bonhoeffer employ to express some of their deepest theological convictions, and thereby demonstrate how the resonance of musical thinking in their contrasting theological pursuits assists us in effecting some *rapprochement* at a point where much misunderstanding and dispute exists. Each in his own way — through metaphors of polyphony and parables — articulates a vision of Christian life lived out as witness to God in Christ that is fully engaged with the richness and diversity of worldly existence.

Roseanne Cash, Johnny Cash's daughter and an accomplished singer in her own right, observed that all of her father's music seems to combine both elements of "light" and "darkness" at the same time without negating or adulterating the truth and significance of either.[112] Barth makes largely the same point about the peculiar theological genius of Mozart in hearing "the whole context of providence":

> [H]e heard the harmony of creation to which the shadow also belongs but in which the shadow is not darkness, deficiency is not defeat, sadness cannot become despair, trouble cannot degenerate into tragedy and infinite melancholy is not ultimately forced to claim undisputed sway. Thus the cheerfulness in this harmony is not without its limits. But the light shines all the more brightly because it breaks forth from the shadow. The sweetness is also bitter and cannot therefore cloy. Life does not fear death but knows it well.[113]

The exploration of musical analogues in the theology of Barth and Bonhoeffer points us toward some of the ways in which — as is evident in the work of artists like Johnny Cash and Bruce Springsteen — music may bear "witness, *in the Christian sense of the word.*" Music is a participatory experience that links worldly existence with its transcendent ground in God's loving, reconciling self-revelation in Christ — but in the form of "parables"

112. In the CD sleeve notes to *Cash Unearthed* (American Recordings, 2003).
113. *CD* III/3, p. 298.

or "polyphony" so as not to confuse the otherness of divine existence with the integrity of human creativity and experience. Music helps us do theology in a way that respects the fact that music testifies to the ways of God, but must never be mistaken for an aesthetic idolatry.

In one of Barth's most purple passages from the *Church Dogmatics*, he articulates a theological vision of human existence that even Bonhoeffer might say "Amen!" to:

> What is lacking to the self-attestations of the creature as such . . . they can acquire as and when God Himself begins to speak and claims and uses them in His service. . . . They can blend their voices with that of God. He could hardly be the God who has lent them these voices if they could not do this as commanded and empowered by Him. What they say can so harmonize with what He Himself says that to hear Him is to hear them, and to hear them to hear Him, so that listening to the *polyphony* of creation as the external basis of the covenant . . . is listening to the symphony for which it was elected and determined from eternity and which the Creator alone has the power to evoke, yet according to His Word the will also. Nor has He only the will. For when He speaks His one and total Word concerning the covenant which is the internal basis of creation, this symphony is in fact evoked, and even the self-witness of creation in all the diversity of its voices can and will give its unanimous applause.[114]

114. *CD* IV/3.1, pp. 159-60; my italics.

11. Musical Time and Eschatology

Alastair Borthwick, Trevor Hart, and Anthony Monti

Preliminary Contexts

Studies in the psychology of music have often been conducted in the context of a post-Enlightenment, pre-twentieth-century repertoire. A similar emphasis is beginning to emerge in the interdisciplinary area of theology and music, although occasional forays into more recent classical music are to be found.[1] The place of popular music in discussions is also well established. While not as culturally biased as the notion that God is an Englishman (Austro-German would be nearer the mark, if the predominant repertoire is taken as an indicator), interdisciplinarity involving music does appear to be predisposed toward a particular set of cultural values. In this context, general statements about the theological significance of "music" need to be carefully located: What kind of music is being referred to? Who is listening to it? World music, early music, popular music: all of these are likely to offer a range of complementary or contradictory insights into theology that require our attention. However, the focus of this essay is on that other neglected area of music, and what it has to offer our engagement with eschatological issues: modern music since the tail-end of the nineteenth century, specifically the transitional works of Mahler and other music associated with the modernist aesthetic.

What will be attempted in this essay is perhaps most helpfully described

---

1. Jeremy Begbie, for example, includes a study of John Tavener, Boulez, and Cage in *Theology, Music and Time* (Cambridge: Cambridge University Press, 2000), pp. 128-47.

in terms of a distinction drawn, for example, by Jürgen Moltmann between "natural theology" and a "theology of nature." Natural theology, Moltmann observes, is about the "the self-evidence of nature as God's creation,"[2] presuming that anyone can "read-off" certain truths about God by paying careful attention to the natural and human worlds. Yet, Moltmann notes, the biblical traditions do not see things this way at all. For them, "The world does not disclose itself as God's creation just by itself. It is only because he reveals himself as its creator, preserver and saviour that God manifests the world as his creation."[3] This is precisely where a "theology of nature" begins; for its concern is "to interpret nature in the light of the self-revelation of the creative God."[4] If there is "theology" to be had at all from nature apart from faith, Moltmann suggests, then it is in the form of a world which points beyond the horizons of its own possibilities, containing "traces" and "parables" of a future together with God which, for now, tantalize without satisfying, leaving us hungry for the reality itself.[5]

The existence of the arts must be acknowledged among those aspects of finite existence which, on the presupposition of a merely finite source and destiny for the world, are the most enigmatic and raise questions of a properly religious and theological sort. In this paper we shall suggest that certain formal properties of modernist music in particular chafe deliberately at the edges of our experience of finitude in this way. This chafing may and should be felt in one way or another by any sensitive participant in the music, whether composer, performer, or listener. Faith, as such, is not required (though where it exists it makes the chafing worse).[6] Knowledge of the world "as" creation, Moltmann suggests, might therefore be said to exist under the conditions of unbelief as well as those of faith; but in the form of unbelief such knowledge has (and can have) no awareness of its own true identity. It depends on the testimony of faith to reveal this to it. Faith, meanwhile, (in the form of theology) is called not just to state *that* but to suggest, at least, *how* the world points beyond itself as a "true and real parable and promise of the kingdom."[7] Such is part of the task of a "theology of

2. Jürgen Moltmann, *God in Creation: A New Theology of Creation and the Spirit of God,* trans. Margaret Kohl (London: SCM Press, 1985), p. 54.

3. Moltmann, *God in Creation,* p. 54.

4. Moltmann, *God in Creation,* p. 53.

5. Moltmann, *God in Creation,* p. 58.

6. See Moltmann, *Theology of Hope: On the Ground and the Implications of a Christian Eschatology* (London: SCM Press, 1967), p. 21.

7. Moltmann, *God in Creation,* p. 59.

nature" in Moltmann's terms, and it is to this task that this essay, with its concentration on "eschatological" resonances in modern music, is intended as a contribution.

As a form of art rooted more obviously than some in temporality as well as physicality, music has *prima facie* resonances with Christian theology's concern with questions about cosmic beginnings and endings, and some of these have been taken up and explored deliberately by musicians in the modern era. So, for example, the idea of composition itself as creation *ex nihilo* was exposed as a fallacy by the very short-lived experiment of integral serialism, as practiced by Pierre Boulez and Karlheinz Stockhausen.[8] The annihilation of historical precedence is only partially achieved (genre, for instance, is unaffected by serial processes), and the loss of individual creative freedom is the price paid for this dubious prize. In some instances, modernist music evinces a preoccupation with *a posteriori* nihilism. Theodor Adorno draws attention to this aspect of Alban Berg's music,[9] and the deliberate divergence of such music from the hopefulness which characterizes Christian faith should not be underestimated; but for the purposes of justifying entry into the hermeneutic circle of theology and modern music such examples are more than counteracted by a roll-call of twentieth-century composers whose work-lists include pieces that are explicitly Christian: Stravinsky, Messiaen, Penderecki, and Arvo Pärt, to name just a few. In one sense, this opposition of twentieth-century composers either sympathetic or antagonistic toward Christianity only highlights the most obvious connections or disjunctions between modern music and Christianity: explicitly Christian music tends to affirm what we already know theologically (Stravinsky's *Canticum Sacrum* is not intended to be ironic, for instance);[10] and Berg's nihilistic conclusion to *Wozzeck* really is unrelentingly hopeless within the framework of the opera. The emphasis in this essay, while acknowledging these explicit distinctions, is equally geared toward the way in which

8. For discussion, cf. Begbie, *Theology, Music and Time*, ch. 7, esp. pp. 191-98. Ironically, Boulez was pursuing an idea he had first encountered in the piano piece *Mode de valeurs et d'intensités* by his teacher Olivier Messiaen (a devout Christian). The most significant pieces written using integral serialism fall within a period of approximately eighteen months.

9. Theodor Adorno, *Alban Berg: Master of the Smallest Link*, trans. Julie Brand and Christopher Hailey (Cambridge: Cambridge University Press, 1994).

10. Michael Hall's *Leaving Home: A Conducted Tour of Twentieth-Century Music* (London: Faber and Faber, 1996), though not especially concerned with the relationship between modern music and Christianity, points to the continuing presence of hope in at least some works in this direct sense. See the discussion of Luciano's Berio's *Laborintus II*, pp. 227-30.

some modern music might be *implicitly* consonant with or evocative of the shape of Christian hope and the movement of the present into God's promised future, even to the extent of contradicting the apparent intentions of the composer; to quote Jacques Maritain, "the artist, whether he knows it or not, is consulting God when he looks at things."[11]

Temporality and Teleology

One way in which music is particularly suitable for representing eschatological reality is its ability to accommodate different modes of temporal engagement. As Günter Thomas points out: "Jesus was resurrected not just into the eternal life of God but into a new existence that happens to include such a rich variety of times that created time is not excluded."[12] As *the* essentially temporal art form, music is perhaps uniquely capable of embodying the "rich variety of times" that characterize the new creation inaugurated by the resurrection of Jesus.

Temporality is one of two related concepts, along with teleology, in terms of which the case for a fundamental consonance between modern music and Christian eschatological hope may be argued. The theological implications of both of these concepts have been studied in depth elsewhere in a tonal context, and their relevance to eschatology has been made abundantly clear, but in music of the twentieth century composers have attempted to re-engage with these concepts in new ways. The linear time that is characteristic of tonal music (or, more precisely, of *conceptions* of tonal music), often in highly sophisticated, multi-layered forms, has, for composers such as Harrison Birtwistle, given way to a dualistic conception in terms of linear and circular time.[13] Similarly, the teleological processes that underlie tonal music, as evidenced by their centrality to Heinrich Schenker's understanding of tonality,[14] have been replaced by non-teleological processes in the work of a wide-ranging group of composers, most of whom have been influenced by either Stravinsky or Mahler. The effect of this latter change lies

11. Jacques Maritain, *Art and Scholasticism* (New York: Sheed and Ward, 1933), p. 64.

12. Günther Thomas, "Resurrection to New Life: Pneumatological Implications of the Eschatological Transition," in *Resurrection: Theological and Scientific Assessments*, ed. Ted Peters, Robert John Russell, and Michael Welker (Grand Rapids: Eerdmans, 2002), p. 264.

13. Jeremy Begbie has discussed the limitations of a linear view of musical time in *Theology, Music and Time*, e.g., pp. 56-59.

14. Heinrich Schenker, *Free Composition*, trans. E. Oster (New York: Longman, 1979).

at the heart of musical modernism itself: "the tension between the attempt to embody fragmentation and the impulse to transcend it."[15]

How are these technical differences to be reconciled with the hermeneutic interpretations of tonal music? The perspectives are undoubtedly new, but are they contradictory or paradoxical in relation to the tonal ones? And what of other technical categories such as the superimposition of musical ideas without harmonic unity (Tippett), or the reconfiguration of musical time in relation to musical space as an aspect of psychological time (itself leading to a superimposition of ideas)? Such developments appear to place a question mark against too easy an appeal, for instance, to fugal writing as a metaphor for the eternal "perichoresis" that is the Triune God.[16] By drawing our attention to the conventional nature of fugue as a form, they compel recognition of the fact that while such musical parallels may indeed be theologically instructive, the instruction they provide is sometimes by way of contingent illumination rather than rooted in any necessary link between musical form and heavenly archetype. Not all music need be a creaturely "vestigium trinitatis." And, as we shall see, the "modeling" or remodeling of eschatological ideas in musical form, too, where it occurs, can embrace different musical possibilities, drawing out different facets of a dense and complex expectation.

Tonal Closure and Hope

We may begin by looking at closure. Perhaps no musical figure more fully embodies the tension between "common practice" and "modern" techniques of closure than Gustav Mahler (1860-1911). As Robert G. Hopkins observes, "Mahler was a composer of tonal music, but there is general agreement that his works exemplify the gradual breakdown of tonal syntax — especially tonal *harmonic* syntax — during the late nineteenth and early twentieth centuries."[17] Although there are several ways in which Mahler's

---

15. Arnold Whittall, "Modernist Aesthetics, Modernist Music," in *Music Theory in Concept and Practice,* ed. James M. Baker, David W. Beach, and Jonathan W. Bernard (Rochester, NY: University of Rochester Press, 1997), p. 158.

16. See Anthony Monti, *A Natural Theology of the Arts: Imprint of the Spirit* (Aldershot, Hampshire: Ashgate, 2003) pp. 119-20, 143-44. Also see Robert W. Jenson, *Systematic Theology,* vol. 1: *The Triune God* (Oxford: Oxford University Press, 1997), pp. 234-36.

17. Robert G. Hopkins, *Closure and Mahler's Music: The Role of Secondary Parameters* (Philadelphia: University of Pennsylvania Press, 1990), p. 64.

music contributes to the breakdown of common practice era tonality, the most important way is undoubtedly the composer's eschewing of strong authentic cadences. Such strong cadences are the traditional means for establishing closure in tonal music, and offer a natural musical parable for a similarly "strong" and satisfying end to the world and its history. Mahler's avoidance of these cadences entails that he must resort to different means to establish musical closure. These different means, in their turn, we suggest, can model an alternative kind of eschatological "closure" entirely consonant with the wider shape of Christian hope.

To appreciate the significance of Mahler's move away from strong cadences as devices of closure, we should recall their function in the music of such common practice era giants as the eighteenth-century composers Haydn and Mozart. In their works, strong cadences create a sense of anticipation or expectation, either of new material, the return of familiar material, or of an implication (such as a variation or repetition) of that material. In classical tonal music, these figures of anticipation, expectation, and implication point to their resolution in a final moment of closure in the tonic (or "home") key — a strong authentic cadence which constitutes the ultimate point of arrival, the "goal" *(telos)* of the work for which it was designed from the beginning.

One can readily see why this model of closure has sometimes been appealed to in modeling an eschatological hope which, in broad terms anyway, has an essentially goal-oriented or teleological dimension. From the Christian perspective, all of history has its proper origin and *telos*, its Alpha and Omega, its beginning and end, in him through whom and for whom all things were created, and in whom all things hold together (see Col. 1:15ff.). Yet this claim is misunderstood if we simply identify history's temporal "end" with this appointed *telos* in Christ or, we might say, conflate the logic of mere *chronos* with that of *kairos*.[18] From one angle (though by no means a privileged one), a Christian account of the world's history may be plotted as

---

18. The distinction indicated by these respective Greek terms is drawn from Moltmann's characteristic use rather than that of the New Testament. See, for example, Jürgen Moltmann, *Science and Wisdom*, trans. Margaret Kohl (London: SCM Press, 2003), pp. 95-97. For Moltmann, *chronos* is the irreversible linear sequence of homogeneous points in time, flowing irretrievably from the past into the future, "devouring its children" as it goes (see Moltmann, *The Coming of God*, trans. Margaret Kohl [London: SCM Press, 1996], p. 24). *Kairos* is time *sub specie aeternitatis*, time in which the power of eternity is experienced as present, breaking the stranglehold of transience and creating genuinely new possibilities, and anticipating the final fulfillment of time in God's promised future.

a linear temporal movement under God from beginning to end, from something that occurred "in the beginning" to a climactic point in "the last days." From another perspective, though, the world's temporal end is anything but final, being rather a point of transition from one stage of creaturely existence to another, and one in which the world finds its actual fulfillment through redemptive transformation (death, and resurrection into a new creation). Furthermore, Christian teleology needs to be decisively distinguished from the "myth of progress" which has so dominated the imagination of modernity.[19] The myth conflates the physical fact of the passage of time with the idea of a progress in intellectual, technological, social, moral, and spiritual terms, so that we expect things inevitably to get better in the future than they have been in the past, culminating in some shattering climax of projected (but usually only dimly imagined) "perfection." This, then, is an "immanent teleology," one which sees nature and history themselves as already containing the resources and processes needful for evolution toward their own eventual fulfillment. Christian faith, though, has a rather different story to tell about the world and its prospects. It is a story which faces squarely (1) a deep-rooted moral and spiritual recalcitrance manifest in our humanity (one apparently indifferent to variations of time and place) and (2) the relentless entropic movement of all things toward death and decay, swallowing up even our best and most noble achievements in the futility of transience. Curiously, while modernity generally prefers to deny the former reality (despite abundant empirical testimony to it) it wholeheartedly endorses the latter, but does not permit this in any way to disrupt its essential optimism. Yet left to its own devices, this account tells us, the world actually has little to hope for, being destined to peter out in a return to that nothingness out of which it was, in the beginning, summoned into existence.

"Real life is always misrepresented by those who wish to make it lead up to a conclusion," the novelist Gustave Flaubert once observed; "God alone," he continued, "can do that."[20] And it is in this vital apprehension, of course, that the source of Christian hope lies, a fact which renders it wholly incompatible with optimism or the scientistic projection of progress.[21] Flaubert

19. See on this Richard Bauckham and Trevor Hart, *Hope against Hope: Christian Eschatology at the Turn of the Millennium* (Grand Rapids: Eerdmans, 1999), pp. 1-25.

20. Cited in P. T. Forsyth, *The Justification of God* (London: Duckworth, 1916), p. 223.

21. Strictly speaking, of course, scientism has no place for teleology in these terms, the categories of value being ones imported into rather than derived from its observations of pattern in the natural sphere. See on this, e.g., Philip Davis, *The Victorians* (Oxford: Oxford University Press, 2002), pp. 70-97.

was thinking on the scale of the individual life, but for Christian theology the same is true of the cosmos. Its hope rests on the fact of resurrection, not on a refusal to contemplate that unpalatable truth about the world of which the crucifixion is both a concrete instance and a supreme symbol. This, the corpse of Jesus on Golgotha tells us, is the most the world is capable of without God. This is a judgment we may not want to hear, but hear it we must. For unless and until we come to terms with the incapacity manifest here, we shall constantly be tempted to fix our hope in places unable to sustain its weight. Without the obduracy which denies that some things do indeed progress with the passage of time, and that we therefore have some reason to be thankful that we live in the twenty-first rather than twelfth century (or, perhaps more accurately, in modern Western rather than other societies), we must nonetheless put things in a bigger perspective than this, and admit that human life (on the individual and cosmic scales) cannot itself provide that "sense of an ending" which alone grants it meaning. God alone can do that. In other words, the object of Christian hope is properly finally a *transcendent* one, looking both upward and forward, beyond the imaginable range of this world's possibilities, to an action of God so drastic and radical that the biblical writers are finally compelled to picture it as a "new creation," something of which God alone is capable, and which will leave the world as we know it difficult to recognize.

One problem with appeal to the parable of strong musical closure in the tonic, therefore, is that, unqualified, it may reinforce the supposition that this familiar world will reach its climactic fulfillment in the "home" key, on the basis of themes, variations, and developments leading naturally (if sometimes unexpectedly) up to it, after which the performance of the work is complete and our aesthetic expectations with respect to it duly satisfied. Yet, we have just suggested, there is a vital sense in which this is not so. History's proper goal does not and cannot lie within its own temporal boundaries (its "end" in terms of the logic of *chronos*), but beyond them in the new creation of God. And the intersection of these two spheres of reality (now, in so far as there are already identifiable anticipations of this new creation in history's own midst, or at the point of its eventual advent) is one experienced not in the terms of this world, but precisely as an interruption of it,[22] a consideration suggestive, perhaps, of other musical parables. For now, though, our point is to draw attention to the fact that not all dimensions of Christian eschatology are exhaustively characterized by the teleological

22. See further, Bauckham and Hart, *Hope against Hope*, pp. 174-210.

model. Like all parables or metaphors, this one captures only part of the truth, and demands to be supplemented by others. And here is where Mahler comes in. For even as he contributes to the breakdown of tonal syntax as teleologically conceived, Mahler begins to develop new, non-cadential gestures of closure. Once we have examined examples of these gestures, we shall be in a position to discern their potential to shed light on a hitherto relatively neglected aspect of eschatology.

One example of such a gesture of closure is the conclusion to the third movement of Symphony No. 4 (measures 338-53).[23] This passage begins with an authentic cadence in the first three measures; from this cadence, the second violins, with their *pppp* melody, gradually fall from F♯6 in measure 338 to G4 in measure 344. This fall implies that the movement is about to achieve final closure on the tonic, G; yet such is not the case, for the movement will in fact end on the dominant chord. Thus the sense of final closure must be created through other means, which Robert G. Hopkins refers to as "secondary parameters."[24] One such parameter involves duration, as one of the motifs is repeated with gradually longer durations in measures 343-46 and still longer durations in measures 347-50, as though the passage were slowing down to a stop. Another such parameter involves instrumental timbre: in measures 351-52, first the basses and then the clarinets fall away, leaving a pure, ethereal compound timbre of flute and strings (all but one part of which are playing harmonics) for the final two measures. Together the lengthening of duration, the purifying of timbre, and (as yet another "secondary parameter") the softening of dynamics bring the music to silence following a dominant chord.

Thus, although the movement does not end on the expected tonic, giving a sense of arrival at a goal, it does produce an unmistakable effect of completion, due to the cumulative effects of the parameters described above. Indeed, the combination of these factors with the lack of the tonic may be said to generate its own distinctive kind of qualified "completion" — one that is not in

23. As with other musical examples, the authors urge readers to obtain recordings of the pieces discussed. Printed examples have not been included because the authors believe that these privilege the non-temporal aspects of the music, contrary to the essay's intentions. To understand musical time it is necessary to experience it through listening. Many of the music examples can be located straightforwardly in a wide range of recordings when, for example, they refer to the beginning or end of a movement. A small number will make reference to particular time points in specific recordings.

24. Hopkins, *Closure and Mahler's Music*. "Secondary parameters" is part of the subtitle of Hopkins's book.

fact closed and definitive, but instead points beyond itself, anticipating something more still to come, opening out into the potentially infinite. No wonder,
then, that this passage has been described as a form of heavenly "dissolution"
— and this impression is reinforced when we note that, after the silence, the
final dominant chord is resolved into the tonic in the opening measure of the
following movement, "A Child's View of Heaven."

Another example of a non-cadential gesture of closure, this time at the
conclusion to a symphony, occurs in the coda to the final movement of
Mahler's Symphony No. 9. Although, unlike the previous example, this coda
does end on the tonic in the final three measures, this tonic comes not as the
goal of a full emphatic "arrival" but as the end point of a process of fragmentary dissolution that fades into silence — in such a way that the silence itself
becomes part of the music. In a coda marked *Adagissimo* — the slowest possible speed, further slowed by additional directions in the score — both isolated pitches and thematic fragments are extended in duration to such an extent as to suggest that Mahler is loath to take leave of them. Perhaps the most
significant of these fragments is the motif for the viola (B♭-A♭-G♯-A♭) in
measure 180, which has featured prominently earlier in the movement. Repeated in eighth-notes in measure 182, it undergoes a remarkable final transformation in the last two measures when it is not only augmented to half-
notes but, more significantly, inverted, so that it now recalls the motif for
harps at the start of the symphony that recurs throughout the first movement. After this allusion to the beginning, "The rest is silence."

No wonder, then, that Leonard Bernstein describes this coda as "the
closest we have ever come, in any work of art, to experiencing the very act of
dying, of giving it all up":

> It *is* terrifying, and paralyzing, as the strands of sound disintegrate. We
> hold on to them, hovering between hope and submission. And one by one
> these spidery strands connecting us to life melt away, vanish from our fin-
> gers even as they dematerialize; we are holding two — then one. One, and
> suddenly none. For a petrifying moment there is only silence. Then again,
> a strand, a broken strand, two strands, one . . . none. . . . And in ceasing,
> we lose it all. But in letting go, we have gained everything.[25]

This last point deserves further comment. Bernstein describes the Ninth
as "a sonic presentation of death itself . . . which paradoxically reanimates us

25. Leonard Bernstein, *The Unanswered Question: Six Talks at Harvard* (Cambridge,
MA: Harvard University Press, 1976), p. 321.

every time we hear it."[26] Thus we experience this coda not as life denying but as life affirming — and perhaps not merely of past or present life. Recently another conductor, Benjamin Zander, in his recorded commentary on the Ninth, cites in this coda a brief quotation in the violins from one of Mahler's *Kindertötenlieder* ("The Songs for Dead Children"). According to Zander, this quotation suggests that Mahler may have had his daughter's death in mind when writing this coda and that therefore it may not be a straightforward expression of resignation or even farewell:

> The words in the song: "O be not afeard. The day is beautiful. They are only on their way to yonder height." We are too numb to move. But this brief vision of children seems to point mysteriously, not towards death, but towards life. The sound begins to evaporate; and then it ends very, very quietly, with a kind of peace that is not given to us often.[27] [Dare one suggest, "the peace which passeth understanding"?]

These two examples (from among many others that might have been cited) of Mahler's gestures of closure that avoid the return to a traditional strong cadence certainly suggest a different understanding of "closure" from that traditionally applied to eschatology by tonal analogies. The earlier notion of closure, which has come in for severe criticism in contemporary theology, is usefully summarized (and criticized) by Günter Thomas:

> Overall, the general understanding of the eschatological transition is more a deep sense of *ending* than of joyful life. The key metaphor is *closure*. Nothing new can happen since creation comes to its end. Transience is basically equated with perishability. Yet this notion of an ending is only one aspect of the concept of consummation. The other notion of *perfection* is not necessarily coupled with closure, and completion need not imply an ending.

In short, certain traditional views of closure, according to Thomas, rule out "temporality with an open future."[28]

Here we run up against some huge issues to do not just with metaphysics, but with the nature and function of language in contexts where what is at issue lies beyond the range of expectations ordinarily placed upon it.

26. Bernstein, *The Unanswered Question,* p. 318.

27. Benjamin Zander, "On Performing and Listening to Mahler: Symphony No. 9," Philharmonia Orchestra, Telarc, CD-80527C (1999).

28. Thomas, "Resurrection to New Life," p. 261.

Whether or not there will actually be something analogous to created space and time in the new creation of God is one question. It is certainly important to acknowledge, with Augustine, that time *as we know it* is "in creation" rather than creation being "in time." Temporality, in other words, is something which God calls into existence with the world, and not some absolute state of affairs to which he himself is subject. Whether we choose to answer the question about time and the new creation positively or negatively, or with apophatic reserve, though, it ought to be clear that *we are bound to think and speak in temporal terms* whenever we reach imaginatively beyond the limits of this world to picture how things may or may not be in the next. We cannot help doing so, and any attempt not to do so collapses quickly into meaninglessness and nonsense. If, therefore, we would speak of the new creation at all, then it can only be in terms of an imagined temporal relation to this world (in some sense it will come "after" this world has reached its temporal end) and something analogous to temporality pertaining there as here.

Just as it obliges us to speak of the unspeakable, so, too, Scripture, by its evocation of an analogy with creation, seems to require us to acknowledge the finitude and transience of the world we currently know, and encourages us to be bold rather than inhibited in our eschatological imagining of the promise of God. If there is indeed "temporality with an open future" to be reckoned with and made sense of, therefore, it cannot be supposed to lie in any open-ended extension of the current state of things. In that sense, the image of cosmic "completion" is an important one which cannot be let slip. The "last times" are indeed the last, viewed from the perspective of this old order. Yet Christian hope, rooted in the imagery of Old and New Testaments, looks for a *transcendent renewal of* this world rather than its wholesale replacement with some other world. This means that our world does indeed have a "future," even if that future does not lie (and cannot be understood) within the terms of its own mode of temporality. But such things cannot even be thought or said unless we are prepared to indulge the imaginative supposition of an open future. For completion and fulfillment are inextricably temporal categories, as, indeed, is "new." In short, we cannot both affirm (as Christian eschatology requires us to) that the true completion and fulfillment of this world lies "beyond" it (a temporal rather than a spatial metaphor in eschatological contexts) and simultaneously eschew the metaphorical projection of temporality into this transcendent "future." For what it is worth, we think there are very good reasons for supposing that something analogous to created time will indeed characterize the new creation, just as, on the basis of the doctrine of resurrection, we must suppose that something analogous to our current embodied (and thus spatial) existence will. But we need not establish that case here in order to make our basic point.

It is this very possibility of "temporality with an open future," on the other hand, that is suggested by the model of closure we have seen in Mahler. Whether by fading into an ethereal dominant, as in the Fourth, or by dissolving into a palpable silence, as in the Ninth, Mahler's gestures of closure suggest, in Thomas's words, that "completion need not imply an ending." Rather, completion may suggest an opening out onto that which is without end or limit — that is, onto infinity or, better perhaps, the transcendent future of God's promise.

To comprehend the significance of this, we may turn for help to one of the Cappadocian Fathers, Gregory of Nyssa (c. 330-395 C.E.). Arguing from the infinity of God — an infinity he understands not spatially, but temporally — Gregory maintains that the perfection to be attained in the life of the world to come is not one of a state of static timelessness. Rather, it is one of unlimited, temporal progress in the knowledge of God, since "at each stage the greater and superior good holds the attention of those who enjoy it and does not allow them to look at the past."[29] Thus on Gregory's view, the world to come is not a world where we finally "arrive" and all loose ends are tied, but instead is one of infinite progression into the unfathomable mystery of God. It is this ancient, yet strangely neglected, dimension to eschatology that is modeled by the sort of non-cadential gestures of closure that we find in Mahler.

Non-tonal Closure and an Eschatological Paradox

The loss of certain cadential features associated with long-range voice-leading in Mahler that is suggestive of a more open temporality is taken a step further in the music of Michael Tippett (1905-1998), specifically in the second period of his mature work. If Mahler's music is located in an era of musical transition, then in Tippett this historical tension is re-enacted at the level of the individual. In the music up to and including his Symphony no. 2 (1957) some significant characteristics of tonal music remain. Specifically, goal-directed motion still finds its conclusion in recognizable patterns of harmonic closure, but with the composition of his second opera, *King Priam*

29. Gregory of Nyssa, *Song of Songs*, trans. Casimir McCambley (Brookline, MA: Hellenic College Press, 1987), p. 128.

(1958-61), many of these common practice characteristics are either abandoned or radically re-interpreted. The music is now characterized by fragmentation, discontinuities, the statement rather than development of ideas, and a predisposition toward non-teleological patterns of organization. Closure through a return to a home key, for instance, does not even exist in the negative Mahlerian sense (ending on the dominant necessarily implies the existence of a tonic, even if arrival at the tonic is ultimately denied). If the discredited progressivist understanding of eschatology rooted in the modern myth of linear time (see the discussion of Bauckham's critique of Moltmann below, pp. 286-87) is further brought into question by Mahler's techniques of closure, then Tippett's radical alternatives to tonal closure *might* be thought to imply a complete denial of all that contributes to the concept of linear time, and thence progressivism, but this is not straightforwardly the case.

In his music of the 1960s and early 1970s, rather than abandon the possibility of closure and goal-directedness Tippett sought to find non-tonal counterparts to them. Some of these invoke tonal relationships but apply them to non-tonal objects. One of the most striking of these is the relationship of identity — fundamental to harmonic closure in most tonal music (the return to the home key) — between pitch material at the beginning and end of *The Vision of Saint Augustine* (1963-65). Though texturally and timbrally distinct, the two sections are based on the decidedly non-tonal pitch combinations of C_2, $B\flat_2$, E_3, F_3, $F\sharp_3$, B_3 and C_2, $F\sharp_2$, B_2, F_3, $B\flat_3$, E_4, respectively, though this identity is a consequence of the piece's preoccupation with circularity, as a later discussion will show (see below). As with other counterparts this one involves an element of "gesture" in the sense that its effectiveness depends not so much on perceptual properties as its context within Western music as a whole, a factor that will prove to be crucial in the theological exploration of Tippett's teleology. In contrast, Mahler's techniques of closure remain perceptual in the sense that the operation of secondary parameters is in accord with widespread, possibly even universal, psychological phenomena (such as becoming slower or quieter).[30]

One of the most significant gestures of closure employed by Tippett involves chords of "higher consonance" which, according to Arnold Whittall, "while giving some priority to [tonally] triadic elements, no longer require the exclusive presence of those elements in any privileged contexts: their

---

30. The universality of these phenomena is considered in Fred Lerdahl and Ray Jackendoff, *A Generative Theory of Tonal Music* (Cambridge, MA: MIT Press, 1983), as well as in more recent work by Lerdahl.

function is mediation rather than resolution."[31] While the function of such chords *is* wide-ranging within Tippett's music as a whole (such chords even appear in the pre–*King Priam* music, although here resolution is still a frequent outcome), within particular pieces, especially in the period under consideration, Tippett's use of these chords often corresponds to a sense of closure, though a contextual rather than perceptual one. Some examples rely on dramatic context, such as the higher consonance used to set the protagonists' "Goodbye" at the end (fig. 500 in the score) of Tippett's third opera, *The Knot Garden* (1966-69). Others assign an exclusive role to higher consonances so that the accumulation of associations within the piece and the historical resonances of their triadic elements combine to establish a syntax of closure. This kind of closure is to be found extensively in Tippett's Sonata no. 3 for Piano (1972-73).[32] Chords containing triadic elements are located exclusively at phrase or section endings, and, as if to confirm the function of such chords, the piece ends with the superimposition of two forms of one of the most widespread higher consonances to be found in Tippett's *oeuvre*, the so called Z' chord.[33] In this case it consists of, in the left hand, an A major triad with an added upper B3 and, four octaves higher in the right hand, an A major triad with an added lower D6. Significantly, the appearance of these chords does not follow from longer-range process, in the way that even the dominant chord at the end of the third movement of Mahler's Symphony No. 4 is at least located at the end of a falling line: there is a harmonic abruptness about Tippett's closures, more an interruption than a natural development of what precedes them, and in this sense, perhaps, more akin to the sort of eschatological interruption alluded to above.[34]

It would be easy to surmise from these dislocated higher consonances that teleological processes have been abandoned by Tippett in this period, but this is not so. Teleological processes are still relatively widespread; it is only their connection with closure that has been revoked. Sonata No. 3 begins with a perceptually clear process based on a contour pattern: the two contrapuntal elements of the music begin at the extreme registers of the pi-

31. Arnold Whittall, *The Music of Britten and Tippett: Studies in Themes and Techniques* (Cambridge: Cambridge University Press, 1990), p. 5.

32. See Alastair Borthwick, "Tonal Elements and Their Significance in Tippett's Sonata No. 3 for Piano," in *Tippett Studies*, ed. David Clarke (Cambridge: Cambridge University Press, 1999), pp. 117-44.

33. See David Clarke, *Language, Form, and Structure in the Music of Michael Tippett*, 2 vols. (New York and London: Garland Publishing, 1989), pp. 8, 81-82.

34. See the discussion on p. 278 above.

ano and gradually, though not mechanically, work their way into the middle of the piano keyboard, at which point the texture gradually fans out again, this time using a chordal texture. In Symphony No. 3 (1970-72) an initial opposition between two musical ideas (called "arrest" and "movement" by Tippett in the score) is subjected to a geometric expansion, each reappearance being approximately double the duration of the previous one. In both of these examples what is striking from the point of view of teleology is that the processes are unrelated to endings. Progress is not projected over the continuum of the piece; it comes and goes, it is even (in the case of both the sonata and the symphony) shown to be reversible by the presence of palindromic sections.

The use of higher consonances as endings tends to reinforce the theological interpretation presented above of Mahler's closures. Mahler's use of dominant chords, while not dissonant in the vertical plane, is undoubtedly dissonant in a horizontal or linear sense. To this, Tippett's higher consonances add a vertical dissonance (despite the superficially conflicting terminology!) which further undermines the necessity for closure at the end of the piece. Beyond this affirmation, the dislocation of teleological processes from endings offers a new conceptual engagement with eschatology in general.

Jürgen Moltmann classifies eschatology according to two theological categories: "the transposition of eschatology into time"[35] and the "transposition of eschatology into eternity,"[36] both of which he attempts to distance himself from inasmuch as they claim to offer a sufficient explanation of the eschaton.[37] The first category involves the "reduction of eschatology to historical time,"[38] an eschatology deeply rooted in the modern myth of linear progress discussed above in relation to tonal teleology. The second category "adds a vertical dimension of eternity to the horizontal linear dimension in such a way that the former constantly impinges on the latter, encountering believers in a way that detaches them from historical time."[39]

Despite Moltmann's attempts to distance himself from these twin eschatological conceptions, Bauckham identifies some abiding similarities between Moltmann's own eschatology and the positions he rejects. In particu-

35. Moltmann, *The Coming of God,* p. 6.
36. Moltmann, *The Coming of God,* p. 13.
37. See Richard Bauckham, "Time and Eternity," in *God Will Be All in All: The Eschatology of Jürgen Moltmann,* ed. Richard Bauckham (Minneapolis: Fortress Press, 2001), pp. 155-226.
38. Bauckham, "Time and Eternity," p. 174.
39. Bauckham, "Time and Eternity," p. 175.

lar, there is, then, an inbuilt tension in his thought between the eschaton's situation (1) *at* the end of time (i.e., as part of the temporal future) and (2) *as* the end *(telos)* of every particular moment of historical time, in some sense already "present to" every moment, and into which every moment will duly be taken up and transformed. But, Bauckham suggests,

> Moltmann does not seem to have faced the problem of how the simultaneity of the eschaton to all time can be understood from the perspective of a moment within historical time, which would somehow have to be understood as *both* a moment within the flow of time *and* as in immediate relationship with the transcendent future in which it will be transformed into eternity. The concern to retain real eschatological futurity . . . has obscured an issue which Moltmann's own eschatological conceptuality seems to raise.[40]

Without presuming to offer an adequate resolution, it does seem that the peculiar interaction of teleology and temporality invoked by Tippett in pieces like Sonata No. 3 might provide one way of modeling, and getting to grips with, the problem which Bauckham identifies here.

The endings or "non-endings" employed by Tippett in the 1960s and early 1970s are not arbitrary whims, they have "to be earned and sought after,"[41] as Ian Kemp has claimed. Their meanings depend on what has preceded them, but not in the sense that they represent a realization or culmination of an earlier implicatory process. Cadential preparation has no place here any more than progressivism did in Tippett's ambivalent response to the idea of "perfectability" through social and political change in the 1960s.[42] Likewise, the eschaton can be understood as an event that will occur in historical time (as an ending) and will be meaningful in relation to it (its moment of occurrence is not arbitrary), but it will not depend on the outcomes of historical progress. Furthermore, its occurrence in historical time is meaningful in relation to all history, just as Tippett's gestures of closure depend on the wider context of Western music. The relationship with the transcendent future follows, analogically, from those incomplete closures identified in the endings of composers such as Mahler and Tippett: that which has become meaningful is revealed as temporally open, even infinitely so. Con-

40. Bauckham, "Time and Eternity," p. 176.

41. Ian Kemp, *Tippett: The Composer and His Music* (Oxford: Oxford University Press, 1987), p. 330.

42. Kemp, *Tippett*, p. 330.

ceptualized in this way, the tension between the two eschatological categories identified by Moltmann is not necessarily problematic: temporal linearity can coexist with temporal associations, the historically "final" one of which is temporally open.

Non-tonal Temporalities and Eschatological Times

While a transcendent future is conceivable in these metaphorical terms, the question of what kind of temporality it involves remains unanswered and, perhaps, finally unanswerable. Moltmann's own proposed distinction between the "*absolute eternity* of God" and the "*relative eternity* of the new creation," or the "time of creation" and "aeonic" time (the time of the new creation)[43] suggests, though, that musical modernism's exploration of linear and circular (or cyclical) time may provide some fruitful approaches to the task of modeling this transcendent future. Aeonic time (which Moltmann also refers to variously as "the time of Angels," "the invisible creation, which is called heaven,"[44] and "time filled with eternity"[45]) is distinguished in Moltmann's account from the purely linear time of creation by, among other things, its essentially cyclical pattern. It is not *timelessness* (which would amount to eternal *lifelessness*), but a pattern of time in which the relevant vital movement sees things "changed from glory into glory without perishing, without growing, and without diminution." This attempt to imagine the unimaginable is not without its problems. John Polkinghorne, for example, criticizes Moltmann for a vision of eternity characterized by "repetitive dullness," and sees the need for something more "dynamic."[46] Moltmann certainly intends dynamism, but whether the model he adopts really furnishes it is, perhaps, another question. Can a scenario in which nothing *more* or *new* ever actually happens finally escape the taint of that "dullness" generated by over-familiarity? Is it possible, we might ask, to imagine instead a mode of linearity in which sequence does not lead irrevocably to the sort of transience which Moltmann wishes to exclude from the new creation? Can there be "new things" added to the pattern of our experience in the eschaton,

43. Jürgen Moltmann, *The Way of Jesus Christ: Christology in Messianic Dimensions,* trans. Margaret Kohl (London: SCM Press, 1990), p. 330.

44. Moltmann, *The Way of Jesus Christ,* p. 330.

45. Moltmann, *Science and Wisdom,* p. 109.

46. John Polkinghorne, *The God of Hope and the End of the World* (London: SPCK, 2002), p. 119.

that is to say, without the corresponding loss of all that we value and hope to enjoy eternally?[47] Might music help us to imagine such a thing?

In *The Vision of Saint Augustine* (1963-65), Tippett was confronted with Augustine's vision of eternity, and however Augustine (and his mother) understood the precise nature of the temporality experienced within the vision, Tippett's representation of it inevitably focuses on what Moltmann would describe as aeonic time which, as David Clarke has commented, "is at least a less terrifying prospect than what might have been had Tippett indeed succeeded in musically mapping time and eternity as absolutes."[48] Significantly, Tippett's own discussion of this work is found in an essay entitled "Music of the Angels."[49] If, indeed, the sphere of creaturely existence as a whole is marked by some form of temporality, then angels (as created beings not belonging to our cosmos) might be supposed to dwell in Moltmann's aeonic time-zone. At a technical level Tippett's representation of eternity consists of eight superimposed ostinati of varying durations (16, 21, 26, 32, 34, and 34⅔ crotchets, some durations being shared by more than one ostinato) that are introduced out of phase and repeated cyclically. The design ensures that the ostinato figures will remain out of phase for an inordinately long period, far in excess of the one minute of clock time occupied by the music in the work as a whole.[50] Unlike tonal polyphonic textures, the combination of these ostinato figures does not take place within a unified harmonic context. Clarke interprets this passage as "a possible metaphor for Augustine's understanding of God's view of time from his position of eternity, in which all events, past, present and future, are simultaneously available."[51] The specifically Christian subject of this work might easily lead to an inappropriate conflation of the composer's own intentions and the existence

47. See the criticism along these lines by Richard Bauckham in *God Will Be All in All*, p. 184.

48. David Clarke, *The Music and Thought of Michael Tippett: Modern Times and Metaphysics* (Cambridge: Cambridge University Press, 2001), p. 96. Clarke's chapter on *The Vision of Saint Augustine* is most significant for its attempt to account for transcendence without recourse to theism.

49. Michael Tippett, "Music of the Angels," in *Music of the Angels: Essays and Sketchbooks*, ed. Meirion Bowen (London: Eulenberg Books, 1980), pp. 60-66.

50. The passage can be heard in Michael Tippett, *The Vision of St. Augustine*, London Symphony Orchestra, conducted by Sir Colin Davis, Conifer Classics CD 75605 52304 2, track 14, 8'34".

51. Clarke, *The Music and Thought of Michael Tippett*, p. 116. Kemp shares a similar understanding about the meaning of superimposition in *The Vision* generally. See Kemp, *Tippett*, p. 397.

within his work of patterns which lend themselves readily to such eschatological modeling. We do not need to commit the genetic fallacy, though, in order to sustain our inter-disciplinary engagement. As the nineteenth-century novelist and critic George MacDonald observes, from a theological perspective there is no need to limit the meaningfulness of any work of art to that which the author or composer intends. On the contrary, he insists, "there is *always* more in a work of art . . . than the producer himself perceived while he produced it,"[52] a fact which MacDonald traces to the provenance of all creative endeavor and every artistic possibility in the primordial plenitude of God's own creative relation to the world (in theological terms a more satisfying and adequate basis on which to proceed than mere "postmodern" insistence that the author has no claim upon the meaning of his text).

While Clarke's interpretation of Tippett's piece is largely unproblematic, apart from its telling displacement from the absolute ("God's view") to the relative ("Augustine's understanding"), it is the pattern of temporality that is most significant for the purposes of this essay. On this level it is noteworthy that the superimposition of ideas is constructed out of ostinati, without a unifying harmony. Might this offer a parable of humanity's own place in aeonic time (which is, according to Moltmann, a form of creaturely correlation with the shape of God's uncreated existence)? If we suppose, for example, that fugal textures may provide a metaphor for the eternal *perichoresis* proper to God's triune being as Father, Son, and Holy Spirit, might we allow, too, that the dissonant superimposition of musical lines "sounds out" helpfully the notion of individuals caught up in God's presence, their differences both from each other and from God being part and parcel of the dynamic of finite progression toward and "into" his eternal triune life?[53]

There is, of course, a sense in which all appeal to such eschatological patterns remains speculative and provisional, and this provisionality needs to be stressed by the provision of musical counterexamples. Harrison Birtwistle's orchestral piece *The Triumph of Time* (1972) represents a first attempt to bring his understanding of the concepts of linear and circular time into a single work as organizing principles. Before the composition of this piece, Birtwistle's use of block repetitions had suggested a preoccupation

---

52. George MacDonald, *A Dish of Orts, Chiefly Papers on the Imagination, and on Shakespere (sic)*, enlarged edition (London: Sampson Low Marston & Co. Ltd., 1893), p. 25.

53. See, e.g., Jürgen Moltmann, *The Trinity and the Kingdom of God* (London: SCM Press, 1981), p. 157.

with cyclical organization, a preoccupation that has scarcely been diminished by his incorporation of linear patterns. As recently as November 2003 Birtwistle reaffirmed that he was "concerned with time that is circular. Time is not linear, though it expresses itself that way. . . . In the end you understand music through your memory. You go back to the same thing again and again and experience it differently."[54] The role of memory is, of course, central to both Augustine's and, in the same tradition, Moltmann's conception of time.[55] Only through memory can circular time begin to approach a literal meaning, as Birtwistle suggests. In practice, circularity tends to involve spatial rather than temporal manipulations. Birtwistle's explanation of the interaction of linear and circular time in the *Triumph of Time* in terms of the recurrent properties of musical objects demonstrates this point. One object "is circumscribed and never changes, one descends through a sequence of potentially unlimited degrees of change to the musical object which is a permanent state of change."[56] Hence, circularity is evinced by objects (spatially defined!) that recur without change, and linearity by those subjected to change with each recurrence.[57] The combined effect might be referred to by the more subtle geometric metaphor of helical time. The coexistence of different modes of temporality here may provide a useful model for the perichoretic interplay between a God who is in some sense unchanging (not subject to the processes attaching to creaturely time) and a world which is constantly changing, even as it is drawn deeper into union and communion with this God.

Proliferating Parables

As was pointed out at the outset of this study, general statements about the theological significance of "music" need to be located within precise historical and cultural contexts. We have seen that this is especially true of the concept of "closure." In common practice era music, closure speaks of a final point of arrival — ultimately, of our death. In Mahler, closure suggests that

54. Harrison Birtwistle's interview with Stuart Jeffries, in *The Guardian* (8 November 2003).

55. See Moltmann, *God in Creation,* p. 129.

56. Harrison Birtwistle, quoted in Michael Hall, *Harrison Birtwistle* (London: Robson Books, 1984), p. 175.

57. For a more detailed analysis of *The Triumph of Time,* see Robert Adlington, *The Music of Harrison Birtwistle* (Cambridge: Cambridge University Press, 2000), pp. 100-103.

death leaves our lives intrinsically unfinished and open-ended. In Tippett, closure goes so far as to suggest a kind of transcendence, in a way that nevertheless makes sense only in relation to the wider history of Western music.

Closure itself, of course, is inseparable from what has been a central theme of this study, namely, time (however this might be conceived). Here again, despite modernity's repeated denials of God, one can discern theological significance in the cumulative "progress" of music in the sense described by Gregory of Nyssa: an ever-expanding vision of eschatological possibilities, as we move ever more deeply into the eternal, infinite mystery of God. If this essay has focused on linear and circular conceptions of time then this should not be taken as an adequate description of musical time in general, and all that it might offer the understanding of eschatological time. Even allowing for more sophisticated concepts of linear time that include the out of phase parallel lines implied by the tension between continuity and fragmentation (characteristic of modernist music, as discussed above), and related manifestations of circular time, there are other conceptions that might allow for an ebb and flow of time, even to the extent of the reversal of time's arrow.[58] Beyond general concepts of musical time there are, of course individual compositions. Since each piece embodies a unique temporal pattern, it could be argued that each one offers a distinctive metaphorical engagement with eschatological time: the piece as parable, if you will.

Another dimension to the theological significance of time is the distinction between creation *ex nihilo* (the creation of something totally new, out of nothing) and creation *ex vetere* (the creation of something new out of what already is). As we have already suggested, there is a tension here in the logic of Christian hope. What is hoped for is indeed something so radically "new" that its provenance can only adequately be pictured by tracing an analogy with God's original creative act "in the beginning." There will be a new heaven and a new earth, not merely a polishing of this world's rough edges. And yet in a profound and equally important sense it is nonetheless a creation *ex vetere*, a radical *renewal* of *this* world rather than its replacement by another. And this, in the words of John Polkinghorne, "invests the present created order with the most profound significance, for it is the raw material from which the new will come."[59] By fashioning the "raw material" of sound

---

58. For an example of this on a cosmological scale, listen to Anthony Payne's orchestral piece *Time's Arrow*, BBC Symphony Orchestra, conducted by Andrew Davis, London: CD NMC D037S (1996).

59. John Polkinghorne, *Science and Christian Belief* (London: SPCK, 1994), p. 167.

(including sound as previously fashioned by others) into new works, composers perhaps anticipate this creation *ex vetere* much more obviously than they ever parallel the primordial creative activity of God. With regard to modern music in particular, those experiments which failed did so by rejecting the past for the sake of pursuing a rival creation *ex nihilo* — a prerogative that belongs solely to God.[60] On the other hand, those exponents of modernism (such as Schoenberg, Berg, and Stravinsky) who succeeded did so precisely by brilliantly reworking the traditions out of which they emerged.

Indeed, modern music can be said to be a commentary on earlier music — even going so far as to highlight those discontinuities, paths not taken, etc., that earlier interpretations of such music avoided.[61] Neoclassicism is an obvious example of music "commenting" on earlier styles, but to a greater or lesser extent, this kind of commentary is widespread in modern music. In his Symphony No. 3, Tippett comments critically on Beethoven's Ninth with regard to what he saw as its unqualified affirmation of Schiller's *Ode to Joy.* He criticizes it precisely by incorporating it into his own symphony, juxtaposing it with material characterized by what he (Tippett) calls "the strengths and the viciousness of all that is involved in a positive act of almost violence."[62] The extraction of the "Schrekensfanfare" from Beethoven's Ninth into context that is bereft of teleological resolution brings into question the progressivist optimism evinced by Schiller.

At least one critic, Allen Thiher, has characterized modernism in general as "a quasi-theological response . . . to a crisis in the interpretation of temporality." This response, according to Thiher, takes the form of a search for "an ontologically superior realm, transcending time and history," leading ultimately to "an ontological plenitude that exists as an atemporal presence."[63] In a sense, then, modernism, this account suggests, might be regarded as the search for a lost Eden. From a Christian perspective, though, we have seen that some examples of modern music are more fruitfully regarded not as lingering "traces" harkening back to some lost paradisal state, but as parabolic

60. "Everything of man must have been of God first" notes MacDonald in his reflection on this theme, and the human artist is in truth more *trouvère* than he is a poet. *A Dish of Orts,* p. 3; pp. 19-20.

61. See Alan Street, "Superior Myths, Dogmatic Allegories: The Resistance to Musical Unity," in *Music Analysis* 8, no. 1 (1989): 77-123.

62. Michael Tippett, *The E. William Doty Lectures in Fine Arts,* 2nd series, 1976 (Austin: College of Fine Arts, University of Texas at Austin, 1979), p. 57.

63. Allen Thiher, *Words in Reflection: Modern Language Theory and Postmodern Fiction* (Chicago: University of Chicago Press, 1984), p. 37.

anticipations, pointing forward in new and unexpected ways, modeling suggestively the enigmatic relation between life in this world and "the life of the world to come." Music's insistence on accommodating both sequential and recurrent patterns, and in particular modern music's self-consciously ambiguous treatments of aural closure may help us to resist any easy resolution or classification of this relationship, enabling us, perhaps, to "hear" and to feel something of the paradox of eschatological "newness," and of a coming kingdom in which genuine movement, development, and desire will somehow coexist forever with the joy and resolution of the final crashing chords.

12. Improvising Texts, Improvising Communities: Jazz, Interpretation, Heterophony, and the *Ekklēsia*

Bruce Ellis Benson

In the beginning, there was improvisation. For creation is precisely God setting in motion a reality of "ceaseless alterations."[1] Thus, the very being of life is improvisatory — by which I mean that it is a mixture of both structure and contingency, of regularity and unpredictability, of constraint and possibility. Further, if God is indeed still at work in the world, then God, too, is part of that improvisatory movement. Being part of that reality, we take part in that improvisatory movement in all that we do. Since we are creatures embedded in multiple and ever-changing historical and cultural milieus, our identities and very being arise from our relations to others and the world which we inhabit.[2]

As improvisers, we constantly reshape that which is at hand rather than "create." Here I am deliberately juxtaposing the notion of improvising defined as to "fabricate out of what is conveniently on hand" to that of creating defined as "to produce where nothing was before."[3] But, if we are improvisers in our very being, what implications does that ontological reality have for

---

1. John Milbank, "'Postmodern Critical Augustinianism': A Short *Summa* in Forty Two Responses to Unasked Questions," *Modern Theology* 7 (1991): 227.

2. Hegel may be the first to show how intersubjectivity — the interconnected nature of human persons — is constitutive of human subjectivity, though he is certainly not the last. See Georg Wilhelm Friedrich Hegel, *Phenomenology of Spirit,* trans. A. V. Miller (Oxford: Clarendon, 1977), pp. 178-96.

3. *Merriam-Webster's Collegiate Dictionary,* 11th ed. (Springfield, MA: Merriam-Webster, 2003), s.v. "improvise," and *The Oxford English Dictionary,* 2nd ed. (Oxford: Oxford University Press, 1989), s.v. "create." I will return to this distinction shortly.

hermeneutics? Toward a possible beginning of an answer to that question, I will consider four aspects, around which this paper is structured:

1. why "improvisation" is an appropriate metaphor for interpretation
2. how Gadamer's notion of "play" illuminates improvisation
3. the role of the Holy Spirit in biblical interpretation and the *cantus firmus* that underlies improvisation
4. how the development of jazz improvisation illumines the development of Christian interpretation

But, first, to see why "improvisation" is a helpful way of thinking about interpretation, we need to see how it differs from the notion of "performance."

Performance and Improvisation

Consider Stephen Barton's observation:

> In recent study of the nature of NT interpretation, considerable attention in certain circles has been given to the possibility that there is one metaphor that is particularly appropriate for articulating what NT interpretation involves. It is the metaphor of *performance*.[4]

There are a couple of crucial implications to construing New Testament interpretation (and biblical interpretation in general) in terms of performance. First, to say that interpretation takes the form of "performance" is to claim that scriptural texts are "brought to life" by way of performance in the sense that they do not *fully* exist except in the moments either of being authored or of being read and understood. Without doubt, texts certainly exist apart from being read and understood. For our purposes here, I will take a text to be "the putting into writing of an author's intended meaning." But "un-interpreted" texts — while they exist — are only "potential" mean-

---

4. Stephen C. Barton, "New Testament Interpretation as Performance," *Scottish Journal of Theology* 52, no. 2 (1999): 179. Barton discusses Nicholas Lash, "Performing the Scriptures," in *Theology on the Way to Emmaus* (London: SCM, 1986), pp. 37-46; and Frances Young, *The Art of Performance: Towards a Theology of Holy Scripture* (London: Darton, Longman and Todd, 1990), republished as *Virtuoso Theology: The Bible and Interpretation* (Cleveland: Pilgrim, 1993).

ings. It takes an interpreter to "revive" their meaning (i.e., "bring them to life"). This ontological claim concerning the being of a text inevitably leads us to a second ontological claim, viz., that interpreters or readers are necessary not only for a text to have meaning but also for it simply to *be* in its fullest sense.[5] If written texts are dependent upon both authors and interpreters for their existence *as texts*, then texts do not have an independent but rather a *dependent* existence — yet still an existence in which text and interpretation do not merely collapse into one another.

Second, in the same way that performance of musical or theatrical works can be characterized as having varying levels of fidelity, so biblical "performances" have varying levels of fidelity. Some performances are simply more faithful to the text than others. However, establishing "fidelity" is not quite as simple as it initially sounds. Given what we know about the different ways of defining "fidelity" to texts that can be found in the history of performance practice of, say, Bach's *St. Matthew Passion* or plays of Shakespeare, it is hardly surprising that the definition of "fidelity" to biblical texts has been construed in various *ways* over the past two millennia.[6] So the question is not just one of *levels* of fidelity but also one of *kinds* of fidelity. I think Frances Young is right in comparing disagreements in biblical interpretation to those in the "authenticity movement" in music.[7] But, in making that comparison, we have not necessarily *solved* any interpretational difficulties. For, as I have argued elsewhere, disagreements between those in the "authenticity movement" and "mainstream" performers tend to be about the true meaning of fidelity.[8] As we will see, questions of fidelity can only be answered from *within* the interpretive community.

5. Kevin J. Vanhoozer asks: "Does the canon have a reality independent of the church, and from the history of its reception, or does it have its being, to paraphrase Bishop Berkeley, only in being *received?*" My response is that, while the canon (i.e., Scripture) is not identical to its reception (which is why one can make a distinction between better and worse "receptions"), its being is very strongly tied to reception (so that speaking of better or worse receptions is not possible *apart* from reception). In other words, we do not have access to a "reception-free text" by which to judge receptions. See his *The Drama of Doctrine: A Canonical-Linguistic Approach to Christian Theology* (Louisville: Westminster John Knox, 2005), p. 146.

6. Typically, the debate in music has revolved around the issue of spirit and letter, i.e., being faithful to the "spirit" of the piece or to the "letter" (or, more specifically, notes).

7. Young, *Virtuoso Theology*, p. 24.

8. See my discussion of differing notions of "fidelity" in the authenticity movement in *The Improvisation of Musical Dialogue: A Phenomenology of Music* (Cambridge: Cambridge University Press, 2003), pp. 96-124.

BRUCE ELLIS BENSON

While the metaphor of performance is undoubtedly helpful in thinking about the act of interpretation, it seems to me that it *almost* gets interpretation right — but not quite. In one sense, the idea of "performance" seems appropriate for thinking about interpretation because "to perform" is defined as "to finish making, to complete the construction of."[9] Even though performance requires "execution" of what is notated (whether in words or musical notes), performers clearly *add* something to whatever they interpret. In terms of musical pieces, performers may need to make decisions regarding tempi, attack, vibrato, instrumentation, and many other aspects. Roman Ingarden describes this aspect of musical texts in terms of *"Unbestimmt-heitsstellen"* — places of indeterminacy.[10] But it is not just musical texts that have such points of indeterminacy. Even E. D. Hirsch, Jr. — a strong advocate of construing textual meaning by way of the intent of the author — recognizes this point. Although Hirsch points out that any communication requires a certain degree of "determinacy," he is all too well aware that such determinacy only goes so far. To quote him:

> Determinacy does not mean definiteness or precision. Undoubtedly, most verbal meanings are imprecise and ambiguous, and to call them such is to acknowledge their determinacy: they are what they are — namely ambiguous and imprecise — and they are not univocal and precise.[11]

In regard to musical scores, musicologists often refer to this lack of precision as "underdetermination." That is, scores do not provide enough information to actually perform the work. One must know what to do with the notes on the page, and that knowledge comes only by being steeped in a performance practice or tradition. But the imprecision of texts — musical and otherwise — could likewise be construed by what I term "overdetermination." In other words, scores and texts generally provide *more* possibilities than could be realized in simply *one* interpretation. So a symphony can be performed with deep feeling or machine-like precision and a novel like *Middlemarch* can be read as a character study or a discourse on morals. The

9. For the various definitions of "perform" or "performance" used in this and the following paragraph, see the *Oxford English Dictionary*, s.v. "perform."
10. Roman Ingarden, *Ontology of the Work of Art: The Musical Work — The Picture — The Architectural Work — The Film*, trans. Raymond Meyer with John T. Goldthwait (Athens: Ohio University Press, 1989), p. 90.
11. E. D. Hirsch Jr., *Validity in Interpretation* (New Haven, CT: Yale University Press, 1967), p. 44.

298

degree of "over-" and "under"-determination, of course, is dependent upon the genre. Whereas writers of technical manuals attempt — as much as possible — to avoid both aspects, poets often exploit them. Yet interpretation always requires determination. Hans-Georg Gadamer points out that this need for "determination" is particularly evident in translations. No matter how much the translator wishes to remain faithful to the original text, "every translation that takes itself seriously is at once clearer and flatter than the original."[12] Similarly, we can say that every interpretation says both more and less than the original text.

In light of what is involved in interpreting a text, one might well ask whether the metaphor of performance is *strong* enough to describe interpretation. The answer partially depends upon what we mean by "performance." One might, for instance, appeal to a somewhat older definition of "perform": "to make up or supply (what is wanting)." Such a definition fits well with baroque (and Renaissance and medieval) performance practice, for baroque musicians were given considerable leeway in performance (so much so that the line between "composer" and "performer" was not nearly as clear as it is today). In contrast, performers today are expected to follow scores much more closely (and scores in turn are much more precisely notated).[13] Given the way that we currently define the notion of "performance" (i.e., in a much more narrow sense than in previous ages) perhaps "improvisation" might be a more apt metaphor for interpretation.[14] For, if interpretation is rightly seen as "transformative" (in the sense that it both adds to and narrows a text), then interpreters might better be thought of as "improvisers."

Of course, the very idea of "improvising" upon a text — particularly a biblical text — is likely to cause anxiety among those who (rightly) view Scripture as sacred. Should one be *improvising* on holy writ? One might simply respond by pointing out that — descriptively speaking — that is what interpreters actually *do* (however much they might think or contend otherwise). But, more important, let me point out that I do not intend to suggest anything like the "spontaneous creation" that often characterizes our current — and usually quite inaccurate — notion of "improvisation." Instead of

12. Hans-Georg Gadamer, *Truth and Method,* 2nd rev. ed., trans. Joel Weinsheimer and Donald G. Marshall (New York: Crossroad, 1989), p. 386.

13. Regarding baroque performance practice, see David Fuller, "The Performer as Composer," in *Performance Practice,* vol. 2, ed. Howard Mayer Brown and Stanley Sadie (Houndsmills, UK: Macmillan, 1989), pp. 117-46.

14. I discuss the performance/improvisation distinction at length in *The Improvisation of Musical Dialogue.*

this Romantic picture of improvisation, I have in mind what classical rheto-ricians term *"inventio,"* which can be literally translated as "invention" but not inaccurately as "improvisation."[15] *Inventio* is both a repetition and a transformation, for it is the art of taking that which already exists and devel-oping or elaborating upon it. As such, it involves *imitatio* but it goes beyond simple imitation. Likewise, this *inventio* is only inventive in a very limited sense. Obviously, interpretations can be more imitative and less inventive or more inventive and less imitative. But there is neither pure imitation nor pure invention. Rather, the interpreter is situated between *imitatio* and *inventio.*[16] Here I side with the classical rather than the Romantic sense of improvisation.[17]

To say that interpretation of a text requires improvisation is to say that interpretation of a text — which involves making the text intelligible by ex-plaining what the text says[18] — involves more than simply *repeating* the text. One must make it come alive. True, performers make music come alive in a performance. Yet performance — at least as we currently define it — is too restrictive a model for what interpreters do. To be sure, performers are al-lowed a little leeway in how they perform. But their role is relegated more to repetition than creation. On my account, interpretation of texts *is* a repeti-tion but with the kind of variation found in classical improvisation. In other words, performance is too *narrow* a model for interpretation. But if, in con-trast, Romantic improvisation is too *wide* a model, then how might we de-scribe the improvisation of interpretation? I think Gadamer's notion of play provides us with a helpful model, one much closer to the classical concep-tion of improvisation than the Romantic one.

15. See, for instance, Quintilian, *Institutio Oratia,* IV, trans. H. E. Butler (Cambridge, MA: Harvard University Press, 1922), book X; and Cicero, *De inventione,* trans. H. M. Hubbell (Cambridge, MA: Harvard University Press, 1949).

16. Even Quintilian notes that pure repetition is impossible: "there is nothing harder than to produce an exact likeness, and nature herself has so far failed in this endeavour that there is always some difference which enables us to distinguish even the things which seem most like and most equal to one another" (*Institutio Oratia,* IV, 10.2.10).

17. As Gerald Bruns deftly contrasts them, classical improvisation works "with what is received, which it then proceeds to color, amplify, alter, or fulfill," whereas Romantic impro-visation "begins with a blank sheet of paper." See his *Inventions: Writing, Textuality, and Un-derstanding in Literary History* (New Haven: Yale University Press, 1982), p. 147.

18. Here I have in mind the threefold distinction of hermeneutics: *subtilitas intelligendi* (understanding), *subtilitas explicandi* (interpretation), and *subtilitas applicandi* (applica-tion). See Gadamer, *Truth and Method,* p. 307.

Gadamer and Play

In *Truth and Method*, Gadamer uses play to explain how texts come into being, how they continue to exist, and how we interpret them. In effect, the *ergon* — a product, whether an artwork, a jazz tune, or a biblical text — has its existence within the *energeia* (activity) or play of a community. Gadamer sees texts as ontologically constituted by this interactive play between text and community. Thus, although texts are "things," their "thinghood" is inextricably wrapped up with their connection with the play that surrounds them. To interpret a text is to enter into this play. Although Gadamer is speaking particularly of the artwork in the following passage, he clearly intends to describe interpretation generally in saying that "*all encounter with the language of art is an encounter with an unfinished event and is itself part of this event*" (Gadamer's italics).[19] If texts are connected with both compositional and interpretational "play," then their being is in motion and so they can never quite be described as "finished" or "complete." Even though Gadamer explicitly claims that the original experiences "*an increase in being*," it is quite clear that this is likewise true for the piece of art. Texts and artworks are always affected by interpretation. Rather than the relationship being simply "*one-sided*," in the sense that only our understanding or experience of the text is affected, Gadamer thinks that this relationship works both ways.[20] We are affected by the text; but the text is also affected (ontologically) by us. Obviously, this complicates the identity of the text. In effect, the text becomes an historical entity that can change — and *does* change — over time. While that description may sound strange, note that we encounter such entities every day in the form of human persons. Although my identity today is the "same" as when I was a child in one sense (the sense to which my birth certificate and passport attest), I am not the "same" person. And yet I'm not simply different either.[21] In the case of both texts and human persons, we have examples of entities that are both "the same" and yet also "different" (here we might appeal to Jacques Derrida's logic of *différance*, as a way of explaining how something can change and yet "remain the same").[22]

19. Gadamer, *Truth and Method*, p. 99.

20. Gadamer, *Truth and Method*, p. 140.

21. Paul Ricoeur makes this distinction in terms of "identity as *sameness* (Latin, *idem*)" and "identity as *selfhood* (Latin, *ipse*)." It is within this second sort of identity that development and change are possible — while still maintaining an identity. See his *Oneself as Another*, trans. Kathleen Blamey (Chicago: University of Chicago Press, 1992), p. 116.

22. *Différance* is Derrida's neologism for expressing a "logic" characterized by a difference that is not merely "different" and a deferring that refers to the *eschaton* (or what in his

It is important, though, to note that Gadamer's dynamic conception of the artwork or text differs quite significantly from that of Paul Valéry, whom Gadamer accuses of an "untenable hermeneutic nihilism."[23] The problem with Valéry's account is that he (unwittingly) thinks of artistic creation in terms of Kant's genius. Given that the genius "himself does not know" how the creative process works, he is unable to provide any rules for creating or continuing a work of art.[24] In contrast, although Gadamer does not put it in quite these terms, he sees the creation of art as improvisatory in the classical sense (i.e., the sense I am using here). An artwork or a text comes to be amid the play, which also sustains it. And that play is only possible if there are rules of the game. Without such constraints, there can be no game, no play, and thus no text.[25] Interpretation for Gadamer, then, is not hermeneutic nihilism.

Of course, games themselves are not unchanging Platonic objects. They *too* come into being, are maintained by being played, and change over time. So both object and game (or text and community) are in motion. Yet how does all of this happen? In one sense, it is highly understandable that Gadamer provides no real answer this question. No two games are exactly the same; each has a different history. And the history of any particular game is crucial to understanding both the being of any given text and the ways in which that text is interpreted. While Gadamer does not say that play is "improvised," that seems to be implied.[26] That is, a game comes into being in an improvised way and is constantly being improvised upon as the play takes shape. Thus, it is not *just* the text that undergoes the improvisatory movement; it is also the game itself. One only need think of how literal games

---

later writing he refers to as the "messianic"). Here I particularly have the first aspect (that of "differing") in mind. Later, I will turn to the aspect of "deferring." See "Différance," in *Margins of Philosophy,* trans. Alan Bass (Chicago: University of Chicago Press, 1982), pp. 7-8.

23. Gadamer, *Truth and Method,* p. 95.

24. Immanuel Kant, *Critique of Judgment,* trans. Werner Pluhar (Indianapolis: Hackett, 1987), p. 175, §46.

25. Jeremy S. Begbie speaks of "liberating constraints" in ch. 8 of *Theology, Music and Time* (Cambridge: Cambridge University Press, 2000). Although Begbie does not use this terminology per se, it strikes me that he is speaking of what philosophers generally call "positive freedom," or being free *to* do something. The constraints Begbie discusses are those that make human action (in this case, jazz improvisation) possible precisely by "providing a space" for action.

26. In an early conversation with Gadamer, I suggested to him that interpretation — on his account — could be described in terms of jazz improvisation. He resisted that possibility. Yet, in subsequent conversations, he came to agree with me that what takes place in jazz improvisation is similar to what takes place in interpretation in general.

change over time for that to be evident. Even well-established sports have, from time to time, changes in their rules.

The Holy Spirit and the *Cantus Firmus*

While we will see that there are helpful and striking parallels between the improvisation found in jazz and Christian interpretation, it is crucial to note in advance that there are at least two fundamental dissimilarities. First, Christian texts have both human and divine authorship. While it is hardly simple to work out exactly what it means to say that human authors were "inspired" by the Holy Spirit as they wrote, that belief is absolutely central to Christianity. Moreover, it is just as important a Christian doctrine that the Holy Spirit guides us in interpretation. So the Holy Spirit plays a role in *both* the improvisational writing and the improvisational interpretation of Scripture. While certainly not all interpretations of Scripture are valid — and we would do well to heed the Johannine admonition to "test the spirits" (1 John 4:1), as well as "test the interpretations" — there is no reason to think that the Holy Spirit may not be saying new things through the locutions of Scripture. Vanhoozer notes that God "uses the book of Jonah to satirize religious ethnocentricism" and then goes on to say "God may be doing new things with Jonah and other biblical texts too by virtue of their being gathered together in a canon."[27] But, if God can speak in new ways through canon formation, cannot the Holy Spirit *continue* to speak in new ways as the Word goes forth throughout the world?

At this point, of course, we've changed perspectives: for improvisation focuses on the improviser or interpreter. Yet, if a text only exists by way of *both* author and interpreter, then both of these perspectives are necessary. One alone is insufficient. If we see the improviser as *working with* something (or perhaps *someone*) that (who) already exists, then improvisation is hardly one-sided. Indeed, from a Christian perspective, we can speak of improvisation as taking place by the guidance of the Holy Spirit. Of course, that there are differing interpretations also attests to the possibility of *mis*interpretation. But, given the richness of Scripture, it is hardly surprising that different groups would emphasize different aspects (even if, unfortunately, at times to the exclusion of others).

27. Kevin J. Vanhoozer, *First Theology: God, Scripture and Hermeneutics* (Downers Grove, IL: IVP, 2002), p. 194.

In any case, there is no reason to think that Scripture's meaning has already been fully mined. One way of thinking about what takes place in the ongoing improvisation upon Scripture is in terms of what the pianist Tommy Flanagan says about jazz improvisation: "soloists elaborate upon what the structure of the piece has to say; what it tells them to do."[28] Scripture provides a structure upon which interpreters elaborate. That there are so many elaborations upon Scripture attests to its rich counterpoint. But here we must be clear as to what makes this improvisation possible. Alan J. Torrance's observations on worship are helpful in understanding what takes place in interpretation. Torrance rightly criticizes Jürgen Moltmann's conception of worship as something that *we* do. In contrast, taking his cue from an important distinction made by Begbie between "worship as task" and "worship as gift," he says the following: "Christian worship shares in a human-Godward movement that belongs to God and which takes place *within* the divine life. It is precisely into and within *this* that we are brought by the Spirit to participate as a gift of grace" (Torrance's italics).[29] Our improvisational interpretation is made possible as gift, which in turn is made possible by our being incorporated within the *ekklēsia*. Being part of the *ekklēsia* makes communion *(koinōnia)* possible not only with those in Christ's body but also with the *perichoresis* of the Trinity.

Second (though clearly related to this first point), in that this improvisational motion is created and sustained by God, there is a *cantus firmus* that supports and guides it. That is not to say there is no *cantus firmus* in jazz improvisation. It is not just that the rhythm section of a jazz combo — for example — provides the undergirding structure that makes improvisation possible. The constraints of chord progressions, jazz style, performance traditions, and much more provide the "space" for the "spontaneous" to take place. In many ways, those same kinds of constraints provide the bedrock of orthodoxy from which Christian textual improvisation can take place. Dietrich Bonhoeffer claims that "where the *cantus firmus* is clear and plain, the counterpoint can be developed to its limits."[30] The *cantus firmus* of which Bonhoeffer speaks is our love for God that is made possible by God's love for us. We are bound together

28. Paul Berliner, *Thinking in Jazz* (Chicago: University of Chicago Press, 1994), p. 170.

29. Alan J. Torrance, *Persons in Communion: As Essay on Trinitarian Description and Human Participation* (Edinburgh: T&T Clark, 1996), p. 314. Torrance is criticizing Jürgen Moltmann's discussion in *The Trinity and the Kingdom of God: The Doctrine of God,* trans. Margaret Kohl (London: SCM Press, 1981), p. 152.

30. Dietrich Bonhoeffer, *Letters and Papers from Prison,* ed. Eberhard Bethge (New York: Macmillan, 1971), p. 303.

in love, and no calamity can break that bond. With that sense of the *cantus firmus* in mind, perhaps we might say — paraphrasing Augustine — "love God, and interpret as you please." Yet here we would do well to expand and modify this notion of the *cantus firmus* to include not merely the love for and being in communion with God but also (and even more important) the *cantus firmus* of the revelation of God to us by way of the Hebrew Scriptures, the New Testament, and — most significant of all — Jesus Christ himself. That revelation is further refined by such early documents of the *ekklēsia* as the Apostolic and Nicene creeds. Christian interpretation — much like jazz improvisation — does not occur in an historical vacuum but is situated in the rich tradition of the Christian *ekklēsia*, which is further situated in God's revelation.

Although improvisation has barely been used as a way to think about biblical interpretation *per se*, it is increasingly becoming a metaphor to illustrate how we live the Christian life in a faithful way and even how doctrine has developed.[31] N. T. Wright suggests that one way of thinking about what it means to live out the biblical narrative in a faithful way is to think of the *ekklēsia* as improvising a lost fifth act of a Shakespeare play. Instead of simply writing out a fifth act, skilled actors — well versed in Shakespeare, the play itself, and acting in general — would *"work out a fifth act for themselves."*[32] More recently, Vanhoozer has used improvisation as a way to think about the development of Christian doctrine.[33] In terms of interpretation, Young points out the need for improvisation in the cadenzas in pieces of classical music in the last chapter of *Virtuoso Theology*. There she notes how one must be steeped in the tradition of classical music and be truly a virtuoso in order to improvise a cadenza that is "fitting" for a given piece of mu-

31. My own thinking about jazz and interpretation goes back to my article "Ingarden and the Problem of Jazz," *Tijdschrift voor Filosofie* 55, no. 4 (December 1993): 677-93. For how jazz might be a way of thinking about community, see my article "The Harmony that Creates Community," *Kettering Review* (1996): 46-53. *The Improvisation of Musical Dialogue* is my attempt to show how improvisation is foundational to all of musical life, even in the performance of classical music.

32. N. T. Wright, "How Can the Bible Be Authoritative?" (The Laing Lecture for 1989), *Vox Evangelica* 21 (1991): 18; Wright's italics. Improvising upon Wright's idea, Samuel Wells has provided a provocative account of what it means to live as faithful Christians in an improvisational manner. See his *Improvisation: The Drama of Christian Ethics* (Grand Rapids: Brazos, 2004).

33. Kevin J. Vanhoozer, *The Drama of Doctrine*. Although Wells and Vanhoozer are largely influenced by theatrical improvisation (whereas my emphasis on improvisation comes from my own avocation as a jazz musician), the similarities between improvisation in jazz and theater are far more significant than their differences.

sic. She also addresses the understandable concerns of those who think that, somehow, improvising a cadenza seems inappropriate — a kind of sacrilege. To those who insist that we need merely "replay the classic texts," she rightly responds that "a genuinely 'neutral' performance has never been available." Of course, that no neutral performance has ever been possible means that there is always "the problem of loss of identity, the danger of syncretism."[34] But, while syncretism is most certainly a danger, actual church history is *filled* with syncretism. As Lamin Sanneh reminds us, syncretism is "the term we use for the religion of those we don't like."[35] So the question is not *whether* the church adapts and adopts particular cultural practices but how *appropriate* that adoption is. Since interpretation always takes place within a given context, that context will always have some effect on an interpretation. We could rue that as a kind of "infection" to avoid, or else recognize with Gadamer that, without context, *there would be no understanding at all.*

In what follows, my goal will be to show how jazz illumines Christian improvisation in terms of (1) how they both develop improvisationally, (2) how that development leads to canonical texts and ways of interpreting them that take on a kind of authority, and (3) how that continuing development allows for improvisation upon both their texts and the traditions themselves. My claim is that both jazz and Christian texts arise through improvisation and that subsequent interpretation of them is in turn improvisational. Moreover, I will be particularly attending to the role of alterity in the development and continuance of both the jazz and Christian communities.

Improvising Jazz

At what point does jazz become "jazz," rather than the blues or ragtime, out of which it clearly grew? To the extent that we can meaningfully speak of a "beginning" of jazz, we must immediately acknowledge that it is improvised from the start out of two types of alterity — musical and ethnic. On the one hand, there are striking similarities between jazz and ethnic European music.[36] On the other hand, jazz contains distinctly African American and African elements, such as syncopation and call-and-response patterns. African

34. Young, *Virtuoso Theology,* pp. 163-64.
35. Lamin Sanneh, *Whose Religion Is Christianity? The Gospel Beyond the West* (Grand Rapids: Eerdmans, 2003), p. 44.
36. William H. Youngren, "European Roots of Jazz," in *The Oxford Companion to Jazz,* ed. Bill Kirchner (Oxford: Oxford University Press, 2000), pp. 19 and 26.

music tends to negate precisely the regularity sought in European music — such aspects as steady pitch, timbre, vibrato, and directness of attack — as does jazz.[37] More important for our concern here, jazz operates musically by way of alterity or heteronomy.[38] Multiple voices in jazz do not necessarily produce a "polyphony" based on harmonious counterpoint but a "heterophony."[39] Although the ancient Greek term *heterophōnia* literally meant the simultaneous performance of differing versions of a melody, in jazz heterophony is used more loosely to describe differing voices, dissonance, cross-rhythms, and multiple versions of melodies.[40]

If games are improvised out of elements on hand, then what is on hand in the case of jazz are Black spirituals, ragtime, European folk music, and even opera. For instance, in an interview Louis Armstrong sings the beginning of "Serenade" from Romberg's *The Student Prince* and then says: "That's jazz. That's the way I look at it. Anything you can express to the public is jazz."[41] The heterophony of jazz is due to its fundamental openness to heteronomy or alterity in which new improvisational possibilities are continually opening up. And the alterity within jazz is as much ethnic as musical. Although the history of jazz has usually been written in terms of Black and white, there are at least three racial identities early on in jazz. It is this third category — Creoles of color or *gens du couleur* — that undermines the binary of racial opposition. Whereas Creole musicians were often very familiar with the European musical tradition and thus better at reading music,

37. Ernest Borneman, "The Roots of Jazz," in *Jazz: New Perspectives on the History of Jazz by Twelve of the World's Foremost Jazz Critics and Scholars*, ed. Nat Hentoff and Albert J. McCarthy (New York: Holt, Rinehart and Winston, 1959), p. 17. Also see Gunther Schuller, *Early Jazz: Its Roots and Musical Development* (New York: Oxford University Press, 1968), ch. 1.

38. Following Emmanuel Levinas, I am using "heteronomy" in the broad sense of "otherness" (not in the strict sense of a law that comes from outside of oneself). See Emmanuel Levinas, "Philosophy and the Idea of Infinity," in *Collected Philosophical Papers*, trans. Alphonso Lingis (Pittsburgh: Duquesne University Press, 1987), pp. 47-59.

39. I borrow the term "heterophony" from Samuel A. Floyd Jr., "African Roots of Jazz," in *The Oxford Companion to Jazz*, p. 14. Note that Gunther Schuller speaks of "uncontrolled polyphony" (*Early Jazz*, p. 179). But a polyphony that lacks control (and so allows for alterity) is probably better described as "heterophony."

40. See *The Oxford English Dictionary*, 2nd ed., s.v. "heterophony."

41. In this same interview, Armstrong goes on to sing, "Ah! ah! Rido ben di core, Che tai baie costan poco," from Verdi's *Rigoletto*. See Joshua Berrett, "Louis Armstrong and Opera," *Musical Quarterly* (1992): 216-41. Berrett analyzes various solos by Armstrong that have been influenced by listening to and playing opera, including *Rigoletto*. Similarly, Jelly Roll Morton (on his Library of Congress recordings made in 1938 — available as Rounder Records 10914) plays the "Miserere" from Verdi's *Il trovatore* "straight" and then plays it as jazz.

Blacks were better at improvising.[42] As Creoles and Blacks were allowed to integrate (in the 1890s), they began to influence one another musically; the result was a musical "Creolization." Creole culture serves as a metaphor for understanding the development of jazz. *Musically,* Creoles occupied a space somewhere between white European and African American music — and that "betweenness" helped open up a space for white musicians.[43] While we think of improvisation in jazz as improvisation upon "tunes," the improvisation on musical styles is both historically and ontologically prior — and key to understanding how jazz operates. Moreover, the development of jazz (including the improvisation upon tunes) is the story of continual improvisation upon itself.

Improvising Christianity

This sort of improvised beginning is remarkably similar to that of what we now call Christianity. Like the story of jazz, it's hard to know exactly where to begin. Jesus appears in the midst of a heteronomous Judaism comprised of Sadducees, Pharisees, Herodians, and Essenes — all of whom took the Torah as their text but each with varying interpretations. Jesus himself takes no stand with any of these groups. Instead, demonstrating a keen knowledge of the Torah, he improvises upon the conventional readings of it. Of course, in so doing, Rabbi Jesus is continuing a long-established Jewish practice of textual improvisation. What distinguishes his improvisations is their radicality and the authority with which he speaks. Jesus' voice does not merely join a polyphony of rabbinic voices but proves heterophonic. One of his constant refrains is "You have heard that it was said. . . ," followed by "But I say unto you. . . ."[44] Even though Jesus qualifies these radical statements with the statement "Do not think that I have come to abolish the law or the prophets; I have come not to abolish but fulfill" (Matt. 5:17), to his audience this would

42. For more on these differences between Black and Creole musicians, see David Ake, *Jazz Cultures* (Berkeley: University of California Press, 2002), ch. 1.
43. We have remarkably little information regarding white musicians in New Orleans, but they were clearly present. See, for instance, Bruce Raeburn, "Jewish Jazzmen in New Orleans, 1890-1940: An Overview," *Jazz Archivist* 12 (1997): 1-12. For various reasons, it was actually the (white) Original Dixieland Jazz Band that made the first jazz recordings (in 1917) and thus popularized the term "jazz" (or "jass," as it was then spelled).
44. Matthew 5 is filled with such sayings (see, for example, verses 21-22, 27-28, 31-32, 33-34, 38-39, 43-44).

have sounded like a strange fulfillment indeed. And Jesus does not merely confine his improvising to the commandments of the Torah. He likewise appropriates its imagery for his own stories. The parable of the vineyard (Mark 12:1-12), for example, is clearly based on the "song of the vineyard" in Isaiah 5:1-7. While there are important points of similarity, Jesus does not merely retell the same story. For Jesus' version is primarily about *himself.* Thus, Jesus — a master improviser on Old Testament texts — inscribes a new reading within an old one, affirming both but transforming the old so that it can no longer be read in the same way. The improvisation that Jesus exemplifies could be described in terms of Derrida's "iterability," which he describes as "alterability of this same idealized in the singularity of the event, for instance, in this or that speech act. It entails the necessity of thinking *at once* both the rule and the event, concept and singularity."[45] The point of iterability is that citation is always at once repetition and transformation.[46] In effect, Jesus repeats and alters. Such is the nature of improvisation.

Of course, it is crucial to note that Jesus is not just any ordinary improviser: he is the Son of God. So his improvisations have an ultimate authority. And here we come to the fundamental question of authority, of what makes an improvisation not just "good" but *valid.* For the question of "validity in interpretation" (to borrow Hirsch's phrase) is central in biblical interpreta-

45. See Jacques Derrida, *Limited Inc* (Evanston, IL: Northwestern University Press, 1988), p. 119. Although Jacques Derrida explicitly works out the notion of "iterability" in "Signature Event Context" and "Limited Inc a b c . . ." (both in *Limited Inc*), the *idea* is already present in his discussions of Husserl, particularly *Edmund Husserl's Origin of Geometry: An Introduction,* trans. John P. Leavy (Stony Brook, NY: Nicolas Hays, 1978) and *Speech and Phenomena and Other Essays on Husserl's Theory of Signs,* trans. David B. Allison (Evanston, IL: Northwestern University Press, 1973). Certainly it is connected to the notion of *différance* (and Derrida explicitly connects them in "Signature Event Context"). So we might say that the concept of iterability is an example of iterability.

46. Note that Derrida says that "everything begins with reproduction," in "Freud and the Scene of Writing," in *Writing and Difference,* trans. Alan Bass (Chicago: University of Chicago Press, 1978), p. 211, and likewise that "everything 'begins,' then, with citation," in "Dissemination," in *Dissemination,* trans. Barbara Johnson (Chicago: University of Chicago Press, 1981), p. 316. Of course, one *might* argue that Jesus is simply bringing out the "real" meaning or "a" meaning of Isaiah 5:1-7 that had been there all along. I find such an interpretation implausible, since Jesus' parable differs significantly from the allegory of Isaiah 5:1-7.

Why this explanation is included in Matthew 21:33-46 but missing in Mark 12:1-12 and Luke 20:9-19 is for New Testament scholars to dispute. A further difference worth noting is that between the synoptic Gospels and the version found in the *Gospel of Thomas* 93:1-16, which is free of allegorical elements. For more on this, see C. S. Mann's commentary on Mark (Garden City, NY: Doubleday, 1986), pp. 455-67.

tion. The simple answer to the question of what makes an interpretation valid — though hardly a simple answer in practice — is that improvisations that are authorized by the Holy Spirit are precisely those that are valid and provide the *rule* for future interpretations. As such, they prove *canonical,* either in the literal sense of forming the biblical canon or in the more metaphorical sense of providing a measure against which to measure other interpretations.

The improvisatory interpretive practice exemplified by Jesus necessarily becomes part of the very fabric of Christianity as it grows. For, as Christ's followers fulfilled the great commission of Matthew 28, the gospel spread to increasingly wider and differing circles. Whereas Jesus had preached largely in the countryside and to peasant Jews, the fledging *ekklēsia* took Jerusalem as its center. With the conversions of Barnabas and Paul, the faith spread considerably wider. This expansion required a new interpretation of the faith and a new ethnic conception of *who* could be included in the *ekklēsia.* In effect, Paul served as the Christian "Creole" — a Hellenized Jew, educated in the Torah, a Roman citizen, and a missionary to Greeks and Romans alike. It is this "betweenness" of Paul and the conception of Christianity upon which he insists that makes it possible for many of us today to be included. But this "betweenness" is what made Christianity "translatable" beyond narrow Jewish boundaries. As Sanneh puts it:

> Christianity, from its origins, identified itself with the need to translate out of Aramaic and Hebrew, and from that position came to exert a dual force in its historical development. One was the resolve to relativize its Judaic roots. . . . The other was to destigmatize Gentile culture and adopt that culture as a natural extension of the life of the new religion.[47]

In proclaiming that "there is no longer Jew or Greek" (Gal. 3:28), in effect Paul pushes for what has been recently called a "'kreolized' identity — a revolutionary new cultural and social identity."[48]

Of course, this transition from Jewish sect to world religion does not

---

47. Lamin Sanneh, *Translating the Message: The Missionary Impact on Culture* (Maryknoll, NY: Orbis, 1989), p. 1.

48. Fred Wei-han Ho, "'Jazz,' Kreolization and Revolutionary Music for the 21st Century," in *Sounding Off! Music as Subversion/Resistance/Revolution,* ed. Ron Sakolsky and Fred Wei-han Ho (Brooklyn: Autonomedia, 1995), p. 134. Although Wei-han Ho borrows this concept from Dorothy Désir-Davis to describe new hybrid identities forged by way of jazz, it is entirely appropriate as a description of the new hybrid identities forged by the *ekklēsia.*

come without a fight. Even after Peter's vision in which he comes to see that the *euangelion* was for Gentiles as well as Jews (Acts 10), some Jews in Jerusalem still insisted that Gentile converts needed to follow the Torah.[49] Yet Paul insists that there is a fundamental difference between following the Torah and following the *euangelion*. To follow the latter is to be freed from the former. Paul's claim does not merely open up the *ekklēsia;* it likewise opens up biblical interpretation. For if the distinction between Jew and Greek no longer matters, then the Torah becomes a text that can be interpreted by Gentiles. Indeed, while the Christian faith came to generate its own text, that text was grafted on to that of the Torah in such a way so that the new text became an improvisation upon the old.

Even the texts of the New Testament itself are improvisatory, the four Gospels being particularly good examples. While they all tell the story of Jesus, each was written for different audiences to serve different needs. They can be rightly characterized as "polyphonic," but they are also heterophonic — they have somewhat contrasting melodies that cannot *simply* be harmonized with one another, except by overemphasizing similarities and underemphasizing differences. If the Gospels can be read as answers to Jesus' question "who do you say that I am?" then each has a different "take" on Jesus, and none of these "takes" is simply reducible to any other (even though they are not fundamentally at odds with one another either).[50] Their stories emphasize different elements of Jesus' life and teaching and also have markedly different tones. Mark presents us with a Jesus who is constantly shattering the expectations of his followers, whereas Matthew's overarching argument is that Jesus' authority is not that of just any rabbi. Thus, Jesus inaugurates a new Israel, one whose center is the *ekklēsia* not the synagogue. In contrast to the straightforward narrative style of the Synoptic Gospels, John gives us much more of a symbolic portrayal of Jesus. Whereas Mark's Jesus seems remarkably human, John's seems more divine and in control of all that happens to him. Taken together (as opposed to one by one), these voices give us a richer, fuller picture of Jesus. We can rightfully speak of the Holy Spirit as "orchestrating" their contrasting voices polyphonically and heterophonically.

---

49. Note that Luke's account of this dispute in Acts 15 is considerably more sanguine than Paul's in Galatians 2.

50. Although these differences have long been recognized by scholars, they are ably articulated in Robin Griffith-Jones, *The Four Witnesses: The Rebel, the Rabbi, the Chronicler, and the Mystic* (San Francisco: HarperSanFrancisco, 2000).

The Coalescence of Canon and Orthodox Interpretation

Having briefly considered how jazz and Christianity came into being by improvising an identity, we need to turn to what Gadamer terms the *"transformation into structure."*[51] By the time that Armstrong says that "anything" can be jazz,[52] that claim is both true and yet in need of significant qualification. For the roughly six decades that preceded that statement helped codify what counted as "jazz" and yet also showed that it was still remarkably fluid. Something similar happens in Christianity. We need to trace the bare outlines of this twofold development, and then see how that development continues today. All along we will see that the improvisations of and upon the texts of each discourse have a marked influence on the texts themselves.

The jazz diaspora from New Orleans to cities across the United States brought about the development of differing styles of jazz — swing, Bebop, cool, free, fusion — and an ever-widening ethnic inclusivity. The result was a growing collection of texts and ways of interpreting those texts. True, some of those texts are so strongly associated with a particular style that they are generally only played in that idiom. But many jazz tunes could be — and have been — played in a variety of styles. And, within a given style, there is always a good deal of "space" for improvisation. Moreover, for at least a half century (judging by numerous recordings of so-called "standards"), there has been something like a "canon" in jazz. While that canon continues to evolve, it clearly would include Gershwin tunes like "A Foggy Day," Kern tunes like "All the Things You Are," Porter tunes like "Night and Day," Ellington tunes like "Satin Doll," and, say, Monk's "'Round Midnight." Of course, jazz is not merely defined by its primary texts but also by its secondary texts or "commentaries" — which each improvisation ends up being. As Michel Foucault observes, discourses are partially defined by their primary and secondary texts — and the space that is allowed between them.[53] Some discourses — jazz being one of them — allow for a great deal of space for improvisatory movement between text and commentary. Even after only a century of development, jazz has already become more than simply polyphonic. For the various styles of jazz are truly "other," neither reducible to some common "essence" nor necessarily even simply "complementary."

51. Gadamer, *Truth and Method*, p. 110; Gadamer's italics.

52. In an interview from 1962.

53. Michel Foucault, "The Discourse on Language," in *The Archaeology of Knowledge and the Discourse on Language*, trans. A. M. Sheridan Smith (New York: Pantheon, 1972), pp. 220-21.

Moreover, there is a continuing controversy — one that shows no sign of abating — over who "owns" jazz. While this might seem to be merely a sociological or political problem, it is deeply hermeneutical. For it is a question of who counts among the "rightful" or "faithful" interpreters of jazz.

The two millennia of Christian improvisation are even more difficult to sketch, since it is much longer and considerably more varied. So we will need to concentrate on just a few of the more important moments of Christian improvisational history. That the early part of Christian interpretation is improvisational is a claim not likely to be contested. But, one might ask, what about later periods of Christian interpretation? Or, more pointedly, what about our time? Are biblical texts still being "improvised" upon?

The early centuries of the Christian church were ripe with interpretational variations. If one considers the early preaching of Christians and their interpretation of the Old Testament, it becomes clear that they "made no sharp distinction between literalist treatments of the text, Midrash exegesis, Pesher interpretation, and the application of accepted predictive prophecies. All of these were employed."[54] Yet the Christian diaspora to parts of what are now Asia, Africa, and Europe only multiplied these interpretational possibilities as the *ekklēsia* diversified. By about A.D. 100, the Gospels and epistles of Paul, Peter, and John were circulating in places such as Polycarp's Smyrna and being quoted in a way that shows they were known among some believers.[55] But exactly what counted as orthodox interpretation was still being decided. For instance, although Matthew's Gospel, the *Didache*, Ignatius's letters, and the *Gospel of Thomas* all originate in Syria, they give us significantly different views of the faith and the *ekklēsia*.[56] The emergence of differing theories regarding the exact ontological status of Christ that were subsequently deemed heretical also attests to this uncertainty. But, much as improvisations in jazz proved crucial in defining the contours of interpretation, Christological interpretational disagreements proved crucial in helping determine the contours of orthodox belief. That Arianism came to be de-

---

54. Richard Longenecker, *Biblical Exegesis in the Apostolic Period* (Grand Rapids: Eerdmans, 1975), p. 103.

55. W. H. C. Frend, *The Rise of Christianity* (Philadelphia: Fortress, 1984), p. 135.

56. For instance, to quote Frend: "If for [Matthew] Christ is the lawgiver of the new covenant, the *Didache* represents him as the Servant and Vine of David. Matthew sees the church as a hierarchical community (like Qumran) based on Peter as the rock on which it was founded; the *Didache* does not refer to Peter, but portrays a community in which there is no single monarchial bishop, but a number of officeholders" (Frend, *The Rise of Christianity*, pp. 144-45).

nounced as a heresy showed that not just any interpretation or improvisation could be accepted as valid or orthodox. Further, the development of the doctrine of the Holy Spirit enabled interpreters to read passages in both Testaments in a new way. Seeing the writing of both Testaments as inspired by the Holy Spirit meant that they had a common author.

Even with the formation of the canon and the clarification of major Christian doctrine brought about by early church councils, the improvisational interpretation upon Scripture continued, though it was obviously progressively more circumscribed. A particularly good example of this is the development of the allegorical method of interpretation. Although allegorical interpretation can be seen as complementary to "literal" interpretation (since interpreters such as Origen thought that the real truth of Scripture was "concealed beneath the literal expression"[57]), the need for allegorical interpretation was frequently occasioned by the fact that the literal reading of many Old Testament texts was deemed simply unacceptable to certain early exegetes. Augustine's conversion to Christianity, for instance, was made possible only by his discovery of the allegorical method from Ambrose, for it made certain portions of Scripture palatable to him that he had earlier found impossible to accept. Note that Augustine stands as one of the strong "improvisers" in the Christian tradition, one whose interpretations have had a monumental influence on subsequent interpretation of Scripture.[58] In other words, these two ways of reading texts — literal and allegorical — were sometimes seen as polyphonic, in the sense that one complemented the other. But they were sometimes seen as simply heterophonic, in the sense that commentators felt forced to choose one over the other (because one seemed simply unacceptable). Whatever we make of the allegorical method today, there can be no doubt that it counts as a significant improvisation upon the Old Testament, as well as the New.

Even though Luther and Calvin are associated with literal interpretations of Scripture, their interpretations represent significant improvisational moments in the history of scriptural interpretation. One might argue that

57. Manlio Simonetti, *Biblical Interpretation in the Early Church: An Historical Introduction to Patristic Exegesis,* trans. John A. Hughes (Edinburgh: T&T Clark, 1994), p. 42.

58. Although allegorical interpretation tends to be associated with Alexandria, it actually was imported into the West and eventually became the dominant mode of exegesis there. As Gerald Bray puts it: "By the end of the patristic period, exegetical methods had been fairly securely established. Allegorical interpretation, shorn of the philosophical extremes of Origen, was the norm in *almost every case*" (my italics). See his *Biblical Interpretation: Past and Present* (Downers Grove, IL: IVP, 1996), p. 110.

they served merely to "bring out" meanings in the text that had "been there all along." Yet it is more plausible to think that their readings were strong improvisations upon the text — *based upon the text,* of course, but not *simply* limited to it. Although Luther's reading of Romans now seems intuitively obvious to many of us (especially Protestants), it would not have been obvious to many of Luther's contemporaries. Moreover, that particular reading has had enormous and continuing influences upon Protestant thought, so much so that it is not too much to say that Protestants are virtually *unable* to read Romans apart from Luther's interpretation of it.[59] Similarly, although Calvin puts particular emphasis on a literal reading of Scripture, the covenant theology that he develops is far more than simply a "literal" reading of the text. One may argue that it is a reading that is truly *faithful* to the text, but it is still an improvisation.

This improvisation of interpretation continues in our own day. We have no trouble, for instance, singing "His Banner Over Me Is Love" and thinking of this in terms of God's love for us today.[60] Similarly, American evangelicals are perfectly comfortable explaining salvation in terms of "letting Jesus into your heart" or "accepting Jesus as your personal savior," even though such language and even such concepts are clearly an improvisation on Scripture. I do not in any way mean to suggest that such ways of expressing Christianity are inappropriate or unfaithful to Scripture. But we must see them for what they are: cultural and historical improvisations on Scripture. Perhaps, though, the improvisational nature of our interpretations is seen most clearly in our conceptions of Jesus. As we noted, the Gospels can be seen as answers to the question "Who do you say that I am?" Stephen Prothero has recently provided a remarkable assemblage of American answers to this question that include the "meek and mild" Jesus, the "friend" Jesus, the "moral example" Jesus, and even variations of Jesus found in other religions.[61] There are pictures of Jesus as social activist, like that given by John Howard Yoder,[62] and a

---

59. And, since Luther's reading has now become dominant even in Roman Catholic theology, that influence has spread considerably further.

60. I borrow this example from Bray, who quotes Song of Songs 2:4 ("He brought me to the banqueting house, and his banner over me was love") and then says: "In the original context, it appears that what the author had in mind was a night of sexual bliss following an orgy of heavy drinking, but no modern congregation singing the chorus based on these words ever thinks of that." See Bray, *Biblical Interpretation,* p. 159.

61. Stephen Prothero, *American Jesus: How the Son of God Became a National Icon* (New York: Farrar, Straus & Giroux, 2003).

62. John Howard Yoder, *The Politics of Jesus,* 2nd ed. (Grand Rapids: Eerdmans, 1994).

growing number of pictures of Jesus that are no longer dominated by Europeans and Americans. Much like the early church, we are in the midst of important changes in ways of thinking about Jesus. What began in the East as a Jewish sect that spread from the countryside to the cities and then to various parts of the world is currently dominated by the West. Yet that dominance is slowly disappearing as a new diaspora to the East and the South replaces the old. These rapid changes in the configuration of the *ekklēsia* are resulting in significant changes in the ways in which Scripture is interpreted and even translated. As formerly colonized groups come to read Scripture and theologize in light of their situations, new readings of biblical texts are already emerging and will undoubtedly continue to emerge. For instance, it is understandable why the Indian theologian Russell Chandran says:

> Please do not use the word "Lord" when you speak of Jesus in Asia. This idea of the lordship of Christ carries echoes of Western aggressiveness, of colonialism, and imperialism. It is the humble Christ, the Christ who quietly serves and sacrifices, it is this Christ who reaches towards our hearts.[63]

It is important to note that the problem here has less to do with the notion of "lordship" per se than with the fact that the "lordship of Christ" all too easily translated into something like the "lordship of the British Empire" during colonial rule. Of course, the idea of lordship as "aggressiveness, of colonialism, and imperialism" is actually quite *foreign* to the biblical notion of the lordship of Christ, who explicitly says: "You know that the rulers of the Gentiles lord it over them, and their great ones are tyrants over them. It will not be so among you; but whoever wishes to be great among you must be your servant" (Matt. 20:25-26). Or, to use a different example, in many parts of Africa the vision of Jesus as "great Ancestor" is the one that resonates most with believers. Accordingly, some contemporary African Roman Catholic Eucharistic prayers begin with addresses like "O Father, Great Ancestor."[64]

These improvisational changes are apt to make evangelicals in the West uncomfortable, but we must not forget that we *too* have been engaged in improvisation upon Scripture (and, truth be told, some of our discomfort may stem from the fact that *our* improvisations are losing their hegemony in the

63. Quoted in R. S. Sugirtharajah, *Postcolonial Criticism and Biblical Interpretation* (Oxford: Oxford University Press, 2002), p. 168.

64. Philip Jenkins, *The Next Christendom: The Coming of Global Christianity* (Oxford: Oxford University Press, 2002), p. 116.

global church).[65] To those who might complain that some of the examples that I've included here are ones that "distort the text," I would reply: "Perhaps they do. Or perhaps it is *you* who distort the text." My goal here is not that of adjudicating between (to use Ricoeur's memorable phrase) "the conflict of interpretations."[66] Rather, it is to make clear that *all* of us who interpret Scripture are engaged in an improvisational practice. Such improvisation may be more faithful or less faithful to the gospel, but it is no less an improvisation for that. Further, I have attempted to show that *dissonance* is not only a driving mechanism of improvisation but also an inevitable result. We interpret Scripture in ways that make it less foreign to us (less *dissonant*), which is to say that we are always engaged in intra-lingual translation.

Moreover, these differing ways of interpreting cannot *simply* be described as polyphonic. John Milbank is almost right in envisioning a community in which there is "an infinite differentiation that is also a harmony."[67] In such a community, says Milbank, "the possibility of consonance is stretched to its limits, and yet the path of dissonance is not embarked upon."[68] Milbank clearly conceives the Christian community in terms of polyphony and harmony. While he is willing to stretch that harmony "to its

---

65. Or to give a different example, it is quite sobering that members of the Anglican Communion in the global south and east — what were once marginalized regions of the communion — are now particularly vocal in their criticism of the current course of the Episcopal Church in the United States of America (my denomination).

66. Paul Ricoeur, *The Conflict of Interpretations,* trans. Don Idhe (Evanston, IL: Northwestern University Press, 1974).

67. John Milbank, *Theology and Social Theory: Beyond Secular Reason* (Oxford: Blackwell, 1990), p. 427.

68. Milbank, *Theology and Social Theory,* p. 429. Note that Milbank does go on to say the following: "To say (with Deleuze) that dissonance and atonality are here 'held back' or 'not arrived at,' would be a mistake of the same order as claiming that nihilism is evidently true in its disclosure of the impossibility of truth. Instead, one should say, it is always possible to place dissonance back in Baroque 'suspense'; at every turn of a phrase, new, unexpected harmony may still arrive. Between the nihilistic promotion of dissonance, of differences that clash or only accord through conflict, and the Baroque risk of a harmony stretched to the limits — the openness to musical grace — there remains an undecidability." Open discourses do not *simply* have a harmony "stretched to its limits." They also have dissonances that may resist harmonization — or at least harmonization in the here and now. While "new, unexpected harmony may still arrive," there must be the openness and even the promotion of creativity that creates dissonance. Without such openness to such dissonance, we would not have the late Beethoven quartets or Stravinsky's *Rite of Spring.* Harmony may *arrive,* but that arrival may well have to do with a change in *us* as listeners, and perhaps a radical revision of what counts as "harmony" (as in the case of Peter's vision).

limits," harmony remains the dominant metaphor. For the ancient Greeks, *polyphōnia* carried the idea of multiple tones and *polyphōnos* multiple voices. That characterization of the Christian community seems right, both descriptively and prescriptively. But it does not go quite far enough. In juxtaposition to (that is, *in addition to*) the notion of "polyphony," we need to set the notion of heterophony — both descriptively and prescriptively. First, while polyphony gives us the idea of *multiple* voices, heterophony emphasizes the *otherness* of those voices. From the start, the Christian community has had this otherness at its core, and has continually been in the process of coming to terms with it. Second, heterophony emphasizes the idea of differing voices that do not simply blend or produce a pleasing harmony but remain distinct and sometimes dissonant, sometimes precisely when we would rather they were not.[69]

Neither interpretations nor the communities that produce them are always harmonious. Indeed, creative interpretations often produce dissonance, and that dissonance does not necessarily simply pass away. For instance, Luther's insistence on salvation by faith alone was a very dissonant message in his time to many, one so dissonant that it led to a deep and lasting ecclesiastical break. Today, even the Roman Catholic Church recognizes Luther's insistence on justification by faith to be the right interpretation of Romans. But such was not the case at the time. In other words, in order to take a stand for orthodoxy, Luther was forced to be a heteronomous voice. Yet there are other kinds of heteronomy in the *ekklēsia* that remain and probably will not disappear. There is no easy reconciliation of, say, Calvinism and Arminianism. Despite the fact that some would denounce one of these as heretical (thus Tim LaHaye has infamously claimed that "Calvinism . . . comes perilously close to blasphemy"),[70] most Christians see them both as within the realm of Christian orthodoxy. But these two views represent significantly *differing* views regarding how salvation takes place and exactly

69. David Cunningham rightly points out that "polyphony" and "harmony" are *not* synonymous, even though they are often taken to be such. Given that difference, he thinks the notion of polyphony is sufficient, since "polyphony could theoretically be either 'harmonious' or 'dissonant.'" Yet it is precisely because I want to emphasize the existence of (and *need for*) dissonance and difference that I think we need the notion of heterophony. See David S. Cunningham, *These Three Are One: The Practice of Trinitarian Theology* (Malden, MA: Blackwell, 1998), p. 128.

70. This remarkable quotation comes from an endorsement by LaHaye on the back cover of Dave Hunt, *What Love Is This? Calvinism's Misrepresentation of God* (Sisters, OR: Loyal, 2002).

who is saved. These views can hardly be reconciled with one another, any more than the pacifism of Mennonites with the views of Christians who hold to just war theory. Of course, there are also views — such as Gnosticism and Arianism — that the *ekklēsia* has decidedly denounced as heretical (even though, in both cases, that denunciation came over a long time of sorting through their respective claims). So there is only so much room within the *ekklēsia* for heteronomy. Some heter*onomy* is simply heter*odoxy*.

To conclude, we need to emphasize *both* polyphony and heterophony, as well as consonance and dissonance, in order to do justice to differing interpretational voices within the *ekklēsia*. Part of living within the *ekklēsia* is learning to accept the reality that there are differing voices that we must not simply dismiss or ignore but instead take seriously. While we seek harmony as brothers and sisters, we must also recognize that dissonance is often productive and, in any case, an inevitable result of a continually improvised *ekklēsia*. Yet, even though I've emphasized the role of heterophony in interpretation — the hermeneutical "differing" of *différance* — we must not forget that *différance* is likewise messianic in nature. For *différance* also entails "deferring" and so points us to a future time. That time may not be one in which all difference is "resolved." Certainly, there will be no erasure of difference, as in some Buddhist vision in which all becomes undifferentiated One. Instead, there will be a new harmony of those differences, one in which there is true — and not merely contrived — *shalom*. Here and now, though, we can barely begin to imagine how that harmony of heavenly *shalom* might sound.

PART FOUR   MUSIC AND WORSHIP

13. Faithful Feelings: Music and Emotion in Worship

Jeremy S. Begbie

The power of music to engage our emotional life is proverbial. David's lyre soothes Saul; "The Star-Spangled Banner" brings a tear to the eye of the patriotic marine; the fifteen-year-old finds solace from a broken heart in a moody ballad. A psychologist observes: "Some sort of emotional experience is probably the main reason behind most people's engagement with music."[1] Although this cannot be said of all music worldwide (the functions of music are multiple and highly diverse), it does seem true of a good deal of music in globalized Western society.

And yet music's emotional power is probably its single most controversial feature. Philosophers, psychologists, and music theorists vigorously debate just how it affects our emotions. Many in the Christian church have feared its ability to "get inside" us, not least in worship. Many are anxious that music all too easily turns into a device of manipulation, a tool of moral harm, all the more dangerous because it can work its charms without our being aware of it. Others insist such worries are overplayed, betraying an exaggerated suspicion of anything not amenable to rational control.

In this essay, I want to ask: What is it about musical sounds and the way they operate such that they become emotionally significant and valuable to

1. Patrik N. Juslin and John A. Sloboda, "Music and Emotion: Introduction," in *Music and Emotion: Theory and Research*, ed. Patrik N. Juslin and John A. Sloboda (Oxford: Oxford University Press, 2001), p. 3.

The title of this essay draws on the title of a book by Matthew Elliott, *Faithful Feelings: Emotion in the New Testament* (Leicester: IVP, 2005).

us? And what can we learn from this theologically, with regard to music in worship? We will first offer some general comments about emotion, and set these in the light of a trinitarian theology of worship. Then we explore the emotional power of musical sounds, and go on to situate our findings in the context of this same theology. We will see that certain capacities of music are singularly appropriate for carrying and advancing certain key dimensions of worship. We will also discover that our theology of worship is itself enriched in the process: theology throws light on music, and music throws light on theology.

It should be added that there is no attempt here to offer a comprehensive account of emotion, musical emotion, or musical emotion in worship. But we do highlight what I believe are fruitful possibilities for further exploration and research.

Faithful Feelings

Emotion: Charting the Territory

The literature on emotion is now vast and burgeoning, especially in anthropology, psychology, neuroscience, and philosophy.[2] Here we cannot do jus-

2. See, e.g., Anthony Kenny, *Action, Emotion and Will* (London: Routledge & Kegan Paul, 1963); Robert C. Solomon, *The Passions* (Garden City, NY: Anchor Press/Doubleday, 1976); R. C. Solomon, "The Logic of Emotion," *Noûs* 11 (1977): 41-49; Amelie Rorty, ed., *Explaining Emotions* (Berkeley: University of California Press, 1980); C. E. Izard et al., eds., *Emotions, Cognition, and Behaviour* (Cambridge: Cambridge University Press, 1984); Patricia S. Greenspan, *Emotions and Reasons: An Inquiry into Emotional Justification* (New York: Routledge, 1988); William E. Lyons, *Emotion* (Cambridge: Cambridge University Press, 1993); R. C. Solomon, "The Philosophy of Emotions," in *Handbook of Emotions*, 2nd ed., ed. M. Lewis and J. M. Haviland-Jones (New York: The Guilford Press, 2004), pp. 3-15; Antonio R. Damasio, *Descartes' Error: Emotion, Reason, and the Human Brain* (New York: G. P. Putnam, 1994); Patricia S. Greenspan, *Practical Guilt: Moral Dilemmas, Emotions, and Social Norms* (New York: Oxford University Press, 1995); Michael Stocker and Elizabeth Hegeman, *Valuing Emotions* (Cambridge: Cambridge University Press, 1996); Paul E. Griffiths, *What Emotions Really Are: The Problem of Psychological Categories* (Chicago: University of Chicago Press, 1997); Antonio R. Damasio, *The Feeling of What Happens: Body and Emotion in the Making of Consciousness* (New York: Harcourt Brace, 1999); Richard Wollheim, *On the Emotions* (New Haven: Yale University Press, 1999); Nico H. Frijda et al., eds., *Emotions and Beliefs: How Feelings Influence Thoughts* (Cambridge: Cambridge University Press, 2000); Peter Goldie, *The Emotions: A Philosophical Exploration* (Oxford: Clarendon Press, 2000); Martha C. Nussbaum, *Upheavals of Thought: The Intelligence of Emotions* (Cambridge: Cam-

tice to the complexity of the field, nor to its fervent disputes. But we can at least chart a way through the territory, indicating our reasons for adopting the course we do, and referring to supporting literature and alternative positions as we proceed.

The Classic Triad It is widely held that some "basic" emotions are universal to all members of the human species.[3] Theorists argue about which these are, but they are usually variants of happiness, sadness, anger, fear, and disgust. The presence of such emotions is usually gleaned from three kinds of evidence: self-reports (what people say they feel), overt behavior (the way people act), and physiological phenomena (the way their bodily systems behave). This has led to a fairly standard way of describing emotional states: as involving an interplay between *conscious experience* (we "feel" anger, fear, or whatever); expressive *bodily behavior* (if irritated, we may well tense our bodies or press our lips together; if frightened, we might widen our eyes); and *physiological activation* (people who are emotionally agitated will often perspire, their pulse rate increases, blood gets diverted from internal organs to the larger muscles, pupils dilate, and so on).[4]

We need to bear these three components in mind throughout: there is substantial evidence that our emotional involvement in music involves all three.[5] Together, they call into question two common tendencies in thinking about emotion. The first is to see emotions as essentially private mental states, and the bodily or physiological correlates as quite distinct and contingent. This is clearly mistaken, and in any case, assumes a mind-body dichotomy increasingly recognized as unsupportable.[6] The second tendency is to treat emotions individualistically. Against this, theorists urge that emotions,

bridge University Press, 2001); Peter Goldie, *Understanding Emotions: Mind and Morals* (Aldershot: Ashgate, 2002); K. T. Strongman, *The Psychology of Emotion* (Chichester: Wiley, 2003); Robert C. Solomon, *Thinking about Feeling: Contemporary Philosophers on Emotions* (Oxford: Oxford University Press, 2004); Jenefer Robinson, *Deeper Than Reason: Emotion and Its Role in Literature, Music, and Art* (Oxford: Clarendon Press, 2005).

3. Paul Ekman and Richard J. Davidson, *The Nature of Emotion: Fundamental Questions* (New York: Oxford University Press, 1994).

4. David G. Myers, *Psychology* (New York: Worth Publishers, 2004), ch. 13. Scherer calls this the classic "reaction triad"; K. R. Scherer, "Neuroscience Projections to Current Debates in Emotion Psychology," *Cognition and Emotion* 7 (1993): 3.

5. John A. Sloboda and Patrik N. Juslin, "Psychological Perspectives on Music and Emotion," in *Music and Emotion: Theory and Research,* ed. Patrik N. Juslin and John A. Sloboda (Oxford: Oxford University Press, 2001), pp. 84-85.

6. Damasio, *Descartes' Error.*

insofar as they are publicly recognizable bodily states, can profoundly affect, and be affected by, our relations to others: emotions are "intrinsically social."[7] Indeed, as a crucial non-verbal means of relating to others, emotion is to some extent entailed in nearly all social activity.[8] We have evolved highly developed skills for identifying emotion in others and responding accordingly. Not least, emotions can play a major role in establishing and strengthening human unity, in creating and sustaining profound bonds between even the most disparate people — think of how contagious enthusiasm is in a classroom, or fear in an airplane.

However, the triadic scheme needs to be supplemented by an element that would seem to play an essential role in occurrent emotional states, namely, *cognition*. Much recent discussion has surrounded this matter, and it has led to a distinction often made between "non-cognitive" and "cognitive" accounts of emotion.

Non-cognitive Theories   "Non-cognitive" labels a family of theories that sees emotion as fundamentally separate from, and even opposed to, the rational and intellectual, and as such, having little if anything to do with the mind's pursuit and grasp of truth. Emotions are basically irrational bodily reactions, transient surges of affect quite unrelated to cognition. Reports of an affective experience can be explained entirely in terms of physiological changes and outward bodily movements. This is sometimes tied to a view of human nature that contrasts the "lower," "animal," bodily nature with the "higher," mental faculties.[9] Many thus speak of emotion disdainfully, extol-

---

7. Sloboda and Juslin, "Psychological Perspectives on Music and Emotion," p. 86.

8. Tia DeNora, "Aesthetic Agency and Musical Practice: New Directions in the Sociology of Music and Emotion," in *Music and Emotion: Theory and Research,* ed. Patrik N. Juslin and John A. Sloboda (Oxford: Oxford University Press, 2001), pp. 161-80; Strongman, *Psychology of Emotion,* ch. 10.

9. René Descartes provided one of the first developed accounts of what would today be called a non-cognitivist theory of emotion: see René Descartes, *The Passions of the Soul* (Indianapolis: Hackett, 1989). For discussion, see Lyons, *Emotion,* pp. 2-8. Modern psychological theory of emotion is widely regarded as initiated by William James, whose views in many ways extend those of Descartes. James claimed that the awareness of physiological changes and bodily movement following the perception of a situation *is* the emotion: "we feel sorry because we cry, angry because we strike, afraid because we tremble." William James, "What Is an Emotion?" in *The Nature of Emotion,* ed. M. B. Arnold (Harmondsworth: Penguin, 1968), p. 13. According to the James-Lange theory (so-called because the Danish physician and psychologist Carl Lange came to the same conclusion on his own), emotions are feelings that come about as a result of bodily processes and behavior, rather than being their cause.

ling the curbing power of reason. This outlook commonly links emotions with our "animal nature," as distinct from what makes us human, and some evolutionary accounts of emotion chime in with this: emotions are biological adaptive bodily reactions geared toward survival, both physical and social.[10] Admittedly, not all who hold to a strong distinction between cognition and emotion denigrate the latter. Many encourage emotion in order to "balance out" the rational and intellectual; some feminist theory wants to reinstate our emotional nature against what is seen as a damaging (and typically male) intellectualism,[11] and for the early nineteenth-century Romantics, the presumed irrationality of emotion was generally something to be celebrated (as distinct from scientific rationalism). But underlying these we still find the same dichotomous understanding of reason vs. emotion, intellect vs. passion.

In discussions of worship, non-cognitive approaches to emotion often hold sway. Many are instinctively cautious about sermons that target the emotions, songs that span emotional extremes, exuberant bodily expression. The fear is that we will lose touch with reality, become too preoccupied with the body, open ourselves to unscrupulous manipulation by church leaders. Preaching should be addressed first to the mind and only then to the emotions; bodily movement should be kept to a minimum; songs should be concerned with intellectually graspable truth, only secondarily (if at all) with moving us.

In contemporary studies of emotion, however, non-cognitivism has fallen on hard times.[12] Among other things, there is the problem of satisfac-

---

Implicit here is a separation of cognition and emotion: "Emotion and cognition seem then parted . . . cerebral processes are almost feelingless." William James, "The Emotions," in *The Emotions*, ed. C. G. Lange and W. James (Baltimore: Williams and Wilkins, 1922), pp. 122-23.

10. Classically in Charles Darwin, *The Expression of the Emotions in Man and Animals* (London: HarperCollins, 1998). For an overview of evolutionary approaches, see Strongman, *Psychology of Emotion*, pp. 64-70.

11. See, e.g., Carol Gilligan, *In a Different Voice: Psychological Theory and Women's Development* (Cambridge, MA: Harvard University Press, 1982).

12. See, from the perspective of anthropology, Rom Harré, *The Social Construction of Emotions* (Oxford: Blackwell, 1988); philosophy, John Macmurray, *Reason and Emotion* (London: Faber & Faber, 1935); Ronald De Sousa, *The Rationality of Emotion* (Cambridge, MA: MIT Press, 1987); Martha C. Nussbaum, *Love's Knowledge: Essays on Philosophy and Literature* (New York: Oxford University Press, 1990), pp. 40-43; Nussbaum, *Upheavals of Thought*; M. B. Arnold, "Cognitive Theories of Emotion," in *Encyclopedia of Psychology*, vol. 2, ed. R. J. Corsini (New York: John Wiley and Sons, 1994); neuroscience, Damasio, *Descartes' Error*. For a summary of critiques, see Elliott, *Faithful Feelings*, pp. 27-31.

torily differentiating emotions if they are to be understood solely in terms of bodily changes and movements; of accounting for the way emotions become motives for behavior (we do not say "I ran away because my heart suddenly beat faster," but "I ran away because I was scared of the mugger with a knife"); and from a neuro-scientific perspective, an emotion/cognition dichotomy seems unsupportable.[13]

Cognitive Theories This takes us to "cognitive" theories of emotion.[14] Common to these is the integral role that cognition is thought to have in emotional experience. But there is considerable disagreement about what that role is, and about what constitutes "cognition." The field can be opened up by observing that generally speaking, what we consider to be full-fledged emotions depend on *beliefs* about the world or oneself. My fear of falling off a two hundred-foot cliff is dependent upon my belief that if I fall, I will die. To say "I am angry with you" implies that I believe you have done or said something that has provoked my anger. Beliefs on which emotions are based may be true or false, rational or irrational, superficial or profound, but without them, it is hard to see how an emotion could arise.

These beliefs in turn form the basis of *evaluation* (or appraisal[15]): "Fear

13. Emotional processes are not restricted to subcortical brain regions that are shared with other animals; they recruit parts of the frontal lobes, the largest and latest brain structures to emerge in evolutionary development. Damasio, *Descartes' Error;* Isabelle Peretz, "Listen to the Brain: A Biological Perspective on Musical Emotions," in *Music and Emotion: Theory and Research*, pp. 105-34, esp. pp. 105-6.

14. It is fair to say, within psychology at least, that the tide has recently turned strongly in favor of such theories (paralleling the ascendancy of cognitive psychology). For a survey of the major theorists, see Strongman, *Psychology of Emotion*, ch. 6.

15. Nussbaum, *Upheavals of Thought*, p. 28. The distinction Lyons makes between evaluation and appraisal is, I think, questionable (Lyons, *Emotion*, p. 80); in any case, it is not relevant to us here.

Belief and evaluation are logically distinct, even if in practice intertwined (Lyons, *Emotion*, p. 35). I believe that the shark's teeth are dangerous, but while I may be terrified on seeing a shark ten feet away, my friend next to me may be exhilarated: we both believe the teeth are dangerous, but my friend evaluates the danger in a different way, leading to a different emotion. It is the evaluative component that most accurately specifies and differentiates the emotions, not beliefs. (Essentially the same distinction is made by Lazarus and Smith [R. S. Lazarus and C. A. Smith, "Knowledge and Appraisal in the Cognition-Emotion Relationship," *Cognition and Emotion* 2 (1988): 281-300] when they distinguish between knowledge — consisting of "cognitions about the way things are and how they work," and appraisal — "consisting of evaluations of the significance of this knowledge for well-being" [p. 282]. Knowledge, in this sense, is a necessary but not sufficient condition for emotion, whereas

or anger may arouse fight or attack, but they still depend on a realization that something is threatening or annoying, which is an appraisal, however rudimentary."[16] According to William Lyons, "The evaluation central to the concept of emotion is an evaluation of some object, event or situation in the world about me in relation to me, or according to my norms. Thus my emotions reveal whether I see the world or some aspect of it as threatening or welcoming, pleasant or painful, regrettable or a solace, and so on."[17] Because emotion entails evaluation in this sense, different appraisals of the same situation by different people can give rise to different emotions. Indeed, the evaluative factor is probably the best tool for specifying and differentiating emotions: mere physiological changes are insufficient for the task, reports of "feeling" are notoriously hard to assess, and although bodily behavior may provide clues as to the emotion, one set of bodily movements can invite a variety of interpretations. One needs to seek out how the subject of an emotion is appraising a situation to identify the emotion being experienced with any accuracy.[18]

Even if we hold that belief and evaluation are essential to the very iden-

---

appraisal [so defined] is both necessary and sufficient. I would prefer "belief" to "knowledge" in this context, since it allows for the possibility of false belief.)

16. Arnold, "Cognitive Theories of Emotion," p. 259.

17. Lyons, *Emotion*, pp. 58-59.

18. Lyons, *Emotion*, pp. 62-63. For Lyons's response to objections to this view, see *Emotion*, pp. 80-89. Martha Nussbaum mounts a vigorous case for claiming that evaluative judgment is not only a constituent part of emotion but that emotions are best defined in terms of evaluative judgment *alone*. Emotions *are* evaluative judgments. Nussbaum, *Upheavals of Thought, passim*, but esp. pp. 19-88. She argues that "feelings" are not absolutely necessary as definitional elements in any of the emotion types, nor are bodily processes, whether internal (physiological activation) or external (overt bodily behavior).

I have no quarrel with the notion that evaluative judgment plays a constituent and determinative role in emotional experience; it is essential to emotion, and a sufficient cause of emotion. And we should certainly resist reducing emotions to irrational, blind instincts. But I am equally unconvinced that the definition of emotion should be confined without remainder to evaluative judgment (see esp. Nussbaum, *Upheavals of Thought*, pp. 44-45, 56-64). For the components of the "classic triad" ("feeling," bodily behavior, and physiological activation) would also seem to be constitutive of emotion, and not themselves reducible to evaluative judgment. Aaron Margolis observes: "The continuity between mind and body is an interesting and important insight. But Nussbaum only reaches it by essentially collapsing emotions into cognitive states. It is one thing to say that cognitive states are constituents of emotions, even necessary constituents. But a sufficient condition?" Aaron Margolis, review of Martha Nussbaum, *Upheavals of Thought: The Intelligence of Emotions*, at http://web.archive.org/web/20041010184804/http://www.politicaltheory.org/books/reviews/nussbaum03.html, accessed June 2010.

tity of an emotion, this does not, however, mean that emotions are the result of coolly (non-emotionally) entertaining a judgment and then responding accordingly with an emotion. We do not think before every emotion, deliberately and consciously, "I judge this to be a dangerous situation . . ." or whatever.[19] On the other hand, we are not speaking merely of a physiological reflex — like jerking our hand away from a hot plate. Some might claim that there are such things as "reflex emotions" (e.g., instant embarrassment, the flaring up of jealousy) that seem to include no evaluation. But this is only so if we limit evaluation entirely to deliberate and conscious acts. If we allow a dispositional dimension to evaluations — if we allow that they can be latent and activated instantaneously — the objection seems to be answered. I am afraid of small dogs because some time ago I was bitten by one and from then on evaluated them as dangerous. I am afraid of small dogs even though there is no dog present in my office now. Were one to walk into the office, my fear would "kick in," on the basis of a tendency to evaluate dogs in this way.[20] But whatever we make of this, the important point here is that, even if we allow that actually occurring emotions may not always arise from a deliberate and conscious act of judgment but can arise from a disposition or tendency

19. Jenefer Robinson believes that at the "core" of emotions is a "non-cognitive appraisal" that is produced "automatically," and "automatically" results in physiological changes. However, she goes on to say that, after the initial emotional reaction, there is a more discerning cognitive appraisal: "cognitive monitoring," as she puts it. Here much depends, she stresses, on seeing emotions not as instantaneous "things" but as *processes*. Robinson, *Deeper Than Reason*, chs. 1-3.

This relates to a lively debate among theorists. R. B. Zajonc and R. S. Lazarus focused the issues most sharply, the former arguing that emotion precedes cognition and is independent of it, the latter arguing that the cognitive appraisal of meaning underlies all emotional states, even if the thought process of evaluation may be virtually instantaneous (R. B. Zajonc, "Feeling and Thinking: Preferences Need No Inferences," *American Psychologist* 35 [1980]: 151-75; R. S. Lazarus, "Thoughts on the Relation between Emotion and Cognition," *American Psychologist* 37 [1982]: 1019-24; "On the Primacy of Cognition," *American Psychologist* 39 [1984]: 124-29; R. B. Zajonc, "In the Primacy of Affect," *American Psychologist* 39 [1984]: 117-23; "Feeling and Thinking: Closing the Debate over the Independence of Affect," in *Feeling and Thinking: The Role of Affect in Social Cognition*, ed. J. P. Forgas [Cambridge: Cambridge University Press, 2000], pp. 31-58). To a large extent the debate seems to be about definition (see, e.g., Strongman, *Psychology of Emotion*, p. 91).

20. See Lyons, *Emotion*, pp. 85-89. Nussbaum speaks of "background" emotion-judgments (as opposed to "situational" emotion-judgments). I may be angry over time at some persistent wrong; this may shape and pattern many of my actions (I may be generally withdrawn, irritable), yet only be overtly manifest in particular circumstances (when I lash out or lose my temper). Nussbaum, *Upheavals of Thought*, pp. 69-75.

to evaluate something in a particular way (formed previously and part of our makeup), and that "automatic" appraisal may be followed by a more discriminating and extended cognitive act of judgment, emotions nonetheless depend on evaluation of *some* sort at *some* stage.

Emotions and Objects If emotions necessarily entail beliefs and judgments, they will be *oriented to objects.* I am not angry in the abstract, but angry *about* something or angry *at* someone. Fear arises because something has threatened me, joy because I have encountered something that is good, beautiful, or whatever. Emotions are *of* or *about* or *at* something — they have "particular objects."[21] The object-oriented character of emotions is

21. Lyons proposes we see these "particular objects" as being of two sorts: "material" objects and "intentional" objects. *Emotion,* pp. 106-9. Material objects are simply actually existing things in the world (although not necessarily composed of physical matter); intentional objects are objects not actually existing in the world but in some manner conceived by the mind. Intentional objects need not be illusory: it makes sense to speak of loving someone who has died — he no longer exists in the world (he is an intentional object) — but he is certainly not illusory. (On illusory objects, see n. 26 below.) Or, to take another example, I might not believe in the reality of Harry Potter, but I might well respond emotionally to his unhappy home situation. What Lyons's distinction does not take account of, of course, are theological realities.

It is perhaps worth alluding to a technical term often used in discussions about emotions and objects, and directly linked to what we were saying about evaluation. All emotions, it is said, have a "formal object," distinguishable from a particular object (Lyons, *Emotion,* pp. 49-50, 99-104). A formal object is a *property* implicitly ascribed to a particular object, in virtue of which the emotion can be identified as *this* emotion rather than *that.* Faced with a shark, I construe a number of its features (its razor-sharp teeth, its fin above the water) as being frightening, and it is my evaluation of the shark as frightening that makes my emotion fear, rather than some other emotion. The formal object in this case is the property or category of "the dangerous": I evaluate the shark as having the property of being dangerous. Without this formal object, the emotion simply makes no sense: emotion depends not just on an object "out there," but on an object evaluated in a certain way. The formal object associated with a given emotion is essential to that emotion and to the concept of that emotion. So with regard to fear, for example, "No description of the concept of fear is correct unless it includes the word 'danger' or some synonym for it" (Lyons, *Emotion,* p. 101). Lyons thinks the term "formal object" is a misnomer, and with good reason, since it is not really an object at all but an *evaluative category* employed in the process of appraisal. Even so, understanding the term can help clarify what is involved in the evaluative process we described earlier. (We should acknowledge that as an evaluative category, "the dangerous" is in fact quite a wide one. We might find something "worryingly dangerous" or "excitingly dangerous," for example. But this does not alter the basic point about the necessity of a formal object, and distinguishing an emotion with respect to it.)

JEREMY S. BEGBIE

well brought out in a passage from C. S. Lewis's account of grieving at the loss of his wife:

> I think I am beginning to understand why grief feels like suspense. It comes from the frustration of so many impulses that had become habitual. Thought after thought, feeling after feeling, action after action, had H. for their object. Now their target is gone. I keep on through habit fitting an arrow to the string; then I remember and have to lay the bow down. So many roads lead through to H. I set out on one of them. But now there's an impassable frontier-post across it. So many roads once; now so many *culs de sac*.[22]

That emotions are, by their very character, oriented to objects has been challenged by some. It is pointed out that not only can emotions take vague objects (as when I fear that my plans will come to nothing) but that in some cases there is no object to speak of at all. In depression, a person may be unable to identify the reason for his or her depressed state; there seems to be no particular object, or relevant beliefs about an object. In response, two comments are in order. First, in some cases we might well be unable to *identify* the object or *articulate* it, but this does not exclude the notion of an object altogether. (This is certainly the case in much depression.) Second, with forms of depression that seem directed to no object and impervious to changes of belief, and with other emotion-like states that seem to lack objects — e.g., irritability, equanimity — and that in some cases have no beliefs, I am inclined to agree with those who want to speak of *moods* or *feelings* rather than emotions, reserving the term "emotion" for situations with an object or objects, and associated beliefs and evaluations.[23] Moods become emotions when they latch on to objects: we might "get out the wrong side of the bed," waking up in an irritable mood, this mood becoming an emotion of irritation or anger when someone dares to cross our path and say something annoying.[24]

22. C. S. Lewis, *A Grief Observed* (London: Faber & Faber, 1961), p. 39.
23. See Stephen Davies, "Philosophical Perspectives on Music's Expressiveness," in *Music and Emotion: Theory and Research*, ed. Patrik N. Juslin and John A. Sloboda (Oxford: Oxford University Press, 2001), p. 27; Nussbaum, *Upheavals of Thought*, pp. 132-34. In practice, the boundary between emotions with a vague object and moods/feelings without an object may not be clear-cut, but the basic distinction still holds and preserves what would seem to be true to the way the word "emotion" is commonly used: that emotion is by its nature object-oriented, whereas a mood is not.
24. I owe the example to my colleague Dona McCullagh.

It follows that if emotions have this directional character, arising from beliefs about and evaluations of an object or objects, they can be *appropriate* or *inappropriate*.[25] Emotions can be well-founded or ill-founded, justified or unjustified, warranted or unwarranted. If a mouse crawls into the room and I jump on the desk screaming wildly, my fear is inappropriate — my evaluation of the situation as dangerous is based on the mistaken belief that the mouse is harmful. But if a masked man runs into the room firing an AK-47 in all directions, extreme fear is appropriate, for my evaluation of the situation as dangerous is based on the quite justified belief that the gunman could kill me.[26] Important also to note is that, depending on the context, emotions can be *misdirected*, e.g., as when I am elated at passing an exam and express that elation by laughing at someone who has just tripped up and injured themselves.

Emotions and Truthful Perception   If emotions entail beliefs and evaluations about states of affairs beyond our own making, and can thus be appropriate or inappropriate, we can conclude (against the non-cognitivist) that they are not to be regarded as intrinsically inimical to truthful perception. Indeed, it would seem that they are capable of advancing and assisting our "grasping for the truth,"[27] and as such, not inherently opposed to reason. This has been argued vigorously on several fronts in recent years.[28] For ex-

25. The point was especially well expounded by the Scottish philosopher John Macmurray in his classic book, *Reason and Emotion* (London: Faber & Faber, 1935).

26. Incorporated into the well-founded/ill-founded distinction is the distinction between illusory and non-illusory objects. An illusory object of an emotion is one about which I have a false belief or judgment. If I fear a harmless mouse in the room, then the particular object of my fear is illusory (see n. 21 above), because my fear is based on the belief that the mouse can harm me (though of course there is no illusion about the existence of the mouse in the room). If I love my grandfather, believing him to be alive (when he is dead), and my love for him is dependent on him being alive, the object of my love is an illusory object. Emotions based on non-illusory objects are based upon correct beliefs about those objects, and emotions based upon illusory objects are based upon incorrect beliefs about those objects. Strictly speaking, therefore, emotions themselves cannot be illusory. If I am infatuated with someone who I believe is always kind and the person is in fact being cruel to me, the infatuation is not illusory but the object is, because of the mistaken belief that the person is always kind and the misevaluation that she is being kind to me. The emotion is real, but not properly founded on a true belief and thus inappropriate. See Lyons, *Emotion*, pp. 109-12.

27. Jamie Dow, *Engaging Emotions: The Need for Emotions in the Church* (Cambridge: Grove Books, 2005), p. 9.

28. See, for example, Dylan Evans, *Emotion: The Science of Sentiment* (Oxford: Oxford University Press, 2001); Macmurray, *Reason and Emotion;* Solomon, "The Logic of Emo-

ample, it has been urged that emotions are critical for decision-making: they guide action in contexts where our knowledge is imperfect and we are confronted with multiple, conflicting goals.[29] The philosopher Martha Nussbaum has insisted on the critical place of emotions in making moral choices: they "are not only not more unreliable than intellectual calculations, but frequently are more reliable, and less deceptively seductive."[30]

---

tion"; M. P. Morrissey, "Reason and Emotion: Modern and Classical Views on Religious Knowing," *Horizons* 16 (1986): 275-91; Dylan Evans and Pierre Cruse, *Emotion, Evolution, and Rationality* (Oxford and New York: Oxford University Press, 2004); Elliott, *Faithful Feelings*, pp. 36-48.

29. See Dylan Evans, "The Search Hypothesis of Emotion," *British Journal for the Philosophy of Science* 53 (2002): 497-509. Emotions are one of the principal means whereby attention is focused and decisions accordingly configured.

Anthony Damasio contends that the role of emotions in decision-making depends on "somatic markers." The brain is subject to a kind of emotional conditioning such that when we experience an emotion, the brain retains the memory of the bodily changes or states that occur. When we are faced with a decision and the thought of various response options, a large number will be dismissed almost immediately because of our "gut feelings" about them; solutions that might involve us in unpleasant bodily experience are rejected. The options are thus reduced, protecting us from potentially harmful consequences. Emotionless reasoning (like Mr. Spock in *Star Trek*), often thought to be an ideal, in fact drastically inhibits our powers of effective decision-making and is best seen as pathological and counterproductive. Damasio, *Descartes' Error*, ch. 8.

30. Nussbaum, *Love's Knowledge*, p. 40. Emotions are "intelligent parts of our ethical agency, responsive to the workings of deliberation and essential to its completion . . . there will be certain contexts in which the pursuit of intellectual reasoning apart from emotion will actually prevent a full rational judgment — for example by preventing an access to one's grief, one's love, that is necessary for the full understanding of what has taken place when a loved one dies" (*Love's Knowledge*, p. 41). See also Justin Oakley, *Morality and the Emotions* (London: Routledge, 1992).

One of the most illuminating accounts of the knowledge-bearing character of emotions is provided by the scientist Michael Polanyi. See R. T. Allen, "Polanyi and the Rehabilitation of Emotion," in *Emotion, Reason and Tradition: Essays on the Social, Political and Economic Thought of Michael Polanyi*, ed. R. T. Allen (Aldershot: Ashgate, 2005), pp. 41-54. Against those who habitually regard emotion as entirely passive, irrational, and suspect because of its connection with value, and who recommend an emotion-free attitude in the search for truth, Polanyi insists that emotions are an intelligent response to apprehended realities, that "passion" is a vital component in every act of knowing. Far from inhibiting scientific inquiry and discovery, the passions are indispensable to it. In science the emotions have a threefold function: "selective," "heuristic," and "persuasive." Emotions *enable a scientist to select what is of value:* they indicate that a discovery is intellectually precious, and that it is precious to science. Heuristically, emotions *sustain the process of discovery* by intimating particular discoveries that have yet to be made, and sustaining the ongoing pursuit of them. As for their persuasive function, emotions *enable the scientist to communicate convincingly*

Emotions and Actions Finally, because they involve belief and evaluation, emotions are typically *motivators to action*.[31] I act *out of* fear, sadness, or whatever. I evaluate the shark as dangerous and swim away.[32] N. H. Frijda uses the term "action tendencies" to describe the way emotions do not specify the precise action required but provoke types of behavior, *tendencies* to act in this way rather than that.[33] We should note that emotions become motives to action when they contain *desire* as part of their occurrent states (whether the desire is conscious or unconscious). If I pity someone in pain, I will want to alleviate their suffering; if I take joy in my daughter, I will want to show it to her in some way.

Emotion and Faithful Worship

We have offered a very brief outline sketch of a cognitive account of emotions. How might this be situated within a theology of Christian worship?

By "worship," we mean those regular occasions when the church is gathered by the triune God to receive and celebrate its corporate identity in a focused, concentrated way. More succinctly, in worship we are re-oriented to God. If sin is a rejection of our calling to honor the Creator, a refusal to praise God, in worship we are re-directed (reconciled) to the One worthy of all praise, re-oriented in love to one another and thus built up as the people of God. And as we are built up as God's people, we are re-oriented to God's world in mission. The indwelling agent of this re-orientation is the Holy Spirit, and its mediator is Jesus Christ.[34]

his or her discoveries to others; in the case of a great or significant discovery, this can never be a completely formal and mechanical process, for the formal systems we already have at our disposal will likely be inadequate. Michael Polanyi, *Personal Knowledge: Towards a Post-Critical Philosophy* (New York: Harper & Row, 1964), chs. 6 and 7, esp. pp. 132-60. Polanyi also speaks of another emotional dimension of science — the permanent intellectual *satisfaction* that comes from having made a discovery (*Personal Knowledge*, p. 173).

31. Lyons, *Emotion*, ch. 11, esp. pp. 168-69.

32. The same emotion, it should be noted, can motivate different actions. A mugger with a knife comes running toward me in an alleyway — I may run in the opposite direction, I might try to disarm him or I might jump out of the way.

33. Nico H. Frijda, *The Emotions* (Cambridge: Cambridge University Press, 1986), pp. 69-94.

34. For fuller treatments of the trinitarian character of worship, see James Torrance, *Worship, Community and the Triune God of Grace* (Carlisle: Paternoster Press, 1996); Thomas A. Smail, *The Giving Gift: The Holy Spirit in Person* (London: Hodder & Stoughton,

Worship so understood will be *faithful.* We can expand on this with regard to the emotions. First, worship is faithful in the sense that it is properly
oriented — primarily to God, and, in the power of the Spirit, to others with
whom we worship, and to the world we represent and to which we are sent.
Emotion, therefore, will be rightly directed. Properly oriented, faithful worship will also be *appropriate* — to God, others, and the world. As far as emotion in worship is concerned, the danger does not lie in emotion *per se,* but in
emotion that is not properly directed and/or not appropriate. So, for example, if we are more enthralled by the sound of the choir than by the God they
praise, the emotion is misdirected; if someone spends an entire service trem-
bling and cringing with fear of God, the emotion is inappropriate.[35]

Second, faithful worship is *with and through Christ.* For Christ guarantees its proper orientation (in the Spirit, to God the Father, other worshipers
and the wider world), and he ensures it will be appropriate (true to God's
character and purpose, and because of that, to other worshipers and the
wider world).

Crucial here is the "vicarious humanity of Christ."[36] Christ, as fully human, embodies and enables faithful worship. He is "faith-ful," full of faith in
the Father, not only in his earthly life of loving and obedient self-offering to
the Father, culminating in crucifixion, but also in his continuing risen life —
he is now the human High Priest who, on the ground of his atoning work,
leads us in our worship (Heb. 2:12; 4:14; cf. Rom. 8:34). In him, our humanity
has been taken, and through the Holy Spirit re-formed, re-turned to God, so
that now with him we can know his "Abba, Father" as *our* Abba, Father. So
the church's worship is united with the one perfect response of the incarnate
Son, with his once-for-all offering of worship on the cross, and with his ongoing worship of the Father in our midst as High Priest. And this is possible
through the same Spirit who enabled and undergirded Christ's own earthly

---

1988); Robin Parry, *Worshipping Trinity: Coming Back to the Heart of Worship* (Carlisle: Paternoster, 2005); Christopher J. Cocksworth, *Holy, Holy, Holy: Worshipping the Trinitarian
God* (London: Darton Longman & Todd, 1997).

35. Indeed, in this latter case, the fear is ill-founded, for it is based upon a false belief
about God, namely that he is essentially threatening or destructive.

36. See T. F. Torrance, "The Mind of Christ in Worship: The Problem of Apollinarian-
ism in the Liturgy," in T. F. Torrance, *Theology in Reconciliation: Essays Towards Evangelical
and Catholic Unity in East and West* (Eugene, OR: Wipf & Stock, 1996), pp. 139-214; Graham
Redding, *Prayer and the Priesthood of Christ in the Reformed Tradition* (London: T&T Clark,
2003); Christian D. Kettler, *The God Who Believes: Faith, Doubt and the Vicarious Humanity
of Christ* (Eugene, OR: Cascade Books, 2005).

self-offering. Worship, in short, is a sharing by the Spirit in the Son's communion with the Father by the Spirit.

Understood in this way, worship is an invitation to be re-humanized, as we grow in the likeness of Christ. The axiom of Gregory of Nazianzen pertains here: "What is not assumed is not saved." Christ assumed the whole of our humanness in order to redeem us. Included in this are our *emotions,* likewise our renewal in his image. Emotions are not intrinsically fallen or incidental to our humanness, but part of what God desires to transform, not least in worship. At its best, then, worship is a school of the emotions. Whether confessing with heavy Lenten hearts, or shouting Easter acclamations, we learn to become emotionally mature, to become (so to speak) a little less adolescent.

Third, faithful worship is a *truthful* activity. We have noted that our emotions can play a key part in truthful perception. In worship, when we discover through the Spirit and with Christ a new dimension of the Father's love for us, or the hidden need of the person in the pew next to us, or some new dimension of evil in a terrorist atrocity — our emotions, far from hindering our grasp of truth, enable a clearer discernment of it.

Fourth, faithful worship is a *uniting* activity. To be re-directed to the Father through the Son by the Spirit is to discover the love that is eternally given and received between Father and Son, the love with which we can be bound together (John 17:21). All worship in the Spirit builds up the Body of Christ and encourages unity (1 Cor. 14:5, 12, 26). Emotions can, of course, rupture relations, but (as we have noted) they can also be instrumental in generating and sustaining powerful bonds between people, and as such serve the Spirit's work of bringing about the reconciled unity made possible through the death of Christ.

Fifth and finally, faithful worship is an *ex-centric* activity: to be caught up in the life of the triune God entails being thrown out into the world as agents of transformation. In Miroslav Volf's words, worship happens in the rhythm of "adoration and action."[37] If emotions typically generate "action tendencies," they will likely have a key place in provoking the desire to do God's will, in energizing God's people for mission.

---

37. Miroslav Volf, "Worship as Adoration and Action: Reflections on a Christian Way of Being-in-the-World," in *Worship: Adoration and Action,* ed. D. A. Carson (Grand Rapids: Baker, 1993), pp. 203-11.

Music and Emotion

If our argument has been along the right lines, inasmuch as music is impli-
cated in our emotional involvement in worship, it should promote the features of worship just described. We could speak at length about each feature,
but our focus in this essay is fairly specific: what is it about musical sounds
and the way they operate such that they become emotionally significant and
valuable to us? And what can we learn from this theologically, with regard to
music in worship?[38]

Objects? Immediately, a difficulty presents itself. We have spoken of emotion being oriented to objects. Gentle music in a restaurant might create a
"mood" or "proto-emotion," but to be full-fledged, we have said, an emotion
requires an object of some kind (together with beliefs about, and evaluation
of the object). However, musical sounds do not in any clear or consistent
way represent, denote, or convey objects for us to be emotional *about* (except

---

38. Sloboda and Juslin make a distinction between "intrinsic" and "extrinsic" sources of
emotion in musical experience, the former being features of the musical sounds themselves,
and the latter being factors that belong "outside" the music but by virtue of which an emotional response occurs (Sloboda and Juslin, "Psychological Perspectives on Music and Emotion," pp. 91-96). Here I am concerned with "intrinsic" sources. This is not to deny that a
wide range of emotionally significant extrinsic factors may be operative whenever we make
and hear music. But it is nonetheless quite legitimate to ask: What might be emotionally potent about the sounds themselves and the way they operate?

Therefore, I am not considering the role of emotionally loaded associations that music
may stimulate ("they're playing our tune, darling"), or cases where musical sounds simulate
an object that elicits an emotional response in us (e.g., the thumping of an elephant charg-
ing toward us).

And I am not considering highly dubious theories that posit a *necessary* link between
musical sounds and a person's occurrent emotion. For example, some locate the emotional
content of music in *persons* — which usually means either the creator of music ("expressivist"
theories) or the hearer/listener ("arousal" or "evocation" theories). For extensive criticisms of
the former, see Stephen Davies, *Musical Meaning and Expression* (Ithaca, NY: Cornell University Press, 1994), pp. 170-84; A. H. Goldman, "Emotions in Music (a Postscript)," *Journal of
Aesthetics and Art Criticism* 53 (1995): 59-69; Roger Scruton, *The Aesthetics of Music* (Oxford:
Clarendon Press, 1997), pp. 144-45. And for critique of arousal theories, see Scruton, *Aesthetics
of Music*, pp. 145-48; Davies, *Musical Meaning and Expression*, pp. 184-99. Problematic also are
"representational" theories: where music's expressiveness is said to depend on it representing
emotion. This implies that to be moved by music we must be able to perceive, along with the
sounds, some extra-musical "emotion" to which the music in some manner directs us. Music
may simulate an object that arouses an emotion in us, but in this case it "represents" the object, not the emotion. For discussion, see Scruton, *Aesthetics of Music*, ch. 5.

in the relatively rare cases when extra-musical phenomena are simulated). How, then, can we speak of the experience of genuine emotion in and through musical experience when no objects are attached to the musical sounds?[39]

The answer, I believe, lies in recognizing that music is never heard on its own but as part of a perceptual complex that includes a range of non-musical phenomena: for example, the physical setting in which we hear the music, memories of people associated with it, artificial images (as in the case of film and video), words (the lyrics of a song, program notes, the title of a piece, what someone said about the piece on the radio), and so on. As Nicholas Cook puts it, "Pure music . . . is an aesthetician's (and music theorist's) fiction."[40] Music is perceived in a manifold environment. And this generates a fund of material for us to be emotional "about." Music swims in a sea of potential objects. The problem of how genuine emotion can be felt through music-without-objects only arises if we posit a sealed-off world of pure music. No such world exists.

So, for example, we go to a film. We hear music along with images and words. The music's emotional properties get "hooked onto" those words and images, drawing us deeper emotionally into the drama. Sometimes the music's general emotional properties are nuanced (focused, made more precise) by words and images. More commonly, the words and images supply the general emotional properties, and the music nuances them. For example, to-

---

39. This problem was famously highlighted by the philosopher Eduard Hanslick (1825-1904), who claimed that music (and he is thinking of instrumental music without words) is unable to arouse or represent basic emotion (joy, melancholy, anger, fear, etc.) in an artistically relevant way (Eduard Hanslick, *The Beautiful in Music: A Contribution to the Revisal of Musical Aesthetics* [New York: Da Capo Press, 1974]). Supporting this, he argued that music itself is not capable of providing the materials necessary for emotional arousal — beliefs appropriate to the experiencing of an emotion, and objects of emotion (something to be emotional about). Hanslick was not denying that the experience of music can occasion deep feelings. (He believed this could happen through "personal associations," or through emotionally unstable people being triggered by particular features of music quite arbitrarily.) But he denied that such feelings were relevant to the artistic nature and purpose of music. The expressiveness of music, for Hanslick, lies rather in its play of forms, its own interior logic arising from the patterning of sounds.

40. Nicholas Cook, *Analysing Musical Multimedia* (Oxford: Clarendon Press, 1998), p. 92. This is the point made by Cook against Kivy and Davies, who want to distinguish between emotions that require an object and those that do not, and claim that music can represent the appearance of the latter but not the former (because music cannot convey or represent objects). As Cook rightly points out, this is to treat music as if it were heard in a vacuum (Cook, *Analysing Musical Multimedia*, pp. 86-92).

ward the end of the film *The Mission,* the main theme music returns as the
South American mission station is pictured being burned to the ground
along with its converts. The images and words provide the emotional objects, the music's emotional properties nuance the emotions evoked by
them. In this way, we are pulled into the story all the more profoundly: we
feel more intensely the heart-rending poignancy of this tragedy, one especially devastating given that the mission station was founded by the priest
who played this music's melody on a pipe.[41]

Bodily Behavior

However, even bearing in mind this context of potential objects, it is quite
legitimate to ask what the musical sounds themselves might be bringing to
the emotional experience. To be more specific: how is it that certain types of
musical sound come to be given emotive descriptions ("cheerful," "heart-
rending," etc.)? It has often been shown that a wide variety of listeners can
reach a large measure of agreement about the emotional character of musical stimuli, likewise composers about the kind of music that will generally be
considered appropriate for, say, a scene in a film.[42] What grounds this agreement? Can particular sounds themselves possess features that give them
emotional potency?

This is an immensely complex field, and all answers have to be somewhat partial and provisional. But we can make a start by considering the no-

41. In response to the initial challenge about music and objects, it might well be argued:
the aesthetic configuration of the music constitutes the emotional object. We are moved directly by the qualities of the sounds, their interplay, arrangements, and syntactical structure. I
hear a chord sequence, a guitar riff, an intricate elaboration, the shape of a song, the form of a
sonata, and I find that its patterning, arrangement, and internal "sense" generate emotion — a
feeling of wonder, perhaps, or amazement. Even with melancholy music we will be moved by
how beautifully melancholy it is. (Sloboda and Juslin point out that psychological research has
"embarrassingly little to say" about this kind of aesthetic response; Sloboda and Juslin, "Psychological Perspectives on Music and Emotion," p. 81.) This may well be a component in the
perception of some music, especially in situations where some kind of "aesthetic contemplation" is most easily practiced — in a concert-hall, perhaps. But in culture at large, and worldwide, by far the majority of situations where we hear music will not conform to this pattern.

42. See, e.g., Martyn Evans, *Listening to Music* (Basingstoke: Macmillan, 1990), p. 62;
A. Gabrielsson and P. Juslin, "Emotional Expression in Music Performance," *Psychology of
Music* 24 (1996): 68-91; Sloboda and Juslin, "Psychological Perspectives on Music and Emotion," p. 94. See the extensive discussion of this matter in Davies, *Musical Meaning and Expression,* pp. 243-52.

tion of a "perceived property," as developed by the philosopher Peter Kivy.[43] When I hear joy in the last movement of Beethoven's Seventh Symphony, argues Kivy, I am not hearing it representatively (in the way I see a mountain in a mountain picture), but rather in the way I see the greenness of a leaf — as a quality perceived. Kivy contends that there are distinct (if complex[44]) emotive properties of music, perceived not as representing something else, but as properties of the music itself, and on the basis of which we describe the music as "mournful," "ebullient," or whatever.

What grounds might we have for claiming that music can have such properties? For many, the most promising way to begin answering this question is through "contour theory." Associated in particular with Kivy and Stephen Davies,[45] this holds that music can bear a structural similarity to the heard and seen manifestations of human emotive expression, and that it is this which leads us to ascribe emotive properties to it. A number of emotions have behavioral expressions that are constitutive of their nature, and these expressions have distinctive "physiognomies." Contour theory holds that musical sounds correspond in various ways to bodily expressions characteristic of emotive states. It is not so much that music embodies emotion as that music embodies *bodily behavior* characteristic of emotion. (This highlights the importance of the second element in the "classic triad" of emotion.)

The two forms of bodily expression marked out as most relevant are *vocalization* and *gesture*. It has long been recognized that non-verbal vocaliza-

43. See Peter Kivy, *Introduction to a Philosophy of Music* (Oxford: Clarendon Press, 2002), pp. 31-36.

44. Emotive properties are not simple and uniform. When we ascribe an emotive property like mournfulness to a piece of music, we do so because of a *number* of features that together lead us to ascribe the quality "mournful" to it. If I call my car red, there is nothing I can point to in order to persuade you it really is red except the one color of the red car. I do not say, "It's red because of this or that . . ."; redness is a simple property. But if I say, "This piece of music is mournful," you might ask, "What's mournful about it?", and I would then have to point to several features of the music that would back up the claim: slow tempo, minor key, subdued dynamics, falling melodies, or whatever. Nonetheless, even if complex, its mournfulness is a quality in its own right (an "emergent" quality), distinct from the many qualities that generate it. Kivy, *Introduction to a Philosophy of Music*, pp. 34-36.

45. Peter Kivy, *Sound Sentiment: An Essay on the Musical Emotions, Including the Complete Text of the Corded Shell* (Philadelphia: Temple University Press, 1989), esp. chs. 2-8; Davies, *Musical Meaning and Expression*, pp. 228-77; "Philosophical Perspectives on Music's Expressiveness," pp. 34-37; Kivy, *Introduction to a Philosophy of Music*, chs. 3-7. For critique, see Goldman, "Emotions in Music (a Postscript)"; Geoffrey Madell, *Philosophy, Music and Emotion* (Edinburgh: Edinburgh University Press, 2002), ch. 1.

tion — rhythmic and melodic utterances without words — is a major medium of human emotional communication. Humans have an innate ability to produce and perceive certain rhythms, contours, and timbres that encapsulate an emotional state; indeed, some vocal sounds, in the emotional states they express, are fundamental and the same across cultures (and even across species). This ability is taken into the practice of speech — we can quickly recognize emotion in a speaker by the sound of her or his voice, even if the words are emotionally neutral. Certain musical patterns are heard as emotionally expressive, it is argued, because of this capacity. So, for example, cheerful people tend to speak quickly, often in bright and loud tones, and in a high vocal register. Music we call "cheerful" will likewise often tend to be fast and loud and use upper registers; phrases will tend to rise in pitch more than they fall (e.g., the "Et resurrexit" from Bach's *Mass in B Minor*). Sad or grief-ridden people tend to speak softly, slowly, and hesitatingly; their voices tend to sink at the end of sentences, and they use the lower part of their vocal register. The same often goes for melancholy melodies (e.g., Chopin's "Funeral March"). The empirical evidence supporting the link between vocal and musical expression of emotion is now substantial.[46]

It has been shown that *gesture* associated with emotional states also cor-

---

46. Charles Darwin noted that "when the voice is used under any strong emotion, it tends to assume . . . a musical character" (Darwin, *The Expression of the Emotions in Man and Animals*, p. 92). There are some, such as Davies, who are doubtful that vocalization is crucial for the recognition of music as emotionally significant; Davies, "Philosophical Perspectives on Music's Expressiveness," p. 35 n. 7. But this is to ignore a considerable body of research: see, e.g., A. Kappas et al., "Voice and Emotion," in *Fundamentals of Nonverbal Behavior: Studies in Emotion and Social Interaction,* ed. R. S. Feldman and B. Rime (Cambridge: Cambridge University Press, 1991), pp. 200-238; K. R. Scherer, "Expression of Emotion in Voice and Music," *Journal of Voice* 9 (1995): 235-48; J. Panksepp and G. Bernatsky, "Emotional Sounds and the Brain: The Neuro-Affective Foundations of Musical Appreciation," *Behavioural Processes* 60 (2002); P. N. Juslin and P. Laukka, "Communication of Emotions in Vocal Expression and Music Performance: Different Channels, Same Code?" *Psychological Bulletin* 129 (2003): 770-814; P. N. Juslin and P. Laukka, "Emotional Expression in Speech and Music: Evidence of Cross-Modal Similarities," in *Emotions Inside Out: 130 Years after Darwin's "The Expression of the Emotions in Man and Animals,"* ed. P. Ekman et al. (New York: New York Academy of Sciences, 2003), pp. 279-82; Iain Morley, "The Evolutionary Origins and Archaeology of Music" (PhD thesis [electronic version], University of Cambridge, 2006), pp. 162-73, 177-81; M. M. Lavy, "Emotion and the Experience of Listening to Music: A Framework for Empirical Research" (unpublished PhD thesis, University of Cambridge, 2001), pp. 39-47. Lavy writes: "Humans have a remarkable ability to communicate and detect emotion in the contours and timbres of vocal utterances; this ability is not suddenly lost during a musical listening experience" (p. v).

responds in striking ways to the dynamic features of music. According to Davies, music presents "emotion characteristics in appearances"[47] — a piece of music sounds sad in the way that a weeping willow looks sad, not because it *is* sad, but because it "presents the outward features of sadness."[48] And by far the most important human appearances in this regard are bodily movements, especially gait, bearing, or carriage. Sad people typically walk in a slow, halting way, with drooping bodies. Music we call "sad" tends to be slow and halting, with falling, faltering melodies. By embodying bodily motion, music embodies emotion.

This receives some corroboration from psychological and neuropsychological research. The links between emotion and bodily behavior are very close, something confirmed by the phenomenon known as "proprioceptive feedback": that "going through the motions" of an emotion can, at least to some extent, generate a similar mood.[49] As Anna sings in *The King and I*:

Whenever I feel afraid
I hold my head erect
And whistle a happy tune
So no one will suspect
I'm afraid.

. . . The result of this deception
Is very strange to tell
For when I fool the people I fear
I fool myself as well![50]

That Anna sings is no coincidence. As we shall stress later, although we can rarely provide perfect predictions of music's effects, we can speak of strong tendencies given certain features of the music — singing happy music may well, in the right conditions, engender a happy mood, which, when

47. Davies, *Musical Meaning and Expression*, pp. 221-28.

48. Davies, *Musical Meaning and Expression*, p. 239. See also Olga McDonald Meidner, "Motion and E-motion in Music," *British Journal of Aesthetics* 25 (1985): 349-56; Lavy, "Emotion and the Experience of Listening to Music: A Framework for Empirical Research," pp. 54-57.

49. Morley, "The Evolutionary Origins and Archaeology of Music," pp. 173-77.

50. Richard Rodgers and Oscar Hammerstein, *The King and I*, 1958. Psychologist David Myers asks: "If assuming an emotional expression triggers a feeling, then would imitating others' expressions help us feel what they are feeling? . . . the laboratory evidence is supportive. . . . Acting as another helps us feel what another feels" (Myers, *Psychology*, p. 476).

JEREMY S. BEGBIE

directed to certain objects, may well become a full-fledged emotion. Particularly important here is *rhythm*. Heard rhythm and bodily movement are
closely related in humans — we are able to synchronize auditory beats and
bodily motion with great precision.[51] It is thus not surprising to find that
rhythm often plays a part in our ascribing emotional qualities to music,
given that musical rhythm can evoke qualities of bodily movement characteristic of certain emotions (joyful music will usually tend to be fast, like
the movements of joyful people). But especially crucial to note here is the
power of rhythm to *bind people together* through synchronization: it has
long been known that one of the most powerful ways to unite a group is
through rhythmic music. And, given rhythm's connections with emotion, it
is one of the quickest ways in which emotion is spread and shared. As we
join in the movements of others, through "feedback," a mood is easily generated.[52] This is especially so if the bodily gestures are visible to members of
the group: visual, auditory, and motor elements come together to create a
potent and mutually reinforcing combination, and can lead to fervent emotion when directed toward various objects. We only need think of a protest
march with chanting — combining musical rhythm, vocalization, and gesture (marching and pounding fists); or the rock concert, where it is almost
impossible not to join with the emotionally charged stamping, swaying,
and clapping we see and hear all around us.

This links up with those who want to describe our emotional participation in music as a kind of dance. Roger Scruton writes of a "sympathetic
response" to music in which we find emotional meaning in the sounds and
respond accordingly with movements of our own — whether overt or internal, voluntary or involuntary. We "dance with" or "move with" the
sounds.[53]

We have spoken mainly of melody and rhythm. But what of harmony?[54]

51. According to Aniruddh Patel, "there is not a single report of an animal [apart from
humans] being trained to tap, peck, or move in synchrony with an auditory beat."
Aniruddh D. Patel, *Music, Language, and the Brain* (Oxford: Oxford University Press, 2008),
p. 409. See M. Molinari, M. G. Leggio, M. De Martin, A. Cerasa, and M. Thaut,
"Neurobiology of Rhythmic Motor Entrainment," *Annals of the New York Academy of Science: The Neurosciences and Music* 999 (2003): 313-20.

52. "Rhythm turns listeners into participants, makes listening active and motoric, and
synchronizes the brains and minds (and, since emotion is always intertwined with music
[and with the body, we would add], the 'hearts') of all who participate" (Oliver W. Sacks,
Musicophilia: Tales of Music and the Brain [New York: Alfred A. Knopf, 2007], pp. 244-45).

53. Scruton, *Aesthetics of Music*, pp. 354-64.

54. Against contour theorists, Geoffrey Madell insists that "in introducing the element

344

Take, for example, chords such as major, minor, and diminished, which are widely held to have a particular affective quality (e.g., minor chords are routinely regarded as expressive of negative emotion such as sadness, sorrow, and so forth). How might they gain this emotional character, and how does this square with contour theory?

In part, it seems, these acquire their emotional character through their relation to other chords (or implied chords). In real-world music, chords do not appear in isolation but alongside others, and in Western music they relate to each other through patterns of tension and resolution. In its small-, medium- and large-scale dimensions, at many different levels, and (potentially) engaging every parameter (including melody, dynamics, texture, meter, and timbre), music consists of movements from rest to instability, followed at some stage by a return to rest. One of the most important ways in which this is played out is through harmony: music is heard according to the "gravitational pull" or "attraction" of a target, the "tonic" chord (the "home" key). Chords other than the tonic are heard as drawn toward it in varying degrees depending on their "distance" from the tonic, and a sense of musical motion is generated by the push and pull away from the tonic. Indeed, an extremely common structure is the progression from rest (home key), toward a "distant" place (foreign key), back to rest (home key): home-away-home again.[55]

Many theorists have related this tension-resolution pattern to music's expressiveness.[56] Indeed, "tension" and "resolution" are terms frequently

---

of harmony we introduce something which really does not have any parallel to human behaviour" (Madell, *Philosophy, Music and Emotion*, p. 13). This is too sweeping, but Kivy acknowledges this weakness and confesses he cannot address it satisfactorily (Kivy, *Introduction to a Philosophy of Music*, pp. 43-45).

55. See Joseph Peter Swain, *Musical Languages* (New York: W. W. Norton & Co., 1997), ch. 2. I explicate this more fully in Jeremy Begbie, *Theology, Music and Time* (Cambridge: Cambridge University Press, 2000), ch. 2. For the most thorough treatment of the notion of "distance" in tonal music, see Fred Lerdahl, *Tonal Pitch Space* (New York: Oxford University Press, 2001).

56. For a short survey of some of the relevant literature, see Lerdahl, *Tonal Pitch Space*, pp. 188-92. Stephen Davies speaks of the tensions and resolutions typical of music at some length, but sees their significance for contour theory only in their suggestion of order and purposiveness: "musical movement invites attention to expressiveness because, like human action and behavior . . . it displays order and purposiveness" (Davies, *Musical Meaning and Expression*, p. 229). That is, musical movement is invested with human expressiveness because it possesses a logic akin to human action (rather than to random or fully determined movement). But according to numerous writers it is not simply the overall dynamic of purposiveness that gives musical movement its emotional power but (much more) its *internal*

used in speaking of emotions — my anger "resolves" into acceptance, my
anxiety into peace of mind, and so on. And we should note that the emotional character of the resolution is given a distinctive hue by virtue of its
position: it is the resolution *of a tension*. So, for example, the "joy" of a major
chord resolving minor music is commonly perceived not simply as possessing joy, but "joy-as-resolution."[57]

---

configurations of tension and resolution, the way in which we are moved from stability to instability, "toward" and "away from" centers of rest.

57. It would seem that a particular form of the tension-resolution scheme plays a large
part in the emotional intensity of Western music: the generation and confirmation/viola-
tion of expectations. The first scholar who sought to demonstrate this at length was Leonard
Meyer, who contended that we experience music in the context of stylistic norms that have
their roots in our habitual tendency to resolve ambiguity. Leonard B. Meyer, *Emotion and
Meaning in Music* (Chicago: University of Chicago Press, 1956). In his early work, Meyer held
that emotions are experienced due to violations of expectancy. As we are taken through a
piece of music, we find its patterns converge with and diverge from basic stylistic templates.
Deviations from a musical stylistic norm arouse strong affect (surprise, frustration, and so
forth). "Emotion or affect is aroused when a tendency to respond is arrested or inhibited"
(Meyer, *Emotion and Meaning in Music,* p. 14). (In his later work, *Explaining Music: Essays
and Explorations* [Chicago: University of Chicago Press, 1978], in what would seem to be an
effort to give his theories a more objective leaning, Meyer shifts significantly away from the
notion of "creating expectations" to that of "implication": a musical event is said to imply
another by rendering it more or less probable.) Although some of his contentions have been
widely challenged, Meyer's work spawned a large body of writing that fruitfully follows the
lines opened up by him. His stress on the emotional potential of musical expectation (or implication) has been substantially confirmed and carried forward by psychological research.
See, e.g., J. J. Bharucha, "Melodic Anchoring," *Music Perception* 13 (1996): 383-400; T. Eerola
and A. C. North, "Expectancy-Based Model of Melodic Complexity," in *Proceedings of the
Sixth International Conference on Music Perception and Cognition,* ed. C. Woods et al. (Keele,
Staffordshire, UK: Department of Psychology, 2000); Sloboda and Juslin, "Psychological
Perspectives on Music and Emotion," pp. 91-92; John A. Sloboda, "Empirical Studies of
Emotional Response to Music," in *Exploring the Musical Mind,* ed. John A. Sloboda (Oxford:
Oxford University Press, 2005), pp. 203-14, esp. pp. 209-13; David Huron, *Sweet Anticipation:
Music and the Psychology of Expectation* (Cambridge, MA: MIT Press, 2006); also S. Larson,
"The Problem of Prolongation in Tonal Music: Terminology, Perception, and Expressive
Meaning," *Journal of Music Theory* 41 (1994): 101-36; "Musical Forces and Melodic Expecta-
tions: Comparing Computer Models with Experimental Results," *Music Perception* 21
(2004): 457-98. From a musicological perspective, the significance of the "implication-
realization" model has been explored extensively by Eugene Narmour; see his books *Beyond
Schenkerism: The Need for Alternatives in Music Analysis* (Chicago: University of Chicago
Press, 1977); *The Analysis and Cognition of Basic Melodic Structures: The Implication-
Realization Model* (Chicago: University of Chicago Press, 1990); and *The Analysis and Cognition of Melodic Complexity: The Implication-Realization Model* (Chicago: University of Chicago Press, 1992).

How might these findings relate to contour theory? Further research is needed. But if music recruits the same emotional circuits as other activities associated with emotion, it is hardly fanciful to suggest that there will be correlations made between, on the one hand, the tensions and resolutions of chord sequences and, on the other, the tensions and resolutions of bodily behavior that accompany various emotional states. After all, the terms "tension" and "rest" are clearly applicable to some forms of bodily process characteristic of emotion — fear frequently comes with restlessness, emotional calm with a restful posture, and so forth; and similar things could be said of the move from equilibrium to tension and tension to resolution. Indeed, the very words "tension" and "resolution" (or "relaxation") can describe bodily states connected to emotion.

But this still leaves us with the question: why should particular chords be seen as more or less dissonant and consonant, more or less "resolved" in the first place? Is this entirely a matter of socio-cultural contingency? And how might the emotive correlations of this be accounted for by contour theory; that is, in terms of bodily behavior? In response, some might say that the crying of a baby or the howl of a person in distress (emotional vocalizations) are normally highly dissonant, and that our reaction to extreme dissonance is often to cringe or frown. Maybe; but a more direct physiological explanation is probably more plausible. Simply put, dissonance provokes a less pleasant sensation than consonance. The widely reported experience of a disagreeable "roughness" between tones regarded as dissonant could be cited in this connection,[58] and there is evidence that our description of major chords as emotionally more positive than minor is bound up with similar factors.[59]

Contour theory has considerable advantages over its rivals, perhaps the most important being its focus on emotion's links to the body. But three main qualifications are in order. First, even if there is a correspondence between behaviors and musical sounds, we should avoid implying that being moved by music entails a mental act whereby we "spot the resemblance" between a musical stimulus and a (remembered) bodily expression of emotion. It would seem rather that emotionally significant musical sounds and vocalizations/gestures that express emotions are dealt with by the same neu-

58. On this, see Lerdahl, *Tonal Pitch Space*, pp. 80-82; Donald Hall, *Musical Acoustics* (Pacific Grove, CA: Brooks/Cole, 2002), pp. 393, 439-43.
59. A. J. Blood et al., "Emotional Responses to Pleasant and Unpleasant Music Correlate with Activity in Paralimbic Brain Regions," *Nature Neuroscience* 2 (1999): 382-87; Lerdahl, *Tonal Pitch Space*, pp. 80-81.

rological systems; they relate at the level of brain processing, not at the level of two objects being perceived as similar. Second, contour theory may well be too restrictive. To explain musical expressiveness solely in terms of its links with public bodily behavior (as in Stephen Davies's version) seems too narrow. For one thing, it would appear that emotional gesture and vocalization are virtually inseparable.[60] Moreover, as we have just suggested, in some cases it seems reasonable to believe that music is described in emotional terms chiefly because of its direct physiological effects, rather than because its contours are associated with emotional behavior. The third qualification concerns expression and arousal. One of the strengths and driving forces of contour theory is that it seeks to avoid positing any *necessary* link between musical sounds and a person's occurrent emotion — whether composer, performer, or listener. It purports to show how music can have emotionally expressive properties without that being tied to the producer's or hearer's emotions. To use Kivy's analogy, the Great St. Bernard dog looks sad but as far as we know is no sadder than any other dog, and will not necessarily make us sad. Music can be expressive *of* an emotion without *expressing* or *arousing* that emotion.[61] Nevertheless, in real-world situations, a composer or performer *may* express emotion through music. And with respect to arousal, music frequently *does* (and is frequently intended to) arouse emotions (or at least, moods) in ways that are at least to some extent fairly predictable: given certain conditions, there will be a strong tendency for particular musical sound-patterns to engender this or that mood or emotion. (No film composer would be in business otherwise.)

To summarize: although conclusions in this field have to be somewhat provisional, we are suggesting that when we ascribe emotional properties to

60. Morley, "The Evolutionary Origins and Archaeology of Music," pp. 177-83. For example, as Morley puts it: "A down-turned mouth, slackness of posture, lower voice and reduced pitch contour in vocalisation . . . are all part of a gamut of physiological responses associated with sadness and/or depression" ("The Evolutionary Origins and Archaeology of Music," p. 218).

61. See above, n. 38. "The sadness is to the music rather like the redness to the apple, than it is like the burp to the cider" (O. K. Bouwsma, "The Expression Theory of Art," in *Philosophical Analysis: A Collection of Essays,* ed. Max Black [Englewood Cliffs, NJ: Prentice-Hall, 1950], p. 94). Contour theory also avoids the key drawback of representational/referring theories, for it is not claiming that the music's emotional power depends on hearing musical sounds as representative of/referring to melancholy and cheerfulness, any more than seeing a green bus as green depends on seeing it as representative of/referring to greenness. We hear sadness and cheerfulness not as referents but as properties of the musical sounds.

music we are doing so because of correspondences between the musical sounds and the physical expressions of emotional states, or, to be more accurate, because musical sounds are processed by the same neurological systems as bodily behavior characteristic of emotions. And, it would seem, the most relevant bodily behaviors in this respect are vocalization and gesture. (However, in some cases there may be a more direct link through immediate physiological effect.) We have also stressed that we cannot assume a necessary link between this or that music and a corresponding affect in the music-maker or music-hearer, but music may nonetheless be used to express emotion, and we can frequently speak of the tendency of particular musical sound-patterns to spawn moods and emotions of particular types.

Representative Concentration

Still, however, the question remains: Why do we *value* the emotional expressiveness of music? What benefit do we gain?

We would be foolish to insist on there being one benefit only; again, any answer has to be provisional. But a large part of the answer, I suggest, lies in the notion of *concentration*. Typically, our emotional lives are messy. Emotions are often confused and transient; they are tangled, come and go, jump out at us at odd times. Likewise the bodily movements characteristic of them. If I am angry, I might throw my arms all over the place, stamp my feet, shout things I only half mean, grit my teeth, or mutter intermittently.

Suppose, however, a dancer wants to display anger. She will likely deploy particular movements — a glare perhaps, a clenched fist, a thrust of the head. Such movements are *concentrated,* and in at least three senses. First, and most basic, they will be *purified,* free from irrelevance and off-putting distractions, distilled, pared down. Second, they might also *compress* a range of gestures into one; for instance, condensing complex angry states into a single sweep of the arm. Third, they might *specify* one type of emotion rather than another, *this* emotion rather than *that.*

Something similar applies to music. (And the dancer analogy is especially fitting, given what we have been saying about bodily behavior.[62]) Inso-

---

62. On the very close relation between music and dance with respect to emotion, see Morley, "The Evolutionary Origins and Archaeology of Music," pp. 173-77. Also C. L. Krumhansl and D. L. Schenck, "Can Dance Reflect the Structural and Expressive Qualities of Music? A Perceptual Experiment on Balanchine's Choreography of Mozart's Divertimento No. 15," *Musicae Scientiae* 1 (1997): 63-85.

far as bodily behavior is embodied in music, it is not the inchoate vocalizations and gestures characteristic of our emotional life, but bodily behavior translated into the formalities of music: particular melodic shapes, appoggiaturas, suspensions, falling chromatic lines and so forth. The last movement of Tchaikovsky's "Pathétique" Symphony is not expressive of grief as we normally experience it; it offers concentrated "grief in music." Through carefully structured and ordered devices the piece is pared down, shorn of irrelevance. In some passages, we might speak of grief-emotions compressed, and in others of a particular grief — Tchaikovsky knows how to differentiate reflective grief from despairing grief, for example.[63] When we appropriate these concentrated expressive qualities of music in relation to objects about which we can be emotional, just because the qualities are "concentrated" they have the capacity to transform our emotional involvement ("purifying," "compressing," and "specifying" our emotions); in short, they enable *a more concentrated emotional engagement with the object or objects with which we are dealing.*

Latent here, I suggest, is a dynamic of *representation.* Consider Samuel Barber's "Adagio for Strings" when performed at the funeral of President Kennedy. By embodying concentrated emotional qualities, music could give voice to, or "speak for" thousands. The mourners could be emotionally represented by the music; they could identify with it and be pulled into its concentrated expressiveness and thus grieve more deeply, perhaps more appropriately.[64] Not so long ago, a friend of mine led a funeral service for a young mother who had taken her own life, leaving an only son. Immediately after the formalities at the graveside, her son lifted a set of bagpipes and played a lament for his mother. My friend said that it was as if he summed up for everyone "what we really wanted to say, deep down." At that funeral, they were emotionally represented by music. This may be why people who grieve often do not want cheerful music, nor something that just plays the chaos of their grief back to them, but something that can both connect with their grief as it is and help them find new forms and depths of emotion, perhaps forms that help to set their sorrow in a larger, more hopeful emotional context, and in this way begin to re-form them.

63. This is perhaps the sort of thing Mendelssohn had in mind when he said that music is not *less* but *more* precise than words (as quoted in Nussbaum, *Upheavals of Thought,* p. 251).

64. Of course, music is not some kind of person who represents people; rather, because of its emotional qualities, it can *serve* to represent people as it is taken up and used in particular situations.

Clearly, then, through music we can be *emotionally educated* — for we can be introduced to types of emotion previously unknown to us. Just as unfamiliar muscles are toned in a workout, music can give us an emotional workout ("I never knew I had those muscles there"; "I never knew I could feel that way"). In a Pentecostal service of praise, for example, we may well feel not only a joy in God we have previously felt, but a new depth of joy. Music can help us discover something that we *could* feel, that we have not felt before.[65] And, we might add, we can also be educated emotionally: we might discover what we *should* feel in particular situations, in the presence of particular objects.

This is certainly not intended to be a complete account of the emotional benefit we gain from music. But I am suggesting that "representative concentration" may often belong to the heart of the matter: that in relation to objects of emotion, music can concentrate our emotional engagement (through purification, compression, or specification); and that this dynamic is one of representation, in which music "speaks for us," on our behalf.[66] And just because it involves this process of concentration, music can be a means of emotional education.

Music, Emotion, and Worship

It is time to return to worship and explore the resonances between our findings and the theology of worship outlined earlier. There are many ways in which music may serve the emotional dynamics of worship, but, as we have said, our focus here is quite limited. We have been asking: what is it about musical sounds and the way they operate such that they become emotionally significant and valuable to us? And we have answered: at least in part, they become emotionally significant because they possess qualities corresponding to *bodily behavior* characteristic of emotion. Music can be emotionally valuable because, among other things no doubt, it embodies emotional qualities in a *concentrated* way, and is thus capable of concentrating our

65. The central weakness of theories that suggest music merely resembles, reflects, mirrors, copies (or whatever) our emotions is that they invariably fail to come to terms with the emotionally *transformative* effect of music.

66. It will be objected that other art-forms are capable of operating in similar ways. Indeed they are, but as our argument so far would indicate, music's distinctive contribution is its translation of emotional bodily movement into sound. This makes it neither superior nor inferior to other forms of art, but it does make it distinctive.

emotional engagement with objects, and in a representative way. Further, in the process, we can be emotionally educated.

What can we learn from these findings theologically? The first thing to say relates to bodily behavior. That music's emotional capacities are so closely linked with the body need not be underplayed. Quite the opposite, for bodily renewal is part of God's intention for humanity — the physical body of Jesus is not only the vehicle of salvation but the very site of the promise of our own physical transformation: it is made subject to judgment and death, and raised from the dead as a pledge of the resurrection of our own bodies (1 Cor. 15:35-58). Even now, life is given to our mortal bodies by the Spirit of the Father who raised Jesus from the dead (Rom. 8:11), in anticipation of the Spirit-filled life of the Age to Come. Worship in the Spirit, through Christ, will by its very nature be caught up in this body-transforming momentum.

But we have said that in music, emotionally significant bodily movements are embodied in a concentrated (musical) form, in such a way that the music can represent us and concentrate us emotionally as we are drawn into its life. Here the dynamics of musical emotion and the dynamics of emotion in trinitarian worship come together in a remarkable way, especially when we recall what we said earlier about the vicarious humanity of Christ. In the life of Jesus, emotional "concentration" becomes *redemptive*. As one of us, Jesus lived a life of sinless and perfectly concentrated emotion in the midst of our emotional confusion. In him, we witness emotion shorn of all sinful distraction and confusion. In his anger at Chorazin, Bethsaida, and Capernaum (Luke 10:13-15), we see anger purified of corrupt motives, driven only by an opposition to all that stands against God's love. In his joy when praying to the Father (Luke 10:21) we see joy as it is meant to be, an elation completely centered on the one who sent him and able to meet the worst the world can hurl at him. In his grief at the tomb of Lazarus (John 11:35) we see grief as it could and should be: stinging to the depths and utterly free of sentimentality. And on other occasions we find variegated emotion compressed, and generalized emotion nuanced and focused, made specific — all in the service of his mission. Here in this human being emotion is concentrated; here we are emotionally represented.

Now, by the Spirit, as our risen, human representative, Christ can concentrate our emotional life in the likeness of his — and not least in worship. He is the High Priest, tempted yet without sin, sympathizing with our weaknesses, unashamed to call us his brothers and sisters, and alive to intercede for us, appearing in God's presence on our behalf. We are not required to perfect our offering for it to be accepted, but can rely upon the one who takes our cries before the Father more truly and authentically than we ever could ourselves. This will mean the purging, compressing, and specifying of our emotions, whether directly in relation to God, or in relation to all the other emotional objects relevant to worship: other worshipers perhaps, or a reference in the Creed, the sick friend we pray for, the difficult decision at work.

It would seem, then, that there is a striking correspondence between the dynamics of musical emotion and the dynamics of worship. The upshot for our purposes is twofold. First, it would seem that music is particularly well suited to being a vehicle of emotional renewal in worship, a potent instrument through which the Holy Spirit can begin to remake and transform us in the likeness of Christ, the one true Worshiper.

Of course, this power is open to abuse. If the orientation is askew, or the emotion inappropriate, then manipulation, sentimentality, and emotional self-indulgence are among the ever-present dangers. So for example, an upbeat mood engendered by joyful music, instead of growing into an emotion by being turned appropriately to God or each other, may never get directed anywhere, and never grow into an emotion proper. (When people speak about the danger of music "whipping up the emotions," this is usually what they mean.) Or we may find emotion is misdirected — as when the musical tenderness of a love-song to Jesus is used by a teenager to feed his infatuation for the girl in the next pew (or, indeed, his infatuation with the girl is simply transferred to Jesus via the music). Or an emotion may be specified inappropriately — as when a hymn on the cost of the cross is set to consistently ebullient music. Perhaps the most worrying tendency today is to use music with a very limited range of emotionally significant qualities, or music that cannot specify anything but the most broad and basic emotions — in short, music that can never help to educate congregations as to the enormous range of emotion possible in worship (a range reflecting the width we find, for instance, in Scripture.

But emotional abuse should not lead us into a stultifying anti-emotionalism. To "grow up" into Christ is to grow up emotionally as much as anything else, and carefully chosen music in worship may have a larger part to play than we have yet imagined.

Second, we have seen, I think, that not only does theology illuminate music, but music illuminates and enriches our theology, in this case the theology of worship. Indeed, the dynamic of representative concentration that has emerged in our study of music brings to the fore and helps us understand more deeply not just something crucial to worship's emotional character, but something crucial to all worship. Just as ambassadors on foreign trips carry the needs of their country with them, concentrating their people's concerns and speaking as they would speak if they could, so Christ takes our muddled and often half-meant worship and concentrates it in the presence of "Abba, Father." In prayer "through Jesus Christ our Lord," our own prayer (so often feeble and confused, with sighs too deep for words) is purged, compressed, and specified; and we are educated in the process, discovering not only what we already knew we wanted to say, but also what we could or perhaps should say. Even our "crumpled 'Amens'"[67] are shaped into things of beauty. In saying our creeds, half understood and muttered half-heartedly, we can be confident that Christ will take and perfect what we say and mean, and is at work to purge, compress, and specify our belief, so that in due course we can discover more of what we could and should affirm ("Lord, I believe; help my unbelief"). Such is the liberating momentum at the heart of every gathering of God's people: we have a High Priest who worships in our midst.

67. Murray Rae, "Grace and Its Expectations: Offering up Our Crumpled Amen," *Refresh* 5, no. 1 (Winter 2005): 11-13.

14. Music for the Love Feast:
Hildegard of Bingen and the Song of Songs

Margot Fassler

Hildegard of Bingen's long and extraordinarily productive life began in 1098 and ended in 1179. Her *curriculum vitae* reads like that of no other woman from the Middle Ages, her innovations in several fields making a parallel with her musical achievements.[1] She has more securely attributable monophonic chants assigned to her name than any composer from the entire Middle Ages; she is the only composer in the history of Western music who was also a serious and highly respected theologian; she is the first composer who arranged for the ordering, copying, and preservation of her musical compositions; she was the first to have promoted, and perhaps even planned, visual commentary for a theological treatise that includes song texts;[2] and her morality play was not only the "first," but also the only one of its type to be fully set to music. As an example of someone who can interweave theology and music with consummate skill and proficiency, especially in relation to worship, there can be few from whom we can learn more.

It is useful to place the music she wrote against the backdrop of her three major theological treatises, for her music, always interactive with her

---

1. For an overview of Hildegard's life and works, see Barbara Newman, "'Sibyl of the Rhine': Hildegard's Life and Times," in *Voice of the Living Light: Hildegard of Bingen and Her World*, ed. Barbara Newman (Berkeley: University of California Press, 1998).

2. On the only known illuminated copy of Hildegard's *Scivias*, see Madeline Caviness, "Artist: 'To See, Hear, and Know All at Once,'" in *Voice of the Living Light*, ed. Newman, pp. 110-24. This precious manuscript was lost during World War II, although black-and-white photographs survive.

religious writings, is most profitably understood as a part of her concentrated program of expanding the canon of religious writings and music for the explicit use of communities of religious women. It is not difficult to see that Hildegard, the abbess, teacher, and maker of liturgies, was especially interested in the idea of a unique "female voice" for the rendering of praise to God.[3] In fact, her deliberate and complex attempts to fashion a "female voice" in which to sing, and her many works defining this voice in a multiplicity of ways, constitute yet another first. Her music, received under divine inspiration, could lay claim to such femininity because it flowed through a woman, and first and foremost was for women singers; and because it was from and of God, it was a direct representation of those aspects of the divine nature associated with the feminine. Hildegard composed as a self-styled "poor little woman" for others of her kind, creating a vision of the female as interactive with the divine through her compositions, but also making God "sound" in a woman's voice. Whereas all other medieval liturgical "voices" known to us are generically male, Hildegard's is decisively otherwise. This does not mean that she left the male of the species out; far from it. Communities of men requested music from her, and she produced it, both specific pieces and a planned collection of her compositions. Even though Hildegard's "voice" is essentially female, she is willing and ready for all to join in the lofty and high-pitched song.

Hildegard is a difficult thinker, and she wrote many liturgical song texts of varied natures. In exploring her work one must reach for precise themes, and then hold fast to the cord while being whirled through the cascading images that are typical of her writing in all genres. The difficulty is compounded by the fact that precise dating for many of Hildegard's works, including her songs, is not possible. What we have are a few solid pillars, provided by the time periods for her three major theological treatises (see Table 1). As can be seen, periods of work on these treatises appear to divide her mature life into three stages: early middle age, later middle age, and old age. Because she mentions them in *Scivias*, we can ascribe the largest single block of her compositions to the first period, demonstrating at least that she com-

---

3. On Hildegard's view of women and their importance in the history of salvation, see the pioneering study by Barbara Newman, *Sister of Wisdom: St. Hildegard's Theology of the Feminine* (Berkeley: University of California Press, 1987). Newman speaks of Hildegard's two strategies for coming to terms with the female: one is to develop the humility topos, especially with concentration on God's love for the Virgin Mary, who exemplifies this ideal; the other is to explore aspects of the Divinity itself that are associated with the feminine.

posed from the start, and that her musical creativity was an intimate part of the ways in which she worked as a theologian. We also can compare some songs, those found in *Scivias*, to two groups we know were written later: the songs for St. Ursula and those written in honor of St. Disibod.

The music she wrote and its probable context have occasioned much debate. The circumstances of its production are unique both in the attention given to its copying, and in its attribution to Hildegard through inclusion in a larger body of her works. Both major surviving collections of her music were produced in her own monastic house, the Rupertsberg, most probably during her own lifetime and under her immediate supervision. Thus, although Hildegard's music has not been recorded in any liturgical books known to us, it is gathered into a corpus, sometimes with attention to genre, and commonly with titles supplied for particular pieces. The greater part of Hildegard's compositions were written for the Divine Office, that is, for the hours of monastic prayers that her nuns sang on a daily basis. The most common genres of works in the Office are antiphons, usually fairly short chants sung with intoned psalms and canticles, and responsories, long chants sung at the close of intoned readings, especially at Matins. Hildegard usually wrote these pieces in pairs, and thus they could be used in a variety of ways in a given feast, or throughout the octave, the seven days following the feast. As I have explained elsewhere, the majority of her pieces are written for "commons," that is, for categories of saints, such as apostles or martyrs, or for the Blessed Virgin, and thus they could be sung for the Office repeatedly throughout the church year, whenever the occasion called for such a work, or pair of works.[4] In addition, it is important to note that Hildegard writes infrequently for feasts of the temporal cycle, that is, for feasts commemorating the birth, life, passion, death, resurrection, and ascension of the Lord. She is far more interested in music for feasts venerating the lives and passions of the saints. The reasons for this selection of subjects are complicated, but very important for understanding the feminine voice, especially as it praises God.

In order to move expeditiously through Hildegard's free-verse chant texts, their theological meanings, and her compositional style, I have chosen to focus on her understanding and fusion of two core scenes from the Bible, both of which she encountered in the liturgy: the love feast of the Song of Songs and the song of the Lamb's high court from the Book of Revelation. These two passages of Scripture and their well-established liturgical mean-

4. See my discussion in "Composer and Dramatist: 'Melodious Singing and the Freshness of Remorse,'" in *Voice of the Living Light*, ed. Newman, pp. 149-75.

Table 1: General Dating of Hildegard's Works

Treatise and Date	Events Pertinent to Dating of Music	Musical Works Connected with Treatise and/or Events
I.		
Scivias: 1141-51	Establishment of Rupertsberg: 1150	Songs for St. Rupert: probably by 1150
	Departure of Richardis: 1151	*Scivias* songs: by 1151
	Death of Richardis: 1152	*Ordo virtutum:* by 1151
	Disibod Songs commissioned: 1155	
	Relics of Ursula discovered in Cologne: 1156	Ursula songs: after 1156
II.		
Liber vitae meritorum (Book of Life's Merits): 1158-63		
Book of Simple Medicine: by 1158		
Causes and Cures: by 1158		
III.		
Book of Divine Works: 1163-73	Death of Volmar: 1173	

ings were a great source of inspiration for Hildegard the composer. Hildegard's genius was in taking scriptural readings she knew well from the liturgy, constructing images with liturgical and theological import from these materials, and then transforming these pregnant and powerful images into songs meant to resound within a community. This ongoing process is elemental, and operates in everything that she does. The songs she creates both powerfully represent the highest truths and embody the truths themselves in their very sounding and singing. They capture a particular stream of her divinely inspired visions, allowing her to create treatises that are prophetic and music that is sacramental in its powers.

To explore these ideas, I will first briefly explain Hildegard's view of the Song of Songs and of the Lamb's high court as found in *Scivias,* book 2, vision 6.[5] After this, I will turn first to the songs for St. Ursula as one of the

---

5. See the English translation of *Scivias* by Mother Columba Hart and Jane Bishop, with an introduction by Barbara Newman, in the Classics of Western Civilization series (New York: Paulist Press, 1990), pp. 237-89.

groups of pieces that embodies Hildegard's understanding of the Eucharist (the taking of communion, commemorating the Last Supper and Christ's sacrifice in the Mass)[6] as a love feast, and then in closing will trace some of these same ideas in her musical morality play, the *Ordo virtutum*.

Love Songs and the Making of the Church

The Song of Songs was one of the most commented upon books of the Bible in the Middle Ages. The poetry explores sexual longings — both male and female — within pastoral settings that merge impressionistically, creating a dream-like parade of points of view and images of fertility. In the Middle Ages, the longings were most commonly discussed in terms of the Church as the fertile bride of Christ, both yearning for their final joining at the end of time. The Mariological cast of these commentaries is also well known, and the liturgical use of the texts for Marian feasts and for feasts of the Dedication of the Church has been much explored by scholars.

We should not be surprised to find that Hildegard's interpretation of the Song of Songs is strongly Mariological, with Mary becoming a multilayered image of *Ecclesia*, the Church, and Christ the bridegroom, lifting *Ecclesia/ Mary* out of worldly life and into his eternal and heavenly embrace.[7] All of these themes operate in Hildegard's exploration of the intertwined powers of song and love as she expands on these more common topoi in her writings and in her music, commenting upon the sacramental force of the Eucharist and the importance of her mode of life in the cloister as well as in the Church. Hildegard inherited a tradition of studying the Song of Songs in the context of the feast of the Assumption of the Virgin (the taking up of the Virgin Mary into heaven), where this book of Scripture predominates in the liturgy. Hildegard's theology and her Mariology focus mainly on the Incarnation (the union of divinity with humanity in Jesus Christ), especially as a moment of change, both in history and in the individual soul. In her Marian chants and

---

6. Readers who desire an introduction to standard liturgical structures and theological concepts, and further bibliography, may wish to consult *The Oxford Dictionary of the Christian Church*, ed. F. L. Cross and E. A. Livingstone, 3rd ed. (Oxford: Oxford University Press, 1997).

7. For an introduction to Hildegard's Mariology, see Barbara Newman, *Sister of Wisdom*; Fassler, "Composer"; and Margot Schmidt, "Maria: 'materia aurea' in der Kirche nach Hildegard von Bingen," in *Hildegard von Bingen: Prophetin durch die Zeiten*, ed. Edeltraud Forster (Freiburg im Breisgau, 1997), pp. 262-83.

chants for other female saints, she borrows the language of love as first developed in the liturgy for the Assumption, reshaping it in the process.

Hildegard uses the biblical language of embrace — leading to intercourse and extending to conception — adapted from the Song to refer to moments of change in body and soul, seen and unseen. Several kinds of intercourse, mingling, or exchange are put side by side: the disobedient action that led to sexual shame and the fall from grace in the Garden of Eden, the Annunciation that provoked conception without penetration, the transformation of the elements of the Eucharist at Mass, and the new bridehood of virgins found in the history of the Church and in her own cloister. She can work with such complex imagery because her mode of exploration is so carefully constructed. She takes her essential understanding of the Song out of the context of the Feast of the Assumption, but subsequently both builds upon and transforms the meaning she knew first into a larger and more dramatic picture of God's encounter with human beings through the sacraments, especially the sacrament of the Eucharist.

In her work she fuses her understanding of the sexual power of the Song with the music of the high altar of the Lamb, as found in the Book of Revelation. The text of the "Sanctus," one of the great genres of ordinary Mass chants of the medieval church, is taken from this book of the Bible, and is sung in praise just before the process of consecrating the elements.[8] In her commentary, Hildegard makes it yet another great love song, and one that celebrates the mingling of the human and the divine through and in the eucharistic elements and their taking by the faithful.[9] Her use of two passages from these central scriptural texts in immediate proximity can be found in *Scivias* 2.6. As will be seen, her theological interpretation of the sacrament superimposes the garden of love upon the altar table of the Lamb's high feast.

The Eucharist is procreative, and the song it inspired embodies Christ, just as the action of taking the host also offers "Christ within." Hildegard's view joins the Song of Songs to the song of the virgins who praise the Lamb in the Book of Revelation, offering a picture of the eucharistic sacrifice at the

8. On the "Sanctus," consult the 2nd ed. of the *New Grove Dictionary of Music and Musicians* (London: Macmillan, 2001), 22:228-29, and the appropriate sections in David Hiley, *Western Plainchant: A Handbook* (Oxford: Clarendon Press, 1993).

9. Before reading this discussion of *Scivias* 2.6, it is as well to read both the Song of Songs from the Old Testament and ch. 14 of Revelation (also known as the Apocalypse), the last book in the New Testament, which describes "the Lamb and the virgins that follow him."

end of time, a joining of the two historic songs that had special appeal for her as an artist. Like all medieval exegetes, Hildegard was accustomed to lying between the breasts of scriptural and liturgical images, nurtured from the one verse, and then another, drinking from several spouts of words. To find her mixing metaphors is not to be wondered at, but rather expected — the liturgy was her food, just as the singing of the Office and regular participation in the Eucharist sustained her life and her understanding of what life was about. The Song of Songs, as she came to expound it, relates Mass and Office through common imagery, making the Eucharist a love feast with an incarnational heart, while the Christ who feeds is shaped with both masculine and feminine attributes. Many passages in *Scivias* 2.6 speak of the bride and bridegroom on the altar of the church, joined in the eucharistic sacrifice, but none is so all-encompassing as that of section 34, in which Solomon, in the words of the lover of the Song of Songs, speaks for the Church, and the kiss of the beloved is taken in the act of eating and drinking the elements of the Mass:

> "Who shall give you to me for my brother, sucking the breasts of my mother, that I may find you out of doors and kiss you, and no one will despise me?" (Song of Songs 8.1) What does this mean? With groans and devotion and with sure faith the people of the Church say, "Who will be merciful and give me, a miserable human in tribulation, You, the Bridegroom of the Church? — You, Whom I name my brother because of Your Incarnation, and Who sucks the mercy and truth that nourish humanity from the Divinity, which is my mother in my creation, giving me life and growth?" What does this mean? "The nourishments of the Church too are full of Your grace, for You Who are the Living Bread and the fountain of living water makes her fully abound in the sacrament of Your body and blood. And this You do that I may surely find You out of doors, knowing that You are the Son of God in Heaven but seeing You as a man on earth, for my mortal eyes cannot perceive You in Divinity; and that I may find You in the bread and wine of the divine mystery, the sacrament without deception or artifice. And thus I may kiss You, for You were incarnate for my salvation. . . ."[10]

10. See *Scivias*, 2.6 §35, pp. 259-60. The whole of *Scivias* 2.6 may be usefully read for a fuller understanding of Hildegard's beautiful and unusual understanding of the sacrament. For ready comparison with other thinkers from the Middle Ages, see Gary Macy, *The Theologies of the Eucharist in the Early Scholastic Period: A Study of the Salvific Function of the Sacrament According to the Theologians, c. 1080–c. 1220* (Oxford: Oxford University Press, 1984).

The Garden of the Altar welcomes those who have suffered the Fall to a second chance; the garden of the monastery sustains the lives of nuns who have ventured into a special relationship with God, whose Son is their *Sponsus* — their bridegroom — and their Lamb. In the songs she wrote for St. Ursula, Hildegard fuses all these images; she places a song with new meaning in the mouths of the nuns who sing the Office, and who regularly taste the body and blood of the Lord at the altar of their own church. They offer a special song of love in the sequences Hildegard wrote for them to sing at Mass, one of which will be analyzed in some detail below.[11]

St. Ursula: Archetypal Virgin Martyr and Bride of Christ

The love feast that Hildegard spreads before our eyes in the *Scivias* is a banquet for the daily needs of those who strive on earth. But it is also a spiritual banquet for the saints who feed and drink joyfully, and whose actions call those not yet saintly through the inspiration of their miraculous deeds. Quotations from the Song of Songs are prominent in several of Hildegard's song texts, but none is worked out on the grand scale found in the chants for St. Ursula and her Companions. Here are many parallels between Hildegard's use of the Song to describe the sacrament of the table and the lives of the martyred virgins. This, along with works for the Virgin Mary, is Hildegard's fullest complex of chants: responsories, an antiphon, a set of antiphons for

11. Scholars have explored Hildegard's views of love in interpersonal relationships in the context of her feelings for the nun Richardis. Some have seen Richardis as the model for the straying and subsequently recovered Anima in the *Ordo Virtutum*. Richardis left Hildegard's care to become an abbess herself, and shortly thereafter died, apparently claiming that she was sorry to have left the Rupertsberg. For an introduction to this topic, see Barbara Newman's essay on Hildegard's life in *Voice of the Living Light*, p. 12. The works Newman cites as essential reading are important in further situating Hildegard: Peter Dronke, "Hildegard of Bingen," in his *Women Writers of the Middle Ages* (Oxford: Oxford University Press, 1981), pp. 144-201; Sabina Flanigan, *Hildegard of Bingen, 1098-1179: A Visionary Life* (rev. ed. London and New York: Routledge, 1998); and Edward Peter Nolan, *Cry Out and Write: A Feminine Poetics of Revelation* (New York: Continuum, 1994). In his provocative and elegant study, *Music, Body, and Desire in Medieval Culture: Hildegard of Bingen to Chaucer* (Stanford: Stanford University Press, 2001), Bruce Holsinger interrelates Hildegard's understanding of "musical pleasure" and "musical violence" (p. 101). I agree with Holsinger that music for Hildegard was "a sonorous vehicle of spiritual grace and moral clarity" (p. 101); I will look at other kinds of evidence to show that the sexuality described in Hildegard's song texts has scriptural and liturgical underpinnings, and depends primarily upon her view of the sacraments.

Lauds that includes two extra pieces for other Hours, a sequence for the Mass, and an Office hymn. The entire set of chant texts is bound together by Song of Songs imagery, much of which recollects the themes encountered in *Scivias* as described above. In the chants there is both narrative progression and a harking back to pre-established imagery. In the narrative, Ursula moves from love and the wedding feast to the sacrifice of death, which provides a kind of sacramental consummation: her blood, not that of the hymen in intercourse but that of the slain virgin, mingles with her lover's liquid life. He is the Lamb who was slain, and their life forces mingle in his high court, at the sonorous apex of the Church. I will discuss the texts of individual chants and groups of chants briefly as the poems embody and expand on themes already encountered. At the end I will focus on the sequence, both its text and its music, as a sounding manifestation of Hildegard's themes produced through the action of praise itself, related to her understanding of what music is and how it works within the human person for the purpose of transformation. Hildegard's sequence for St. Ursula is, like all her works in this genre, an exercise in deconstruction of the familiar, a process used not only to take apart but also to create liturgical meaning. It is especially important here because it is an exercise in the only chant genre for the Mass liturgy that has a significant representation in works by Hildegard, who was far more interested in composing for the Office than for the Mass.[12]

According to the story, Ursula was a fourth-century queen of Britain, who renounced her betrothed to join with other virgins in a life consecrated to God. The virgins were commonly wont to sail and to swim near their boat, and one day a sudden gale blew the entire company off to the Continent. There the virgins became famous agents of religious conversion, but their triumphant progress was cut short by Attila the Hun and his soldiers who, when he encountered them near Cologne, slaughtered Ursula and her virgin companions (later counted as 11,000). They had been asked to submit or to die, and only the latter course was acceptable.

Hildegard's texts include references to male companions, defenders who died with the virgins they sought to care for and protect. When bodies assumed to be those of the virgins were uncovered near Cologne in the mid-twelfth century, men were found buried with them. Elizabeth of Schönau wrote to Hildegard about this finding, and Elizabeth's own life of Ursula and her companions emphasizes the mixed character of the company, thus explaining the situation of the newly uncovered relics.

12. See Fassler, "Composer," pp. 150-59.

Hildegard's hagiographical exercise defends this position, which suggests that the songs date from after 1156, when this particular group of relics was discovered. With so many virgins and companions, the discovery provided relics for many churches and monastic foundations. The eagerness for Office music for this group of saints was tied to the recently elevated cult, and it may be supposed that Hildegard's own church received one of the widely dispersed relics from the dig; her songs may have been composed for their reception, as well as in support of Elizabeth's hagiographic ideals.[13] Hildegard, as we have seen, wrote her compositions with practical needs in mind, clearly hoping the works would be of use to religious communities, and especially to her own. But the works are always more than discrete pieces or groups of pieces, and all are tied to a larger theological program. One reads and listens in two ways: to the particular piece and its details, and also with attention to the ways in which the work was known in the context of her larger purpose.

The set of pieces Hildegard wrote for St. Ursula, like all her music, is both functional and deliberately out of keeping with tradition. This is true for carefully conceived theological reasons far too complex to explain here in their entirety. The first responsory and antiphon are appropriate for First Vespers of the feast; the second responsory would then have been used at Matins; the five Lauds antiphons make an appropriate set for the psalms of Lauds, with "Et ideo puellelae istae" serving for the Benedictus of this hour; "Deus enim rorem" might have been used for the Little Hours, including that of Terce, which preceded Mass; and the last of the eight psalter antiphons for Second Vespers. The hymn is a mighty work, which could have served at any of the Office hours, and the sequence would have graced the Mass, set in its traditional place before the reading of the Gospel.

The texts reveal that the plan — if such it can be called — was to offer both a narrative and a time for lofty reflection with steady repeating of the most important imagery, especially that of blood. This is a feast venerating martyrs of the church, but in this case the slaughtered subjects were also a group of virgins. In mentioning the pieces in quasi-liturgical order here, my goal is to emphasize allusions to the Song of Songs and to demonstrate ways

13. In addition to the correspondence between Elizabeth of Schönau and Hildegard regarding St. Ursula, there is a letter to Hildegard from an abbess of the monastery at Cologne, a church dedicated to St. Ursula and near the supposed site of the martyrdom, which reveals great personal intimacy between these two figures. See *The Letters of Hildegard of Bingen*, vol. 2, trans. Joseph L. Baird and Radd K. Ehrman (New York: Oxford University Press, 1998), p. 104.

in which these allusions in the poetry join the pieces to the liturgical commentary of *Scivias* 2, the images and their theological context forming a useful divining rod for a difficult group of song texts.[14]

Just one example of this glorious fusion must suffice, and that is the opening of "Favus distillans." In this responsory, Ursula is seen as a woman who has had a dream in which Christ becomes her lover, causing her to reject her human spouse for union with the Godhead. Both the opening of the poem and the subsequent verse locate the saint in the Song of Songs as the *sponsa,* the bride, but make her spouse the paschal victim, the Agnus Dei, or Lamb of God. From the grove of the sweet lover, Ursula moves to the court of the Lamb, and then, more locally, to the dawn of monastic song and the morning liturgy, taking Hildegard and her community of nuns into this kaleidoscope of the exalted and the intimate, the general and the particular.

> **Response**: A dripping honeycomb was Ursula the virgin, who yearned
> to embrace the Lamb of God, honey and milk beneath her tongue.
> For she gathered to herself a fruitful garden and the choicest flowers
> in a flock of virgins.
> **Verse**: So rejoice, daughter of Zion, in the most noble dawn.

Hildegard also invokes the favored poetic structures of the Song of Songs in the sequence "O Ecclesia," where Ursula becomes the Church as she is the bride of the Lamb. It begins:

> Ecclesia, your eyes are like sapphires, your ears like Mount Bethel; your
> nose like a mountain of incense and myrrh, your voice like the sound of
> many waters.

In the final verses, Ursula and her companions discover a new Cana in their wedding feast, and their blood's wine is a drink of special savor. "O Ecclesia" carries through with the sexual imagery and the jewels described in the Song, as the virgins become a necklace of wounds, blood-gleaming pearls that strangle the throat of the Devil, whose neck and head are charac-

---

14. Before turning to a study of the sequence "O Ecclesia," readers are advised to read the entire set of poems for St. Ursula and the eleven thousand virgins, noting the several allusions to the Song of Songs and to the high court of the Lamb from Revelation. The Ursula poems are found in Barbara Newman's edition of Hildegard's *Symphonia: A Critical Edition of the Symphonia armonie celestium revelationum (Symphony of the Harmony of Celestial Revelation),* 2nd ed. (Ithaca, NY: Cornell University Press, 1998), pp. 230-47.

teristically described through phallic imagery in Hildegard's play and other writings. That they "surround" his throat and choke out his life is a richly textured reversal of the Fall, with its introduction of carnal intercourse and the devil's triumphant seduction of Eve, a scene that is most skillfully exploited in the Anglo-Norman "Ordo Representationis Ade."[15] The virginal pearls represent the newness that is briefly tasted by all who approach the communion table rightly.[16] The devil's *symphonia* that mocked the virgins as they were slain becomes the new symphony of triumph played round the altar, the high throne of the Agnus Dei.

The reversal celebrated in the sequence text is also reflected in the music, which appears as a deconstructed and refashioned example of the genre with some features preserved and others not. Hildegard's music is generative, much of it coming out of stock motives that she employs constantly. Hildegard creates a sonic fabric in which she can include motives from well-known chants borrowed from the liturgy, as well as develop particular twists and motivic details that bind pieces together or that allow for tone painting on certain words. She is also deeply sensitive to liturgical genre, using formal considerations to make further theological points. When considering her music, any group of pieces has to be understood on several levels: as a part of a sonic whole, as part of the context of the smaller group of works to which it relates, and then, of course, as part of the well-defined genres of liturgical chant that she knew so well from a lifetime of singing, and bent and twisted to her will. So it is with the hymn and the sequence for St. Ursula, both of which are part of a set of pieces that relate musically as well as textually, the opening motive of a fifth (which, of course, she uses elsewhere) being exploited throughout, regardless of the tonal center of the piece.

All of Hildegard's sequences rely on double-versicle structure, with texts in the free art prose employed by Notker and later poets who take their inspiration from him.[17] As is well known, Hildegard's sequences are much more

15. For discussion of the Mariology in this play, see Fassler, "Composer," and Schmidt, "Maria."

16. The importance of circumcision as a foreshadowing of the sacrament of baptism is developed at great length in Hildegard's *Scivias*. She sees the taming of lust beginning with circumcision, which points toward the salvific action of baptism. The Virgin Mary completed the task, and Christ and the Church perpetuate her action, extending it to all with the grace to accept it. See, for example, *Scivias*, 3.2, pp. 332-33. For the association of ring imagery with sexual intercourse, see Holsinger, *Music, Body, and Desire*, pp. 142-52.

17. For discussion of the sequence in Hildegard's region during the early twelfth century, see Lori Kruckenberg, "The Sequence from 1050-1150: Study of a Genre in Change" (PhD diss.,

melismatic and formally far freer than any other surviving works in the genre.[18] She buried kernels of similar melodic phrases within paired versicles in torrents of notes, reinventing the form as she went. Yet, although it may be difficult to discern at first, even "O Ecclesia" — the freest of all Hildegard's works in this genre — is tightly controlled, and her departures from the form she established and the musical language she chose to employ allow for heightened proclamation of the text and underscore poetic meanings. The nature of Hildegard's liturgical songs, the powerful interdependence of word on song and formal structure, and of music upon textual sense, reveal that she conceived both dimensions of her work as parts of a single process, singing as she verbalized, verbalizing as she sang. We can, as is common in contemporary scholarship, comprehend Hildegard's texts apart from their music, and study her music apart from the texts, but this was neither the manner in which she wrote the works nor the way she intended them to be known. Song, as she defines it, is made of music and words, and the two create parts of a breathing sonic organism, which, in the mouths of the praising faithful, make church, make Divinity: "And so the words symbolize the body, and the jubilant music indicates the spirit; and the celestial harmony shows the Divinity, and the words the Humanity of the Son of God."[19]

In Table 2, the Latin text of "O Ecclesia," organized into the poetic units found in the original sources, appears next to a literal English translation based on Newman.[20] The musical units are indicated in the left column.

University of Iowa, 1998). Analysis of the text-music relationship in the Notkerian sequence is provided in Richard Crocker, *The Early Medieval Sequence* (Berkeley: University of California Press, 1977). Although the sequence texts by Notker are a securely attributable body of poems, the melodies are later, and the ways in which they were adapted to the texts are complex.

18. Several scholars have produced analyses of Hildegard's sequences, such as Michael Klaper in the commentary to Lorenz Welker, *Lieder: Faksimile Riesencodex (Hs. 2) der Hessischen Landesbibliothek Wiesbaden fol. 466-481v* (Wiesbaden, 1998), English translation by Lori Kruckenberg. Klaper compares his own analysis of the piece with that by Marianne Richert Pfau, "Hildegard von Bingen's 'Symphonia Armonie Celestium Revelationum': An Analysis of Music Process, Modality, and Text-Music Relations" (PhD diss., State University of New York at Stony Brook, 1990), demonstrating how two capable scholars arrive at different understandings of its formal structure. For another view of several works in the genre, see Hildegard of Bingen, *Sequences and Hymns,* ed. Christopher Page (Lustleigh: Antico Edition, 1983).

19. *Scivias,* 3.13, §12, p. 533.

20. *Symphonia,* pp. 238-43, with notes on pp. 311-12. Newman provides two translations of all Hildegard's liturgical poetry, one free, the other literal and close to the structure of the original. I have provided the latter here, but encourage reference to both when studying Hildegard's poetry.

Table 2: Text of "O Ecclesia": Hildegard's Sequence for St. Ursula

Music	Text	Translation

I.1	1. *O Ecclesia,*
	oculi tui similes
	saphiro sunt,
	et aures tue monti Bethel,
	et nasus tuus est
	sicut mons mirre et thuris
	et os tuum quasi sonus
	   aquarum multarum
		1. O Church,
		your eyes are
		like sapphire,
		and your ears like Mount Bethel,
		your nose like
		a mountain of incense and myrrh,
		and your mouth like the sound of
		   many waters

I.2	2. *In visione vere fidei*
	Ursula Filium Dei amavit
	et virum cum hoc seculo
	   reliquit
	et in solem aspexit
	atque pucherrimum iuvenem
	vocavit, dicens:
		2. In a vision of true faith,
		Ursula fell in love with the Son of God
		and renounced a husband along with
		   this world.
		She gazed upon the sun
		and called to the fairest youth,
		saying:

I.3	3. *In multo desiderio* *desideravi ad te venire* *et in celestibus* *nuptiis tecum sedere,* *per alienam viam ad te currens* *velut nubes que in purissimo aere* *currit similis saphiro.*	3. In great yearning I have yearned to come to you and at the heavenly wedding feast sit with you, racing to you by a strange path like a cloud that, in the purest sky, races like sapphire.
II.1	4. *Et postquam Ursula* *sic dixerat,* *rumor iste* *per omnes populos exiit.*	4. And after Ursula had spoken thus, this report went out among all peoples.
II.2	*Et dixerunt:* *Innocentia puellaris ignorantie* *nescit quid dicit.*	And they said: In the innocence of girlish ignorance, she knows not what she says.
III (I.3cc, ee)	5. *Et ceperunt ludere cum illa* *in magna symphonia,* *usque dum ignea sarcina* *super eam cecidit.*	5. And they began to sport with her in great harmony, until the fiery burden fell upon her.
(II.3)	*Unde omnes cognoscebant* *quia contemptus mundi est* *sicut mons Bethel.*	Then all people recognized that scorn for the world is like Mount Bethel.
IV.1	6. *Et cognoverunt etiam* *suavissimum odorem* *mirre et thuris,*	6. And they recognized also the sweetest fragrance of incense and myrrh,
IV.2	*quoniam contemptus mundi* *super omnia ascendit.*	because scorn for the world mounts above all.

Music	Text	Translation
V.1	7. *Tunc diabolus* *membra sua invasit,* *que nobilissimos mores* *in corporibus istis* *occiderunt.*	7. Then the devil entered into his members, who, in those bodies, slaughtered the noblest way of life.
V.2	8. *Et hoc in alta voce* *omnia elementa audierunt* *et ante thronum Dei* *dixerunt:*	8. And in a high voice all the elements heard and before the throne of God said:
VI	9. *Wach! rubicundus sanguis* *innocentis agni* *in desponsatione sua* *effusus est.*	9. Wach! The scarlet blood of an innocent lamb at her betrothal is spilled.
VII.1	10. *Hoc audiant omnes celi* *et in summa symphonia* *laudent Agnum Dei,*	10. Let all the heavens hear this and in supreme harmony praise the Lamb of God:
VII.2	*quia guttur serpentis antiqui* *in istis margaritis* *materie Verbi Dei* *suffocatum est.*	for the throat of the ancient serpent in these pearls from the matter of the Word of God is strangled.

Sequence poetry, whether set in the style of Notker from the late ninth century or Adam of St. Victor from the twelfth century, is dependent on melodic repetition.[21] The sequence is a through-composed chant form, with different music for every poetic unit, and yet with each sense unit (stanza or strophe) falling into two — or sometimes more — parts, each of which is sung to the same melody. Thus, the most typical musical form of the sequence is AABBCCDDEE, etc., with each letter representing a melodic unit, and, as can be seen, with each of them rendered twice. Hildegard respects this feature of the sequence as a genre. The text of "O Ecclesia," adapted to use my style of indicating versicles according to a musical plan, is organized as follows:[22]

21. For comparison of the early sequence with the late sequence, see Margot Fassler, *Gothic Song: Victorine Sequences and Augustinian Reform in Twelfth Century Paris* (Cambridge: Cambridge University Press, 1993).

22. Study of the music can bring a completely different formal understanding of a piece such as this one, which, in comparison with Hildegard's other sequences, is even freer and more difficult to analyze. For another analysis of this work, see Janet Martin and Greta Mary Hair, "'O Ecclesia': The Text and Music of Hildegard of Bingen's Sequence for St. Ursula," *Tjurunga* 30 (1986): 3-62. The piece has been chosen for discussion here because so much work of varying kinds has been done on it. My own work is the first to place it in the larger theological context of the *Scivias*, using the lens of the Song of Songs for closer readings. Many of the details I do not have time to emphasize can be found in Martin and Hair's excellent study.

I.1, I.2, I.3; II.1, II.2; III. II.3; IV.1, IV.2; V.1, V.2; VI; VII.1, VII.2

Or, if each melodic unit is represented by a letter:

AAA, BB, CB, DD, EE, F, GG

As with "O Jerusalem," the sequence for St. Ursula needs to be interpreted as the music "cuts" the text into units, binding some sections together very strongly and giving independence to other stanzas, even casting them out of the established musical framework.[23] Hildegard has joined the opening stanzas — those dependent on the Song of Songs — together, folding three sense units one upon the other (see Example 1). In the singers' (or listeners') minds, the Church described as "the beloved" in the Song becomes Ursula as she sees her bridegroom in a vision of true faith, and then in the third statement, as she joins him in the love feast of heaven, the sapphire sky (the jewel of his belly in the Song, as well as that of Ezekiel 1:26). The opening is especially powerful, given that the sequence was understood in Hildegard's time as a commentary on the "Alleluia" of the Mass liturgy. Hildegard's reference to this form in the elaborate opening gestures toward a common understanding of this sequence as a human translation of angelic sound, the Church on earth resounding with the Church above, and Ursula joining the former to the latter through her vision of a mystical union with the Lamb. Barbara Newman has written about the association of the eagle with mystical experience, and here Ursula, like the eagle, can look straight into the sun.[24] The price she will pay for her joining is suggested only by the myrrh, whose precious perfume was used to anoint the dead, making it a symbol of Christ's passion, and here of Ursula's death as well. The melody soars to its loftiest point both at the mention of the mouth of the beloved, which has the sound of many waters *(os tuum quasi sonus aquarum)*, and of the purest air of the blue heavens *(in purissimo aere)*, which calls Ursula to the nuptial kiss, through music's ability to raise the words on high.

23. The sequence "O Ecclesia" (from Wiesbaden, Hessische Landesbibliothek, Hs. 2, fol. 477[r-v]) is performed along with others of the Ursula set on Anonymous IV's recording "Eleven Thousand Virgins: Chants for the Feast of St. Ursula," 1997 (Harmonia Mundi 907200). The useful notes to the performance do not emphasize formal structures and their meaning. Readers are encouraged to listen with Example 1 in hand, exploring the ways in which the music is organized, and the way in which it orders the text. For a performance of "O Ecclesia" that mirrors the reading presented here more closely, see Gothic Voices, conducted by Christopher Page, "A Feather on the Breath of God: Sequences and Hymns by Hildegard of Bingen," 1984 (Hyperion CDA 66039).

24. See Newman, *Symphonia*, p. 311.

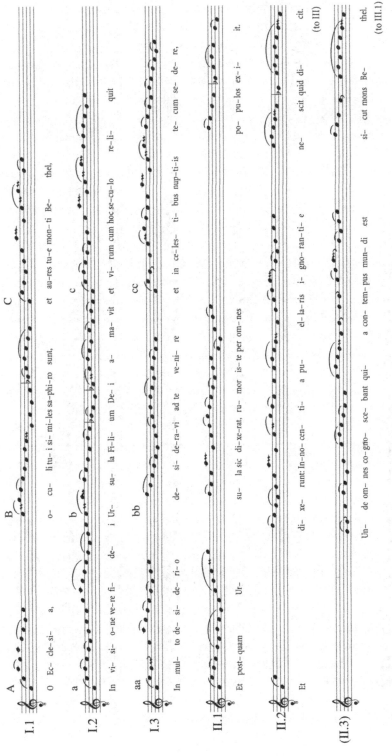

Example 1. Hildegard of Bingen, "O Ecclesia": sequence for St. Ursula (continued on following pages)

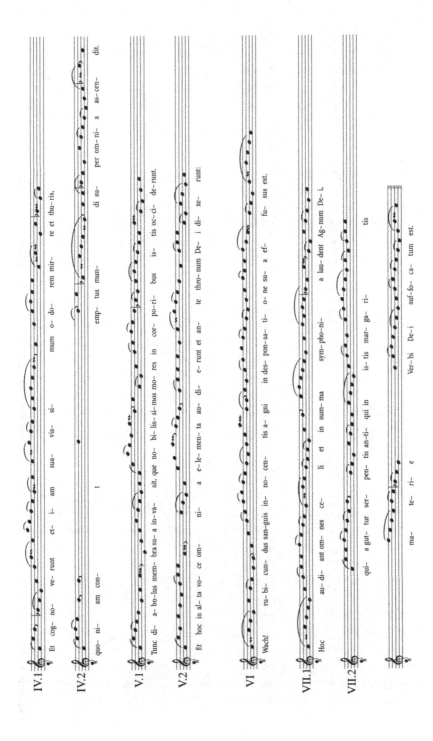

D

E

I.1   et na- sus tu- us est si- cut mons mir- re   et   thu- ris et os tu- um qua- si so- nus a-   qua- rum mul- ta-   rum

d

e

I.2   et in   so- lem a- spe- xit at-   que   pul- cher-ri- mum iu- ve- nem   vo-   ca- vit, di-   cens:

dd

ee

I.3   per a- li- e- nam vi- am ad te cur- rens   ve- lut nu- bes que in pu- ris- si-mo a- e- re cur- rit si- mi- lis sa- phi- ro.

(to II.1)

III

I.3ccee)   Et ce- pe-runt lu- de- re cum il- la in   ma- gna sym- pho-ni- a, us- que dum i- gne- a sar- ci- na   su- per e- am ce- ci-   dit.

(to II.3)

The female voice is naturally a higher voice than the male, and Hildegard wrote music for this sound, putting her notes in a range that only women could comfortably sing, especially young women. John of Salisbury and others were disgusted by the "feminization" of music, by lofty ranges and flexible melismas then prevalent in much new music of the period; Hildegard flies in the face of any assumption that the female is somehow silly, somehow less worthy. In her sonic landscape, the ideal *is* female, and yet, of course, men are welcome to join this world of song, if they play by the rules of its unique harmonies. There is one masculine voice, however, that cannot join in the game, and that voice is the Devil's. He cannot sing (as in *Ordo Virtutum*), and when his works are represented in song, the voice is often low and growling, a point made in "O Ecclesia" at a dramatic moment.

The lofty and bejeweled opening of "O Ecclesia" is followed by the challenge of the world and of the Devil; this comes in words that Hildegard crafted to inspire and defend her nuns, who clearly were often scorned for their love of a bridegroom they could not see. The world says "you do not know what you say" when Ursula claims her lover; but the virtue of contempt for the world itself inspires respect, as she takes the fiery burden of her martyrdom, with reference to the passion of the bloody joining to follow. As can be seen, Hildegard uses repetition to bind the next three stanzas together as well, beginning with "Et postquam" and continuing through the end of what I have labeled as musical unit III. Unit III is a melodic hybrid. The opening notes are like those of I.3cc. The music shifts to elaborated material from I.3ee as the mocking symphony described in the text leads to Ursula's fiery burden. The music makes the connection between this and the mouth that sounds like many waters and the sapphire heavens.[25] In order to establish the structure for the sound and the violation of that framework, Hildegard must work carefully with convention. After two blocks of musically interconnected texts, and a third musical unit that borrows from each, she makes a true shift away from the opening music, all the while keeping to the large framework of the arch that is found in every line, a steady rising from the opening *a*, up to the highest ranges of the tessitura, and then a return at the end to the lower *a*, motion that can be seen (and heard!). In almost every poetic stanza this rising and falling occurs, and with some regularity.

25. Hildegard's sophisticated uses of contrafacta technique are not surprising for a twelfth-century poet/composer. For an introduction to the technique and its central role in twelfth-century music, see Fassler, *Gothic Song*, esp. ch. 8: "Contrafacta in the Parisian Sequence Repertories: An Introduction," pp. 161-84.

When the Devil's minions kill Ursula's companions in Unit V, the musical openings are invaded by his base propensity for rape. Unit V, as can be seen in the example, begins low but then descends even lower, the *a* to *g*, and then down to *e*, a note that could only be sung by the male voice (or very low female voices). The word here is "membra," a veiled reference to the male sex organ that has been filled with the Devil's sound, the sound of a fallen race. The high voices of the entire universe protest this action, beginning in the parallel stanza in the low range, but not as low as the notes on "membra," and then rising at the ends of the texts found in Unit V to the throne of the Lamb, who hears the universal cry of woe. We hear it too in Unit VI, on the dramatic "Wach!" that reaches to the high court where the blood streams into the chalice of the Church, making the food of the communion feast. Unit VI stands by itself, characteristically presenting a mingling of two martyrs' bloods in the heavenly bed of the Lamb's altar. Ursula is wed and her union consummated. The sorrowful "wach" turns to joy of understanding: suffering begets a new joy, and the wholeness of the virginal body kills the Devil himself. The point is made graphically through the device of repetition in Unit VII, and in two especially significant places. The "wach" of Unit VI becomes the "hoc" of Unit VII, joining these two musically different units with a rhyming pun, as the lament is introduced twice, the second time to do its work of salvation. The pitches, making a low arch from *a* to *c'* and back to the lower neighbor note of *g*, are transposed higher several times, both in Unit VI and then in Unit VII as the "wach" moves to "hoc" and then to the highest *symphonia*. This music joins with the Lamb and Ursula and her virgins become made of him, the matter of the Word of God. In this eucharistic action, they are fed and become food, joining his body to offer *Ecclesia* to those who take it into themselves. Their transformed bodies become pearls, a new necklace for the Devil's phallic throat, squeezing him with unblemished muscles that strangle him. The new sexuality is eucharistic; as discussed above, the host-like pearls are made of a new substance that transforms and saves. The notes for "materie" are the same as those for "guttur serpentis," and Hildegard uses the repetition to literally stuff the maw with substance (see Units VII.1 and VII.2).

Hildegard's music constantly interrelates and interprets her texts, and understanding and actually hearing the connections she makes would have required the years of practice that were possible within the monastic community. Knowing her subtle tricks depends on memory and deep knowledge of the pieces. Once one grasps her tonal idioms, her music is not hard to sing, not at all, for it is highly formulaic and generative. But the inner sense of the texts and melodies takes as much deep reflection to appreciate as any sophisticated art music. Repetition is her favored device, and she uses it not only here in a sequence (as would be expected), but throughout her music — both on the largest of organizational levels as well as in the smallest details. Her musical devices depend on the texts, but the meanings of the texts depend on the musical devices, large and small. The genres she explores are all rooted in liturgical convention, as with "O Ecclesia" with its repeating pairs or triples. But the genre does get altered, and the reasons for doing this have to do with a theology of newness and transformation. The music became the nuns' food; their partaking of it was expected to change them, and to prepare them for the reception of the bridegroom they encountered not only in the prayer and praise of the Divine Office, but face to face in the Mass. The sequence for Ursula served as preparation for this event, and so too, I believe, did the *Ordo Virtutum*.

Ordo Virtutum as Preparation for the Sacramental Love Feast

The *Ordo Virtutum* is a complex work, drawing on traditions from the liturgical drama of the Prophets' plays and the battles of good and evil as found in several classical and medieval texts.[26] The purposes and settings of the play have been much discussed. Peter Dronke has suggested that the play was designed for the dedication of Hildegard's new church at the Rupertsberg.[27] Pamela Sheingorn has proposed that the play would have served to initiate the nuns into the Benedictine way of life.[28] Gunilla Iversen has focused on

26. See Fassler, "Composer," pp. 168-75. An introduction to the play's meaning and its reliance on the Song is found on p. 169.

27. For summaries of his arguments and further bibliography, see his notes to the translation of the play in *Nine Medieval Latin Plays* (Cambridge: Cambridge University Press, 1994), esp. pp. 152-53. He attacks the idea advanced by Eckehard Simon that Hildegard's play was not meant for performance; see Eckehard Simon, *The Theatre of Medieval Europe: New Research in Early Drama* (Cambridge: Cambridge University Press, 1991), p. xiii. All references to the play in this paper are from Dronke's edition and translation. The music for the play can be found in Hildegard of Bingen, *Lieder*, ed. Pudentiana Barth, M. Immaculata Ritscher, and Joseph Schmidt-Görg (Salzburg, 1969), and in a performance edition of the play by Audrey Ekdahl Davidson (Kalamazoo: Western Michigan University Press, 1985), which also has an English translation.

28. See her "The Virtues of Hildegard's *Ordo Virtutum;* or It *Was* a Woman's World," in *The* Ordo Virtutum *of Hildegard of Bingen: Critical Studies*, ed. Audrey Ekdahl Davidson (Kalamazoo: Western Michigan University Press, 1992), pp. 43-62.

the play in the context of Hildegard's life, especially with reference to her relationship with the nun Richardis von Stade.[29] I do not dispute the idea that the play may have been performed on highly festive occasions such as the Dedication of the Church or upon the occasion of the Consecration of Nuns, but I think its use by Hildegard and the women in her convent was probably far more common than the circumstances these once-in-a-lifetime situations would have offered. The Virtues of the play appear in the costumes of Hildegard's convent, with freely flowing hair and special attributes. The illuminated *Scivias* shows them repeatedly, and both Madeline Caviness and Sarah Bromberg have commented on the correspondences between the visualized representations and the Virtues in the play.[30] The play also appears in prose form in *Scivias* as the introduction to the final scene of joy and glory that ends the treatise with a commentary on Psalms 148–150. The play's action and featured characters — so central to Hildegard's theology — needed to be encountered on a regular basis. The Song of Songs is a useful key to Hildegard's dramatic work, especially when her use of the text in the play is joined with her exploration of it elsewhere. Anima, the Everywoman character whose fall from grace and whose redemption after confession is the active purpose of the work, is here engaged in a healing service with Christ as both her doctor and her spouse. She prepares for a marriage that is the joining of his body in Eucharist as defined in both the *Scivias* and the Ursula songs. The play serves as a kind of group confession for the entire community, as they both forgive and embrace the fallen soul, who, once more, is given another chance to be redeemed.[31]

In his introduction to the play, Dronke refers to the importance of the Song and lists several places where the text is cited:

Royal Wedding Chamber: lines 75 and 104
The Kiss of the King: line 90
Burning in the King's embraces: line 105
The Flower in the Meadow: line 109

---

29. See "Réaliser une vision: La dernière vision de *Scivias* et le drame *Ordo virtutum* de Hildegarde de Bingen," *Revue de Musicologie* 86 (2000): 37-63. The idea was also proposed by Julia Holloway in "The Monastic Context of Hildegard's *Ordo Virtutum*," in *The* Ordo Virtutum, ed. Davidson, pp. 63-77, and by Barbara Newman in *Sister of Wisdom*, pp. 222-24.

30. See, for example, Caviness's discussion in her "Artist" (n. 2 above).

31. Dronke says in his introduction to the text, "At the opening, an image drawn from the parables of repentance (the lost sheep and the lost drachma) in Luke 15 offers a glimmer of hope that the errant Anima may be found again" (p. 149).

The Embraces of the Princess: lines 125 and 129
The Royal Nuptials: line 131
The Rocky Cavern (where the hiding dove becomes a warrior): line 154

The themes of love and joining also emerge at other crucial points in the play. The opening prologue, sung by the Patriarchs and Prophets, speaks of the beautiful body of the Word of God; both the men of old and the Virtues of the new order work to shine with him, "building up" the body (line 5). From the outset, this is a play encouraging the "joining" Hildegard describes in the eucharistic feast. The first chorus is of the embodied souls who wish to be a "daughter of the King" (11). Anima is ready to have her love feast: "O let me come to you joyfully, that you may give me the kiss of your heart!" (24). The Virtues are ready to serve as handmaidens to this daughter of the king (25), but she wants to take off her garment, the new flesh of the conse-crated virgin, the only robe worthy for this bridegroom's chamber. She can-not complete the mortification of flesh needed to "make the robe" of glory: "Woe is me, I cannot complete this dress I have put on. Indeed, I want to cast it off!" (39-40). This Song of Songs has a reluctant bride who ignores the song of longing issuing from the throne of the Lamb, the primal song of the Creator sung to all his flock: "Ah," the Virtues sing, "a certain wondrous vic-tory already rose in that Soul, in her wondrous longing for God, in which a sensual delight was secretly hidden" (51-52).[32]

In the middle section of the play, the Virtues call the lost soul to the rightful love feast of the garden of bliss, to the royal *thalamus* (74-75). The flower of the garden is blasted, yet another flower calls it to join in radiant light. The mystical experience of Ursula, who like the eagle could stare into the sun, is invoked here as well, as the Virtues claim they can make the soul ready for the encounter with the Christ. Fear of God says: "I, Fear of God, can prepare you, blissful daughters, to gaze upon the living God and not die of it" (80-81). The gazing is part of joining and longing, a union that never will be severed. But, like the mockers in the Ursula songs, the Devil accuses the Virtues of a false theology. They have invented this mystical marriage with an unseen God. He croaks and mocks in words that are supremely chal-lenging: "Bravo! Bravo! What is this great fear, and this great love? Where is the champion? Where the prize giver? You don't even know what you are worshipping" (84-85).

---

32. On the two kinds of songs Hildegard creates, of sorrow and of joy, see Fassler, "Composer," pp. 168-75 and notes.

The Devil hits the nuns in the solar plexus of their beliefs in a mystical union. As with the transformation of the elements at Mass, their bride-groom cannot be seen and is a figment; their offspring are not real human beings. The altar is a barren stone table with no food, and with no actual host to serve the meal. But in their next lines, the Virtues extol the beauties of the love feast, which the Devil cannot see, to the befuddled Anima. Obedience offers "the kiss of the king" (89-90); Faith promises the leaping fountain (95); and Chastity takes the company by the hand to the garden of the Song of Songs: "Maidenhood, you remain within the royal chamber. How sweetly you burn in the King's embraces, when the Sun blazes through you, never letting your noble flower fall. Gentle maiden, you will never know the shadow over the falling flower!" (104-8). The sexual imagery is reversed, for the blasted and impregnated human body will be wet with a new liquid, and also be freed from the curse of sin and death, as the Virtues promise, singing all together: "The flower in the meadow falls in the wind, the rain splashes it. But you, Maidenhood, remain in the symphonies of heavenly habitants: you are the tender flower that will never grow dry" (109-11). And further:

> **Virtues**: Royal daughter, you are held fast in the embraces the world shuns: how tender is your love in the highest God.
> **Discipline**: I am one who loves the innocent ways that know nothing ignoble: I always gaze upon the King of Kings, and, as my highest honour, I embrace him.
> **Virtues**: Angelic comrade, how comely you are in the royal nuptials.
> (125-31)

Anima, who has fallen and whose festering wounds stink of sin (170-71), crawls back; she has seen the royal virtues, graceful and beautiful, in the highest Sun (161-64). The Devil croaks again, this time in rage as his prey slips away: "You were in my embrace, I led you out. Yet now you are going back . . ." (210). One lover will be replaced by another.

Even as they bind him, the Devil rages against their unseen lover and his unseen offspring: "You don't know what you are nurturing, for your belly is devoid of the beautiful form that woman receives from man: in this you transgress the command that God enjoined in the sweet act of love; so you don't even know what you are!" (235-37).

The Devil's challenge, taken in the context of the love imagery of *Scivias*, especially as developed in the Ursula songs, strikes at the heart of the Christian mystery and belief in the power of the sacrament of the Eucharist. The answer to his challenge, as Chastity argues in her final retort, is belief in the presence of God's Son in human life: "I did bring forth a man, who gathers up mankind to himself, against you, through his nativity" (240-41).

The magnificent finale of the play includes a call from Christ to the Father to let the faithful come to him in order to bring the triumphant completion of the Holy Jerusalem that is the Church. Here Christ speaks for the lost souls, pleading as victim, and begging God that his suffering for their good be triumphant. When Christ ceases speaking, the play closes with a plea for all to bend their knees. I believe the play to be a call to the altar, to the royal nuptials of the eucharistic feast. It makes great sense for such a work, filled as it is with the imagery Hildegard used in *Scivias* 2.6, and in her liturgical poetry, to be a community enactment of confession and forgiveness, the themes and rhythms of which are especially appropriate before the mystical union that the faithful soul could find regularly in the Mass liturgy.

In Hildegard's interpretation, the virgins offer the song of longing to their bridegroom, rather than the other way around. Yet, he is the song they sing, and he is present as the longed-for food that they take inside their bodies, making *Ecclesia* as they do so, making him who is *Ecclesia* as well. So he leads them on, beckoning to them — at the end of the play — when he calls them to the Cross and to the end of time. The *Ordo Virtutum* as a genre builds on the modes of praise exercised in the Office, and leads to and prepares for the sacrament as explored both through the *Scivias* and in the Office texts and the sequence discussed here.

The lush gardens of Hildegard's thought open most readily through a honeycombed multiplicity of interconnected passageways, and these different genres — liturgical commentary, Office texts, sequence text and music, and play — offer liturgical perspectives on the Mass, the Office, and the drama, this last a genre that, I would argue, serves to make a deliberate bridge from cloister, to choir, to altar. The texts define the singing of the nuns and help characterize the symphony of praise they offer, making a new love through the sacramental feast that was a climax to their lives of prayer and praise. In Hildegard's world of images, human/divine love is conditioned by a beautiful and efficient sexuality, a restored sense of longing and fulfillment that is both the means and the end of a salvific union with the divine. In order to achieve this sense in a practiced liturgy, Hildegard engages in a studied and serious "genre bending," making the familiar into the unfamiliar to craft a theological statement about singing and its importance, especially as the music is made by nuns.[33] In the *Ordo Virtutum*, the nuns had a transformed play of the Prophets to sing, one in which the female Virtues replaced the old patriarchy and became the new agents leading the faithful to God, in a language that especially suits the love life of consecrated Virgins.

33. The phrase "genre bending" was used by my colleague Harold Attridge in his presidential address to the Society of Biblical Literature, 2001. His topic was the Gospel of John, the book of the Bible that, along with Revelation (which Hildegard also believed was by John the Evangelist), was Hildegard's favored text. Genre bending is characteristic of all she does as both theologian and artist.

15. The Wisdom of Song

Steven R. Guthrie

Knowledge of the truth of God or the truth of the Gospel is not given in an abstract or detached form but in a concrete embodied form in the Church, where it is to be grasped within the normative pattern of faith imparted to it through the teaching of the apostles, and is therefore to be grasped only in unity and continuity with the faith, worship, and godly life of all who are incorporated into Christ as members of his Body.[1]

In the world Christian community today, nothing defines "brotherhood" more obviously than singing.[2]

1. Thomas F. Torrance, *The Trinitarian Faith: The Evangelical Theology of the Ancient Catholic Church,* as quoted in James J. Buckley and David S. Yeago, "A Catholic and Evangelical Theology?" in *Knowing the Triune God: The Work of the Spirit in the Practices of the Church,* ed. James J. Buckley and David S. Yeago (Grand Rapids: Eerdmans, 2001), p. 9.

2. Mark Noll, "Praise the Lord: Song, Culture, Divine Bounty and Issues of Harmonization," *Books & Culture: A Christian Review* (November-December 2007): 14.

I am grateful to the following friends, who read earlier drafts of this essay and contributed helpful comments: Jeremy Begbie, Oliver Crisp, Tim Gombis, Julie Guthrie, Bruce Hansen, Trevor Hart, and Pat Manfredi.

Singing and Knowledge

What does music contribute to corporate Christian worship? Calvin writes that singing "has the greatest value in kindling our hearts to a true zeal and eagerness to pray";[3] and this seems right. Most of us who have joined in Christian worship will have experienced the power of music to "kindle the heart" — to move and stir our emotions. Song engages us at the level of feeling and passion, and this is one of its great gifts to corporate worship.

There is potentially a "dark side" to this affirmation, however. Calvin continues in the next sentence: "Yet we should be very careful that our ears be not more attentive to the melody than our minds to the spiritual meaning of the words."

Calvin's assessment of music (at least in this passage) would seem to be not only: "singing engages the emotions"; but also: "singing engages the emotions and *not* the mind." While music "kindles the heart," it is the "meaning of the words" that is perceived by "our minds." If this is so, then Christians must use music with care. Music on this account strengthens the church's heart but not its mind. Excessive attention to "the melody" (the *music* of music, as it were) means the relative neglect of meaning.[4]

This segregation of music's service to the church continues to find currency. Some contemporary churches divide their services into a "worship time" (a time when music is played and sung) and a "teaching time" (a time when words are spoken and heard). The implication seems to be that music has to do with something other than the teaching ministry of the church. In general, while it is widely assumed that music has to do with emotion, feeling, or passion, it is rarely associated with growth in wisdom and understanding.

Early Christian writers also recognized the affective power of music, but just as often they associated music with "harmony." Music seemed to them a sounding image of rightly ordered relationships. "The importance of singing 'with one voice' was a constant refrain among the early Christian writers,"[5] writes Calvin Stapert. "Almost from the beginning music was an ex-

3. John Calvin, *Institutes of the Christian Religion,* ed. John T. McNeill, trans. Ford Lewis Battles (Philadelphia: Westminster Press, 1960), 3.20.32, p. 895.

4. Of course, this concern also reflects a deficient understanding of emotion and its relation to cognition. See Jeremy Begbie's essay in this collection, "Faithful Feelings: Music and Emotion in Worship," esp. pp. 328-31.

5. Calvin Stapert, *A New Song for an Old World: Musical Thought in the Early Church* (Grand Rapids: Eerdmans, 2007), p. 25.

pression of, a metaphor for, and a means toward unity."[6] The following passage from Ignatius of Antioch's (died c. A.D. 108) letter to the Ephesians is a good example of this association.

> In your concord and harmonious love, Jesus Christ is sung. And do ye, man by man, become a choir, that being harmonious in love, and taking up the song of God in unison, ye may with one voice sing to the Father through Jesus Christ, so that He may both hear you, and perceive by your works that ye are indeed the members of His Son. It is profitable, there-fore, that you should live in an unblameable unity, that thus ye may always enjoy communion with God.[7]

For Ignatius the harmony of believers is not simply a good organiza-tional principle, or even a right behavior to be encouraged. The existence of the church is a theological statement. When the church is a concord, then "Jesus Christ is sung" — the person and character of Jesus is declared. In fact, Ignatius is simply repeating an idea found in the "Farewell Discourse" of John's Gospel. Jesus prays that his disciples, "may all be one."

> As you, Father, are in me and I am in you, may they also be in us, so that the world may believe that you have sent me. The glory that you have given me I have given them, so that they may be one, as we are one, I in them and you in me, that they may become completely one, so that the world may know that you have sent me and have loved them even as you have loved me. (John 17:20-23)

Again, the idea is not simply that it is better to avoid conflict. Rather, Je-sus' prayer assumes that the unity of his followers will declare the glory of the Son, as well as the unity of Father and Son. The church's unity has both a doxological and a pedagogical function. Paul's metaphor for the church — the Body of Christ — suggests these same dimensions. As the "Body of Christ," the unified community of believers is *imago Christi*, a living image of Jesus Christ, the One who is himself the "image of the invisible God" (Col. 1:15).

---

6. Stapert, *A New Song*, p. 26.

7. Ignatius, *Epistle to the Ephesians*, in *The Ante-Nicene Library*, vol. 1: *The Apostolic Fathers*, ed. Alexander Roberts and James Donaldson (Edinburgh: T&T Clark, 1870), pp. 149-50. See also the discussion and quotations in James McKinnon, ed., *Music in Early Christian Literature* (Cambridge: Cambridge University Press, 1987), and Stapert, *A New Song*, pp. 25-27.

This vision of the church provides the foundation for the argument I will develop in this essay. The activity of singing, I will argue, is both an enactment and an exposition of the church's unity. Singing, we might say, is a sounding image of the unified church — which (in turn) is the image of Jesus Christ, who is the self-revelation of God. If these affirmations are valid, then we can venture the very bold claim that the singing of the church is one way by which God is made known. The church's singing does not only "kindle the heart"; it is also a means by which the church grows in wisdom and understanding of God. Music (I am arguing) strengthens not only the "heart" of the church, but its "mind" as well.

In exploring this line of argument, we will give close attention to another letter to the Ephesians — the one written by the Apostle Paul.[8] In this letter, Paul urges Christians to sing (Eph. 5:18-21). Moreover, two themes we have already mentioned — wisdom and knowledge; and the unity of the church — are also central concerns of Paul's letter. The first question we will pursue is simply: why might have Paul urged Christians to sing at this particular point in the letter? Some have suggested that in these verses Paul, like a farmer wandering his field, simply scatters handfuls of general exhortations to do good. Is this the most we can say from these references to singing? Or is there a more organic connection between this exhortation and the larger concerns of Ephesians?

Singing and the Filling of the Holy Spirit

In chapter 5 of Ephesians, Paul writes:

> Do not get drunk with wine, for that is debauchery; but be filled with the Spirit, as you sing psalms and hymns and spiritual songs among yourselves, singing and making melody to the Lord in your hearts, giving thanks to God the Father at all times and for everything in the name of our Lord Jesus Christ. Be subject to one another out of reverence for Christ.[9] (Eph. 5:18-21)

---

8. Ephesians is often identified as pseudo-Pauline, but the letter's authorship is not directly relevant to my argument. For the sake of convenience, in this essay I will refer to the author of Ephesians as Paul.

9. Unless otherwise indicated, all scriptural citations are from the New Revised Standard Version.

STEVEN R. GUTHRIE

These references to song are often treated as a throwaway comment — one good thing in a list of good things. Eric Routley has this passage in view when he observes that the New Testament has relatively little to say about music — aside from "a stray remark in two of the Epistles about the singing of hymns and spiritual songs."[10] A close reading of Ephesians, however, suggests a much richer connection between this command and the rest of the letter. This is not a stray remark.[11]

"Be Filled with the Spirit"

The references to music in Ephesians 5 are preceded by the imperative command, "be filled with the Spirit." This imperative "is not just another in a long string; rather, it is the key to all the others."[12] Indeed, this command can be seen as the culmination of the first five chapters.

Throughout the letter Paul wants to impress upon his audience their identity as "a holy temple in the Lord; in whom you also are built together spiritually into a dwelling place for God" (Eph. 2:21-22). Paul here identifies the multi-ethnic church with the temple in Jerusalem.

The temple (and before it, the tabernacle) is at the center of the Jewish universe, specifically because it is the place on earth where God makes his dwelling and manifests his glory.[13] During his ministry, Jesus shockingly identifies his own body with the temple: "'Destroy this temple, and in three days I will raise it up.' The Jews then said, 'This temple has been under construction for forty-six years, and will you raise it up in three days?' But he was speaking of the temple of his body" (John 2:19-21). Jesus, the passage suggests, is (like the Old Testament tabernacle and temple before him) the place on earth where God's presence and glory are made manifest.

Jesus' claim is startling enough, but in Ephesians Paul makes the even more remarkable claim that *the church of Jew and Gentile* is being "built together" into the dwelling of God's Holy Spirit. The people of God are now

10. Eric Routley, *Church Music and the Christian Faith* (London: Collins, 1980), p. 15. Routley is referring to this passage in Ephesians and the parallel passage in Colossians.

11. David Ford's *Self and Salvation* is an outstanding exception to the tendency to gloss over this passage. See "Communicating God's Abundance: A Singing Self," in *Self and Salvation: Being Transformed* (Cambridge: Cambridge University Press, 1999), pp. 107-36.

12. Gordon Fee, *God's Empowering Presence: The Holy Spirit in the Letters of Paul* (Peabody, MA: Hendrickson, 1994), p. 721.

13. See, for example, Exodus 19:42-43.

the temple — like the tabernacle, like Jesus — the place on earth where God's presence and glory are made manifest. The command in chapter 5 to "be filled with the Spirit," then, is not simply an exhortation to individual piety. It is a charge to be "joined together" (Eph. 5:21) as the people of God, and so, to be the temple. They are to be the dwelling place of God's glorious presence; filled — indwelt — by God's own Spirit.

At just this point Paul urges the church to sing, and he does so in a way that excludes any characterization of this injunction as a "stray remark." Singing and the filling of the Holy Spirit are bound together grammatically. Verses 19-21 comprise a single grammatical unit, controlled by the main verb, "be filled" *(plērousthe)*. This command is a passive imperative, followed by four subordinate participial clauses: (1) *speaking (lalountes)* to one another in songs, hymns, and spiritual songs; (2) *singing (adontes)* and *making music (psallontes)* in your hearts; (3) *giving thanks (eucharistountes)* to the Lord; and (4) *submitting (hypotassomenoi)* to one another.[14] These five participles are grammatically dependent upon the verb. Conversely, the participles also support the verb, giving substance and content to the command to be filled with the Spirit.[15] Structurally, we might set out the passage in the following way:

Be filled with the Spirit:
> — *speaking* to one another in songs, hymns, and spiritual songs
> — *singing*
> and
> *making music* in your hearts
> — *giving thanks* to the Lord . . .
> — *submitting* to one another . . .

Five participles elaborate the command to be filled with the Holy Spirit. Three of these have to do with music: *speaking* to one another *in songs,*

14. I have learned a great deal about recent scholarship on Ephesians through conversations with my friend Timothy Gombis (see Timothy G. Gombis, *The Divine Warrior in Ephesians* [PhD diss., University of St Andrews, 2005]). In particular, the analysis in this essay has been guided by his article, "Being the Fullness of God in Christ by the Spirit: Ephesians 5:18 in Its Epistolary Setting," *Tyndale Bulletin* 53, no. 2 (2002): 259-72.

15. There is some disagreement whether these are participles of means (i.e., "be filled with the Spirit, *by means of* . . .") or effect (i.e., "be filled with the Spirit, *which will result in* . . ."). For further discussion, see Gombis, "Being the Fullness of God in Christ by the Spirit." In either case, we can say that Paul sees a close and vital relation between being filled with the Spirit and the actions mentioned in verses 19 to 21.

hymns, and spiritual songs; singing; and *making music.* Given the importance of the filling of the Holy Spirit in the theology of this letter, it is fascinating that the author should make such a strong connection between Spirit and song. How can we account for this?

"Speaking to One Another"

One way of making sense of this passage is to read "singing" or "music" as simply another way of saying "worship." Considering this passage, one New Testament scholar observes that the filling of the Spirit "manifests itself in several ways. One is in worship."[16] This gloss absorbs the very particular command to "sing and make music" into a general exhortation to worship.[17] No doubt Paul does want his readers to worship God, but the text argues against a simple equation of "singing" with "worship." Ephesians 5:19 urges Christians to speak *to one another (lalountes heautois)* in songs, hymns, and spiritual songs. The focus of the first participial clause is not the praise of God.[18] Rather "songs, hymns, and spiritual songs" are means by which the believers are to address *one another.*

This idea emerges even more clearly in a parallel passage:[19]

Let the word of Christ dwell in you richly in all wisdom; *teaching and admonishing one another in psalms and hymns and spiritual songs,* singing with grace in your hearts to the Lord. (Col. 3:16, Authorized Version)[20]

16. Arthur G. Patzia, *Ephesians, Colossians, Philemon,* New International Biblical Commentary, vol. 10 (Peabody, MA: Hendrickson, 1984), p. 264.

17. This same substitution crops up in some churches where "the time of worship" comes to mean "the portion of the service that includes music."

18. Andrew Lincoln observes this point. See Andrew T. Lincoln, *Ephesians,* Word Bible Commentary (Dallas: Word Books, 1990), p. 345.

19. However one dates the letters and whether or not one attributes Ephesians to the apostle Paul, there clearly are relationships of dependence between Ephesians and the letter to the Colossians. One instance of this is Ephesians 5:18/Colossians 3:16.

20. Here the Authorized Version follows the sense of the original more closely than some modern translations. So for instance, the NIV groups "teaching" and "admonishing" with "wisdom," separating "singing" into a separate clause: "Let the word of Christ dwell in you richly as you teach and admonish one another with all wisdom and as you sing psalms, hymns and spiritual songs." This organization is driven less by the syntax of the original than it is by a twentieth-century sense of what activities can legitimately be considered means of teaching and admonishing. See the discussion in Fee, *God's Empowering Presence,* p. 652.

Commenting on this passage, Gordon Fee observes that the singing and worship of the early church was "two dimensional" — addressed both to God and to one another; meant for both the "worship of [Christ] and for the continuing instruction of God's people."[21]

Singing toward Wisdom

There is then a didactic, pedagogical character to New Testament song. If this is the case, then Paul's commendation of song is connected to one of the other principal concerns of the letter: wisdom.

Ephesians depicts the spiritual life in cosmic dimensions, contrasting those who are children of light with those who belong to darkness. The darkness that once enshrouded the children of light was (among other things) the darkness of ignorance. So Paul urges them to "no longer live as the Gentiles live, in the *futility of their minds*" (Eph. 4:17).

> They are darkened in their *understanding,* alienated from the life of God because of their *ignorance* and hardness of heart. (Eph. 4:18)

The children of light on the other hand "have *learned* Christ" (Eph. 4:20). You "were *taught* in him, as truth is in Jesus," Paul continues in verse 21. Therefore Christians should no longer be "deluded" by the lusts of the old self (v. 22), but rather "renewed in the spirit of your *minds*." As people of truth, who have turned from delusion, we should "[put] away *falsehood*," and "speak the *truth* to our neighbors" (v. 25).

The language of wisdom, knowledge, and truth continues through chapter 5. Those in the light should "let no one deceive [them] with empty words" (Eph. 5:6). Since "the fruit of the light is found in all that is good and right and true" they should "try to find out what is pleasing to the Lord" (v. 9). They should live, not as the unwise, but as the wise *(sophoi)* (v. 15). Nor should they be foolish, but rather they should

> *understand* what the will of the Lord is. Do not get drunk with wine, for that is debauchery; but be filled with the Spirit, as you sing psalms and hymns and spiritual songs among yourselves. (vv. 17-19)

---

21. Fee, *God's Empowering Presence,* p. 656; see also p. 653 n. 68, and Stapert, *A New Song,* pp. 21-22.

In their epistolary context, the songs, hymns, and spiritual songs of verse 19 are connected with the long string of commands found in chapters 4 and 5: to learn the truth, to be wise, to know what is right. Paul says in effect:

— *Put away ignorance . . .*
— *Let no one deceive you . . .*
— *Know the truth . . .*
— *Be wise . . .*
— *Sing!*

If singing is a means of teaching and admonishing, that the Christian may attain wisdom (Col. 3:16), then we can also better understand why song should be linked so strongly with the filling of the Spirit. Paul urges Christians to be people of wisdom and knowledge, and in the theology of Ephesians it is the Holy Spirit who is particularly associated with giving knowledge and understanding, and revealing the wisdom of God.[22]

The command to be filled with the Holy Spirit (Eph. 5:18) is also a command to be filled with the wisdom and understanding that come from the Spirit. And the singing of the church — speaking to one another, admonishing and teaching one another, in songs, hymns, and spiritual songs — is one means by which the Spirit reveals the wisdom of God.

The New Human

Another important theme in Ephesians is the unity of the church. In fact, there is an organic connection between this theme and that of wisdom. The multi-ethnic church of Jesus Christ in all its diverse unity *is* the "wisdom of God" revealed by the Spirit. Paul describes the ethnically and socially diverse church as "the mystery hidden for ages" (Eph. 3:9), "the mystery . . . made known to me by revelation" (Eph. 3:3).

The creation of this community is no secondary benefit of God's redemptive work. Rather, "this was in accordance with the eternal purpose

22. Fee observes that in Pauline theology generally, "wisdom and revelation in the ongoing life of the believing community are expressly associated with the Spirit. In 1 Corinthians in particular wisdom is one of the Spirit's charismata (12:8), and the Spirit is the means of revelation whereby believers come to understand the wisdom that lies in the folly of the cross (2:10-13). . . . In Ephesians the Spirit is explicitly noted as the source of the revelation of God's mystery (3:5), which Paul wants his recipients also to understand" (Fee, *God's Empowering Presence,* p. 676).

that he has carried out in Christ Jesus our Lord" (Eph. 3:11). The cross of Christ has brought together Jew and Gentile, abolishing the hostility that existed, not only between them and God, but between one another. This reconciled community is nothing less than a New Humanity:

> For he is our peace; in his flesh he has made both groups into one and has broken down the dividing wall, that is, the hostility between us. He has abolished the law with its commandments and ordinances, that he might create in himself one new humanity *(hena kainon anthrōpon)* in place of the two, thus making peace, and might reconcile both groups to God in one body through the cross, thus putting to death that hostility through it. (Eph. 2:14-16)

God, "who created *(ktisanti)* all things" (Eph. 3:9) has now created *(ktisē)* a New Human (2:15). This "new self" is "created *(ktisthenta) according to the likeness of God*" (4:23).

These gestures toward the Genesis creation account reveal the horizon against which Paul understands the church. God's eternal purpose has been to create the kind of community — to create the kind of humanity — made manifest in the church. In Christ and through the church, God is re-creating humanity in his image.

"Created According to the Likeness of God"

Ephesians 3 and 4 echo the beginning of the biblical story, where God creates the Human Being in his image and according to his likeness.

> Then God said, "Let us make humankind in our image, according to our likeness; and let them have dominion over the fish of the sea, and over the birds of the air, and over the cattle, and over all the wild animals of the earth, and over every creeping thing that creeps upon the earth." So God created humankind in his image, in the image of God he created them; male and female he created them. (Gen. 1:26-27)

The *imago Dei* has been variously understood by the theological tradition and has been associated with everything from the capacity for reason to an upright posture.[23] Whatever else it may mean to say human beings are

---

23. See the discussion in Jürgen Moltmann, *God in Creation: An Ecological Doctrine of*

created in God's image, the passage itself seems to connect "image and likeness" with humanity's role as God's representative among the created order.[24] In an ancient society the one who bears the king's image (on a seal, for instance, or a signet ring) carries his authority, relays his commands, and acts on his behalf. In Genesis 1 then, God invites humanity to share in the care and administration of his creation, to act as his representative.

As the bearer of God's image, humanity also declares God's wisdom and glory to the created order. If "the heavens declare the glory of God" (Ps. 19:1), then how much more clearly is God's glory announced by those made according to his likeness? "Human beings are created as the image of God for the divine glory," writes Moltmann. "They themselves are God's glory in the world."[25] Taking these two points together, we may say that there is a didactic or pedagogical dimension to the *imago Dei*. Humanity is created to manifest — to declare, make plain, and enact — the purposes and glory of God.

In addition to this, the passage in Genesis suggests that this "likeness" to God is not simply an individual endowment or capacity. Rather, there is a sense in which *the human community* bears the image of God: "Let Us make man in Our image, according to Our likeness," reads the Genesis account, "and let *them* rule. . . . So God created man in His own image, in the image of God He created him; *male and female He created them*."[26] It is as male and female — as a community of persons in relationship — that humanity is the image of God.[27] "Human beings are *imago trinitatis*" writes

Creation, The Gifford Lectures 1984-1985 (London: SCM, 1985), pp. 219-25; and in Gordon J. Wenham, *Genesis 1–15*, Word Biblical Commentary (Waco, TX: Word, 1987), pp. 29-32.

24. See, for instance, Walter Brueggemann, *An Introduction to the Old Testament: The Canon and Christian Imagination* (Louisville: Westminster John Knox, 2003), pp. 34-35; Wenham, *Genesis*, p. 32.

25. Moltmann, *God in Creation*, p. 228.

26. Moltmann reads Genesis 1 through the lens of trinitarian theology: "These shifts between singular and plural at this particular point are important: 'Let *us* make human beings — *an* image that is like *us*.' That is to say, the image of God (singular) is supposed to correspond to the 'internal' plural of God, and yet be a *single* image. In the next verse the singular and plural are distributed in the opposite way: God (singular) created the human being (singular), as man and woman (plural) he created them (plural). Here the human plural is supposed to correspond to the divine singular. Whereas the self-resolving God is a plural in the singular, his image on earth — the human being — is apparently supposed to be a singular in the plural. The one God, who is differentiated in himself and is at one with himself, then finds his correspondence in a community of human beings, female and male, who unite with one another and are one" (Moltmann, *God in Creation*, pp. 217-18).

27. "The 'sacred story' begins with God's eternal purpose for man. . . . His eternal purpose was that mankind should be 'one body,' with the unity of a perfect organism: a higher

Moltmann, "and only correspond to the triune God when they are united with one another."[28]

If our likeness to God is not just individual but communal *(in his image — male and female he created them)* then the divisions and hatred among humanity are nothing less than a destruction of the image of God. One part of humanity lashes out against another and in so doing destroys and continues to destroy God's image.[29] This is the pattern of sin that unfolds across the early chapters of Genesis. In the Garden, Adam and Eve recognize one another as "bone of my bones and flesh of my flesh." The last words from an unspoiled Eden are: "the man and his wife were both naked, and were not shamed" (Gen. 2:25). After the fall, however, Adam defends himself by ac - cusing Eve (3:12). Cain — the first Man born of Man and Woman — raises his hand to kill his brother (4:1-16). Genesis 4 lists the seven generations from Adam to Lamech, and then records Lamech's words to his wives: "I have killed a man for wounding me, a young man for striking me. If Cain is avenged sevenfold, truly Lamech seventy-sevenfold" (4:23-24). In seven generations a sevenfold vengeance has increased to seventy-sevenfold. The growing wickedness of humanity is expressed in terms of an exponential increase in violence and division. God looks at the human beings he has created and is grieved. He determines to send a great flood specifically because "the earth is filled with violence."

> Now the earth was corrupt in God's sight, and *the earth was filled with violence.* And God saw that the earth was corrupt; for all flesh had corrupted its ways upon the earth. And God said to Noah, "I have determined to make an end of all flesh, for *the earth is filled with violence because of them;* now I am going to destroy them along with the earth." (6:11-13)

One of the characteristic marks of sin in the early chapters of Genesis, then, is the loss of peace and human community. Rather than showing forth God's image as his representative, fallen humanity has *mis*represented God.

---

kind of organism, indeed than any that we know . . . a free and harmonious fellowship of persons united in the love of God. . . . That is God's plan for mankind: that it should be 'one body'" (D. M. Baillie, *God Was in Christ: An Essay on Incarnation and Atonement* [London: Faber and Faber, 1948], p. 203).

28. Moltmann, *God in Creation*, p. 216.

29. "But something has gone wrong. The organism has somehow failed to function as one body. It has come to be divided into countless little bits of life, each person trying to be a quite independent cell, a self-sufficient atom" (Baillie, *God Was in Christ*, pp. 203-4).

Rather than reflecting the glory of Father, Son, and Holy Spirit in eternal community, humanity has defiled God's image through the destruction of community.

The Revelation of a Harmonized Humanity

This is why Paul finds such cosmic significance in the multi-ethnic church. From Jew and Gentile God has made a New Human Being, created in the likeness of God. This restored image is, as God intended, a declaration of his character and glory. Paul writes that

> this grace was given to me to bring to the Gentiles the news of the boundless riches of Christ, and to make everyone see what is the plan of the mystery hidden for ages in God who created all things; *so that through the church the wisdom of God in its rich variety might now be made known* to the rulers and authorities in the heavenly places. (Eph. 3:8-10)

The church enters into lived experience of this New Humanity as it "puts on" Christ.[30] Jesus is the perfect image of God — "the exact representation of his being" (Heb. 1:3). In Jesus, the invisible God is made known (John 1:18). The church, in turn, is remade in the image of the perfect humanity of Christ. Just as Christ is the image of the invisible God (Col. 1:15) and "the radiance of God's glory" (Heb. 1:3), so the church, Christ's body, is restored to humanity's rightful role as God's image-bearer and the declaration of his glory.[31]

30. "You were taught, with regard to your former way of life, to put off your old self, which is being corrupted by its deceitful desires . . . and to put on the new self, created to be like God in true righteousness and holiness" (Eph. 4:22, 24). Cf. Colossians 3:9-10: "Do not lie to each other, since you have taken off your old self with its practices and have put on the new self, which is being renewed in knowledge in the image of its Creator."

31. In his commentary on Genesis Walter Brueggemann draws out these connections between (a) humanity created in the image of God; (b) Jesus Christ as the perfect image and likeness of God; and (c) the church as the body of Christ, in which God is at work recreating the image. "In Jesus Christ, we are offered a new discernment of who God is and of who humankind is called to be. . . . And as Jesus models a new disclosure of God, so he embodies *a call for a new human community.* Paul urges an abandonment of the old life for an embrace of the new: 'Put off your old nature which belongs to your former manner of life and is corrupt through deceitful lusts, . . . put on the new nature created after the *likeness of God* in true righteousness and holiness' (Eph. 4:22-24). The idea of the 'image of God' in Gen. 1:26-29 and in Jesus of Nazareth is not an idea which lives in a cosmological vacuum. It

There is in fact a reciprocal relationship between our two themes of (1) wisdom and understanding; and (2) the unity of the church. On the one hand, wisdom and understanding lead to community. As "pastors and teachers . . . equip the saints" those saints "come to the unity of the faith and of the knowledge of the Son of God" (Eph. 4:11-13). As the love of God and the self-giving of Christ are revealed, believers come to understand the love they are to show one another.[32]

On the other hand, the unity of the church is itself a "theological statement" — a declaration of the wisdom and purposes of God (Eph. 3:8-10). The church of Jew and Gentile bears the likeness of God, and as image-bearer, represents God to the created order. As the socially and ethnically diverse church is "built up in love" (4:13) it shows forth the shape of the triune life — a community of self-giving love and differentiated unity.

The Voice of the Body

To this point we have identified two of the central themes in Ephesians — and wisdom and understanding; the unity of the church. We have also seen that the command to sing is bound up with these themes. Since (as we acknowledged at the outset) singing is not often in our culture paired with "wisdom" or "understanding," before going on we may need to make clear just what is meant by these terms. What might it mean to say that singing contributes to the wisdom and understanding of the church?

The wisdom and understanding we are describing here is a deepened awareness that may or may not become fully (verbally) articulate; an awareness that arises from *sharing in the practices of the community.* It is what Susan Wood refers to as "participatory knowledge" (a knowledge which she in turn likens to Polanyi's "tacit knowledge"). She writes:

> Our participation in the liturgy gives us access to a certain kind of knowledge of God, which I am identifying as participatory knowledge. This

---

is an explicit call to form a kind of human community in which the members, after the manner of the gracious God, are attentive in calling each other to full being in fellowship" (Walter Brueggemann, *Genesis,* Interpretation: A Bible Commentary for Teaching and Preaching [Louisville: Westminster John Knox, 1982], pp. 34-35; emphasis in original).

32. "Put away from you all bitterness and wrath and anger and wrangling and slander, together with all malice, and be kind to one another, tenderhearted, forgiving one another, as God in Christ has forgiven you" (Eph. 4:31-32).

knowledge is mediated through the symbol system of the liturgy, including the scriptures, liturgical actions, sacraments and prayers.[33]

In song, we share in the life and activity of the church. We learn — we come to *know* — its ways, not by having these articulated for us verbally and conceptually, but by participating in them. We come to a lived and (we might say) a kinesthetic understanding of what the church *is*, by taking part in what the church *does*. Wood employs a famous example from Polanyi to illustrate this point:

> We learn what balance feels like by riding a bicycle rather than listening to explanations. By being fed, by hearing the words of forgiveness, by being caught up in the paschal events of the death and resurrection liturgically made present, we learn God's sustaining, self-diffusive love. By entering into praise and thanksgiving we know who we are in relationship to God and God's sovereignty. Within the liturgy we come to know ourselves and God because the liturgy orders our relationships: my relationship to others within the body of Christ sacramentally constituted within the Eucharist, my relationship to God as recipient of God's graciousness.[34]

This is not to deny that there is cognitive content to the Christian gospel. Knowledge of God can be expressed verbally and conceptually: *we believe in God the Father almighty, maker of heaven and earth.* And yet, this knowledge of God is received and can only be properly understood within the setting of the life and practices of the church.[35] The "core practices" of the church — including the activities of prayer, reading Scripture, sharing in the Lord's Supper, and singing — are the means by which the Holy Spirit mediates knowledge of God.[36] By sharing in these practices members of the Body are instructed in the shape, trajectory, and cadence of the church's common life. The participatory knowledge gained may shape future behav-

33. Susan K. Wood, "Participatory Knowledge of God in the Liturgy," in *Knowing the Triune God,* ed. Buckley and Yeago, p. 95.

34. Wood, "Participatory Knowledge," p. 96.

35. "Knowing is articulated in teaching, and in teachings about teachings. But to revise Austin Farrer's proverb, we cannot know that which we can *only* know. Knowing is an ingredient of our dealings with things — and, in this sense, an ingredient of our practices. The Church can state its faith, but what Christians say about the triune God cannot be adequately explicated without reference to what Christians most characteristically *do* in worship and obedience to that God" (Buckley and Yeago, "A Catholic and Evangelical Theology?" p. 9).

36. See especially Reinhold Hütter, "The Church: The Knowledge of the Triune God: Practices, Doctrine, Theology," in *Knowing the Triune God,* ed. Buckley and Yeago, pp. 23-47.

ior and *action*. As I speak with the church, I learn how the church and its members speak. This participatory knowledge also conditions the way in which the words and actions of the church are *received*. Through the teaching ministry of the church, we learn that God is Holy, and that we should come before him in reverence (to take one example). Through the liturgy of the church however, we learn the *enacted content* of "reverence." In song and prayer and public reading of Scripture we come to know the meaning of reverence by indwelling it; we come to know its posture and intonation. We might say that singing (along with the other core practices of the church) provides the prosody of the church's proclamation.

Returning to Ephesians, in Paul's letter a certain kind of unity is described and articulated. Congregational singing in turn allows us to *indwell* the unity that Ephesians *describes*. Singing does this by enacting that unity and modeling some of its most distinctive aspects.

An Enactment

Singing is an enactment of the differentiated unity of the body of Christ. It is the Voice of the New Humanity — One Voice composed of many voices; the "one new humanity out of the two" (Eph. 2:15). As Jew and Gentile sing together they sound out the reality of the new person fashioned in Christ. The restored image of God is made sensible, manifest in time — and that is important. An image is fashioned to be displayed and perceived. In the same way, the unity of the church — the restored image — is to be a declaration (Eph. 3:8-10). The singing of the church embodies and declares the New Humanity.

Of course, the power of song to embody community is not limited to the *Christian* community. Anthropologists, psychologists, and sociologists have drawn attention to the way in which across human history "joint music-making [has] served to facilitate cooperative behaviour by advertising one's willingness to cooperate, and by creating shared emotional states."[37] William McNeill argues that singing together leads to the experi-

---

37. Steven Mithen, *The Singing Neanderthals: The Origins of Music, Language, Mind, and Body* (Cambridge, MA: Harvard University Press, 2006), p. 218. The chapter from which this quotation is taken ("Making Music Together") is a helpful summary of recent research in the area. See also John Blacking, *How Musical Is Man?* (Seattle: University of Washington Press, 1973); Tia DeNora, *Music in Everyday Life* (Cambridge: Cambridge University Press, 2000), esp. pp. 109-63; and David J. Hargreaves and Adrian C. North, eds., *The Social Psychology of Music* (Oxford: Oxford University Press, 1997).

ence of "boundary loss" — "a blurring of self-awareness and the heightening of fellow feeling with all who share in a dance."[38] "This is the process," says Steven Mithen, "in which football crowds, church choirs and children in the playground are all engaging."[39]

What was unique about the New Testament church, then, was not that it was a group of people experiencing community, nor that this community manifested itself in song. What was extraordinary was those among whom the "boundaries" were being crossed and which parties were experiencing "fellow feeling." In its congregational song one would have been able to *hear* the gathered church of Jew and Gentile — with all of its various regional accents, all the distinctive pronunciations of aristocrats, slaves, and free people; male and female voices, voices of young and old — all of these perceived at once in a single melody. This congregational song is not a *metaphor* of the socially and ethnically diverse church. It *is* this gathered body; or at least, this body's voice, this body made audible. The church's song is one way that the church and the Spirit announce this unity — to one another and to the wider world. It is one way that the Spirit reveals this community to its members, and continues to call its members to community. The members of the chorus literally participate in the one Body that is created out of many bodies. As they do, they *instruct* one another, saying: "Listen: this is the body of Christ — a chorus of Jew and Gentile, slave and free. Listen: this is the Image of God — a melody sung by male and female, impoverished and wealthy. Listen: this is the kind of life Christ brings — a harmony resonating through the bodies of these brothers and sisters, so lately aliens and enemies."

In addition to enacting the church's unity (something which other shared activities also do), singing also manifests the *distinctive shape* of the church's unity. I will mention three aspects of this shared life that one may hear elaborated in music.

Differentiated Unity

In the Garden God created Humanity, male and female, in his own image. The two are created out of one,[40] yet without loss of unity. In Jesus Christ, God creates a New Humanity, in his own image. The one is created out of

---

38. Mithen, *Singing Neanderthals*, p. 209.
39. Mithen, *Singing Neanderthals*, p. 215.
40. Cf. Genesis 2:21-24.

two (Jew and Gentile)[41] yet without loss of distinction. Both the first Humanity and the New Humanity, then, are a unity that maintains the distinctiveness of its members.

"[Make] every effort to maintain the unity of the Spirit in the bond of peace," writes Paul. For "there is one body and one Spirit" (Eph. 4:3-4). This unity, however, is facilitated through the very diversity of the body and its varied gifts: "The gifts he gave were that some would be apostles, some prophets, some evangelists, some pastors and teachers" (4:11). The New Human Being is no monolithic Unity. Rather, in Christ, many disparate, competing voices are drawn into consonance through the Spirit's ingenious work of reharmonization. "Spirit," writes Colin Gunton, "is that which, far from abolishing, rather maintains and even strengthens particularity. It is not a spirit of merging or assimilation — of homogenization — but of relation in otherness, relation which does not subvert but establishes the other in its true reality."[42]

Music provides a compelling sounding image of this differentiated unity and unified diversity. When we sing together we hear *"simultaneous voices which are nevertheless also one voice."*[43] We might say equally: when we sing together we hear one voice which is nevertheless the voice of many. Miroslav Volf argues that a truly trinitarian ecclesiology will affirm both person and community. The self in Christian community therefore "is a self that is always 'inhabited' or 'indwelled' by others."[44] Music, it would seem, is equipped to make sensible — as few other activities can — a self that is "'inhabited' or 'indwelled' by others." When I sing among others, I hear a voice that is both mine and not mine; a voice that is both in and outside of me. I hear my voice and your voice — and this third thing — our voices together: a sound which has properties which belong neither to your voice nor to my voice alone, but one that is nevertheless shaped and takes its substance from the individual voices comprising it.

Freedom in Submission

We have already seen that the command "be filled with the Holy Spirit" is joined to five dependent participles. The first three have to do with singing

41. Cf. Ephesians 2:15.

42. Colin E. Gunton, *The One, the Three and the Many: God, Creation and the Culture of Modernity* (Cambridge: Cambridge University Press, 1993), p. 182.

43. Roger Scruton, *The Aesthetics of Music* (Oxford: Clarendon Press, 1997), p. 339.

44. Miroslav Volf, *After Our Likeness: The Church as the Image of the Trinity* (Grand Rapids: Eerdmans, 1997), p. 3.

and making music. The fifth and last is "submitting to one another out of
reverence for Christ" (Eph. 5:21). The section that follows (5:22–6:9) considers how this "submitting to one another" is to work itself out — in relationships between wives and husbands, parents and children, slaves and masters.[45] We should not miss the fact, however, that *singing* to one another, *giving thanks* to God, and *submitting* to one another are all part of *the same
command.* All of these together fill out the dimensions of the imperative "be
filled with the Spirit."[46] Singing and mutual submission, then, are two parallel manifestations of the New Humanity in Christ.[47] Those who are filled
with the Spirit both sing to one another *(lalountes heautois psalmois)* and
submit to one another *(hupotassomenoi allēlois),*[48] and — marvelously — in
the grammatical structure of the passage "submitting to one another" is informed and conditioned by "singing to one another." What a difference it
might make if we were to take *music* as the model of "mutual submission"
between husbands, wives, parents, children, slaves, and masters; if song were
the school we attended to learn this kind of submission! Music immerses us
in the event of mutual submission and so helps us to learn the submission
Paul describes.

What kind of mutual submission happens in song? For one thing, singing words together involves *synchronicity* — staying in time with one an-

45. Paul urges the Christians "to be filled with the Spirit (v. 18) . . . they need to be full
of the Spirit for their corporate worship (vv. 19-20) . . . [and] they need to be full of the Spirit
in order to maintain the 'unity of the Spirit' in their several relationships in a believing
household (v. 21), which are then spelled out in detail in 5:22–6:9" (Fee, *God's Empowering
Presence,* p. 719).

46. "All of verses 19-21 take the form of a series of participles that modify the primary
imperative in verse 18" (Fee, *God's Empowering Presence,* p. 719).

47. See, for example, Ephesians 5:28-32, in which the marriage relationship enacts the
New Humanity: "In this same way, husbands ought to love their wives as their own bodies.
He who loves his wife loves himself. After all, no one ever hated his own body, but he feeds
and cares for it, just as Christ does the church — for we are members of his body. 'For this
reason a man will leave his father and mother and be united to his wife, and the two will become one flesh.' This is a profound mystery — but I am talking about Christ and the
church."

48. Unfortunately verse 21 is often treated as the point at which Paul concludes the preceding material and turns to a new theme. The New International Version along with some
other modern translations actually breaks up the five participles that are grammatically dependent on verse 17, and inserts a paragraph break after verse 20: "Instead be filled with the
Spirit. 18. Speak to one another with psalms, hymns and spiritual songs. 19. Sing and make
music in your heart to the Lord, 20. always giving thanks to God the Father for everything in
the name of our Lord Jesus Christ 21. Submit to one another out of reverence for Christ."

other. The singers submit themselves to a common tempo, a common musical structure and rhythm. In addition to this, those who sing surrender to the constraints of a particular melody and harmony, a common key and tonal hierarchy. As they submit in this way they discover limits that are not oppressive; limits that do not frustrate but facilitate the participants' intention to sing. If this mutual submission entails the loss of one sort of freedom (the freedom to sing whatever notes one wants, in whatever way one chooses), it also enables freedom of another sort — the freedom to sing *this* tune; the freedom to be part of a chorus.

Musical submission also involves genuine participation. It is not and cannot be the silencing of a weaker by a dominant voice. The chorus is a society whose life depends upon its members contributing their voices. In a multi-voiced harmony, privileging some voices and excluding others does not mean that the louder voices "win." Rather, the harmony as a whole fails. The chorus depends on its members (acoustically) "making room" for other voices, allowing the other voices in the choir to sound out. Nor can the submission be imposed on the group by some of its members. If one voice persistently "enforces the rules" — insisting upon a particular tempo by drowning out the others, for instance — the chorus then ceases to be a chorus, the music suffers and ensemble is lost.[49]

In song, then, we learn about a kind of mutual submission in which we do not lose, but discover our voices. This is a submission that is creative; which does not eliminate but opens up possibilities. Moreover, music manifests a mutual submission that is winsome and appealing, rather than dull, oppressive, and burdensome.

Sensitivity to and Awareness of Others

Finally, and perhaps most obviously, music may help us to understand what it means to listen and respond to others. Roger Scruton contends that hearing music *as* music means moving in "a dance of sympathy" with the imag-

---

49. In any chorus, as in the body of Christ, "different gifts are apportioned to each." It may well be that one or more among those singing (a singer with a better ear or a stronger voice) will take the lead — in securing pitch, dynamics, tempo, and so on. (Many of us, when singing in a choir, will have been grateful for the more accomplished, more experienced singer nearby — discretely piping out the correct note, or with her finger underlining the appropriate place in the score!) The point is simply that if this "leading out" obliterates the others, if there is no blend of voices, then the chorus is not musically successful.

ined life in the sounds, hearing a series of musical tones as gesture and movement in phenomenal space. "In responding to a piece of music," he writes, "we are being led through a series of gestures which gain their significance from the intimation of community."[50] And again, "through melody, harmony, and rhythm, we enter a world where others exist besides the self."[51] The American philosopher Kathleen Higgins advances a similar idea, maintaining that "musical hearing . . . makes us aware of the world as a place of encounter and interaction between what is within and what is outside us."[52] If the character of sin is that it is *incurvatus se* — turned in upon itself — then living as children of light means precisely becoming aware of "a world where others exist besides the self."

Paul writes that those in darkness are characterized — ironically — by both sensuality and a lack of sensitivity. They are separated from God and lost in ignorance *"because of the hardness of their heart"* (Eph. 4:18, NASB). "They have lost all sensitivity" he continues, "and have abandoned themselves to licentiousness" (Eph. 4:19). *Young's Literal Translation* renders the verse: "who, *having ceased to feel,* themselves did give up to lasciviousness."[53] Fee observes that in the chapters of Ephesians that follow, "most of the sins mentioned express the self-centeredness that contradicts love and disrupts the unity of the body."[54] Those in darkness attend and respond to only their own desires: "gratifying the cravings of [their] sinful nature and following its desires and thoughts" (Eph. 2:3, NIV).

At the most basic level singing together reminds us that there are others in the room, that the people seated to my right and to my left have voices. In song I participate in the experience of using my voice alongside and in concert with the voices of others. We have all attended musical performances where one poor soul in the choir makes the shift from fortissimo to pianissimo — one note too late. When singing in a group we instinctively avoid such embarrassing moments. If the others in the room are singing softly and slowly, I do as well. Unremarkable though this may seem, in these instances we *indwell* a kind of sensitivity and responsiveness to others. We gain experience in hearing one another; we learn to move in "a dance of sympathy" with those around us. And if we have ears to hear, we are reminded that the

50. Scruton, *Aesthetics of Music,* p. 357.

51. Scruton, *Aesthetics of Music,* p. 502.

52. Kathleen Marie Higgins, *The Music of Our Lives* (Philadelphia: Temple University Press, 1991), pp. 33-34.

53. The original reads: *hoitines apēlgēkotes heautous paredōkan tē aselgeia.*

54. Fee, *God's Empowering Presence,* p. 709.

New Humanity in Christ includes voices other than our own — voices of different quality, timbre, and register to which we must tune our own song.

All of this, I have suggested, we may learn *in the act of singing.* The singers may or may not be able to articulate these lessons fully, but they are realities learned (I have argued) through being indwelt. But we can say more: the church may grow in wisdom and understanding not only *in* the act of singing, but through deliberate and discursive *reflection on* the act of singing — the sort of reflection we are engaged in now, in this essay. Music provides an experience of unity; a participatory knowledge of unity; and also, conceptual resources that allow us more fully to appreciate and articulate that unity.

Back to the Choir Loft

Do these descriptions of music bear any meaningful relation to our actual experience of church music? While acknowledging the importance of the church's unity, we still may feel as if there is some distance between this talk of music as a "sounding image of the New Humanity" and the more mundane — and potentially contentious — world of choir rehearsals, music committees, and choosing music for Sunday morning. Does the preceding conversation really "touch down" in the world of the contemporary church's musical practice?

Which Music?

We might ask, for instance: *what kind of music are we talking about?* Does each and every possible instance of "music" potentially embody the unity of the church and lead it toward wisdom? Christian rap and Palestrina; Fanny Crosby's revival hymns and urban gospel choirs; the *St. Matthew Passion,* Southern Harmony "square-note" singing, and contemporary "lite-rock" worship teams — do all of these sound out the mystery of the church with equal fidelity? Or does Paul have some specific sort of music in mind?

We can venture a few broad statements. The music Paul refers to is vocal and communal. The command to speak "to one another" in song also suggests that the participants could hear one another. It also seems apparent that the songs Paul commends reflect the teaching of the church. We cannot go too far beyond this, nor do we need to — the ideas we have developed to this point would apply to nearly any form of communal singing.

The little we know about the liturgy of the early church suggests that the singing of the earliest Christians would most likely have been simple, unaccompanied, unison singing and chanting.[55] It may be that the hymnody of the modern church with its multi-voiced harmonies is even better suited to communicating the "unified diversity" of the church. And it may be that there are some types of music that express this less well, but have other gifts to bring to corporate worship.

But another, even more pointed question may come to mind.

What Unity?

Over the last twenty-five years churches in North America have waged countless battles, skirmishes, congregational revolts, and clerical counterattacks over the practice of music — hostile engagements that are often collectively described as "The Worship Wars." Anyone who has ever directed a choir, served on a music committee, or played in a worship band (or even made the mistake of asking at Sunday dinner: "What did you think of the music at this morning's service?") will be forgiven for reading the last several pages with a wry smile. Music seems to split churches more often than it unifies them. It is also not difficult to think of counter-examples — instances in which excellent choral music is generated by thoughtless, mean-spirited people. Where then is this "sounding enactment of unity" we have been describing?

(1) In response, we might note that the same complaint might be made about many if not all of the practices of the church. Preaching, the reading of Scripture, the sacraments — all of these are good gifts given to the church for its life and health; none of these infallibly bring about the good for which they are intended. The Lord's Supper is meant to embody the unity of the church,[56] but has also been the source of disunity, debates, and divisions.[57] Such failures simply bear witness to the sad but uncontroversial truth that humanity is able to misuse God's good gifts. That music should be the source of discord is sadly ironic, but this is not an irony unique to music.

55. See the discussion in Jeremy Begbie, *Resounding Truth* (Grand Rapids: Baker Academic, 2007), pp. 73-74.

56. Cf. 1 Corinthians 10:17: "Because there is one bread, we who are many are one body, for we all partake of the one bread."

57. In fact, it was a source of division in the Corinthian church to whom Paul wrote concerning "one loaf" and "one body." See 1 Corinthians 11:17-22.

The sexual union of husband and wife *really is* an enactment of their unity. Is it possible for sexual intercourse to continue where there is no love or unity? Of course. Do these instances negate the reality of the union that is embodied in healthy sexual relationships? Absolutely not. In the same way, we may acknowledge that music often causes divisions in the church without calling into question its power to embody Christian unity.

The church's singing, like its teaching and preaching, calls men and women to live differently. And, as with the teaching and preaching of the church, some respond to this call, while others disregard it.

(2) The very disagreements we are considering should also serve as a reminder that it is not music which creates the church, or which transforms individuals into the likeness of Christ. It is God's Spirit. I have suggested some of the reasons why music is a powerful means through which God's Spirit may enact his purposes for the church. But we should not make the mistake of thinking that music itself exercises some sort of magical power — as if the Kingdom will come if only our choir is sufficiently rehearsed or our worship band sufficiently polished. In some instances, the singing of the church may act as a testimony against its own behavior.

(3) It is also worth mentioning that most of the "music wars" are battles *about* music, not battles *in the midst of* music. I grew up singing nineteenth-century revival hymns in church, many of which had little appeal for me musically. Nevertheless, the experience of singing them gave me a powerful sense of belonging in that community. When I remember the church I grew up in, I remember first of all Sunday night "Song and Testimony" services. Those evenings spent singing together expressed more clearly than anything else the warmth, sincerity, and mutual commitment of that Christian community; and I became aware of the church's unity and identity as a result of sharing in the songs. This happened, again, even though I didn't care much for the songs musically. In a similar sort of way, I have on more than one occasion watched a choir under my direction develop a sense of camaraderie and unity, while learning a piece they dislike. The point is simply that the experience of *shared song* is not the same thing as *shared musical tastes* or *a shared aesthetic*.

Tuning the Music Committee: A Report from the Field

Ambrose, the fourth-century bishop of Milan, knew the wisdom of song we have been describing. He wrote:

STEVEN R. GUTHRIE

[A psalm is] a pledge of peace and harmony, which produces one song from various and sundry voices in the manner of a cithara. . . .

A psalm joins those with differences, unites those at odds and reconciles those who have been offended, for who will not concede to him with whom one sings to God in one voice? It is after all a great bond of unity for the full number of people to join in one chorus. The strings of the cithara differ, but create one harmony.[58]

Does this ever happen? Does a psalm ever "join those with differences, unite those at odds and reconcile those who have been offended"? I can relate at least one such instance.

For several years I worked as a minister of music, serving on the pastoral staff of various churches. One of these churches in particular struggled through a series of contentious disagreements about music. There were disputes about musical style, about the place of music within the services of the church, and (especially) about which people were and were not being used in the music ministry. Generals and armies had been recruited and armed, and trenches had been dug. I chaired a music committee composed of members of the different factions, and sat through week after week of tense, irritable, and unproductive meetings.

One week — feeling as if I had nothing to lose — I suggested that we begin our meeting by singing a couple of hymns together, *a cappella*. We had the same discussions, the same disagreements, and reached the same stalemates — but, the conversation seemed to me a little more gracious, the atmosphere a bit more open. Encouraged, I once again began the next week's meeting with several minutes of singing, and then did so again the following week, and again — each week through the rest of the committee's tenure. No one will be surprised to learn that our problems were *not* solved immediately. The conflicts and differences of opinion did not disappear. There was, however, a noticeable change. Our meetings "warmed" considerably. There was a greater sense of camaraderie and we became better at listening to one another. We compromised and made slow, steady progress on our disagreements. We came to enjoy our time together and (remarkably) over several months even began to resemble something like a Christian community (all the while continuing to disagree about issues of musical style)! No doubt, part of the change simply came about as we got to know one another better. Certainly, there were people praying for greater unity among the committee

58. Quoted in Stapert, *A New Song,* p. 26.

members, and I believe those prayers were effective. But it seemed to me (and to others on the committee, when we discussed it some months later) that our singing had played a part in bringing about a change. The singing had been not so much "moving" or "inspiring" as *instructive.*

The members of the music committee were all church stalwarts — long-time Christians who had served the church in various capacities. It is safe to assume that all of them had read Paul's description of the church as the Body of Christ, had heard sermons on loving one another, and, if pressed, could have offered a few helpful thoughts on the unity of the church. As we sang together, however, we came to understand what the unity of the church might mean and sound like in *this* room, in the midst of *these* issues, among *these* people with *these* voices. Even in the midst of our bickering, we all would have affirmed the wisdom of Paul's command: "submit yourselves to one another out of reverence for Christ." With each week's opening hymns, however, we were forced to *rehearse* this mutual submission, and as we did, we learned how such submission is enacted in song. What we had understood before — conceptually and at the level of conviction — we came to understand through indwelling and participation. As Christians we already knew we had been called to unity; in song we came to understand the distinctive shape of that unity. Harsh and irritable tones of voice were more quickly revealed as such when set immediately alongside our four-part singing. We seemed to remember more readily that each one around the table had a voice, and that it was best for the whole group if each voice were heard. And we discovered that the sound of all of our voices together could be beautiful, not just frustrating. Week after week our singing modeled the kind of community to which God was calling us; week after week melody and harmony intoned tuition in the wisdom of song.

16. The Truth Shall Set You Free:
Song, Struggle, and Solidarity in South Africa

C. Michael Hawn

I was a seminary professor in a small North Carolina town in 1986. Its location was barely an hour from Greensboro, where on February 1, 1960, the Greensboro Four, as they were later called, began a new movement of peaceful demonstrations. These four black freshmen at North Carolina A&T University initiated pacifist activities, including sitting in restaurants unofficially designated for whites, drinking at posted white-only public water fountains, and moving beyond the back of public buses. Though removed by over twenty-five years from the events of 1960, I was aware that racial tensions remained just under the surface of daily activities in the town where I lived. Vestiges of the decades of racism were visible in the inadequate housing conditions and public services available to African Americans. The segregation of blacks from whites — literally across the railroad tracks from each other — further deepened the cultural chasm. Given this history, I was particularly disturbed by an announcement that the state leader of the Ku Klux Klan had requested, and was granted, a permit to hold a demonstration down the main street of this small town of six thousand residents. I joined my seminary colleagues in concern about the effects that a KKK rally might have on our community — a community that needed healing rather than a public display of racism. As a result many of us encouraged the seminary students to join us in a silent protest against the KKK.

The day of the march came on a clear spring Saturday. Well in advance, the main street was lined with many representatives from the seminary as well as townsfolk. In addition I recognized some clergy from nearby Raleigh, people who had the experience of marching in civil rights demonstrations in the 1960s and 1970s, some even with Martin Luther King Jr. At the appointed hour a military-style procession slowly made its way up the street to a drum cadence. The participants were dressed in army-style fatigues and carried rifles. I assumed (prayed) they were not loaded. Riding in a lone jeep was the North Carolina state leader of the KKK surrounded by his "honor" guard. Having grown up in Iowa, a state with a relatively homogeneous racial population in the northern Midwest, I had never experienced anything like this. I was paralyzed by what I saw. I sensed the presence of evil more strongly than at any previous point in my life. I watched in silence and disbelief as local high school students ran out to join the macabre parade, chanting racist slogans in support of the stated principles of the KKK. Some seminary students began to attempt to restrain the teenagers, leading to struggles between the two groups. It looked as if a brawl might ensue, providing the possibility for publicity and deepening the long-established racial rifts that plagued the community.

Suddenly, I felt a hand from behind on my shoulder. A retired Baptist minister from Raleigh, long known for his participation in the Civil Rights movement and public stance against war in Viet Nam, whispered to me, "Mike, help me sing." At first I thought he was crazy. Having no experience in these kinds of events, I felt that I was in a large theater watching a breaking news story in slow motion. Though a trained singer, no sound would come out. Then I heard the minister start to sing with a voice full of the confidence of many peaceful demonstrations, "We shall overcome." Though he was not a vocal soloist by anyone's estimation, the sound was one of the most beautiful that I have ever heard. He helped me and those close by find our voices and our song grew. Our ill-conceived strategy of silence in the face of evil gave way to full-bodied song. As the procession passed, we found not only our voice, but also our feet and spontaneously closed ranks behind the demonstrators, ushering the KKK band out of the town on the wings of our song. Somehow, the incipient struggles between the seminary students and the local teenagers subsided almost immediately and the sound of song replaced racial epithets. Reflecting later on the experience with students, some noted that our singing not only demonstrated overt support for the African Americans in our community, but functioned as a musical exorcism, taking back our town. What might have happened if that Baptist minister had not started singing this venerable song of the Civil Rights movement? Silence led to paralysis; singing led to solidarity.

Participating in communal singing is an act of will. Lifting one's voice at a rugby or baseball game unites a disparate group behind a favorite team.

Lifting voices in an environment of oppression is an act of unified opposition to injustice. In the defiance that prompts the singing, there is the understanding that one is not alone. Others acknowledge the injustice and raise their voices in dissent. More importantly, singing in defiance of injustice is a sign of hope that evil power used to provoke pain will not ultimately prevail. Hoping for justice is a point of intersection between political protest in the streets and eschatological expectation that sustains Christian liturgy. This essay explores the intersection of song and political protest in South Africa, with the hope that the discussion will inform our *theological* understanding of music in worship in other parts of the world.

A funeral for a black African in apartheid South Africa was an event at the intersection of personal grief and public politics. The loss of a loved one or national hero such as Steven Biko on September 12, 1977, was cause for personal grief. The torture and unnecessary death of a political leader placed his mourners in a position of intense scrutiny by police who had been sent by local authorities to observe the event. Experiences like the Sharpeville Massacre (March 21, 1960) were always in the minds of the mourners who knew that the police were ready to respond against a large gathering of blacks with extreme force at any perceived sign of provocation. The demonstration on the day of the Sharpeville Massacre was a peaceful protest against the apartheid Pass Laws prohibiting the freedom of movement by black South Africans into white population centers except with careful documentation for prescribed reasons. Fifty-six blacks were killed and many more injured on that day, cementing this occasion in the minds of those who have been victims of later police actions.

In the decades that followed right up until the election of Nelson Mandela, any gathering of blacks, even for — especially for — funerals of slain black South Africans was subject to unprovoked violence. Even the appearance of white priests and nuns could not guarantee that a black mourner would not be shot during the funeral march.[1] During the "Emergencies" of 1960 and 1986 when all civil rights were suspended for blacks and "coloureds,"

---

1. David Dargie, a white South African, then a Roman Catholic priest, recalls one tragedy when a young black mourner, Bigboy Mginywa, was shot and killed in front of him at a funeral. On another occasion he attended a political funeral in the 1980s where a group of Black Sash women (a white women's organization, though not excluding black membership, known for their silent, non-violent protests) were threatened by police for singing Sontonga's song outside the gate of a black township. It is no wonder that "Nkosi sikelel' iAfrika" carries the unifying power that it does today. This episode was cited by Dargie in "Thinking Back to Tiyo Soga," *East London Daily Dispatch* (June 13, 1997).

the threat of violence increased.[2] Although large gatherings of black South Africans were illegal, these funerals were defiantly held in large soccer fields, capable of holding thousands of mourners, under the watchful eye of heavily armed South African police who were ready to move in at the slightest provocation. Closed caskets were illegally draped in the black, green, and gold flag of the banned African National Congress (ANC). Following angry speeches and the sounds of wailing, Enoch Mankayi Sontonga's anthem "Nkosi Sikelel' iAfrika" ("Lord, Bless Africa"), the proscribed anthem of the ANC, was sung. The sound of its strains unified the oppressed protestors and gave them the courage to continue their peaceful march in the face of evil.

As the cause of blacks in South Africa came increasingly to the forefront of the world's attention in the 1980s and early 1990s, evening newscasts often displayed the demonstrations of blacks against apartheid. Almost invariably singing songs of freedom seemed to be a part of the international news clips. For many in the United States, singing during peaceful demonstrations in South Africa was reminiscent of Civil Rights marches where "We Shall Overcome" rallied the demonstrators and gave them hope to continue the struggle. Just as in my personal experience of a KKK rally in a small North Carolina town, the silence of most in the white South African community against apartheid led to paralysis. The singing of black and some white South Africans in defiance of apartheid led to solidarity and the eventual dismantling of one of the most evil systems of oppression the modern world has seen.

Songs of protest often flow freely from the streets to the church and back again, whether among blacks in South Africa or African Americans in the United States. Were freedom songs composed for protests in the streets or worship in the church? The origin of these songs is difficult to discern in cultures where oppression is ubiquitous in every sphere of life, blurring the dichotomy between the sacred and secular. The question for the African is not one of appropriateness in one setting or another. The question is one of singing as a means of inspiring solidarity — whether in the streets or in the pews — and seeking hope in a community where individual freedoms were virtually nonexistent.

What purpose did the singing serve? What texts were sung by the peaceful demonstrators? What kind of music provided the vehicle for these texts?

2. Two powerful novels by Richard Reve provide a sense of life for "coloured" South Africans during the Emergencies in Cape Town where some of the violence was most brutal. They are *Emergency* (Capetown: David Philip, 1964), an account of the Emergency in 1960 following the Sharpeville Massacre, and *Emergency Continued* (Cape Town: David Philip, 1990), an account of conditions leading to the second Emergency in 1986.

How were they a part of the worship of black South Africans? These are valid questions for researchers of music and liturgy in South Africa. However, South African Freedom Songs, as they became known, came to the attention of the broader European community and the United States during the 1980s. Why should Europeans and North Americans, for example, sing South African Freedom Songs, collectively forged by black Africans in the heat of oppression in a country thousands of miles away, and what do these songs have to do with the liturgies of people, many of whom may never have suffered from political oppression or social injustice? This essay advances the thesis that liturgical experiences in solidarity with the other expose our vulnerable edges — an uncomfortable meeting that opens us to the possibility of a much broader and profound sense of encounter with the Creator.

Prototypes for South African Freedom Songs

To understand the singing that accompanied the antiapartheid movement in South Africa, two songs in particular are pivotal, constituting as they do a major foundation for the nascent cultural and national identity of black South Africans. The first is the earliest Christian hymn composed by a black South African, usually considered to be the first Xhosa Christian, the prophet Ntsikana son of Gaba (c. 1780-1821). The second is the hymn "Nkosi Sikelel' iAfrika" (1897) composed by Enoch Mankayi Sontonga (c. 1873-1905), a song that provided the basis for the current multilingual South African national anthem. Both of these songs have their roots in the Xhosa language and culture. Together they provide a musical heritage for the famous Freedom Songs of South Africa.

The hymn of the prophet Ntsikana is the prototype of church music in a traditional Xhosa style. David Dargie describes the prophet as

> an attractively mysterious figure in Xhosa history. A Cirha, and son of a councillor of the famous chief Ngqika, he was the first Xhosa Christian. It was probably as a herd-boy that he heard the preaching of the first missionary among the Xhosa, Dr. J. T. van der Kemp of the London Missionary Society, who worked in Ciskei from 1799 to 1801. The missionary, however, made no Xhosa converts; it was only years later, about 1815, that Ntsikana underwent a conversion experience without the presence of any missionary or white person.[3]

3. David Dargie, "The Music of Ntsikana," *South African Journal of Musicology* 2 (1982): 7.

Ntsikana's vision was dramatic. He was standing outside his hut when he saw a strange light strike his ox, called Hulushe, as the sun rose. A boy nearby could not see this light. Later in the day he went to a celebration with his family and miraculous occurrences continued. Janet Hodgson describes the vision as follows:

> Three times, as he started to dance, a raging wind arose out of clear blue sky forcing all dancers to stop. Tradition has it that he now became aware that the Holy Spirit had entered him, but the people thought him bewitched. He promptly took his family home and they were amazed when on the way he washed the red ochre from his body in the Gqora river, as a sign of his entry into a new life.[4]

The effects of this revelation continued the next day as he prayed and chanted, using the words "elelele homna," which may have been a Xhosafication of "Alleluia Amen." Eventually he gathered a group of disciples and settled into a new life, teaching them his hymns. These hymns included the theology of the Creator and one true God, the coming Messiah who suffered for all people, and reconciliation among opposing groups. The latter theme was particularly timely due to the increasing tension between the Xhosas and the white settlers during this time.

Ntsikana practiced an ascetic lifestyle, sending one of his wives back home. As a messenger of reconciliation, he warned Chief Ngqika and Chief Ndlambe to seek peaceful resolutions to conflict and tension within the Xhosa nation between factions of Ndlambe and Ngqika, which Ntsikana saw as particularly dangerous. Ntsikana was correct and both leaders later regretted that they did not heed his counsel. While Ntsikana was wary of the influence of the whites coming into Xhosa lands, he was opposed to the prophet Makanda Nxele who predicted that the Xhosa would conquer the whites in war. When Nxele's prophecy was not fulfilled, Ntsikana became revered as a true prophet.

The authenticity of Ntsikana's hymns ultimately may be discerned only by their abiding influence on the spiritual life of the Xhosas, their persistent presence as a living artifact of Xhosa cultural heritage, and, therefore, the embodiment of hope for liberation for the Xhosa people.

In 1909 Ntsikana was chosen over several past chiefs and heroes of the tribe as a national patron of the Xhosa people, and the St. Ntsikana Memorial

---

4. Janet Hodgson, "Ntsikana's 'Great Hymn,' A Xhosa Expression of Christianity in the Early 19th Century Eastern Cape," *Communications* 4 (1980): 4.

Association was founded. Following the election of Nelson Mandela, a Thembu Xhosa, as the first black president of South Africa in 1994, Ntsikana's hymns have experienced a revival of interest as a symbol of African heritage.

Ntsikana's hymn (sometimes presented as four songs) is rooted in the traditional music culture of the Xhosa people.[5] The music is in the style of the musical bow tradition,[6] alternating around a progression of two major chords a step apart. This is a vocal music culture of overtone singing as well as bows that through various means provide subtle overtones. Thomas Turino notes that the "traditional music of the Nguni (Zulu-, Swazi-, Sotho-, Xhosa-speaking) peoples of [South Africa] is itself stylistically distinct from the music of other African areas. For example, in contrast to [most] African musical styles . . . , Nguni music is a predominately choral-vocal style using slower tempos and lacking the polyrhythmic percussion accompaniments found in, say, West Africa."[7] Though traditional Xhosa music has become increasingly influenced by the drumming cultures of nearby tribes as well as the use of marimbas from the Shona in Zimbabwe, Xhosa music has historically been almost entirely vocally oriented.[8]

John Knox Bokwe (1855-1922), who studied with William Kolbe Ntsikana, grandson of Ntsikana Gaba, and was ordained as a Presbyterian minister in Scotland (1906), was a member of the Ngqika Mbamba clan (Xhosa). He was born at Ntselamanzi, near Lovedale, the Presbyterian mission.[9] Bokwe provided the first transcriptions of Ntsikana's songs (1878) from the

5. In correspondence (April 7, 2004), David Dargie notes: "It is not clear whether Ntsikana composed one song in a variety of versions or several songs for worship. There are a number of survivals of his song(s). I have transcriptions of 11 versions, including JK Bokwe's written version and his son ST Bokwe's performed version, in my *Ntsikana* booklet. Ntsikana was not literate, and composed orally."

6. There are a variety of musical bows among the Xhosa of South Africa. They usually consist of a single wire tied to the ends of a stick approximately three feet or one meter in length. When the wire string is pulled tight, the stick bends. The sound of various bowed instruments is amplified by the different means of a calabash *(uhadi)*, a tin can *(inkatari)* used by the Sotho, and the oral cavity of the player *(umrhubhe)*. The string may be bowed or struck with a stick. The resulting sounds include two fundamental pitches one step apart and simultaneous overtones made by the resonator.

7. Thomas Turino, "The Music of Sub-Saharan Africa," in *Excursions in World Music*, ed. Bruno Nettl et al. (Englewood Cliffs, NJ: Prentice Hall, 1992), p. 191.

8. For more detailed information on Ntsikana's hymn, see C. Michael Hawn, *Gather into One: Praying and Singing Globally* (Grand Rapids: Eerdmans, 2003), ch. 4, "Singing Freedom: David Dargie and South African Liberation Song."

9. J. A. Millard, "John Knox Bokwe," in *Malihambe — Let the Word Spread* (Pretoria, South Africa: Unisa Press, 1999).

Ahomna
Ntsikana's Song

Example 1

"Ahomna" (song No. 20 from *Halle, Halle*) © 1999 Choristers Guild, Garland, Texas. Used by permission. All rights reserved.

oral tradition using sol-fa transcription.[10] Selborne T. Bokwe, his son, known as a choir leader, recorded versions of Ntsikana's songs for Hugh Tracey, legendary for his recordings of African music throughout southern, central, and eastern Africa from the 1920s through the 1950s. Both the written version and oral variants live side by side today as they continue the heritage of the prophet Ntsikana's hymn, a song that might be called the "Ein feste Burg" of the Xhosa people. The story of this great African hymn is one of the richest in all of hymnody.[11] See "Ahomna" (Example 1 above).

10. David Dargie, "Thank God for Music of uMdengentonga," *East London Daily Dispatch* (July 11, 1997). The texts of Ntsikana's hymn were written down in 1822 after the group came to the mission following Ntsikana's death in 1821.

11. For an excellent summary of the Ntsikana story and a compact disc of variant recordings, see David Dargie, *Ntsikana Music Collection 2000: Songs of the First Christian Xhosa* (Alice, South Africa: University of Fort Hare, 2000), a collection of music transcriptions and scores of the songs of the Xhosa prophet St. Ntsikana, for study and performance, with an introduction to the life of Ntsikana, and photographs (including performers). Contact Prof. Dr.

"Ahomna" is a word of respect addressed to royal persons or Deity. Note the root movement one step apart between the F and G major chords. This follows the style of "harmony" found in the musical bows of the Xhosa people. The additive rhythm (3+3+2) is very typical of Xhosa traditional music and may be found in other South African music, including popular urban styles. The melody, a descending pattern, follows the outline of the overtones made by the musical bow player with the mouth over the end of the bow. The text, a reduction of the complete great prayer, has the quality of a petition. The plea to God for peace and freedom reflects the context of British oppression at the turn of the nineteenth century during which the hymn was created.[12]

Sontonga's anthem, on the other hand, was written in a nineteenth-century Western musical style. Unlike the traditional Xhosa musical style of Ntsikana's hymn, "Nkosi sikelel' iAfrika" draws upon the musical style of colonial powers in melodic structure, harmonic movement, and rhythm. "Nkosi" sounds in its earliest version similar to European national anthems such as "God Save the Queen." While this may seem unusual for a group struggling for African cultural identity, three observations not only clarify this situation, but also provide an understanding for how an anthem strongly influenced by a Western style of music could foster the emergence of South African Freedom Songs.

First, a truly national anthem in countries with a colonial history usually does not reflect the music of any of the indigenous cultures, but is derived from musical styles beyond the provincial boundaries of the country. Drawing from Benedict Anderson's concept of "unisonance," Philip Bohlman discusses the role of music in nationalism as "the sonic moment that occurs when people throughout the nation gather in a shared performance of music. . . . The unisonant moment may occur when a national anthem is being sung at a state ceremony."[13] This experience produces cultural intimacy, an experience that allows each person in the nation to join with all other citizens

---

David Dargie in Germany (Phone-Fax: **49089-49 16 92; Email: dave.dargie@t-online.de), or the International Library of African Music (ILAM) at Rhodes University, 6140 Grahamstown, South Africa.

12. Ntsikana was a legendary prophet for peace among the Xhosas during the early nineteenth century, a crucial time in their history when the Xhosas were engaged in a series of wars against the British. See Noël Mostert, *Frontiers: The Epic of South Africa's Creation and the Tragedy of the Xhosa People* (Johannesburg: Pimlico, 1992), pp. 461-66, for an account of Ntsikana's role in this struggle.

13. Philip V. Bohlman, *World Music: A Very Short Introduction* (New York: Oxford University Press, 2002), p. 94.

in unified singing moment. Michael Herzfeld notes that it is not usually the folk music of one particular group that produces cultural intimacy.[14] South Africa is a country that currently consists of twenty-five living languages.[15] "Nkosi silelel' iAfrica" reflects the paradox of the principle of unisonance. It is a national anthem that borrows heavily from the Western hymn style of the European colonials and draws minimally on African musical compositional practices. Bohlman states that folk songs tend to be incorporated into symphonic movements while sacred songs provide the basis for national anthems.[16] "Nkosi" has its roots in the sacred realm. Consider an earlier version of "Nkosi" below. Note the petition to the Lord (Nkosi) to "Hear our prayers and bless us." "Descend Holy Spirit" is an invocation, the language of liturgy. The Xhosa with the original Lovedale Press English translation follows:

Nkosi sikelel' iAfrika,	Lord, bless Africa.
Malupakam' upondo lwayo,	May her horn [of power] rise up.
Yiva imitandazo yetu, Usisikelele	Hear our prayers, and bless us.

Refrain:	
Yihla Moya, Yihla Moya,	Descend Holy Spirit, Descend Holy Spirit,
Yihla Moya Oyingcwele.	Descend Holy Spirit.

Sontonga's music is reminiscent of a Victorian hymn. The music echoes the style of Great Britain, one of South Africa's colonizers, and the melody carries the petitions and invocation to the Holy Spirit with a solemn majesty. Though added to and modified numerous times, Sontonga's hymn became the South African national anthem in 1994. Its musical style is in keeping with many national anthems around the world. Achieving unisonance, it seems, requires finding a song with sacred sensibilities that do not reflect the roots of any particular culture within the nation and, therefore, may be sung by all.

The second aspect of "Nkosi" in the South African context to bear in mind is that it was subject to processes of *adaptation* from the beginning.[17]

---

14. See Michael Herzfeld, *Cultural Intimacy: Social Poetics in the Nation-State* (New York: Routledge, 1997).

15. See http://www.ethnologue.com/show_country.asp?name=South+Africa (accessed October 15, 2007).

16. Bohlman, *World Music,* p. 95.

17. The information for the following section is a compilation from several of the many websites devoted to "Nkosi" and its many versions. Two helpful sources are cited in nn. 21 and 22.

Adaptation is one of the principles of African composition. Though initially composed in a traditional Western literate process, as it spread throughout South Africa (and beyond), "Nkosi" was increasingly affected by the practices of oral composition. The natural variations of oral musical composition were eventually incorporated into various written arrangements of the anthem, blending the original Western hymn with specific African compositional techniques. Sontonga was a teacher at a Methodist mission school in Johannesburg who often composed songs for his students. It was out of these humble origins that this song was adopted for broader use.[18] "Nkosi" was first sung in a broader public forum in 1899 at the ordination of Rev. Boweni, a Shangaan Methodist minister. Sontonga's choir and other choirs spread "Nkosi" to the Johannesburg and Natal regions. On January 8, 1912, at the first meeting of the South African Native National Congress (SANNC), the forerunner of the African National Congress (ANC), "Nkosi" was sung following the closing prayer. By 1925 the ANC officially adopted "Nkosi" as a closing anthem for its meetings.

Solomon Plaatje, whose *Native Life in South Africa* (1916) is one of the most important accounts of the events that led to the systematic institutionalization of apartheid,[19] is thought to be the first to record the song. This recording was made in London in 1923. Plaatje was one of South Africa's most respected writers and a founding member of the ANC. Seven additional Xhosa stanzas were later added by poet Samuel Mqhayi. In 1927 the Lovedale Press, in the Eastern Cape, published all the verses in a pamphlet form. It was included in the Presbyterian Xhosa hymn book, *Ingwade Yama-culo Ase-rabe* (1929). Moses Mphahlele published a Sesotho version in 1942.

For decades black South Africans have regarded "Nkosi Sikelel' iAfrika" as the unofficial national anthem of South Africa and it was sung regularly as an act of defiance against the apartheid regime in churches and at rallies and funerals. A proclamation issued by the state president on April 20, 1994,

18. It is interesting to note that at approximately the same time as "Nkosi," "Lift Every Voice and Sing" (sometimes called "The Negro National Anthem") was written by brothers James Weldon Johnson (text) and J. Rosamond Johnson (music) in the United States. This hymn also grew out of similar humble origins at the turn of the twentieth century as a song sung by children for a school assembly in Florida celebrating Abraham Lincoln's birthday. The author and composer did not originally conceive it as a song with wider possibilities. It is also in a hymn-like musical style (not in the style of an African American spiritual or gospel song) with a text that invokes God and lists petitions, a common practice in hymns.

19. Solomon T. Plaatje, *Native Life in South Africa* (1916; Randburg, South Africa: Ravan Press, 1982).

just before the election of Nelson Mandela in May, stipulated that both "Nkosi Sikelel' iAfrika" and "Die Stem van Suid-Afrika" ("The Call of South Africa"), the Afrikaans national anthem, would be the national anthems of South Africa. In 1996 a shortened, combined version of the two anthems was released as the new South African National Anthem.[20]

Therefore, as one source states, "There are no standard versions or translations of Nkosi Sikelel' iAfrika so the words vary from place to place and from occasion to occasion. Generally the first stanza is sung in Xhosa or Zulu, followed by the Sesotho version."[21] Another source attests to the multiplicity of translations: "The song spread beyond the borders of South Africa and has been translated and adapted into a number of other languages. It is still the national anthem of Tanzania and Zambia and has also been sung in Zimbabwe, Namibia and South Africa for many years."[22]

The third driving force that needs to be borne in mind for understanding the manner in which South African Freedom Songs could emerge in conjunction with Western musical styles is the unusual role of choral music in South African life. Because of the length of Western colonialism in South Africa, a strong choral tradition developed in the country that was virtually unknown in most other areas of the continent. "Nkosi" spread not only as an anthem sung at political meetings and funerals, but by church and community choirs. It was noted above in the discussion of Xhosa traditional music that a choral-vocal approach, void of drums used by other neighboring tribes, was an unusual, perhaps unique, South African musical style. In addition, according to Turino, the "music taught by Christian missionaries, also a choral tradition, had a particularly strong impact in South Africa,"[23] and the distinctive sound that belongs to the South African Freedom Song is clearly a synthesis of traditional Xhosa choral-vocal styles and British cathedral choral tradition. The combination of the two results in a style of African music with which Euro-North Americans can find a particular affinity.

---

20. An official sheet music version of "Nkosi" is available on the South African government website at http://www.info.gov.za/aboutgovt/symbols/anthem.pdf (accessed February 6, 2008). A sound file of the anthem is available at the same site: http://www.info.gov.za/aboutgovt/symbols/anthem.htm#sheetmusic (accessed February 6, 2008).

21. From http://www.info.gov.za/aboutgovt/symbols/anthem.htm#sheetmusic (no author given). (Accessed February 6, 2008.)

22. See Geneveve Walker, "Enoch Mankayi Sontonga" (National Monuments Council, 1996), http://www.endarkenment.com/kwanzaa/nkosi/sontonga.htm (accessed February 6, 2008).

23. Turino, "The Music of Sub-Saharan Africa," p. 191.

In the drive for conversion, missionaries taught religious songs translated into local languages and set to diatonic melodies (i.e., melodies based on the standard *do-re-mi* scale) and harmonies with basic Western chords (I, IV, and V). Hymn-based music can now be heard all over Africa, and it is certainly an element in the style of the famous Ladysmith Black Mambazo, as it is among the other urban vocal groups composed of Zulu, Xhosa, Swazi, and other migrants in South Africa.[24]

"Nkosi" is composed in the African popular choral music style *makwaya* (choir). John Knox Bokwe used this style to support his ministerial study in Scotland and to provide a bridge between Scottish Presbyterians and South Africans, hoping for continued support for mission work there. Bokwe's interest in Ntsikana was part of a broader nationalism concerned about cultural advancement among black South Africans. He was a leader in this movement that "preserved semantic tones while achieving a high musical literacy — a happy marriage of African and European compositional principles."[25] Many notable South African composers found their home in the *makwaya* style, including Benjamin Tyamzashe, A. A. Khumalo, Hamilton Masiza, Marks Radebe, Rueben Cluza, Joshua Mogapeloa, and Michael Moerane. *Makwaya* is a popular music that can be found in both church and civic life. David Coplan notes that *makwaya* "supported the traditional attachment of black South Africans to choral song . . . , [r]eflecting the secular use of the emotional and spiritual catharsis provided in sacred pieces."[26] Sontonga's "Nkosi Sikelel' iAfrica" is a prime example of *makwaya* style, conveying religious fervor in a popular choral form that may be sung at church services, civic concerts, political rallies, union meetings, and even weddings. Valmont Layne, a South African performer educated at the University of Cape Town, describes the *makwaya* and its influence:

> Formally, makwaya, even though based on the western hymn, is not performed according to the western aesthetic system. This is a deliberate choice and is born of syncretism. Congregational singing was attractive to westernising African communities. But, they negotiated this westernisation. African choirs made harmonies not on the basis of a dominant melodic line, but by polyphonically embellishing a bass ostinato. Melodic

24. Turino, "The Music of Sub-Saharan Africa," p. 189.
25. David B. Coplan, "Popular Music in South Africa," in *Africa: The Garland Encyclopedia of World Music*, vol. 1, ed. Ruth M. Stone (London: Routledge, 1997), p. 763.
26. Coplan, "Popular Music in South Africa," p. 764.

parts tend to follow the tonal patterns of the song words. Makwaya has, in turn, influenced new urban working class forms such as isicathamiya (made famous by Paul Simon and Ladysmith Black Mambazo). It also influenced other forms of vocal and instrumentalised music, including . . . South African ragtime and early jazz, plus the rearrangement of indigenous folk songs for choral performance in four-part harmony.[27]

The synthesis between Western hymns and African choral practice was most evident during this eyewitness account of an historic moment in post-apartheid South Africa:

On October 29, 1998 former Archbishop Desmond Tutu officially presented President Mandela the five volumes of the report of the Truth and Reconciliation Commission (TRC). Tutu, head of the TRC, had heard long hours of personal testimony from the victims of the atrocities committed under the tyranny of apartheid. The first stage of the investigation was complete. When Mandela received the TRC Report from Tutu, the South African National Choir broke into jubilant song. Then, before a global audience, Mandela and Tutu danced in celebration, not because the recovery from apartheid was complete — far from it. These two winners of the Nobel Peace Prize danced and sang in solidarity with those who marched and sang before them in the face of unspeakable injustice. They danced in celebration of what had transpired to bring them to this point. They danced in the hope that the songs that had carried them this far along the "long walk to freedom"[28] would sustain them in the difficult days ahead when political change would hopefully lead to transformation in the attitudes and lives of people.[29]

The combination of the superbly trained South African National Choir singing choral versions of Freedom Songs with traditional dancing by Tutu and Mandela was electrifying. The musical traditions of the oppressed and the oppressor came together at that memorable moment, symbolic of the hope for a new South Africa where whites and blacks could live together in equality. Of course, the closing anthem was Sontonga's "Nkosi sikelel' iAfrika."

27. Valmont Layne, "Township Music," in *Townships in South Africa: A Brief History* (CD Booklet: Colophon Records, c. 2000). The recording is entitled *Townships: From Segregation to Citizenship*, published with the support of International Co-operation — Ministry of Foreign Affairs of Belgium (DGCI/DGIS).
28. This is the title of Nelson Mandela's autobiography, *Long Walk to Freedom* (Boston: Little, Brown, 1994).
29. Hawn, *Gather into One*, p. 105.

Nkosi Sikelel' iAfrica

Enoch Mankayi Sontonga (c.1873-1905)
Arr. Karl Aloritias

Notes on pronunciation:
   "Ph" is a cross between the English "p" and "ph" ("f") sounds.
   "Th" is a cross between the English "t" and "th" sounds.
   "Ch" is a cross between the English "ch" and "sh" sounds.

Example 2

The choral arrangement of "Nkosi" shown in Example 2, above, by Australian composer Karl Alortias (2003) demonstrates both the spread of this anthem to other parts of the world and a synthesis of black African and European musical styles. During the first ten measures, the bass part moves in a strong hymn-like manner typical of the common practice of period Western hymn styles. The step-wise movement of the melody is similar to that of many Victorian hymns. The upper three parts, however, move in parallel fashion, typical of African harmonizing. In the second section, an African call-response pattern is set up with the soprano part serving as the call. Throughout most of the anthem the vertical harmonies change together, recalling the familiar, chorale style of Western hymns. Music has the capacity to embody diversity non-verbally through a fusion of styles.

Singing and Praying for the World

While most of our discussion has centered on the origin of songs and their role in political struggle, these songs also find fulfillment in liturgy. One of the most important and earliest characteristics of Christian liturgy is the inclusion of the prayers of the people. Christians have the responsibility to pray for the needs of the world. In an age of instant communication and vivid portrayals in the media, the injustices of the world — political oppression, civil war, genocide, rampant disease, illiteracy, poverty, displaced persons, homelessness, and many others — may overwhelm us. One response to the flood of unbearable news is to become numb and seek sanctuary in a liturgy that shields us from suffering or, at least, makes it more acceptable. For much of the Christian world, singing and praying are a unified action. Singing in solidarity with those who suffer is one way to keep the needs of the world before us so that our prayers reach beyond those who are near and dear and extend to all of humanity. We look now at how the song of South Africans gained recognition around the world and found a place in the song repertoire of congregations thousands of miles from South Africa.

Philip Bohlman stresses the significance of "encounter" in his amazing "Very Short" introduction to world music. Permit me to quote Bohlman at length from a section that sets well the stage for the closing section of this chapter:

Asserting that there is music everywhere in the world is . . . a Western concept, if it is also, however, a concept that results from Western encounters with the world. . . . Encounters mark important historical moments; encounters bring about change, even revolution; encounters create the conditions for exchange. . . .

At the beginning of the 21st century, then, world music is not simply the music of the exotic "other." Our encounters with the world have become quotidian, and music mediates these encounters, whether we perceive that or not. It is not simply a matter that television advertisement regularly draws on South Asian and West African drumming; it is not the weaving of world-music tracks into film sound tracks; it is not only the fact that Protestant hymnals are increasingly multicultural or that the Catholic Mass is musically familiar to every ethnic community in the metropolis; nor is it that Sufism has become a world religion mediated by world music; it does not even stop with the legal cases about musical ownership or the limits of downloading music from the Internet. It is, rather, the confluence of all these phenomena, which too must be understood as encounters are imagined and mediated by the West. World music is an inescapable everyday experience, whether or not we understand what that means.[30]

The spread of Freedom Songs to the world church through various international assemblies has created "the conditions for exchange" between South Africa and cultures around the world. As Europeans and North Americans became increasingly aware of the apartheid struggle in South Africa, singing these songs gave them a way of joining in solidarity with black South Africans. To borrow Bohlman's words, sharing South African Freedom Songs across cultures marked an important historical encounter between cultures that brought about change, "even revolution," a revolution that led to the downfall of apartheid and the inauguration of black majority rule in 1994.

Our ultimate concern is with what these songs, as they are used in worship by Christians around the world, might mean for a deeper sense of being bound together as the body of Christ, and a more profound encounter with God. The musical and liturgical challenge then is to facilitate an encounter with the struggle of South Africans mediated by the songs from this struggle. The encounter we seek goes beyond a superficial, even subliminal, awareness of another culture through popular media or noting, in passing, bilingual hymns in our hymnals. It is an encounter that seeks to open oneself up to another's way of praying — praying in the fullest sense of that word: invoca-

30. Bohlman, *World Music: A Very Short Introduction*, p. xvi.

tion, praise, adoration, petition, intercession, and blessing. These prayers are mediated through the songs of another culture. Receiving these sung prayers from others' struggles adds an awe-full sense to our encounter with those who send us these gifts.

Part of the challenge for the church and its liturgy is to move from a co-lonial sense of missions where the "best of the West is shared with the rest" to a reciprocal posture in which the West (or the northern world) receives the witness of the world church in song and prayer. In a world so thoroughly connected through travel and communications, authentic worship in the twenty-first century seeks to explore the dynamic between parochial per-spectives and global worldviews, between local needs and global injustice, between a congregation gathered around a eucharistic table on Sunday morning and a cosmic table where the faithful of all times and places gather in eternal thanksgiving. This dynamic between local and global challenges the norm of worship as a place where individual comfort is the first and foremost criterion. Worship is also a place to encounter the other and the Other, exposing our vulnerable edges and risking our personal comfort in hope of a broader understanding of the incarnation — understanding the human face of God as reflected in others' experiences.

Three examples from the South African Freedom repertoire follow. These songs came to the northern church primarily by means of an encoun-ter in 1978 between Fjedur, a Swedish youth choir, and South Africans suffer-ing under apartheid. Through the efforts of Anders Nyberg, the perfor-mances of Fjedur in Sweden and Europe, Fjedur's recordings that presented the songs with authenticity and vitality, and the publication of South Afri-can Freedom Songs, especially in the collection *Freedom is Coming: Songs of Protest and Praise from South Africa* (1984), these songs have become avail-able to the world church.[31]

We begin with perhaps the most frequently sung export from the Freedom Song struggle, "Siyahamba." "Siyahamba"[32] is a well-known Zulu/ Xhosa song that has been incorporated into several recent hymnals and has

31. *Freedom Is Coming* was a joint publication by the Swedish publisher Utryck, SKm (The Church of Sweden Mission), and Walton Music in the United States. Two additional volumes came out in Sweden, *We Shall Never Die* (1986) and *Imisa* (1987). A more recent publication collected and arranged by Anders Nyberg is *Freedom Is in Your Hand* (Sweden: Utryck; United States: Walton Music, 2003). The recording is by a group of musicians from Johannesburg.

32. Dargie comments that the text is basically the same in Siswata (the Swazi people), Xhosa, and Zulu.

become widely sung in North America.[33] South African ethnomusicologist David Dargie notes that "Siyahamba" was a Freedom Song originating with Amadodana, a Methodist young men's group.[34] Usually translated as "We are marching in the light of God," the simple text contains layers of meaning. "We" may be seen as a word of community, the community of those living and the community of the living dead. "Marching" is an action that unifies the community as they move physically and spiritually in the same direction. It is a physical, kinesthetic response to the Spirit, not a passive acquiescence. The "light of God" has meaning on several levels. While it is a symbol of creation and of Jesus Christ, "the light of the world," it is also a common refrain in songs of healing or *ngoma* throughout Southern and Central Africa. This refrain, "Let darkness be replaced with light," is coded language for "seeing clearly."[35] God is the source of clear sight in the midst of the struggle, i.e., the source of discernment and truth. As we march we can see our way ahead. Our path is clear. Where there is light, there is hope.

When this message is mediated with the music, the words become embodied in the lives of the community that sing and dance it. The accessibility of the musical form draws all present into the song's cyclic structure immediately. Its portability allows the song to be taken to places of "darkness" where its message can illuminate evil in its myriad forms and offer the singers hope as they see clearly the path ahead. Its flexibility allows for the performers/participants to add to the basic song a message that draws into it the existential reality of the situation. "We" grow in number as we "march," for

33. For examples in North America, see *The United Methodist Hymnal* (1989), "Thuma Mina" (497); *Hymnal: A Worship Book* (1992), "Asithi: Amen" (64), "Thuma Mina" (434); *Chalice Hymnal* (1995), "Masithi" (30), "Siyahamba" (442), "Thuma Mina" (447); *Covenant Hymnal* (1996), "Siyahamba" (424), "Hallelujah! Pelo Tso Rona" (499), "Thuma Mina" (626); *Voices United* (1996), "Sanna Sannanina" (128), "Thuma Mina" (572), "Siyahamba" (646); *The New Century Hymnal* (1995), "Masithi" (760), "Siyahamb'" (626), "Thuma Mina" (360), "We Shall Not Give Up the Fight" (437); *The Book of Praise* (1997), "Thuma Mina" (777), "Siyahamba" (639), "Asithi Amen" (264), "Freedom Is Coming" (725). Recent African American hymnals such as *This Far By Faith* (1999) from the Evangelical Lutheran Church of America (ELCA) make extensive use of South African sources. Current hymnal supplements continue to expand this literature into common usage. See *With One Voice* (1995) from the ELCA; *Wonder, Love and Praise* (1997), Episcopal Church, USA; and *The Faith We Sing* (2000), United Methodist, for more examples.

34. In a visit to Dallas on March 21, 2000, Dargie mentioned that this and another song in Nyberg's collection *Freedom Is Coming*, "Singabahambayo" (17), were from this group.

35. John M. Janzen, *Ngoma: Discourses on Healing in Central and Southern Africa* (Berkeley: University of California Press, 1992), pp. 111-18.

C. MICHAEL HAWN

there are those who join us — literally — on the way. The song accommodates and even facilitates a growing, evolving community of believers. "We are marching," knowing that the living dead are singing with us. If this song is taken into the liturgy as a processional, it brings with it the struggle of the streets and sanctifies it. Liturgy is not hermetically sealed from daily life, rather it sanctifies daily struggle in the lives of the *ekklesia*.[36]

The harmonies of "Siyahamba" are accessible to anyone who sings Western harmony. The harmonic progression (I-V-I-V7-I-IV-I-V-I) is familiar to anyone who has sung American gospel songs. It lends itself to harmonizing by ear; indeed the written music is almost confusing because of repeats, and the use of a musical score inhibits a physical response dictated by the active verb, "marching." Its steady beat embodies a sense of marching. "Siyahamba" is a natural processional at the commencement of the liturgy or at the conclusion of the service when the choir can lead the entire congregation out in the streets to spread Christ's light in the darkness. No hymnals are needed. The flexible cyclic musical form allows the song to continue as long as necessary.

Part of the popularity of "Siyahamba" resides undoubtedly with the infectious joy of the music. When singing with South Africans in their struggle, however, it is necessary to include songs of petition and songs that confront evil. The danger always exists that encounters between South Africans and Westerners will be relegated to the commercial arena in which the commodity of music provides an emotional fix drawn from "happy Africans." Such a cross-cultural encounter is not worthy of liturgy. Rather than exploring alterity, differences are minimized by choosing only the repertoire that fits most comfortably with our preconceived biases. Alterity gives way to assimilation into our established worldview. We have substituted liturgical ethnotourism for the possibility of a revolutionary encounter, all the while congratulating ourselves for our multiculturalism. If we join South Africans in joyful song — and we should because there is so much to celebrate — then we must also join them in petitions for mercy and defiance against evil structures.

"Nkosi, Nkosi, yiba nenceba" (Example 3, below) is a Xhosa *Kyrie eleison*.[37] Unlike the energy generated by singing and moving to "Siyahamba," "Nkosi, Nkosi" is a mournful petition for mercy in the face of injustice. Rather than being influenced by Western harmonic progressions, this song is a direct descendant of Ntsikana's traditional hymns. The harmony alternates between

36. Most of the analysis of "Siyahamba" appears in Hawn, *Gather into One*, pp. 144-45.
37. Nyberg, *Freedom Is Coming*, p. 29. See also "Azisenzeni Na?" ("What Have We Done?"), in Nyberg, *Freedom Is in Your Hand*, p. 15.

428

NKOSI, NKOSI

Music by G. M. Kolisi

Nkosi, Nkosi, yiba nenceba
Krestu, Krestu, yiba nenceba

Lord have mercy, have mercy upon us
Christ have mercy, have mercy upon us

Example 3

two major chords, a full step apart. The alternating major chords, recalling the alternating harmonies of the soft musical bows of the Xhosa people, provide a monotony[38] over which one may pray for the needs of the world. The music is quite accessible by the congregation, who only needs to hear it a few times to add their voices to the petition. When hummed, spoken petitions can easily be heard as the community responds continuously with their petition.

"Siph' Amandla Nkosi"[39] ("Lord, give us power"; Example 4, below) is a song in the mold of South African protest songs such as "Vula Botha siya ngqongqoza" ("Open Botha, we are a-knocking"). Rather than a mournful petition for mercy, this is a defiant demand for power to break the bonds of oppression and restore wholeness. "Amandla" (power) is a pervasive theme of those suffering injustice and tyranny. "Amandla" is also a pervasive word in the Freedom Songs of South Africa. The syncopated rhythm of "amandla" adds to the defiance, giving energy. The English translation specifies the use of the power to "rip down prisons," "lift up people," "withstand hatred," "not to be bitter," "make us fearless," and "because we need it." It is a text punctuated with implicit exclamation points, a quality the jagged rhythms and energetic rests help to emphasize. The harmonic rhythm moves quickly, changing on virtually every syllable, emphasizing the impatience and urgency of the singer. Other songs about power make it clear that those experiencing political oppression do not have the luxury of separating politics and faith. In "Akanamandla"[40] ("He has no power"), the power of Satan must be overcome.[41] These songs blur the distinction between the power to overcome satanic power and the political leaders of tyranny.

Where Does the Revolution Take Place?

The spirit of the Freedom Songs continues to live on in liturgies all around South Africa after more than a decade of black rule in South Africa. A Xhosa

---

38. Ronald Grimes makes a clear distinction between boredom and monotony. "Liturgy as a form of work does not surprise, though it may keep us open to serendipitous moment by its very monotony. . . . Liturgy is a full emptiness, a monotony without boredom, a reverent waiting without expectation." See Ronald Grimes, *Beginnings in Ritual Studies* (Lanham, MD: University Press of America, 1982), p. 44.

39. Nyberg, *Freedom Is Coming*, p. 19.

40. Nyberg, *Freedom Is Coming*, p. 21.

41. There are many other songs in *Freedom Is Coming* that stress the unity of politics and faith in the struggle for power, including "We Shall Not Give Up the Fight" (36) and "Freedom Is Coming" (8).

SIPH' AMANDLA

Siph' amandla Nkosi
Wokungesabi
Siph' amandla Nkosi
Siyawadinga

O God give us power
To rip down prisons
O God give us power
To lift the people

O God give us courage
To withstand hatred
O God give us courage
Not to be bitter

O God give us power
And make us fearless
O God give us power
Because we need it

Example 4

Methodist congregation that I visited in a city in the Eastern Cape is like many black congregations throughout South Africa. In post-apartheid South Africa, members of this church sing a variety of genres that include colonial hymns in translation, Africanized Anglican chant, and South African Freedom Songs. Just as singing the Freedom Songs was a means of sustaining hope that led to social change during the apartheid years, singing these songs in the post-apartheid era continues to nurture congregations as the country pursues equality in the face of difficult odds. South Africans are not the only ones changed, however.

Earlier in this essay, I referred to the work of Anders Nyberg and his musical ensemble Fjedur under the sponsorship of the Church of Sweden Mission. Fejdur made a trip to South Africa in 1978 to join in song with South African choirs. The choral cultures from opposite ends of the globe found a bond in a common song, the Freedom Songs of South Africa. In subsequent years members of Fjedur took these songs to churches throughout Sweden and the songs became a part of their liturgical vocabulary. Through international gatherings such as the Lutheran World Federation meeting in Bucharest in 1984, Fjedur spread these songs throughout Europe and to the far reaches of the globe. Publication of the songs along with Fjedur's authentic recordings spread the sound of the Freedom Songs to congregations and choirs who not only sang them but also learned of black South Africans' struggle against apartheid. The connection between these songs and the struggle from which they were born provided the congregations with a means of singing in solidarity rather than participating in enervating silence. Singing in solidarity has the potential to transform not only those in the midst of the struggle but also those far removed from places of oppression.

Anders Nyberg commented on the effect of these songs on Fjedur:

> Making the connection between the struggle and the songs was an important part of the choir's development. We learned the songs as we witnessed the struggles in South Africa. These songs, in turn, freed the Swedish churches to dance and sing in less restrained ways as Fjedur traveled throughout Sweden. Through these songs we made the Church aware of the struggle. Songs of sadness, such as "Senze ni na?" ("What have we done?"), and songs directly confronting the apartheid authorities, such as "Vula Botha siyanqungqoza" ("Open Botha, we are a-knocking"), were as important as the more familiar ones that are now sung in churches.[42]

Over twenty-five years after their trip to South Africa, I met with three former members of Fjedur. I asked them how their encounters with South Africans and their music — their journey to South Africa, learning the songs of South Africans, teaching these songs throughout Sweden and beyond — had changed them. Did their encounters leave them with more than good memories? Their response indicated that they had experienced both a musical and a personal revolution. Speaking primarily from a musical perspec-

42. Correspondence from Anders Nyberg, May 12, 2004.

tive, choral director Karin Eklundh articulated how the encounter with South African musicians had changed her perspective on music making in Sweden with her choral ensemble:

> This experience has colored our sense of how we do all music. Music has to be authentic — not just beautiful — but related to the lives of people. All music has to have a quality of authenticity and connection with people — not just music for music's sake. [In Fjedur] we learned Swedish folksongs and South African music by ear. This is a different kind of musical experience. Using the ear — not just the eye — to learn music is important now. There should be a physical response to music. My community choir in Uppsala said they want to sing only with [written] music and did not want to dance. I get them doing it all. African music breaks down the distance between choir and people. This idea is especially important in Sweden where the choir is the group with the talent and others should listen.[43]

The musical revolution that she experienced has its parallels in the performance of liturgy. Liturgy is not something done to and for people, but achieves authenticity when it facilitates an encounter between the people's struggles and the Creator of wholeness. Authentic liturgy involves the entire body — the entire physical body of each worshipper and the entire body of believers, the *ekklesia*. It is not a one-way encounter performed by some and observed by others.

Encounters like this one between South Africans and the church around the world are potentially as close as our neighbors in most of our communities. Liturgy in the twenty-first century awaits Christians who will build bridges between cultures, mediated by the sung prayers of Christians around the world. Rather than being paralyzed by silence in the face of injustice, let us sing in solidarity with those whose burdens are heavy and, in doing so, discover that our own worship finds a more authentic voice to praise the Creator of all song.

43. This quotation comes from an interview arranged by Per Harling with three former members of Fjedur, Karin Eklundh, Karin Olsson, and Anne-Marie Nilsson, on January 28, 2004, in Uppsala, Sweden.

17. The Singing of Jesus

Michael O'Connor

Images of Jesus Christ singing are virtually unknown in Christian art and hymnody. I am not aware of any icon or fresco that shows him at prayer-in-song, nor of any hymn that meditates on this theme. When I asked a number of intelligent, church-going musicians why they thought this was so, their consistent response was, "Oh, did Jesus sing?" (Admittedly, the sample was not large, but the responses were virtually identical.)[1] Yet Jesus was fully human. We have no trouble imagining that Jesus ate, drank, and slept just like the rest of us; that is what people do. But singing? Why do Christians, who devote a great deal of time to singing, overlook their Lord's practice in this regard?[2]

With very few exceptions, Christians have prayed in song for their entire history. For most religions, for most of the time, the same is true. Like posture and gesture, singing has been seen not as a decoration or an add-on to the "real prayer" (supposedly delivered in spoken words) but as something which can be prayer in itself. This conviction is attested in the tag attributed to Augustine, "Who sings, prays twice" ("Qui cantat bis orat"). And as Rowan Williams observes, engaging with music is one way of engaging with God: "To listen seriously to music and to perform it are

---

1. I am disregarding the likes of *Jesus Christ Superstar, Godspell,* and Bach's Passions since these are sung portrayals of Jesus rather than portrayals of Jesus singing.

2. Reggie M. Kidd's recent book, *With One Voice: Discovering Christ's Song in our Worship* (Grand Rapids: Baker, 2005), is a signal exception. The present study bears resemblances to and complements Kidd's creative and committed work.

among our most potent ways of learning what it is to live with and before God."[3]

It ought to come as no surprise that Jesus, the teacher and leader of Christian prayer, should himself pray in song. In this chapter I will draw from a variety of sources and present the theme in three steps: first, the singing of Jesus during his earthly life, as found in the Gospels and deduced from what we know about musical culture of the time; second, the risen Jesus singing in the earthly liturgy of the church, i.e., the singing of the high priest who leads the singing church, his body, in prayer and intercession; and third, music and the Parousia, or how the resurrection and Second Coming of Christ have musical and cosmological consequences (especially against the background of a Pythagorean musical cosmology). The sources are wide-ranging, including biblical texts, sermons, biblical commentaries, poems, apologetic and devotional literature. My methodological assumptions are largely pre-critical, following practices typical of patristic and medieval writers, enshrined in liturgical texts and lectionaries and continued by hymn writers and poets.[4] I shall not so much be presenting an argument, as pointing out and contemplating a theme, one whose presence has been largely *sotto voce* in Christian tradition. The reasons for this neglect are not clear, though they might be related to the reasons why Christians have sometimes marginalized the "laughing Jesus" too. My aim is above all to spotlight the image of Jesus as a singing person. From this, we may then derive a sense of the intrinsic goodness of singing and of the fittingness of our practice of singing prayers to God — in our worship here on earth and in the praise offered in heaven.

The Singing of Jesus during His First Coming

Like any other child, Jesus would have experienced singing and chanting in the home and at play. And like any other faithful Jew, he would have experienced singing in public worship. Israel's worship presented two complementary approaches to music. The worship of the Temple made use of a dedi-

3. Rowan Williams, "Keeping Time," in *Open to Judgement: Sermons and Addresses* (London: Darton, Longman and Todd, 1994), pp. 247-50, here 249.

4. For a forthright defense of such an approach, see David C. Steinmetz, "The Superiority of Pre-Critical Exegesis," *Theology Today* 36 (1980): 27-38, reprinted in *The Theological Interpretation of Scripture*, ed. Stephen E. Fowl (Oxford: Oxford University Press, 1997), pp. 26-38.

cated group of "musicians," instrumentalists and choral singers whose role in worship followed a definite routine. The worship of the synagogue and the home, by contrast, was entirely vocal and less "professional"; this would have been Jesus' more frequent experience of organized prayer. While we speak of this worship as *sung worship,* Edward Foley warns against anachronistic assumptions about its musical style: "The performance of synagogal, word-centred worship continuously migrated back and forth between what we might call speech and song. While it was always lyrical, in the broad sense of that term, the modern hearer (especially from western cultures) might not always classify it as musical."[5] There are parallels today with the patterned intonation of street vendors, horse-racing commentators, and rap artists.

Here a note about vocabulary is in order: this fluidity of practice is reflected in the New Testament by a fluidity of terminology. The New Testament often uses the verb "to say" in contexts where we might assume something more stylized than plain speech, something more akin to singing: the canticles of Mary, Zechariah, and Simeon (Luke 1:46; 1:67, 2:28), the angels' words to the shepherds on Christmas night (Luke 2:13), the crowd's greeting of Jesus on his entry into Jerusalem (Luke 19:38; Matt. 21:9), and throughout the book of Revelation (e.g., 4:8 and 5:12-14). Most significantly, the song of the four living creatures and the twenty-four elders is introduced as follows: ". . . they sang a new song, saying . . . [*adousin ōdēn kainēn legontes*]" (Rev. 5:9). If it is possible here to "say" a "song," then other instances of "saying" (such as those of Mary, Zechariah, Simeon, and the angels already noted) should not be construed as exclusive of singing; on the contrary, "to say" "can be interpreted broadly to include 'to sing.'"[6] Nowadays, we *either* "sing" *or* "say"; in the Greek of the New Testament, it is possible to do both *at the same time.* There is probably more singing in early Christianity than at first meets the eye (or ear), particularly in the context of worship and prayer.

Whatever this lyrical quality, in Jewish worship it was invested with a religious importance: according to the Babylonian Talmud (which contains

5. Edward Foley, *Foundations of Christian Music: The Music of Pre-Constantinian Christianity* (Collegeville: Liturgical Press, 1996), p. 49. See also his entry "New Testament, Music in the," in *Worship Music: A Concise Dictionary,* ed. Edward Foley (Collegeville: Liturgical Press, 2000), pp. 216-17, and Joseph Gelineau, "Music and Singing in the Liturgy," in *The Study of Liturgy,* ed. Cheslyn Jones, Geoffrey Wainwright, and Edward Yarnold (New York: Oxford University Press, 1978), p. 144.

6. Thomas Allen Seel, *A Theology of Music for Worship Derived from the Book of Revelation* (Metuchen, NJ, and London: Scarecrow Press, 1995), p. 110.

rabbinical material from the early third century A.D. onward), "Whosoever reads Scripture without a melody or studies law without a tune, of him [the prophet] says: 'Moreover I gave them statutes that were no good.'"[7] Against this background, Foley asserts that "It would be difficult to imagine any public reading in the synagogue that was not fundamentally lyrical."[8] When Jesus stands up in the synagogue at Nazareth to read from the scroll of Isaiah (Luke 4:16-20), it is reasonable to assume that he proclaimed the text using some form of heightened speech or cantillation. It should be stressed that Jesus was not taking this role because he was considered a talented singer, or had a good voice; the role of "cantor" was shared among the members of the community, and Jesus was simply doing what was expected. Likewise at times of prayer with his disciples, perhaps even when teaching them the Our Father, it can be assumed that Jesus would have used some kind of cantillation.

Alongside these general assumptions about the musical experiences of Jesus, the Gospels tell us explicitly only once that Jesus sang — and it is far from a trivial occasion. It comes at the end of his last supper with his disciples, in the face of imminent suffering and death: "When they had sung the hymn [*hymnēsantes*], they went out to the Mount of Olives" (Mark 14:26; also Matt. 26:30).

How is this "hymning" to be interpreted?

a. The most common explanation, and that favored by modern scholars, derives from an examination of the Passover ceremony itself: if the meal was a Passover meal (and Mark and Matthew present it as one, as does Luke), then the "hymning" would have encompassed the psalms of praise appointed for the end of that ritual meal (the second and final part of the Hallel Psalms, which some scholars give as Psalms 114–118, others as 115–118).[9] According to this view, Jesus and his disciples were faithfully carrying out the rituals of Passover. This, however, is not the only explanation to be found.

b. For Justin Martyr (c. 100–c. 165), anxious to demonstrate to the Jews the fulfillment of the Old Testament by Christ, this text from the "memoirs of the

7. *Babylonian Talmud* (Megillah 32a), cited in "Jewish Music, §III, 2(ii)(a): Synagogue Music and Its Development: Biblical Cantillation," in *The New Grove Dictionary of Music and Musicians*, ed. S. Sadie and J. Tyrrell (London: Macmillan, 2001), vol. 13, p. 41. The biblical quotation is Ezekiel 20:25.

8. Foley, *Foundations*, p. 55.

9. Morna D. Hooker, *The Gospel According to Mark*, Black's New Testament Commentaries (London: A. & C. Black, 1991), p. 344.

Apostles" is the fulfillment of a verse in the messianic Psalm 22: "I will proclaim your name to my brothers and sisters, in the midst of the congregation I
will praise you" (Ps. 22:22).[10] What David foretold in song, the Son of David
fulfills by singing. Justin is the first of a number of writers to draw on this verse
(especially as quoted in Heb. 2:12), but, as we shall see, they are few and far between and their interpretations amount to less than a consensus.

c. Two further explanations are offered by Bede (673-735). First, he
opines that Jesus and his disciples were simply praising the Lord in
thanksgiving after having had their fill, as set forth in the Psalter ("The afflicted shall eat and be satisfied; those who seek him shall praise the Lord,"
Ps. 22:26). As an alternative, he offers the thought that the "hymn" in question might be the so-called "priestly prayer" of John 17, in which Jesus sang,
giving thanks to the Father, raising his eyes to heaven, praying for himself
and his disciples, and for those who were to believe, through their words.[11]
This suggestion of Bede's enjoyed wide circulation beyond its original context, being incorporated into at least two widely used collections of biblical
commentary, the *Glossa ordinaria* and the *Catena aurea* of Aquinas.

d. The apocryphal Acts of John offers yet another slant on the singing at
the end of the last supper. Here the hymning has been transformed into a lit-
any or mantra accompanying a mystical dance:

> Before his arrest by the lawless Jews, who were given their laws by the law-
> less serpent, he gathered us all together and said: "Before I am given over
> to them, let us sing a hymn to the Father, and thus go to meet what lies
> ahead." So he bade us form a circle, as it were, holding each other's hands,
> and taking his place in the middle he said: "Answer Amen to me." Then he
> began to hymn and to say:
>
> "Glory be to thee, Father."
>
> And we, forming a circle, responded "Amen" to him.

10. Justin Martyr, *Dialogue with Trypho*, CVI, in *The Ante-Nicene Fathers: The Writings
of the Fathers Down to A.D. 325*, ed. Alexander Roberts and James Donaldson, vol. 1 (New
York: Christian Literature Publishing Company, 1885; repr. Peabody, MA: Hendrickson Publishers, 1994), p. 252.

11. "Et hymno dicto, exierunt in montem Olivarum. Hoc est, quod in psalmo legimus:
'Edent pauperes et saturabuntur, et laudabunt Dominum, qui requirunt eum' (Psal. XXI).
Potest autem hymnus etiam ille intelligi quem Dominus, secundum Joannem, Patri gratias
agens, decantabat, in quo et pro seipso, et pro discipulis, et pro eis qui per verba eorum
credituri erant, elevatis sursum oculis precabatur" (*Opera*, Corpus Christianorum, Series
Latina [Turnholt: Brepols, 1955-], vol. 120, pp. 612-13).

"Glory be to thee, Word, Glory be to thee, Grace." "Amen."
"Glory be to thee, Spirit: Glory be to thee, Holy One,
Glory be to thy glory." "Amen." . . .

After dancing this with us, my beloved, the Lord went out, and we confused and asleep, as it were, fled one way and the other.[12]

Whatever we make of this curious song and dance, it is clear that the experience unsettles the disciples. The use of music and ritual by no means
dulls the edge of the coming crisis.

Though each commentator approaches the text differently, there is a cumulative effect to these interpretations: Jesus, the new David, fulfilling the
demands of the old covenant, and preparing for the sacrifice of the new covenant, turns to the Father with songs of praise, obedience, and intercession.

One final group of Gospel texts calls for attention when considering the
singing of Jesus during his earthly life. According to Matthew and Mark, the
last words of Jesus on the cross were the first words of Psalm 22 (Matt. 27:46;
Mark 15:34). For David Ford, the interpretation of this passage must not be
sentimentalized or unrealistic: Jesus "did not sing on the cross. His 'loud cry'
is the extremity of speech, beyond talk and song."[13] Paul Westermeyer does
not go quite so far: "At the darkest moment on the cross, Jesus was not reduced to silence, but to the musical moan of Psalm 22, 'My God, my God,
why have you forsaken me?'"[14] In Luke, the loud voice of Jesus recites a different Psalm verse (31:5), commending his spirit into his Father's hands
(Luke 23:46). In each of these narratives, a reminiscence of musical prayer
accompanies the final moments of Jesus' life; his paschal sacrifice is offered,
"it is accomplished" (John 19:30), with the sounds of Jewish prayer. What Jesus learned in the regular worship of his people springs to his lips as his life
comes to an end. Then with death comes silence; he sings no more.

In conclusion: Jesus grew up in a lyrical culture and worshiped in a setting that used musical/lyrical forms regularly and with ease. It would have
come naturally to him to sing at prayer; indeed, it would have been *unnatu-
ral* not to do so. When praying to his Father in heaven, Jesus, the Word incar-

12. Acts of John, 94-97, translation in James McKinnon, *Music in Early Christian Literature* (Cambridge: Cambridge University Press, 1987), p. 25. McKinnon notes that this hymn
provided the text set by Gustav Holst in his "Hymn of Jesus."

13. David Ford, *Self and Salvation: Being Transformed* (Cambridge: Cambridge University Press, 1999), p. 129.

14. Paul Westermeyer, *Te Deum: The Church and Music* (Minneapolis: Fortress, 1998),
pp. 39-40.

nate, did not shun the use of human words, human gestures, and human postures; likewise he did not shun human music. His relationship with the Father was thoroughly translated at the incarnation so that his loving and obedient orientation to the Father finds apt expression in Jewish ritual songs; and verses from the Psalms hang on his lips as he yields up his Spirit.

The Singing of the Risen Jesus in the Church's Earthly Liturgy

When Jesus is raised from death, a song returns to his lips ("You have turned my mourning into dancing . . . and so my soul will praise you and not be silent. O Lord my God, I will praise you for ever" [Ps. 30:11-12]). But before considering the song of the risen Jesus, it will be helpful to consider the background of eschatological singing in the Old Testament. Singing is an act of faith, and music is an integral part of the human response to the gift of salvation.[15] After the Jews are delivered out of Egypt and cross the Red Sea to safety, their immediate reaction is to sing to the Lord (Exod. 14:31–15:1). A connection between resurrection and singing is foreshadowed in Isaiah: "Your dead shall live, their corpses shall rise. O dwellers in the dust, awake and sing for joy" (Isa. 26:19; see also Isa. 51:11). The singing of a "new song" (Pss. 33:3; 40:3; 96:1; 98:1; 144:9; 149:1; Isa. 42:1) here and now looks forward to the singing of a new song in the new creation. This pattern is echoed in the New Testament vision of deliverance (Rev. 15:2-3). The new song is the song of heaven — the "four living creatures" and the "elders" (5:9), and the 140,000 on Mount Zion (14:3). A new song celebrates the victory of the Lamb over death and the ransoming of the elect (Rev. 5:9 and 14:2). Singing is what redeemed people do and in doing so they anticipate a consummation of their song in a future glory. Addressing the newly baptized, Augustine links their rebirth and eschatological hope with their new song:

> So anyone who knows how to love the new life knows how to sing the new song. So for the sake of the new song we need to be reminded what the new life is. All these things, you see, belong to the one kingdom — the new person, the new song, the new testament or new covenant. So the new person will both sing the new song and belong to the new covenant.[16]

---

15. Joseph Ratzinger, *The Spirit of the Liturgy* (San Francisco: Ignatius, 2000), p. 137.

16. Augustine, *Sermons,* The Works of St Augustine: A Translation for the 21st Century, Part III, vol. 2, trans. Edmund Hill (New York: New City Press, 1990), Sermon 34, p. 166.

If this is true of those born to new life in Christ, it is also true of Christ himself, the first-born, the fruit fruits of the new creation. He too gives thanks for life restored, for heaven opened. But it is not a song he sings in isolation: he witnesses to his brothers and sisters and invites them to join in his song. He is the high priest who leads the priestly prayer of his body the church.

Jesus taught his disciples to pray; he prayed with them, and he sang with them. They evidently continued this practice among themselves after his ascension. From all that we can see in the apostolic writings, there is nothing to contradict this view, and much to support it (e.g., Acts 16:25-26; Eph. 5:18-20; Col. 3:16-17; James 5:13). When they gathered to pray, the first Christians were assured that the risen Christ remained among them: "For where two or three are gathered in my name, I am there among them" (Matt. 18:20). The Spirit of Christ, sent from on high, not only gave them speech for witness and preaching (Acts 2), but prayed in them, with "sighs too deep for words" (Rom. 8:26), and with the gift of singing (I Cor. 14:15). Even though Jesus had left their sight, the Christian community sang and prayed in the memory of the risen Lord who was present with them through his Spirit. That Christ is present and *sings* among his (singing) people is attested by a psalm text already quoted, which is taken up in the Letter to the Hebrews: "I will proclaim your name to my brothers and sisters, in the midst of the congregation [*en meso ekklēsias*] I will praise [*hymnesō*] you" (Heb. 2:12, quoting Ps. 22:22).

This quotation appears in a passage which speaks of the suffering and exaltation of Jesus. The psalm is quoted because of what it says about the kinship of Jesus with humanity: having become human, he is not ashamed to call us his family. Having entered into our condition, and having made the first part of the psalm his own, most dramatically on the cross ("My God, my God, why have you forsaken me?"), he now takes up the second part of the psalm in his resurrection. The demonstration and experience of this solidarity is expressed musically: the singing of praise to the Father among the assembly of his brothers and sisters reveals the fellowship of Jesus with his kin.[17]

And just as the singing of Jesus is a revelation of redemptive solidarity with the disciples, so the singing of the disciples in imitation of the master can be a witness to the world. John Calvin (1509-64) reads this verse as an encouragement to the Christian community to persevere in acts of public praise which not only honor God but also witness to others: "And it is a truth, which may serve as a most powerful stimulant, and may lead us most fervently to

17. See Friedrich Doormann, "Deinen Namen will ich meinen Brüdern verkünden (Hebr 2,11-13)," *Bibel und Leben* 14 (1973): 245-52.

praise God, when we hear that Christ leads our songs [*nobis praecinere*], and is the chief composer of our hymns [*primum hymnorum modulatorem*]."[18]

John Wesley (1703-91) echoes comments already mentioned, seeing Jesus not only as the leader of the apostolic choir at the end of the last supper (with Justin), but also more generally among the Christian community (with Calvin):

> Christ declares the name of God, gracious and merciful, plenteous in goodness and truth, to all who believe, that they also may praise him. "In the midst of the church will I sing praise unto thee" — as the precentor of the choir. This he did literally, in the midst of his apostles, on the night before his passion. And as it means, in a more general sense, setting forth the praise of God, he has done it in the church by his word and his Spirit; he still does, and will do it throughout all generations.[19]

Other commentators likewise place the "moment" of this verse in the life of the church and particularly in its worship: "The glorified Saviour is not only the Church's brother, revealing to it the Father; he is also the Church's precentor, leading its worship."[20]

Christ sings among his people when they are gathered to worship on earth. This is part of his promise to remain among them even to the ends of the age (Matt. 28:20). The singing of Jesus in the church shows who he is (Son of the Father) and who his disciples are (no less than his brothers and sisters). Christ is the leader and initiator of Christian worship, the High Priest of the sacrifice of praise offered to the Father by those who serve him

18. *Commentaries on the Epistle to the Hebrews by John Calvin,* translated from the original Latin and edited by John Owen (1853; Grand Rapids: Eerdmans, 1949), pp. 66-67. "Atque haec doctrina acerrimi stimuli vice nobis est, quo ferventiore studio feramur ad laudandum Deum, quum audimus Christum nobis praecinere, et primum esse hymnorum modulatorem" (T. H. L. Parker, ed., *Commentarius in epistolam ad Hebraeos,* Iohannis Calvini Opera Exegetica, vol. XIX [Geneva: Droz, 1996], p. 40). Reggie Kidd draws out the missionary aspect of the singing of Jesus in remarks on a parallel text (Rom. 15:6 quoting Ps. 57:9): Paul "thinks of the church's evangelism as Jesus singing among the nations, drawing Gentiles and Jews together so they might offer a chorus of praise to the Father. Through Paul's own mission, he hears Jesus *singing* nations into submission by singing them into *life*" (*With One Voice,* p. 107).

19. John Wesley, *Explanatory Notes on the New Testament,* vol. 2 (Grand Rapids: Baker Books, 1986; "Reprinted from an undated edition published by the Wesleyan-Methodist Book-Room London"), no page numbers.

20. C. J. Vaughan, *The Epistle to the Hebrews with Notes* (London: Macmillan, 1891), p. 45.

(see Heb. 8:1-2). The eternal Son's loving obedience toward the Father, translated into human form in the incarnation (which is his priesthood) is now shared with all of his brothers and sisters. In Reggie Kidd's evocative expression, the song of the church on earth is "antiphon" to Christ's voice from heaven.[21] For Augustine, this leads to joyful exclamations about the interweaving voices of the one Christ, head and members: "He prays for us as our priest, prays in us as our head, and is prayed to by us as our God. Let us therefore acknowledge our voice in him and his voice in us."[22]

Liturgical singing thus exists in two times at once: the time of this present age, which is passing away, and the time of Christ, which is both "above" and "before" us.[23]

The Beginning and End of Music

So far our theme has been explored with respect to the earthly life of Jesus and the present time of the church, in-between Pentecost and Parousia. The song of Jesus has, however, been detected both earlier and later in the story. For the bishops at Second Vatican Council (1962-65), the incarnation brings heaven's song to earth so that earthly singers can join, even now as they worship, in the high priest's heavenly song of praise and intercession:

> Christ Jesus, high priest of the new and eternal covenant, taking human nature, introduced into this earthly exile that hymn which is sung throughout all ages in the halls of heaven. He joins the entire community of humanity to himself, associating it with his own singing of this canticle of divine praise. For he continues his priestly work through the agency of his Church, which is ceaselessly engaged in praising the Lord and interceding for the salvation of the whole world.[24]

21. Kidd, *With One Voice*, p. 115.

22. *Enarrationes in Psalmos* 85, 1 (PL 37).

23. See Jeremy Begbie, *Theology, Music and Time* (Cambridge: Cambridge University Press, 2000), p. 151.

24. Second Vatican Council, *Constitution on the Sacred Liturgy (Sacrosanctum concilium)*, §83. See also Christopher Cocksworth, *Holy, Holy, Holy: Worshipping the Trinitarian God* (London: Darton, Longman and Todd, 1997), p. 159: "He calls us to join his voice and to share in his song. God in Christ gives us words for worship. They are divine words, which have been accurately translated into human language by the movement to us in the incarnation and they are words which are authentically returned to the divine life by the movement to God in the priesthood of Christ."

Here the song of the heavenly priest, echoed in the earthly liturgy, reflects an eternal song of the heavenly places, a "pre-existent" song that has been sung for as long as there have been voices to offer praise. In his earthly life, Jesus taught and rehearsed this eternal canticle, in and for the world.

In a largely overlooked treatise on heavenly music, the Lutheran composer and music theorist, Johann Mattheson (1681-1764) extends the range about as far as it will go. Drawing together suggestive texts from Old and New Testaments, he seeks to establish both the origins and the endurance of the song of Jesus.[25] First, in the book of Proverbs, Wisdom speaks of being "at play" in God's presence at the creation of the world, "delighting in the children of the human race" (Prov. 8:31); Mattheson remarks that this "playing" is the playing (and singing) of music; the Son of God (who is the Wisdom of God), is the divine "Oberkapellmeister" of the angelic hosts.[26]

Second, in the book of Job, God demands to know from Job: "Where were you when I laid the foundation of the earth . . . , when the morning stars sang together and all the children of God shouted for joy?" (Job 38:4-7). Here Mattheson observes that, in the book of Revelation, Jesus describes himself as the bright morning star (Rev. 22:16), and so — Mattheson believes — implicitly counts himself among those singing at the foundation of the world. He is the chorus-leader *(choragus)* of the heavenly princes.[27]

Since Christ is the first-born Son, he must have been among the "children" on the earth; and since he is *the* morning star, he must have been among the morning stars too. If then he was among the musical hosts at the foundation of the world, and sang also in this vale of tears, so much more must we hold that in eternity, with the chorus of angels and saints, he will praise the Father's glory in song.[28] Concerning the singing of Jesus in the midst of the congregation (Heb. 2:12), Mattheson is clear where this scene is to be located: it is "the coming world, about which we are speaking" (Heb. 2:5).

Mattheson's exegesis has brought together a number of diverse texts to present a continuity between the music of Christ and the angels at the beginning of creation and the music led by Christ in the world to come. Biblical authority has been brought to bear on liturgy and also on cosmology. And

25. Johann Mattheson, *Behauptung der Himmlischen Musik aus den Gründen der Vernunft, Kirchen-Lehre und Heiliger Schrift* (Hamburg, 1747). I am grateful to Joyce Irwin for alerting me to its existence. On Mattheson, see *The New Grove Dictionary of Music and Musicians,* vol. 16, pp. 139-44.

26. Mattheson, *Behauptung,* p. 67.

27. Mattheson, *Behauptung,* pp. 99-100.

28. Mattheson, *Behauptung,* pp. 121-22.

while liturgical theology is hospitable to this idea, the impact on Christian cosmology is more problematic.

Old Creation, New Creation

The music of heaven in Christian tradition is heavily influenced by Greek ideas about cosmic harmony and unity.[29] For Pythagoras, the order and meaning of the cosmos can be perceived in the proportions found within nature and revealed in musical ratios. Music brings to bear the "number" that is the principle of order and balance in the cosmos. The planets, rotating in their crystal spheres, make musical sounds corresponding to these primal ratios, engendering the "music of the spheres." Music quite literally makes the world go round. This text from Isidore of Seville is typical of Christian Pythagoreans.

> Thus without music no discipline can be perfect, for there is nothing without it. The very universe, it is said, is held together by a certain harmony of sounds, and the heavens themselves are made to revolve by the modulation of harmony.[30]

In Christian thought, the music of the spheres is closely linked to the mission of the angels: they are the spirits who drive the astrological music machine.[31] So when they sing at the nativity of the Word made flesh, it is the music of cosmic harmony that breaks briefly (and, for once, audibly) into the sublunary world. It follows that heavenly music in this scheme is predominantly angelic music. So we seek to come into tune with heaven by craning our necks and straining to hear the angelic chant and joining in. Referring to an all-too-brief "glimpse" of heavenly music, Milton (1608-74) would write:

29. For a more detailed treatment of these ideas, see the essays in this volume by Carol Harrison and John Ito. For concise surveys of this tradition, see Wayne D. Bowman, *Philosophical Perspectives on Music* (New York: Oxford University Press, 1998), pp. 19-68, and the entertaining account in Jamie James, *The Music of the Spheres: Music, Science, and the Natural Order of the Universe* (London: Abacus, 1993).

30. Isidore of Seville, *Etymologiarum* III, 17, translated in *Strunk's Source Readings in Music History*, ed. Oliver Strunk (1950; New York: W. W. Norton, 1998), p. 150.

31. Quentin Faulkner, *Wiser than Despair: The Evolution of Ideas in the Relationship of Music and the Christian Church* (Westport, CT: Greenwood, 1996), p. 94. Faulkner cites examples from Gregory the Great and Dante.

O may we soon again renew that song,
And keep in tune with Heaven, till God ere long
To His celestial concert us unite,
To live with Him, and sing in endless morn of light.[32]

This scheme privileges the on-going (mostly inaudible) music of creation. Beatitude is somehow concerned with recovering this "original music." But, for Christianity, salvation is to come not from a return to some pristine beginning, but as the outcome of a cataclysmic end. The nostalgia for heavenly music must be eschatologically redefined. Milton himself was aware of the tension and in another poem, "Ode on the Morning of Christ's Nativity," he powerfully dramatizes it. Writing on Christmas Day itself, he begins by evoking the angelic chorus singing to the shepherds. Their music is an echo of the music first heard at creation (alluding to Job 38:7):

Such music (as 'tis said)
Before was never made,
But when of old the sons of morning sung,
While the Creator great
His constellations set,
And the well-balanced world on hinges hung,
And cast the dark foundations deep,
And bid the welt'ring waves their oozy channel keep.[33]

Milton is captivated by this music and wonders whether, if we could only hear this music, its power to transform us would be complete: sin and death would be rolled back and the first golden age of innocence and glory would be restored:

For if such holy song
Enwrap our fancy long,
Time will run back and fetch the age of gold,
And speckled Vanity
Will sicken soon and die,
And leprous Sin will melt from earthly mould;

---

32. "At a Solemn Music," lines 25-28. For the context of this and similar texts, see John Hollander, *The Untuning of the Sky: Ideas of Music in English Poetry, 1500-1700* (Princeton, NJ: Princeton University Press, 1961); and Diane Kelsey McColley, *Poetry and Music in Seventeenth-Century England* (Cambridge: Cambridge University Press, 1997).

33. John Milton, "Ode on the Morning of Christ's Nativity" (1629), stanza XII.

And Hell itself will pass away,
And leave her dolorous mansions to the peering Day.[34]

The vision is beautiful, the possibility seemingly within reach. But, in this poem at least, Milton remains unconvinced: he is bound to affirm that such music, however divinely ordered, cannot take away the sin of the world. Such a view would neglect the one whose coming is the very reason for this manifestation of angelic delight: the baby in the manger who is to be the redeemer. So Milton fixes on a contrasting, forward-looking musical image. While the music at Jesus' first coming was a sweet and holy song, the music that will accompany his latter appearing will not be so sweet; instead of a journey backward in time to the pristine music of the first day, Milton whisks us forward to the "trump of doom" of the last day. The eschatological music is an overture to judgment, awesome and dreadful, issuing from the throne of the crucified and risen King:

But wisest Fate says no:
This must not yet be so;
The Babe lies yet in smiling infancy,
That on the bitter cross
Must redeem our loss,
So both himself and us to glorify:
Yet first to those ychained in sleep,
The wakeful trump of doom must thunder through the deep,

With such a horrid clang
As on Mount Sinai rang
While the red fire and smould'ring clouds outbrake:
The aged Earth, aghast
With terror of that blast,
Shall from the surface to the centre shake,
When at the world's last session,
The dreadful Judge in middle air shall spread his throne.[35]

Milton's poem has taken us from the music of the first creation to the music that ushers in the revealing of the new creation, from a metaphysical scheme built on speculation about creation's primordial music, to a scheme

34. Milton, "On the Morning of Christ's Nativity," stanza XIV.
35. Milton, "On the Morning of Christ's Nativity," stanzas XVI-XVII.

based on God's dealings with his people throughout history, attentive to the sounds that accompany the forging of the covenant — on Sinai and at the Parousia. The final victory over death, the overthrowing of all idolatry, and the remaking of all things in Christ, is *signaled* by a dreadful music. A similar conclusion is reached by John Dryden in "A Song for St Cecilia's Day" (1687):

> So when the last and dreadful hour
> This crumbling Pageant shall devour,
> The TRUMPET shall be heard on high,
> The Dead shall live, the Living die,
> And MUSICK shall untune the Sky.

So far our musical considerations of the Parousia have centered on the last trumpet. While this has been going on, what has happened to singing? We have seen how the quotation from Psalm 22 in Hebrews 2:12 has received a variety of interpretations in Christian tradition. Unlike Justin, Calvin, and Wesley, William Lane places the "moment" of this verse quite precisely at the Second Coming:

> The statement is taken from that part of the psalm where lament is exchanged for an expression of joyful thanksgiving. It is appropriate to an experience of vindication and exaltation after suffering and affliction. The writer to the Hebrews locates here a reference to the exalted Lord who finds in the gathering of the people of God at the parousia an occasion for the proclamation of God's name and who as the singing priest leads the redeemed community [*en mesō ekklēsias*] in songs of praise.[36]

The terrifying judge of idolatry is also the high priest perfected through suffering, who leads his brothers and sisters to the banquet prepared by the Father, with a song of rejoicing. His resurrection is to be their resurrection; his Father is their Father; his song theirs. This too appears to be the interpretation of the writer of the pseudepigraphical Odes of Solomon, a Christian wisdom-poet possibly of late first century. Ode 31, which in a number of details mirrors Psalm 22, contemplates the Son's offering of the elect to the Father at the Last Day:

---

36. William Lane, *Hebrews 1–8*, Word Biblical Commentary, vol. 47A (Dallas: Word Books, 1991), p. 59. In this quotation I have transliterated the Greek text.

Chasms vanished before the Lord, and darkness dissipated before His
appearance.
Error erred and perished on account of Him; and contempt received
no path, for it was submerged by the truth of the Lord.
He opened His mouth and spoke grace and joy; and recited a new
chant to His name.
Then He lifted his voice towards the Most High, and offered to Him
those that had become sons through Him.
And His face was justified, because thus His Holy Father had given to
Him.
Come forth, you who have been afflicted, and receive joy.
And possess yourselves through grace, and take unto you immortal
life.[37]

With this moment, the redeemed participate fully in, by being enveloped in,
the song of Jesus. What is anticipated in liturgical singing here below is possessed in the resurrection in the world to come.

This eschatological understanding of the song of Jesus is elaborated in
the most sustained piece of theological writing on the New Song among
early Christian writers, that provided by Clement of Alexandria. His concentrated meditation on this theme is a Christian response to the prevailing
musical cults and myths of enchanting deities in the milieu of ancient Egypt.
Clement compares the false enchantments of Orpheus and the like with the
music-making of the true Orpheus, who is Jesus Christ. And alone among
the early Christian writers, Clement not only refutes this power, but offers a
theological reflection on the Orpheus image and develops a counter-image
of Christ the New Song.[38]

For Clement, Christ was the true musical enchanter, accomplishing
through the Spirit what "Orpheus had failed to do with his kithara: creating
order."[39] While Orpheus tamed the beasts, Christ converted sinners and led

37. *The Odes of Solomon: The Syriac Texts,* edited with translation and notes by James
Hamilton Charlesworth (Missoula, MT: Scholars Press, 1977), Ode 31.1-7, pp. 116-17.
38. Robert A. Skeris, *Chroma Theou: On the Origins and Theological Interpretation of
the Musical Imagery Used by the Ecclesiastical Writers of the First Three Centuries, with Special
Reference to the Image of Orpheus,* Publications of the Catholic Church Music Associates, vol.
1 (Altötting: Coppenrath, 1976), p. 157. See also John Block Friedman, *Orpheus in the Middle
Ages* (Cambridge, MA: Harvard University Press, 1970), pp. 53-56; and Eleanor Irwin, "The
Songs of Orpheus and the New Song of Christ," in *Orpheus: The Metamorphoses of a Myth,*
ed. John Warden (Toronto: University of Toronto Press, 1982), pp. 51-62.
39. Skeris, *Chroma Theou,* p. 131.

them in a song of praise to the Father. Thomas Merton sums up Clement's comprehensive musical imagery: "Here he shows us the cosmos as a hymn of glory to the Father, in which Christ has descended to sing to God, accompanying his song with the many-voiced instrument, the human nature He assumed in the Incarnation."[40]

Clement multiplies the imagery on three levels. Christ plays the instrument of the creation (especially the human part of it); Christ sings the true song; and Christ himself *is* the new song (played by the Father). Later writers would develop other parallels: Orpheus went into the underworld and brought back Eurydice, so Christ went among the dead and brought back his bride the church.[41] But Clement's signal contribution is to dwell on the singing and the song which are Christ. Christ is the resurrection and the life, and he is therefore the New Song in person.

It is often unclear whether Clement intends his words to be taken metaphorically or literally. In the following passage, Clement compares the power of the music of Orpheus (who tamed wild beasts) with that of the New Song (who tames those human beings allegorically represented by different kinds of wild beasts): "See how mighty is the new song! It has made men out of stones, and men out of wild beasts. They who were otherwise dead, who had no share in the real and true life, revived when they but heard the new song."[42]

Although the Orpheus myth employs the sounding of actual music, it is not clear whether the New Song stands here for a real song of Christ, or as a metaphor for the gospel message proclaimed and heard in faith. Some of what Clement writes, however, does seem to suggest that music itself, the medium of Orpheus, has become a sacred medium in the hands (and voice) of Christ; the singing of praise in faith can be as much an experience of grace as the preaching and hearing of the gospel. The joy of the redeemed will be captured in few words shared by many voices:

> And the union of many into one, bringing a divine harmony out of many scattered sounds, becomes one symphony, following one Leader [*choreigo:* chorus-leader] and Teacher, the Word, and never ceasing till it reaches the Truth itself, with the cry, "Abba, Father." This is the true

40. Clement of Alexandria, *Selections from the Protreptikos*, with an essay and translation by Thomas Merton (Norfolk, CT: New Directions, 1962), p. 12.

41. Irwin, "The Songs of Orpheus," p. 56.

42. *Protreptikos* I, 4. The translation is that of Butterworth in the Loeb Classical Library edition of Clement's work (London, 1919), p. 11.

speech which God welcomes from His children. This is the first-fruits of God's harvest.[43]

Clement's starting point was the enchanting power of music, abused by Orpheus in the myths of the idolaters. His conclusion is the song of praise which fills the heavens, directed unerringly to the one true God by the heavenly chorus-leader, Jesus Christ. Clement has gone a stage further than Milton. He has not only imagined a heavenly music that is marked by the history of redemption, but he has made Christ the leader of its performance. The angels are members of a chorus of which Christ is the leader and director, and it is he, not they, who initiates the music.

There is a tendency in Clement to identify Christ and the New Song; the power of one is the power of the other. This is not surprising — the New Testament pictures Jesus as person and as Word, as Word-in-Person. Clement is simply moving from Jesus as Word-incarnate, to Jesus as Song-incarnate, risen and glorified. In an illuminating commentary on the Christological psalms, Cajetan (1469-1534) makes a different and complementary move: to Jesus as Prayer-in-Person. Prayer, he says, is not an isolated activity, but the underlying category of all that Jesus does. All that he did and suffered was on account of the Father; the whole life of Christ was of God. His whole life, day and night, as it were, comes before God. Indeed, in a remarkable piece of exegesis, it can be said that prayer is not so much what he *does*, but what he *is:* "I myself am my prayer to you, since all that I am is a prayer."[44] He, for whom existence means to be a Word spoken *by* the Father, is also a prayer returned *to* the Father. With his whole life, he sings the returning prayer which answers to the Father's originating love.

Concluding Remarks

How are we to understand such an eschatological singing? Some will choose to take these remarks entirely metaphorically: to speak of heavenly music is to use a metaphor that evokes harmony and beauty, but not actual sound or musical performance. (This is the sort of treatment sometimes given to eating too: many profess that the Eucharist is a foretaste of the heavenly banquet,

43. *Protreptikos,* IX, 88. Butterworth, p. 195.
44. "Vere tota vita Christi erat Dei." On Ps. 109:20, *Opera Omnia quotquot in sacrae scripturae expositionem reperiuntur* (Lyons, 1639) vol. III, 373a. "Ego ipse sum oratio mea tibi, quia totum quod sum, sum oratio." On Ps. 69:13, vol. III, 240b.

but far fewer actually expect to be eating in heaven.) Others replace heavenly music with heavenly silence. Joseph Gelineau suggests that "After this life the only music that will be able to satisfy the soul will be the music of silence."[45] And in a similar vein, in his work on the meaning of the Psalter in the prayer life of Christians, Thomas Merton asserts: "The Psalms are more than language. They contain within themselves the silence of high mountains and the silence of heaven. . . . The Liturgy of heaven is a most perfect harmony which, like the music of the spheres, sees song transfigured into silence."[46]

Still others, however, may want to insist on an actual, audible, heavenly music-making. John Donne (1571-31) writes of "no noise nor silence, but one equal music." John Polkinghorne draws on the insights of general relativity theory to affirm that "The new creation will not be a timeless world of 'eternity,' but a temporal world whose character is everlasting. (It will contain music, that specifically temporal art.)"[47] And Paul Westermeyer wonders whether the expectation of jubilant song in heaven (rather than silence) is a typically Lutheran trait.[48] Lining up with the typically Lutheran position, and in contrast to the Catholic Gelineau and Merton, Joseph Ratzinger (now Pope Benedict XVI) sees faith-filled speech and contemplative silence eventually yielding to song: "But wherever God's word is translated into human words there remains a surplus of the unspoken and the unutterable which calls us to silence — into a silence that in the end lets the unutterable become song and also calls on the voices of the cosmos for help so that the unspoken may become audible."[49]

Sweeping aside the scruples of theologians and pastors such as Augustine and Calvin, Ratzinger lets the Bible make the case: "In contrast to theology, the psalms manifested an utterly unpuritanical delight in music."[50] The Psalter not only provides the command to sing ("Sing praises to God, sing praises," Ps. 47:6), but it also furnishes inspired songs to enable the fulfillment of that command.[51] Singing enables praise because it involves the

45. Joseph Gelineau, *Voices and Instruments in Christian Worship* (Collegeville: Liturgical Press, 1964), pp. 27-28.

46. Thomas Merton, *Bread in the Wilderness* (London: Burns and Oates, 1953), p. 125.

47. John Polkinghorne, *The God of Hope and the End of the World* (New Haven, CT: Yale University Press, 2002), p. 117.

48. Westermeyer, *Te Deum*, p. 99.

49. Joseph Ratzinger, *A New Song for the Lord* (New York: Crossroad, 1996), p. 137; translation amended.

50. Joseph Ratzinger, *Feast of Faith* (San Francisco: Ignatius, 1981), p. 114.

51. Ratzinger, *Spirit of the Liturgy*, p. 140.

whole person: it is at once mental, emotional, and muscular, a work of the spirit and a work of the flesh, a work of individuals and a work that fosters fellowship.[52] As such is it a fitting testimony to the incarnation of the Son of God, whose humanity was complete in every way. But singing is also an ecstatic act, in which the singer reaches out to others, becomes vulnerable before them, becomes a gift to them. And as such, it is a fitting testimony to the eternal life of the Son before the Father, a self-emptying life of prayer, love, trust, and obedience.

The contemplation of the singing of Jesus raises questions in Christology, eschatology, and trinitarian theology. It also offers a chance to consider the Christological and eschatological character of music in worship: our liturgical song is not created by us, but given us by our high priest. He translated heaven's song into a truly earthly song at his incarnation, in order that he might make such an earthly song, together with a host of earthly singers, part of the worship of heaven. The singing of Jesus offers a rich link between the way we pray and the life we hope for, putting the music we use to a considerable challenge, and inspiring us in the way we use it.

52. See Thomas Aquinas, *Summa Theologiae,* II-IIae, q. 91, a. 1 and 2.

Afterword
Mr. Holland's Advice: A Call to Immersive, Cross-Disciplinary Learning

John D. Witvliet

This volume represents a burst of cross-disciplinary energy and insight that can be celebrated by musicians and theologians, music-lovers and God-lovers alike. At its best, this exchange between music and theology at once points both to thought-provoking conceptual innovations and to a transformation of the ethos in which musical and theological reflection takes place.

As I studied these essays, I found myself pondering what both their specific contributions and their approach might mean for any number of other topics, themes, and intellectual and pastoral challenges. To select only one small example: consider the prospects of this volume for all who ponder the meaning and significance of human death, whether biologically, pastorally, clinically, philosophically, or personally. After reflecting on Bach's treatment of death (chapter 9), the multiple musical ways of depicting eschatological time (chapter 11), and the power of musical worship to heal emotion (chapter 13), it is difficult to imagine wanting to engage in any substantive reflection on death apart from reflective engagement with musical experiences. And in preparing our own musical response to death, how can we not be struck by the power of music to instruct us in ways of healing the breaches of communal life (chapter 15)? How can we not wonder about how the funeral musics of the world's cultures might challenge assumptions and open up possibilities for our own improvisatory responses (Hawn)? What challenge or comfort might we discover in someone like Messiaen — with his preference for music that is "iridescent, subtle, even voluptuous," for music that "expresses the end of time, ubiquity, glorified bodies and the divine and supernatural mysteries" (see Sholl, p. 163)? In what registers and modes might music preach the real sermon at most funerals, and if so, what kinds of disciplines would we need to focus its homiletic potential (chapter 3)? How does the singing of the ascended Christ (chapter 17) offer a language in which to understand and picture what lies beyond the grave?

At the same time, reading this book is a humbling experience. This is a book that pushes all of us to the edges of our competency. It is one thing for theologians to master the Old and New Testaments, Augustine and Chrysostom, Aquinas and Luther, Barth and Rahner — or for musicians to master Palestrina and Bach, Mahler and Stravinsky, the Beatles and Bono, the gamelan and drumming circles. It is quite another to gain even amateur expertise in both worlds. Most of us who read this book may well find our view of any given essay marred by our own astigmatisms: we will see each essay through one stronger disciplinary eye and one weaker one. Thus, for most of us, this book is an invitation to a challenging, but deeply rewarding trajectory of learning. Most of us need to strengthen at least one disciplinary eye to help us achieve the kind of musical-theological binocular vision that offers so much promise for new insight.

For this reason it seems wise to reflect on the best way to proceed with the learning task this book invites. How should we act upon the yearning that this book creates? How can we best engage in the learning necessary to both benefit from and contribute to the music-theology conversation? What should we do if we feel both compelled and intimidated by this book?

As I worked my way through this book, I found myself wondering what Mr. Holland would say about that. I take Glenn Holland to be a good representative for a special class of people, the kind of world-class music teachers that their students both respect and love. Glenn Holland was an aspiring composer, committed to writing a masterpiece, who despite a lifetime's worth of frustrations, discovered the joy and honed the craft of teaching music. The film about him, *Mr. Holland's Opus* (1995), ends with a remarkable scene in which his students over many years plan a surprise celebration of his life's work, giving his composition its first performance. Among its many interwoven themes, the film powerfully conveys that writing a symphony is not the only masterpiece that matters, and that the practical wisdom that enables teaching and learning is among the most splendid gifts that God bestows. What, then, would Mr. Holland say about the kind of learning this volume requires of us?

Immersive Learning

First, I suspect that Mr. Holland would remind us of a point that may be obvious, but one that is also remarkably easy to ignore or take for granted: learning music, learning about music, and learning from music best happen if we actually make and listen to music. All music-related learning is ultimately derivative of musical experiences. This, not surprisingly, is a fundamental tenet in the field of music education. One summary of the most prominent music learning methodologies puts it this way:

> Music learning begins with active, holistic experiences that combine the seeing and hearing of models with doing and experimenting, and that doing, experimenting, verbalizing, and comparing oneself with models leads to the acquisition of skills in performing and discriminating, and finally to skills in conceptualizing musical sound and relating it to printed symbols.[1]

The experience of music is irreducible, never fully explored by reflection or analysis. And without the experience of music, our learning about or from music is likely to be either misguided or senseless. Bennet Reimer, a leading music theorist and philosopher, says it this way:

> Music educators, in the "music" aspect of that term, help their students experience the meaning of music by immersing them directly and personally in its meanings — the felt sounds they are helped to experience. The music they make and respond to yields its mysteries — its immediately experienced ways to know. . . . So by taking our students into musical sounds, in all the ways our culture provides for, we allow music to speak its mystery.[2]

The actual experience of music offers much that essays about music cannot offer as richly: a participatory knowledge, the heightened capacity to remember a particular musical experience or layer of musical meaning, a depth of perception into a fundamental area of musical meaning, or a sense

---

1. Richard Colwell, ed., *Handbook of Research on Music Teaching and Learning* (Schirmer Books, 1992), 541. This is a summary of the common elements in five of the most prominent leading methods of music education: Delcroze, Orff, Kodaly, Suzuki, and Gordon. Each of these five famous methods is, in some way, a protest against musical education that was insufficiently grounded in musical experiences.

2. Bennett Reimer, *A Philosophy of Music Education*, 3rd ed. (Upper Saddle River, NJ: Prentice Hall, 2003), 159.

of the affect that a given layer of musical meaning entails. Learning music apart from making or listening to music is about as complete as lectures on "how to ride a bike" or "how to swim."

With respect to one of the aims of this volume: even if the primary gain of a particular resonance between areas of musical and theological meaning is conceptual, the experience of the music itself remains essential. If Mahler and Tippett offer music that helps us think more deeply about eschatological time (see chapter 11), then that knowledge is best gained not only by reading about it but by experiencing this music, and by creating a conversation between that musical experience and the essay about it. Alert students might pause to wonder about what kind of performance of the music might be especially effective at evoking a particular layer of theological resonance, or what linguistic register would be most apt for describing the area of new theological insight. In this way, this volume offers us all a potent (and welcome!) excuse for attending concerts, purchasing recordings, joining a musical ensemble, or learning to play an instrument.

Learning through Apprenticeship

Second, I suspect that Mr. Holland would caution against any attempt to engage in this learning by ourselves. He would urge us to find the best mentor possible to guide our learning. Anything as richly nuanced and complex as music is best learned through apprenticeship. In the frequently cited words of Michael Polanyi:

> An art which cannot be specified in detail cannot be transmitted by prescription, since no prescription for it exists. It can be passed on only by example from master to apprentice. This restricts the range of diffusion to that of personal contacts, and we find accordingly that craftsmanship tends to survive in closely circumscribed local traditions.[3]

Person-to-person learning helps us absorb ways of perceiving multiple layers of meaning at once, helping us pay attention to elements or aspects of musical experience that would otherwise escape us. Part of the value of a master mentor is that we can witness a good model up close — and not only a model of good music, but a model of encountering music. A good music

---

3. Michael Polanyi, *Personal Knowledge* (Chicago: University of Chicago Press, 1962), 53.

teacher not only identifies worthy music to study, but also models how to select it, how to encounter it, and how to reflect upon it. Good music teachers
teach technique, musicality, and musical understanding all at once.

Participating in this music-theology exchange is no different. Musicians
or theologians are not likely to make much progress in this field by the
power of their own will or by making more trips to formerly unexplored sections of a research library. But they will by spending time together, by reading theology together, by listening to music together, by seeking out mentors
(like the authors in this volume) who are pushing each other toward richer,
more faithful exchanges across disciplinary lines. After reading this volume,
I could purchase a recording of Bach Cantata 56 or 106, but the experience
would be far richer if I could listen to it with Rick Plantinga. I have always
been impressed that Michael Hawn's approach to sabbatical research has often been to seek out a musical mentor in a different region of the world. And
while this luxury may not be possible for all readers, I suspect that most
readers live in proximity to a surprising number of those with expertise in
modes of both music making and theology (do not forget the young people
around you who may be ideal docents for their own identity-shaping musical cultures).

Training the Imagination through Drills

Third, Mr. Holland, like every good music teacher, would identify some appropriate drills to practice. Musicians practice scales and technical exercises.
Music theorists practice techniques for musical analysis. Composers often
challenge themselves with compositional drills that involve tight, if arbitrary
constraints ("sketch an evocative 30-second piece for tuba and ukulele on
the theme from your favorite film"). Even the best professional musicians
spend hours each day cajoling their muscles into ever more precise technique through elaborate technical drills.

What most outstanding teachers intuitively realize (and what many
young students may never expect) is that such drills involve a lot more than
muscle memory. They inculcate a way of conceiving the art form, a way of
"thinking in" and "thinking through" the art form. Listen to three prominent theorists lauding the virtue of aptly designed technical drills:

> **Arts educator Elliot Eisner:** "Techniques represent ways of doing some-
> thing, but techniques also reflect ways of thinking about the thing to be

done. Thus the acquisition of technique is not merely a technical achievement; it is a mode of thought."

Philosopher of music education Bennett Reimer: "Technique now, musicianship later [is a misconception that] has plagued performance teaching in music education throughout its history, accounts for much of the convergent, rule-learning-and-following, technique-dominated, rote nature of the enterprise. . . . The solution is to recognize and cultivate their interdependence right from the start."

Philosopher V. A. Howard: effective drills and rehearsal techniques lead to an "education of an understanding that ranges from physical dexterity, to emotive discovery, to perceptual insight, to pattern recognition, to associative hunches, to logical argument — in no particular order and in every combination"; the result "stands in marked contrast to two extremes: drudgery, on the one hand, or means without dreams; and fantasy, on the other, or dreams without means."[4]

The question for readers of this volume, then, might be: "What kind of drills might be needed to train us to learn from and participate in the conversation described in this book?" Here are a few I can envision for fairly standard courses in music or theology:

- Select a brief piece of music from ordinary experience. Write a 6-line poem about it that includes at least one theological question. Repeat this exercise daily for a week. Then choose the best two examples, and explain what qualities help them stand out. What aspects of the music drew your attention? Lacking further instruction, how did you go about identifying a theological question to pose?
- Select a biblical text or theological theme. In a music store or library, spend one hour searching for three pieces of music from vastly different genres that offer some potential resonance with your topic. With a group of other students, listen to each piece of music daily for a week, and write a 2-page reflective essay on the connections (or lack thereof) between the music and your selected topic.

4. Elliott W. Eisner, *Arts and Creation of Mind* (New Haven: Yale University Press, 2002), 146; Bennett Reimer, *A Philosophy of Music Education,* 128; V. A. Howard, *Learning by All Means: Lessons from the Arts* (Peter Lang, 1992), 21, xiv.

- Find a biblical text and musical piece that treat the very same (preferably narrow) subject. After playing or listening to the music and contemplating the text, conduct every kind of analysis that you are equipped to offer (e.g., clausal analysis of the text, harmonic analysis of the music). Then list any points of resonance or dissonance you discover about their respective treatments of the subject. Pay attention to the ethos, the register, the tone, the conceptual content, the background assumptions, and the ultimate purpose of each. You may have many false starts in this open-ended search, but celebrate the moment of discovery when you discover resonance between these two worlds.

There is, obviously, some level of arbitrariness to these exercises. They are merely preparatory exercises, the "scales" that prepare us to receive and contribute to the "performances" represented by the essays in this book. But they may be indispensable tools to develop the capacity for engaging in this work. If musicians would not even think of ignoring the disciplined drills that sharpen the skills, dispositions, and ways of thinking needed for their way of being, it seems foolhardy at best to attempt work at the intersection of music and theology apart from developing drills suited to the task.

The Juxtapositions of Interdisciplinary Cross-Training

Fourth, I suspect that Mr. Holland would advise that the learning that this conversation requires can be honed only through intentional cross-training. This volume is testimony to the kind of learning that happens when enough energy is built up on both sides of an interdisciplinary synapse. Intentionally juxtaposing two energy-laden subject areas creates the space for insight. This works, in part, because insight and imaginative gains often occur in the context of conflict, dissonance, dissimilarity, and unfamiliarity. A lot of learning within the field of music already consists of juxtaposition. Even young piano students are now often taught a set of different skills at the same time, juxtaposing work in reading notation, strengthening the finger skills, listening to intervals, improvising simple melodies. This volume suggests taking this kind of juxtaposition-oriented learning to a new level.

I would suspect that if we were to assign Jeremy Begbie the task of studying a theologian he had never read and a composer he did not know, Jeremy would, after a week's immersion in each, be able to offer rich and insightful comments that did not merely rehash material that he has already published and that could not be predicted ahead of time. The insight would emerge, in part, because Jeremy's encounter with the material would be immersive. The insight would also emerge because those two reflective tasks were done in stark juxtaposition, by someone intent upon and with proven experience in looking for connections, similarities, differences, and resonances between them.

This is not to suggest that our choice of materials to juxtapose should be arbitrary or random (though working at juxtaposing apparently random subjects could well be a fruitful drill or exercise). Instead, we rightly ask about what kind of music would best promise to open up insight into a given theological theme or topic that puzzles or surprises us, as well as what theological themes, metaphors, and images might help us make sense of any given piece of music we might be studying. Indeed, the music of Bach nearly begs for reflection on the theological meaning of death and resurrection. Similarly, pondering the relationship of divine and human activity in theology nearly begs for reflection on the varieties of musical counterpoint.

Happily, the nearly infinite possibilities for creative juxtaposition free us from the presumption that this conversation will ever be exhausted. Those who have mastered the fields of Hebrew poetry, the music of Bach, the theology of Barth, and the practice of organ playing are likely to explore juxtapositions far different from those who know the syntax of Pauline Greek, the music of the gamelan, the theology of Chrysostom, and the practice of jazz singing.

Training Both Perception and Pedagogy

Fifth, I suspect that Mr. Holland would take care to coach two fundamentally different but interrelated skills: experiencing music and communicating about it instructively. It is one thing to notice something profound in the exchange between theology and music and another to explain it to someone in illuminating ways.

Elliot Eisner, quoted on pp. 458-59, has been especially attentive to the dynamics of these interrelated tasks. He notes that arts education is sharpened through two indispensable kinds of tasks: the task of connoisseurship and the task of criticism. He describes connoisseurship as "the ability to see, to perceive what is subtle, complex, and important . . . to know how to look, to see, to appreciate," an ability honed through reflective engagement with artistic (in our case, musical) experiences. In terms of this volume, connoisseurship involves learning to pay attention not to every element and aspect of music, but to certain elements that are theologically significant. It also involves powers of recognition: the ability to notice and celebrate a particularly compelling resonance or flash of insight.

But to become an effective contributor to this discussion requires not only recognition, but also communication, the capacity to elicit in others, including those with little musical or theological knowledge, the same kind of attentiveness and capacity for discovery. Thus, Eisner goes on to speak of criticism as "the art of disclosing the qualities of events or objects that connoisseurship perceives." Criticism does not best proceed by trying to translate what happens in an artistic medium into words, but rather attempts "to create a rendering of a situation, event, or object that will provide pointers to those aspects of the situation, event, or object that are in some way significant." Eisner notes that this kind of disclosive task is often best accomplished by non-discursive rather than by discursive speech. That is, it is often best evoked or elicited through metaphor, poetry, and less direct forms of communication. That is not to say that criticism is ad hoc or undisciplined. Indeed, Eisner describes four (disciplined) tasks of the effective critic: description, interpretation, evaluation, and "thematizing" (the distillation of what is most essential).[5] Just as an expert docent at an art museum must be not only an art lover but also an effective teacher, and just as an effective liturgical catechist must not only love God and be deeply compelled by liturgical participation, but must also have the ability to lead others to do the same, so too an outstanding teacher must both grasp an insight and elicit that grasping in others.

I linger over Eisner's extended phenomenological descriptions of these basic tasks because they help us see what kind of learning is most important for us to cultivate. For his part, Eisner uses this framework to offer a devastating critique of educational reform efforts in which too many critics of arts education are not really connoisseurs (often being blinded to truly effective teaching by overuse of quantitative data and by a lack of time spent in arts classrooms) and are too taken up with discursive rather than non-discursive speech. As Eisner notes, reams of statistical data about arts education is simply insufficient for eliciting better teaching. What is needed are more people like Glenn Holland, people who are masters of not only musical understanding, performance, or composition but also the poetic and practical wisdom that leads to masterful instruction.

5. Elliott W. Eisner, *The Educational Imagination*, 3rd ed. (Upper Saddle River, NJ: Merrill Prentice Hall, 2002), 215, 219, 220-23.

It is not difficult to translate this insight into the conversation modeled for us in this volume: the best work done at the intersection of theology and music is done by those who are both attentive connoisseurs of their subject — whose love for the subject is infectious, whose awareness of subtle moments of insight is well cultivated — as well as effective critics and pedagogues, with the capacity to elicit, disclose, and awaken insight in others. In general, what is true in arts education is also true at the intersection of music and theology: eye-opening criticism, while taking care to draw upon every apt analytical and discursive tool, is never content with this analysis, but presses on to make disciplined choices of apt and savory metaphors that help others experience a lightbulb moment of insight. Look back at pages you've read in this book, and I suspect that the texts you underlined and pages you earmarked are those which break open, even for a moment, into poetry.

Future Work in This Field

All of this has implications for how we can best enter into the movement this book is meant to inspire: experience music while being attentive to its theological implications, find mentors to guide your encounters with the disciplines and repertoire you do not know, practice creating juxtapositions of subject areas and skill sets, attend not only to recognizing and savoring new insight but also to evoking it in others.

There is nearly an infinite number of pathways that work in this emerging interdisciplinary field might follow: addressing particular theological or musical topics; generating an ever-wider set of interdisciplinary encounters with work in dance, visual arts, theater, and philosophy; producing new approaches to musical and theological composition and creativity. But little is likely to be sustained over time without the kind of immersive, mentor-led, disciplined, juxtaposition-oriented connoisseurship and criticism contained in this book.

In sum, the question this volume poses is not limited to the particular claims of any given essay, but to the way of being the book as a whole commends: How might each of us live in more attentive and disclosive ways, attuned to the God of triune majesty and the utter musicality of the world we are graced to inhabit?

Contributors

JEREMY S. BEGBIE is the inaugural holder of the Thomas A. Langford Research Professorship in Theology at Duke Divinity School, North Carolina. He teaches systematic theology, and specializes in the interface between theology and the arts. His particular research interest is the interplay between music and theology. He is also Senior Member at Wolfson College, Cambridge, and an Affiliated Lecturer in the Faculties of Divinity and Music at the University of Cambridge. He is the author of a number of books, including *Voicing Creation's Praise: Towards a Theology of the Arts* (T&T Clark, 1991); *Theology, Music and Time* (Cambridge UP, 2000); and most recently, *Resounding Truth: Christian Wisdom in the World of Music* (Baker/SPCK, 2007), which won the Christianity Today 2008 Book Award in the Theology/ Ethics Category. He has taught widely in the UK, North America, and South Africa, specializing in multimedia performance-lectures.

BRUCE ELLIS BENSON is Professor of Philosophy at Wheaton College in Illinois. He is a co-founder of the Society for Continental Philosophy and Theology and currently serves as its Executive Director. He is also co-chair of the steering committee of the Theology and Continental Philosophy Group of the American Academy of Religion. His authored books are *Graven Ideologies: Nietzsche, Derrida and Marion on Modern Idolatry* (InterVarsity, 2002); *The Improvisation of Musical Dialogue: A Phenomenology of Music* (Cambridge UP, 2003); and *Pious Nietzsche: Decadence and Dionysian Faith* (Indiana UP, 2008). He is co-editor of *The Phenomenology of Prayer* (Fordham UP, 2005); *Hermeneutics at the Crossroads* (Indiana UP, 2006); *Transforming Philosophy and Reli-*

gion: Love's Wisdom (Indiana UP, 2008); *Evangelicals and Empire: Christian Alternatives to the Political Status Quo* (Brazos, 2008); and *Words of Life: New Theological Turns in French Phenomenology* (Fordham UP, 2009). He is the author of a forthcoming book on improvisation and the arts in the Church and Postmodern Culture series (Baker Academic).

ALASTAIR BORTHWICK is a composer, musicologist, and Head of Department (Drama and Music) at the University of Hull, UK. He has an undergraduate degree in physics (BSc, ARCS, Imperial College London), a diploma in piano performance (LTCL), and postgraduate degrees in music (MMus, University of Sheffield; PhD, King's College London). He has published a book entitled *Music Theory and Analysis: The Limitations of Logic* (Garland, 1996) and articles on music theory, analysis, and music since 1900, particularly British music. His compositions — for choirs (many to Christian texts), soloists, chamber ensembles, and orchestra — have been performed in festivals around the world. He was a featured composer at the Beijing Modern Music Festival in 2006.

DANIEL K. L. CHUA was the Professor of Music Theory and Analysis at King's College London and has recently become the Head of the School of Humanities and Professor of Music at the University of Hong Kong. He is the author of *The "Galitzin" Quartets of Beethoven* (Princeton UP, 1995) and *Absolute Music and the Construction of Meaning* (Cambridge UP, 1999). Recent articles include "Untimely Reflections on Operatic Echoes: How Sound Travels in Monteverdi's L'Orfeo and Beethoven's Fidelio, with a Short Instrumental Interlude" *(Opera Quarterly)*, "Rioting with Stravinsky: A Particular Analysis of the Rite of Spring" *(Music Analysis)*, and "Beethoven's Other Humanism" *(Journal of the American Musicological Society)*.

MARGOT FASSLER is the Keough-Hesburgh Professor of Music History and Liturgy, University of Notre Dame, and Robert Tangeman Professor Emerita, Yale University. She is the author or editor of numerous articles and books, including *Gothic Song: Victorine Sequences and Augustinian Reform in Twelfth-Century Paris* (Cambridge UP, 1993; 2nd ed., NDP, 2009), which won the Nicholas Brown Prize of the Medieval Academy and the Otto Kinkeldey Prize of the American Musicological Society, and *The Virgin of Chartres: Making History through Liturgy and the Arts* (Yale UP, 2010). She also makes documentary films on sacred music, including *Joyful Noise: Psalm Singing in Community,* and, while a Henry Luce III Fellow in Theology and in residence at the Center of Theological Inquiry, is writing a book on Hildegard of Bingen.

STEVEN R. GUTHRIE is Associate Professor of Theology at Belmont University in Nashville, Tennessee, and leads Belmont's "Religion and the Arts" program. From 2000 to 2003, Dr. Guthrie was the postdoctoral research fellow of the Institute for Theology, Imagination and the Arts, at the University of St Andrews. He earned his undergraduate degree in music theory from the University of Michigan School of Music, and has worked as a professional musician and a church minister of music. His publications include *Creator Spirit: The Holy Spirit and the Art of Becoming Human* (Baker Academic, 2011); *Faithful Performances: Enacting Christian Tradition* (ed. with Trevor Hart, Ashgate, 2006); and the entry "Theology and Music" in the *Encyclopedia of Christianity* (Eerdmans-Brill).

CAROL HARRISON went up to Lady Margaret Hall, Oxford, in 1979, and completed her doctorate in Oxford and Paris (Sorbonne) (1987). She taught in the Department of Theology, University of Hull, for one year (1988-89) before taking up her current post as Lecturer in the History and Theology of the Latin West, in the Department of Theology and Religion, in the University of Durham. She is now a University Reader. Her publications include three books on Augustine: *Beauty and Revelation in the Thought of Saint Augustine* (Oxford UP, 1992); *Augustine in Context: Christian Truth and Fractured Humanity* (Oxford UP, 2000); and *Rethinking Augustine's Early Theology: An Argument for Continuity* (Oxford UP, 2006). She is editor of the Routledge *Early Church Fathers* series and is currently serving as President of the International Association of Patristic Studies.

TREVOR HART is Professor of Divinity and Director of the Institute for Theology, Imagination and the Arts in the University of St Andrews. His publications include *Faith Thinking: The Dynamics of Christian Theology* (SPCK, 1995), *Hope Against Hope: Christian Eschatology in Contemporary Context* (with Richard Bauckham, Eerdmans, 1999), *Faithful Performances: Enacting Christian Tradition* (ed., with Steven Guthrie, Ashgate, 2006), and *Tree of Tales: Tolkien, Literature and Theology* (ed., with Ivan Khovacs, Baylor, 2007). His current project is a study of human artistry from the standpoint of a Christian theology of creation.

C. MICHAEL HAWN is University Distinguished Professor of Church Music and Director of the Sacred Music Program at Perkins School of Theology, Southern Methodist University, Dallas, Texas. His undergraduate and graduate degrees are from Wheaton College (BME) and Southern Seminary (MCM and DMA). He has received several fellowships for study in Africa, Asia, and Latin America in the area of world Christian music and liturgical encultur- ation. He has published over 250 articles, chapters in books, reviews, and cur- riculum materials. His books include *Gather into One: Praying and Singing Globally* (Eerdmans, 2003) and *One Bread, One Body: Exploring Cultural Di- versity in Worship* (Alban Institute, 2003). Recently, his chapter "Praying Globally — Pitfalls and Possibilities of Cross-cultural Liturgical Appropria- tion" appeared in *Christian Worship Worldwide: Expanding Horizons, Deepening Practices*, ed. Charles Farhadian (Eerdmans, 2007).

JOYCE IRWIN is Research Affiliate in the Department of Religion at Colgate University and Director of Music at St. David's Episcopal Church, DeWitt, New York. She received her PhD in Religious Studies from Yale University and has taught at the University of Georgia and at Colgate University. Her publications include *Sacred Sound: Music in Religious Thought and Practice* (Scholars Press, 1983) and *Neither Voice nor Heart Alone: German Lutheran Theology of Music in the Age of the Baroque* (P. Lang, 1993) as well as contri- butions to Carol Baron's *Bach's Changing World: Voices in the Community* (University of Rochester Press, 2006). Currently she is working on theologies of music in eighteenth-century music, particularly in the writings of Johann Mattheson.

JOHN PAUL ITO teaches music theory in the conservatory at Lawrence Univer- sity. His interdisciplinary interests are reflected in his training: he holds an SB from the Massachusetts Institute of Technology, an MM in viola performance from Boston University, and a PhD in music theory from Columbia Univer- sity. His dissertation, which he is currently converting to book form, deals with the role of meter in performance and its relationship to physical coordination and the expressive shaping of sound. His more recent research looks at how music theory can operate in an epistemological middle ground between the sciences and the humanities, drawing on models from cognitive linguistics.

ANTHONY MONTI received his PhD in English Literature from Fordham University in New York. Before his untimely death, he was an adjunct lec- turer at Rampao College, The Newark School of Theology, and Bergen Community College in New Jersey and Rockland Community College. His book, *A Natural Theology of the Arts: Imprint of the Spirit*, is published by Ashgate Press.

DAVID J. R. S. MOSELEY is a Lecturer in the Department of Theology and Religious Studies at the University of San Diego, and Chair of the Religious Studies Department at The Bishop's School in La Jolla, California. He holds undergraduate and graduate degrees in law, theology, and philosophy from Magdalen College, Oxford University, and a PhD in theology and music from Jesus College, Cambridge University, writing his thesis on Karl Barth's theological evaluation of Mozart's music. He currently serves as Theologian-in-Residence at St. Paul's Episcopal Cathedral, San Diego. During his career, he has also worked for non-profit agencies that provide local social services, international health and development programming, and human rights advocacy, which has allowed him to travel throughout the developing world. He has articles on "Prosperity Gospel" and "Globalization" appearing in the forthcoming edition of the *IVP New Dictionary of Theology.*

MICHAEL O'CONNOR is a lecturer at St Michael's College in the University of Toronto and a pastoral musician. He studied philosophy and theology at the Pontifical Gregorian University in Rome and historical theology at the University of Oxford. A former Warden of the Royal School of Church Music (RSCM) in the United Kingdom, he is a member of the Board of the newly established RSCM Canada. He was a member of the international Advisory Board of the Theology Through the Arts Project. His interests include the relationship between the Bible and the arts (especially music), the theology of worship, and the theology of music.

CATHERINE PICKSTOCK is a University Reader in Philosophy and Theology at the Faculty of Divinity, University of Cambridge, and a Fellow and Tutor of Emmanuel College, Cambridge. She held a research fellowship at Emmanuel College and was then elected to a British Academy postdoctoral fellowship before taking up her lectureship in Philosophy of Religion at Cambridge. She has published several books and articles in the area of philosophical theology that focus upon theology, philosophy, and music.

RICHARD J. PLANTINGA is Professor of Religion at Calvin College in Grand Rapids, Michigan. His chief area of research and teaching lies in the area of Christian responses to non-Christian religious traditions. His publications in this area include *Christianity and Plurality* (Blackwell, 1999). He is also engaged by the relationship between theology and music, on which subject he teaches, lectures, and conducts research.

ROBERT SHOLL is a Lecturer in Academic Studies at the Royal Academy of Music and has taught at King's College, London, and at The Royal College of Music. His doctorate, *Olivier Messiaen and the Culture of Modernity,* is currently being revised for publication. He was a member of the Theology through the Arts research group and is a founding co-editor of oliviermessiaen.net. Most recently, he edited *Messiaen Studies* (Cambridge UP, 2007). He has recently given papers on Messiaen at Washington, DC (AMS), Princeton, Brown and Boston Universities, King's College London, the Royal Academy of Music, and the Royal College of Music. In 2008, he organized a major conference at London's Southbank Centre on Contemporary Music and Spirituality as the first event in Southbank's Messiaen Festival, and he is the editor (with Sander van Maas, University of Amsterdam and Utrecht) of a forthcoming set of related studies. He was the organizer of a conference, *Arvo Pärt: Soundtrack of an Age,* held at the Southbank Centre in September 2010, and he is also the organizer of a conference on the music of Pierre Boulez at the Southbank Centre in October 2011. He studied the organ with Olivier Latry (Titulaire Organiste de Notre Dame de Paris), and currently tutors for the Royal College of Organists. He has recently given recitals in the Festival de la Musique Sacrée at the Cathedral of St.-Malo and at La Madeleine (Paris), Westminster Abbey, St. Paul's Cathedral, and Notre-Dame de Paris. Future plans include more recitals in Paris and Australia and a disc of commissioned electroacoustic music.

NANCY VAN DEUSEN is Louis and Mildred Benezet Chair in the Humanities at Claremont Graduate University, California. Her publications include *Music and Theology at the Early University,* which explores the concept of a university, as well as music's place as an analogical bridge between the natural sciences and philosophy within that concept. As a musicologist and music theorist with ongoing interest in music analysis, van Deusen's teaching activities and scholarly publications have transcended the boundaries between music theory, history, and practice within a cultural context. She is a Fellow of the Medieval Academy of America and has received a National Endowment for the Humanities Grant, several Fulbright Research Grants, and an American Philosophical Society Research Grant. Her teaching career has included positions at California State University, Northridge, and the Institute for Musicology at the University of Basel, Switzerland.

JOHN D. WITVLIET is Director of the Calvin Institute of Christian Worship and teaches worship, theology, and music at Calvin College and Calvin Theological Seminary. His responsibilities include oversight of the Worship

Institute's practical and scholarly programs, including the annual Calvin Symposium on Worship and the Worship Renewal Grants Program, funded by Lilly Endowment. He is the author of *The Biblical Psalms in Christian Worship* (Eerdmans, 2007) and *Worship Seeking Understanding* (Baker Academic, 2003) and co-editor of *Worship in Medieval and Early Modern Europe* (University of Notre Dame Press, 2004). A graduate of Calvin College, Dr. Witvliet holds graduate degrees in theology from Calvin Theological Seminary, in choral music from the University of Illinois, and the PhD in liturgical studies and theology from the University of Notre Dame.

Glossary of Musical Terms

absolute frequency   The identifiable frequency of a tone (measured in hertz).

absolute music   Music that is not meant to be "about" anything but rather enjoyed for its own sake, without reference to extramusical ideas, images, etc.

absolute pitch   The identification of a note without the help of another (named) note for reference. Compare RELATIVE PITCH.

accidental   A symbol (sharp ♯, flat ♭, or natural ♮) used to raise or lower a note from the pitch indicated by the current KEY SIGNATURE, or to reinstate a key signature pitch changed by a preceding accidental.

appoggiatura   A type of melodic embellishment.

arpeggiac   The adjective from ARPEGGIO.

arpeggio   A chord whose notes are played in succession instead of together.

art music   See CLASSICAL MUSIC.

atonal music   Music that is not written in a key. See also ATONALITY.

atonality   A style of music that avoids gravitation toward a specific KEY.

augmentation   The lengthening of note values in a melody to slow it down, often to half the original speed (compare DIMINUTION). Augmentation can also apply to chords and intervals.

bar   The British term for MEASURE.

beat frequency   The rate of BEATING that occurs between two tones very close in frequency.

beating   An audible pulse that occurs between two tones very close in

471

frequency. Since it fades and disappears as the pitches unite in frequency, it is used to help tuning. See also ROUGHNESS.

cadence   A series of notes or chords that brings a phrase, section, or piece to a sense of rest or CLOSURE.

cadenza   Originally improvised, and retaining its improvisatory nature even when written by a composer, a cadenza is a passage toward the end of a piece designed to give free expression to a soloist's technical skills.

cantillation   The chanting of sacred texts.

cantus firmus   Latin for "fixed song," a *cantus firmus* is a pre-existing melody which medieval and Renaissance composers often used as a structural foundation for a CONTRAPUNTAL composition.

chord progression   A sequence of chords.

chromatic music   Music that makes use of notes that do not belong to the prevailing major or minor KEY.

chromatic scale   A scale of the twelve SEMITONES in an OCTAVE played or sung consecutively.

cithara   The Latin spelling for the Greek *kithara* — an ancient stringed instrument in the lyre family.

classical music   The classical era is usually understood as dating from the mid-eighteenth to the early nineteenth centuries. More widely, classical music — sometimes called "high art" music — refers to any music in the concert-operatic tradition of the West.

closure   Bringing about a sense of ending or completion, closure can have varying strengths, with weaker points of closure marking the ends of phrases or sections within a piece.

coda   Italian for "tail," a coda is a section added to the end of a piece to enhance the sense of CLOSURE.

col legno   A direction to a string player to use the (wooden) back of the bow.

color   Tone color, or sound color, is another term for TIMBRE.

common practice   A term that refers to an era encompassing the baroque, classical, and Romantic periods, often contrasted with the modern era.

complex tone   Almost all tones are complex tones — that is, comprised of a FUNDAMENTAL PITCH and OVERTONES.

concordance   A state of harmonious balance, or CONSONANCE.

consonance   Consonant tones sound pleasing to the ear when combined, and have a sense of stability. Compare DISSONANCE.

continuo Common in the baroque era, the continuo was a part embellished from a basic bass line, providing a piece with a sense of harmonic continuity.

contrapuntal The adjective from COUNTERPOINT — that is, composed according to the principles of counterpoint.

counterpoint Two or more independent lines of melody that are played or sung simultaneously.

cross-rhythm A rhythmic device in which beats are shifted forward or back from their expected position in METER.

crotchet The British term for a QUARTER NOTE.

da capo An instruction on a musical score to return to the beginning and repeat part or the whole of a piece.

development The elaboration of musical material, for example, by changing its key or altering its note or rhythmic patterns.

diabolus in musica Meaning "the devil in music," a Latin nickname for the TRITONE.

diachrony Literally "through time" — something that is diachronic happens through a succession of events. Compare SYNCHRONY.

diatonic music Melody or harmony that, in contrast to CHROMATIC MUSIC, confines itself to the notes of the prevailing key.

diminished chord Generally including the interval of the diminished fifth, diminished chords (e.g., the diminished triad) are heard as lacking a tonal center.

diminished interval A diminished interval is one semitone narrower than a PERFECT or MINOR INTERVAL.

diminution The opposite of AUGMENTATION, diminution is the process of shortening the length of notes in a theme, often resulting in the melody being sung or played at twice the speed. Diminution also applies to chords and intervals.

dissonance Dissonant tones sound discordant when combined, or have a sense of instability which seems to demand RESOLUTION into CONSONANCE. Compare SENSORY DISSONANCE.

dominant The fifth note of a major or minor scale.

dominant chord A chord built on the fifth note of a major or minor scale.

dynamics The gradations of volume in music.

eighth note Called a *quaver* in British terminology, an eighth note lasts one-eighth the length of a whole note, or semibreve.

enharmonic   Enharmonically equivalent tones are identical notes called by different names (e.g., B♭ is the enharmonic equivalent of A♯).

equal temperament   A system of tuning where the distance between every pair of adjacent notes is equal.

figural music   Frequently used to draw contrast with the simplicity of plainchant, figural denotes more florid — often polyphonic — musical composition. See also POLYPHONY.

figure   A short musical element (melodic or rhythmic) which may be used as a basis of a composition or used recurrently as background accompaniment to a melody.

fugue   A musical form popular in the baroque period and notably explored and celebrated by J. S. Bach, the fugue is a CONTRAPUNTAL composition, where two or more parts are layered, "answering" and overlapping each other as they introduce alterations in melody or pitch to the original theme.

fundamental pitch   The first tone of an OVERTONE SERIES.

glissando   A direction to play a passage by sliding from one pitch to another.

ground-bass   A term used interchangeably with OSTINATO BASS.

harmonic (n.)   Often used interchangeably with OVERTONE, the term can also be used more specifically of an overtone whose frequency is a whole number multiple of its fundamental. See also HARMONICS.

harmonic progression   An alternative name for CHORD PROGRESSION.

harmonic series   Frequently used interchangeably with OVERTONE SERIES, it can refer more specifically to a series whose overtones are whole number multiples of the FUNDAMENTAL PITCH.

harmonic syntax   As syntax in language allows us to understand how words work together to convey meaning, harmonic syntax concerns the "rules" which govern how TONAL MUSIC in the COMMON PRACTICE era "works."

harmonics   Harmonics (see HARMONIC above) can be played, for example, on a violin by touching a string very lightly at a specific point, preventing some of the main OVERTONES present in a tone from sounding, leaving a very pure, thin tone in a high register.

home key   The key that functions as a piece's "center of gravity."

horizontal   In music, horizontal — or linear — generally refers to the melodic aspect of a piece (notes sounding one after the other). Compare VERTICAL.

integral serialism   See SERIALISM.

intermezzo   A piece for performance between acts of a play or opera, or between movements of larger works, frequently composed for solo piano.

interval   The distance in pitch between two tones, usually named according to the number of STEPS it spans.

interversion   Coined by Messiaen, interversion is the systematic reordering of elements of a motif — note durations or tone pitches, for example — according to a set of rules.

inversion   An inverted melody, chord, or interval is one sung or played "upside-down" (e.g., the switching around of upper and lower melodies in COUNTERPOINT).

isicathamiya   A style of vocal music from South Africa, traditionally sung by an unaccompanied all-male choir.

key   A system of notes that takes its name from the first note of its major or minor scale.

key signature   The written indication of the KEY of a piece.

legato   Italian for "tied together," legato is an instruction to play with no noticeable breaks between the notes.

leitmotif   A recurring theme that represents an element in a drama (e.g., a person, place, idea, etc.).

linear   See HORIZONTAL.

major chord   A chord consisting of the intervals of the major third and perfect fifth above the ROOT (sometimes with further notes added to this triad), and considered "stable" (see RESOLUTION).

major interval   Some INTERVALS built out of the MAJOR SCALE are given the name "major," such as the major third, major fourth, and so on.

major key   A key based on a MAJOR SCALE.

major scale   A set of notes with a pattern of whole and half STEPS, equivalent to that of the white notes of the keyboard from C to C.

measure   Each measure (or *bar*) — indicated by a vertical bar-line — divides notated music into a set number of beats.

melisma   A passage of music where one syllable is sung across many notes.

meter   Meter — indicated in written music by a TIME SIGNATURE — is the division of music into patterns of regular stressed and unstressed beats, marked as MEASURES.

minimalism   A musical movement of the second half of the twentieth century that focuses on creating a sense of stasis through the use of repeated themes and motifs which are subject to slow transformation.

minor chord   A chord consisting of the intervals of the minor third and perfect fifth above the ROOT (sometimes with further notes added to this triad).

minor interval   Some intervals built out of the minor scale are given the name "minor," such as the minor third, minor sixth, and so on.

minor key   A key based on a minor scale.

mode   Originating in ancient Greece and used widely in the Middle Ages, a mode is essentially a group of notes, or scale, from which music is made, the relations between the notes generating (as we might say today) a certain "mood."

modes of limited transposition   A term coined by Messiaen. Modes of limited transposition are modes arranged symmetrically around a central note or notes, and built in such a way that they can only be transposed up or down a SEMITONE a limited number of times before resulting in the same notes as the original.

monochord   Used by Pythagoras to demonstrate the theory of musical intervals, the monochord was an instrument consisting of one string stretched over two fixed bridges, with a third, moveable bridge to change the pitch.

monody   Originating in the baroque period, monody is a style of vocal composition for solo singer with instrumental accompaniment.

monophony   A single line of melody without accompaniment.

motet   A polyphonic vocal composition especially important in the medieval and Renaissance periods. See also POLYPHONY.

motif   A recurring pattern of notes that runs thematically through a piece. It is shorter than a theme, of which it may be a part. See also LEITMOTIF.

neoclassicism   A style particularly associated with the early twentieth century, and exemplified in some of Stravinsky's music, neoclassicism draws on techniques from earlier classical or baroque periods.

non-retrogradable rhythm   Messiaen's term for palindromic rhythms — which read the same forward or backward.

octatonic scale   An eight-note scale, but usually referring specifically to one that alternates between whole and half steps as it ascends — Messiaen counted it among his MODES OF LIMITED TRANSPOSITION.

octave   The simplest INTERVAL in music — one note being double the frequency of the other.

Ondes Martenot   An electronic keyboard instrument invented by

Maurice Martenot in 1928, and notably utilized by the composer Messiaen. It produces haunting, wavering tones.

ostinato Italian for "obstinate," an ostinato is a pattern of melody, harmony, or rhythm that is repeated many times.

ostinato bass An OSTINATO in the bass line.

overtone A higher tone present in the sounding of a FUNDAMENTAL PITCH.

overtone series A sequence of frequencies above the FUNDAMENTAL PITCH of a tone. See also HARMONIC SERIES.

partial A component of a complex tone, such as its FUNDAMENTAL or an OVERTONE.

pentatonic mode A MODE comprising five notes.

perfect interval The musical INTERVALS of the UNISON, fourth, fifth, and OCTAVE are called "perfect" due to their simple pitch relationships producing highly consonant sounds.

pizzicato An instruction to a string player to play the instrument by plucking the strings with the fingers instead of using the bow.

polycoloration The simultaneous use of two or more distinct sound colors (TIMBRES).

polydynamics The simultaneous use of two or more distinct DYNAMICS.

polyphony Music with two or more melodic and independent voices, in contrast to music with one voice (monophony) or with one dominant voice with accompaniment (homophony).

polyrhythm The simultaneous use of two or more distinct rhythms.

polysonority The simultaneous use of two or more distinct sonorities.

polytonality The simultaneous use of two or more KEYS.

programmatic music In contrast to ABSOLUTE MUSIC, programmatic music is often given a descriptive title and is intended to express or indicate a non-musical subject such as a place, emotion, or story.

quarter note Called a *crotchet* in British terminology, a quarter note lasts one quarter the length of a whole note, or semibreve.

recitative A type of speech-like solo singing, generally loose in rhythm and lacking structured melodies.

relative pitch The identification or hearing of notes in terms of their relationships to one another. Compare ABSOLUTE PITCH.

resolution The progression from a sense of musical tension to a sense of musical stability or conclusion.

retrogradation The use of RETROGRADE as a musical device.

retrograde   A device where a group of notes or rhythmic pattern is sung or played backward.

ritornello   A ritornello (lit. "little return"; pl. ritornelli) is an instrumental passage that occurs in varying guises during a work, common with baroque composers such as Bach and Handel.

root   The note from which a chord takes its name and on which the chord is based.

root movement   An alternative term for CHORD PROGRESSION, where the chords are labeled according to their ROOTS.

roughness   The SENSORY DISSONANCE that may be heard when the frequency of BEATING between two tones becomes too low to be audible, or when the beating occurs between OVERTONES of the two tones.

semitone   Also called a half step, the smallest INTERVAL (e.g., C to C♯) used in modern Western music.

sensory consonance   The absence of SENSORY DISSONANCE in musical sounds.

sensory dissonance   The BEATING or ROUGHNESS heard when two tones (or a combination of their overtones) are close together in pitch. Determined by physiological reaction to sound, sensory dissonance is distinct from DISSONANCE, which is in part culturally defined.

serialism   Serialism is a highly controlled method of composition whereby tones (usually the twelve semitones of the octave) are ordered in a fixed series which is then subject to various permutations. *Integral* or *total* serialism extends the procedure to other elements of music such as timbre, rhythm, and dynamics.

staccato   Usually indicated by a dot above or below the note, staccato (lit. "detached") notes are cut short of their full time value to keep them audibly separate from the adjacent notes.

step   A small INTERVAL, between two close pitches — C to C♯ is a half step, and C to D a whole step.

stochastic music   A method of composition developed by Iannis Xenakis that uses computers or mathematical processes (such as probability theory) to produce randomly generated musical elements.

suspension   A suspension is a tone that is foreign to its chord — it is suspended, or held over, from the previous chord where it "belongs" — and the resulting dissonance is resolved when the tone moves a step downward to "join" the current chord.

sympathetic vibration   The vibrations of one sound-producing body causing another body to vibrate at the frequency of its fundamental or overtones.

symphonic poem   A single-movement orchestral piece that develops a programmatic theme, often inspired by a painting, story, or poem. See PROGRAMMATIC MUSIC.

synesthesia   The experiencing of one sense as a result of the stimulation of another (e.g., when someone hears a chord and describes it in terms of a visible color).

synchrony   Literally "timed together," sychronic events occur simultaneously.

syncopated rhythm   See SYNCOPATION.

syncopation   The deliberate disruption of meter so that naturally strong beats become weak or unexpected emphasis is placed on weak beats.

temperament   A system of tuning that makes slight compromises to strict tuning for the practical purposes of music-making. An example is EQUAL TEMPERAMENT.

tension and resolution   See RESOLUTION.

tessitura   Broadly defined as the natural range of a voice or instrument, it can specifically refer to the note range used in a vocal or instrumental part.

tetrachord   A set of four notes spanning the interval of a perfect fourth.

through-composition   Through-composed music tends to be non-repetitive and continuous, or — if divided into sections — has different music for each section.

timbre   The quality of a sound that allows us to distinguish one instrument or voice from another.

time signature   A two-number symbol in written music, indicating meter.

tonal music   Music composed or written in a key. See also TONALITY.

tonality   A system of making-music in which note pitches are arranged in relation to a KEY.

tone   A sound of identifiable pitch, "tone" is also sometimes used of the particular expressive quality of a sound. The term can also be used to mean an interval of a whole STEP.

tone painting   A technique in which musical notes imitate the meaning of the words they accompany — for example, lyrics about rising may be sung to an ascending scale.

tone row   Used in SERIALISM, a tone row is a series of the twelve notes of the chromatic scale in a particular order which does not repeat any one note.

tonic   The tonic, or key note, is the first tone of a major or minor scale, toward which the other pitches gravitate.

tonic chord   A TRIAD built on the TONIC note. The tonic chord plays an important role in the composition of TONAL MUSIC.

tonic key   Another name for the HOME KEY.

total serialism   See SERIALISM.

transposition   The process of moving music to a different pitch level or key.

triad   A three-note chord that combines, in its most basic form, a ROOT and the notes a third and a fifth above it.

tritone   An interval of three whole steps. As its nickname — DIABOLUS IN MUSICA — suggests, it is known in Western music for its dissonant quality. See DISSONANCE.

twelve-tone scale   See TONE ROW.

unison   Widely used synonymously with UNISONANCE, unison is also the name given to the interval (0 steps) between two notes from different sources but sounding at the same pitch.

unisonance   Concordance or oneness of sound — or, more specifically, two or more parts singing or playing the same notes ("in unison").

variation   The repetition of a theme with changes or additions to its melody, rhythm, or harmony.

vertical   In music, vertical generally refers to the harmonic aspect of a piece (notes sounding simultaneously). Compare HORIZONTAL.

vibrato   A very small and rapid fluctuation in the pitch of a note giving a more expressive tone color.

voice exchange   A technique whereby two different musical phrases are sung or played in COUNTERPOINT then "swapped" between the two parts.

Index

Boldface page numbers cite figures or musical examples.

Absolute music, 137, 153, 157, 160, 210
Absolute pitch, 126
"Abyss" of modernity, 172-73, 176, 178
Acts of John, apocryphal, 438-39
Adams, John, 187, 208
Additive rhythm, 416
"Aesthetic existence," 255, 267
Aesthetics, 84. *See also* Beauty; Creation (human)
Affects, theory of, 175, 175n.41
Affektenlehre. See Affects, theory of
African musical styles, 414, 416, 419-20; synthesis of with Western styles, 416-24
African National Congress (ANC), 418
"Ahomna," 412, 415-16, **415**
"Akanamandla," 430
Alienation of humanity, 142, 153, 170, 177, 181, 186-87, 189
Allegorical interpretation, 43n.11, 314
Alterity. *See* Heteronomy
Ambrose, Saint, 405-6
Angels: music of, 82, 247-48, 445, 451; and time, 198, 288, 289
Anhalt theologians, 72-73
Anthropic principle, 116-17

Anthropology, 117-18, 147, 151, 187
Anticipation, 145, 276, 280, 293, 294, 440. *See also* Hope
Antirealism, 115. *See also* Realism
Apartheid, 408-33 *passim*
Aquinas, Saint Thomas, 168, 175, 177, 181, 185, 186n.73. *See also* Thomism
Arcadia, 144, 145. *See also* Eden; Utopia
Ariès, Philippe, 223-24, 225
Aristotle, 50-52; Philip the Chancellor and, 49, 50, 53, 56-57; prominence of his *Physics* in Middle Ages, 49-50
Armstrong, Louis, 307, 312
Arndt, Johann, 75-76
Arnoldi, Philipp, 74
Arousal theories of emotion, 338n.38, 348
Atonality: in combination with tonality, 209-10, 211
Atonement, theories of, 221, 227, 228
Augustine, Saint, 27-45 *passim*, 58, 63, 69, 282, 289, 291, 314, 434, 440, 443; and ambivalence toward music, 36, 41-43; on faith, 40-41, 44; as "improviser," 314; and the liberal arts, 29-31, 40, 44-45; and the Manichees, 36, 38; on mu-

481

abuse, 323, 353; as witness, 11, 240-70
passim (esp. 240-41, 254, 264, 269-70).
See also under Philip the Chancellor
Music (as related to culture and society): in classical education, 27, 28; in
the contemporary church, 404; and
cross-cultural engagement, 412, 424-
26, 432-33; and cultural identity, 416-
17; and culture, 17-20, 137-211 *passim;*
and film, 339-40, 348; in late antiquity, 27; and politics, 208, 260, 261,
408-33 *passim;* and religion, 189, 190,
192-93, 208; role of in modernity, 138;
and social justice, 408-33 *passim;* and
social unity, 397-98. *See also* Freedom
songs; Protest songs; Singing; Worship
Music (as related to emotion), 323-54
passim (esp. 323-24, 325, 338-51); emotional power of, 69-71, 148, 192, 205,
254, 323, 339-40, 383; emotional value
of, 349-51; emotive "properties" of,
340-49. *See also* Augustine, Saint: on
power of music
Musical bow tradition, 414, 416, 430
Music of the spheres, 81, **140**, 157, 445,
452. *See also* Cosmic harmony; Enchantment
Musicology, 4n.10, 6-7, 8
Music-theology dialogue, 1-13; difficulties and dangers of, 3, 11-13, 137, 159;
fruitfulness for music, 9-10; fruitfulness for theology, 10-11, 20-22, 63-64;
future possibilities for, 159-61; history
of, 2-3, 271
Myth of progress. *See* Progress, modernist

Narcissism, 152
Narrative: and music, 166, 169, 195, 208.
See also Grand narratives
National anthems, 416-17. *See also titles
of individual anthems*
Natural theology, 245, 261, 263, 265, 272.
See also Theology: of nature
Nature. *See* Creation (divine);

Supernature vs. nature; Theology: of
nature
Necessity. *See* Constraint
"Negro National Anthem," 418n.18
Neoclassicism, 293
Neoplatonism, 32, 69, 139, 158
Neurophysiology: and music, 123-24,
131, 343, 347-48
"New humanity," 391, 397, 398-99, 400
Newman, Barbara, 367, 370
"New musicology," 7
"New song," 440; Jesus Christ as, 448-51
New Testament: as heterophony, 311;
and improvisation, 311; and instru-
mental music, 71
Nicolai, Philipp, 75, 76
Nietzsche, Friedrich, 137, 138, 139, 159,
259
Nihilism, 273
"Nkosi, Nkosi, yiba nenceba," 428-30,
429
"Nkosi Sikelel' iAfrika," 411, 412, 416-24,
422-23
Nonretrogradable rhythm, 204, 211
Notation, rhythmic, 124, 133
Novelty, 94. *See also* Innovation; Origi-
nality
Ntsikana son of Gaba, 412-16, 420, 428
Number. *See* Mathematics; Number
symbolism
Number symbolism, 99-100, 210
Nussbaum, Martha, 328n.15, 329n.18,
330n.20, 334
Nyberg, Anders, 426, 432

Occult. *See* Magic
Octatonic scales, 171n.27
Octave equivalence, 113n.7, 127n.39
O'Donovan, Oliver, 153
Old Testament: and instrumental mu-
sic, 71, 75-76
"Open Botha, we are a-knocking," 430,
432
Open systems, 131-32. *See also* Order:
open vs. closed
Opera, 77, 79, 144-45, 147, 164-65;

Pygmalion, 149-50, **150**; *Tristan and Isolde,* 191. *See also* Messiaen, Olivier: Works: *St. François d'Assise*
Oppression, political, 408-33 *passim*
Order: cosmic, 111, 117, 126; mathematical, 109-34 *passim;* open vs. closed, 93-94, 103; and return, 203-4
Organ music, 68, 71-74
Oriental music, 197
Origen, 314
Originality, 107-8, 163. *See also* Novelty
Orpheus, 144, 449-51
Orthodoxy in interpretation, 304, 313-14, 318. *See also* Validity: in biblical interpretation
"Overdetermination" of scores or texts, 298-99
Overtone playing. *See* Musical bow tradition
Overtones, 121-23, **122**. *See also* Overtone series
Overtone series, 106, 122, **122**, 127n.40, 131; as metaphor for music-theology dialogue, 138. *See also* Corps sonore
Overtone singing, 414

Palindromes, 206, 209n.37, 286. *See also* Non-retrogradable rhythm
Parables. *See* Barth, Karl: and "parables of the kingdom"; Music (conceptions of): as parable
"Parables of the kingdom." *See under* Barth, Karl
Parousia: music and, 435, 447-49
Pärt, Arvo, 193, 208
Participation, 9, 90-91. *See also* Church music: congregational participation in; *Koinōnia*
Participatory knowledge, 395-97
Pastorals, 144
Paul, Saint, 310-11. *See also* Colossians, Letter to the; Ephesians, Letter to the
Penrose, Roger, 117-18
Pentatonic modes, 210
Perfection, 277, 281, 283. *See also* Holy Spirit: as perfecter

Performance. *See under* Biblical interpretation
Perichoresis, 264, 275, 290, 291, 304
Perpetual variation. *See* Continuous variation
Personnages rythmiques, 168, 169
Philip the Chancellor, 46-64 *passim;* and Aristotle's *Physics,* 49, 50, 53, 56-57; as Chancellor, 48, 58; as composer, 49, 59; and creation in Genesis, 57; on material (invisible and visible properties of), 53, 55, 63; on material (motion of), 57; on material (opacity of), 54, 58; on material (potentiality of), 53, 56; methodology in *Summa de Bono,* 50, 53, 56-57, 58; and music, as exemplifier, 53, 55n.13, 58-61; on preexistence, 53, 54-55, 59, 63; Works (attributable compositions): "Laudes Referat," 59-61, **60-62**; Works (written): *Summa de Bono,* 49, 50, 53-58
Physiology. *See* Emotion: and physiological changes; Music: and physiological responses; Neurophysiology; Psychoacoustics
Pietism, 77, 79n.55
Pitch class, 113, 127, 128, 129
Plaatje, Solomon, 418
Plainchant. *See* Chant
Plato, 111. *See also* Platonism
Platonism, 90, 91, 117
Play, 267-68, 296, 300-303. *See also* Games
Pleasure. *See* Augustine, Saint: on music and pleasure
Pneuma, cosmic: and instrumental sound, 149-50, **150**
Poetry, 175. *See also individual poets*
Polanyi, Michael, 334n.30, 395, 396
Politics: and music, 208, 260, 261, 408-33 *passim*
Polkinghorne, John, 110, 115-17, 119, 126, 129, 134, 288, 292, 452
Polycoloration, 200
Polydynamics, 200, 211